Microsoft®

# Microsoft® PowerPivot for Excel® 2010: Give Your Data Meaning

*Marco Russo*

*Alberto Ferrari*

PUBLISHED BY
Microsoft Press
A Division of Microsoft Corporation
One Microsoft Way
Redmond, Washington 98052-6399



Library of Congress Control Number: 2010933009

Printed and bound in the United States of America.

Microsoft Press books are available through booksellers and distributors worldwide. For further information about international editions, contact your local Microsoft Corporation office or contact Microsoft Press International directly at fax (425) 936-7329. Visit our Web site at www.microsoft.com/mspress. Send comments to mspinput@microsoft.com.



**Acquisitions Editor:** Rosemary Caperton
**Developmental Editor:** Maria Gargiulo
**Project Editor:** Rosemary Caperton
**Editorial and Production:** Kathleen Atkins (editorial) and Online Training Solutions, Inc. (production)
**Technical Reviewer:** Todd Meister; Technical Review services provided by Content Master, a member of CM Group, Ltd.
**Cover:** Twist Creative

Body Part No. X17-09967

*I wish to dedicate this book to my parents.*

*Thank you for everything.*

*—Alberto*

# Contents at a Glance

# Table of Contents

# Preface

## Marco Russo

On November 4, 2009, Alberto and I had dinner with many other Analysis Services experts from all around the world, including many people from the Microsoft development team. We were in Seattle for the PASS Summit 2009, a conference for SQL Server professionals, and because Redmond, Washington is very near to Seattle, events like this often give you a chance to meet people you know only through e-mail. At that time, PowerPivot had just become the official name for what we had been calling Gemini for the past year, and we were continuing to call it Gemini. That dinner was very pleasant; I admit we were very geeky conversationalists, but everyone was very interested in Analysis Services–related topics and there were no guests outside the discipline, so we talked.

We were discussing the future of Analysis Services, and if you wonder why this is relevant to PowerPivot, it might help to know that PowerPivot was developed by the same team that produced Analysis Services, and these two products share a lot of technology. So Gemini (well, we were still not used to the new name) was part of many discussions.

Alberto, Chris Webb, and I were also celebrating the publishing of another book, *Expert Cube Development with Microsoft SQL Server 2008 Analysis Services*, which we wrote in 2009 without having a single physical meeting. (Alberto and I live in Italy and Chris lives in the U.K.) I was at a table with Edward Melomed and happened to say something like "PowerPivot is just too simple, it doesn't deserve a book by itself," which induced Edward to list all the PowerPivot topics that could justify a book (and more!). I was not convinced, but just as a joke I started writing the table of contents of a PowerPivot book on the paper table cover. At that time, I was still unfamiliar with PowerPivot, and DAX was still relatively new to me. However, after an hour of brainstorming about this book, I had the schema of its contents on the table. At the end of the dinner, I cut the piece of table cover containing my table of contents and started wondering about this book. To write or not to write it?

Well, you already know the answer. After a few weeks (maybe days), I fully understood why this book was necessary and why PowerPivot is not a gadget for Excel, but rather is a tool that will grow in importance and will be adopted by many people who need to analyze their data without the aid of experts to design a complete BI solution in the standard way.

*Marco Russo*

## Alberto Ferrari

Whenever I learn about new technologies, I like to try to figure out whether and how they will be adopted by people in the near future so that I can keep up with the market. After many years of this exercise and a great many tests, I can now state a solid truth about my power to predict the future: I am always wrong. I am not alone in this; Marco will never openly admit that, back in 1995, he thought that the Internet would not survive the end of the year but you know, nobody is perfect.

When I first heard about PowerPivot during the keynote of PASS Summit 2009, I leaped to my prediction of the future of PowerPivot, and anyone could have read on my face what I thought of it: "Do you really believe that Business Intelligence can be left to the masses as Self-Service BI? Come on, Microsoft, you are kidding? No one will ever be able to produce his personal reports with this toy."

During dinner, I heard Marco and Edward talking about a book and, honestly, I was more interested in food and beer than in another book, especially if that book had to be about that useless technology. Nevertheless, I let them talk. When Marco spoke to me about the book again, I decided to study PowerPivot a bit because knowing your enemy is mandatory. I downloaded the first betas and started playing with it. I hate to admit it, but it was pure fun. I loaded huge tables inside this small toy and I was able to produce reports with minimal effort. I tried to make some complex calculations and found them hard to produce, but I felt that PowerPivot was not a toy; it was the start of a new era in Business Intelligence.

I have been working with PowerPivot for a year, more or less, and I think that it is capable of producing great analysis and reports. It surely will bring Business Intelligence to the masses. Nevertheless, as with any tool, PowerPivot requires that you study it, and that you understand the philosophy that underlies it, which is quite different from the classic approach to BI.

Moreover, even if PowerPivot is powerful, you need to remember that it is nothing but a tool. BI projects always require a creative mind. You need to be able to model data and provide information to the tool in such a way that reporting is easy, no matter which tool you are using. In the opening era of Self Service BI, remember that this creative mind is yours, so roll up your sleeves and start studying: PowerPivot is here to serve your reporting needs. You are probably missing only some skills to start having fun with it, and I hope this book will help you fill the gap in your knowledge.

*Alberto Ferrari*

# Acknowledgments

We have to thank so many people for this book that we know it is impossible to write a complete list. So thank you so much to all of you who contributed to this book without even being aware that you did. Blog comments, forum posts, e-mail discussions, chats with attendees and speakers at technical conferences: everything has been useful to us and many people have contributed many ideas to this book. That said, there are people we need to cite personally here because of their particular contributions.

As you might have seen in our Preface, we have to start with Edward Melomed: he inspired us, and we probably would not have started this book without a passionate discussion with him one year ago.

We have to thank Microsoft Press, O'Reilly, and other publishing people who contributed to the project: Ben Ryan, Rosemary Caperton, Todd Meister, Jaime Odell, Maria Gargiulo, and probably many others behind the scene. But a particular mention goes to Kathleen Atkins: she has been our project manager and editor. It has been a pleasure to work with her. We enjoyed the accuracy of her comments and corrections. We are not native English speakers, and she deserves all the credit if you can read this book. But, remember, all the errors are still the responsibility of the authors!

The only job longer than writing a book is studying, in preparation for writing it. A group of people that we (in all friendliness) call ssas-insiders helped us in this work of getting ready to write this book. A few people from Microsoft deserve a special mention because they spent precious time teaching us important concepts about PowerPivot and DAX. Their names are Marius Dumitru, Jeffrey Wang, and Akshai Mirchandani. Your help has been priceless, guys!

We also want to thank Amir Netz and Ashvini Sharma for their contribution to the discussion about how to position PowerPivot. We feel they helped us in some strategic choices we made in this book.

Finishing a book in the age of the Internet is challenging because there is a continuous source of new inputs and ideas. A few blogs have been particularly important to our book, and we want to mention their owners here: Chris Webb, Kasper de Jonge, Rob Collie, Denny Lee, and Dave Wickert.

Finally, we want to thank all the reviewers of early drafts and thank other people who discussed specific issues with us. They are really too many to list, but we need to make a particular mention of Tomislav Piasevoli, Darren Gosbell, Vidas Matelis, and Greg Galloway.

Thank you so much, guys!

# Introduction

Since we first began thinking about Microsoft PowerPivot for Excel 2010, we have had to revise our thoughts a number of times. First we needed to be persuaded to look at the tool seriously. Then when we decided to write about it, we had to decide how to do that. Writing a book is a hard work. Two authors writing a book together is much harder. You might think at first that the project requires of each person half the time it would take either author to write the whole book himself. As it turns out, a joint project requires a lot of communication because each person discusses the drafts written by the other, which leads to long conversations about what the final results should be. Despite our misunderstanding of the time it would take us to write this book, we think that the final result is much better for the reader, who can read a more balanced and accurate description of our topic in these pages than either of us might have produced otherwise.

That said, there is a point where enough is enough and you do not want to negotiate a shared vision anymore. For this reason, you can read our two separate points of view in the Preface, which records our personal, uncensored, biased, and conflicting thoughts. But both of us agree on an important point: PowerPivot is not a gadget. A first impression of PowerPivot might mislead you. We made this wrong evaluation too, at the beginning of our acquaintance with PowerPivot. Do not make the same mistake. PowerPivot is powerful and useful, and it defines a new path for the era of self-service Business Intelligence (BI).

## Who Is This Book For?

We wrote this book for Excel users who are interested in using PowerPivot to produce Business Intelligence reports by themselves. In the book, we take for granted that you have a good understanding of Excel. Business Intelligence skills are not required; we provide insights and descriptions of what is useful if you are just entering the world of self-service BI, covering the required topics more fully in cases we thought greater detail might be necessary.

The book is composed of 11 chapters. We suggest that you read the book from cover to cover even if we understand that many of you will probably jump directly to find the most appropriate information for your business. Nevertheless, so that you understand at least the PowerPivot basics, Chapters 1 through 5 are mandatory. Chapters 1, "First Steps with PowerPivot," and 2, "PowerPivot at Work," are introductory and explain the basics of PowerPivot; you see some simple examples and focus on the differences between classical PivotTables made with Excel and the new PowerPivot engine. Chapter 3, "Introduction to DAX," introduces the DAX programming language, which is the language used by PowerPivot to compute formulas.

We devote Chapter 4, "Data Models," to data modeling, which is an important topic because good data modeling helps you to get the results you want faster and with minimal use of DAX, exploiting all of the PowerPivot features. Chapter 5, "Loading Data and Models," covers all of the many different options for loading data into PowerPivot. Whether you are using a SQL server, Microsoft Access, an OLAP cube on Microsoft SQL Server Analysis Services, or any other media that stores your company information, you will find detailed instruction on how to load data from there to PowerPivot.

Chapter 6, "Evaluation Context and CALCULATE," is all about DAX, and you will find yourself reading it more than once. We devote considerable attention to the evaluation context and the most powerful function in PowerPivot, which is CALCULATE. Although you have seen many calculations before this chapter, only here do you begin to understand how they really work. You might find Chapter 6 hard to understand at first glance, but do not worry about it. Whenever you feel the need, go back and give it a second and maybe third read. Every time you wonder why a formula does not return the result you intended, this chapter is likely to contain the explanation of the behavior and the keys for writing a better and faster formula for your calculation.

Chapters 7 through 11 can be read separately because, even if their topics increase in complexity from Chapters 7 through 11, each one treats specific topics. Chapter 7, "Date Calculations in DAX," deals with date calculations, such as Year To Date, Parallel Period In Prior Year, computation of working days, and many other very useful and frequently necessary date calculations. We strongly suggest that you learn this material well because a correct calendar table is mandatory for performing date intelligence in PowerPivot. Chapter 8, "Mastering PivotTables," covers interesting Excel and PowerPivot features aimed at the production of reports. It describes a mix of Excel 2010 and PowerPivot features, with many examples of how to use them. The chapter also offers many ideas that you can use to build your reports. Chapter 9, "PowerPivot DAX Patterns," demands your close attention. You come to it with basic knowledge about DAX; in the course of reading Chapter 9, you learn many complex patterns of formulas, such as ratios, percentages, ranking, and ABC analysis. When you complete this chapter, you deserve the rank of DAX expert. Chapter 10, "PowerPivot Data Model Patterns," is the logical continuation of Chapter 9: after you become a DAX expert, you need to move a step further and become a data modeling expert. You see some examples of common scenarios for which you need to use both the DAX programming language and a specific data model. Chapter 11, "Publishing to SharePoint," is the only chapter dedicated to the Microsoft SharePoint integration with PowerPivot. It presents basic SharePoint functionalities and shows how to extend PowerPivot features using its SharePoint integration.

# System Requirements

You need the following software and hardware to build and run the code samples for this book:

- Windows XP with Service Pack (SP) 3 (32-bit), Windows Vista with SP1, Windows Server 2003 R2 with MSXML 6.0, Windows Server 2008 or later (32-bit or 64-bit), or Windows 7 or later operating systems.
- Microsoft Excel 2010 and PowerPivot for Microsoft Excel 2010 (which is a free Excel add-in downloadable from *http://www.powerpivot.com*).
- 500 MHz 32-bit or 64-bit processor or higher .
- Minimum of 1 GB of RAM. (Two GB or more is recommended.)
- 5400-RPM hard drive (with three GB of available hard disk space).
- Display with a 1024 × 576 or higher resolution.

# About the DVD

The companion DVD that ships with this book contains tools and resources to help you get the most from *Microsoft PowerPivot for Excel 2010: Give Your Data Meaning*.

## What's on the DVD

The companion DVD for *Microsoft PowerPivot for Excel 2010: Give Your Data Meaning* includes the following:

- A complete electronic version of this book.
- All of the workbooks we used to produce this book, which you can use to follow the many examples in the book on your computer.
- An Access version of the AdventureWorks database, which might be useful for readers who do not have access to the SQL Server version of this database.

**Digital Content for Digital Book Readers**

If you bought a digital-only edition of this book, you can enjoy select content from the print edition's companion DVD.

Visit *http://go.microsoft.com/fwlink/?Linkid=200417* to get your downloadable content. This content is always up to date and available to all readers.

## Errata & Book Support

We have made every effort to ensure the accuracy of this book and its companion content. If you do find an error, please report it on our Microsoft Press site at Oreilly.com:

1. Go to *http://microsoftpress.oreilly.com*.
2. In the Search box, enter the book's ISBN or title.
3. Select your book from the search results.
4. On your book's catalog page, under the cover image, you will see a list of links.
5. Click View/Submit Errata.

You will find additional information and services for your book on its catalog page. If you need additional support, please e-mail Microsoft Press Book Support at *mspinput@microsoft.com*.

Please note that product support for Microsoft software is not offered through the addresses above.

## We Want to Hear from You

At Microsoft Press, your satisfaction is our top priority, and your feedback our most valuable asset. Please tell us what you think of this book at:

*http://www.microsoft.com/learning/booksurvey*

The survey is short, and we read *every one* of your comments and ideas. Thanks in advance for your input!

## Stay in Touch

Let us keep the conversation going! We are on Twitter: *http://twitter.com/MicrosoftPress*

Chapter 1

# First Steps with PowerPivot

Microsoft SQL Server PowerPivot for Excel is a new technology aimed at providing self-service Business Intelligence (BI). PowerPivot is a real revolution inside the world of data analysis because it gives you all the power you need to perform complex analysis of data without requiring the intervention of BI technicians. This tool, an Excel add-in, implements a powerful in-memory database that can organize data, detect interesting relationships, and give you a swift way to browse information.

These are some of the most interesting features of PowerPivot:

- The ability to organize tables for the PivotTable tool in a relational way, freeing the analyst from the need to import data as Excel worksheets before analyzing the data.
- The availability of a fast, space-saving columnar database that can handle huge amounts of data without the limitations of Excel worksheets.
- DAX, a powerful programming language that defines complex expressions on top of the relational database. DAX allows you to define surprisingly rich expressions, compared to those that are standard in Excel.
- The ability to integrate different sources and almost any kind of data, such as information from databases, Excel worksheets, and sources available on the Internet.
- Amazingly fast in-memory processing of complex queries over the whole database.

Some people might think of PowerPivot as a simple replacement for the PivotTable, some might use it as a rapid development tool for complex BI solutions, and others might believe it is a real replacement for a complex BI solution. PowerPivot is a great tool for exploring the BI world and implementing BI solutions. It is not a replacement for a complex BI solution, such as the ones built on top of Microsoft Analysis Services, but it is much more than a simple replacement for the Excel PivotTable.

PowerPivot fills the gap between an Excel workbook and a complete BI solution, and it has some unique characteristics that make it appealing to both Excel power users and seasoned BI analysts. This book examines all the features of PowerPivot, but as with any big project, we need to start from the beginning. This chapter offers a simple introduction to the basic features of PowerPivot. We suggest that you follow the step-by-step instructions we give you in this chapter so that you can see on your own computer the results that we show in the book. In the chapters that follow, we do not use step-by-step instructions because we think that it is better to focus most of the book on concepts rather than on "click Next" instructions.

PowerPivot comes as an add-in for Excel 2010. To use PowerPivot, you need to download the installer from *http://www.powerpivot.com/download.aspx* and follow the instructions from the installation program.

After you install PowerPivot, you can see it—and use it—by means of a new section on the Excel ribbon named, obviously, PowerPivot.

## Working with Classic Excel PivotTables

Since the Excel 97 release, Excel spreadsheet users have been able to analyze data using the PivotTable. Prior to the availability of PowerPivot, using PivotTables was the main way to analyze data. The PivotTable tool is an easy and convenient way to browse huge amounts of data that you collect into Excel sheets. This book does not explain in detail how the PivotTable tool works; you can find a lot of good descriptions elsewhere. However, it is helpful to recall the main features of the PivotTable tool to compare it with PowerPivot.

Let us suppose you have a standard Excel table, imported from a query run against a database that contains all the data that you want to analyze. To get this data, you probably asked someone in your IT department to provide some means to access the database and a specific query, to retrieve the information. Your Excel sheet would look like the one in Figure 1-1. Because the table contains raw data, it is very difficult to analyze. You can look at this worksheet on the companion DVD under the name CH01-01-StandardPivotTable.xlsx.

| OrderType | SalesPerson | OrderTerritoryGroup | OrderTerrito | OrderID | OrderDate | Order | Ord | OrderSubT |
|---|---|---|---|---|---|---|---|---|
| Internal | Tsvi Michael Reiter | North America | Southeast | 43659 | 7/1/2001 0:00 | 2001 | 7 | 24643.9362 |
| Internal | Tsvi Michael Reiter | North America | Southeast | 43659 | 7/1/2001 0:00 | 2001 | 7 | 24643.9362 |
| Internal | Tsvi Michael Reiter | North America | Southeast | 43659 | 7/1/2001 0:00 | 2001 | 7 | 24643.9362 |
| Internal | Tsvi Michael Reiter | North America | Southeast | 43659 | 7/1/2001 0:00 | 2001 | 7 | 24643.9362 |
| Internal | Tsvi Michael Reiter | North America | Southeast | 43659 | 7/1/2001 0:00 | 2001 | 7 | 24643.9362 |
| Internal | Tsvi Michael Reiter | North America | Southeast | 43660 | 7/1/2001 0:00 | 2001 | 7 | 1553.1035 |
| Internal | José Edvaldo Saraiva | North America | Canada | 43661 | 7/1/2001 0:00 | 2001 | 7 | 39422.1198 |
| Internal | José Edvaldo Saraiva | North America | Canada | 43661 | 7/1/2001 0:00 | 2001 | 7 | 39422.1198 |
| Internal | José Edvaldo Saraiva | North America | Canada | 43661 | 7/1/2001 0:00 | 2001 | 7 | 39422.1198 |
| Internal | José Edvaldo Saraiva | North America | Canada | 43661 | 7/1/2001 0:00 | 2001 | 7 | 39422.1198 |
| Internal | José Edvaldo Saraiva | North America | Canada | 43661 | 7/1/2001 0:00 | 2001 | 7 | 39422.1198 |
| Internal | José Edvaldo Saraiva | North America | Canada | 43661 | 7/1/2001 0:00 | 2001 | 7 | 39422.1198 |
| Internal | José Edvaldo Saraiva | North America | Canada | 43661 | 7/1/2001 0:00 | 2001 | 7 | 39422.1198 |
| Internal | José Edvaldo Saraiva | North America | Canada | 43661 | 7/1/2001 0:00 | 2001 | 7 | 39422.1198 |
| Internal | José Edvaldo Saraiva | North America | Canada | 43674 | 7/1/2001 0:00 | 2001 | 7 | 3149.2584 |
| Internal | Jillian Carson | North America | Central | 43675 | 7/1/2001 0:00 | 2001 | 7 | 6835.9493 |
| Internal | Jillian Carson | North America | Central | 43675 | 7/1/2001 0:00 | 2001 | 7 | 6835.9493 |
| Internal | Michael G Blythe | North America | Southeast | 43676 | 7/1/2001 0:00 | 2001 | 7 | 17040.8246 |
| Internal | Michael G Blythe | North America | Southeast | 43676 | 7/1/2001 0:00 | 2001 | 7 | 17040.8246 |
| Internal | Michael G Blythe | North America | Southeast | 43676 | 7/1/2001 0:00 | 2001 | 7 | 17040.8246 |
| Internal | Michael G Blythe | North America | Southeast | 43676 | 7/1/2001 0:00 | 2001 | 7 | 17040.8246 |
| OnLine | OnLine | Pacific | Australia | 45166 | 1/16/2002 0:00 | 2002 | 1 | 3578.27 |
| OnLine | OnLine | Pacific | Australia | 45168 | 1/16/2002 0:00 | 2002 | 1 | 3578.27 |
| OnLine | OnLine | North America | Southwest | 45175 | 1/17/2002 0:00 | 2002 | 1 | 3578.27 |
| OnLine | OnLine | Europe | United Kingdon | 45186 | 1/19/2002 0:00 | 2002 | 1 | 3578.27 |

**FIGURE 1-1** Sample data for the PivotTable.

Having all the data available in a sheet, we can now choose to insert a PivotTable. The wizard prompts us for the table to use as the source of the Pivot and for where to put the PivotTable, and then it provides the standard Excel PivotTable interface shown in Figure 1-2.

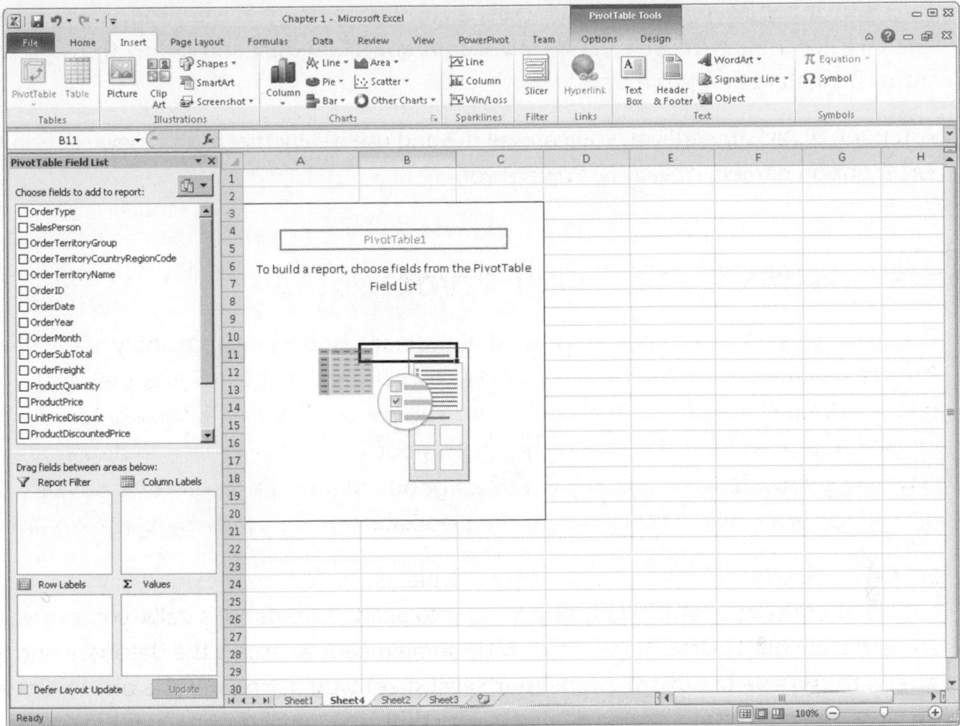


**FIGURE 1-2** The standard PivotTable interface.

From here, you can choose to take, for example, the OrderYear and put it in columns and the SalesPerson in the rows, and display the OrderSubTotal in the intersection of the rows and columns. After properly formatting your numbers, you get a nice report (as you can see in Figure 1-3) showing how salespeople performed over time.

| Sum of OrderSubTotal | Column Labels | | | | |
|---|---|---|---|---|---|
| Row Labels | 2001 | 2002 | 2003 | 2004 | Grand Total |
| Amy E Alberts | | 3,680,772.68 | 23,220,800.52 | 2,428,929.89 | 29,330,503.09 |
| David R Campbell | 7,918,246.94 | 40,012,866.45 | 61,182,091.03 | 24,023,131.94 | 133,136,336.35 |
| Garrett R Vargas | 9,347,642.66 | 37,296,045.05 | 48,568,957.76 | 15,377,197.36 | 110,589,842.83 |
| Jae B Pak | | 131,903,843.42 | 190,111,404.96 | 71,699,902.70 | 393,715,151.09 |
| Jillian Carson | 28,941,083.66 | 144,735,036.84 | 151,920,734.56 | 47,322,586.54 | 372,919,441.60 |
| José Edvaldo Saraiva | 23,516,216.01 | 59,809,321.95 | 88,230,115.11 | 51,065,965.83 | 222,621,618.90 |
| Linda C Mitchell | 22,291,810.28 | 126,596,553.49 | 187,014,820.08 | 75,661,785.09 | 411,564,968.94 |
| Lynn N Tsoflias | | | 26,576,864.23 | 22,106,501.57 | 48,683,365.80 |
| Michael G Blythe | 15,202,066.62 | 122,654,831.24 | 164,183,279.39 | 49,787,115.93 | 351,827,293.17 |
| OnLine | 3,266,373.66 | 6,530,343.53 | 22,037,506.26 | 27,392,957.48 | 59,227,180.92 |
| Pamela O Ansman-Wolfe | 12,267,747.58 | 41,643,418.50 | 43,019,493.67 | 26,562,675.92 | 123,493,335.68 |
| Rachel B Valdez | | | 51,134,655.06 | 34,606,110.20 | 85,740,765.26 |
| Ranjit R Varkey Chudukatil | | 43,735,751.48 | 110,826,883.14 | 51,574,585.19 | 206,137,219.81 |
| Shu K Ito | 20,937,204.43 | 87,803,922.17 | 99,734,758.79 | 37,221,052.42 | 245,696,937.81 |
| Stephen Y Jiang | 296,030.14 | 13,555,086.55 | 24,790,569.89 | 11,071,061.46 | 49,712,748.04 |
| Syed E Abbas | | | 8,789,724.49 | 360,990.31 | 9,150,714.79 |
| Tete A Mensa-Annan | | 12,107,154.10 | 41,973,848.67 | 23,206,378.50 | 77,287,381.28 |
| Tsvi Michael Reiter | 26,100,552.89 | 75,000,783.27 | 82,019,121.65 | 33,660,601.06 | 216,781,058.87 |
| **Grand Total** | **170,084,974.87** | **947,065,730.73** | **1,425,335,629.26** | **605,129,529.39** | **3,147,615,864.24** |

**FIGURE 1-3** Example of a report with the PivotTable tool.

By changing the way data is organized in rows and columns, you can easily produce different and interesting reports, with an intuitive, fast interface that helps you navigate the information.

Figure 1-3 shows what a standard PivotTable looks like. Users all around the world have been using this tool for many years with great success, analyzing their Excel data in many different ways and producing reports according to their needs.

One of the best characteristics of the PivotTable tool is its ease of use. Excel analyzes the source table, detects numeric values, and provides us with the ability to display their total slicing data over all other columns. Clearly, totals are aggregated using the SUM function because this is what is normally needed. If we want a different aggregation function, we can choose it by using the various PivotTable options.

As easy as it is to use, PivotTables have some limitations:

- PivotTables can analyze only information coming from a single table stored in an Excel worksheet. If you have different worksheets, containing different information, there is no easy way to correlate information coming from them.
- It is not always easy to get the source data into a format that is suitable for analysis. In the previous example, you saw a table that is extracted from a SQL query run against the AdventureWorks database and that you build to analyze data. The skills needed to build such a query are somewhat technical because you need to know the SQL syntax and the underlying database structure. Situations like this often force you to ask your IT department to develop such queries before you even start the analysis process.
- Because only one table can be analyzed at a time, you can often end up building the queries needed for a specific analysis, and, if for any reason you want to perform a different analysis, you need to build different queries. If, for example, you have a query that returns sales figures at the month level, you cannot use it to perform further analysis at the "day of week" level; to do that, you need a new query. This requirement, in turn, might prompt you to contact IT again, which can become expensive if the IT department charges for the amount of work it does.

When PivotTables are not enough, as is the case for medium-size companies, it is very common to start a complete BI project with products like SQL Server Analysis Services, which provide the same pivoting features on complex data structures known as OLAP cubes. OLAP cubes are difficult to build but provide the best way to freely analyze complicated company data. We talk briefly about OLAP cubes later, in Chapter 4, "Data Models;" at this point, it is enough to point out that they are the definitive solution to BI requirements but they are expensive and still require a strong effort from the IT department.

## Working with PivotTables in PowerPivot

Standard PivotTables are good tools. Nevertheless, to let you analyze more complex data, Microsoft introduced the so-called *self-service BI*. The goal of this technology is to let you build complex data structures and analyze them with pivot tables, removing the current limitations of the PivotTable. PowerPivot is the first tool available from Microsoft to handle self-service BI.

PowerPivot enables you to analyze data without needing to contact IT staff to produce complex queries. Further, it removes the limitation that a PivotTable can analyze only a single table. You want to be able to query more tables at the same time, producing reports that easily integrate information coming from different sources.

### Working with the AdventureWorks Sample Database

To provide examples, we use the AdventureWorks database throughout this book. We have chosen AdventureWorks because it is a well-known database, freely available on the Web, and contains sample data that you can easily use for complex analysis. The database contains information about AdventureWorks Cycles, which is a large, multinational, fictitious company that manufactures and sells metal and composite bicycles to North American, European, and Asian commercial markets.

You can download the AdventureWorks database from *http://www.codeplex.com/SqlServerSamples*, where you will find different versions of the database, depending on the release of SQL Server that you have installed. If you do not have SQL Server on your computer, you can use the Microsoft Access version of AdventureWorks that is provided on the companion DVD. Moreover, all the demos in this book are available on the companion DVD as Excel workbooks. So you can follow most of the examples even if you do not have access to a database.

Moreover, for the interested reader, Microsoft provides sample data in Excel workbooks that can be used to test PowerPivot at this URL: *http://tinyurl.com/PowerPivotSamples*. Even if we do not use these files in this book, you might be interested in loading them to have some data to perform your tests.

## Importing Data

We want now to create an Excel workbook that performs some analysis on the AdventureWorks database using PowerPivot. The first step is to import data from the external database. You can choose from several options for doing that, but this first example simply covers importing data from the SQL Server database containing AdventureWorks. Later, in Chapter 5, "Loading Data and Models," we discuss other options in greater detail.

From the Launch group on the Excel ribbon, click the PowerPivot Window button, shown in Figure 1-4, and launch the PowerPivot window, which is the most important tool we will use to get and arrange all the data we need to analyze. That window is separated from the Excel window, but it is strictly integrated, nevertheless, because you are still operating on the same Excel document.

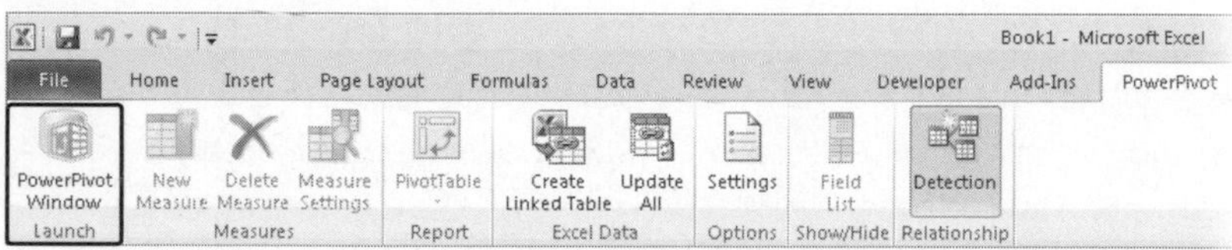


**FIGURE 1-4** The PowerPivot Window button on the Excel ribbon.

When you open the PowerPivot window, you are ready to load some data. The first step is to establish a connection between the Excel sheet and the database. To do that, on the From Database drop-down menu, choose From SQL Server, as shown in Figure 1-5.

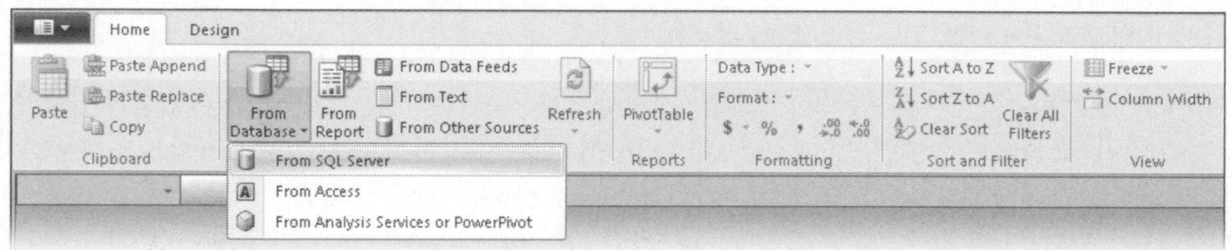


**FIGURE 1-5** The menu option to import data from a SQL Server database.

Selecting this menu option opens a dialog box, which allows you to specify the connection option. In the example shown in Figure 1-6, we are loading data from the local instance of SQL Server. Your specific configuration might be different from this, requiring a different name for the SQL Server instance.

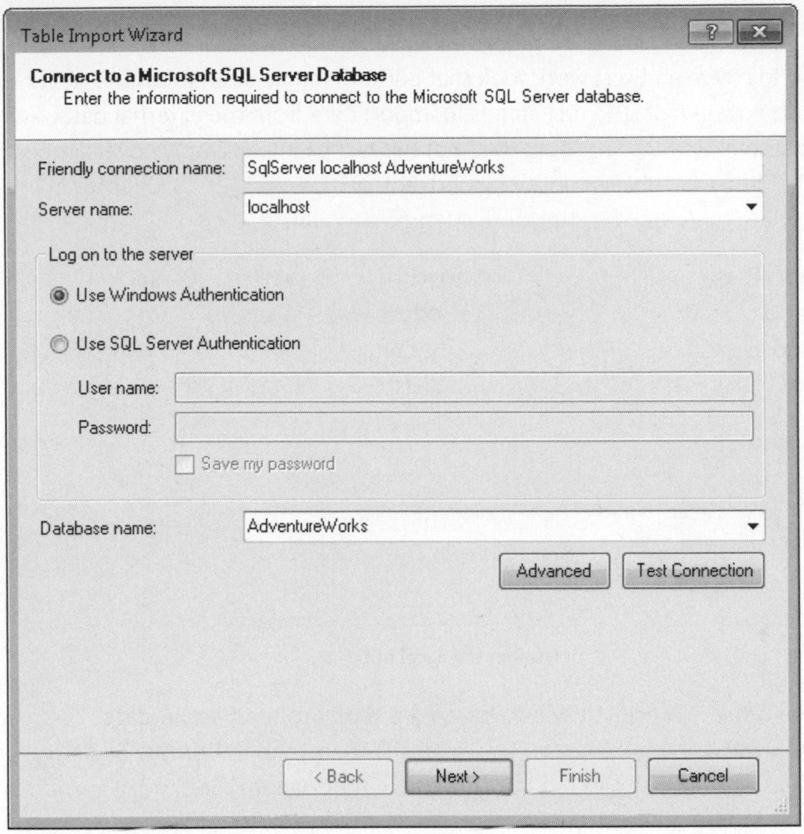

FIGURE 1-6 The Table Import Wizard, the first step.

Clicking Next, we move to the next window. Because we want to ignore the option to write a query, let us click Next to go directly to the next page, where we can select the tables to import. This window (see Figure 1-7) shows all the available tables that can be imported in PowerPivot. The tables are sorted by Schema and then by Source Table name.

**FIGURE 1-7** Choosing the tables to import.

We want to load three tables:

- **Product** Contains all the details about products sold by AdventureWorks.
- **Sales Order Header** Contains header information about the orders.
- **Sales Order Detail** Contains the detailed information about all the rows inside the orders and acts as a bridge between the sales order header and the products.

After you select these three tables, you can perform basic analysis about which products have been sold. The orders header provides information about the date of the order, the customer, the order total, and other information. Clicking Finish after having selected those tables launches the process of loading data from the database, which completes in a few seconds.

After the tables load, the PowerPivot window changes, showing all the data that has been loaded, as you can see in Figure 1-8.

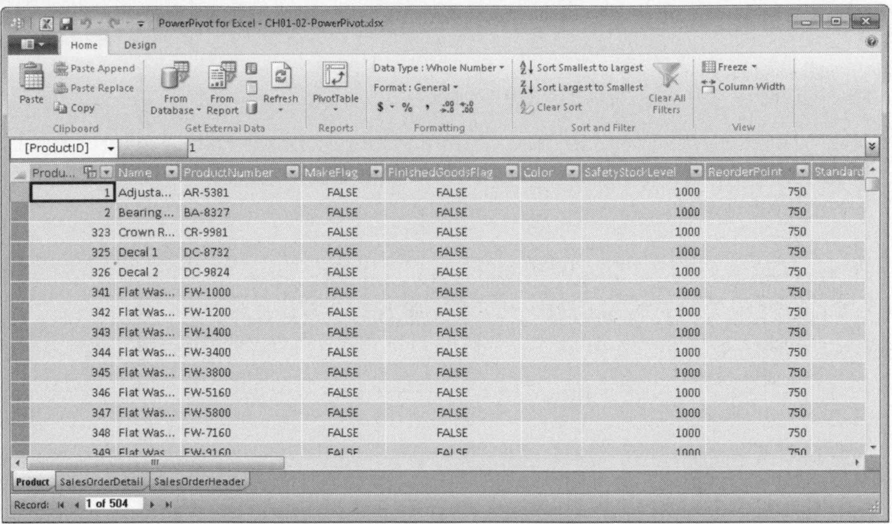


| Produ... | Name | ProductNumber | MakeFlag | FinishedGoodsFlag | Color | SafetyStockLevel | ReorderPoint |
|---|---|---|---|---|---|---|---|
| 1 | Adjusta... | AR-5381 | FALSE | FALSE | | 1000 | 750 |
| 2 | Bearing... | BA-8327 | FALSE | FALSE | | 1000 | 750 |
| 323 | Crown R... | CR-9981 | FALSE | FALSE | | 1000 | 750 |
| 325 | Decal 1 | DC-8732 | FALSE | FALSE | | 1000 | 750 |
| 326 | Decal 2 | DC-9824 | FALSE | FALSE | | 1000 | 750 |
| 341 | Flat Was... | FW-1000 | FALSE | FALSE | | 1000 | 750 |
| 342 | Flat Was... | FW-1200 | FALSE | FALSE | | 1000 | 750 |
| 343 | Flat Was... | FW-1400 | FALSE | FALSE | | 1000 | 750 |
| 344 | Flat Was... | FW-3400 | FALSE | FALSE | | 1000 | 750 |
| 345 | Flat Was... | FW-3800 | FALSE | FALSE | | 1000 | 750 |
| 346 | Flat Was... | FW-5160 | FALSE | FALSE | | 1000 | 750 |
| 347 | Flat Was... | FW-5800 | FALSE | FALSE | | 1000 | 750 |
| 348 | Flat Was... | FW-7160 | FALSE | FALSE | | 1000 | 750 |

**FIGURE 1-8** The PowerPivot window with some tables loaded.

The central pane contains the data and looks very similar to an Excel table inside a worksheet. Nevertheless, do not be confused: PowerPivot tables are completely different objects from Excel tables. PowerPivot implements a very fast and space-saving columnar database that stores tables in memory; it compresses data and uses much less memory than Excel tables. Moreover, PowerPivot tables can be related to other tables to build complex data models that can be easily queried with pivot tables.

We spend a lot of pages through the whole book describing all the features of this window but, at this time, we want to examine only the basic functionality of PowerPivot. So let us choose the PivotTable option from the PivotTable button on the ribbon and, when prompted, let us specify New Worksheet as the target of the pivot table. In Figure 1-9, you can see the look of the PivotTable working on a PowerPivot database.

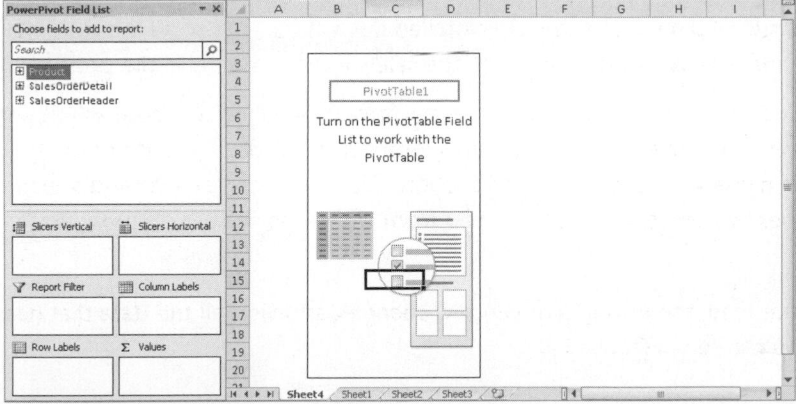


**FIGURE 1-9** The pivot table on a PowerPivot database.

We can see that this pivot table is very similar to the one used to analyze simple Excel tables, but it contains some basic differences:

- In the field list, we have three tables, not just one, as with the classic PivotTable. This means that you can select attributes and values from all the three imported tables. Moreover, if you add more tables later, all the PowerPivot tables will be available for you to select values and attributes.
- You have two more areas in which to put attributes, the so-called *slicers*, which we will use later.

Apart from these two differences, the PowerPivot field list looks similar to the standard PivotTable field list even if, under the hood, it acts as an interface to a very different engine.

## Querying Data

Now that you have loaded some tables, you can start analyzing data. Let us start with a basic analysis: we want to see the total amount sold online versus the same total sold directly. The SalesOrderHeader contains a True/False column (OnlineOrderFlag) that contains True for orders placed online and False for orders placed internally; you can select it and place it on the rows. After that, you can select the LineTotal value from the SalesOrderDetail table, which contains the total of the single line of an order.

When you have done that, the Excel worksheet looks like Figure 1-10.

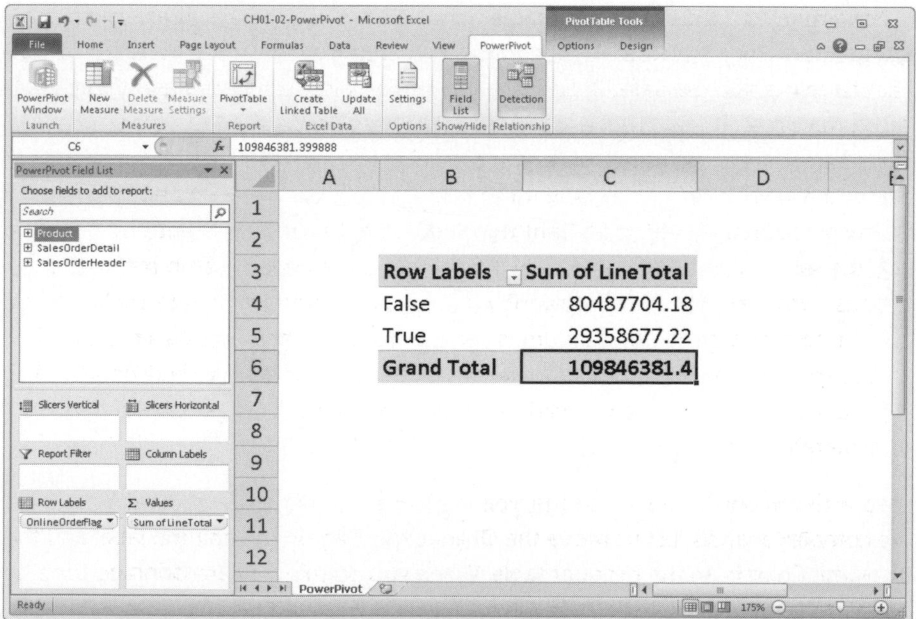


**FIGURE 1-10** A simple query against a PowerPivot database.

Even if it seems intuitive, this simple operation hides one of the most important features of PowerPivot. You have chosen an attribute from the SalesOrderHeader table and one from the SalesOrderDetail table. Even if they belong to two different tables, you can slice the total of the details by using attributes from the header. How is PowerPivot able to do that? The key is in relationships.

A relationship, as its name suggests, is used to tie together two tables. A relationship is graphically shown as a line between the source table and the destination one. The relationship shown in Figure 1-11 can be read as "for each sales order detail, there is a header containing it."

**FIGURE 1-11** Relationship between SalesOrderDetail and SalesOrderHeader.

The AdventureWorks database resembles almost any relational database in containing relationship information between tables. PowerPivot, reading these tables, is able to determine that each row inside the SalesOrderDetails table contains a column (SalesOrderId) that relates to a column with the same name inside the SalesOrderHeader table. In other words, whenever you read a row from the detail table, you can link it to its header by searching inside the header table for a row with the same value for the column SalesOrderId. It is not yet time to discuss relationships in detail; the important thing now is to understand that two tables can work inside the same pivot table if and only if there is a known relationship between them. If this is the case, you can rely on the PowerPivot database engine to analyze the relationship and allow you to slice a table using columns coming from another one. As simple as this feature might seem, it is one of the most powerful capabilities of PowerPivot because it lets you combine many different tables inside a single pivot table. You can explore your database in complete freedom.

Armed with this powerful knowledge, you might want to play with your tables and perform a more complex analysis. Let us move the OnlineOrderFlag on the column label and then choose the column Color from the product table. When you do this, you are bringing together three different tables in a single pivot table. Nevertheless, the result is not exactly what you would expect, as you can see in Figure 1-12.

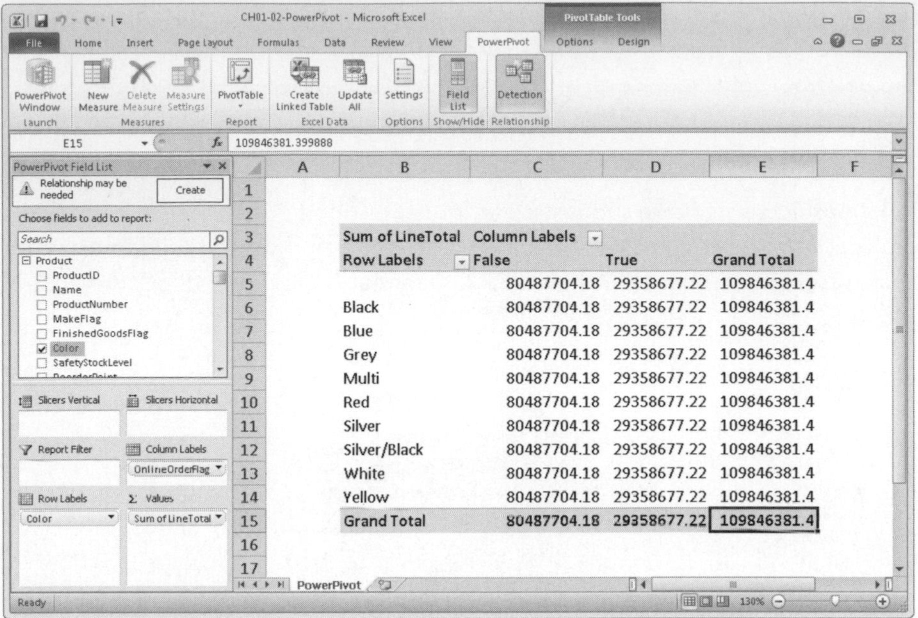


**FIGURE 1-12** If no relationship exists, the result is wrong.

There are two important things to note here:

- The result is the same for all the rows, and it is identical with the grand total, no matter what the color is.
- A warning yellow window appeared inside the task pane, warning you that you need to establish relationships if you want to analyze data using these three tables together.

What happened here? The source database does not contain the definition of any relationship between SalesOrderDetail and Products. Because there are no relationships among the tables, PowerPivot cannot correctly slice values from the detail using the color, which is an attribute of the product table. This produces both the warning and the result that, regardless of the color, the same value is always shown.

Because this is a common situation (the fact that the source database lacks some sort of relationship), PowerPivot provides a sophisticated algorithm that can automatically detect relationships, even if they are not present in the database. Clicking the Create button inside the yellow warning icon starts this algorithm. It runs for a few seconds and then shows the window you see in Figure 1-13.

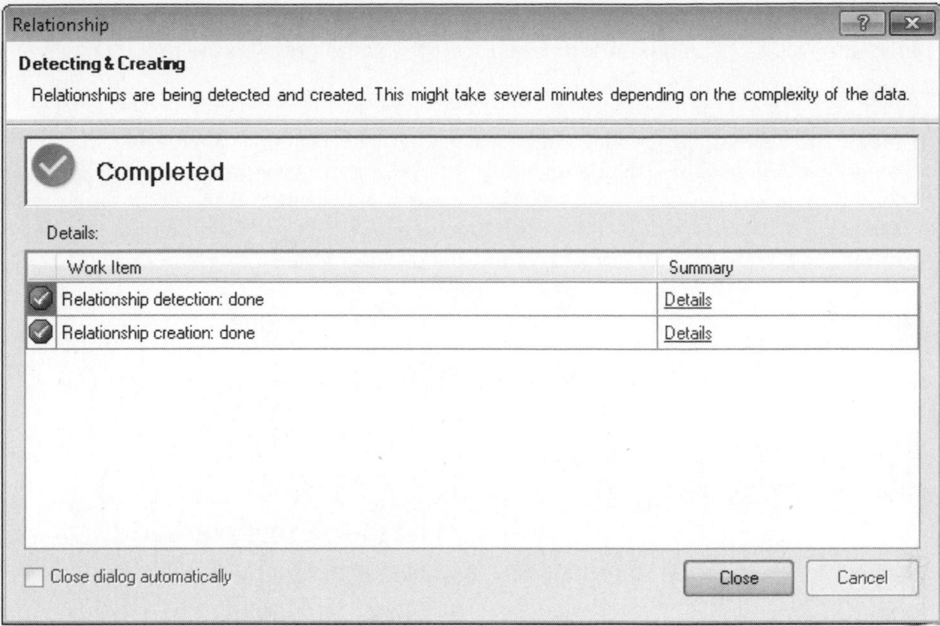


**FIGURE 1-13** Summary window of detected relationships.

The algorithm detected some relationships and then created them for you. Clicking the Details link on the creation line, you can see (Figure 1-14) the details of the relationships that have been created.

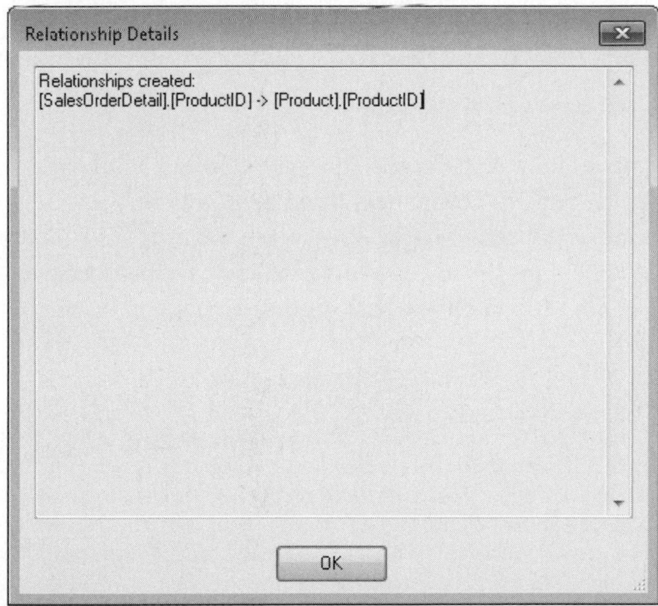


**FIGURE 1-14** Detailed description of the relationships found.

The relationship detected by PowerPivot starts from the ProductID column of the SalesOrderDetail table, and it links this column with the one of the same name in the product table.

**Note** All relationships have the same format: they link a column in a table with a column in another one. Two rows are considered linked if they share the same value for the column values. We will return later to consider the relationship-detection algorithm. At this point, we do not want to spend too many words on it; our focus is on the requirement of relationships to get meaningful results, not on the internal workings of this complex algorithm.

When you close this window, the pivot table is automatically refreshed and shows the grid, with the relationships active, as you can see in Figure 1-15.

| Sum of LineTotal | Column Labels | | |
|---|---|---|---|
| Row Labels | False | True | Grand Total |
| | 664202.2176 | 435116.69 | 1099318.908 |
| Black | 29408606.67 | 8838411.958 | 38247018.63 |
| Blue | 7323754.678 | 2279096.28 | 9602850.958 |
| Multi | 543378.4203 | 106470.74 | 649849.1603 |
| Red | 13898939.02 | 7724330.524 | 21623269.54 |
| Silver | 14663950.86 | 5113389.082 | 19777339.95 |
| Silver/Black | 147483.9098 | | 147483.9098 |
| White | 24638.80758 | 5106.32 | 29745.12758 |
| Yellow | 13812749.59 | 4856755.627 | 18669505.22 |
| Grand Total | 80487704.18 | 29358677.22 | 109846381.4 |

**FIGURE 1-15** With relationships accounted for, the values are now correctly computed.

Now the grid looks much more interesting because the relationship is working and the data is sliced correctly by color. You are now joining three different tables inside the same pivot table and you are slicing order details using values from the order header and the product table. Moreover, as you might already have noticed, you have been able to analyze data without building any queries to the database; it is obvious that you do not need to know SQL to use PowerPivot.

**Note** All this work has been completed without your ever asking IT a single question. Believe it or not, this is the very heart of self-service BI: you are building a BI solution by yourself, without needing to ask for help from anybody else. Of course, later on you will surely encounter some trouble in this process, and maybe some help from the IT team will be welcome. Nevertheless, the effort you ask them to exert on your behalf is likely to be greatly reduced when compared with what you would have asked when trying to analyze data with the Excel PivotTable tool alone.

Clearly, because you want to build the complete solution by yourself, you need to learn some basics of data modeling. And, sometimes, you need to ask for help in building some queries to the database, when simply importing them in PowerPivot is not the best way to analyze data. Moreover, because you have just scratched the surface of the real power of PowerPivot, you will soon discover some useful tools that are available to build complex and meaningful reports from the basic data provided by the database.

# Summary

This chapter introduced you to PowerPivot so that you can begin to understand the difference between a standard pivot table and PowerPivot. It is now time to summarize what you learned.

- Standard Excel pivot tables can work on a single table; PowerPivot, on the other hand, lets you work on many tables, tied together through relationships.
- PowerPivot is a database, so it can store huge amounts of data; Excel is a spreadsheet, and its reason for being is to make computations, not to store data.
- When PowerPivot detects the need for relationships, it uses a relationship-detection algorithm that finds them automatically. It is not magic—sometimes you must define relationships manually—nevertheless, this tool is a big help.

Chapter 2

# PowerPivot at Work

We are now going to introduce some of the most interesting features of Microsoft SQL Server PowerPivot for Excel. The goal of this chapter is to show the most frequently used PowerPivot features for transforming a simple Excel workbook into a complex report that helps you perform analysis on data. This is not yet the place for more advanced topics, such as the DAX programming language or complex relationships. Nevertheless, after you read this chapter, you will be able to perform complex analysis on a relational database and—we hope—still feel the need to go forward in your reading to discover the most advanced uses of PowerPivot.

Please note that we sometimes refer to *the end user* or *the user experience* as if we think that your PowerPivot workbook might be used by somebody else. To make a good report, you always need to think in this way. Even if you are the only user of a specific report, a user-friendly report is easier to read and update even after some time has passed since its creation.

## Using the PivotTable to Produce Reports

Let us start with a very simple report, based on the same three tables that you loaded in the previous chapter: Sales Order Header, Sales Order Detail, and Product.

If you create a PivotTable with PowerPivot and put OnlineOrderFlag and SizeUnitMeasureCode on the Report Filter pane, Size on Column Labels, Color on Row Labels and the OrderQty as the value to sum up, you end up with the report shown in Figure 2-1, which you can find in the workbook named CH02-01-FirstSample.xlsx in the companion content.

| OnlineOrderFlag | True |
|---|---|
| SizeUnitMeasureCode | CM |

| Sum of OrderQty | Column Labels | | | | | | | | | | | | | |
|---|---|---|---|---|---|---|---|---|---|---|---|---|---|---|
| **Row Labels** | **38** | **40** | **42** | **44** | **46** | **48** | **50** | **52** | **54** | **56** | **58** | **60** | **62** | **Grand Total** |
| Black | 631 | 48 | 708 | 812 | 620 | 834 | | 835 | | | 680 | 76 | 65 | 5309 |
| Blue | | | | 53 | 274 | | 304 | | 303 | | 57 | 228 | 64 | 1283 |
| Red | | | | 497 | | 587 | | 496 | | 295 | 380 | 53 | 411 | 2719 |
| Silver | 802 | 173 | 776 | 88 | 718 | 86 | | 48 | | | | | | 2691 |
| Yellow | 270 | 512 | 541 | 562 | 172 | 493 | 210 | | 206 | | 47 | 140 | 50 | 3203 |
| **Grand Total** | **1703** | **733** | **2025** | **2012** | **1784** | **2000** | **514** | **1379** | **509** | **295** | **1164** | **497** | **590** | **15205** |

**FIGURE 2-1** A simple report using PowerPivot.

Before analyzing more advanced features, let us recall briefly what is going on:

- The OnLineOrderFlag, coming from the SalesOrderHeader table, is a TRUE/FALSE value. PowerPivot found only two possible values for it, so it has been able to fill the combo box of the filter with the values True and False. By choosing True, you selected only the orders placed online.
- The same process happened for the SizeUnitMeasureCode, this time coming from the Product table. It can contain only two distinct values (empty and CM). You have selected CM as the measure unit for the size.
- Placing Color on the rows, Size on the rows, and finally OrderQty as the value, PowerPivot analyzed all the rows containing the value (which is OrderQty, contained in the SalesOrderDetail table). Then it followed the relationship between Order Detail and Products and filtered out all the rows from the detail that do not satisfy the filter condition. In the meantime, it removed all the rows that do not satisfy the condition on the OrderHeader table, which contains the OnlineOrderFlag.
- Having detected the set of rows that you want to analyze, PowerPivot followed the relationship between SalesOrderDetail and Product to find out the color and the size of each product sold, summarized up all the quantities, and displayed the final PivotTable.

Do not worry if the process described here is not perfectly clear; it will become easier to understand as you continue reading, thanks to the many examples we are going to provide. But remember this important point: the presence of relationships is essential for PowerPivot to detect the set of rows it must take into account from the source tables.

**Important** You can easily understand why relationships are an important concept in PowerPivot when you remember this significant difference between PowerPivot and the classic Excel PivotTable: the older tool analyzes only one table and so it does not need to relate it with anything else—its analysis is carried on a single object. On the other hand, PowerPivot can analyze more than one table at a time but to do that, it needs to relate the tables to produce useful results.

In the next chapters, we spend several pages in the analysis of different kinds of relationships and how to master them. Nevertheless, before diving into complex analysis, let us solve some minor problems in this sample report to make it more appealing and a smoother introduction to all of the PowerPivot features.

## Formatting Numbers

Even if the report shown in Figure 2-1 contains interesting information, it has a problem: it lacks a format for numbers. In Excel worksheets, the formatting of numbers is one of the functions of the worksheet itself. So, to format the numbers properly, you select the data area of the report and choose a proper formatting. If you follow this procedure in a PivotTable, the first result is not very appealing, as you can see in Figure 2-2.

| OnlineOrderFlag | True |
|---|---|
| SizeUnitMeasureCode | CM |

| Sum of OrderQty | Column Labels | | | | | | | | | | | | | |
|---|---|---|---|---|---|---|---|---|---|---|---|---|---|---|
| Row Labels | 38 | 40 | 42 | 44 | 46 | 48 | 50 | 52 | 54 | 56 | 58 | 60 | 62 | Grand Total |
| Black | 631.00 | ### | ##### | ##### | ##### | ##### | | ##### | | | ##### | ### | ### | 5,309.00 |
| Blue | | | | 53.00 | ##### | | ### | | ### | | 57.00 | ### | ### | 1,283.00 |
| Red | | | | ##### | | ##### | | ##### | | ### | ##### | ### | ### | 2,719.00 |
| Silver | 802.00 | ### | ##### | 88.00 | ##### | 86.00 | | 48.00 | | | | | | 2,691.00 |
| Yellow | 270.00 | ### | ##### | ##### | ##### | ##### | ### | | ### | | 47.00 | ### | ### | 3,203.00 |
| **Grand Total** | **1,703.00** | **###** | **#####** | **#####** | **#####** | **#####** | **###** | **#####** | **###** | **###** | **#####** | **###** | **###** | **15,205.00** |

**FIGURE 2-2** Wrong display of numbers if format strings are applied to the PivotTable.

Because you applied the formatting after you created the PivotTable, none of the columns were large enough to accommodate the new representation of numbers, which now contain dots and commas, resulting in larger columns. You can solve this easily by resizing all the columns. Nevertheless, if you decide to change the measure displayed and use a different one (for example, ListPrice), you probably need a different format and different column sizes, and you probably have to resize the entire worksheet.

The correct procedure to follow is to use the PivotTable field settings to define a number format for the OrderQty column. To perform this, you can right-click inside a cell containing the OrderQty value and, from the menu, choose Value Field Settings, as you can see in Figure 2-3.

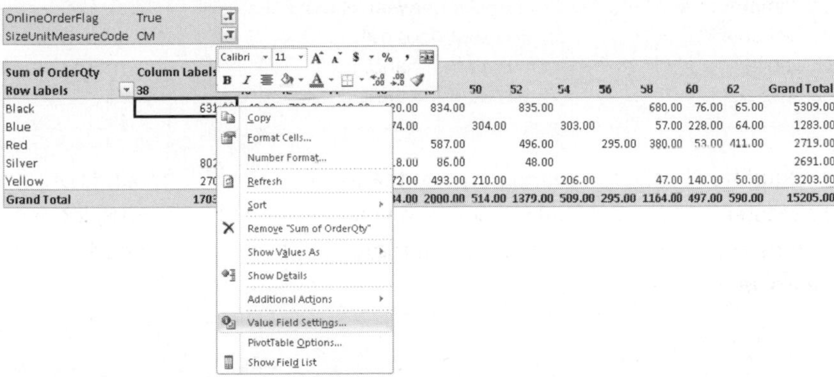


**FIGURE 2-3** The Value Field Settings menu.

This option opens the Value Field Settings dialog box, shown in Figure 2-4, which contains many options. We are interested, for now, only in the number format, which you can view by clicking the Number Format button.

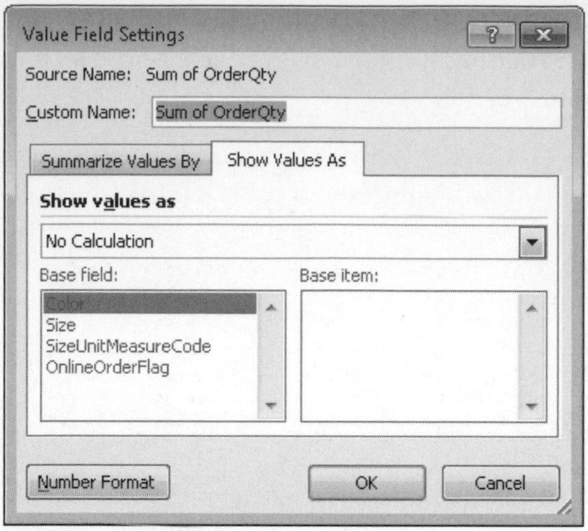

**FIGURE 2-4** The Value Field Settings dialog box.

The Format Cells dialog box (see Figure 2-5) lets you choose a number format for the column in this PivotTable.

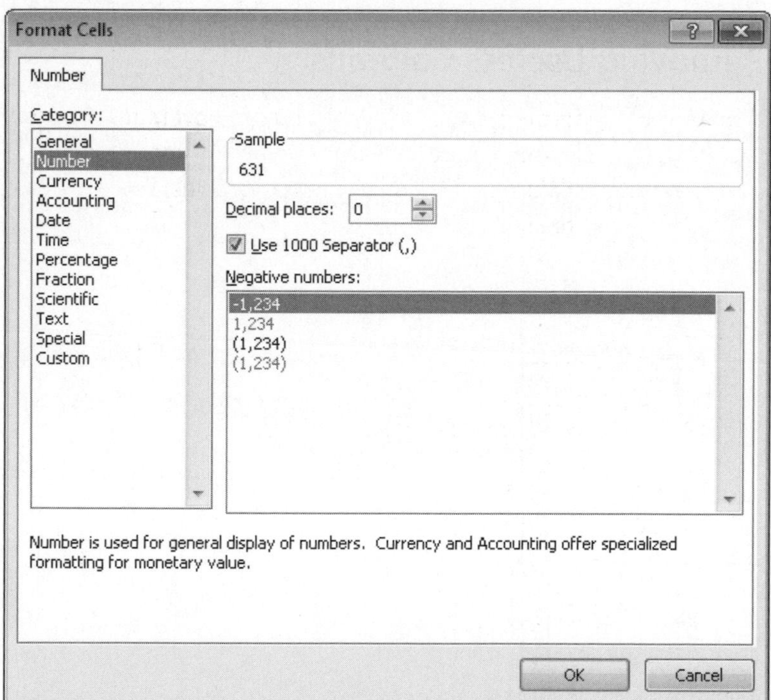


**FIGURE 2-5** The Format Cells dialog box.

When you choose the number format you want (in this case, we have selected a number format with a thousand separator and no decimal places), the PivotTable resizes all the columns automatically, as you can see in Figure 2-6.

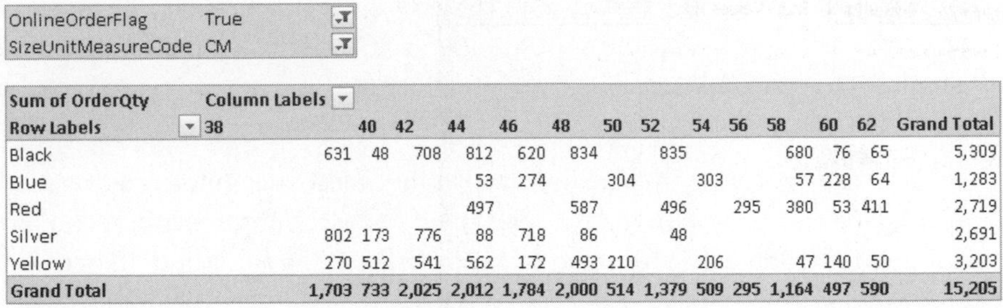

| OnlineOrderFlag | True |
|---|---|
| SizeUnitMeasureCode | CM |

| Sum of OrderQty | Column Labels | | | | | | | | | | | | | |
|---|---|---|---|---|---|---|---|---|---|---|---|---|---|---|
| Row Labels | 38 | 40 | 42 | 44 | 46 | 48 | 50 | 52 | 54 | 56 | 58 | 60 | 62 | Grand Total |
| Black | 631 | 48 | 708 | 812 | 620 | 834 | | 835 | | | 680 | 76 | 65 | 5,309 |
| Blue | | | | 53 | 274 | | 304 | | 303 | | 57 | 228 | 64 | 1,283 |
| Red | | | | 497 | | 587 | | 496 | | 295 | 380 | 53 | 411 | 2,719 |
| Silver | 802 | 173 | 776 | 88 | 718 | 86 | | 48 | | | | | | 2,691 |
| Yellow | 270 | 512 | 541 | 562 | 172 | 493 | 210 | | 206 | | 47 | 140 | 50 | 3,203 |
| **Grand Total** | **1,703** | **733** | **2,025** | **2,012** | **1,784** | **2,000** | **514** | **1,379** | **509** | **295** | **1,164** | **497** | **590** | **15,205** |

**FIGURE 2-6** The PivotTable correctly resized.

This procedure applies number formatting to the current PivotTable only. If the same column is used somewhere else in other PivotTables, your choice in this PivotTable does not affect them.

Please note that, if you change the measure shown, you must repeat the procedure to determine the number format of the new column used.

## Hiding or Removing Useless Columns

In the process of making the report more user-friendly, you can now focus on another small problem: the PowerPivot Field List (see Figure 2-7), from which you choose values to put on rows and columns, shows all the columns of all the PowerPivot tables. You see a large set of columns, many of which are not really useful.

PowerPivot Field List

Choose fields to add to report:

Search

- rowguid
- ModifiedDate
- SalesOrderDetail
  - SalesOrderID
  - SalesOrderDetailID
  - CarrierTrackingNumber
  - OrderQty
  - ProductID
  - SpecialOfferID
  - UnitPrice
  - UnitPriceDiscount
  - LineTotal
  - rowguid
  - ModifiedDate
- SalesOrderHeader

**FIGURE 2-7** The field selector.

Although it is certainly useful to see everything during the process of data discovery, several columns distract us rather than help us. Let us see a couple of examples:

- The column SalesOrderID in SalesOrderDetail is very useful because it makes the relationship between SalesOrderDetail and SalesOrderHeader. Nevertheless, selecting it for reporting purposes produces no useful result. We refer to this kind of column as a technical column—that is, a column mandatory for the data model to work but that has no meaning at all for the reports.
- The columns rowguid and ModifiedDate, in the SalesOrderDetail table, are columns used by the source system that handles the database, but they do not contain any useful information either from the technical or from the reporting point of view. We refer to these columns as useless columns because you can easily remove them without affecting the data model.

**Note** Please note that useless columns are not simply columns that you believe are of no use in the current report. Columns like SpecialOfferID, which is a technical column, contain interesting information that seems not to be useful at a certain point in time. If you plan to use the same source for many reports, you need to think twice before tagging a column as useless and maybe deleting it. But even if you remove a column from the PowerPivot table, you can always reload it later by changing the table properties.

To make the user experience better, you should hide technical columns and remove useless ones so that the names shown in the field selector refer only to columns that can be used in the report to provide useful results. When you remove a column from a table, that column is physically deleted from the PowerPivot data model, is no longer available for any operation, and reduces the memory and disk space taken up by the table. On the other hand, when you hide a column, it still exists in the PowerPivot data model, although the user cannot select it in a report. It is now clear why we choose to hide technical columns (if we remove them, we would not be able to use them for relationship, for instance) and remove useless ones.

To perform this task, you can open the Hide And Unhide Columns dialog box, which you can see in Figure 2-8, from the Design tab on the ribbon of the PowerPivot window. From here, you can choose to hide or show any columns of the table.

If you choose to hide a column in PowerPivot, it does not appear in the PowerPivot tables but is still available in the PowerPivot Field List. This decision might help you achieve a cleaner view of data when you are browsing in the PowerPivot window.

On the other hand, we are not interested in hiding any columns from the PowerPivot window because we want to browse all data. We hide columns only in the PowerPivot Field List.

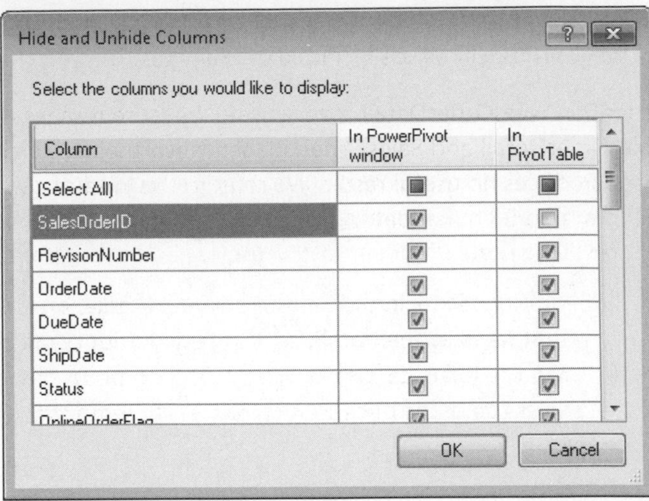


**FIGURE 2-8** Hide and unhide columns.

**Note** As you might have noted, there is no option that allows you to hide a full table. The PowerPivot Field List hides a table if all of its columns are hidden in the PivotTable. Even if hiding a table might seems useless at this point, later on you will discover several data models that contain not only technical columns but technical tables too. For those models, the option to completely hide a table is useful because it lets you hide the complexity of the model when you are browsing data.

After you have hidden technical columns, you still need to delete the useless ones, which are, in our example, the two columns rowguid and ModifiedDate. To do that, you need to select the column in the PowerPivot window and click the Delete button on the Design tab of the ribbon. After you click it, a confirmation message box appears, like the one in Figure 2-9.

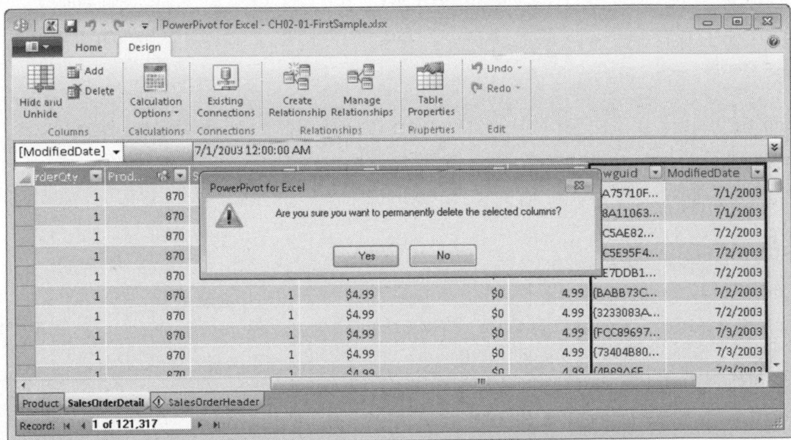


**FIGURE 2-9** When you delete columns, PowerPivot raises a message box.

When you delete a column, it is no longer available for any tasks inside PowerPivot. You can still add it back later, if you edit table properties, but this effort requires that you reload the table, which, for large tables, might be a long process.

You should consider the task to hide and delete technical and useless columns as both a cosmetic and operational change in the PowerPivot functionality. It has some very good impact on the usability of PowerPivot, because fewer columns are available for selection. Moreover, the size of the Excel file is reduced by removing useless data from the tables, speeding up all the operations.

After the cleaning of these columns, the field selector, shown in Figure 2-10, looks much better and user friendly.

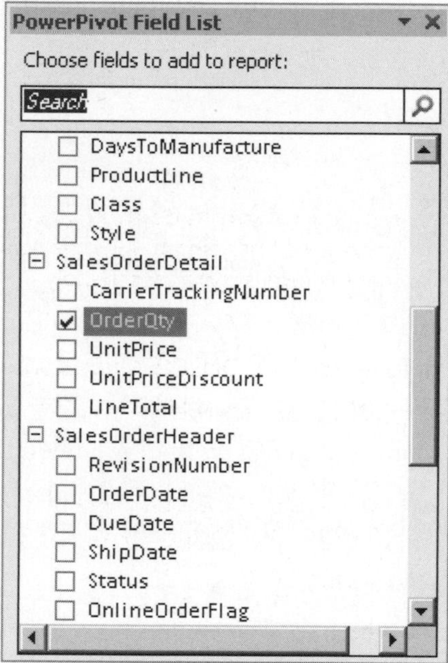


**FIGURE 2-10** The field selector with fewer columns.

## Adding Calculated Columns

Now that you have hidden or deleted unwanted columns, you can continue the work to make the report easier to use and read. You might notice that there are some fields that have a technical meaning and are not easy to understand at a first glance. The OnlineOrderFlag, for example, is one of them. OnlineOrderFlag is a TRUE/FALSE value and, even if it is pretty understandable by itself, it does not look very nice if used in reports. Take a look, for example, at the report in Figure 2-11, where we simply removed the OnlineOrderFlag from the filter of the report and added it to the rows.

SizeUnitMeasureCode CM

| Sum of OrderQty | Column Labels | | | | | | | | | | | | | |
|---|---|---|---|---|---|---|---|---|---|---|---|---|---|---|
| Row Labels | 38 | 40 | 42 | 44 | 46 | 48 | 50 | 52 | 54 | 56 | 58 | 60 | 62 | Grand Total |
| **False** | **11,126** | **5,989** | **10,737** | **16,221** | **6,527** | **14,920** | **3,387** | **9,391** | **3,743** | **369** | **6,410** | **8,122** | **5,220** | **102,162** |
| Black | 4,885 | 1,086 | 4,582 | 6,299 | 1,491 | 6,254 | | 5,886 | | | 3,933 | 1,153 | 579 | 36,148 |
| Blue | | | | 264 | 1,380 | | 1,948 | | 2,559 | | 429 | 2,083 | 232 | 8,895 |
| Red | | | | 4,912 | | 3,792 | | 2,613 | | 369 | 1,766 | 3,525 | 3,267 | 20,244 |
| Silver | 3,872 | 2,235 | 4,503 | 1,265 | 2,736 | 1,093 | | 892 | | | | | | 16,596 |
| Yellow | 2,369 | 2,668 | 1,652 | 3,481 | 920 | 3,781 | 1,439 | | 1,184 | | 282 | 1,361 | 1,142 | 20,279 |
| **True** | **1,703** | **733** | **2,025** | **2,012** | **1,784** | **2,000** | **514** | **1,379** | **509** | **295** | **1,164** | **497** | **590** | **15,205** |
| Black | 631 | 48 | 708 | 812 | 620 | 834 | | 835 | | | 680 | 76 | 65 | 5,309 |
| Blue | | | | 53 | 274 | | 304 | | 303 | | 57 | 228 | 64 | 1,283 |
| Red | | | | 497 | | 587 | | 496 | | 295 | 380 | 53 | 411 | 2,719 |
| Silver | 802 | 173 | 776 | 88 | 718 | 86 | | 48 | | | | | | 2,691 |
| Yellow | 270 | 512 | 541 | 562 | 172 | 493 | 210 | | 206 | | 47 | 140 | 50 | 3,203 |
| **Grand Total** | **12,829** | **6,722** | **12,762** | **18,233** | **8,311** | **16,920** | **3,901** | **10,770** | **4,252** | **664** | **7,574** | **8,619** | **5,810** | **117,367** |

**FIGURE 2-11** The values *True* and *False* are difficult to decode without a description.

Ask yourself this question: What do the labels False and True mean in the report? You can assign a meaning to False only if you remember that its value comes from the OnlineOrderFlag but, in the report itself, there is no clear evidence of the fact that the value True means *The order has been placed online*. Clearly, having a different and more understandable description would greatly improve the report readability.

**Note** Please note that the OnlineOrderFlag is not a technical column. Its description is cryptic, but we definitely want to slice data using this column. So we are not going to hide the column at all. Instead, we will provide it a better description so that the field is more user friendly.

So we are going to describe some standard techniques to show ONLINE ORDER when the value of the column is True and INTERNAL ORDER when the value is False. In order to perform this task, you have two choices:

- You can add a new calculated column to the OrderDetails table, assigning to it a descriptive value for the OnlineOrderFlag. Then you can hide the TRUE/FALSE column and provide only the new column for filtering and slicing.
- You can add a new table to the data model, which has a TRUE/FALSE column as the key and another column that holds the description. Then you can create a relationship between OrderDetails and this new table to let PowerPivot slice the original data with this new table.

Both these operations deal with a much wider topic—*data modeling*. Because they are both interesting and instructive solutions, we describe both of them, first to get a feeling of what a data model is and also to see how a good data model might affect the user experience. We cover data models in full detail in Chapter 4, "Data Models." Nevertheless, this first look now is useful for understanding data models.

The first option is the easier one. To add a column to the SalesOrderHeader table, you need to provide a name and an expression for it so that PowerPivot knows how to select that column and how to compute its values. To add a new column, you need to select the Add Column button on the Design tab of the PowerPivot ribbon, as you can see in Figure 2-12. This operation moves the cursor to the end of the current table and places the cursor inside the formula editor.

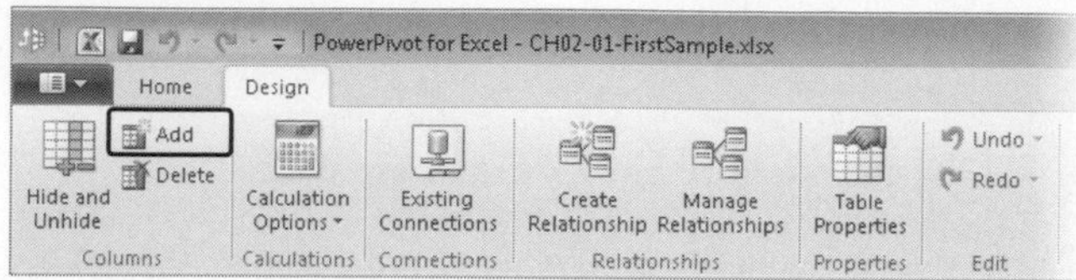


**FIGURE 2-12** The Add button creates a new calculated column.

You can now write the formula for the new column in the formula bar of PowerPivot. The formula bar looks very similar to the formula bar of Excel. Nevertheless, formulas for PowerPivot are very different from formulas in Excel. PowerPivot does not use the Excel formula language. Instead, it uses a new language called DAX, which we introduce in Chapter 3, "Introduction to DAX." But for this simple example, we can ignore the complexities of DAX and enter a simple formula, which is understandable by itself (moreover, it looks similar to Excel) and is shown in Figure 2-13.

**FIGURE 2-13** The formula for the new column, shown in the formula bar.

This code uses the DAX function IF, which looks and works like the IF function in Excel. If the value of the first parameter evaluates to True, it returns its second parameter; otherwise, it returns the third one. In other words, if the OnlineOrderFlag is true, the formula returns ONLINE ORDER; otherwise, its value is INTERNAL ORDER.

The newly added column has been named CalculatedColumn1 by PowerPivot, which is not really user friendly. To rename the column, it is enough to select the column, right-click the column name, and choose Rename from the menu, as you can see in Figure 2-14. You can choose, for example, to name it OrderType.

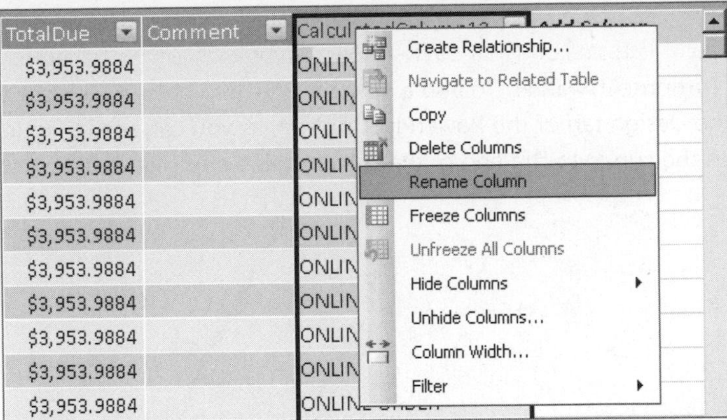


**FIGURE 2-14** The Rename Column option of the column menu, available with a right-click.

In Figure 2-15, you can see the final result, showing both the new column and the formula bar for the calculated column.

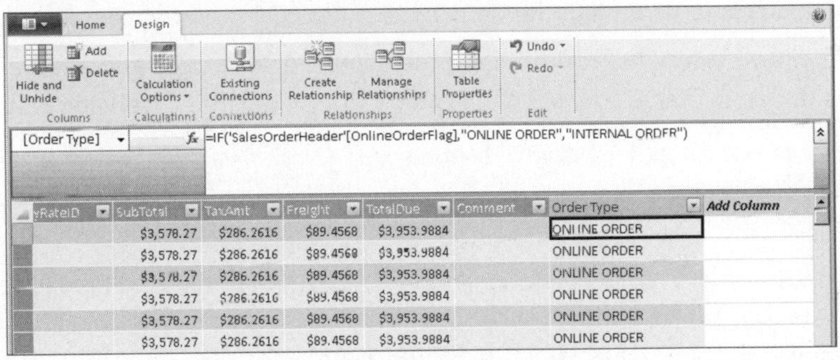

**FIGURE 2-15** The formula bar with the calculated column.

Now that you have a good description of the order type, you can safely hide the column OnlineOrderFlag, which now has become a technical column. (It contains a value needed to compute the description, but you want to browse and slice data using the description defined in the new Order Type column and not the original value.) After you do that, you can use the new OrderType field in a PivotTable, and the result looks like Figure 2-16.

SizeUnitMeasureCode CM

| Sum of OrderQty | Column Labels | | | | | | | | | | | | | |
|---|---|---|---|---|---|---|---|---|---|---|---|---|---|---|
| Row Labels | 38 | 40 | 42 | 44 | 46 | 48 | 50 | 52 | 54 | 56 | 58 | 60 | 62 | Grand Total |
| **INTERNAL ORDER** | **11,126** | **5,989** | **10,737** | **16,221** | **6,527** | **14,920** | **3,387** | **9,391** | **3,743** | **369** | **6,410** | **8,122** | **5,220** | **102,162** |
| Black | 4,885 | 1,086 | 4,582 | 6,299 | 1,491 | 6,254 | | 5,886 | | | 3,933 | 1,153 | 579 | 36,148 |
| Blue | | | | 264 | 1,380 | | 1,948 | | 2,559 | | 429 | 2,083 | 232 | 8,895 |
| Red | | | | 4,912 | | 3,792 | | 2,613 | | 369 | 1,766 | 3,525 | 3,267 | 20,244 |
| Silver | 3,872 | 2,235 | 4,503 | 1,265 | 2,736 | 1,093 | | 892 | | | | | | 16,596 |
| Yellow | 2,369 | 2,668 | 1,652 | 3,481 | 920 | 3,781 | 1,439 | | 1,184 | | 282 | 1,361 | 1,142 | 20,279 |
| **ONLINE ORDER** | **1,703** | **733** | **2,025** | **2,012** | **1,784** | **2,000** | **514** | **1,379** | **509** | **295** | **1,164** | **497** | **590** | **15,205** |
| Black | 631 | 48 | 708 | 812 | 620 | 834 | | 835 | | | 680 | 76 | 65 | 5,309 |
| Blue | | | | 53 | 274 | | 304 | | 303 | | 57 | 228 | 64 | 1,283 |
| Red | | | | 497 | | 587 | | 496 | | 295 | 380 | 53 | 411 | 2,719 |
| Silver | 802 | 173 | 776 | 88 | 718 | 86 | | 48 | | | | | | 2,691 |
| Yellow | 270 | 512 | 541 | 562 | 172 | 493 | 210 | | 206 | | 47 | 140 | 50 | 3,203 |
| **Grand Total** | **12,829** | **6,722** | **12,762** | **18,233** | **8,311** | **16,920** | **3,901** | **10,770** | **4,252** | **664** | **7,574** | **8,619** | **5,810** | **117,367** |

**FIGURE 2-16** Sample report with OnlineOrderFlag decoded.

You can see that no value has changed but the report is now easier to understand because you have a clear knowledge of the meaning of the rows. In other words, the values are now self-explanatory, so the report is easier to use.

**Important** Whenever you create a PowerPivot workbook, you need to remember that textual descriptions of columns are always much easier to understand when compared to the underlying code. It is a bad idea to use code inside PivotTables because it makes the final PivotTable harder to use.

After you delete useless and hidden technical columns, you normally need to decode some columns and create new ones with better descriptions. Then you need to hide the original columns to allow users to choose only among self-describing columns.

We do not want, at this point, to investigate further how to define more complex columns because this first technique is straightforward. We prefer to spend some time showing a different solution to the same issue, which is to create a new related table. This second technique is interesting to study because, in developing it, you are going to change the data model, something you should learn as soon as possible.

There is no table in the database that provides a description for the OnlineOrderFlag, so you need to create an Excel worksheet that contains the table and then make PowerPivot aware of this new information. To create the table, simply type in an Excel worksheet the information (see Figure 2-17) and then, after having selected the six cells, choose Format As Table on the Home tab of the Excel ribbon. You can find the example in the workbook CH02-02-Related.xlsx in the companion content.

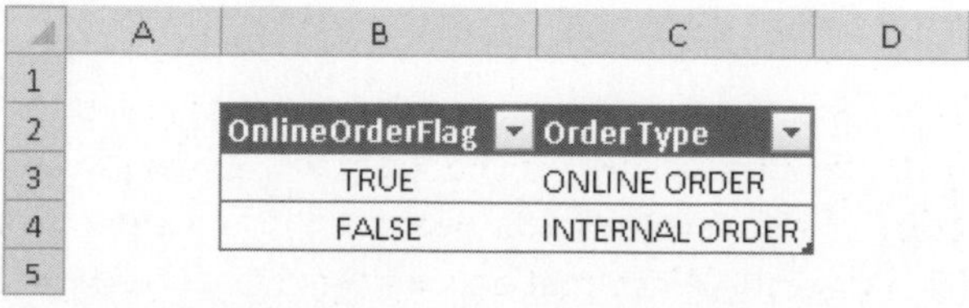

| | A | B | C | D |
|---|---|---|---|---|
| 1 | | | | |
| 2 | | OnlineOrderFlag | Order Type | |
| 3 | | TRUE | ONLINE ORDER | |
| 4 | | FALSE | INTERNAL ORDER | |
| 5 | | | | |

**FIGURE 2-17** Decoding table for the OnlineOrderFlag.

Now that you have an Excel table, all you need to do is to let PowerPivot know of its existence. From the PowerPivot tab on the Excel ribbon, choose the Create Linked Table button with the cursor inside the table (see Figure 2-18). Please note that, if the cursor is not in the table, you need to manually provide the table boundaries, a tedious task that PowerPivot carries out for you if the cursor is inside the table.

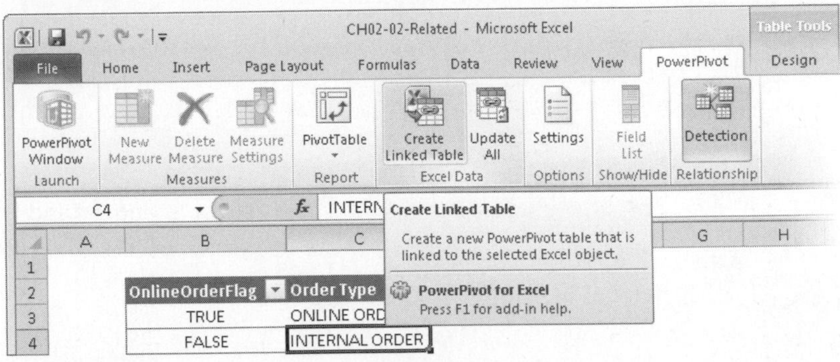


**FIGURE 2-18** The Create Linked Table command imports an Excel table inside PowerPivot.

This operation opens the PowerPivot window in which you can see your Excel table exactly as if it were a standard imported table. The only difference is in the small chain before its name, indicating that this is an Excel linked table and not an imported one. The table can be renamed a more appropriate name if you need to do that—for example, you can rename it SalesOrderHeader_OnlineOrderFlag. You can see this in Figure 2-19.

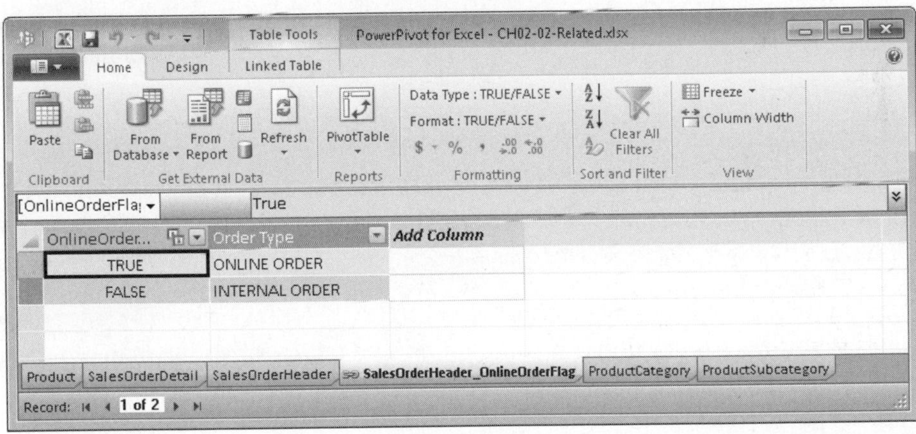


**FIGURE 2-19** The decoding table imported in PowerPivot.

Maybe the power of what we are doing is not immediately evident, so it is worth spending some words on it. We are mixing, in the same PowerPivot model, tables coming from a SQL database with an ad-hoc table created in Excel to suit our needs. In other words, we are extending the existing model with our personal information. This simple fact helps us build complex and interesting data models.

The only missing point is a relationship between the SalesOrderHeader and this new table. To create the relationship, you need to go to the SalesOrderHeader table, choose the column OnlineOrderFlag, and click the Create Relationship button on the Design tab of the ribbon. This action opens a dialog box in which you describe the relationship. It should look like Figure 2-20.

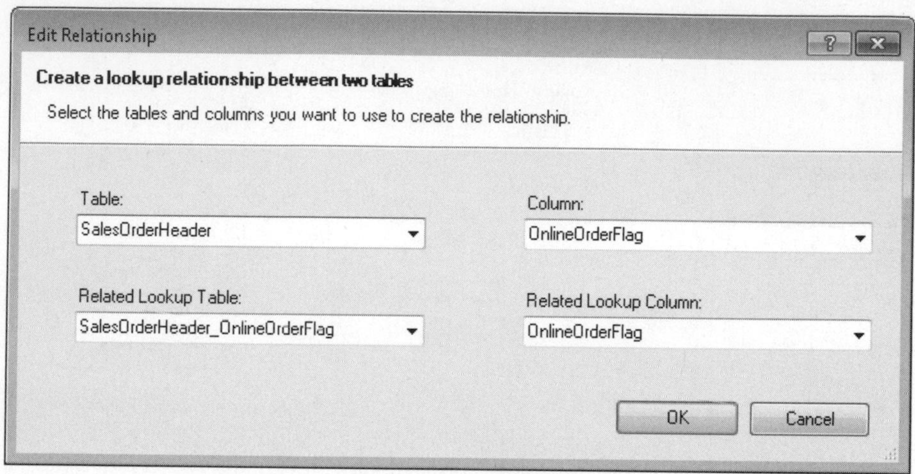


**FIGURE 2-20** Definition of the relationship with the decoding table in PowerPivot.

In Figure 2-20, you are stating that the OnlineOrderFlag in the SalesOrderHeader table is related to the column OnlineOrderFlag in the SalesOrderHeader_OnlineOrderFlag table. Because the related columns have the same type (a TRUE/FALSE value), the relationship can be created. Clicking Create is enough to make PowerPivot analyze data and create the relationship.

## Lookup Tables

This kind of table, which contains keys and values describing them, is normally called a *Lookup Table* because it allows you to give a name to a code by looking up the code in the table.

Lookup tables are very similar to the Excel VLOOKUP functions. If, in a standard Excel worksheet, we want to provide a description to a particular code, we might use a VLOOKUP function in a cell that refers to a decoding area. Lookup relationships work much the same way even if, with PowerPivot, we use relationships to create much more complex models.

Now that you have completed the creation of a linked table and defined the relationship with this new table, it is time to return to the PivotTable and click the Refresh button to see what has changed (see Figure 2-21).

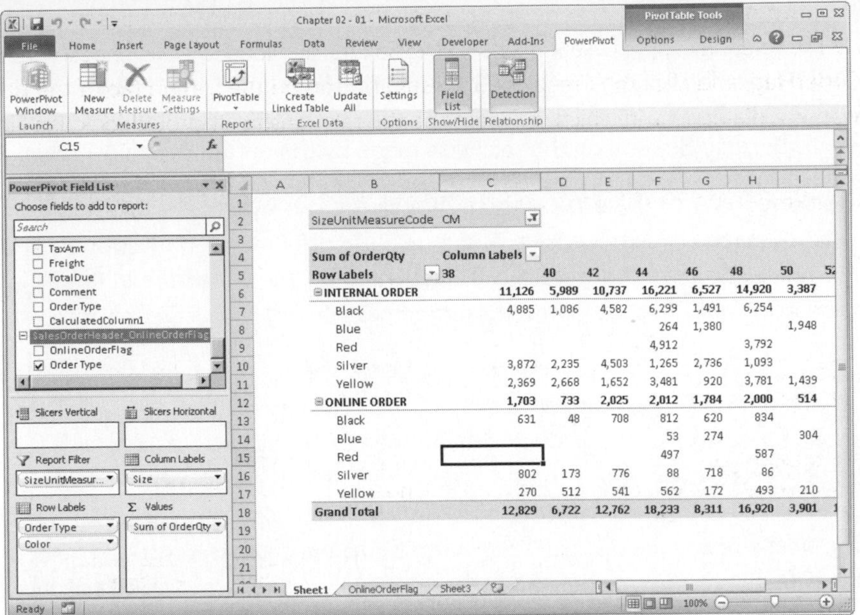

**FIGURE 2-21** The new decoding table in the PowerPivot selector.

You now see a new table inside the Field List, named SalesOrderHeader_OnlineOrderFlag, with two columns (one of which is a technical one that you should hide later). The Order Type column in this new table does the same task that was accomplished by the Order Type in the SalesOrderHeader table. The difference now is that it is much easier to change the descriptions because they are not hard-coded in a DAX formula but contained in a table hosted inside the Excel workbook. This means that changing the descriptions is now a simple task for anyone, and no one has to understand what is going on with the code.

Let us stop for a few seconds and think about what you have done.

- You have been able to mix different sources of data into a single coherent view of information, shaping the data model to make it fit your needs.
- You have provided your users (and yourself) an easy way to give descriptions to technical values, making the process of browsing the PivotTable and producing reports more intuitive.
- You created your first piece of a data model—that is, a model of data that describes the entities you intend to browse.

The only drawback of this solution is that, if many fields require a lookup table, the field selector of the PivotTable might become a little messy because too many tables start to appear inside it. Luckily, there is a simple solution to this: you can use the RELATED function in DAX, something you are going to learn later in this chapter.

## Adding Measures

Even if you can perform many interesting calculations working at the row level of the tables, some calculations cannot be defined at this level because they depend on the query context. (In other words, they depend on the selection made by the user in the PivotTable.)

You will explore many of these calculations later in this book (see Chapters 3, 6, 7, and 8), and to do that, you need to learn the DAX language. But right now we want to show you a simple example of the differences between a calculated column and a measure in PowerPivot. We also briefly investigate why measures are sometimes needed.

You are going to implement a column that calculates the distinct count of products sold. A *distinct count* computes the number of distinct values of a specific column and is very useful, for example, for customers or products that happen to appear several times inside a table such as SalesOrderDetails. This formula cannot be computed at the row level because, for each sale, its value is 1 (one product sold) while, for many sales, its value is not the sum of all the values at the row level. Instead, it needs to be computed based on user selection. Such types of calculation cannot be defined at the row level, so they are called *measures* and need to be defined at the PivotTable level.

To create a new measure, we need to right-click the PowerPivot Field List and choose Add New Measure as in Figure 2-22. You can find this example in the companion file CH02-03-Measures.xlsx.

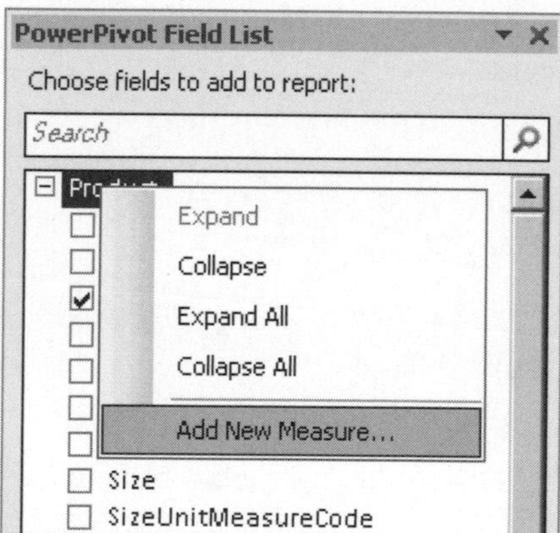


**FIGURE 2-22** The context menu with which you add a new measure to the PowerPivot model underlying the PivotTable.

At this point, a new dialog box appears (see Figure 2-23) in which you need to provide the new measure properties. Type a name for the new measure—say, **DistinctProducts,** and then you need to write the DAX formula that calculates the value.

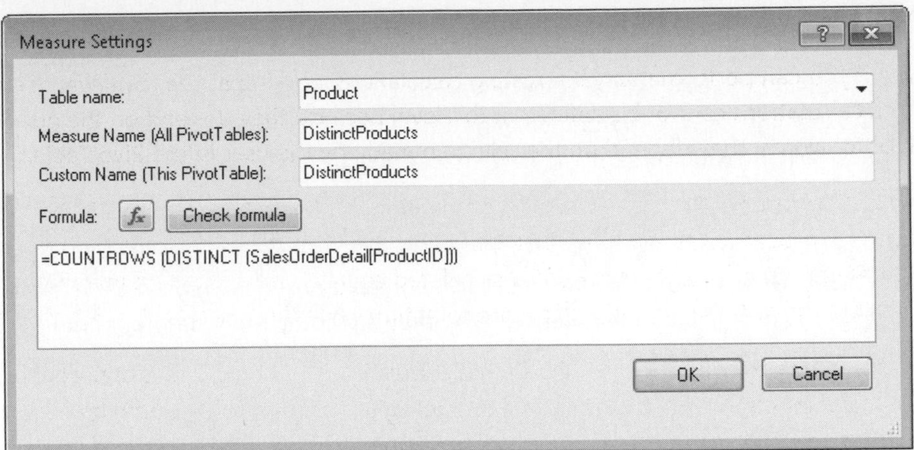


**FIGURE 2-23** The dialog box in which you add a new measure to the PowerPivot model.

Although easy to read, the DAX formula actually hides much of the power of DAX. We are not interested in understanding now the details of how it works. Let us just take a look at it:

```
COUNTROWS (DISTINCT (SalesOrderDetail[ProductID]))
```

You can read it as "count the number of rows that are in a table containing only the distinct values of the column ProductID of the table SalesOrderDetail". To compute the value of this measure, PowerPivot makes the calculation in the context defined by the PivotTable query and provides the correct distinct count of products for each cell of the PivotTable. For example, you can produce an interesting report like the one in Figure 2-24, which computes the number of distinct products sold, slicing data by color.

| DistinctProducts | Column Labels | | |
|---|---|---|---|
| **Row Labels** | **INTERNAL ORDER** | **ONLINE ORDER** | **Grand Total** |
| | 28 | 18 | 42 |
| Black | 79 | 33 | 79 |
| Blue | 26 | 17 | 26 |
| Multi | 7 | 5 | 8 |
| Red | 31 | 16 | 31 |
| Silver | 35 | 17 | 35 |
| Silver/Black | 7 | | 7 |
| White | 4 | 2 | 4 |
| Yellow | 33 | 22 | 34 |
| **Grand Total** | **250** | **130** | **266** |

**FIGURE 2-24** Query of the distinct products.

As you can see, for each cell there is a calculation of the number of unique products sold. Moreover, it is worth noting that the aggregation of distinct count is not the sum. If you look, for example, at the row for the color Yellow, we have sold 33 distinct products with internal orders, 22 online, but the grand total of distinct products is 34. In other words, out of 34 yellow products sold, 22 were sold online, 33 were sold directly, and only one of them has been sold online and not directly, thus giving you the grand total of 34. This might seems confusing at first glance, but it is indeed the correct behavior to expect when you are using distinct counts.

From the PivotTable point of view, measures and columns look very similar even if, for what concerns the internal engine of PowerPivot, they are completely different items. Starting in Chapter 3, you begin to learn the DAX language and the exact difference between calculated columns and measures.

## Adding More Tables

All the reports shown up to now relied on three tables only, and they already have shown some interesting data. Nevertheless, the AdventureWorks database contains a lot of other tables that you can add to the PowerPivot data model to improve reporting. You might have noticed, for example, that the Products table contains a ProductSubcategoryID. This column is a key in the ProductSubcategory table, which we have not loaded yet. It happens, in turn, that the ProductSubcategory table contains a key, called ProductCategoryID, which relates to the ProductCategory table. This chain of relationships lets us retrieve the product category, by means of walking two steps, from a product to its subcategory and then from the subcategory to its category.

Graphically, the relationship can be seen in Figure 2-25.

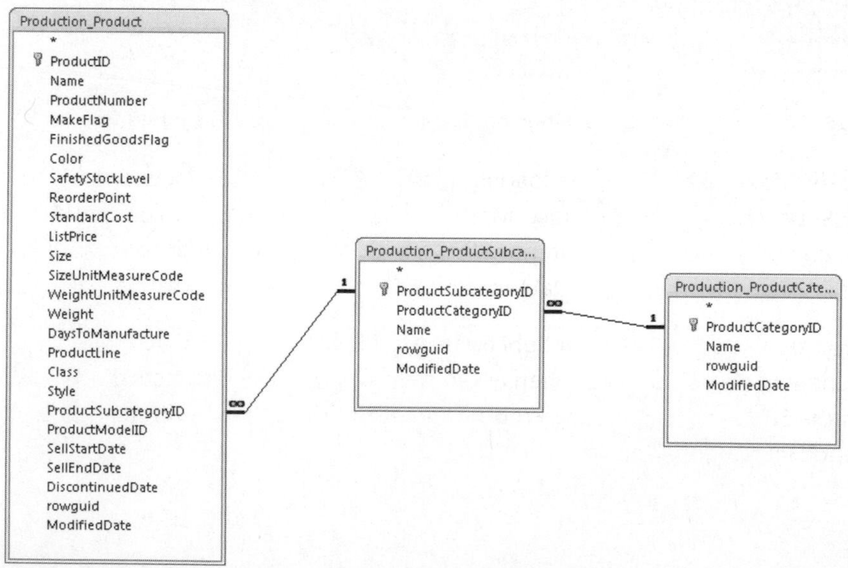


**FIGURE 2-25** The chained (or cascading) relationship between three tables.

These kinds of relationships, which appear very often in the database world, are called *chained relationships* because they form a chain that you can follow from the beginning to the end to relate many tables.

**Note** Please note a curious phenomenon that often appears in the world of databases. Even if we plan to slice data by category first, then by subcategory, and finally by products, following a very natural path, in reality the chain of the relationships is reversed, starting from the more detailed table and going into the less detailed one. This is absolutely normal—it concerns how data is modeled in relational databases. Throughout the book, we discover many other relationships that need to be read in this reversed way.

To make PowerPivot allow you to slice data with the columns of these new tables, you need to import them into your data model. To do that, it is enough to repeat the loading process you did before to import the first three tables. This time, instead of using the From Database button, you should use the Existing Connections button, which is located on the Design tab of the PowerPivot ribbon, as you can see in Figure 2-26. You can do this because the connection to the database has been already saved inside the Excel workbook and you can now use it to import all the useful tables without needing to create a new connection. You can find this example, with the tables already loaded, in the workbook CH02-04-NewTables.xlsx.

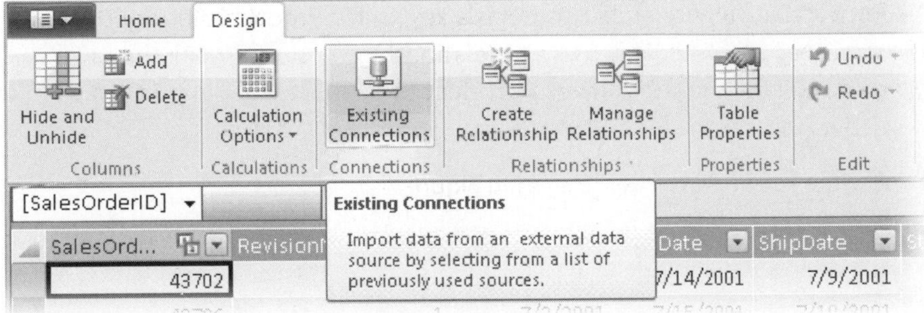


**FIGURE 2-26** The Existing Connection button opens a connection to a previously used database.

You already know that during the loading process PowerPivot detects the relationship between Subcategory and Category. Moreover, you also know that you need to hide technical columns (ProductSubcategoryID, ProductCategoryID) and to remove the useless ones (rowguid and UpdatedDate in both tables) to create a clean data model.

Now, if you try to add Category or Subcategory to the PivotTable, PowerPivot detects the need for new relationships and, when asked to, it automatically detects the relationship between the SubcategoryID in the Products table and the column with the same name in the ProductSubcategory one.

**Note** You might wonder why PowerPivot is so good at finding relationships during the loading of tables and did not detect the relationship between Product and ProductSubcategory, even if this relationship is already stored in the database metadata. The reason is that, during loading of data, PowerPivot searches for relationships among the tables it is currently loading, ignoring tables that are already present in the PowerPivot data model. These other relationships (between existing and new tables) need to be detected later, through the relationship-detection algorithm.

Now that you have empowered the PowerPivot data model with these two tables, you easily can produce complex reports like the one shown in Figure 2-27, in which we mix columns from products, categories, subcategories and orders, letting PowerPivot resolve the complex relationships that make the browsing process possible.

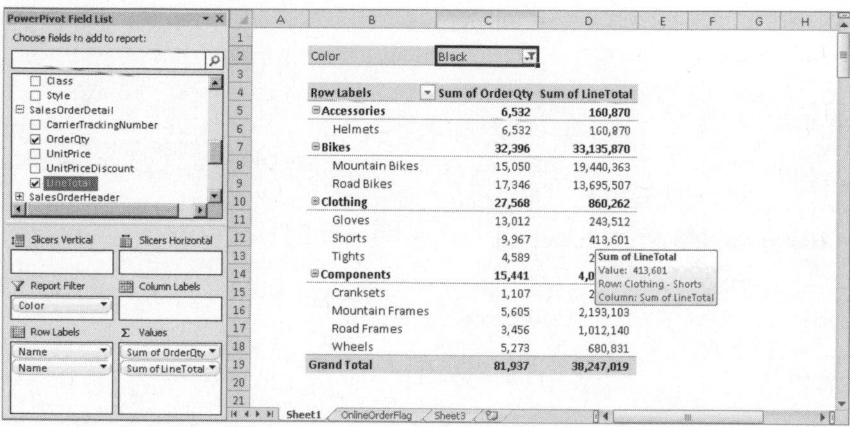


**FIGURE 2-27** Sample report with categories and subcategories.

The report, as it looks now, is quite nice. Nevertheless, because you are surely striving for perfection, you notice a couple of small issues:

- Both tables (ProductCategory and ProductSubcategory) have the same description for the column name, as you can see in the Row Labels list in Figure 2-27. This is not very user friendly because it is hard to understand whether you correctly put subcategory under category or vice versa (apart, clearly, from the rule of common sense as soon as you see wrong data).
- ProductCategory and ProductSubcategory are separated from the Products table, even if they are strictly related to products. In a small pivot table like this one, this is not a big issue. However, as the data model gets larger, you should try to reduce the number of tables shown to the user as much as possible, to make it easier to find the columns. A rule of thumb in the Business Intelligence world dictates that you should never browse more than 15 different tables. If you let tables spread at a speed of one table per lookup, you reach that limit very quickly.

Although the solution of the first point is straightforward (it is enough to change the nan the columns as displayed by PowerPivot in the PowerPivot window), the second one is m more interesting because it lets us introduce a very simple yet powerful DAX formula: RELATED.

You are now going to remove the tables ProductCategory and ProductSubcategory from the field list in the PivotTable editor, replacing them with two new columns in the Product table, named Category and Subcategory. Moreover, in doing this, you will solve both the points stated above.

The problem you need to face is that the original Product table does not contain the textual description of category or subcategory, it only contains the ProductSubcategoryID, which is a technical column used to create the relationship with the ProductSubcategory table. You definitely need a way to create a calculated column in a table that contains the value of a column in another table, following a relationship. This is exactly what the RELATED function has been built for.

The RELATED function returns the value of a column from another table if it has a valid relationship with the current one. You can define two new columns inside the Product table using these formulas, as shown in Table 2-1.

**TABLE 2-1 Using the RELATED function.**

| Column | Formula |
| --- | --- |
| SubCategory | =RELATED (ProductSubcategory[Name]) |
| Category | =RELATED (ProductCategory[Name]) |

The SubCategory calculated column contains the value of the Name column in the ProductSubcategory table, while the Category calculated column contains the name of the category, taken from the ProductCategory table.

**Note** We do not need to worry about the fact that the relationship between Products and ProductCategory is a chained one, which makes it necessary for PowerPivot to follow two relationship steps to gather the correct category value. PowerPivot already knows about the existence of chained relationships and handles this complexity by itself.

This simple definition leads to a much better user experience because now you see two new columns inside the Products table that hold the value of the category and subcategory. So you can safely hide all the columns in the lookup tables (which, in turn, makes both tables disappear from the field list). The report looks like the one in Figure 2-28.

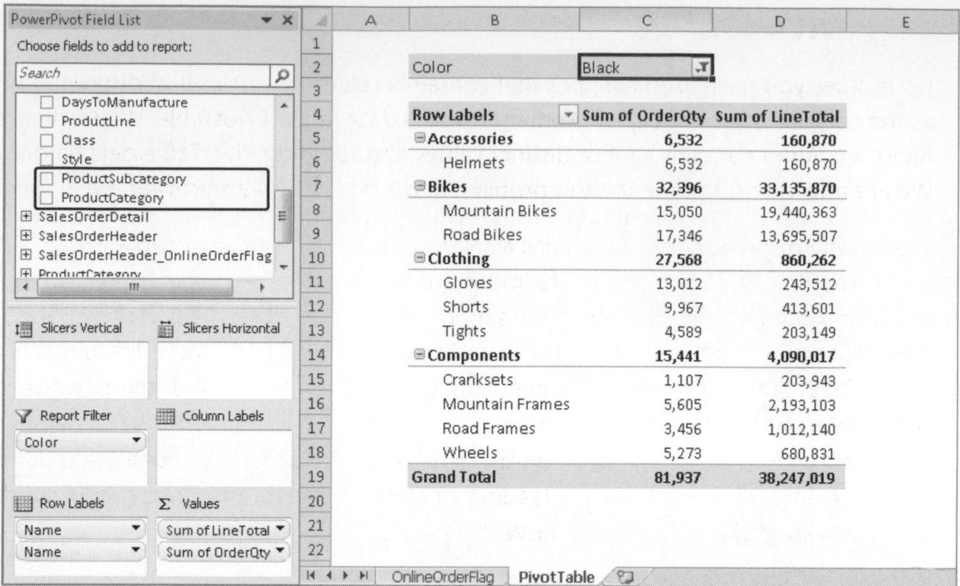


**FIGURE 2-28** Sample report with categories and subcategories tied to the product.

Although this might seem a simple enhancement, it is a very important one because it lets us introduce the concept of Data Modeling, to which we are going to dedicate the whole of Chapter 4. The user queries the Data Model, and the simpler it is, the better will be his experience. One of the most complex abilities of a data modeler is to create models that, even if complex in their implementation, look very easy to the end user.

**Note** Even if the original data model of AdventureWorks has two distinct tables for category and subcategory (which is the right choice for a standard database system), the data model is much easier to query if you hide these two tables and transform their content into columns inside the Product table, which is exactly what you have done. By modifying the data model, you have reduced the number of tables shown to the user and given a meaningful name to the columns.

The two tables still exist in the data model, but they are hidden from the user, who can have access to their values through the new computed columns. This is the first sample situation in which you use an internal data model while showing a different one to the user. You will get acquainted with this technique because we use it throughout the book.

An interesting exercise, which we leave to you to try, is to use the RELATED function to remove the technical table we previously used to give a description of the online order flag. The technique is exactly the same one you used in this section and the exercise gives you greater confidence using the RELATED function. Moreover, you should use the same technique whenever the purpose of a table is to provide lookup values and that table is not a part of the data model you want to show to the user.

## Working with Dates

Up to now, you have used columns that contain a relatively small set of distinct values, such as the color or the category of products, to slice data in the PivotTable. When, on the other hand, a column contains a lot of distinct values, the resulting PivotTable gets harder to use. We are now going to describe this problem in greater detail and provide a solution for it.

The SalesOrderHeader table contains a column, OrderDate, which records the date of the order. The details in this column are important but, for the purpose of reporting, the column contains too much information. If you simply put the OrderDate data in columns, you end up with a report that contains all the information you need but is very difficult to read (see Figure 2-29) because of the high fragmentation of values. In technical terms, we say that the order date column is not a good aggregator because it does not let us focus on interesting information. A good aggregator, on the other hand, groups together a huge number of distinct elements of information, leading to interesting results. You can find this example in the workbook CH02-05-WorkingWithDates.xlsx.

| Color | Black |
|---|---|

| Sum of OrderQty | Column Labels | | | | | | | | | | | |
|---|---|---|---|---|---|---|---|---|---|---|---|---|
| Row Labels | 7/1/2001 | 7/2/2001 | 7/5/2001 | 7/7/2001 | 7/8/2001 | 7/9/2001 | 7/15/2001 | 7/18/2001 | 7/22/2001 | 7/23/2001 | 7/27/2001 | 7/28/ |
| ⊟Accessories | 27 | | | | | | | | | | | |
| Helmets | 27 | | | | | | | | | | | |
| ⊟Bikes | 165 | 1 | 1 | 1 | 1 | 1 | 2 | 1 | 2 | 1 | 2 | |
| Mountain Bikes | 81 | 1 | | | | 1 | 1 | 1 | 2 | | 2 | |
| Road Bikes | 84 | | 1 | 1 | 1 | | 1 | | | 1 | | |
| ⊟Clothing | | | | | | | | | | | | |
| Gloves | | | | | | | | | | | | |
| Shorts | | | | | | | | | | | | |
| Tights | | | | | | | | | | | | |
| Grand Total | 192 | 1 | 1 | 1 | 1 | 1 | 2 | 1 | 2 | 1 | 2 | |

**FIGURE 2-29** Date columns are not good aggregators; the report is sparse.

As you can see, browsing information at the date level produces a sparse report. A much better aggregator would be the year or the month level. Both of those aggregators greatly reduce the fragmentation of the report and result in a better understanding of the data.

PowerPivot can aggregate data, but to do that, it needs columns. So you need to add new columns to the SalesOrderHeader table that contains the year and to the table that contains the month of the order. Aggregating for these columns produces the result you want.

**Note** As you can see, we are shifting our concern from the problem of the sparse report to that of adding new calculated columns, and because we already know how to add new calculated columns, we are now finding our way to the solution of our problem.

You can add two new calculated columns to the SalesOrderHeader table in the PowerPivot window, following the already described procedure, and use Table 2-2 to get the formulas.

**TABLE 2-2 Using the date/time functions.**

| Column | Formula |
|---|---|
| Order Year | =YEAR (SalesOrderHeader[OrderDate]) |
| Order Month | =MONTH (SalesOrderHeader[OrderDate]) |

You are using two DAX functions: YEAR and MONTH, which, as their name suggests, return the year and the month of the date they receive as the parameter. Now you have two new columns that let you slice the data by year and month. You can use these columns to produce interesting reports, like the one in Figure 2-30, which aggregates at the year level.

| Color | Black |
|---|---|

| Sum of OrderQty | Column Labels | | | | |
|---|---|---|---|---|---|
| **Row Labels** | **2001** | **2002** | **2003** | **2004** | **Grand Total** |
| **Accessories** | **331** | **1,279** | **2,858** | **2,064** | **6,532** |
| Helmets | 331 | 1,279 | 2,858 | 2,064 | 6,532 |
| **Bikes** | **2,361** | **10,507** | **13,380** | **6,148** | **32,396** |
| Mountain Bikes | 1,286 | 4,824 | 6,120 | 2,820 | 15,050 |
| Road Bikes | 1,075 | 5,683 | 7,260 | 3,328 | 17,346 |
| **Clothing** | | **8,722** | **13,398** | **5,448** | **27,568** |
| Gloves | | 4,552 | 6,450 | 2,010 | 13,012 |
| Shorts | | 1,378 | 5,157 | 3,432 | 9,967 |
| Tights | | 2,792 | 1,791 | 6 | 4,589 |
| **Grand Total** | **2,692** | **20,508** | **29,636** | **13,660** | **66,496** |

**FIGURE 2-30** Aggregating by year produces more interesting reports.

Or combining month and years, you can produce the report shown in Figure 2-31.

| Color | Black |
|---|---|

| Sum of OrderQty | Column Labels | | | | |
|---|---|---|---|---|---|
| **Row Labels** | **2001** | **2002** | **2003** | **2004** | **Grand Total** |
| 1 | | 281 | 1,746 | 1,774 | 3,801 |
| 2 | | 633 | 2,777 | 2,316 | 5,726 |
| 3 | | 529 | 2,052 | 2,259 | 4,840 |
| 4 | | 379 | 2,888 | 2,519 | 5,786 |
| 5 | | 851 | 4,179 | 3,095 | 8,125 |
| 6 | | 681 | 3,212 | 3,105 | 6,998 |
| 7 | 246 | 3,830 | 2,560 | 221 | 6,857 |
| 8 | 616 | 5,437 | 4,026 | | 10,079 |
| 9 | 442 | 4,467 | 3,910 | | 8,819 |
| 10 | 386 | 2,856 | 2,446 | | 5,688 |
| 11 | 874 | 4,118 | 3,089 | | 8,081 |
| 12 | 658 | 3,277 | 3,202 | | 7,137 |
| **Grand Total** | **3,222** | **27,339** | **36,087** | **15,289** | **81,937** |

**FIGURE 2-31** Combining years and months on the same report.

You might have noticed that the report shows the numbers of the months and not their names, which surely needs to be fixed. In Chapter 7, "Date Calculations in DAX," where we cover date handling in much more detail, you learn how to show the month names. Nevertheless, faster help comes in Chapter 3, where you find a "Date and Time Functions" section with a list of the functions available to you for manipulating dates. You also find in Chapter 3 a simple formula for getting both the number and the name of a month from a date.

The technique of adding more columns to the table to produce aggregates when the data inside the table is too detailed is frequently used with dates. Moreover, dates are so important a topic in the BI analysis that we will spend all of Chapter 7 on it. That said, there are many columns that are not good aggregators. For example, in Chapter 10, "PowerPivot Data Model Patterns," you see a complete banding system that performs aggregations by price bands and, as you will learn, the technique is similar to the one we just used: whenever a column is not a good aggregator, you need to add new columns that group more data so that aggregated values get interesting.

# Refreshing Data

Now that we have scratched the surface of some of the many PowerPivot features, it is time to understand what happens to your reports when the underlying data changes, something that happens rapidly because of the normal life cycle of data.

A report is nothing but an Excel file with a PivotTable that queries data and provides interesting results. Our current model is already a good source that produces nice reports like the one in Figure 2-32. As you might notice, we used the date year and month in columns, so we can expect this report to change over time.

| Color | Black |
|---|---|

| Sum of LineTotal | Column Labels | | | | | | | | | | | |
|---|---|---|---|---|---|---|---|---|---|---|---|---|
| | ⊞2001 | ⊞2002 | ⊞2003 | ⊟2004 | | | | | | | 2004 Total | Grand Total |
| Row Labels | | | | 1 | 2 | 3 | 4 | 5 | 6 | 7 | | |
| **⊟INTERNAL ORDER** | **2,847,408** | **8,833,401** | **9,789,576** | **434,321** | **717,503** | **636,374** | **536,587** | **768,124** | **755,295** | | **3,848,204** | **25,318,589** |
| **⊟Accessories** | **6,682** | **24,866** | **38,406** | **1,722** | **2,288** | **2,435** | **3,092** | **4,149** | **4,276** | | **17,962** | **87,915** |
| Helmets | 6,682 | 24,866 | 38,406 | 1,722 | 2,288 | 2,435 | 3,092 | 4,149 | 4,276 | | 17,962 | 87,915 |
| **⊟Bikes** | **2,840,727** | **8,547,582** | **9,389,254** | **418,664** | **695,427** | **613,796** | **512,554** | **734,951** | **723,798** | | **3,699,190** | **24,476,753** |
| Mountain Bikes | 2,417,625 | 5,178,278 | 4,977,202 | 224,807 | 339,157 | 346,771 | 264,336 | 382,805 | 429,703 | | 1,987,579 | 14,560,685 |
| Road Bikes | 423,101 | 3,369,304 | 4,412,052 | 193,857 | 356,270 | 267,025 | 248,218 | 352,146 | 294,095 | | 1,711,611 | 9,916,068 |
| **⊟Clothing** | | **260,954** | **361,916** | **13,935** | **19,787** | **20,143** | **20,941** | **29,024** | **27,221** | | **131,052** | **753,921** |
| Gloves | | 88,796 | 102,576 | 2,093 | 1,994 | 1,623 | 3,774 | 3,818 | 3,817 | | 17,119 | 208,491 |
| Shorts | | 49,262 | 179,379 | 11,842 | 17,793 | 18,521 | 16,972 | 25,108 | 23,403 | | 113,640 | 342,281 |
| Tights | | 122,896 | 79,961 | | | | 195 | 97 | | | 292 | 203,149 |
| **⊟ONLINE ORDER** | **345,815** | **1,728,252** | **3,851,091** | **426,666** | **439,629** | **457,998** | **467,241** | **558,343** | **554,213** | **9,164** | **2,913,254** | **8,838,412** |
| **⊟Accessories** | | | **31,176** | **5,248** | **5,983** | **5,773** | **7,243** | **6,963** | **7,313** | **3,254** | **41,778** | **72,954** |
| Helmets | | | 31,176 | 5,248 | 5,983 | 5,773 | 7,243 | 6,963 | 7,313 | 3,254 | 41,778 | 72,954 |
| **⊟Bikes** | **345,815** | **1,728,252** | **3,775,240** | **413,023** | **425,080** | **443,750** | **449,906** | **541,894** | **536,157** | | **2,809,810** | **8,659,117** |
| Mountain Bikes | 300,374 | 842,059 | 1,962,004 | 243,674 | 269,054 | 271,754 | 279,584 | 354,778 | 356,398 | | 1,775,241 | 4,879,678 |
| Road Bikes | 45,441 | 886,192 | 1,813,237 | 169,350 | 156,026 | 171,996 | 170,322 | 187,116 | 179,759 | | 1,034,569 | 3,779,439 |
| **⊟Clothing** | | | **44,674** | **8,395** | **8,566** | **8,475** | **10,092** | **9,486** | **10,742** | **5,910** | **61,666** | **106,341** |
| Gloves | | | 14,229 | 2,865 | 3,037 | 2,596 | 3,233 | 3,747 | 3,673 | 1,641 | 20,792 | 35,021 |
| Shorts | | | 30,446 | 5,529 | 5,529 | 5,879 | 6,859 | 5,739 | 7,069 | 4,269 | 40,874 | 71,320 |
| **Grand Total** | **3,193,224** | **10,561,653** | **13,640,667** | **860,987** | **1,157,132** | **1,094,372** | **1,003,828** | **1,326,467** | **1,309,507** | **9,164** | **6,761,458** | **34,157,001** |

**FIGURE 2-32** A report that contains current dates probably needs to be refreshed periodically.

You probably want to produce reports like this one and then refresh their values periodically to get the newest data and cover the latest periods in time. Nevertheless, when you import data to PowerPivot, you do not create a live link between the source table and the Excel workbook. Instead, you copy data to PowerPivot, which stores the information in its columnar database and works separately from the original data source. For this reason, if you want to refresh data, you need to reload the information directly from the source.

To reload data, you need to click the Refresh button on the Home tab of the PowerPivot ribbon, shown in Figure 2-33.

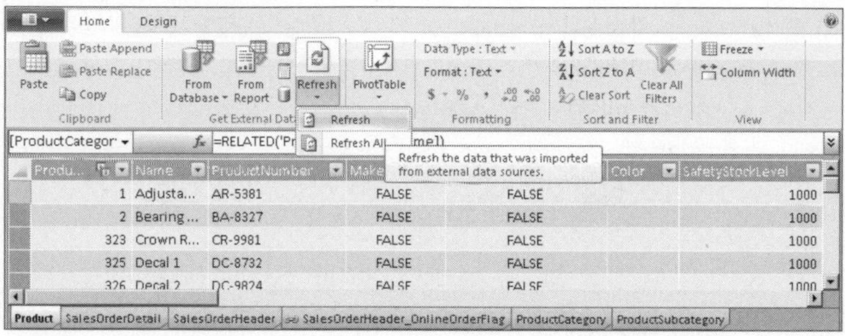

**FIGURE 2-33** To refresh data, we need to use the PowerPivot window.

Because refreshing a table really means reloading it from the database, it can sometimes take time. It is a pretty fast operation for small tables (less than one million rows, for instance), but it gets more time-consuming as the table becomes larger.

**Note** This PowerPivot operation works very differently from the behavior of an Excel PivotTable linked to a SQL Server Analysis Services database. When you connect Excel to Analysis Services, Excel stores only the results, not the original data. So whenever the underlying dataset in the Analysis Services database changes, you can simply refresh the PivotTable to make Excel query the database again and retrieve the new information. The basic difference is that a PowerPivot workbook stores data whereas a classic PivotTable is just a presentation layer over data stored somewhere else (in the example, in the Analysis Services database).

The only kind of tables that are automatically refreshed are Linked Tables—that is, tables that exist in the Excel workbook and are imported inside PowerPivot through the Create Linked Table button. You can switch automatic updates of linked tables on or off, using the options available on the Linked Table tab of the PowerPivot ribbon. The option Update Mode on the Linked Table tab is set to Automatic by default, and there are very rare cases where it might be useful to turn it off.

## Using Slicers

So far, we have looked at PowerPivot features. Now we would like to end this chapter by discussing a standard Excel feature that is very useful when you are working with PowerPivot. Excel 2010 can add slicers to a PivotTable. Although slicers have been introduced mainly for PivotTables linked to PowerPivot data, they are a feature with range: you can define slicers for PivotTables linked to Analysis Services databases or simple PivotTables linked to data in the same Excel workbook. Because slicers are so useful for reports, it is surely worth mentioning them in a PowerPivot book.

Slicers are graphical items that let the user easily define filters on a PivotTable. Take a look at the report in Figure 2-34, which contains a PivotTable and a couple of slicers. You can find this example in the workbook CH02-06-Slicers.xlsx.

| Sum of OrderQty | Column Labels | | | | |
|---|---|---|---|---|---|
| Row Labels | 2001 | 2002 | 2003 | 2004 | Grand Total |
| **Accessories** | **684** | **4,021** | **23,858** | **24,342** | **52,905** |
| Bike Racks | | | 1,858 | 1,308 | 3,166 |
| Bike Stands | | | 119 | 130 | 249 |
| Bottles and Cages | | | 4,827 | 5,725 | 10,552 |
| Cleaners | | | 1,844 | 1,475 | 3,319 |
| Fenders | | | 883 | 1,238 | 2,121 |
| Helmets | 684 | 2,644 | 5,750 | 4,197 | 13,275 |
| Locks | | 676 | 411 | | 1,087 |
| Pumps | | 701 | 429 | | 1,130 |
| Tires and Tubes | | | 7,737 | 10,269 | 18,006 |
| **Bikes** | **2,361** | **10,507** | **17,823** | **10,161** | **40,852** |
| Mountain Bikes | 1,286 | 4,824 | 6,120 | 2,820 | 15,050 |
| Road Bikes | 1,075 | 5,683 | 7,260 | 3,328 | 17,346 |
| Touring Bikes | | | 4,443 | 4,013 | 8,456 |
| **Clothing** | **1,503** | **16,359** | **27,842** | **13,675** | **59,379** |
| Bib-Shorts | | 1,903 | 1,214 | 8 | 3,125 |
| Caps | 520 | 1,853 | 3,562 | 2,376 | 8,311 |
| Gloves | | 4,552 | 6,450 | 2,010 | 13,012 |
| Jerseys | 983 | 3,881 | 5,777 | 2,996 | 13,637 |
| Shorts | | 1,378 | 5,157 | 3,432 | 9,967 |
| Tights | | 2,792 | 1,791 | 6 | 4,589 |
| Vests | | | 3,891 | 2,847 | 6,738 |
| **Grand Total** | **4,548** | **30,887** | **69,523** | **48,178** | **153,136** |

**FIGURE 2-34** Slicers are graphical items that perform one-click filtering.

The two slicers on the left show all the possible values of the Color and Category columns. You can click a single cell and activate a filter for a specific value or press the Ctrl key and click to activate the filter for multiple values. Slicers are clearly useful when a column contains a small number of different values, such as color and category. Slicers for columns that have a lot of different possible values are difficult to use. Nevertheless, because the filtering normally happens on columns with a small number of distinct values, slicers are graphically appealing and very easy to use.

Slicers behave exactly like filters, but they are more elegant and easier to use. It is worth noting, moreover, that slicers can show columns that already appear in the PivotTable, as is the case in our example for the category column. We put the category on rows, in the first place, and then put the category on the slicers. The same column can appear in slicers and in the report. This is a feature that standard filters of a PivotTable do not support.

Moreover, slicers have another significant difference with filters: whereas filters apply to a single PivotTable (they are, after all, part of the query sent to the data source), slicers can be tied to more than one PivotTable, filtering them all with a single click. Let us look at the report in Figure 2-35.

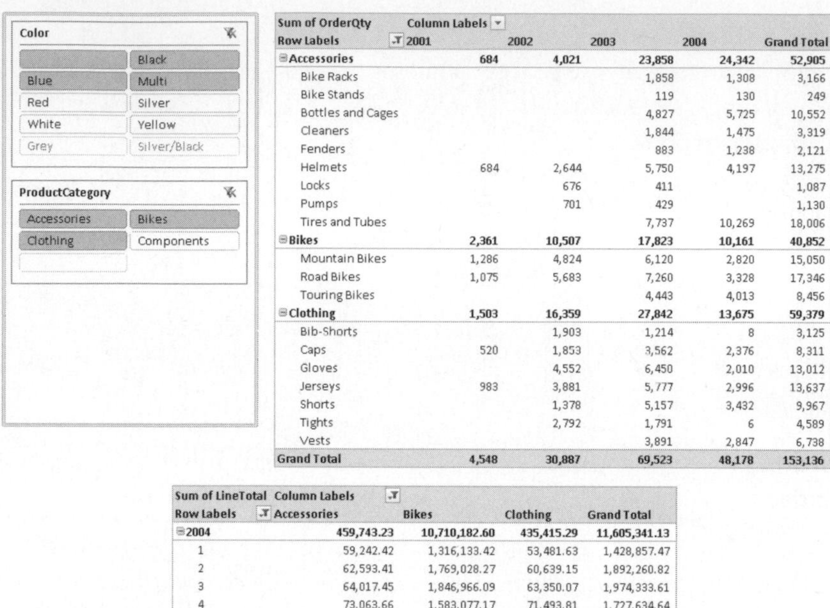


| Sum of OrderQty | Column Labels | | | | |
|---|---|---|---|---|---|
| Row Labels | 2001 | 2002 | 2003 | 2004 | Grand Total |
| Accessories | 684 | 4,021 | 23,858 | 24,342 | 52,905 |
| Bike Racks | | | 1,858 | 1,308 | 3,166 |
| Bike Stands | | | 119 | 130 | 249 |
| Bottles and Cages | | | 4,827 | 5,725 | 10,552 |
| Cleaners | | | 1,844 | 1,475 | 3,319 |
| Fenders | | | 883 | 1,238 | 2,121 |
| Helmets | 684 | 2,644 | 5,750 | 4,197 | 13,275 |
| Locks | | 676 | 411 | | 1,087 |
| Pumps | | 701 | 429 | | 1,130 |
| Tires and Tubes | | | 7,737 | 10,269 | 18,006 |
| Bikes | 2,361 | 10,507 | 17,823 | 10,161 | 40,852 |
| Mountain Bikes | 1,286 | 4,824 | 6,120 | 2,820 | 15,050 |
| Road Bikes | 1,075 | 5,683 | 7,260 | 3,328 | 17,346 |
| Touring Bikes | | | 4,443 | 4,013 | 8,456 |
| Clothing | 1,503 | 16,359 | 27,842 | 13,675 | 59,379 |
| Bib-Shorts | | 1,903 | 1,214 | 8 | 3,125 |
| Caps | 520 | 1,853 | 3,562 | 2,376 | 8,311 |
| Gloves | | 4,552 | 6,450 | 2,010 | 13,012 |
| Jerseys | 983 | 3,881 | 5,777 | 2,996 | 13,637 |
| Shorts | | 1,378 | 5,157 | 3,432 | 9,967 |
| Tights | | 2,792 | 1,791 | 6 | 4,589 |
| Vests | | | 3,891 | 2,847 | 6,738 |
| Grand Total | 4,548 | 30,887 | 69,523 | 48,178 | 153,136 |

| Sum of LineTotal | Column Labels | | | |
|---|---|---|---|---|
| Row Labels | Accessories | Bikes | Clothing | Grand Total |
| 2004 | 459,743.23 | 10,710,182.60 | 435,415.29 | 11,605,341.13 |
| 1 | 59,242.42 | 1,316,133.42 | 53,481.63 | 1,428,857.47 |
| 2 | 62,593.41 | 1,769,028.27 | 60,639.15 | 1,892,260.82 |
| 3 | 64,017.45 | 1,846,966.09 | 63,350.07 | 1,974,333.61 |
| 4 | 73,063.66 | 1,583,077.17 | 71,493.81 | 1,727,634.64 |
| 5 | 89,639.39 | 2,014,607.80 | 87,528.18 | 2,191,775.36 |
| 6 | 81,726.20 | 2,180,369.85 | 85,236.63 | 2,347,332.68 |
| 7 | 29,460.71 | | 13,685.83 | 43,146.54 |
| Grand Total | 459,743.23 | 10,710,182.60 | 435,415.29 | 11,605,341.13 |

**FIGURE 2-35** Slicers can be tied to more than one PivotTable, creating interactive reports.

The upper PivotTable shows the number of items sold over time, whereas the lower one shows a detail of the year 2004 and displays the money value of sales. It would be nice to be able to link the slicer to both PivotTables so that we produce an interactive report in which you can select color and category and update both PivotTables quickly.

To link a slicer to more than one PivotTable, you can move the cursor inside the PivotTable you want to link to a slicer and then choose the Slicer Connections option from the Insert Slicer button on the Options tab of the Excel ribbon. The dialog box in Figure 2-36 appears.

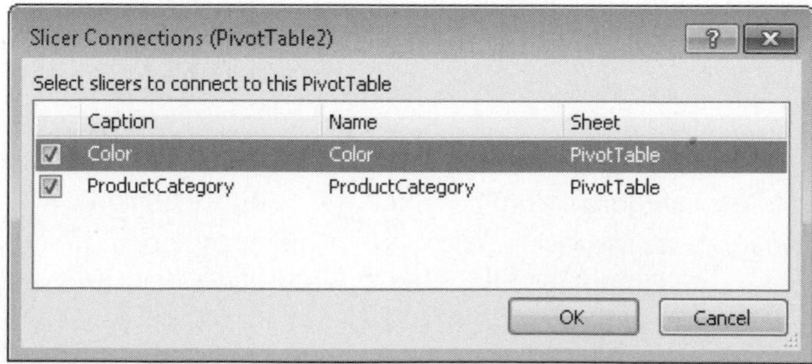


**FIGURE 2-36** With this dialog box, we can tie one slicer to more than one PivotTable.

You can link both slicers (Category and Color) or make a selection of which slicer to link to the PivotTable and which ones not to use. If you link both slicers to both PivotTables, both tables are updated to reflect the filters when you make a selection in the slicers. This simple characteristic of slicers makes them a great option when you need to create interactive reports.

**Caution** Whenever you place more than one PivotTable on the same worksheet, you need to guard against overlapping them. PivotTables, by nature, change their size depending on the selections you make. (As you change the number of categories, the PivotTable containing the categories increases its height to accommodate the new categories selected.) If you want to place PivotTables side by side, for example, you need to make sure that they cannot grow to the point of overlapping. If this happens, Excel raises an error.

# Summary

In this chapter, you learned some of the most useful features of PowerPivot:

- Format strings should be set in the PivotTable field settings so that resizing of columns is carried on by the PivotTable itself.
- Useless columns should be deleted from the PowerPivot data model, and technical ones should be hidden so that you have fewer columns to search to produce the report.
- You can add simple calculated columns or use more complex functions, such as RELATED, to enrich a table with information computed on related tables. RELATED is a very useful function because it allows us to reduce the number of tables and move columns to locations the user expects them.
- You created your first linked table, which enriches the original data model with other information directly stored inside the Excel workbook.
- You learned the basic difference between calculated columns and measures, something we discuss in greater detail in the next chapter.
- Whenever the data inside the data model is too detailed, you should create aggregating columns to avoid slicing too many details. You saw a demonstration of this technique on date columns, but it can be easily extended to other types.
- Data that needs to be refreshed needs to be reloaded from the database because PowerPivot tables are a copy of the original data, not a link to them. This might be an issue with very large databases.
- Slicers are graphical tools to make filters for one or more PivotTables. They are useful and good looking, and they allow you to build interactive reports by combining more than one PivotTable in the same Excel workbook.

Chapter 3

# Introduction to DAX

Now that you have seen some examples of Microsoft SQL Server PowerPivot for Excel worksheets, it is time to learn the fundamentals of PowerPivot expressions. PowerPivot has its own syntax for defining calculation expressions. It is conceptually similar to an Excel expression, but it has specific functions that allow you to create more advanced calculation on data stored in multiple tables. The PowerPivot language is called Data Analysis Expressions, but we always use the shorter DAX acronym.

In this chapter, you learn the basics of DAX and also discover how to use it to solve some typical problems in business scenarios.

## Understanding Calculation in DAX

Just as it does in Excel, any calculation in DAX begins with the assignment operator. The main difference is that DAX never uses cell coordinates like A1, C2, and so on. In DAX, you always specify coordinates using column and table names. Moreover, DAX does not support the concept of range as Excel does: to use DAX efficiently, you need to learn to work with columns and tables.

Please note that in a DAX expression, you can get the value of a column only for a single row or for the whole table—that is, you cannot get access to a specific row inside a table. To get a range, you need to use DAX functions that filter a table, thus returning a subset of the rows of the original table, corresponding to the needed range.

To express complex formulas, you need to learn the basics of DAX, which includes the syntax, the different data types that DAX can handle, the basic operators, and how to refer to columns and tables. In the next few sections, we are going to introduce these concepts.

### DAX Syntax

A relatively simple way to understand how DAX syntax works is to start with an example. Suppose that you have a PowerPivot table like the one shown in Figure 3-1. Two measures, SalesAmount and TotalProductCost, are helpful here.

| Date | Year | Month | Day... | DayName | EnglishProductName | ModelName | OrderQua... | SalesAmount | TotalProductCost |
|---|---|---|---|---|---|---|---|---|---|
| 6/1/2008 | 2008 | 06 - June | 1 | Sunday | Water Bottle - 30 oz. | Water Bottle | 1 | 4.99 | 1.8663 |
| 6/1/2008 | 2008 | 06 - June | 1 | Sunday | Water Bottle - 30 oz. | Water Bottle | 1 | 4.99 | 1.8663 |
| 6/1/2008 | 2008 | 06 - June | 1 | Sunday | Water Bottle - 30 oz. | Water Bottle | 1 | 4.99 | 1.8663 |
| 6/1/2008 | 2008 | 06 - June | 1 | Sunday | Water Bottle - 30 oz. | Water Bottle | 1 | 4.99 | 1.8663 |
| 6/1/2008 | 2008 | 06 - June | 1 | Sunday | Water Bottle - 30 oz. | Water Bottle | 1 | 4.99 | 1.8663 |
| 6/1/2008 | 2008 | 06 - June | 1 | Sunday | Water Bottle - 30 oz. | Water Bottle | 1 | 4.99 | 1.8663 |
| 6/1/2008 | 2008 | 06 - June | 1 | Sunday | Water Bottle - 30 oz. | Water Bottle | 1 | 4.99 | 1.8663 |
| 6/1/2008 | 2008 | 06 - June | 1 | Sunday | Water Bottle - 30 oz. | Water Bottle | 1 | 4.99 | 1.8663 |
| 6/1/2008 | 2008 | 06 - June | 1 | Sunday | Water Bottle - 30 oz. | Water Bottle | 1 | 4.99 | 1.8663 |
| 6/1/2008 | 2008 | 06 - June | 1 | Sunday | Water Bottle - 30 oz. | Water Bottle | 1 | 4.99 | 1.8663 |
| 6/2/2008 | 2008 | 06 - June | 2 | Monday | Water Bottle - 30 oz. | Water Bottle | 1 | 4.99 | 1.8663 |
| 6/2/2008 | 2008 | 06 - June | 2 | Monday | Water Bottle - 30 oz. | Water Bottle | 1 | 4.99 | 1.8663 |
| 6/2/2008 | 2008 | 06 - June | 2 | Monday | Water Bottle - 30 oz. | Water Bottle | 1 | 4.99 | 1.8663 |

Sales

**FIGURE 3-1** You can see DAX syntax in this sales table.

Using this data, you now want to calculate the margin, subtracting the TotalProductCost from the SalesAmount. To do that, you need to write the DAX formula shown in Figure 3-2 in a new column, which you can call GrossMargin.

[GrossMargin] =Sales[SalesAmount]-Sales[TotalProductCost]

| OrderQuantity | SalesAmount | TotalProductCost | GrossMargin | Add Column |
|---|---|---|---|---|
| 1 | 4.99 | 1.8663 | 3.1237 | |
| 1 | 4.99 | 1.8663 | 3.1237 | |
| 1 | 4.99 | 1.8663 | 3.1237 | |

**FIGURE 3-2** Definition of GrossMargin.

This new formula is repeated automatically for all the rows of the table, resulting in a new column in the table. In this example, you are using a DAX expression to define a calculated column. (Later we see that DAX is used also to define measures.) This DAX expression handles numeric values and returns a numeric value, too.

## DAX Data Types

You saw in the previous formula how to handle numeric values. DAX can perform computations with different numeric types, of which there are five:

- Integer
- Real
- Currency
- Date (datetime)
- TRUE/FALSE (Boolean)

PowerPivot has a powerful type handling system so that you do not have to worry much about data types: when you write a DAX expression, the resulting type is based on the type of the terms used in the expression. You need to be aware of this in case the type returned from a DAX expression is not the expected one: then you must investigate the data type of the terms used in the expression itself. For example, if one of the terms of a sum is a date, the result is a date too while, if the same operator is used with integers, the result is an integer. This is known as *operator overloading* and you can see an example of its behavior in Figure 3-3, where the DatePlusOneWeek column is calculated by adding 7 to the value in the Date column. The result is, as we said, a date.

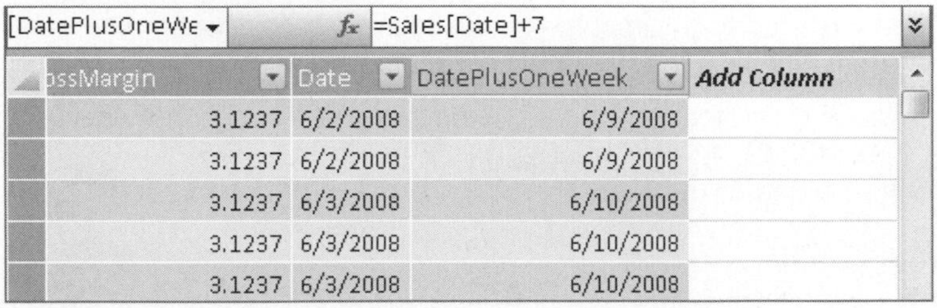

[DatePlusOneWe ▾ fx =Sales[Date]+7

| ossMargin | Date | DatePlusOneWeek | Add Column |
|---|---|---|---|
| 3.1237 | 6/2/2008 | 6/9/2008 | |
| 3.1237 | 6/2/2008 | 6/9/2008 | |
| 3.1237 | 6/3/2008 | 6/10/2008 | |
| 3.1237 | 6/3/2008 | 6/10/2008 | |
| 3.1237 | 6/3/2008 | 6/10/2008 | |

**FIGURE 3-3** Adding an integer to a date results in a date increased by the corresponding number of days.

In addition to operator overloading, PowerPivot automatically converts strings into numbers and numbers into strings whenever it is required by the operator. For example, if you use the & operator, which concatenates strings, PowerPivot automatically converts its arguments into strings. If you look at the formula

```
= 5 & 4
```

it returns a "54" string result. On the other hand, the formula

```
= "5" + "4"
```

returns an integer result with the value of 9.

As you have seen, the resulting value depends on the operator and not on the source columns, which are converted following the requirements of the operator. But even if this behavior is convenient, later in this chapter you see what types of errors might happen during these automatic conversions.

### Inside DAX Data Types

DAX data types might be familiar to people used to working with Excel. However, we need to review a few considerations about two of these data types because of the frequency they are used in PowerPivot data models.

#### Date data type

PowerPivot stores dates in a datetime data type. This format uses a floating point number internally, wherein the integer corresponds to the number of days (starting from December 30, 1899) and the decimal identifies the fraction of the day. (Hours, minutes, and seconds are converted to decimal fractions of a day.) Thus, the expression

```
= NOW() + 1
```

increases a date by one day (exactly 24 hours), returning the date of tomorrow at the same hour/minute/second of the execution of the expression itself.

#### TRUE/FALSE data type

The data type TRUE/FALSE is used to express logical conditions. For example, a calculated column defined by the following expression is of type TRUE/FALSE:

```
= Sales[TotalProductCost] > Sales[Amount]
```

The behavior of this data type is similar to the behavior of data types in Excel and it is usually called a Boolean data type. Usually a column of this type is not made visible to the end user, but is used internally for DAX calculations.

## DAX Operators

Having seen the importance of operators in determining the type of an expression, you can now see a list of the operators available in DAX in Table 3-1.

Moreover, the logical operators are available also as DAX functions, with syntax very similar to Excel syntax. For example, you can write

```
AND( [Country] = "USA", [Quantity] > 0 )
OR( [Country] = "USA", [Quantity] > 0 )
NOT( [Country] = "USA" )
```

that corresponds, respectively, to

```
[Country] = "USA" && [Quantity] > 0
[Country] = "USA" || [Quantity] > 0
!( [Country] = "USA" && [Quantity] )
```

**TABLE 3-1 Operators.**

<table>
<tr><th>Operator Type</th><th>Symbol</th><th>Use</th><th>Example</th></tr>
<tr><td>Parenthesis</td><td>( )</td><td>Precedence order and grouping of arguments</td><td>(5 + 2) * 3</td></tr>
<tr><td>Arithmetic</td><td>+</td><td>Addition</td><td>4 + 2</td></tr>
<tr><td></td><td>-</td><td>Subtraction/negation</td><td>5 – 3</td></tr>
<tr><td></td><td>*</td><td>Multiplication</td><td>4 * 2</td></tr>
<tr><td></td><td>/</td><td>Division</td><td>4 / 2</td></tr>
<tr><td>Comparison</td><td>=</td><td>Equal to</td><td>[Country] = "USA"</td></tr>
<tr><td></td><td><></td><td>Not equal to</td><td>[Country] <> "USA"</td></tr>
<tr><td></td><td>></td><td>Greater than</td><td>[Quantity] > 0</td></tr>
<tr><td></td><td>>=</td><td>Greater than or equal to</td><td>[Quantity] >= 100</td></tr>
<tr><td></td><td><</td><td>Less than</td><td>[Quantity] < 0</td></tr>
<tr><td></td><td><=</td><td>Less than or equal to</td><td>[Quantity] <= 100</td></tr>
<tr><td>Text concatenation</td><td>&</td><td>Concatenation of strings</td><td>"Value is " & [Amount]</td></tr>
<tr><td>Logical</td><td>&&</td><td>AND condition between two Boolean expressions</td><td>[Country] = "USA" && [Quantity] > 0</td></tr>
<tr><td></td><td>||</td><td>OR condition between two Boolean expressions</td><td>[Country] = "USA" || [Quantity] > 0</td></tr>
<tr><td></td><td>!</td><td>NOT operator on the Boolean expression that follows</td><td>! ([Country] = "USA")</td></tr>
</table>

## DAX Values

You have already seen that you can define a value through a literal (like "USA" and 100) or through a reference to a column of a table. Although using literals is straightforward, the syntax for referencing a column needs some attention. Here is the basic syntax:

```
'Table Name'[Column Name]
```

The table name can be enclosed in single quote characters. Most of the time, quotes can be omitted if the name does not contain any special characters, such as spaces. In the following formula, for example, the quotes can be omitted:

```
TableName[Column Name]
```

The column name, on the other hand, always needs to be enclosed in square brackets. Please note that the table name is optional and can be missing. If the table name is omitted, the column name is searched in the current table, which is the one to which the calculated column or measure belongs. However, we strongly suggest that you always specify the complete name (table and column) to avoid any confusion.

### IntelliSense

Whenever you write a formula in Excel or PowerPivot, IntelliSense, a special help feature, shows all the possible function names and references you can use in a formula. When you write a formula in the PowerPivot window, the table name is not displayed by IntelliSense when the database contains only one table. In this case, to get the list of columns using IntelliSense, you must type in the opening square bracket, which calls up the display of all the columns of the current table, as shown in Figure 3-4.

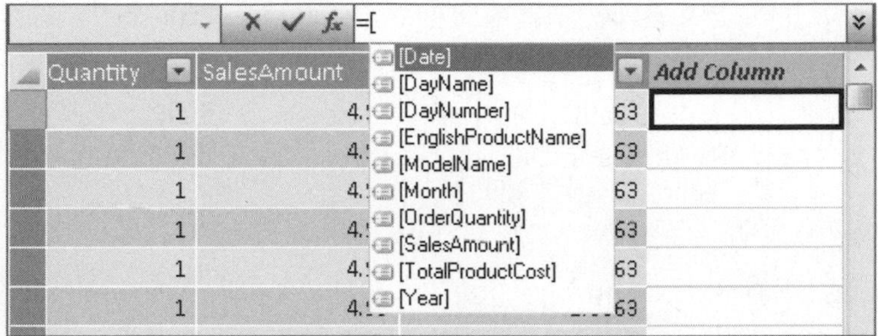


**FIGURE 3-4** IntelliSense shows all the fields of the current table when you type the opening square bracket in the PowerPivot window.

# Understanding Calculated Columns and Measures

Now that you know the basics of DAX syntax, you need to learn one of the most important concepts in DAX: the difference between calculated columns and measures. Even though they might appear similar at first sight because you can make some calculations both ways, you will see that you need to use measures to implement the most flexible calculations, and this is a key to becoming a powerful PowerPivot user.

## Calculated Columns

You saw in Chapter 2, "PowerPivot at Work," how to define a calculated column. You can do it by using the Add Column button on the Column column tab of the ribbon, or you can simply move to the last column, which is named Add Column, and start writing the formula. The DAX expression has to be inserted into the formula bar and IntelliSense helps you during the writing of the expression.

A calculated column is just like any other column in a PowerPivot table and can be used in rows, columns, filters, or values of a PivotTable. The DAX expression defined for a calculated column operates in the context of the current row of the table it belongs to. Any reference to a column returns the value of that column in the current row. You cannot access directly the values of other rows.

**Note** As you see later, there are DAX functions that aggregate the value of a column for the whole table. The only way to get the value of a subset of rows is to use DAX functions that return a table and then operate on it. In this way, you aggregate column values for a range of rows, and possibly operating on a different row by filtering a table made of only one row.

Calculated columns are easy to create and use. You have already seen in Figure 3-2 how to define the GrossMargin column to compute the amount of the gross margin.

```
[Gross Margin] = Sales[SalesAmount] - Sales[TotalProductCost]
```

But what happens if you want to show the gross margin as a percentage of the sales amount? You could create a calculated column with the following formula:

```
[Gross Margin Perc] = Sales[Gross Margin] / Sales[SalesAmount]
```

This formula computes the right value at the row level, as you can see in Figure 3-5.

[Gross Margin Pe ▾ | fx =Sales[Gross Margin]/Sales[SalesAmount]

| OrderQuantity | SalesAmount | TotalProductCost | Gross Margin | Gross Margin Perc |
|---|---|---|---|---|
| 1 | 769.49 | 419.7784 | 349.7116 | 45.45 % |
| 1 | 9.99 | 3.7363 | 6.2537 | 62.60 % |
| 1 | 63.5 | 23.749 | 39.751 | 62.60 % |

**FIGURE 3-5** Calculation of Gross Margin as a percentage calculated row by row.

Nevertheless, when the number is aggregated in the PivotTable, you do not see a correct result. In fact, the results shown in Figure 3-6 are aggregated using the Sum operation (see column F, Sum of Gross Margin Perc), which is the default PowerPivot behavior when you put a numeric column into a PivotTable.

| | B | C | D | E | F |
|---|---|---|---|---|---|
| 3 | Row Labels | Sum of SalesAmount | Sum of TotalProductCost | Sum of Gross Margin | Sum of Gross Margin Perc |
| 4 | 2005 | 3,266,373.66 | 1,954,767.79 | 1,311,605.87 | 407.7815578 |
| 5 | 2006 | 6,530,343.53 | 3,883,493.37 | 2,646,850.15 | 1084.566884 |
| 6 | 2007 | 9,791,060.30 | 5,718,327.17 | 4,072,733.12 | 13146.3482 |
| 7 | 2008 | 9,770,899.74 | 5,721,205.24 | 4,049,694.50 | 17584.6298 |
| 8 | **Grand Total** | **29,358,677.22** | **17,277,793.58** | **12,080,883.65** | **32223.32644** |

**FIGURE 3-6** The Gross Margin Perc column is wrongly aggregated by Sum.

You can try to change the aggregation formula to Average using the Summarize By context menu for the item in the Values list of the PowerPivot Field List. (See Figure 3-7.)

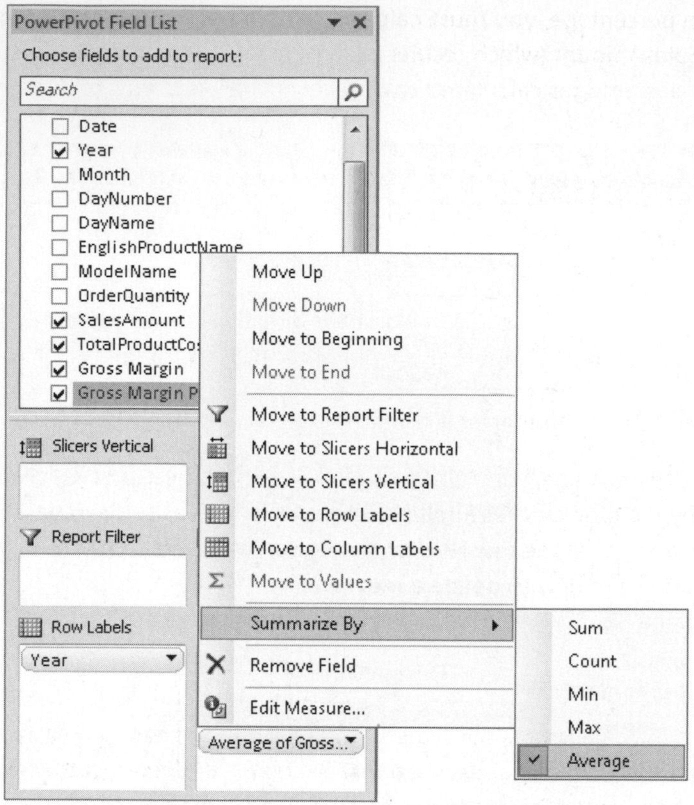


**FIGURE 3-7** Average is selected in the Summarize By context menu for the item in the Value list.

Nevertheless, even using the Average aggregator, the final result is not yet the right one. In fact, in Figure 3-8 you can see that the average of Gross Margin Perc (column F) is internally calculated as the following:

```
= SUM( Sales[Gross Margin] / Sales[SalesAmount] ) / COUNTROWS( Sales )
```

That number is not equal to column G, which is calculated in this other way:

```
= SUM( Sales[Gross Margin] ) / SUM( Sales[SalesAmount] )
```

This last effort is the correct way to perform the calculation of this average.

| | B | C | D | E | F | G | H | I |
|---|---|---|---|---|---|---|---|---|
| 3 | Row Labels | Sum of SalesAmount | Sum of TotalProductCost | Sum of Gross Margin | Average of Gross Margin Perc | Calculated Gross Margin % | | |
| 4 | 2005 | 3,266,373.66 | 1,954,767.79 | 1,311,605.87 | 40.25% | 40.15% | | |
| 5 | 2006 | 6,530,343.53 | 3,883,493.37 | 2,646,850.15 | 40.51% | 40.53% | | |
| 6 | 2007 | 9,791,060.30 | 5,718,327.17 | 4,072,733.12 | 53.78% | 41.60% | | |
| 7 | 2008 | 9,770,899.74 | 5,721,205.24 | 4,049,694.50 | 54.50% | 41.45% | | |
| 8 | Grand Total | 29,358,677.22 | 17,277,793.58 | 12,080,883.65 | 53.35% | 41.15% | | |

**FIGURE 3-8** The GrossMarginPercentage calculated column is different from column G calculated in Excel.

The reason for the wrong calculation is simple: aggregating the row level gross margin computes the average above all the transactions and gives 50 percent of a $10 sale the same weight as a $100 sale. If you look at Figure 3-9, you can understand the issue: to calculate the right Gross Margin percentage, you must calculate a ratio between aggregated values of Gross Margin and SalesAmount (which results in 25 percent in the example), instead of making an average of percentages calculated row by row (which is a wrong 36 percent).

| | A | B | C |
|---|---|---|---|
| 1 | SalesAmount | Gross Margin | Margin% |
| 2 | 20 | 10 | 50% |
| 3 | 180 | 40 | 22% |
| 4 | **200** | **50** | |
| 5 | | | |
| 6 | **Average of Margin** | **=AVERAGE(50%, 22%)** | 36% |
| 7 | **Total Margin** | **=50 / 200** | 25% |

**FIGURE 3-9** Compare wrong and right calculations of Margin percentage over two transactions.

So to calculate the right percentage, you need a way to calculate percentage by dividing the total of gross margin by the total of sales amount. This calculation has to be done at the cell level of the pivot table and not at the row level of the PowerPivot table. To do that, you need to take a step further and learn how to define a measure.

## Measures

A *measure* is a DAX expression that uses the same syntax as calculated columns; the difference is the context of evaluation. A measure is evaluated in the context of the cell of the pivot table, while a calculated column is computed at the row level. The cell context depends on the user selections on the pivot table. So when you use SUM(SalesAmount) in a measure, you mean *the sum of all the cells that are aggregated under this cell,* whereas when you use [SalesAmount] in a calculated column, you mean *the value of SalesAmount in this row.*

When you create a measure, you can define a value that changes according to the filter that the user applies on a pivot table. In this way, you can solve the problem of calculating the gross margin percentage. To define a measure, you can click the New Measure button on the PowerPivot tab of the ribbon, shown in Figure 3-10, whenever a cell in a PivotTable is selected.

**FIGURE 3-10** New Measure button in the PowerPivot ribbon.

Alternatively, you can also right-click a table name in the PowerPivot Field List, choosing the Add New Measure menu item, as shown in Figure 3-11.

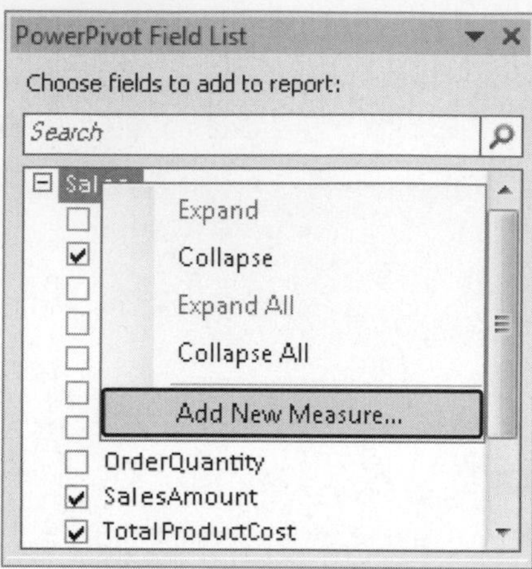


**FIGURE 3-11** The Add New Measure menu item on the context menu on a table in the PowerPivot Field List.

At this point, the Measure Settings dialog box (see Figure 3-12) opens and you can choose the table name that contains the new measure, the name of the measure (which can be customized for each PivotTable), and finally the DAX formula.

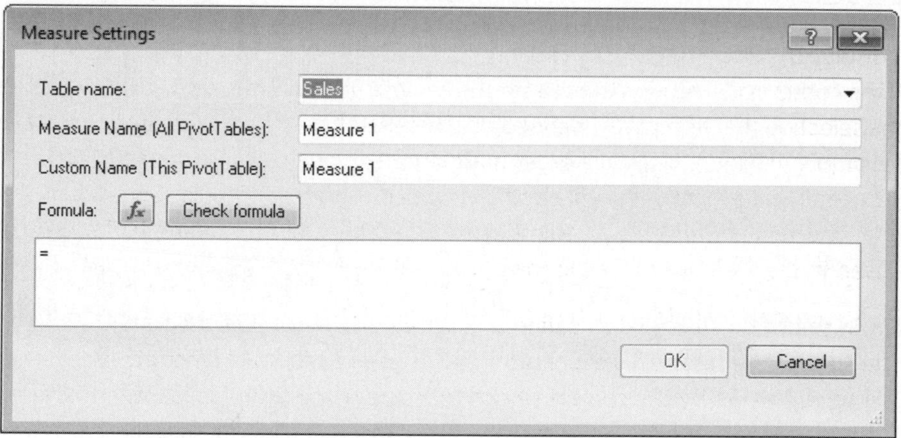


**FIGURE 3-12** Measure Settings displayed to create a new measure.

Now, let us focus on the formula to define a new measure. In a first attempt, you might try to define it by using the same DAX expression used in the calculated column, but you would get the error shown in Figure 3-13.

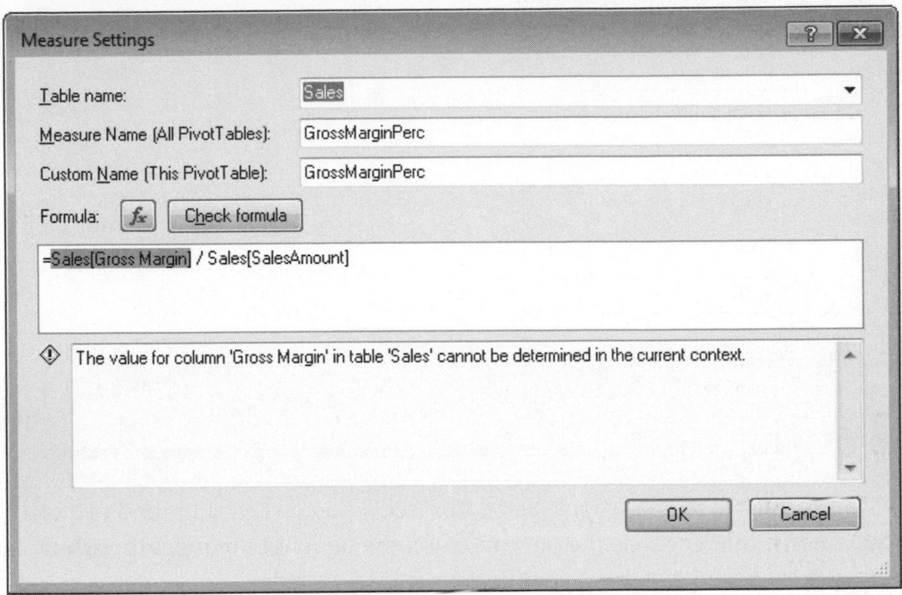


**FIGURE 3-13** Error defining GrossMarginPerc measure with the same DAX expression as calculated column.

You display the error message by clicking the Check Formula button. The reason for the error is that the context of execution is not a single row, but a group of rows. That group corresponds to the selection that is implicitly defined by the cell that has to be calculated in the pivot table. For example, in Figure 3-8, each gross margin percentage cell corresponds to the set of rows that have the same year. In such a context, which contains multiple rows, there is no way to refer to the value of the column Sales[SalesAmount] because a column has a value only when it is used in the context of a single row.

To avoid the error, you need to define an expression that divides the sum of the gross margin by the sum of the sales. This expression makes use of the SUM function, which aggregates all the rows filtered by the current selection in the pivot table (which will be the year, as we said before). The following is the correct DAX expression for the measure; it is also shown in Figure 3-14.

```
= SUM( Sales[Gross Margin] ) / SUM( Sales[SalesAmount] )
```

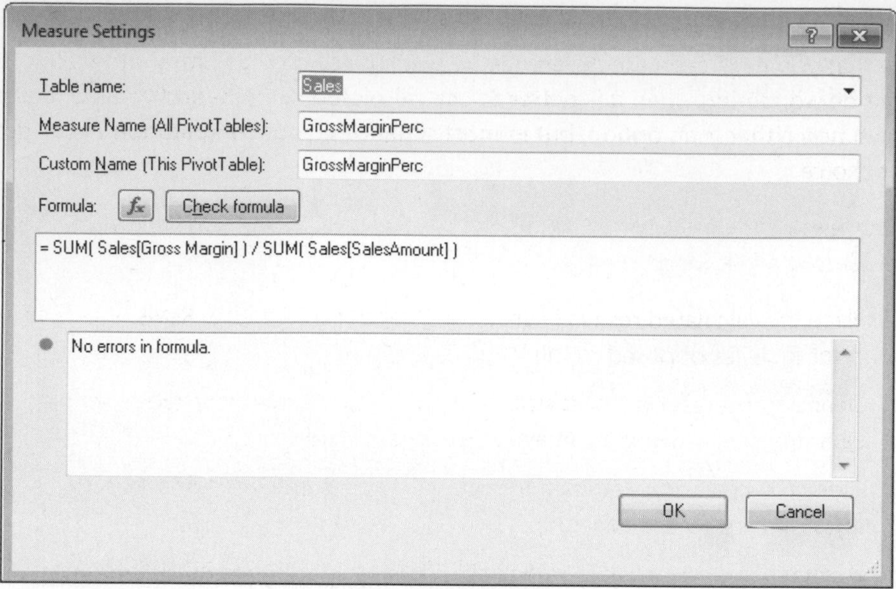


**FIGURE 3-14** Correct definition of the GrossMarginPerc measure.

Finally, you can check that the measure works correctly by comparing the data, as shown in Figure 3-15.

| | B | C | D | E | F | G | H | I |
|---|---|---|---|---|---|---|---|---|
| 3 | Row Labels | Sum of SalesAmount | Sum of TotalProductCost | Sum of Gross Margin | GrossMarginPerc | Calculated Gross Margin % | | |
| 4 | 2005 | 3,266,373.66 | 1,954,767.79 | 1,311,605.87 | 40.15% | 40.15% | | |
| 5 | 2006 | 6,530,343.53 | 3,883,493.37 | 2,646,850.15 | 40.53% | 40.53% | | |
| 6 | 2007 | 9,791,060.30 | 5,718,327.17 | 4,072,733.12 | 41.60% | 41.60% | | |
| 7 | 2008 | 9,770,899.74 | 5,721,205.24 | 4,049,694.50 | 41.45% | 41.45% | | |
| 8 | **Grand Total** | **29,358,677.22** | **17,277,793.58** | **12,080,883.65** | **41.15%** | 41.15% | | |

**FIGURE 3-15** GrossMarginPerc, correctly computed, returns the same value as the G column calculated in Excel.

It is worth noting that if you use the same DAX expression you see in Figure 3-14 in a calculated column, it would calculate the gross margin of all the rows in the table, duplicating the same number for each row. In fact, in a calculated column, the SUM function gets all the rows of the current table, without being filtered by the user selection on the pivot table.

## Differences Between Calculated Columns and Measures

Even if they look similar, there is a big difference between calculated columns and measures. The value of a calculated column is calculated during data refresh and uses the current row as a context; it does not depend on user activity on the pivot table. A measure operates on aggregations of data defined by the context of the current cell: source tables are filtered according to the coordinates of the cell, and data is aggregated and calculated using this filter. In other words, a measure always operates on aggregations of data under the evaluation context and for this reason there is no way to reference a single row in a DAX expression. The evaluation context is explained further in Chapter 6.

## Choosing Between Calculated Columns and Measures

Now that you have seen the difference between calculated columns and measures, you might be wondering when it is better to use calculated columns and when to use measures. Sometimes, either is an option, but in most situations, your computation needs determine your choice.

You have to define a calculated column (in the PowerPivot table grid window) whenever you want to do the following:

- Place the calculated results in an Excel Slicer or see results in Rows or Columns in a pivot table (as opposed to the Values area).
- Define an expression that is strictly bound to the current row. (For example, Price * Quantity cannot work on an average of the two columns.)
- Categorize text or numbers (for example, a range of values for a measure, a range of ages of customers, and so on).

On the other hand, you have to define a measure (in the PowerPivot Field List in the pivot table) whenever you want to display resulting calculation values that reflect pivot table selections made by the user and see them in the Values area of pivot tables—for example:

- When you calculate profit percentage of a pivot table selection
- When you calculate ratios of a product compared to all products but filter both by year or region

Some calculations can be covered both by calculated columns and measures, even if different DAX expressions have to be used in these cases. For example, you can define the GrossMargin as a calculated column:

```
= Sales[SalesAmount] - Sales[TotalProductCost]
```

but it can be defined as a measure too:

```
= SUM( Sales[SalesAmount] ) - SUM( Sales[TotalProductCost] )
```

The final result is exactly the same. We suggest you to favor the measure in this case because it does not consume memory and disk space, but this is really important only in large data-sets. When the size of the workbook is not an issue, you can use the method you are more comfortable with.

**Cross References**

It is obvious that a measure can refer to one or more calculated columns. It might be less intuitive that the opposite is also true. A calculated column can refer to a measure: in this way, it forces the calculation of a measure for the context defined by the current row. This operation transforms and consolidates the result of a measure into a column, which will not be influenced by user actions. Obviously, only certain operations can produce meaningful results because usually a measure makes calculations that strongly depend on the selection made by the user in the pivot table.

# Handling Errors in DAX Expressions

Now that you have seen some basic formulas, it is time to learn how to gracefully handle invalid calculations, in case they happen. A DAX expression might contain invalid calculations because the data it references is not valid for the formula. For example, you might have a division by zero or a column value that is not a number and is used in an arithmetic operation, such as multiplication. You need to learn how these errors are handled by default and how to intercept these conditions in case you want some special handling.

Before you learn how to handle errors, it is worth spending a few words on describing the different kinds of errors that might appear during a DAX formula evaluation. They are

- Conversion Error
- Arithmetical operations
- Empty or missing values

Let us explain them in more detail.

## Conversion Errors

The first kind of error that we are going to analyze is the conversion error. As you have seen before in this chapter, DAX values are automatically converted between strings and numbers whenever the operator requires it. To review the concept with examples, all these are valid DAX expressions:

```
"10" + 32 = 42
"10" & 32 = "1032"
10 & 32 = "1032"
DATE(2010,3,25) = 3/25/2010
DATE(2010,3,25) + 14 = 4/8/2010
DATE(2010,3,25) & 14 = "3/25/201014"
```

These formulas are always correct because they operate with constant values. But what about the following one?

```
SalesOrders[VatCode] + 100
```

Because the first operator of this sum is obtained by another DAX expression, you need to be sure that all the values in that column are numbers to determine whether it will be converted correctly. If the content of a column cannot be converted to suit the operator needs, you will incur a conversion error. Here are typical situations:

```
"1 + 1" + 0              = Cannot convert value '1+1' of type string to type real
DATEVALUE("25/14/2010")  = Type mismatch
```

To avoid these errors, you need to write more complex DAX expressions that contain error detection logic to intercept error conditions and always return a meaningful result.

## Arithmetical Operations

The second category of errors that we want to analyze is that of arithmetical operations, such as the division by zero or the square root of a negative number. These kinds of errors are not related to conversion; they are raised whenever you try to call a function or use an operator with invalid values.

The division by zero, in PowerPivot, requires a special handling because it behaves in a way that is not very intuitive (except for mathematicians). When you divide a number by zero, PowerPivot usually returns the special value *Infinity*. Moreover, in the *very* special cases of 0 divided by 0 or Infinity divided by Infinity, PowerPivot returns the special NaN (not a number) value. Because this is a strange behavior for Excel users to encounter, it is worth summarizing in Table 3-2.

**TABLE 3-2 Special result values for division by zero.**

| Expression | Result |
|---|---|
| 10 / 0 | Infinity |
| 7 / 0 | Infinity |
| 0 / 0 | Infinity |
| (10 / 0) / (7 / 0) | NaN |

It is important to note that Infinity and NaN are not errors but special values in PowerPivot. In fact, if you divide a number by Infinity the expression does not generate an error but returns 0:

```
9954 / (7 / 0)      = 0
```

Apart from this special situation, arithmetical errors might be returned when calling a DAX function with a wrong parameter, such as the square root of a negative number.

```
SQRT( -1 )       = An argument of function 'SQRT' has the wrong data type
                   or the result is too large or too small
```

If PowerPivot detects errors like this, it blocks any further computation of the DAX expression and raises an error. You can use the special DAX ISERROR function to check if an expression leads to an error, something that we are going to use later in this chapter. Finally, even if special values as NaN are displayed in such a way in the PowerPivot window, they are displayed as errors when shown in an Excel PivotTable and will be detected as errors by the error detection functions.

## Empty or Missing Values

The third category that we examine is not a specific error condition, but the presence of empty values, which might result in unexpected results or calculation errors. You need to understand how these special values are treated in PowerPivot.

DAX handles missing values, blank values, or empty cells in the same way, using the value BLANK, which is not a real value but a special way to identify these conditions. The value BLANK can be obtained in a DAX expression by calling the BLANK function, which is different from an empty string. For example, the following expression always returns a blank value, which is displayed as an empty cell in the PowerPivot window:

```
= BLANK()
```

The expression above is useless, but the BLANK function itself becomes useful every time you want to return an empty value. For example, you might want to display an empty cell instead of 0, as in the following expression that calculates the total discount for a sale transaction, leaving the cell blank if the discount is 0:

```
= IF( Sales[DiscountPerc] = 0, BLANK(), Sales[DiscountPerc] * Sales[Amount] )
```

If a DAX expression contains a BLANK, it is not considered an error but an empty value. So an expression containing a BLANK might return a value or a blank, depending on the calculation required. For example, the following expression

```
= 10 * Sales[Amount]
```

returns BLANK whenever `Sales[Amount]` is BLANK. In other words, the result of an arithmetic product is BLANK whenever one or both terms are BLANK. This propagation of BLANK in a DAX expression happens in several other arithmetical and logical operations, as you can see in the following examples:

```
BLANK() + BLANK()       = BLANK()
10 * BLANK()            = BLANK()
BLANK() / 3             = BLANK()
BLANK() / BLANK()       = BLANK()
BLANK() OR BLANK()      = BLANK()
BLANK() AND BLANK()     = BLANK()
```

However, the propagation of BLANK in the result of an expression does not happen for all formulas. Some calculations do not propagate BLANK but return a value depending on the other terms of the formula. Examples of these are addition, subtraction, division by BLANK, and a logical operation between a BLANK and a valid value. In the following expressions, you can see some examples of these conditions, along with their results:

```
BLANK() - 10            = -10
18 + BLANK()            = 18
4 / BLANK()             = Infinity
0 / BLANK()             = NaN
FALSE OR BLANK          = FALSE
FALSE AND BLANK         = FALSE
TRUE OR BLANK           = TRUE
TRUE AND BLANK          = TRUE
```

**Empty Values in Excel**

Excel has a different way of handling empty values. In Excel, all empty values are considered 0 whenever they are used in a sum or in multiplication, but they return an error if they are part of division or of a logical expression.

Understanding the behavior of empty or missing values in a DAX expression and using BLANK() to return an empty cell in a calculated column or in a measure are also important skills to control the results of a DAX expression. You can often use BLANK() as a result when you detect wrong values or other errors, as you are going to learn in the next section.

## Intercepting Errors

Now that you have seen the various kinds of errors that can occur, it is time to learn a technique to intercept errors and correct them or, at least, show an error message with some meaningful information. The presence of errors in a DAX expression frequently depends on the value contained in tables and columns referenced in the expression itself. So you might want to control the presence of these error conditions and return an error message. The standard technique is to check whether an expression returns an error and, if so, replace the error with a message or a default value. To perform this operation, you use a few DAX functions that have been designed for this.

The first of them is the IFERROR function, which is very similar to the IF function, but instead of evaluating a TRUE/FALSE condition, it checks whether an expression returns an error. You can see two typical uses of the IFERRROR function here:

```
= IFERROR( Sales[Quantity] * Sales[Price], BLANK() )
= IFERROR( SQRT( Test[Omega] ), BLANK() )
```

In the first expression, if either Sales[Quantity] or Sales[Price] are strings that cannot be converted into a number, the returned expression is an empty cell; otherwise the product of Quantity and Price is returned.

In the second expression, the result is an empty cell every time the Test[Omega] column contains a negative number.

When you use IFERROR this way, you follow a more general pattern that requires the use of ISERROR and IF:

```
= IF( ISERROR( Sales[Quantity] * Sales[Price] ), BLANK(), Sales[Quantity] * Sales[Price] )
= IF( ISERROR( SQRT( Test[Omega] ) ), BLANK(), SQRT( Test[Omega] ) )
```

Of course, you ought to use IFERROR whenever the expression that has to be returned is the same tested for an error: you do not have to duplicate the expression in two places, and the resulting formula is more readable and safe in case of future changes. You should use IF, on the other hand, when you anticipate the existence of an error of an unwanted condition.

For example, the ISNUMBER can be used to detect whether a string (the price in the first line) can be converted to a number and in that case calculate the total amount; otherwise, an empty cell can be returned.

```
= IF( ISNUMBER( Sales[Price] ), Sales[Quantity] * Sales[Price], BLANK() )
= IF( Test[Omega] >= 0, SQRT( Test[Omega] ), BLANK() )
```

The second example simply detects whether the argument for SQRT is valid or not, calculating the square root only for positive numbers and returning BLANK for negative ones.

A particular case is the test against an empty value, which is called BLANK in DAX. The ISBLANK function detects an empty value condition, returning TRUE if the argument is BLANK. This is important especially when a missing value has a meaning different from a value set to 0. In the following example, we calculate the cost of shipping for a sales transaction, using a default shipping cost for the product if the weight is not specified in the sales transaction itself:

```
= IF( ISBLANK( Sales[Weight] ),
      RELATED( Product[DefaultShippingCost] ),
      Sales[Weight] * Sales[ShippingPrice] )
```

If we had just multiplied product weight and shipping price, we would have an empty cost for all the sales transactions with missing weight data.

# Common DAX Functions

Now that you have seen the fundamentals of DAX and how to handle error conditions, let us take a brief tour through the most commonly used functions and expressions of DAX. Writing a DAX expression is often similar to writing an Excel expression because many functions are similar, if not identical. Excel users often find using PowerPivot very intuitive, thanks to their previous knowledge of Excel. In the remaining part of this chapter, you see some of the most frequently used DAX functions, which you are likely to use to build your own PowerPivot data models.

## Statistical Functions

Almost every PowerPivot data model needs to operate on aggregated data. DAX offers a set of functions that aggregate the values of a column in a table and return a single value. We call this group of functions *statistical functions*. For example, the expression

```
= SUM( Sales[Amount] )
```

calculates the sum of all the numbers in the Amount column of the Sales table. This expression aggregates all the rows of the Sales table if it is used in a calculated column, but it considers only the rows that are filtered by slicers, row, columns, and filter conditions in a pivot table whenever it is used in a measure.

**Note** The syntax of aggregation functions in a DAX expression is identical to the one used by Excel formulas. Moreover, in Excel you can specify a range of cells by using the same syntax table[column] used also by DAX.

In Table A-1 of the Appendix, you can see the complete list of statistical functions available in DAX. The main four aggregation functions (SUM, AVERAGE, MIN, and MAX) operate only on numeric values. These functions are identical to the corresponding Excel functions both in name and in behavior: any data that is not numeric is ignored in the operation. In PowerPivot, these functions work only if the column passed as argument is of numeric or date type. In Figure 3-16, you can see an example of measures defined by these statistical functions.

CountryRegionCode US

| Row Labels | SUM LineTotal | AVG LineTotal | MIN LineTotal | MAX LineTotal |
|---|---|---|---|---|
| Central | 7,909,009.01 | 1,356.14 | 1.37 | 27,055.76 |
| Northeast | 6,939,374.48 | 1,189.06 | 1.37 | 14,880.00 |
| Northwest | 16,084,942.55 | 953.75 | 1.37 | 21,101.79 |
| Southeast | 7,879,655.07 | 1,318.55 | 1.37 | 24,938.48 |
| Southwest | 24,184,609.60 | 943.09 | 1.37 | 27,893.62 |
| **Grand Total** | **62,997,590.71** | **1,047.29** | **1.37** | **27,893.62** |

PowerPivot Field List
Choose fields to add to report:
OrderQty
ProductID
SpecialOfferID
UnitPrice
UnitPriceDiscount
LineTotal
rowguid
ModifiedDate
MIN LineTotal
SUM LineTotal
MAX LineTotal
AVG LineTotal
Sales_SalesOrderHeader
Sales_SalesTerritory

**FIGURE 3-16** Different measures using statistical functions aggregate LineTotal.

As in Excel formulas, DAX offers an alternative syntax to these functions to make the calculation on columns that can contain both numeric and non-numeric values, such as a text column. That syntax simply adds the suffix *A* to the name of the function, just to get the same name and behavior as Excel. However, these functions are useful only for columns containing TRUE/FALSE values because TRUE is evaluated as 1 and FALSE as 0. Any value for a text column is always considered 0. Empty cells are never considered in the calculation. So even if these functions can be used on non-numeric columns without retuning an error, their results are not always the same as Excel because there is no automatic conversion to numbers for text columns. These functions are named AVERAGEA, COUNTA, MINA, and MAXA, and you can see in Figure 3-17 an example of their usage in measures operating on a TRUE/FALSE column of the sample table shown in the same worksheet: the table is used as a linked table in PowerPivot, and the lower part of the picture is a PivotTable based on that PowerPivot data.

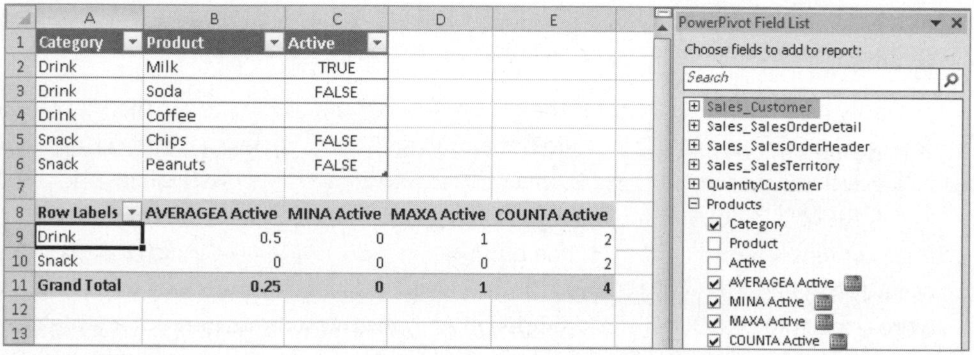

| | A | B | C | D | E |
|---|---|---|---|---|---|
| 1 | Category | Product | Active | | |
| 2 | Drink | Milk | TRUE | | |
| 3 | Drink | Soda | FALSE | | |
| 4 | Drink | Coffee | | | |
| 5 | Snack | Chips | FALSE | | |
| 6 | Snack | Peanuts | FALSE | | |
| 7 | | | | | |
| 8 | Row Labels | AVERAGEA Active | MINA Active | MAXA Active | COUNTA Active |
| 9 | Drink | 0.5 | 0 | 1 | 2 |
| 10 | Snack | 0 | 0 | 0 | 2 |
| 11 | Grand Total | 0.25 | 0 | 1 | 4 |
| 12 | | | | | |
| 13 | | | | | |

PowerPivot Field List
Choose fields to add to report:
Search
- Sales_Customer
- Sales_SalesOrderDetail
- Sales_SalesOrderHeader
- Sales_SalesTerritory
- QuantityCustomer
- Products
  - [x] Category
  - [ ] Product
  - [ ] Active
  - [x] AVERAGEA Active
  - [x] MINA Active
  - [x] MAXA Active
  - [x] COUNTA Active

**FIGURE 3-17** TRUE/FALSE are evaluated as 1/0 in A-suffixed statistical functions.

Despite the same name of statistical functions, the difference in the way they are used in DAX and Excel exists because in PowerPivot a column has a type and its type determines the behavior of aggregation functions. Excel handles a type for each cell, whereas PowerPivot handles a type for each column. PowerPivot deals with data in tabular form (technically it is called relational data) with well-defined types for each column, whereas Excel formulas work on heterogeneous cell values, without well-defined types. If a column in PowerPivot is of a number type, all the values can be only numbers or empty cells. If a column is of a text type, it is always 0 for these functions, even if the text can be converted to a number, whereas in Excel the value is considered a number on a cell-by-cell basis. For these reasons, these DAX functions are not very useful for Text type columns.

Figure 3-18 shows a comparison of the calculation made by the same functions in Excel and PowerPivot, using the same data you can see in the table on the left of the worksheet. The text value N/A in the Quantity column in Excel is considered 0 by calculations of AVERAGEA, MINA, MAXA, and COUNTA made by Excel 2010, as you can see in the second row of the worksheet. However, the calculation of the same measure in PowerPivot considers the value to be 0 for any cell (see the fifth row) because the whole Quantity column is imported as Text in the corresponding PowerPivot table.

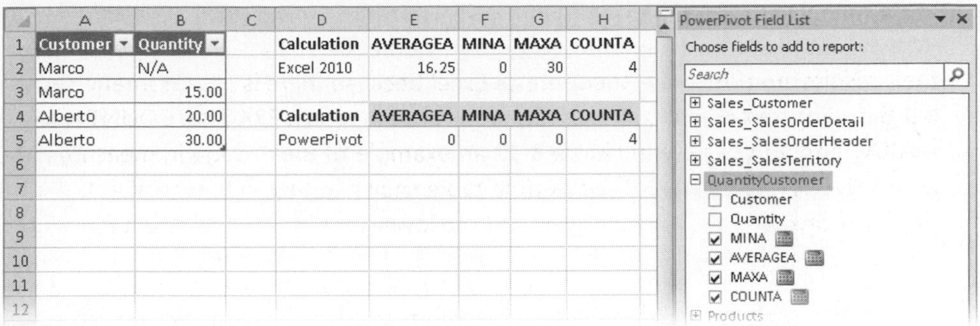

| Customer | Quantity | | Calculation | AVERAGEA | MINA | MAXA | COUNTA |
|---|---|---|---|---|---|---|---|
| Marco | N/A | | Excel 2010 | 16.25 | 0 | 30 | 4 |
| Marco | 15.00 | | | | | | |
| Alberto | 20.00 | | Calculation | AVERAGEA | MINA | MAXA | COUNTA |
| Alberto | 30.00 | | PowerPivot | 0 | 0 | 0 | 4 |

**FIGURE 3-18** Different measures using statistical functions aggregate LineTotal.

The only interesting function in the group of A-suffixed functions is the COUNTA one. It returns the number of cells that are not empty and works on any type of column. If you are interested in counting all the cells in a column containing an empty value, you can use the COUNTBLANK functions. Finally, if you want to count all the cells of a column regardless of their content, you want to count the number of rows of the table, which can be obtained by calling the COUNTROWS function. (It gets a table as a parameter, not a column.) In other words, the sum of COUNTA and COUNTBLANK for the same column of a table is always equal to the number of rows of the same table, as you can also see in Figure 3-19:

```
COUNTROWS( Sales ) = COUNTA( Sales[SalesPersonID] ) + COUNTBLANK( Sales[SalesPersonID] )
```

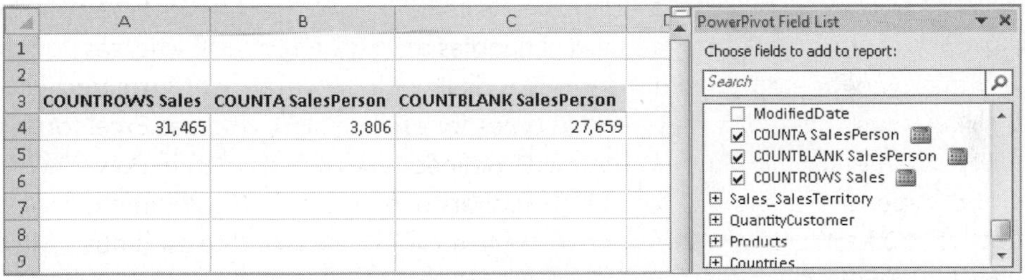

| COUNTROWS Sales | COUNTA SalesPerson | COUNTBLANK SalesPerson |
|---|---|---|
| 31,465 | 3,806 | 27,659 |

**FIGURE 3-19** The COUNTROWS function returns the sum of COUNTA and COUNTBLANK of the same column.

So you have four functions to count the number of elements in a column or table:

- COUNT operates only on numeric columns
- COUNTA operates on any type of columns
- COUNTBLANK returns the number of empty cells in a column
- COUNTROWS returns the number of rows in a table

There is a last set of statistical functions that can apply an expression to each row of a table and then operate an aggregation on that expression. This set of functions is very useful, especially when you want to make calculations using columns of different related tables. For example, if a Sales table contains all the sales transactions and a related Product table contains all the information about a product, including its cost, you might calculate the total internal cost of a sales transaction by defining a measure with this expression:

```
[Cost] = SUMX( Sales, Sales[Quantity] * RELATED( Product[StandardCost] ) )
```

This function calculates the product of Quantity (from Sales table) and StandardCost of the sold product (from the related Product table) for each row in the Sales table, and it returns the sum of all these calculated values. In Figure 3-20, you can see an example of this calculation in the Cost measure of the PivotTable.

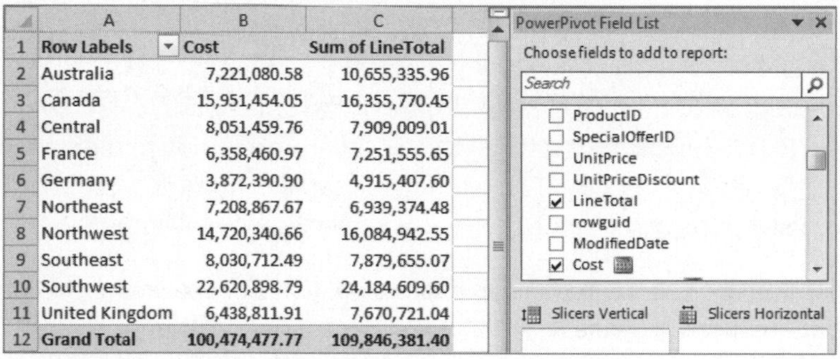

| | A | B | C |
|---|---|---|---|
| 1 | Row Labels | Cost | Sum of LineTotal |
| 2 | Australia | 7,221,080.58 | 10,655,335.96 |
| 3 | Canada | 15,951,454.05 | 16,355,770.45 |
| 4 | Central | 8,051,459.76 | 7,909,009.01 |
| 5 | France | 6,358,460.97 | 7,251,555.65 |
| 6 | Germany | 3,872,390.90 | 4,915,407.60 |
| 7 | Northeast | 7,208,867.67 | 6,939,374.48 |
| 8 | Northwest | 14,720,340.66 | 16,084,942.55 |
| 9 | Southeast | 8,030,712.49 | 7,879,655.07 |
| 10 | Southwest | 22,620,898.79 | 24,184,609.60 |
| 11 | United Kingdom | 6,438,811.91 | 7,670,721.04 |
| 12 | Grand Total | 100,474,477.77 | 109,846,381.40 |

PowerPivot Field List
Choose fields to add to report:
Search
ProductID
SpecialOfferID
UnitPrice
UnitPriceDiscount
LineTotal
rowguid
ModifiedDate
Cost
Slicers Vertical
Slicers Horizontal

**FIGURE 3-20** Using SUMX to calculate standard cost of products sold.

Generally speaking, all the aggregation functions ending with an *X* suffix behave this way: they calculate an expression (the second parameter) for each of the rows of a table (the first parameter) and return a result obtained by the corresponding aggregation function (sum, min, max or count) applied to the result of those calculations. We explain this behavior further in Chapter 6, "Evaluation Context and CALCULATE"; evaluation context is important for understanding how this calculation works. The *X* suffixed functions available are SUMX, AVERAGEX, COUNTX, COUNTAX, MINX, and MAXX.

## Logical Functions

Sometime you might need to build a logical condition in an expression—for example, to implement different calculations depending on the value of a column or to intercept an error condition. In these cases, you can use one of the logical functions in DAX. You have already seen in the previous section, "Handling Errors in DAX Expressions," the two most important functions of this group, which are IF and IFERROR. In Table A-2 of the Appendix, you can see the list of all of these functions (which are AND, FALSE, IF, IFERROR, NOT, TRUE, and OR) and their syntax. In Figure 3-21, you can also see an example of using the IFERROR function: the Price column is of type Text because it contains a N/A value, and the Amount and CheckedAmount columns are calculated using the following formulas:

```
Amount = Sales[Quantity] * Sales[Price]
CheckedAmount = IFERROR( Sales[Quantity] * Sales[Price], BLANK() )
```

[CheckedAmoun ▾ | fx | =IFERROR(Sales[Quantity]*Sales[Price],BLANK())

| Product | Quantity | Price | Amount | CheckedAmount | Add Column |
|---|---|---|---|---|---|
| Bike | 2 | 100 | #ERROR | 200 | |
| Hat | 1 | 15 | #ERROR | 15 | |
| Notebook | 1 | 399 | #ERROR | 399 | |
| Gadget | 3 | N/A | #ERROR | | |

**FIGURE 3-21** Using IFERROR to avoid conversion errors.

The Amount column returns an error because of the N/A value contained in the Gadget row because even if a single row generates a calculation error, the error is propagated to the whole column. The formula used in CheckedAmount column, on the other hand, intercepts the error and replaces it with a blank value.

## Information Functions

Whenever you need to analyze the type of an expression, you can use one of the information functions that are listed in Table A-3 of the Appendix. All of these functions return a TRUE/FALSE value and can be used in any logical expression. They are: ISBLANK, ISERROR, ISLOGICAL, ISNONTEXT, ISNUMBER, and ISTEXT.

It is important to note that when a table column is passed as a parameter, the functions ISNUMBER, ISTEXT, and ISNONTEXT always returns TRUE or FALSE, depending on the data type of the column and on the empty condition of each cell. In Figure 3-22, you can see how the column Price (which is of Text type) affects the result of these calculated columns:

```
ISBLANK = ISBLANK( Sales[Price] )
ISNUMBER = ISNUMBER( Sales[Price] )
ISTEXT = ISTEXT( Sales[Price] )
ISNONTEXT = ISNONTEXT( Sales[Price] )
ISERROR = ISERROR( Sales[Price] + 0 )
```

| Product | Price | ISBLANK | ISNUMBER | ISTEXT | ISNONTEXT | ISERROR |
|---|---|---|---|---|---|---|
| Bike | 100 | FALSE | FALSE | TRUE | FALSE | FALSE |
| Clock | | TRUE | FALSE | FALSE | TRUE | FALSE |
| Hat | 15 | FALSE | FALSE | TRUE | FALSE | FALSE |
| Notebook | 399 | FALSE | FALSE | TRUE | FALSE | FALSE |
| Gadget | N/A | FALSE | FALSE | TRUE | FALSE | TRUE |

**FIGURE 3-22** Results from information functions are based on column type.

You might be wondering whether ISNUMBER can be used with a text column just to check whether a conversion to a number is possible. Unfortunately, you cannot use this approach; if you want to test whether a text value can be converted to a number, you need to try the conversion and handle the error if it fails. To get a TRUE result from the ISERROR function, for example, we tried to add a zero to the Price, to force the conversion from a Text value to a number. The conversion fails for the N/A price value, so you can see that ISERROR is TRUE for that row only.

## Mathematical Functions

The set of mathematical functions available in DAX is very similar to the same set in Excel, with the same syntax and behavior. You can see the complete list of these functions and their syntax in Table A-4 of the Appendix. The mathematical functions of common use are ABS, EXP, FACT, LN, LOG, LOG10, MOD, PI, POWER, QUOTIENT, SIGN, and SQRT. Random functions are RAND and RANDBETWEEN. Finally, there are several functions to round numbers that deserve an example; in fact, you might use several approaches to get the same result. Consider these calculated columns, along with their results in Figure 3-23:

```
FLOOR = FLOOR( Tests[Value], 0.01 )
TRUNC = TRUNC( Tests[Value], 2 )
ROUNDDOWN = ROUNDDOWN( Tests[Value], 2 )
MROUND = MROUND( Tests[Value], 0.01 )
ROUND = ROUND( Tests[Value], 2 )
CEILING = CEILING( Tests[Value], 0.01 )
ROUNDUP = ROUNDUP( Tests[Value], 2 )
INT = INT( Tests[Value] )
```

| Test | Value | FLOOR | TRUNC | ROUNDDOWN | MROUND | ROUND | CEILING | ROUNDUP | INT |
|---|---|---|---|---|---|---|---|---|---|
| A | 1.12345 | 1.12 | 1.12 | 1.12 | 1.12 | 1.12 | 1.13 | 1.13 | 1 |
| B | 1.265 | 1.26 | 1.26 | 1.26 | 1.26 | 1.27 | 1.27 | 1.27 | 1 |
| C | 1.265001 | 1.26 | 1.26 | 1.26 | 1.27 | 1.27 | 1.27 | 1.27 | 1 |
| D | 1.499999 | 1.49 | 1.49 | 1.49 | 1.5 | 1.5 | 1.5 | 1.5 | 1 |
| E | 1.51111 | 1.51 | 1.51 | 1.51 | 1.51 | 1.51 | 1.52 | 1.52 | 1 |
| F | 1.000001 | 1 | 1 | 1 | 1 | 1 | 1.01 | 1.01 | 1 |
| G | 1.999999 | 1.99 | 1.99 | 1.99 | 2 | 2 | 2 | 2 | 1 |

**FIGURE 3-23** Summary of different rounding functions.

As you can see, FLOOR, TRUNC, and ROUNDDOWN are very similar, except in the way you can specify the number of digits to round on. In the opposite direction, CEILING and ROUNDUP are very similar in their results. You can see a few differences in the way the rounding is done (see row B, where 1.265 number is rounded in two different ways on the second decimal digit) between MROUND and ROUND function. Finally, it is important to note that FLOOR and MROUND functions do not operate on negative numbers, whereas other functions do.

## Text Functions

Almost all of the text functions available in DAX are similar to those available in Excel, with only a few exceptions, which are noted in the Appendix. Table A-5 of the Appendix contains a complete description of the text functions available in DAX: they are CONCATENATE, EXACT, FIND, FIXED, FORMAT, LEFT, LEN, LOWER, MID, REPLACE, REPT, RIGHT, SEARCH, SUBSTITUTE, TRIM, UPPER and VALUE. These functions are useful for manipulating text and extracting data from strings that contain multiple values. For example, in Figure 3-24, you can see an example of the extraction of first and last name from a string containing these values separated by commas, with the title in the middle that we want to remove.

We start calculating the position of the two commas and then we use these numbers to extract the right part of the text. The SimpleConversion column implements a formula that might return wrong values if there are fewer than two commas in the string (and it raises an error if there are no commas at all), whereas the FirstLastName column implements a more complex expression that does not fail in case of missing commas.

```
Comma1 = IFERROR( FIND( ",", People[Name] ), BLANK() )
Comma2 = IFERROR( FIND( ",", People[Name], People[Comma1] + 1 ), BLANK() )
SimpleConversion = MID( People[Name], People[Comma2] + 1, LEN(People[Name]) )
                   & " " & LEFT( People[Name], People[Comma1]-1 )
FirstLastName = TRIM( MID( People[Name], IF( ISNUMBER( People[Comma2] ),
                                             People[Comma2],
                                             People[Comma1] ) + 1, LEN(People[Name]) ) )
                & IF( ISNUMBER( People[Comma1] ),
                      " " & LEFT( People[Name], People[Comma1] - 1 ),
                      "" )
```

| Name | Comma1 | Comma2 | SimpleConversion | FirstLastName |
|---|---|---|---|---|
| Russo, Mr., Marco | 6 | 11 | Marco Russo | Marco Russo |
| Ferrari, Mr., Alberto | 8 | 13 | Alberto Ferrari | Alberto Ferrari |
| Ferrari, Alberto | 8 | | Ferrari, Alberto Ferrari | Alberto Ferrari |

**FIGURE 3-24** Extracting first and last names using text functions.

As you can see, the FirstLastName column is defined by a long DAX expression, but you must use it to avoid possible errors that would propagate to the whole column if even a single value generated an error.

## Date and Time Functions

Almost in every type of data analysis, handling time and date is an important part of the job. PowerPivot has a large number of functions that operate on date and time. Some of them correspond to similar functions in Excel and make simple transformations to and from a datetime data type, like the ones described in Table A-6 of the Appendix. These are DATE, DATEVALUE, DAY, EDATE, EOMONTH, HOUR, MINUTE, MONTH, NOW, SECOND, TIME, TIMEVALUE, TODAY,

WEEKDAY, WEEKNUM, YEAR, and YEARFRAC. To make more complex operation on dates, such as comparing aggregated values year over year or calculating year to date value of a measure, there is another set of functions called *Time Intelligence Functions* that will be described later in the book in Chapter 7.

As we said before in this chapter, a datetime data type internally uses a floating point number wherein the integer part corresponds to the day of the month (starting from December 30, 1899) and the decimal part indicates the fraction of the day in time. (Hours, minutes, and seconds are converted into a decimal fractions of the day.) So adding an integer number to a datetime value increments the value by a corresponding amount of days. However, most of the time the conversion functions are used to extract day, month, and year from a date. In the following example, you can see how to extract this information from a table containing a list of dates (see Figure 3-25).

```
Day = DAY( Calendar[Date] )
Month = FORMAT( Calendar[Date], "MM - mmmm" )
Year = YEAR( Calendar[Date] )
```

| Date | Day | Month | Year |
|---|---|---|---|
| 12/29/2010 | 29 | 12 - December | 2010 |
| 12/30/2010 | 30 | 12 - December | 2010 |
| 12/31/2010 | 31 | 12 - December | 2010 |
| 1/1/2011 | 1 | 01 - January | 2011 |
| 1/2/2011 | 2 | 01 - January | 2011 |

**FIGURE 3-25** Extracting date information using date and time functions.

As you can see in Figure 3-25, the Month column is calculated using the FORMAT function, which is classified as a text function but is very useful for building a string that keeps the right sort order of the months by placing the month number before the month name. (Day and Year columns are sorted in the right order because of their numeric data type.)

# Summary

In this chapter, you have explored the syntax of DAX, its data types, and the operators and functions available. You have also learned the following:

- Differences between calculated columns and measures and how to choose between them
- How to handle errors and empty values in DAX expressions using common patterns
- What groups of functions are available in DAX (Statistical, Logical, Information, Mathematical, Text, Date, and Time) and their similarities and differences with Excel formulas

Chapter 4

# Data Models

The first three chapters of this book introduced some basic Microsoft SQL Server PowerPivot for Excel features for generating interesting reports from existing data. In our examples, you discovered the need to model your data to make it easier to understand and manage. Nevertheless, because all the examples were introductory, data modeling was not an issue. It is now time to perform a deeper analysis of data modeling, discover what it is, and how to handle different data models.

Data modeling is not a new concept for database analysts and administrators. These technicians already know that a good data model is the foundation of a good database solution. The PowerPivot world is not exceptional in that regard: a good data model is definitely the foundation of a good reporting system for PowerPivot.

On the other hand, data modeling is somewhat new in the Excel world. Until the introduction of PowerPivot, Excel users could query only one table at a time and so the very concept of relationships was missing. PowerPivot is normally seen as a querying system, a tool that makes it possible to extract certain information from tables. PowerPivot does much more than this, indeed. It is a sophisticated columnar database able to store huge amounts of data. Let us restate this: it is a real database. Because you need to work with a database, you do need to understand how different tables are related to each other and which model is the easiest and most effective at serving your needs. In short, you need to learn the basics of data modeling.

You have already learned in previous chapters the concept of relationships, which is the foundation of data modeling. But because we believe that relationships and data models need to be well understood by the PowerPivot analyst, we are dedicating this entire chapter to data modeling.

# Understanding Data Models

We are now going to introduce data modeling with a simple story. Michelle works in accounting and is an Excel power user. Her manager asked her to perform the sales analysis of different product models, without (clearly) giving any further advice about how to do that. She knows that the first step is always to find all the data needed. So she asks Bill, in the IT department, for some advice. His answer sounds like this:

> *"Well, we have a database with a table named Product, which contains all products. There are several satellite tables that provide descriptions; these are simple domain tables. Moreover, each product has a model, is linked with its photos in different resolutions and, if the price is changed, we hold all the history of price changes in an appropriate table. If you want to focus on models, start looking at Production.ProductModels, and from there you can easily catch all the sales by following very easy-to-see relationships. I think you can get all this data from Excel and then start your analysis."*

## Following the Standard Excel Method

Michelle knows that she needs to load data into Excel worksheets to be able to perform any kind of analysis. Following Bill's instructions, she starts by loading the ProductModel table into an Excel worksheet.

Without knowledge of PowerPivot, she first tries the standard Excel solution. Using the Data menu, choosing the From Other Sources option, and then choosing the From SQL Server option, Michelle establishes a connection with the database, finds the ProductModel table, and loads it into Excel. She ends up with a worksheet like the one shown in Figure 4-1. You can see the example on your computer by using the companion workbook CH04-01-MichelleExcel.xlsx.

| ProductModelID | Name | CatalogDescription | Instructions | ModifiedDate |
|---|---|---|---|---|
| 1 | Classic Vest | | | 6/1/2003 0:00 |
| 2 | Cycling Cap | | | 6/1/2001 0:00 |
| 3 | Full-Finger Gloves | | | 6/1/2002 0:00 |
| 4 | Half-Finger Gloves | | | 6/1/2002 0:00 |
| 5 | HL Mountain Frame | | | 6/1/2001 0:00 |
| 6 | HL Road Frame | | | 5/2/1998 0:00 |
| 7 | HL Touring Frame | | <root xmlns="http://schem | 5/16/2005 16:34 |
| 8 | LL Mountain Frame | | | 11/20/2002 9:56 |
| 9 | LL Road Frame | | | 6/1/2001 0:00 |
| 10 | LL Touring Frame | | <root xmlns="http://schem | 5/16/2005 16:34 |
| 11 | Long-Sleeve Logo Jersey | | | 6/1/2001 0:00 |
| 12 | Men's Bib-Shorts | | | 6/1/2002 0:00 |
| 13 | Men's Sports Shorts | | | 6/1/2002 0:00 |
| 14 | ML Mountain Frame | | | 6/1/2002 0:00 |
| 15 | ML Mountain Frame-W | | | 6/1/2002 0:00 |
| 16 | ML Road Frame | | | 6/1/2001 0:00 |
| 17 | ML Road Frame-W | | | 6/1/2002 0:00 |
| 18 | Mountain Bike Socks | | | 6/1/2001 0:00 |
| 19 | Mountain-100 | <?xml-stylesheet href="ProductDescription.xsl" type | | 6/1/2001 0:00 |

**FIGURE 4-1** The ProductModel table in an Excel worksheet.

Looking at the worksheet, in the Name column, she can see the different product models, but where is the sales information for these products?

Michelle calls Bill again. He answers:

> *"Of course there is no sales data about product models. As I said, products are linked to product models, and sales are about products. If you need to analyze sales by product model, you definitely need to follow the chain of relationship from sales to products, then from products to product model. You may then issue a GROUP BY on the columns you need. By the way, sales are stored in the sales order, which is a standard master/detail structure."*

Michelle follows Bill's instruction to search for a relationship between product models and products, and so she loads the Product table into another Excel worksheet and ends up with a pretty complex spreadsheet that contains all the information about products. Because there are too many columns for her purposes, she removes useless columns and ends up with a worksheet like the one in Figure 4-2.

| ProductID | Name | ProductNumber | Color | StandardCost | ProductModelID |
|---|---|---|---|---|---|
| 1 | Adjustable Race | AR-5381 | | 0 | |
| 2 | Bearing Ball | BA-8327 | | 0 | |
| 3 | BB Ball Bearing | BE-2349 | | 0 | |
| 4 | Headset Ball Bearings | BE-2908 | | 0 | |
| 316 | Blade | BL-2036 | | 0 | |
| 317 | LL Crankarm | CA-5965 | Black | 0 | |
| 318 | ML Crankarm | CA-6738 | Black | 0 | |
| 319 | HL Crankarm | CA-7457 | Black | 0 | |
| 320 | Chainring Bolts | CB-2903 | Silver | 0 | |
| 321 | Chainring Nut | CN-6137 | Silver | 0 | |
| 322 | Chainring | CR-7833 | Black | 0 | |
| 323 | Crown Race | CR-9981 | | 0 | |
| 324 | Chain Stays | CS-2812 | | 0 | |
| 325 | Decal 1 | DC-8732 | | 0 | |
| 326 | Decal 2 | DC-9824 | | 0 | |
| 327 | Down Tube | DT-2377 | | 0 | |
| 328 | Mountain End Caps | EC-M092 | | 0 | |
| 329 | Road End Caps | EC-R098 | | 0 | |
| 330 | Touring End Caps | EC-T209 | | 0 | |

**FIGURE 4-2** The Product table in an Excel worksheet.

There is no information about product models in this table; it contains only product information. Scrolling down, Michelle notices that, in the ProductModelID column, there are several products that contain a value. One of these is the first product in Figure 4-3, which contains *6* as ProductModelID.

| ProductID | Name | ProductNumber | Color | StandardCost | ProductModelID |
|---|---|---|---|---|---|
| 706 | HL Road Frame - Red, 58 | FR-R92R-58 | Red | 1059.31 | 6 |
| 707 | Sport-100 Helmet, Red | HL-U509-R | Red | 13.0863 | 33 |
| 708 | Sport-100 Helmet, Black | HL-U509 | Black | 13.0863 | 33 |
| 709 | Mountain Bike Socks, M | SO-B909-M | White | 3.3963 | 18 |
| 710 | Mountain Bike Socks, L | SO-B909-L | White | 3.3963 | 18 |
| 711 | Sport-100 Helmet, Blue | HL-U509-B | Blue | 13.0863 | 33 |
| 712 | AWC Logo Cap | CA-1098 | Multi | 6.9223 | 2 |
| 713 | Long-Sleeve Logo Jersey, S | LJ-0192-S | Multi | 38.4923 | 11 |
| 714 | Long-Sleeve Logo Jersey, M | LJ-0192-M | Multi | 38.4923 | 11 |
| 715 | Long-Sleeve Logo Jersey, L | LJ-0192-L | Multi | 38.4923 | 11 |
| 716 | Long-Sleeve Logo Jersey, XL | LJ-0192-X | Multi | 38.4923 | 11 |
| 717 | HL Road Frame - Red, 62 | FR-R92R-62 | Red | 868.6342 | 6 |
| 718 | HL Road Frame - Red, 44 | FR-R92R-44 | Red | 868.6342 | 6 |
| 719 | HL Road Frame - Red, 48 | FR-R92R-48 | Red | 868.6342 | 6 |
| 720 | HL Road Frame - Red, 52 | FR-R92R-52 | Red | 868.6342 | 6 |
| 721 | HL Road Frame - Red, 56 | FR-R92R-56 | Red | 868.6342 | 6 |
| 722 | LL Road Frame - Black, 58 | FR-R38B-58 | Black | 204.6251 | 9 |
| 723 | LL Road Frame - Black, 60 | FR-R38B-60 | Black | 204.6251 | 9 |
| 724 | LL Road Frame - Black, 62 | FR-R38B-62 | Black | 204.6251 | 9 |

**FIGURE 4-3** The Product table contains interesting values for ProductModelID.

Looking back at the first worksheet (see Figure 4-1), she discovers that the product model with a ProductModelID that equals 6 is indeed *HL Road Frame*, which happens to be the product model of the HL Road—Red, 58 product. The column ProductModelID in the table of products is actually the value of the ProductModelID in the product models table. To attach the product model description to the product table, it is enough to use a simple VLOOKUP function.

Michelle adds the column name ProductModel just after ProductModelID with this formula:

```
=VLOOKUP([@ProductModelID],Table_PowerPivot_SQL2008R2_AdventureWorks[#All], 2)
```

Now in Figure 4-4, she proudly looks at a more useful worksheet.

| ProductID | Name | ProductNumber | Color | StandardCost | Produc | ProductModel |
|---|---|---|---|---|---|---|
| 680 | HL Road Frame - Black, 58 | FR-R92B-58 | Black | 1059.31 | 6 | HL Road Frame |
| 706 | HL Road Frame - Red, 58 | FR-R92R-58 | Red | 1059.31 | 6 | HL Road Frame |
| 707 | Sport-100 Helmet, Red | HL-U509-R | Red | 13.0863 | 33 | Sport-100 |
| 708 | Sport-100 Helmet, Black | HL-U509 | Black | 13.0863 | 33 | Sport-100 |
| 709 | Mountain Bike Socks, M | SO-B909-M | White | 3.3963 | 18 | Mountain Bike Socks |
| 710 | Mountain Bike Socks, L | SO-B909-L | White | 3.3963 | 18 | Mountain Bike Socks |
| 711 | Sport-100 Helmet, Blue | HL-U509-B | Blue | 13.0863 | 33 | Sport-100 |
| 712 | AWC Logo Cap | CA-1098 | Multi | 6.9223 | 2 | Cycling Cap |
| 713 | Long-Sleeve Logo Jersey, S | LJ-0192-S | Multi | 38.4923 | 11 | Long-Sleeve Logo Jersey |
| 714 | Long-Sleeve Logo Jersey, M | LJ-0192-M | Multi | 38.4923 | 11 | Long-Sleeve Logo Jersey |
| 715 | Long-Sleeve Logo Jersey, L | LJ-0192-L | Multi | 38.4923 | 11 | Long-Sleeve Logo Jersey |
| 716 | Long-Sleeve Logo Jersey, XL | LJ-0192-X | Multi | 38.4923 | 11 | Long-Sleeve Logo Jersey |
| 717 | HL Road Frame - Red, 62 | FR-R92R-62 | Red | 868.6342 | 6 | HL Road Frame |
| 718 | HL Road Frame - Red, 44 | FR-R92R-44 | Red | 868.6342 | 6 | HL Road Frame |
| 719 | HL Road Frame - Red, 48 | FR-R92R-48 | Red | 868.6342 | 6 | HL Road Frame |
| 720 | HL Road Frame - Red, 52 | FR-R92R-52 | Red | 868.6342 | 6 | HL Road Frame |
| 721 | HL Road Frame - Red, 56 | FR-R92R-56 | Red | 868.6342 | 6 | HL Road Frame |
| 722 | LL Road Frame - Black, 58 | FR-R38B-58 | Black | 204.6251 | 9 | LL Road Frame |
| 723 | LL Road Frame - Black, 60 | FR-R38B-60 | Black | 204.6251 | 9 | LL Road Frame |

**FIGURE 4-4** Both products and models in the same worksheet.

In this new worksheet, she has both products and models in the same table, and life looks much better because the final goal seems to be approaching. Bill said to follow the relationship between products and models, and Michelle tried to do that by adding a column to the table that uses the VLOOKUP function. She knows that this might not be exactly what Bill said to do, but she feels that she's on the right path.

Still, she has the first Excel table loaded without any sales at all. Nevertheless, Bill said to follow another relationship (which now Michelle knows is a simple VLOOKUP). He said to remember that sales are stored in orders. It is now time to look for that table.

Michelle searches for something related to sales orders and loads a table called SalesOrderDetail. After cleaning it up a bit, she ends up with the table shown in Figure 4-5.

| SalesOrderID | SalesOrderDetailID | OrderQty | ProductID | UnitPrice | LineTotal |
|---|---|---|---|---|---|
| 43659 | 1 | 1 | 776 | 2024.994 | 2024.994 |
| 43659 | 2 | 3 | 777 | 2024.994 | 6074.982 |
| 43659 | 3 | 1 | 778 | 2024.994 | 2024.994 |
| 43659 | 4 | 1 | 771 | 2039.994 | 2039.994 |
| 43659 | 5 | 1 | 772 | 2039.994 | 2039.994 |
| 43659 | 6 | 2 | 773 | 2039.994 | 4079.988 |
| 43659 | 7 | 1 | 774 | 2039.994 | 2039.994 |
| 43659 | 8 | 3 | 714 | 28.8404 | 86.5212 |
| 43659 | 9 | 1 | 716 | 28.8404 | 28.8404 |
| 43659 | 10 | 6 | 709 | 5.7 | 34.2 |
| 43659 | 11 | 2 | 712 | 5.1865 | 10.373 |
| 43659 | 12 | 4 | 711 | 20.1865 | 80.746 |
| 43660 | 13 | 1 | 762 | 419.4589 | 419.4589 |
| 43660 | 14 | 1 | 758 | 874.794 | 874.794 |
| 43661 | 15 | 1 | 745 | 809.76 | 809.76 |
| 43661 | 16 | 1 | 743 | 714.7043 | 714.7043 |
| 43661 | 17 | 2 | 747 | 714.7043 | 1429.4086 |
| 43661 | 18 | 4 | 712 | 5.1865 | 20.746 |
| 43661 | 19 | 4 | 715 | 28.8404 | 115.3616 |

**FIGURE 4-5** The SalesOrderDetail table.

There is an interesting pattern here. Just as in products, she had the ProductModelID column, here she has a ProductID column that might be related somehow to the product sold. She tries the VLOOKUP function again, but this time she searches the product table for the ProductID column. Moreover, because she has already loaded the product model in the product table, she can use VLOOKUP to load the product model to the SalesOrderDetail table.

The result is very appealing, as is shown in Figure 4-6.

| SalesOrderID | SalesOrderDetailID | OrderQty | ProductID | Product | ProductModel | UnitPrice | LineTotal |
|---|---|---|---|---|---|---|---|
| 43659 | 1 | 1 | 776 | Mountain-100 Black, 42 | Mountain-100 | 2024.994 | 2024.994 |
| 43659 | 2 | 3 | 777 | Mountain-100 Black, 44 | Mountain-100 | 2024.994 | 6074.982 |
| 43659 | 3 | 1 | 778 | Mountain-100 Black, 48 | Mountain-100 | 2024.994 | 2024.994 |
| 43659 | 4 | 1 | 771 | Mountain-100 Silver, 38 | Mountain-100 | 2039.994 | 2039.994 |
| 43659 | 5 | 1 | 772 | Mountain-100 Silver, 42 | Mountain-100 | 2039.994 | 2039.994 |
| 43659 | 6 | 2 | 773 | Mountain-100 Silver, 44 | Mountain-100 | 2039.994 | 4079.988 |
| 43659 | 7 | 1 | 774 | Mountain-100 Silver, 48 | Mountain-100 | 2039.994 | 2039.994 |
| 43659 | 8 | 3 | 714 | Long-Sleeve Logo Jersey, M | Long-Sleeve Logo Jersey | 28.8404 | 86.5212 |
| 43659 | 9 | 1 | 716 | Long-Sleeve Logo Jersey, XL | Long-Sleeve Logo Jersey | 28.8404 | 28.8404 |
| 43659 | 10 | 6 | 709 | Mountain Bike Socks, M | Mountain Bike Socks | 5.7 | 34.2 |
| 43659 | 11 | 2 | 712 | AWC Logo Cap | Cycling Cap | 5.1865 | 10.373 |
| 43659 | 12 | 4 | 711 | Sport-100 Helmet, Blue | Sport-100 | 20.1865 | 80.746 |
| 43660 | 13 | 1 | 762 | Road-650 Red, 44 | Road-650 | 419.4589 | 419.4589 |
| 43660 | 14 | 1 | 758 | Road-450 Red, 52 | Road-450 | 874.794 | 874.794 |
| 43661 | 15 | 1 | 745 | HL Mountain Frame - Black, 48 | HL Mountain Frame | 809.76 | 809.76 |
| 43661 | 16 | 1 | 743 | HL Mountain Frame - Black, 42 | HL Mountain Frame | 714.7043 | 714.7043 |
| 43661 | 17 | 2 | 747 | HL Mountain Frame - Black, 38 | HL Mountain Frame | 714.7043 | 1429.4086 |
| 43661 | 18 | 4 | 712 | AWC Logo Cap | Cycling Cap | 5.1865 | 20.746 |
| 43661 | 19 | 4 | 715 | Long-Sleeve Logo Jersey, L | Long-Sleeve Logo Jersey | 28.8404 | 115.3616 |
| 43661 | 20 | 2 | 742 | HL Mountain Frame - Silver, 46 | HL Mountain Frame | 722.5949 | 1445.1898 |
| 43661 | 21 | 3 | 775 | Mountain-100 Black, 38 | Mountain-100 | 2024.994 | 6074.982 |
| 43661 | 22 | 2 | 778 | Mountain-100 Black, 48 | Mountain-100 | 2024.994 | 4049.988 |
| 43661 | 23 | 2 | 711 | Sport-100 Helmet, Blue | Sport-100 | 20.1865 | 40.373 |
| 43661 | 24 | 2 | 741 | HL Mountain Frame - Silver, 48 | HL Mountain Frame | 818.7 | 1637.4 |
| 43661 | 25 | 4 | 776 | Mountain-100 Black, 42 | Mountain-100 | 2024.994 | 8099.976 |
| 43661 | 26 | 2 | 773 | Mountain-100 Silver, 44 | Mountain-100 | 2039.994 | 4079.988 |
| 43661 | 27 | 2 | 716 | Long-Sleeve Logo Jersey, XL | Long-Sleeve Logo Jersey | 28.8404 | 57.6808 |

**FIGURE 4-6** Product and ProductModel in the sales order detail table.

This Excel table seems to be very near to the final result; she is just missing the date of the order to have a table containing all the data she needs. Michelle now recognizes how valuable VLOOKUP is in this situation: if the date of the order is not in the sales order detail table, it might be in some other table, and she can use VLOOKUP again to put it into the detail table.

It happens that the table SalesOrderHeader contains an OrderDate column, and that table seems to share the column SalesOrderID with the SalesOrderDetail table. It is just a matter of loading the SalesOrderHeader table into Excel, adding one more VLOOKUP column to the sales table and she ends up with the final result, which contains order date, product, product model, quantity, and line total. She needs to slice data for sales year and month, so she adds two new calculated columns to the main table (YEAR and MONTH of the OrderDate) and can now use the PivotTable to produce the required report. In Figure 4-7, you can see the final worksheet, which is the source of the pivot table.

The final Excel workbook file is more or less 16 MB in size. It is pretty slow whenever Michelle wants to update something, yet it works and solves the problem. Without knowledge of data modeling, Michelle has developed a method of performing analysis: using VLOOKUP and loading tables is the way to get reports done.

| SalesOrderID | OrderDate | OrderYear | OrderMonth | OrderQty | Product | ProductModel | UnitPrice | LineTotal |
|---|---|---|---|---|---|---|---|---|
| 43659 | 7/1/2001 | 2001 | 7 | 1 | Mountain-100 Black, 42 | Mountain-100 | 2024.994 | 2024.994 |
| 43659 | 7/1/2001 | 2001 | 7 | 3 | Mountain-100 Black, 44 | Mountain-100 | 2024.994 | 6074.982 |
| 43659 | 7/1/2001 | 2001 | 7 | 1 | Mountain-100 Black, 48 | Mountain-100 | 2024.994 | 2024.994 |
| 43659 | 7/1/2001 | 2001 | 7 | 1 | Mountain-100 Silver, 38 | Mountain-100 | 2039.994 | 2039.994 |
| 43659 | 7/1/2001 | 2001 | 7 | 1 | Mountain-100 Silver, 42 | Mountain-100 | 2039.994 | 2039.994 |
| 43659 | 7/1/2001 | 2001 | 7 | 2 | Mountain-100 Silver, 44 | Mountain-100 | 2039.994 | 4079.988 |
| 43659 | 7/1/2001 | 2001 | 7 | 1 | Mountain-100 Silver, 48 | Mountain-100 | 2039.994 | 2039.994 |
| 43659 | 7/1/2001 | 2001 | 7 | 3 | Long-Sleeve Logo Jersey, M | Long-Sleeve Logo Jersey | 28.8404 | 86.5212 |
| 43659 | 7/1/2001 | 2001 | 7 | 1 | Long-Sleeve Logo Jersey, XL | Long-Sleeve Logo Jersey | 28.8404 | 28.8404 |
| 43659 | 7/1/2001 | 2001 | 7 | 6 | Mountain Bike Socks, M | Mountain Bike Socks | 5.7 | 34.2 |
| 43659 | 7/1/2001 | 2001 | 7 | 2 | AWC Logo Cap | Cycling Cap | 5.1865 | 10.373 |
| 43659 | 7/1/2001 | 2001 | 7 | 4 | Sport-100 Helmet, Blue | Sport-100 | 20.1865 | 80.746 |
| 43660 | 7/1/2001 | 2001 | 7 | 1 | Road-650 Red, 44 | Road-650 | 419.4589 | 419.4589 |
| 43660 | 7/1/2001 | 2001 | 7 | 1 | Road-450 Red, 52 | Road-450 | 874.794 | 874.794 |
| 43661 | 7/1/2001 | 2001 | 7 | 1 | HL Mountain Frame - Black, 48 | HL Mountain Frame | 809.76 | 809.76 |
| 43661 | 7/1/2001 | 2001 | 7 | 1 | HL Mountain Frame - Black, 42 | HL Mountain Frame | 714.7043 | 714.7043 |

**FIGURE 4-7** The final worksheet for pivot table analysis of the sales.

Something to note is that, when Bill spoke about relationships, he really meant that in both tables, there was a column that can be used to perform VLOOKUP. Because the column in the sales details table contains a product ID, Michelle needed to search in the product table for a row with the same value for product ID. This is the product to which the sale refers. Michelle used this pattern whenever Bill told her about a relationship, and she reached her goal.

## Discovering the PowerPivot Way

Maybe you suffered from a sense of déjà vu reading this first story about Michelle. But let us look at what happens if Michelle had PowerPivot available. The story is pretty similar, but the tools she uses are somewhat more advanced.

Knowing that PowerPivot is able to load tables, she directly goes to the PowerPivot window and tries loading the ProductModel table. You can see the final result in PowerPivot using the companion workbook CH04-02-MichellePowerPivot.xlsx.

She opens up a connection with the database and loads it into PowerPivot. She performs some trial and error because the table is not so easy to load. The first loading ends with this error:

```
The size specified for a binding was too small, resulting in table 'ProductModel' column
'CatalogDescription' value being truncated.
The operation has been cancelled.
```

Something is wrong with this column. She is not interested in the catalog description, so she removes the CatalogDescription column by accessing the table preview in the Table Import Wizard by pressing the Preview & Filter button shown in Figure 4-8.

**FIGURE 4-8** The Preview & Filter button in the Table Import Wizard.

The table preview shown in the Table Import Wizard enables her to filter out useless columns by deselecting them with the small check box, as is shown in Figure 4-9.

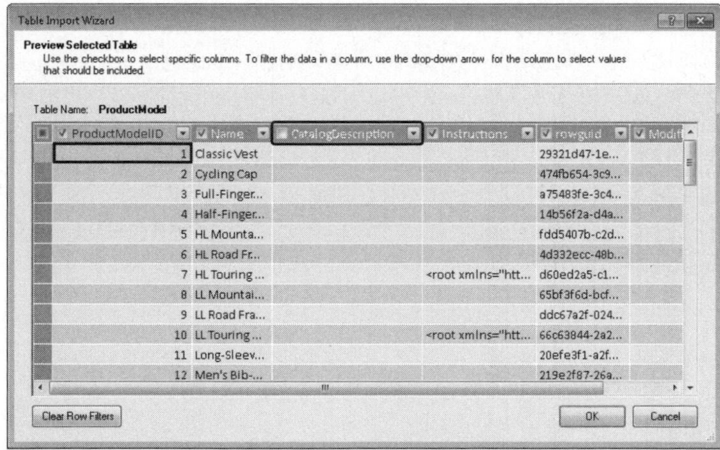


**FIGURE 4-9** The table preview in Table Import Wizard lets you remove columns from the input table.

No luck; she gets another error:

```
The size specified for a binding was too small, resulting in table 'ProductModel' column
'Instructions' value being truncated.
The operation has been cancelled.
```

It seems that another column is creating problems. The solution is the same: she removes that column from the list, tries it again and Bingo! This time, the loading succeeds, and she now has the ProductModel table loaded into PowerPivot, as in Figure 4-10.

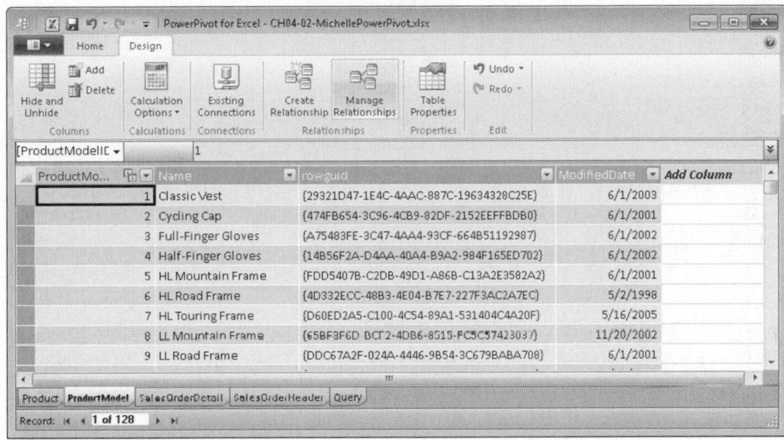

**FIGURE 4-10** The ProductModel table in PowerPivot.

She removes the useless columns from the tables and goes on loading Products, SalesOrderHeader, and SalesOrderDetail by following the very same process. The big difference this time is that the Import Wizard is already able to detect the existence of relationships and loads them into PowerPivot whenever she loads more than one table in the same process.

Now she opens a PivotTable and starts creating her report. After she adds the product model name and the line total from the sales order detail, PowerPivot warns her about the need for relationship, as shown in Figure 4-11.

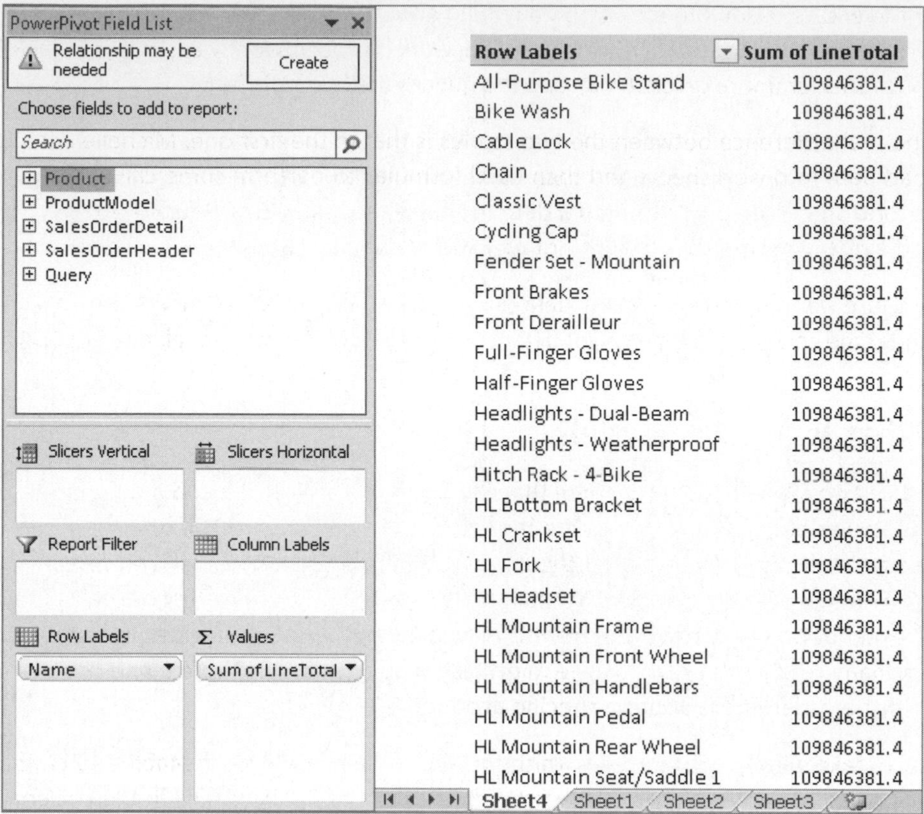


**FIGURE 4-11** PowerPivot detects the need for missing relationships.

She makes PowerPivot detect the necessary relationships, and then because she needs to aggregate the LineTotal by year and month, not by date, she follows the procedure already shown in Chapter 2 to create aggregator columns in the SalesOrderHeader table, which contains the year and the month of the order date. She ends up with the report shown in Figure 4-12.

| Sum of LineTotal | Column Labels | | | | | | | | |
|---|---|---|---|---|---|---|---|---|---|
| | 2004 | | | | | | | 2004 Total | Grand Total |
| Row Labels | 1 | 2 | 3 | 4 | 5 | 6 | 7 | | |
| All-Purpose Bike Stand | 2,544.00 | 3,021.00 | 2,703.00 | 4,611.00 | 3,975.00 | 2,067.00 | 1,749.00 | 20,670.00 | 20,670.00 |
| Bike Wash | 1,278.36 | 1,135.26 | 943.29 | 1,375.82 | 1,673.34 | 1,873.16 | 349.80 | 8,629.03 | 8,629.03 |
| Chain | 291.46 | 473.62 | 777.22 | 473.62 | 655.78 | 1,020.10 | | 3,691.78 | 3,691.78 |
| Classic Vest | 13,635.74 | 15,209.20 | 16,415.67 | 17,588.48 | 26,019.29 | 23,386.71 | 2,222.50 | 114,477.59 | 114,477.59 |
| Cycling Cap | 2,249.48 | 2,479.44 | 2,583.84 | 2,797.24 | 3,157.58 | 3,276.23 | 854.05 | 17,397.86 | 17,397.86 |
| Fender Set - Mountain | 4,352.04 | 3,340.96 | 3,890.46 | 3,868.48 | 4,923.52 | 4,483.92 | 2,351.86 | 27,211.24 | 27,211.24 |
| Front Brakes | 1,661.40 | 2,044.80 | 4,409.10 | 2,300.40 | 3,897.90 | 4,409.10 | | 18,722.70 | 18,722.70 |
| Front Derailleur | 1,921.29 | 2,085.97 | 2,964.28 | 2,305.55 | 3,403.43 | 4,899.98 | | 17,580.50 | 17,580.50 |
| Full-Finger Gloves | | 98.77 | | | 197.55 | | | 296.32 | 296.32 |
| Half-Finger Gloves | 4,958.06 | 4,932.29 | 4,218.46 | 7,006.71 | 7,367.88 | 7,490.83 | 1,640.83 | 37,615.05 | 37,615.05 |
| Hitch Rack - 4-Bike | 10,512.00 | 13,062.29 | 13,560.00 | 14,932.49 | 26,056.22 | 21,704.69 | 2,400.00 | 102,227.69 | 102,227.69 |
| HL Bottom Bracket | 1,749.46 | 2,915.76 | 3,061.55 | 1,749.46 | 2,041.03 | 5,467.05 | | 16,984.30 | 16,984.30 |

**FIGURE 4-12** The final sales report produced with PowerPivot.

In the end, she didn't need to know anything about relationships. PowerPivot handled relationships among tables for Michelle. The overall work has been slightly easier, the Excel file size is much smaller (more or less 8MB), and the queries are blazingly fast.

The real difference between the two stories is that in the first one, Michelle used Excel to load data into worksheets and then used formulas to perform some calculations. In the second story, she really created a data model without VLOOKUP functions and a pivot table querying the data model, not an Excel worksheet.

Because we want to learn what a data model is, we need to better understand what is going on under the cover when PowerPivot detects a relationship and what a relationship is anyway.

## What Is a Data Model?

These two scenarios demonstrate that the Excel way does not need a data model whereas the PowerPivot way creates a data model. But one question is still open: what is a data model? A Data Model is nothing but a list of tables (sometimes referred to as entities) with arrows connecting them. A table, as its name suggests, is a list of columns that hold the real data. The arrows represent the existence of relationships between tables and are normally read as *refers to*. So, we might say that an order line *refers to* a product, meaning that the order line is about a specific product.

Let us take a look at Figure 4-13, which shows the data model for the tables that Michelle has loaded to perform her analysis, which, in turn, is the data model Bill in the IT Department was speaking about.

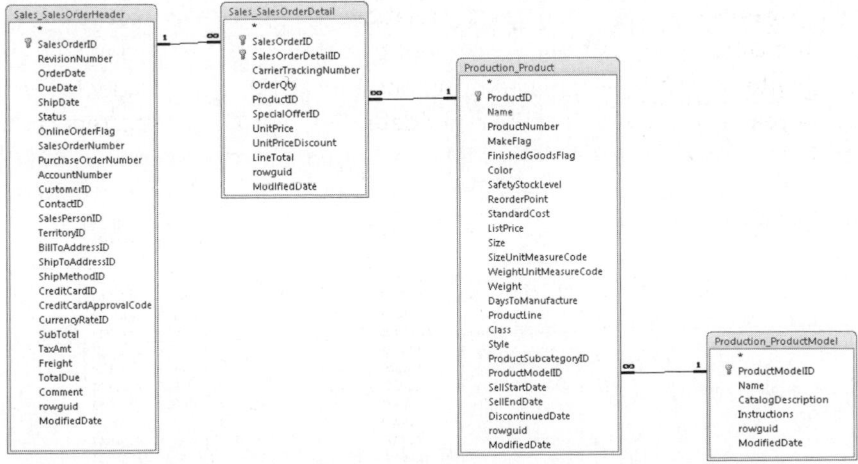


**FIGURE 4-13** The data model of product, models, sales order header, and detail.

You can see that there are four tables (entities) in the diagram:

- **SalesOrderHeader** This contains the global information about an order.
- **SalesOrderDetail** This contains the single lines of the order—that is, the products sold with the order with detailed information about price, quantity, and so on.
- **Product** This table, as its name clearly suggests, contains the product information stored in columns, which are shown in the product box.
- **ProductModel** This contains the different product models.

An arrow starts from the Product table and goes to the ProductModel table. This indicates that there is a column in the Product table whose value needs to be found in the ProductModel table so that you can get the name of the product model. In other words, Product and ProductModel are connected through a relationship.

Although there are many complex ways to define relationships, the standard method is to create a column in both tables (usually the column has the same name in both tables) and state that two rows from the two tables are related when that column contains the same value. In our example, the column ProductModelID exists in both tables, and it is the one responsible for holding the relationship.

**Note** In Excel, we used the VLOOKUP function to perform the lookup; using PowerPivot, we need a relationship between the two tables. The result is the same: using the relationship column, we are able to find product model information and use it in the product table.

It is now easy to read the other arrows: the SalesOrderDetail table shares a relationship with the Product table, which means that a line of an order refers to a product, which is somehow obvious. In this case, the relationship column is ProductID. Moreover, SalesOrderDetail shares a relationship with the SalesOrderHeader table, which means that each line belongs to an order.

To make use of all of the PowerPivot functionalities, you need to learn to read, to understand, and maybe to write some data models—that is, draw boxes and arrows to represent the data you want to describe and use.

As you are about to discover, data modeling is not an easy task and is likely to cause you more than one headache. Nevertheless, because it is the key to building complex analysis, we are going deeper in the discovery of different data models to provide a solid foundation of data modeling problems and solutions.

## Understanding Physical and Logical Data Models

Now that you have taken a first look at what a data model is, you need to learn the difference between the physical and the logical data model. To help you do that, we are going to show an example of a physical data model, describe its limitations and issues, and introduce the new concept of logical data models.

Let us recall the data model you used to analyze products, categories, and subcategories in Chapter 2. There, you had to load into PowerPivot three different tables and connect them by means of the chained relationship shown in Figure 4-14.

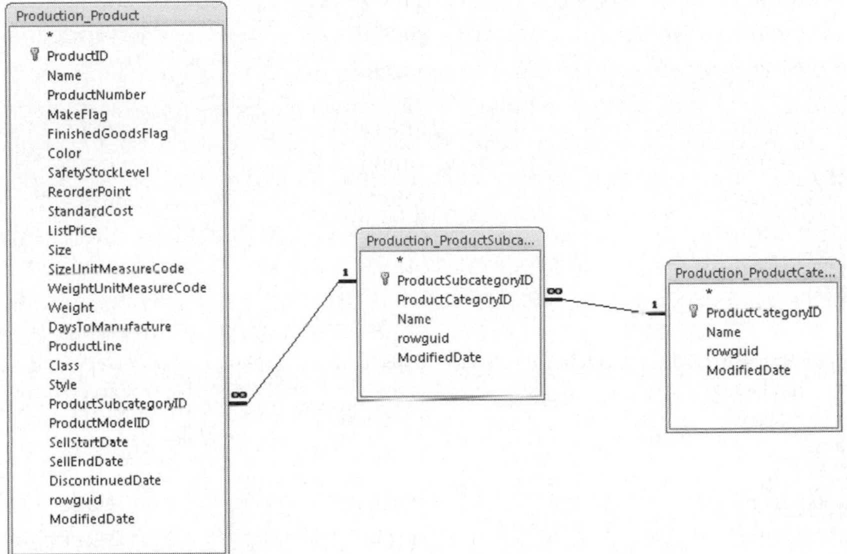


**FIGURE 4-14** The relationships among products, subcategories, and categories.

Probably you don't remember the difficulty we had with this data model, so it might be worth recalling it. When it came to using a pivot table to query this data, you had to query three different tables. Then, because you would normally think of categories and subcategories as simple attributes of the product table, you used the RELATED function to add the new columns ProductCategory and ProductSubcategory to the product table. Then you managed to hide the two lookup tables so that the final data model to query was much more intuitive. In Chapter 2, we called that data model your first; now we are going to describe in much more detail what you did there.

You face a classic problem that arises whenever users and technicians need to speak about a database:

- Users think in a logical way. They divide the database in entities and concepts that are directly related to their view of the topic, which is much related to the real world. In this example, they see products as entities, and categories and subcategories as simple textual descriptions attached to the products. In the user's world, there is no need to think about a table containing all the categories, nor do they understand why any relationships should exist among those tables.
- Technicians, on the other hand, think in a physical way. They divide the database in technical entities that are very much related to the physical representation of data on a disk. In the technical world, it is obvious that if products have categories and subcategories, the most effective way to store this information is through three different tables and a set of relationships among them. The physical representation on a disk aims at the reduction of data duplication, to avoid inconsistencies. This technique is known as *data normalization*. Data normalization is the reason for having so many tables in a relational database. You learn more about normalization in the next paragraphs.

So there are always at least two distinct ways to look at a database. We refer to the two views as the logical (user) versus physical (technician) one. Users think logically; technicians think physically. We can look at Figure 4-15 to better appreciate the difference between the two representations of the same item: a product. On the left side of the figure, you see three tables and two relationships—the technical view. On the right side, you see the simpler user view of a product, which is composed of a single entity.

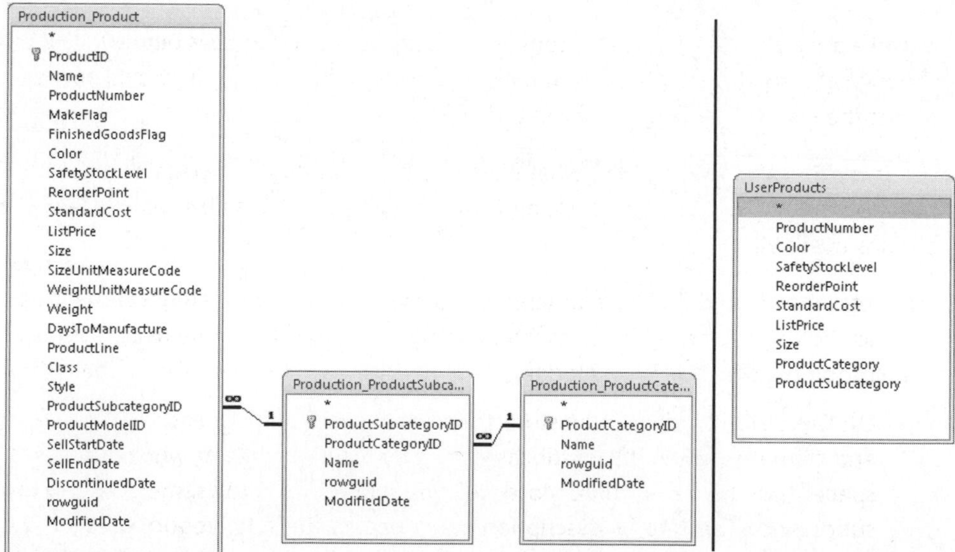


**FIGURE 4-15** Different ways to see products: from the technician (on the left) and the user (right) points of view.

Users are not normally aware of the existence of a technical data model because they interact with the database using an interface—that is, a piece of software that can understand both data models (the user's and the technician's ones), read data from the database in the technical format, and display it to the user in the friendly format. Office workers taking orders therefore do not really need to understand that orders are actually stored in at least these three technical tables that compose the database structure of orders. Moreover, the more complex the structure is, the higher the number of technical tables that you need to model it.

On the other hand, as you might have noticed already, PowerPivot lets you browse the database as it is stored, without trying to make it look simpler. If the data is kept in three tables, PowerPivot shows you columns from all three tables. If a table contains technical columns, the pivot table does not hide them, even if we know that the user makes no use at all of those columns.

For this reason, you need to create a data model in PowerPivot that is nearer to the logical than to the physical type. In this chapter, we show various examples in which you can see prominent differences between the physical and the logical model. Whenever we find such issues, we analyze standard methods to remove them to present the logical model to the user.

If you still remember the content of Chapter 2 (if not, you can always go back a few pages to recall it), you now recognize that when you learned to use the RELATED function to hide technical columns and technical tables, you learned the first steps for turning a physical model into a logical one.

## Normalization and Denormalization

Now we analyze one of the most common causes of the differences between the physical and logical view of a database: *data normalization*. Normalization, in the database world, means the removal of redundancy in the table structure.

Let us try to understand better what we mean by *redundancy*. If you think of the possible ways to store products, categories, and subcategories on a disk file, you have these two options available:

- You can store the textual description of category and subcategory in each product, as the logical model requires. You end up repeating the same description for each product with a specific category.
- On the other hand, you can store the textual description of each category only once and then reference it from subcategories by using a number, which usually takes less space than the description. Moreover, you can perform the same operation with the subcategory, storing its description only once, in the subcategory table, and using a reference from the products table that links to the subcategory. This technique leads to a smaller file, even if it is harder to read.

The first option (to duplicate the category and subcategory value over all rows) is the one required by the logical data model. Because the description of a category is the same for a lot of different products and you have, therefore, a high level of data duplication, the logical model is not optimized. The technical model, on the other hand, is very much optimized because that model removes redundancy, which leads to a smaller size on disk, less use of memory, and—in general—to a higher level of performance of the database. Roughly speaking: the technical model is normalized (redundancy removed), whereas the logical one is denormalized (redundancy present).

Normalization increases the number of tables needed to store the same information, yet it reduces the overall size of the database. The need for normalization has been present in relational databases since their invention, and database analysts are so used to normalization that they look at denormalized databases with disgust. Nevertheless, denormalized databases have the great advantage of being much easier to query and understand because their structure is much more similar to the logical one.

Moreover, with the advent of modern columnar databases, such as PowerPivot, the need to normalize tables is highly reduced. If a single value is repeated several times in a table, PowerPivot does not store the value as it is but provides a kind of automatic normalization by removing the long description and replacing it with numbers that reference the description. In other words, the process of normalization is carried on internally by the PowerPivot database even if you load a denormalized table.

### Is Normalization a Correct Technique?

Please note that normalization is neither good nor bad. The same applies for its contrary: denormalization. The need to normalize data comes from the very nature of the database and follows technical rules that we cannot cover in this small note, yet are very important. An operational database should be normalized, whereas a data model directly browsable by the user should be denormalized.

You should avoid the temptation to think that one model is more correct than the other one. Each one is the right model for the kind of operations that you need to perform on it. The point here is that, when you load data from an operational database, you are likely to find normalized data. Because you need to show that information to a user, you need some techniques to remove normalization and produce a denormalized data model, which is the correct one for the analysis.

Now that you know what normalization is, you still need to learn how to handle normalized tables and how and when you should denormalize them. In the rest of this chapter, we provide several examples for you to follow, taking practical samples from the AdventureWorks database. To give you an advance briefing of these techniques, you always have two options for performing denormalization:

- You can load normalized tables into PowerPivot and then use the RELATED function to provide denormalized columns in the original table.
- You can denormalize the database and load it in a denormalized format into PowerPivot, taking advantage of the fact that PowerPivot automatically normalizes the data, thus optimizing its storage.

Nevertheless, before we dive into a complete treatment of how to denormalize tables, we want to spend some words on another very important difference between the physical and the logical data models so that you get a complete scenario.

## Empty Values

Another big difference between technical and logical structure of the database is in the treatment of empty values. From a purely technical point of view, a missing value is exactly what it is: missing. For example, take a look at the report in Figure 4-16, which is built using the same sales tables that we have shown you up to now and that you can find in the companion workbook CH04-03-EmptyValues.xlsx.

| Sum of OrderQty | Column Labels | | |
|---|---|---|---|
| Row Labels | INTERNAL ORDER | ONLINE ORDER | Grand Total |
| | 19,370 | 28,919 | 48,289 |
| Black | 72,094 | 9,843 | 81,937 |
| Blue | 19,689 | 3,970 | 23,659 |
| Multi | 21,147 | 3,926 | 25,073 |
| Red | 24,280 | 4,949 | 29,229 |
| Silver | 21,599 | 3,424 | 25,023 |
| Silver/Black | 3,931 | | 3,931 |
| White | 4,649 | 568 | 5,217 |
| Yellow | 27,757 | 4,799 | 32,556 |
| **Grand Total** | **214,516** | **60,398** | **274,914** |

**FIGURE 4-16** Empty values, in the database, are empty.

You can see that, slicing for color on the rows, the first line contains all the products for which there is no color defined. No color defined, in the technical world, means that the column color does not contain any value. The lack of a value produces a report in which no label is attached to the color, and this condition is not user-friendly.

The report would look much better if you were able to present data as you see it in Figure 4-17.

| Sum of OrderQty | Column Labels | | |
|---|---|---|---|
| Row Labels | INTERNAL ORDER | ONLINE ORDER | Grand Total |
| <NO COLOR> | 19,370 | 28,919 | 48,289 |
| Black | 72,094 | 9,843 | 81,937 |
| Blue | 19,689 | 3,970 | 23,659 |
| Multi | 21,147 | 3,926 | 25,073 |
| Red | 24,280 | 4,949 | 29,229 |
| Silver | 21,599 | 3,424 | 25,023 |
| Silver/Black | 3,931 | | 3,931 |
| White | 4,649 | 568 | 5,217 |
| Yellow | 27,757 | 4,799 | 32,556 |
| **Grand Total** | **214,516** | **60,398** | **274,914** |

**FIGURE 4-17** Using default values for empty ones, the report looks much more readable.

In this latter report, all rows have a label and, if no color has been supplied for specific products, the report shows a value indicating <NO COLOR>. From the user's perspective, this second report is much more informative than the first one.

Technicians normally refer to empty values as NULL. NULL is a special value used to mean *missing*. In other words, a column containing the special value NULL indicates a column for which no value has been specified because that column was an optional one. In the technical database, NULL values are useful because they do not waste space for missing values. In the logical database, it would be much better to avoid NULL values. Whenever you have a value which has not been specified, you want to show to the user a meaningful message, such as NO COLOR, NO PRODUCT, or something similar that clearly helps the reader understand the meaning of the message.

NULL values are very easy to handle, and for this reason, we prefer to show the technique right here. If you look at the product table, as in Figure 4-18, you can note that the Color column contains some color definition and some empty values. You now know that the empty values correspond to the special value NULL.

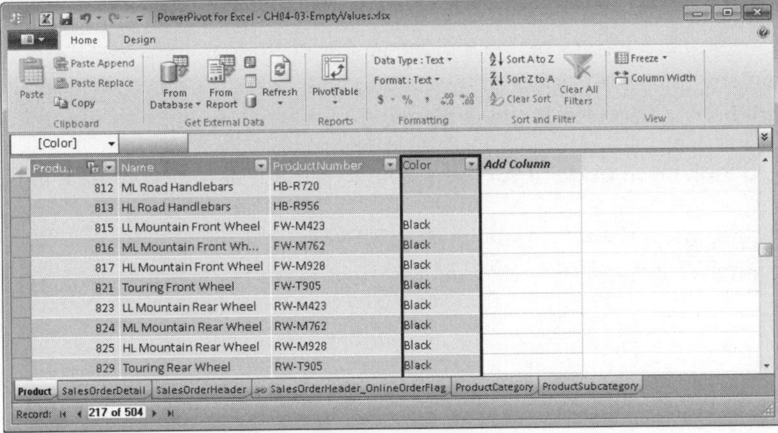


**FIGURE 4-18** The color column contains empty values.

You cannot edit the data in the table to update the empty values with a fixed definition because all data in a PowerPivot table is read-only. Nevertheless, you can easily add a new calculated column that detects whether the Color column is empty and, in that case, it returns our null description.

The formula for the new calculated column is the following:

```
= IF( ISBLANK( Product[Color] ), "<NO COLOR>", Product[Color] )
```

In Figure 4-19, you can see the new CalculatedColor column side by side with the original Color one.

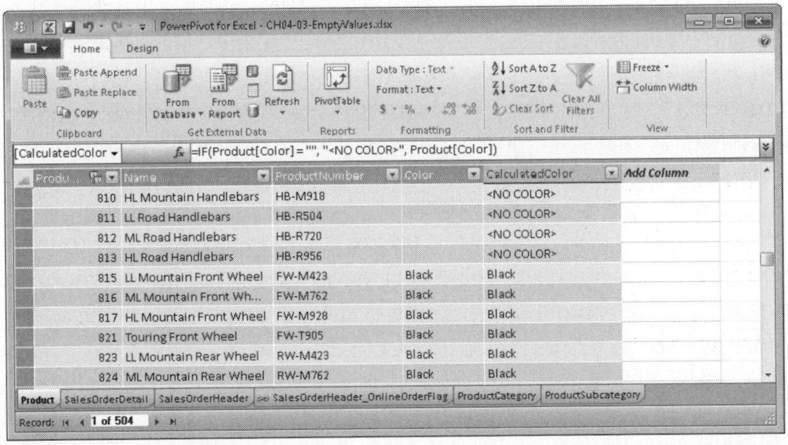

**FIGURE 4-19** The new calculated column replaced the empty values with <NO COLOR>.

Now, you have two columns, each one representing the color but with one containing NULL values and the other one containing meaningful descriptions. To make the PivotTable easier to navigate, you should rename the original Color column something like OriginalColor, and then hide it from the PivotTable browser and let the user navigate the new calculated color column instead (which you should rename Color).

**Note** This solution works fine for removing empty values from all the columns in which they could appear. Nevertheless, the tedious part of the work is that, for each column that might hold empty values, you need to hide the original column and add a new column with a formula similar to the one shown. This work is a bit tiresome, but the reports look much better.

Please note that, in the example, we have enclosed the description for empty values in angle brackets. It is advisable to do so because, this way, this description becomes the first in the report; the sorting order places the character < before any letter or number. Obviously, your needs might be different and, in that case, any description works fine.

# Understanding How and When to Denormalize Tables

Now, after this small digression on empty values, we go back to the issue of normalized tables. To help you get acquainted with the concept of denormalization, we provide some examples of data structures that are (correctly) normalized in the AdventureWorks database, which we need (still correctly) denormalized in the PowerPivot model.

The first example, which we have referred to earlier, concerns products, categories, and subcategories. To denormalize the subcategories, you have seen that you should add a SubCategory column in the Product table and use the RELATED function to fill its value. You perform the same operation with the Category column, and then after hiding the original tables (that is, in our example, ProductCategory and ProductSubcategory), you reach the optimal situation: you can browse a denormalized data model even if the database contains data in a normalized way. In other words, you load a normalized data model into PowerPivot and then you denormalize it by using specific functions and relationships.

Although this technique is pretty easy to implement, it has the disadvantage of being annoying to implement for all the many normalized columns that tend to appear in an operational database. You might be glad to learn at least one different technique to perform the same operation.

This new technique requires that you use the query builder of PowerPivot to perform the process of denormalization in the original data, and so load information into PowerPivot in an already denormalized way. So we are shifting from denormalization in PowerPivot (the previous technique) to denormalization outside of PowerPivot (the new one).

Having more than one technique to solve the same problem brings you the problem later of deciding which one to use under what circumstances, but we talk about that later.

## The PowerPivot Query Designer

If you want to remove normalization from a data model, you can use the query designer of the Table Import Wizard in PowerPivot to produce denormalized SQL queries in the original data model. Nevertheless, before you start designing a query, it is important to understand what a SQL query is.

A SQL query is a statement written in a special language, called SQL, which is understood by most of the modern databases. We are not going to describe in detail how to write a SQL query because there are a lot of good books that cover the topic much better then we could do in a few paragraphs. For the purposes of this book, we are interested in how to use the PowerPivot query designer, which requires that you understand just the basics of SQL and handles much of the hard work for you.

A very simple SQL query looks like this:

```
SELECT
    Prod.ProductId AS ProductID,
    Prod.Name      AS ProductName,
    Sub.Name       AS SubcategoryName
FROM
    Production.Product AS Prod
    INNER JOIN Production.ProductSubcategory AS Sub
        ON Prod.ProductSubcategoryID = Sub.ProductSubcategoryID
WHERE
    Sub.Name = 'Helmets'
```

Let us describe this example in greater detail. A query is composed of several parts, the most common and important of which are these:

- **SELECT** In the first part of the query, you declare which columns you are interested in reading. You can refer to more than one table in the column list of the SELECT element; this is particularly useful when we need to get data from tables that have relationships between them.
- **FROM** In this part of the query, you declare which tables you want the database to read to gather the columns declared in the first section. If more than one table is referenced, as is the case in the example, you should specify how to follow relationships among the different tables. You do this using the JOIN predicate.
- **WHERE** The last part of the query lets you create filtering conditions, so that you do not retrieve all rows. In the example, we asked for rows that contain *Helmets* as the subcategory name.

Now that you have seen the overall structure of a query, you are going to create this query and load its data into PowerPivot to appreciate the difference between the query result and the original tables.

Building a query is always a complex step because it requires a good knowledge of the data model you are querying. SQL technicians normally write queries using a standard text editor because they already know how to retrieve data. Because you are probably not a SQL technician, you are interested in using the PowerPivot query designer, which is a tool that lets you build a SQL query through a visual interface. Even if the query designer handles the hard work for you, understanding the final query structure lets you understand better what the query designer is asking.

To open the query designer, you need to go to the PowerPivot window, click Existing Connections, choose the connection to AdventureWorks and then select Open. In the previous chapters, you always used the first option—that is, you selected the tables you wanted to import from the list of tables. This time you choose Write A Query That Will Specify The Data To Import, and click Next. You reach the query editor dialog box shown in Figure 4-20. In the companion workbook CH04-04-SQL_Query.xlsx, you find the data already loaded and the query ready to be examined.

The query editor is a simple text editor with which you can start to write the SQL query and give it a friendly name. Because you are probably not a SQL expert, it is much better to click on the Design button to invoke the query designer.

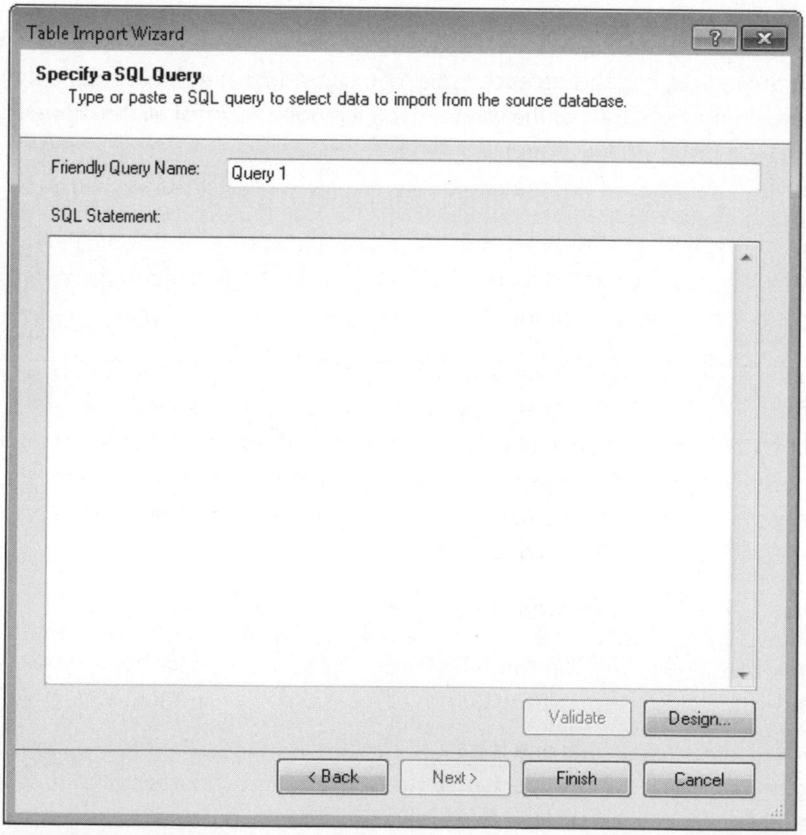

**FIGURE 4-20** The SQL query editor.

In the query designer in Figure 4-21, we have already selected the three tables: Product, ProductSubcategory, and ProductCategory. Moreover, because we want to spend some attention on the Relationship pane, we have expanded it to make it more visible.

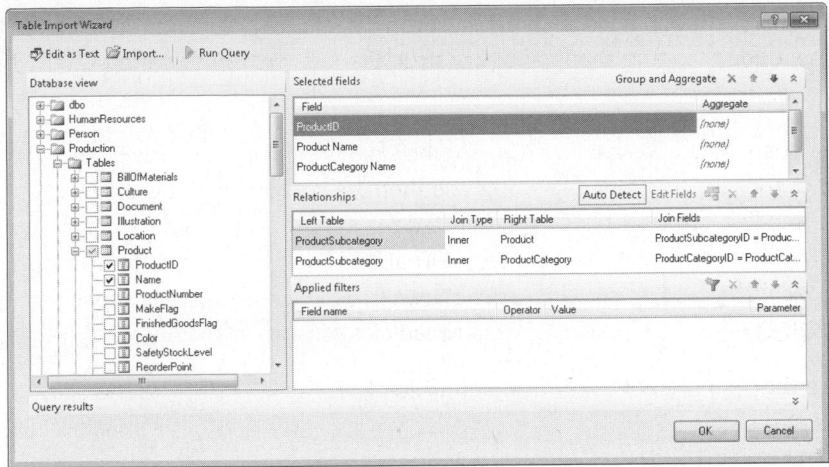


**FIGURE 4-21** The SQL query designer.

Let us explore the query designer in greater detail. In the left pane, you can select the tables to add to the query and, expanding each table, you can select the single columns that you want to retrieve. In the right part of the window, you can see the list of all the columns selected (which is the SELECT part of the query), the list of the tables involved, along with their relationships (that is the FROM part of the query), and in the lower part, the list of filters to apply (that is the WHERE part).

In the example, we selected a small number of columns, to fit the screenshots in the book. In the real world, the number of columns to retrieve is normally much higher.

The less intuitive part of the query designer is the Relationship pane. You can see that after you selected three tables, the designer detected the existence of relationships between them: one between Product and ProductSubcategory and one between ProductSubcategory and ProductCategory. Those relationships have been automatically detected by the engine because they are stored in the database metadata. Later on, we discuss how to define new relationships if the automatic detection algorithm does not find suitable ones.

To understand how relationships work, we need to make some notes:

- A relationship exists between two tables only. It does not matter how many tables are involved in the query, a single relationship relates only two of them at a time.
- The two tables are ordered: one is called *Left table* and the other one is, fantastically, the *Right table*. This is very important, as we see in the next paragraphs, because a wrong table ordering might lead to an incorrect query.

- A relationship has a type (the middle column in the relationship pane) that indicates how to retrieve rows from the database. You definitely need to understand how different types of relationships affect the query result to get the data you need.

So reading the result of the auto detection algorithm, you can see that it detected two relationships: one between Products and ProductSubCategory and one between ProductSubCategory and ProductCategory, and it has chosen the INNER type of relationship for both.

We return later in our exploration of the query designer to analyze how different types of relationships return different results. At the moment, it is enough to click OK to see the query built. PowerPivot returns to the query editor, which is now filled with a complex query that the designer has written for us, as you can see in Figure 4-22.

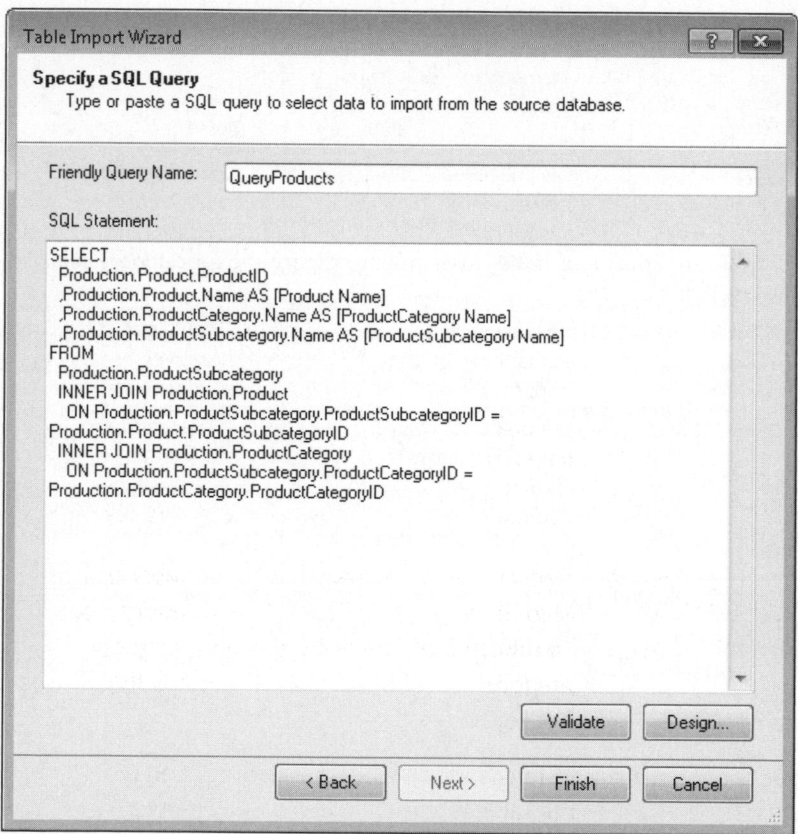


**FIGURE 4-22** The SQL query editor, with a query written by the designer.

If you click Finish, you start the loading process, which means that the query is executed against the database and all the rows are imported into the PowerPivot database. Nevertheless, if you just look at the number of rows returned, you see bad news: only 295 rows have been loaded, while the Products table effectively contains 504 different products.

There is something wrong here: why has PowerPivot lost 209 rows during the loading process? The reason is that the designer is able to understand that a relationship exists between two tables, but it is not as good in determining the type of relationship; having selected the wrong one, the database failed to return all the products. It is definitely time to understand better what kinds of relationship you can set and how they affect the final result.

When you relate two tables (left and right—in the examples, we use left for Products and right for ProductSubcategory) you have four different options, listed in Table 4-1. As you will understand when you study Table 4-1, the big difference among all types of JOIN relationships is in the handling of NULL values in the left or right table.

**TABLE 4-1 Different types of relationships.**

| Relationship | Result |
|---|---|
| INNER JOIN | Only the rows where there is a match between the left and right table are returned. In our example, the query returns only the products that have a subcategory, discarding the ones that have the SubcategoryID column set to NULL. |
| LEFT OUTER JOIN | The left table is preserved. This means that rows coming from the left table that do not have corresponding rows in the right one are returned anyway, leaving all the columns for the right table as NULLs. In our example, all products are returned and, if they have no subcategory, the subcategory name column is left as NULL. |
| RIGHT OUTER JOIN | The right table is preserved. In our example, we would get all the subcategories, even the ones that have no products in them. Moreover, because the left table is not preserved, the products that have no subcategory are not returned. |
| FULL OUTER JOIN | Both tables are preserved. In our example, you receive all the products and all the subcategories. Nonreferenced subcategories contain NULL values for the columns belonging to the product table and, vice versa, products without a subcategory contain a NULL value for the subcategory column. |

If you look carefully at Table 4-1, you can see what happened. The query designer chose the INNER JOIN type for the relationship between Products and Subcategory, and so discarded all the products that do not have a subcategory set. In other words, all the products that contained NULL in the ProductSubCategoryId column are not returned by the query because no subcategory exists with NULL in the key column.

To load all the products, you need to change the relationships to be an OUTER one. You can edit the query again by clicking the Table Properties button in the PowerPivot window. Doing this, PowerPivot opens the query editor again, and from here, you can work again with the query designer.

In Figure 4-23, you can see the query designer again, this time with the correct relationships set.

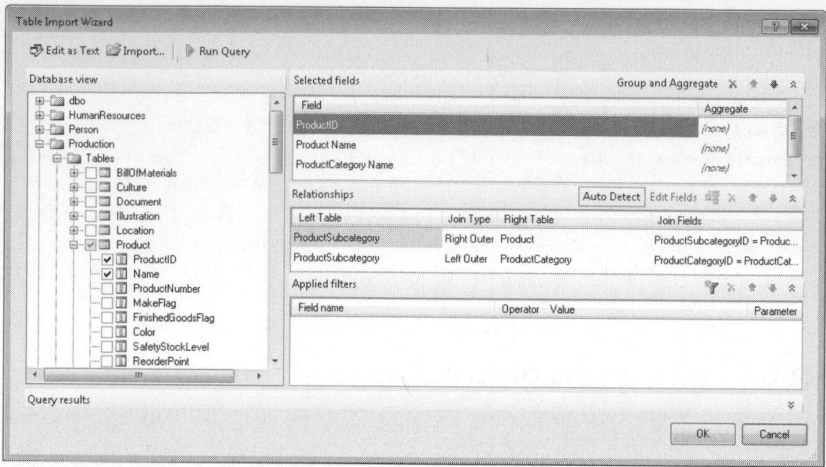


**FIGURE 4-23** The SQL query designer, with the correct relationships set.

Let us review the relationship definition:

- The first relationship is between ProductSubcategory and Product. Please note that ProductSubCategory is the left table, and you want to get all products, even the ones that contain NULL in the ProductSubcategoryID column. So we need a RIGHT OUTER JOIN to exist between the two tables, so that the right table (Product) is preserved.
- The second relationship is between ProductSubcategory and ProductCategory. The ProductSubcategory table is still the left one. Nevertheless, now you want all the subcategories, even if they do not belong to a category. So here you need a LEFT OUTER JOIN type so that the left table (ProductSubcategory) is preserved.

If you now save this query and refresh the table, you get all 504 products in your PowerPivot database, even those that do not have a category or subcategory set.

**Note** LEFT and RIGHT outer joins are interchangeable because both types of join save the rows from one table (the left or right one, depending on the type of join). If you swap the two tables, you need to change the join type. We personally find that it is better to have only one kind of join (that is, left or right—usually, left is our preferred one) in a query definition because it makes it easier to follow the chain. In this example, we would prefer to swap the tables in the first relationship so that we could follow a chain that starts from Products, then LEFT OUTER JOINs to ProductSubcategory that, in turn, LEFT OUTER JOINs ProductCategory. Unfortunately, if you rely on the auto detection algorithm, it chooses the left and right table by itself, making your work a bit harder.

If you now look at the imported table in Figure 4-24, you can appreciate the fact that it is already denormalized, and it merged the three tables into a simpler one, which is much nearer to the logical than to the physical data model.

| ProductID | Product Name | ProductCategory Name | ProductSubcategory Name |
|---|---|---|---|
| 796 | Road-250 Black, 58 | Bikes | Road Bikes |
| 797 | Road-550-W Yellow, 38 | Bikes | Road Bikes |
| 798 | Road-550-W Yellow, 40 | Bikes | Road Bikes |
| 799 | Road-550-W Yellow, 42 | Bikes | Road Bikes |
| 800 | Road-550-W Yellow, 44 | Bikes | Road Bikes |
| 801 | Road-550-W Yellow, 48 | Bikes | Road Bikes |
| 953 | Touring-2000 Blue, 60 | Bikes | Touring Bikes |
| 954 | Touring-1000 Yellow, 46 | Bikes | Touring Bikes |

**FIGURE 4-24** The result of a SQL query is easier to read.

### OUTER JOIN and Chains of Relationships

Please note a subtle yet important point about relationships: if you need to make the type of relationship between Product and ProductSubcategory a LEFT OUTER JOIN, you definitely need to make the relationship between ProductSubcategory and ProductCategory a LEFT OUTER JOIN, too. In fact, if the second join is an INNER one, all the rows without a subcategory are not returned, because when they have no subcategory, they have no category, either. Whenever you handle chained relationships, if the first one is an OUTER JOIN, all the rest need to be of the same type.

Even seasoned SQL programmers often fall into this problem and write wrong queries. Nevertheless, because they are used to making such mistakes, they are used to checking the query results and double-checking the chain of joins, if any exists. PowerPivot users need to conform to the same double-checking strategy whenever they write a query.

You have seen that, using the SQL query designer, you can write queries to the database that transform a simple table into a complex structure, which resolves the relationships at the database level and returns a denormalized table to PowerPivot. So you can use the SQL designer to perform denormalization whenever you need to.

## When to Denormalize Tables

Now that you have learned two distinct techniques for performing denormalization, here is an interesting question about data modeling: when do you need to denormalize tables in queries and when is it better to perform the same operation in PowerPivot? Unfortunately, as with many interesting questions, there is no definitive answer for all situations.

In the example of ProductCategory, the answer is simple: it is much better to denormalize the column in a query because this operation leads to an easier data model to query and lowers the number of tables in PowerPivot. The sole purpose of the ProductCategory table is to provide a description of product categories, and so when you fulfilled this requirement by adding a ProductCategory column to the Products table, the ProductCategory table can be safely removed from the data model without any loss of expressivity. The same, obviously, applies to ProductSubcategory.

Tables whose only job is to provide descriptions are amazingly common in the world of relational databases. So you find a lot of situations where the application of this simple rule drastically reduces the number of tables needed and simplifies the PowerPivot data model. For simple lookup tables, the denormalization through SQL queries is by far the easiest tool.

On the other hand, when a table contains more information than a simple description, you are much more likely to find it difficult to decide whether to import the table and perform the denormalization in PowerPivot or to perform the denormalization in a query and import the result of that query. If, for example, the ProductSubcategory table contains more columns, we need to add all of these columns to the Product table, which might produce a complex Product table that is difficult to use. These situations need to be handled thoughtfully so that you can make correct decisions and produce an easy-to-use model.

Finally, complex tables that represent business entities are the pillars of the data models and so should not be denormalized. If you think, for instance, about the relationship between SalesOrderDetail and Products, you see that the relationship should not be denormalized at all because orders and products are different business entities. Both the entities and their relationship should exist in the PowerPivot database; denormalizing it would produce a wrong data model.

The rationale behind this is that you might be interested in analyzing products without relating them to sales. Think about this: if you denormalize the product name in the sales table, you might want to count the number of products to produce some report. But, if you see the product name only in the sales table, you can count only *sold* products, not products. If a product has never been sold, it does not even appear in the sales table because no sales row exists for it. If you reach the point where you over-denormalize the structure, you might create a data model that returns incorrect answers.

As a rule, you denormalize tables when the number of useful columns in the table is very small (for lookup tables, it is often only one) and you do not denormalize tables when the number of useful columns exceeds three. For two or three columns, it is up to the data modeler (that is, up to you) to choose the best denormalization strategy.

Keep in mind that the task to define a data model is complex, and denormalization is just one of the many hard decisions that need to be made. As a PowerPivot user, you are going to become a data modeler more of your time, so get ready to make difficult decisions and don't be too afraid to take the wrong ones; even seasoned Business Intelligence (BI) experts often have difficulty when it is time to decide whether to keep an attribute normalized or not.

# Complex Relationships

The denormalization process that you have seen up to now works well with simple tables that follow simple or chained relationships. The AdventureWorks database, like any other relational database, often contains much more complex relationships that will really test your judgment.

We are going to use, as an exercise, a diagram for the Customer table, which is implemented in AdventureWorks in a complex way (see Figure 4-25). The purpose of this example is to show how complex the querying of a database might be, so it is a deliberately difficult sample.

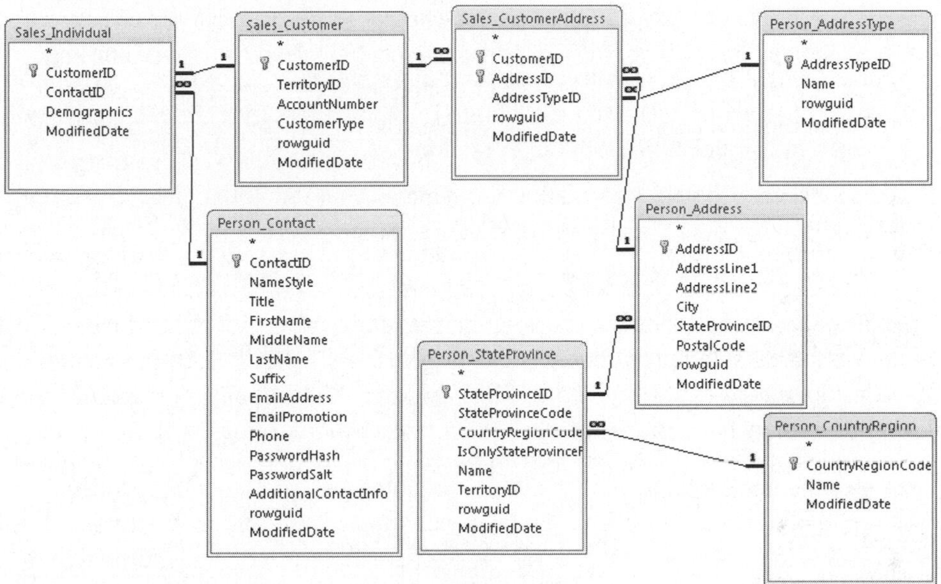


**FIGURE 4-25** The relationship diagram for Customer.

You can see that the business entity *Customer* is represented by several tables that have complex relationships among them.

- Sales_Customer is in relation with Sales_Individual, which stores some demographic information about the customer.
- Sales_Individual, in turn, refers to Person_Contact, through the ContactID column. Person_Contact contains the personal data of any contact, and from the database point of view, a customer is a contact. So Sales_Customer is in chained relationship with Person_Contact.
- A customer row might have different addresses, so the table Sales_CustomerAddress contains all the addresses of a Sales_Customer row.
- All addresses have a related Person_AddressType, which categorizes the address. The main address of the customer has a type (value in AddressTypeID field) called Primary.

- Other information about the address (that is, address line, zip code, and so on) are stored in the Person_Address table, which has a relationship with Sales_CustomerAddress, which in turn has a relationship with Sales_Customer, forming a complex relationship that looks very similar to a chained one.
- Person_Address refers to Person_StateProvince, which in turn is in relation to Person_CountryRegion. They form a chained relationship that lets us recover the name of the country through a couple of steps, from Person_Address to Person CountryRegion.

You cannot expose such a complexity through PowerPivot because it would turn the PivotTable into a nightmare. So let us roll up our sleeves and start the analysis of this topic to understand what to do to make the model easier to query.

- The Sales_Individual table contains some demographic information. When the information is useful, it should be added to the Sales_Customer table, thus removing the Sales_Individual table from our data model.
- The Person_Contact information can be denormalized in the Sales_Customer table so that it is available directly in the Sales_Customer table.
- The Person_AddressType table is a simple descriptive one, so it can be denormalized, if you need to do that. Moreover, if (as we are supposing) we are not interested in having all the addresses of a customer, we can take only the primary address of a customer and then denormalize all of the address information in the Sales_Customer table.
- Because we need to denormalize the address, we denormalize all the chained relationships, starting from the Person_Address and reaching Person_CountryRegion; we move all the information from those tables directly into the Sales_Customer table.

Because a picture is worth a thousand words, in Figure 4-26 you can see the data model as you would like it to appear in PowerPivot.

**FIGURE 4-26** The customer diagram, in its logical form.

You can easily appreciate that this diagram is much easier to understand when compared with the technical one. There is a single entity and all the technical relationships between tables have been removed, leading to a simple structure that makes the user experience much better.

That said, you now have a starting point and a goal to achieve, although the road is pretty hard. Because the structure is complex, you should not even think about loading all the tables into PowerPivot and then using the RELATED function to rebuild the data model because this would be a very time-consuming job. When the starting data model is a complex one, as this is, the best, if not the only way, is to use SQL queries.

Moreover, the query is a complex one because it involves a high number of JOINS, all of which need to be LEFT OUTER JOIN because you want to include all customers, whether or not they have an address stored in the database. Here is the final result of the query:

```
SELECT
    Customer.CustomerID AS CustomerID,
    Customer.AccountNumber AS AccountNumber,
    Customer.CustomerType AS CustomerType,
    Contact.FirstName AS FirstName,
    Contact.LastName AS LastName,
    Contact.MiddleName AS MiddleName,
    Contact.EmailAddress AS EmailAddress,
    Contact.Phone As Phone,
    Address.AddressLine1 AS AddressLine1,
    Address.AddressLine2 AS AddressLine2,
    Address.City AS City,
    StateProvince.StateProvinceCode AS StateProvinceCode,
    StateProvince.Name As StateProvince,
    cr.CountryRegionCode AS CountryRegionCode,
    cr.Name AS CountryRegionName
FROM
    Sales.Customer AS Customer
    LEFT OUTER JOIN Sales.Individual AS Individual
        ON Individual.CustomerID = Customer.CustomerID
    LEFT OUTER JOIN Person.Contact AS Contact
        ON Contact.ContactID = Individual.ContactID
    LEFT OUTER JOIN Sales.CustomerAddress AS CustomerAddress
        ON CustomerAddress.CustomerID = Customer.CustomerID
    LEFT OUTER JOIN Person.AddressType AS T
        ON CustomerAddress.AddressTypeID = T.AddressTypeID AND
           T.Name = 'Primary'
    LEFT OUTER JOIN Person.Address AS Address
        ON Address.AddressID = CustomerAddress.AddressID
    LEFT OUTER JOIN Person.StateProvince AS StateProvince
        ON StateProvince.StateProvinceID = Address.StateProvinceID
    LEFT OUTER JOIN Person.CountryRegion AS CR
        ON CR.CountryRegionCode = StateProvince.CountryRegionCode
```

Even if the query seems strange, its structure is pretty simple. It contains many tables, but the final result has the same structure for the Customer table as you want to show in the user data model. This query can be constructed using the query designer, and you can see in Figure 4-27 the relationships and filters panes of the query designer.

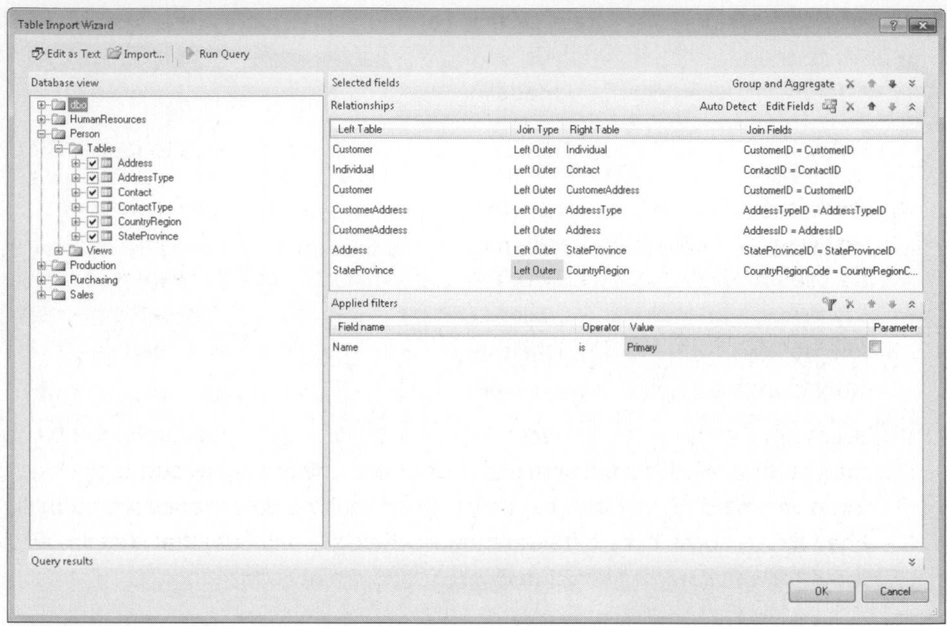


**FIGURE 4-27** The query designer can build complex queries.

In the designer, we have not used the autodetect feature of PowerPivot because, having so many tables, we suggest that you handle relationships by hand. Please, keep in mind that to build such a complex query, you need to have a clear idea of what you are querying, and to get it, you should start from the diagram with boxes and arrows, study it, and then begin to write the query only when you have a clear idea of the goal you are achieving.

**Note** This example has been deliberately a complex one. The goal is not to scare the reader or to direct you to one of the many good SQL books that are on the market. Instead, the focus here is to understand that there is a big difference between how data is stored in the source data model and how you want to handle it for your analytical purposes. Having the data in the correct form makes it easier to produce interesting queries because they are easier to write using the PivotTable. Moreover, if you ever are faced with such a complex architecture, it might be very useful to ask for help from some SQL technician—you might ask that person to write the query for you.

# Understanding OLTP and Data Marts

If you think that many of the preceding topics were pretty complex, well, you are definitely right! The task of creating a data model is taxing. Many decisions need to be made, and it is normal to be missing some of the information you need. Creating a model is more an art than a science: it requires a lot of experience and foresight. Nevertheless, a good data model is the key to producing good analysis, and this is why we believe that a good PowerPivot analyst needs to understand data modeling.

As you have already discovered, there are at least two different ways to look at a data model:

- **Technical view** This is a very compact and normalized way to look at data. This is the best way to model data when it needs to be used by software. Normalized data models are used by OLTP software, which is—more or less—the software that handles everyday tasks for a company. Handling such models is not your task—there are technicians who do it all day long. Nevertheless, you will probably need to read data this way some time or another.
- **User view** This is a highly denormalized view of data, much simpler to query and to analyze. As a side effect, it contains a lot of redundancy, generates bigger databases, and is very hard for software to update. Denormalized data models are normally present when the company has a data warehouse—that is, a database that contains all the data about the company in a structured way, useful for querying.

The task of building a data warehouse usually involves several years of work of highly specialized technicians, whose task is to build both the data warehouse model and the software systems that daily fill it with the information found in the various OLTP systems around the company.

This is not a book about data warehouse modeling, so we are not interested in a complete discussion about how to model a data warehouse. Instead, we would like to give to you the feeling of what a data warehouse is and the differences between querying an OLTP system, as you did up to now, and querying a data warehouse. We are using the data warehouse built on top of AdventureWorks. But, before we look at the examples, it is worth spending some time describing the difference between an operational database and a data warehouse, which requires us to describe how a data warehouse is composed.

## Data Marts, Facts, and Dimensions

The AdventureWorks data warehouse follows the Kimball methodology and is made up of tables called *facts* and *dimensions*. Facts and dimensions are tied together into business units that are called, in Kimball's terminology, *data marts*. Let us quickly review what facts and dimensions are.

The core organizing principle of the data mart structure is that the database is composed of two distinct types of entity:

- **Dimension** A dimension is an analytical object. A dimension can be the list of products or customers, the time space, or any other entity used to analyze numbers.
  - Dimensions have *attributes*. An attribute of a product may be its color, its manufacturer, or its weight. An attribute of a date may be simply its weekday or its month name.
  - Dimensions have both *natural keys* and *surrogate keys*. The natural key is the original product code, customer ID, or real date. The surrogate key is an independent integer number used in the data marts to uniquely identify a dimension entity, joining it to related facts.
  - A dimension has relationships with facts. Its reason for being is that of adding qualitative information to the numeric measures of an event contained in facts. Sometimes a dimension might reference other dimensions, or it might correlate to other dimensions even if its main purpose is that of joining to facts.
- **Fact** A fact is something that happened or that has been measured. A fact may be the sale of a single product to a single customer or the total amount of sales of a specific item during a month. From our point of view, a fact is an event (usually represented by a number) that we want to aggregate in several forms to generate our reports.
  - We normally relate a fact to several dimensions, but we do not relate facts in any way with other facts.
  - Facts definitely have relationships with dimensions via the surrogate keys. This is one of the foundations of Kimball's methodology.

In all the examples you have seen up to now, Product is a dimension table, whereas SalesOrderDetail, for instance, is a fact table. Some tables, such as SalesOrderHeader, behave both as fact and dimension tables, thus violating the Kimball rule that says that a table is either a fact or a dimension, but not both at the same time. This is not an issue because—up to now—we have never queried a data warehouse, and it is normal for OLTP databases to violate the rules of data warehouses because they are not data warehouses.

## Star Schemas

Having seen what facts and dimensions are, you are now ready to learn about a very well-known structure called a Star Schema. A Star Schema is simply the shape taken by data warehouse diagrams. When you define dimensions and create relationships between facts and dimensions, a star schema is the natural result. The fact table is always at the center of the schema, with the dimensions related to the fact table placed around it. Because the fact table is directly related only to the dimensions, you get a shape resembling a star, as you can see in Figure 4-28, where we show a piece of the schema of the AdventureWorks data warehouse.

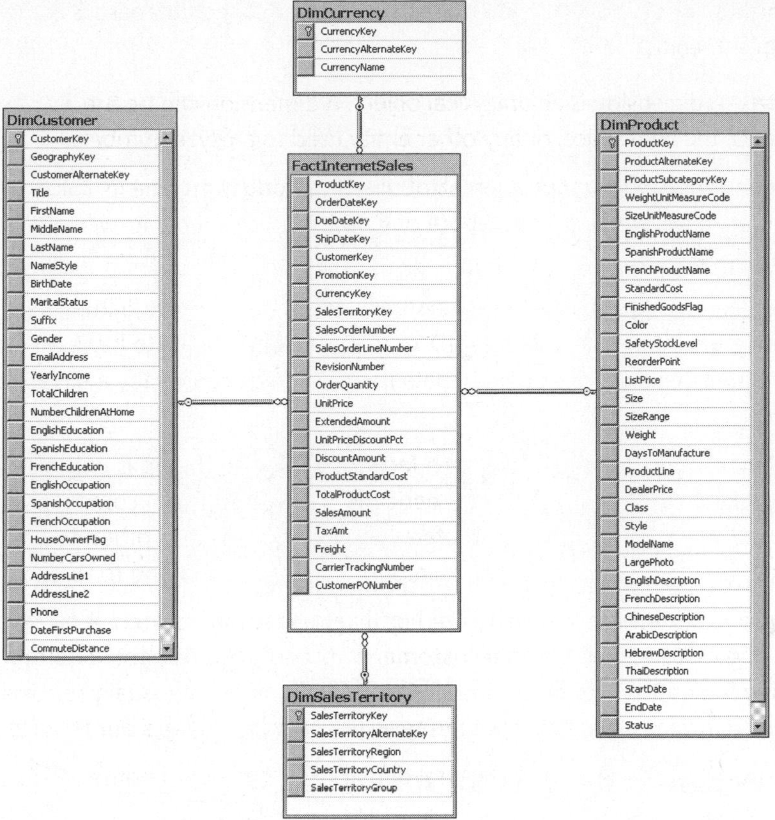


**FIGURE 4-28** A star schema has a fact table at the center and dimensions around it.

When you look at this picture, you can easily understand that a Customer bought a Product with a specific Currency. The sale is pertinent to a specific Territory. Star schemas are easily understandable by almost anybody at first glance.

As long as a data warehouse contains only star schemas created in accordance with the Kimball methodology, it gains several other very useful characteristics:

- There are no chained relationships. Because relationships exist only between facts and dimensions, the maximum depth of a relationship is 1. This makes it easy to generate relationships in PowerPivot because you always know that a dimension is related to a fact.
- All information is highly denormalized. This means that you never need (apart from some very specific cases) to use the RELATED function to load a column from a table into another one.
- If the model is well written, all descriptions in attributes are user-friendly. This means that no columns contain NULLs and the user can slice the data by using attributes in a very easy way.

**Note** The careful reader should have noticed that all the efforts we have made up to now to create a data model for the AdventureWorks database, are—in reality—in the direction of a data warehouse built with data marts. This is not accidental: the rationale behind it is that data marts are by far the best data model to query. Therefore, if we already have a data mart built by our IT department, it is far better to query it than to try to reproduce our personal data mart.

Moreover, we figure that most of the reporting needs in the company are already fulfilled by the data warehouse. When you get your data from there, chances are better that personal reports will be comparable with the corporate ones. If, on the other side, you create your personal reports from scratch, you are in danger of producing computation that differs from that produced by the data warehouse.

Last, but not least, is the fact that by directly querying the OLTP system, we rely on its data model to remain the same over time. Although people building the data warehouse know that their data structure is queried by analysts, OLTP programmers normally do not think that someone is poking around at their data, and so they feel free to change data structure as their needs change, as long as their software works. However, if the underlying OLTP data model changes, you discover it only when someone refreshes your reports for the first time. Chances are that you would need to perform a lot of work to re-create the data model in PowerPivot.

### Which Database Is the Best to Query?

Deciding whether is it better to load data from the OLTP system or the data warehouse is not easy. Using the data warehouse, you receive data already cleaned up and organized, which reduces the hard work of creating your personal data model. On the other hand, data is already organized, so you cannot model it as you would like because a lot of operations have been already carried out.

If you have a data warehouse, we suggest that you start using it. If this is enough to satisfy your reporting needs, you have completed your work with a minimum of effort. If, on the other hand, you still lack some information, you should import new data into PowerPivot tables and try to relate it with the data warehouse facts and dimensions.

Directly querying the OLTP should be seen as a very last resort because the work of creating a clean data model from an OLTP database is not easy. You could spend most of your time cleaning the model, reducing the time you might prefer to dedicate to analyzing the data.

## Querying the Data Warehouse

To see why we recommend querying the data warehouse instead of the OLTP database, we now show you some queries made against the AdventureWorks data warehouse. You can compare these with the previous queries.

Let us say that you want to perform an analysis of customers, products, geography, and time. You have already seen that only one of these entities (customers) is stored in several distinct tables in the OLTP, so you can easily imagine how complex it might be to load four of them plus the fact tables. If you have a data warehouse available, you need to import only the tables shown in Table 4-2 into PowerPivot.

**TABLE 4-2 Tables to load from the data warehouse.**

| Table | Description |
|---|---|
| DimProduct | Dimension containing all the products. |
| DimCustomer | Dimension containing all the customers. |
| DimSalesTerritory | Dimension containing the territories where AdventureWorks sells items. |
| DimTime | Time dimension. We will cover time dimension later in the book. |
| FactInternetSales | Fact table, containing the sales made over the Web. |
| FactResellerSales | Fact table, containing the sales made by resellers. |

You can already appreciate, from this simple list of tables to import, that their number is surprisingly low when compared with the number of tables that you would have needed to load if you had tried to perform the same kind of analysis directly from the OLTP system.

Moreover, because relationships are easily apparent in a star schema data model, PowerPivot can detect them during the loading process. You can create a report for the sales of a specific model of product to people who have a specific occupation, slicing data by year and geography, with just a few clicks.

You can see such a report in Figure 4-29, and although we do not provide here a complete description of how to build it, we strongly recommend that you try to reproduce it on your personal computer to get a real feeling of how easy it is. If you want to see the final sample report for this scenario, you can find it in the companion workbook CH04-05-DataMart.xlsx.

| ModelName | Sport-100 |
|---|---|
| EnglishOccupation | Skilled Manual |

| | Column Labels | | | | | |
|---|---|---|---|---|---|---|
| | 2003 | | 2004 | | Total Sum of SalesAmount | Total Sum of TaxAmt |
| Row Labels | Sum of SalesAmount | Sum of TaxAmt | Sum of SalesAmount | Sum of TaxAmt | | |
| Australia | 3,918.88 | 313.51 | 5,283.49 | 422.68 | 9,202.37 | 736.19 |
| Canada | 4,303.77 | 344.30 | 5,423.45 | 433.88 | 9,727.22 | 778.18 |
| France | 839.76 | 67.18 | 1,224.65 | 97.97 | 2,064.41 | 165.15 |
| Germany | 804.77 | 64.38 | 1,294.63 | 103.57 | 2,099.40 | 167.95 |
| United Kingdom | 1,539.56 | 123.16 | 1,644.53 | 131.56 | 3,184.09 | 254.73 |
| United States | 10,811.91 | 864.95 | 14,485.86 | 1,158.87 | 25,297.77 | 2,023.82 |
| **Grand Total** | **22,218.65** | **1,777.49** | **29,356.61** | **2,348.53** | **51,575.26** | **4,126.02** |

**FIGURE 4-29** A query against the data warehouse provides great reports in just a few clicks.

The really (and we mean *really*) tireless reader might try to reproduce the same report by means of directly querying the OLTP system. Believe us, he would need to spend more time doing that exercise than reading the rest of this book.

### PowerPivot and the Data Warehouse

If the only strength of PowerPivot was the fact that you can build your own reports directly on the data warehouse, the very same purpose could be reached by simply connecting to an Analysis Services OLAP cube, which is probably already present in the data warehouse infrastructure.

Nevertheless, in PowerPivot, this report can be the starting point of your analysis. You can easily add more information by loading it from other tables that you already have in other databases or that reside in simple Excel workbooks where, for example, you might think out the corporate budget.

By using the current data warehouse data model and adding your personal new data, you can build a new data model over the existing data warehouse, adding information and intelligence where you need it. We believe that when a company begins using PowerPivot, the quality of the reports rise. In fact, data that is not yet in the data warehouse can be used immediately by analysts who, in turn, can give good advice to the BI specialists, who can then create a better integration of data in the data warehouse.

In our view, PowerPivot does not replace the corporate data warehouse. PowerPivot gives analysts the ability to extend the existent data warehouse and reach levels of analysis never seen before.

In the rest of this book, you query both the OLTP and the Data Warehouse databases, depending on the kind of analysis you want to perform. In later chapters, you integrate the data warehouse with your personal data.

## Discovering Advanced Types of Relationships

Although standard relationships (that is, relationships between two tables based on a single column, which holds the same value in both tables) are the most popular in relational databases, some other types of relationships can be used to model information and are not so easy to detect and model.

We now discuss some of these other types, using the AdventureWorks data warehouse as an example.

## Role-Playing Relationships

It is not yet time to fully discuss the date dimension; we get to that in Chapter 7, "Date Calculations in DAX." Nevertheless, it is worth pointing out here a very important concept, for which the date dimension serves as a perfect example.

In the previous example, you loaded a dimension called DimTime, which contains all the details about date and time. In Figure 4-30, you can see the PivotTable field selector with the time dimension expanded. You can appreciate that the time dimension contains several useful attributes that can be used to slice your data.

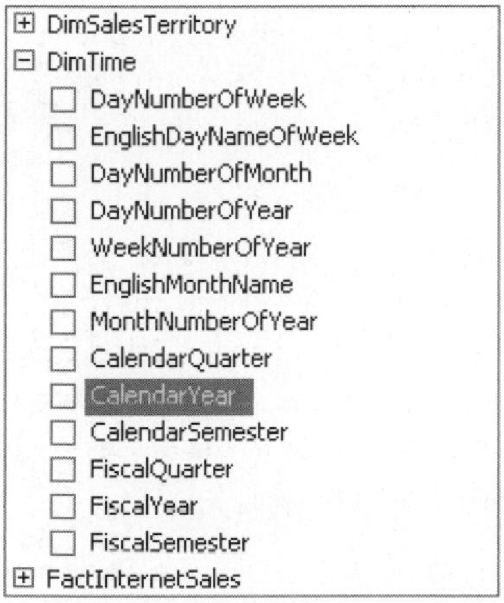

**FIGURE 4-30** The attributes of the time dimension.

In Chapters 2 and 3, you learned that these attributes can be computed directly in the SalesOrderHeader table using the several date and time functions available in DAX. You are now going to learn a different approach to the handling of time attributes, and in general, of aggregators. In fact, in this model, you now have a time dimension with attributes and a relationship between orders and the time dimension. Guess what is changing? The data model.

If you have an entity (in this case the date) for which there are many interesting attributes that you could use to slice data (in the case of the date, you have year, month, day in the year, and so on) you have two options:

- You can add attributes to the original table, as we have done in Chapter 2. This technique is easy to implement. Whenever you want a new attribute, you simply define a computed column in the table holding that attribute. Nevertheless, if you have—for example—many date columns in your database, you need to define many calculated columns, one for each table containing a date column.

- On the other hand, you can create a new table, which has as the key the original datum (in this case a date) and contains all the various attributes. Then, setting up a relationship between the original table and the new one, you get the result you want. You have consolidated the attributes in a dimension. If you have many date columns in different tables, you have many relationships but only one instance of the date table containing attributes.

The main advantage of this new solution is that, if you want to provide new attributes for the date, for instance, you can add fiscal calendar information, it is enough to add this information to the new table and the new attributes work smoothly to slice data wherever a date appears because relationships take this new information to all tables that are related to the consolidated dimension.

This technique, which we refer to as *attribute consolidation*, is common in the data warehouse world and is surely worth using for the date dimension. Attribute consolidation normally leads to a situation where the same table (in this case, the date) needs a relationship with more than one source table or with more than one column in the same table.

If you look carefully, for instance, at the FactInternetSales table, (see Figure 4-31), you can see that there are many columns that contain references to the date. Moreover, please note that the columns contain the surrogate key of the date, not the date itself, following the Kimball rules we stated before.

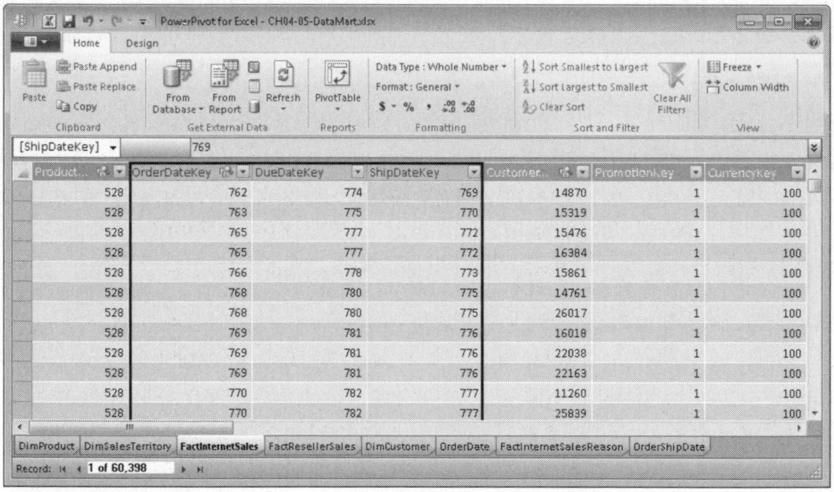

**FIGURE 4-31** The fact table contains three keys for the Date dimension.

In the boxed part of the Figure, you can see three columns that contain a reference to a date:

- **OrderDateKey** The date of the order
- **ShipDateKey** The date of the shipment of the order
- **DueDateKey** The date when the order is due to arrive

The small icon in the OrderDateKey column indicates that this column already has a relationship with another table. So we know, by looking here, that the date dimension has a relationship with the date of the order. Knowing that, you can see that it would be much better to rename the DimTime dimension with a name that indicates the relationship. You can easily do that by right-clicking the table name and choosing Rename to name it, for example, OrderDate.

Now you have a time dimension that has the correct name, but what if you want to slice your data for the shipping date year or the due date month? You could be tempted to create many relationships between FactInternetSales and the date dimension. In a relational model, you are permitted to have more than one relationship between two tables, but this is not the case in PowerPivot. If one table has a relationship with a second table, you cannot set up a new relationship between the same two tables. In other words, two tables can share only one relationship even if a table can have a relationship with other tables.

This situation is well known in the data warehouse world and is known as *role relationship* or *role dimension* (that is, a dimension is referred many times from a fact table and each relationship imposes a role on that dimension). The Time dimension acts as an order date, a shipment date, or a due date. In other words, the same time acts according to different roles, depending on the relationship you follow to get there.

As we said before, role dimensions are not natively supported in PowerPivot. To work around it, you can load the same table more than once and set up relationships from the fact table with those different instances of the same Time dimension, superseding the current limitation.

If you want, for instance, to have a dimension that acts as the ship date, you can open the connection with the database, select the DimTime table again, and load it. It loads as DimTime1. (PowerPivot adds a number after the dimension name to make it evident that this is not the first instance of the table, unless you remember to define a new friendly name.) You should rename it OrderShipDate, to make its meaning evident.

When you add this new dimension to a PivotTable containing some values from FactInternetSales, PowerPivot displays the message Relationship Needed because you still have not defined the relationship between the fact table and the dimension. You now can ask PowerPivot to detect relationship and chances are good that it will detect the relationship between the new time dimension and the ShipDateKey column in the fact table. The relationship you find takes this form:

```
Relationships created:
[FactInternetSales].[ShipDateKey] -> [OrderShipDate].[TimeKey]
```

Does it look easy? It definitely is. Nevertheless, if you think twice about what happened, you discover a strong need to understand how PowerPivot detected that relationship because it seems too easy to be true.

In fact, the FactInternetSales table has three different relationships with the time dimension, for the order, ship, and due dates. After loading the second instance of the time dimension, you had two time dimensions in the database, one of which already had a relationship with the OrderDateKey. So, there is one free time dimension and two candidates for the relationship: ship and due date. PowerPivot detected the correct candidate, selecting the OrderShipDate column. The problem is that it might have found the relationship on the DueDateKey, if the automatic algorithm failed to do its job properly for some reason.

The relationship detection algorithm analyzed not only the data in the tables, but also the names of the columns; this is the reason it detected the relationship with ShipDateKey and not with DueDateKey. Nevertheless, relying only on automatic relationship detection based on heuristics is not a safe option. You need to be sure that the relationship is set up correctly, so even if you can give the automatic algorithm a chance, you definitely need to double-check its work using the Manage Relationship window, where you can verify that all relationships have been found correctly.

**Note** Even if it might be strange for us to say this, we strongly advise never to trust the automatic relationships detector. We suggest that you use it but always verify the relationship the detector finds, and in case of any doubt, double-check it with the Manage Relationship dialog box. A wrong relationship causes the display of wrong data, and if it is not checked at the time of creation, it might be very difficult to find later.

Role dimensions are useful because they lead to an easier model to manage. Attribute consolidation is also welcome because it makes it easier to update the model with new and interesting attributes. You can try, as an exercise, to complete the three roles of the time dimension by adding a new time dimension that has the role of ship date.

## Many-to-Many Relationships

Another interesting kind of relationship, which we use in later chapters, is the many-to-many relationship. Many-to-many relationships are common, and at first sight, pretty complex to understand. Nevertheless, they are powerful and you definitely need to understand them to exploit their power. Later in the book, you will make extensive use of the many-to-many relationship. For now, it is enough to introduce them with an example, to help you understand what they are.

In the AdventureWorks data warehouse, each line of an order might refer to some sale reasons. A Sale reason might be Magazine Advertisement, Review, Demo event, or other reasons that are listed in the table DimSalesReason.

From the data model point of view, each line of an order might refer to more than one reason. Therefore, you cannot add a SalesReasonID column to the SalesOrderDetail table because, when you do that, you can define only a single reason for each line, whereas your data model requires a variable number of reasons for each single line.

You can clearly see the situation in Figure 4-32. If you set up a relationship between FactInternetSales and DimSalesReason, you can slice sales by sales reason, but you are limited to only one sales reason for each order line.

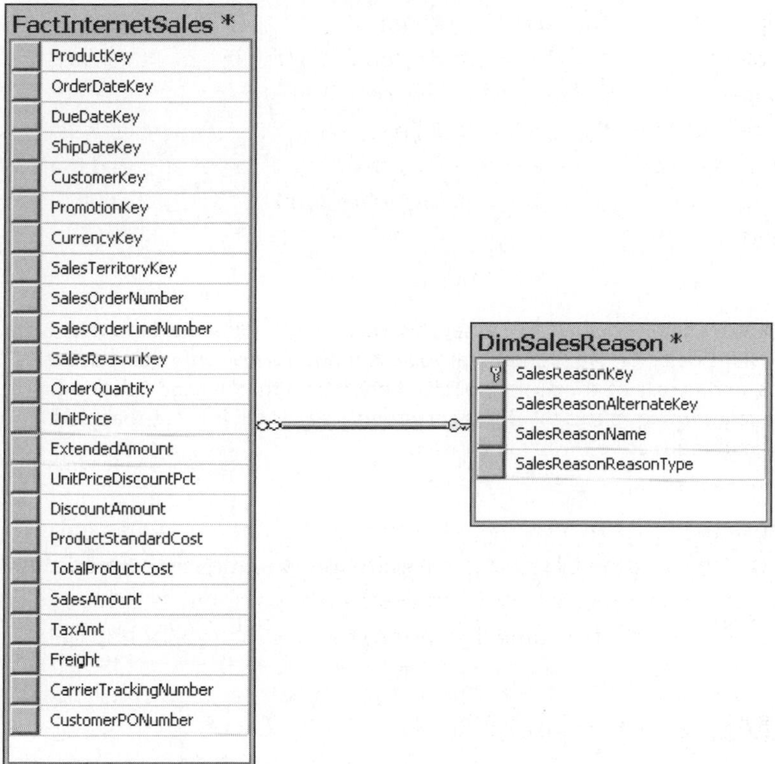


**FIGURE 4-32** The wrong way to model sales reasons.

To set up the relationship correctly, you need an additional table. If you add an intermediate table that contains an order line and a sales reason, you can use this additional table to define both many sales reasons for a single line of an order and many lines of orders for a single sales reason. This is why these kinds of relationships are called many-to-many: if you need to relate many rows in a table with many rows in another one, you can do that using an intermediate table. This intermediate table acts as a bridge between the two original tables: therefore, it is commonly called a *bridge table*.

The correct data model for a many-to-many relationship is shown in Figure 4-33.

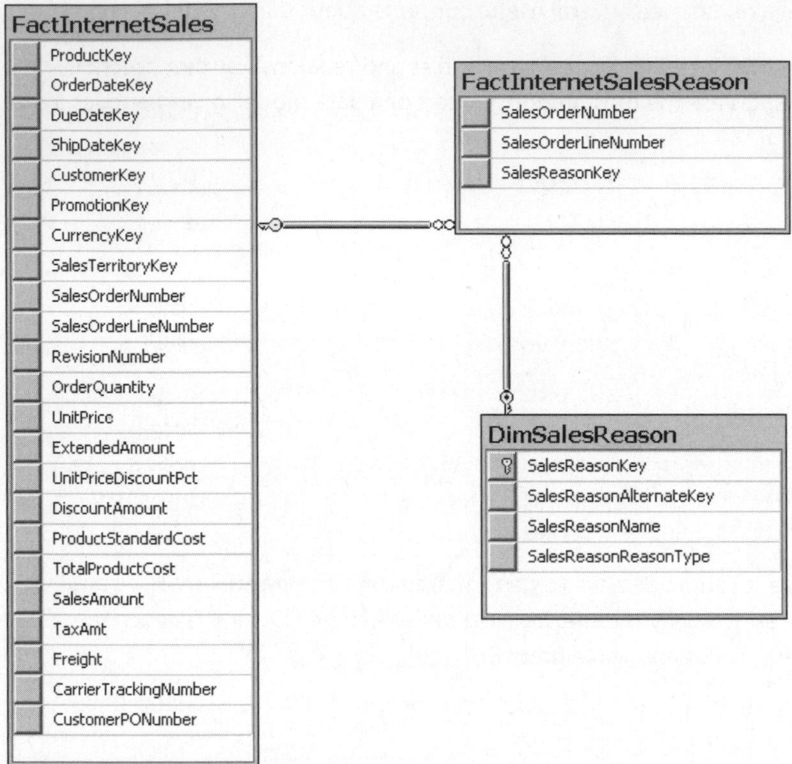


**FIGURE 4-33** The correct way to build the many-to-many data model.

When present, many-to-many relationships violate the rule of the star schema that imposes one as the maximum depth of the chain of relationships between fact tables and dimensions. Nevertheless, you do not absolutely need to conform to that rule. The rule helps you create data models that are easy to understand, but if you need more power to express complex relationships such as many to many, you can safely violate the rule.

Many-to-many relationships are not natively supported in PowerPivot. Later on, in Chapter 10, "PowerPivot Data Model Patterns," you learn how to master many-to-many relationships to make them solve some of the most common patterns of data models.

# Summary

In this chapter, you learned several useful concepts about data models.

- A data model is nothing but a set of tables and relationships that describe some entities. Relationships are the most important part of a data model, giving entities a meaningful position in the data model.
- The same entity structure can be described by different data models, each one having virtues and flaws. The choice of the right data model seriously affects the way we query it.
- PowerPivot is a database, so it is able to understand and use data models. This leads to the necessity, for the PowerPivot user, to understand and correctly use data models.
- The physical data model is often complex because of the normalization process that has been carried on by database administrators to optimize software that runs on it. On the other hand, the logical data model needs to be as simple as possible because it will be queried by humans. The basic process you learned to convert a physical data model into a logical one is called denormalization.
- There are a couple of ways to denormalize data: in PowerPivot or through SQL queries. The PowerPivot way is easier but less powerful; the SQL one is much more powerful, but it requires of you some basic SQL understanding.
- If we have a data warehouse, querying it is the best choice because data in the data warehouse is already denormalized and probably stored as facts and dimensions, a very simple structure to query that provides great results.
- Even a structure as simple as the data warehouse often contains complexities, such as many-to-many relationships or role-playing dimensions. Those advanced dimensions need a specific treatment and understanding.

can be provided by your local administrator of that system and are outside of the scope of this book. Moreover, it is interesting to look at the differences between a text file and a SQL Server query, whereas it of little use to investigate the subtle differences between Microsoft SQL Server and Oracle, which are both relational database servers.

### Data Source Limitations for Refreshing Data

As you will learn later, after data is loaded into PowerPivot, you can refresh it by reloading it again from the data source. Although you can always refresh data on your own personal computer, there are some limitations to this feature when you publish the workbook to SharePoint. For example, if you want to publish your Excel workbook on SharePoint and you want to schedule the refresh of data directly on the server, you have to be aware of the existing limitations of the available data sources. If you import data from text or Excel files stored in a local directory, these files are not accessible by SharePoint and you cannot refresh this data on the server. Moreover, if you are using a 32-bit version of Excel and you access the database by using a third-party provider, you have to be sure that the corresponding 64-bit version is installed on the SharePoint server. Finally, pasting data from the Clipboard is an operation that cannot be refreshed, either on the client or on the server.

# Loading from a Database

We are now going to describe the first option for loading data, which is the From Database button. This option is probably the most frequently used to load data into PowerPivot. This is not an accident because the vast majority of the databases around the world are held in relational databases.

**Note** In the rest of this section, we show examples using SQL Server because this is probably the most frequently used database for PowerPivot users. If you need to connect to a different server, you might need different connection parameters, which you can ask your IT department to give you.

As soon as you select From SQL Server, PowerPivot opens the Table Import Wizard, which you can see in Figure 5-2.

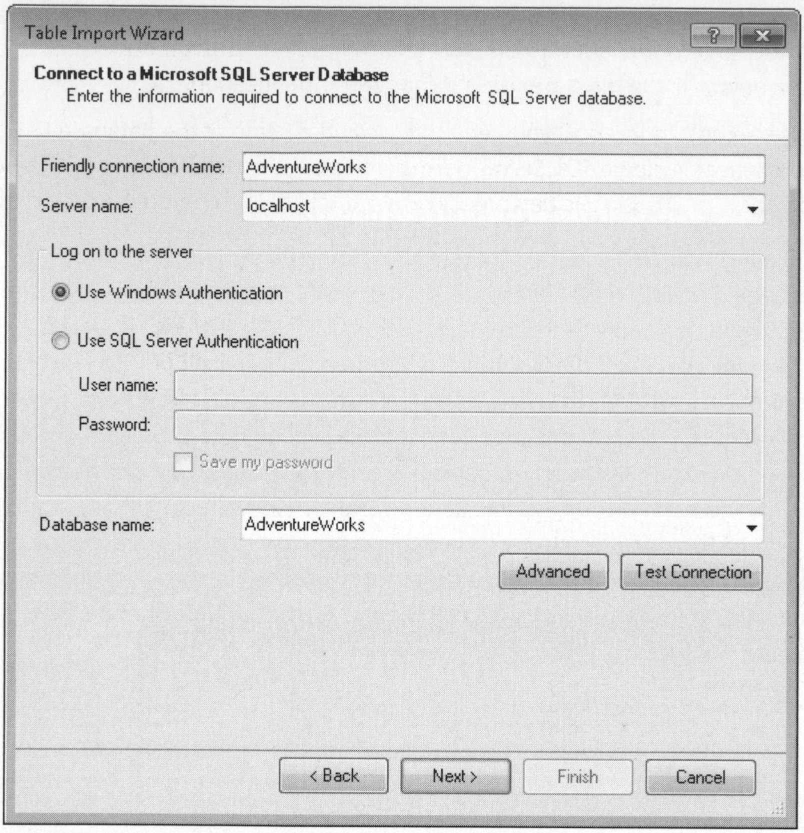

**FIGURE 5-2** The Table Import Wizard, connecting to SQL Server.

The Table Import Wizard guides you step by step during the whole loading process, asking for just a few parameters in each dialog box. These are the important parameters that you need to fill in this first dialog box:

- **Friendly connection name** This is a name that you can assign to the connection to recall it later. We suggest overriding the default name that PowerPivot suggests because using a meaningful name makes your life easier later on, when you need to recall the same connection, for example, to load another table from the same database.
- **Server Name** This is the name of the SQL Server to which you want to connect. In all the examples, we use *localhost*, which is a special name that refers to the local computer, whichever its name is. In your specific environment you will need to write the name of the SQL server, which your IT department will provide you.
- **Log on to the server** This option lets you choose the method of authentication to use when connecting to SQL Server. You can choose between Windows Authentication (which uses your current Windows account to provide the credentials for SQL Server) and

SQL Server Authentication. (In this case, you need to provide user name and password in this dialog box.) Your IT department tells you what authentication method to use; in this book, we always assume we are using Windows Authentication.

- **Database name** In this box, you need to specify the name of the database to which you want to connect. A single SQL Server normally hosts many databases, so you need to provide the name of the specific database of interest to you. Again, you need help from the IT department so that they can give you the name of the database that contains your data.

Before continuing, it is a good practice to test the connection with the Test Connection button so that you can be sure that there are no problems with the connection parameters. If the connection test runs fine, you can confidently save this connection and proceed with the next steps. If, on the other hand, you find any kind of problem, it is better to discover it now and solve it immediately.

Clicking Next brings you to the next window of the wizard (see Figure 5-3), where you need to make an important choice: whether you want to load data directly from tables or views or whether you want to write a SQL query to perform some advanced data loading.

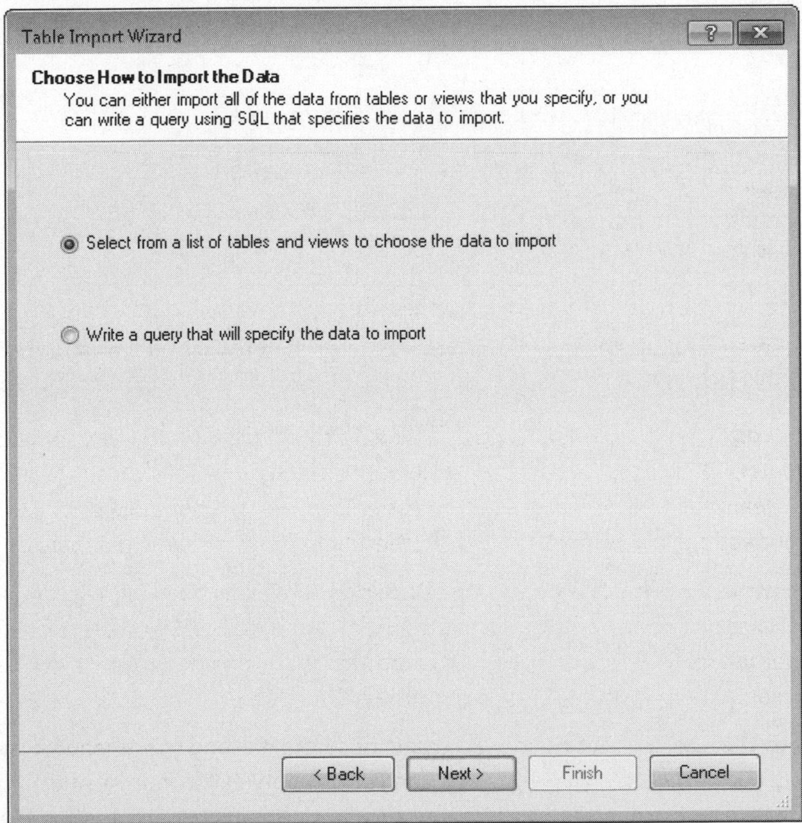


**FIGURE 5-3** Choosing the correct loading method.

These two options lead you to completely different loading paths, which we explore in the following sections.

## Loading from a List of Tables

If you choose to select the tables from a list, PowerPivot reads from SQL Server the list of tables and views available in the database and allows you to choose which one to load, as shown in Figure 5-4.

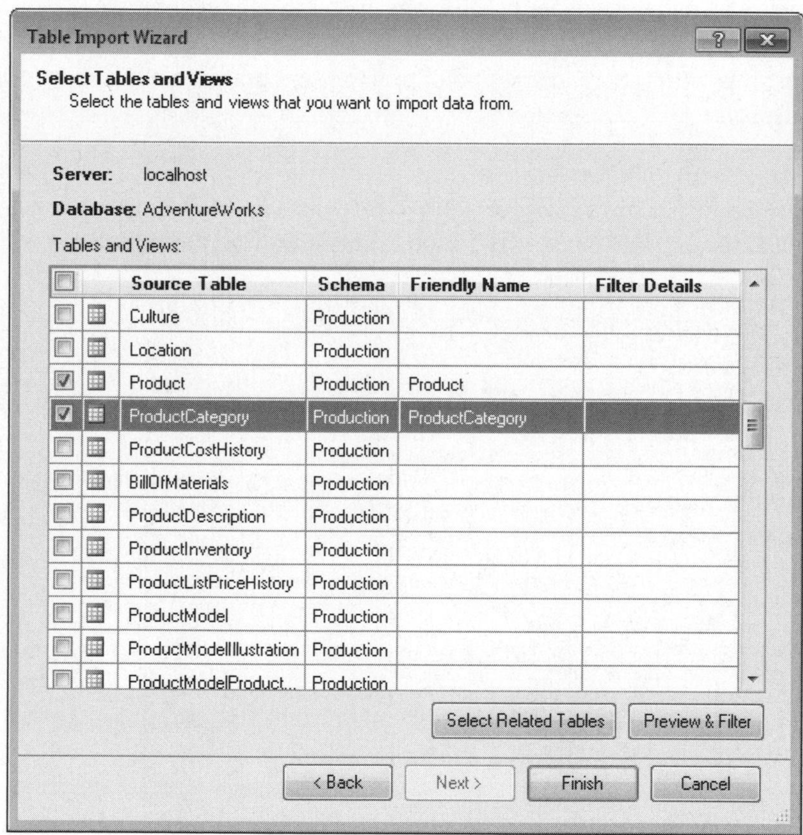


**FIGURE 5-4** List of tables to import.

When you select a table for import, you can give it a friendly name, which is the name that PowerPivot uses for the table after it has been imported. If you like, you can filter to reduce the number of rows you have to read from the table. Filtering is useful when you face very big tables and you are interested in the analysis of only some of the rows.

To access the filtering dialog box (see Figure 5-5), you should use the Preview & Filter button.

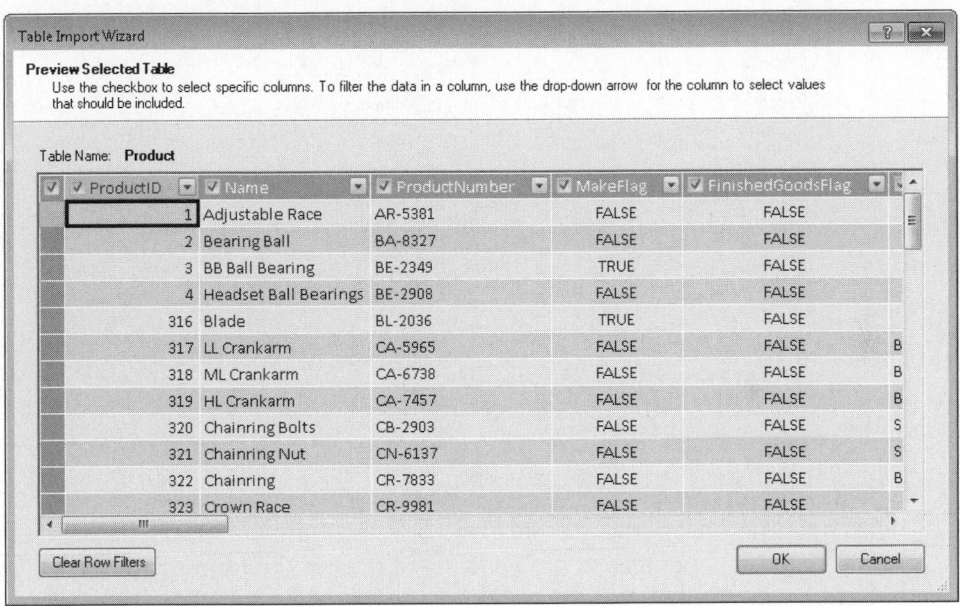


**FIGURE 5-5** Previewing and filtering a table.

To limit the rows in a table, you can apply two different kinds of filters:

- **Colum filtering** You can choose a selection of all the columns of the table for loading. This is convenient when the source table contains technical columns, which are not useful for our analysis. To select or remove a column, you need to use the small check box that appears before each column title in the grid.
- **Data filtering** You can also choose to load only a subset of the rows of the table, specifying a condition that filters out the unwanted rows. In Figure 5-6, you can see the data filtering dialog box open for the Name column.

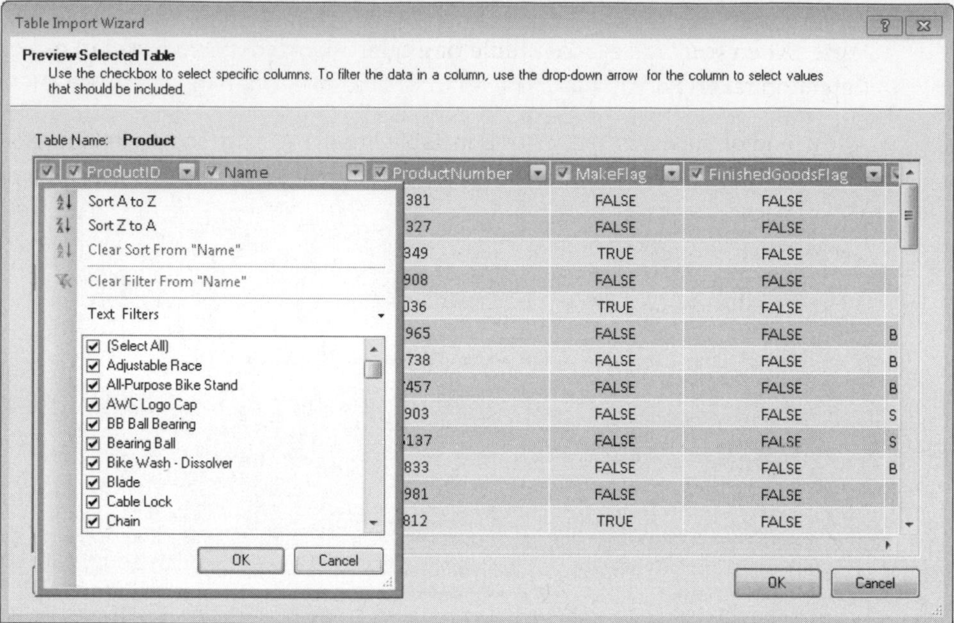


**FIGURE 5-6** Data filtering.

Data filtering is very powerful and relatively easy to use. You can use the list of values, automatically provided by PowerPivot, or if there are too many values, you can use the Text Filters option and provide a set of rules in the forms *greater than*, *less than or equal to*, and so on.

**Note** Both column and data filters are saved in the PowerPivot table definition so that when you refresh the table from the PowerPivot window, they can be applied again.

## Loading Relationships

When you finished filtering the table, clicking OK makes PowerPivot load the tables. As soon as PowerPivot finishes loading data, it detects whether there are any relationships among the tables currently being loaded. Because relational databases are able to store not only data, but also information about existing relationships, PowerPivot queries the database to see whether relationships are stored, and if some exist, PowerPivot replicates them in its internal database.

The relationship detection occurs only when you load data directly from more than one table. When you load a single table or a query (which we discuss later), no relationship detection takes place.

At the end of the list of Work Items in Table Import Wizard, shown in Figure 5-7, you can see an additional step, called Data Preparation, which indicates that relationship detection has taken place.

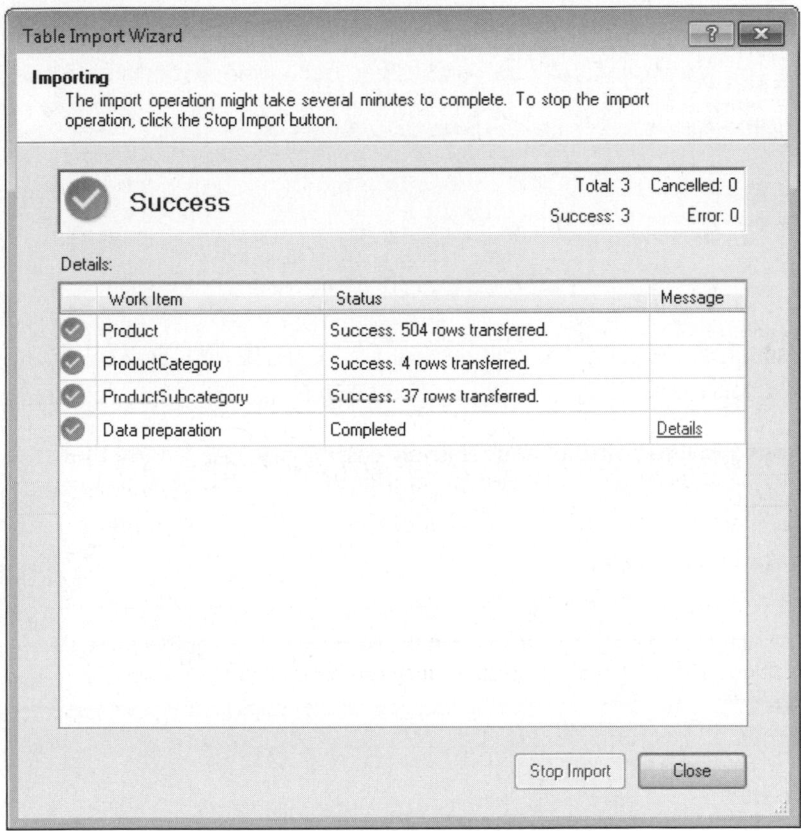


**FIGURE 5-7** The data preparation step of the Table Import Wizard.

If you want to see more details about the relationships that the Table Import Wizard found, you can use the Details hyperlink to open a small window that summarizes the relationships created.

## Selecting Related Tables

During the loading process that we have shown up to now, we have not focused on another useful button in the Table Import Wizard, which is the Select Related Tables button (see Figure 5-8). We dedicate some time to it now.

PowerPivot can analyze the relationships between tables stored in the database and automatically select for us all the tables that have some kind of relationship with the ones already selected.

If, for example, you select only the Product table, you get a window similar to Figure 5-8.

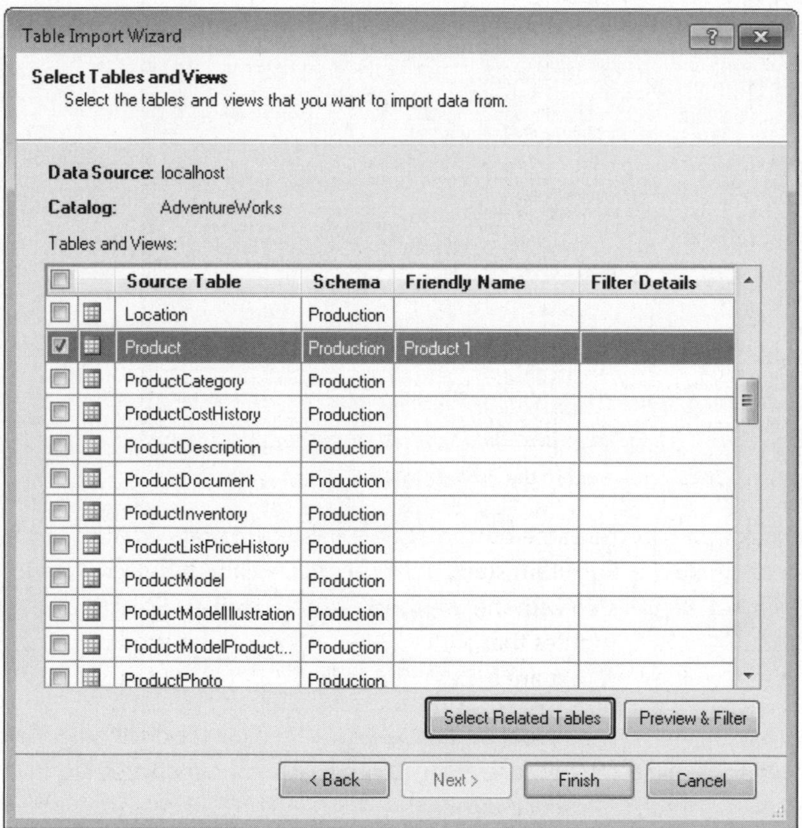


**FIGURE 5-8** PowerPivot lets us quickly select all tables related to the already-selected ones.

If you click the Select Related Tables button, PowerPivot scans all the tables in the database, searching for any that has a relationship with the Product table. As soon as it detects one, it automatically selects it. In Figure 5-9, you can see the result: 16 tables have been selected by this process, which means that the database contains 16 tables that have a direct relationship with Products.

**FIGURE 5-9** There are 16 tables related to the Product table.

Please note that if you click the same button again, PowerPivot finds another 11 tables to select. The second time the algorithm starts, it has 16 tables already selected, so it detects all tables that have a relationship with the previously selected tables. So, to recap, the first time PowerPivot detected the tables that are in relationship with the Product table, and the second time it detected tables that are in relationship with those found during the first step.

This process is more evident if you look carefully at Figure 5-9. The ProductCategory table was not selected during the first step because ProductCategory is not directly related to products. The Product table is related to ProductSubcategory. Then ProductSubcategory, in turn, is in relationship with ProductCategory, which will be selected during the second step.

You could go on repeating this step until all directly and indirectly related tables are selected. Chances are that, if you did that, you would end up selecting the whole database because normally all tables are related in some way with all the others.

## Loading from a SQL Query

In the previous sections, we completed the description of the loading process from a relational database. During the first step of the Table Import Wizard, you chose to select some tables and then you followed all the steps to the end. But, as we have seen before, there was another option: Write A Query That Will Specify The Data To Import (see Figure 5-3).

As you might recall from Chapter 4, SQL is a standard query language for reading information from a database, and when you select the second option in Figure 5-3, PowerPivot opens the query editor, shown in Figure 5-10.

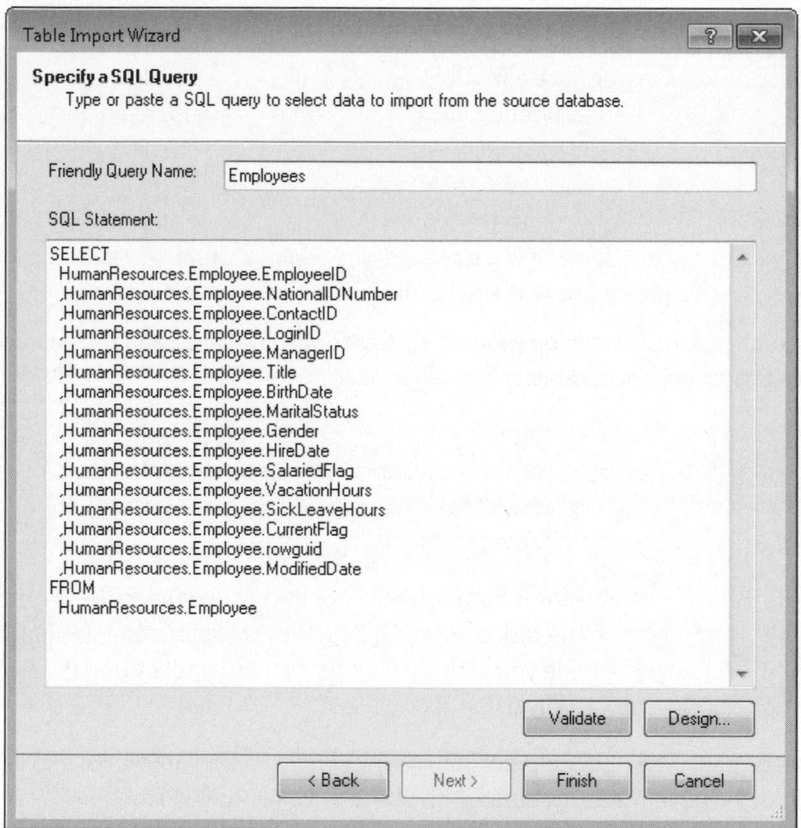


**FIGURE 5-10** The query editor allows us to specify a SQL query as the data source.

You saw a description of how the query designer works in Chapter 4, so we are not going to repeat all that stuff here. The interesting part is the fact that, when working with SQL databases, you always have the option to load tables or queries, whichever looks better for your specific data model.

## Loading from Views

Before leaving the SQL database topic, let us spend some time on another kind of object that you can use to load data from a SQL database: *views*. But before we describe this object, we should briefly review the main characteristics of the two ways to load data we have used so far: tables and queries.

- **Tables** The big advantages of tables are that they are easier than queries to load and that PowerPivot is able to automatically detect most relationships. On the other hand, directly loading tables makes it necessary to understand the source data model and to follow complex chains of relationships in PowerPivot, making the later data modeling process in PowerPivot slightly complex.
- **Queries** SQL queries produce a much cleaner result than tables do because you can use SQL to perform denormalization, follow chains of relationships, and produce a final result that makes the final data model much easier to query in PowerPivot. On the other hand, SQL queries are not easy to write and if you decide to use the query editor, you are likely to have some difficulties expressing exactly the query you want to write. SQL was not written for end users; it is a query language aimed at technicians, and no query editor will ever be able to make it easy to express a really complex query.

All that said, another structure can be exposed by relational databases, and it is an interesting mix between a SQL query and a table: it is called a view.

A view is nothing but a SQL query stored in the database and which has a name. From the PowerPivot point of view, a view is like a table: it contains rows divided into columns. The only difference is that when PowerPivot asks for the data, the database does not return rows stored in a table; instead it executes the SQL query and returns its result.

What makes views first-class citizens is that they address the gap between database technicians and power users. Because the task to write SQL queries is better accomplished by IT staff, you can ask IT staff to provide you with a set of views that handle the complexities of SQL and expose a more user-friendly data model to you.

As an example of how views can help both the IT department and you, we have developed a set of views in the AdventureWorks database under the prefix PowerPivotBook.

**Note** If you want to follow this example on your PC, you need to get access to the AdventureWorks database by using SQL Server Management Studio and run the SQL query, which you can find in CH05-SQL-Views.sql. If you have any problem accessing the SQL database using Management Studio, you probably need to ask your IT department for some help.

If you load the PowerPivotBook.Products view into PowerPivot, for example, you get a very nice data structure for the product table (see Figure 5-11).

| ProductID | Name | ProductCategory | ProductSubcategory | Color | ProductNumber | FinishedGood |
|---|---|---|---|---|---|---|
| 352 | Front D... | <NO Category> | <NO Subcategory> | Silver | FL-2301 | FINISHED GOODS |
| 461 | Lock Ring | <NO Category> | <NO Subcategory> | Silver | LR-2398 | FINISHED GOODS |
| 679 | Rear De... | <NO Category> | <NO Subcategory> | Silver | RC-0291 | FINISHED GOODS |
| 707 | Sport-1... | Accessories | Helmets | Red | HL-U509-R | NON FINISHED ... |
| 708 | Sport-1... | Accessories | Helmets | Black | HL-U509 | NON FINISHED ... |
| 709 | Mounta... | Clothing | Socks | White | SO-B909-M | NON FINISHED ... |
| 710 | Mounta... | Clothing | Socks | White | SO-B909-L | NON FINISHED ... |
| 711 | Sport-1... | Accessories | Helmets | Blue | HL-U509-B | NON FINISHED ... |
| 712 | AWC Lo... | Clothing | Caps | Multi | CA-1098 | NON FINISHED ... |
| 713 | Long-Sl... | Clothing | Jerseys | Multi | LJ-0192-S | NON FINISHED ... |
| 714 | Long-Sl... | Clothing | Jerseys | Multi | LJ-0192-M | NON FINISHED ... |
| 715 | Long-Sl... | Clothing | Jerseys | Multi | LJ-0192-L | NON FINISHED ... |
| 716 | Long-Sl... | Clothing | Jerseys | Multi | LJ-0192-X | NON FINISHED ... |
| 841 | Men's S... | Clothing | Shorts | Black | SH-M897-S | NON FINISHED ... |
| 842 | Touring... | Accessories | Panniers | Grey | PA-T100 | NON FINISHED ... |
| 843 | Cable L... | Accessories | Locks | <NO Color> | LO-C100 | NON FINISHED ... |
| 844 | Minipu... | Accessories | Pumps | <NO Color> | PU-0452 | NON FINISHED ... |
| 845 | Mounta... | Accessories | Pumps | <NO Color> | PU-M044 | NON FINISHED ... |
| 846 | Taillight... | Accessories | Lights | <NO Color> | LT-T990 | NON FINISHED ... |
| 847 | Headlig... | Accessories | Lights | <NO Color> | LT-H902 | NON FINISHED ... |
| 848 | Headlig... | Accessories | Lights | <NO Color> | LT-H903 | NON FINISHED ... |

**FIGURE 5-11** Using views, the data model for products is very simple.

You can appreciate several interesting aspects in this structure:

- When no category or subcategory exists, the view returns a default value for it, indicating the lack of a value. That default value begins with an open angle bracket so that this element shows up first in a sorted list, to make it more evident in any report.
- The same technique has been applied to the color.
- The view contains the complexity of details about the relationships between products, subcategories, categories, and product models; the view shows a data model that already contains denormalized information as attributes of the product table.
- The FinishedGoodFlag Boolean value has been converted by the view into a more user-friendly textual description, which is easier to query and analyze.

As you might notice, the view carries on for us the hard task of denormalization and detection of empty values, along with the handling of relationships.

If you are familiar with SQL, you can see that the SQL query that creates this structure is an easy one and creating it takes just minutes. If you are not, it is enough to understand that your IT people will be more than happy to write these queries for you and expose them as views so that you can easily load data from the database and perform the complex analysis you want to, without ever asking them to produce any software.

Moreover, IT will really like the fact that you are reading data from views because—from their point of view—the view acts as an interface between the database and the users asking for data (you, in this case). When IT people look at views, they are aware of the data you are using.

We recommend that you use views because a view acts as a perfect bridge between the complexity of SQL queries (which is left to IT staff) and the simplicity of tables.

# Opening Existing Connections

In the preceding section, we showed you all the features and stages of data loading, creating a connection from the beginning. After you create a connection with a data source, it will be saved in the PowerPivot workbook so that you can open it again without needing to provide the connection information. Unfortunately, this useful option is not so easy to find because it is on the Design tab of the PowerPivot ribbon, as you can see in Figure 5-12.

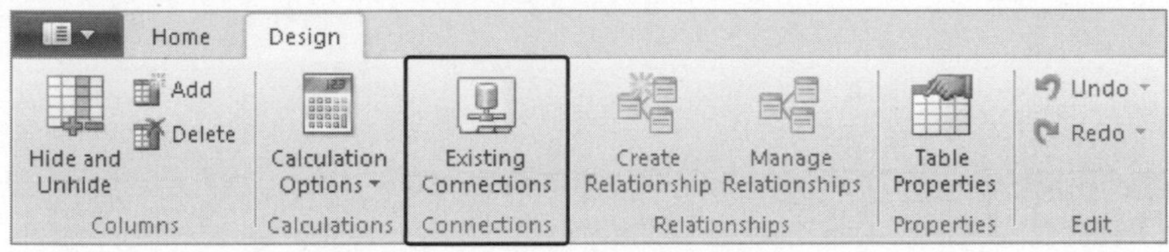


**FIGURE 5-12** The Existing Connection button on the Design tab.

If you click this button, PowerPivot opens the Existing Connection dialog box shown in Figure 5-13, where you can select either the connections saved in the Excel workbook or any local connection previously saved in your document library.

Moreover, if you need to change the properties of a saved connection, you can use the Edit button to open the Edit Connection dialog box again and update its configuration.

**Note** It is very important that you get used to reopening existing connections whenever you need to import more tables from the same database because, if you create a new connection each time you want to load data, you end up with many connections in the same workbook. If you have many connections and you need to modify some of the connection parameters, you will have some extra and unneeded work to update all the different connections. Moreover, if you have fewer connections, performance might improve, and there is less administrative effort in handling external connections whenever the workbook is published on SharePoint.

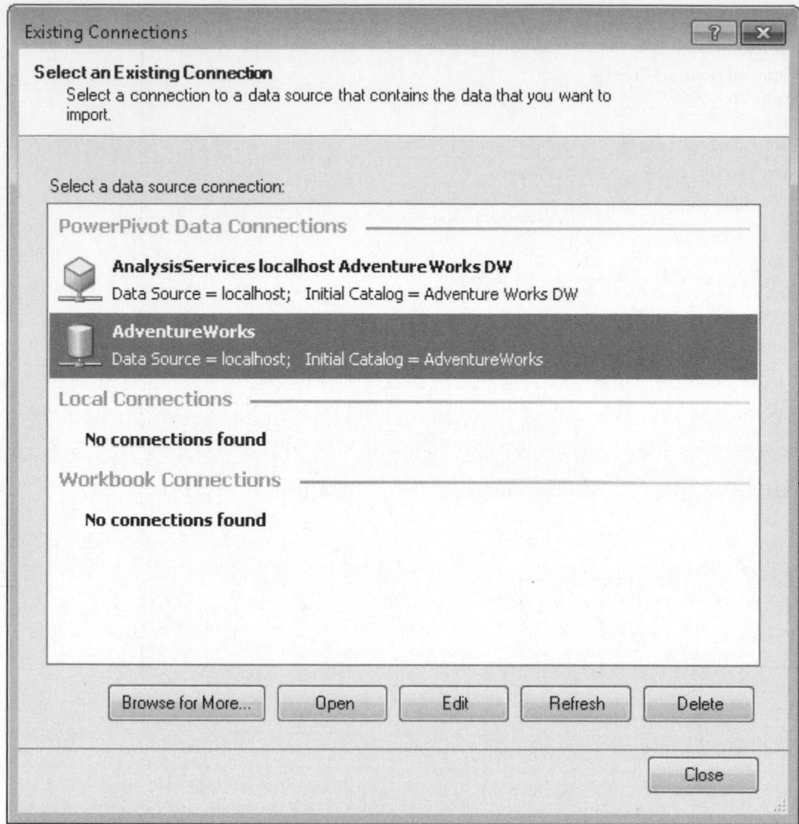


**FIGURE 5-13** The Existing Connection dialog box.

# Loading from Access

Now that you have seen all the ways data can be loaded from relational databases, we can describe other data sources, the first of which is the Microsoft Access data source. Many Microsoft Office users are used to storing information in Access databases, so PowerPivot provides an Access data source that can load data from Access in much the same way you do with SQL Server.

Clearly, when you open the Table Import Wizard with an Access data source, the connection parameters are slightly different because Access databases are stored in files on disk instead of being hosted in server databases. In Figure 5-14, you can see the Table Import Wizard asking for an Access file.

**FIGURE 5-14** The Access Table Import Wizard.

## AdventureWorks Access Database

The AdventureWorks database used in this book is available also in Access format on the companion DVD. You can open the AdventureWorks.zip file and extract the AdventureWorks file in Access format. Copy it to your local disk before using it in PowerPivot.

There is no practical difference between Access and a relational database when it comes to loading tables. On the other hand, the SQL designer of Access is limited because it does not offer a visual designer for the SQL query. When you query Access, you need to write the query in a plain text editor, which you can see in Figure 5-15.

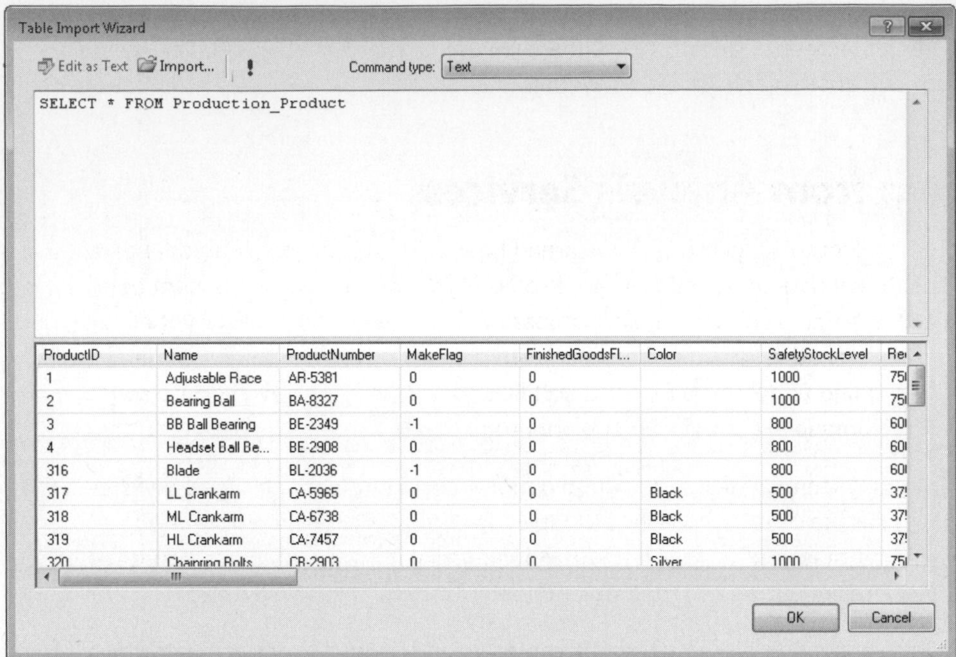


**FIGURE 5-15** The Access query designer in PowerPivot has few features.

Because the query designer of Access is so limited, if you need to load data from Access and need help with SQL, it might be useful to write the query using the Access query designer, directly in the Access application, as shown in Figure 5-16. Then after the query has been built in Access, you can load the data from the query.

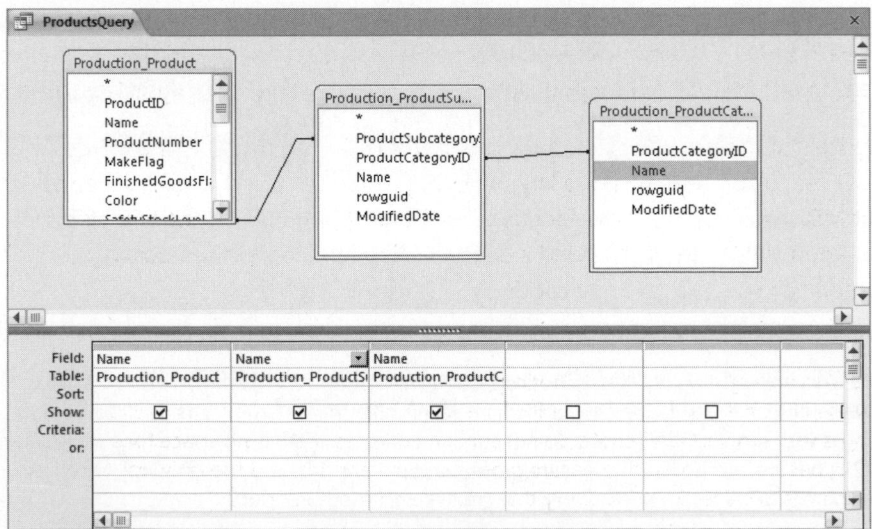


**FIGURE 5-16** The Access query designer can be used to design Access queries.

Remember that after data is loaded in PowerPivot, there are no differences between SQL Server, Access, or any other database we use to import data; all PowerPivot tables can relate to one another and be used together.

## Loading from Analysis Services

In the preceding sections, you learned how to load data from relational databases. Different relational data sources might have some slight difference among them but the overall logic of importing from a relational database remains the same. PowerPivot allows you to load data from other data sources, which are completely different kinds of databases. So we are now going to describe the Microsoft SQL Server Analysis Services data source, which has some unique features, as we are about to discover.

It might seem strange to have the option to load data from Analysis Services, whose main scope is the construction of pivot tables, into PowerPivot, whose scope is to build pivot tables! You might wonder why you ever need to load data from an Analysis Services database when you already can create pivot tables directly from the original source.

Once again, the reason is data integration. Even if you can easily create pivot tables on an Analysis Services OLAP cube, it is not easy at all to integrate different information in the same pivot table. With PowerPivot, you can load data coming from the Analysis Services database, integrate this information with other tables coming from other databases (including your personal Excel workbooks), and then use PowerPivot to create new and interesting pivot tables, as you will do in later chapters.

To connect to Analysis Services, you need to select the From Analysis Services Or PowerPivot option of the From Database button in the PowerPivot window. The Table Import Wizard opens again (see Figure 5-17), and you need to provide the server name and the database to which you want to connect. This time, you also need to point to a valid Analysis Services database.

Clicking Next in this first window brings you to the MDX query editor. The MDX editor is similar to the SQL editor, but this time the language that you need to use to query the database is not SQL but MDX, which is the query language for OLAP cubes. As with the SQL editor, you do not need to know the language to build a query: PowerPivot contains an advanced MDX query designer, which you can open by clicking the Design button.

**Note** As you might have already noticed, you cannot import tables from an Analysis Services database; the only way to load data from an Analysis Services database is to write a query. The reason is very simple: OLAP cubes do not contain tables, so there is no space for a table selection. OLAP cubes are composed of measure groups and dimensions, and the only way to retrieve data from there is to create an MDX query that creates a dataset to import.

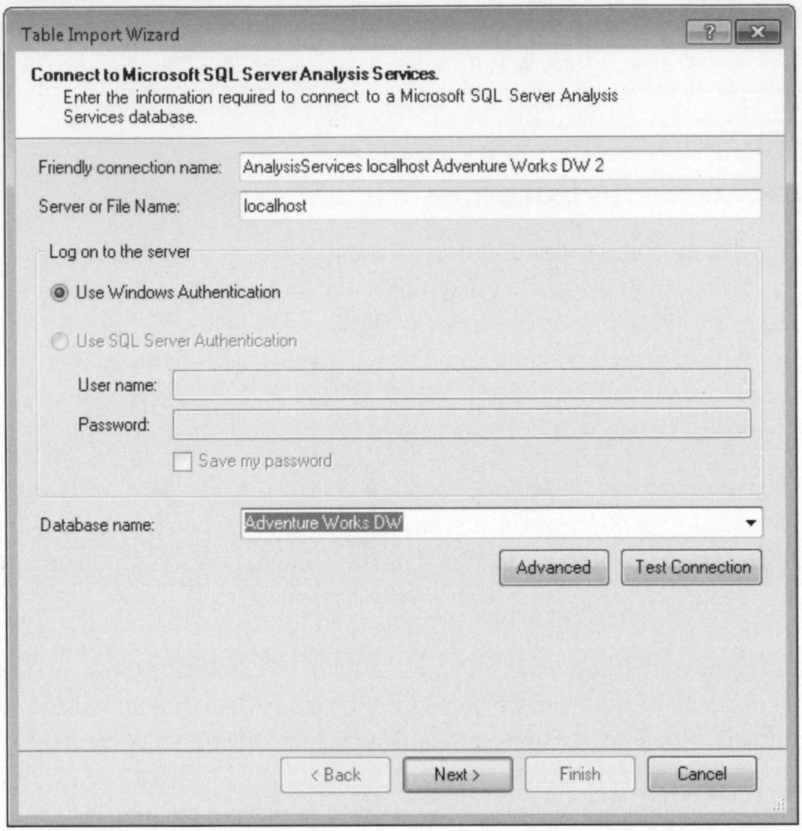

FIGURE 5-17 Connection to an Analysis Services database.

## Using the MDX Editor

Now we describe the MDX editor. Designing an MDX query is much easier than designing a SQL query. The reason emerges partly from their purposes: whereas SQL is a query language intended to be used by IT people, MDX has been created to be easily integrated into rich clients, like PowerPivot. Moreover, as strange as it might seem, MDX editors are powerful and convenient to use because MDX is much more difficult to write than SQL; as a consequence, much more effort went into writing an MDX editor than into writing a SQL editor.

In Figure 5-18, you can see a sample query that provides the sales amount divided by region, category, subcategory, and other dimensions. We are now going to use this example to show some of the most interesting features of the MDX editor. You can find this example in the companion workbook CH05-01-MDX_Loading.xlsx.

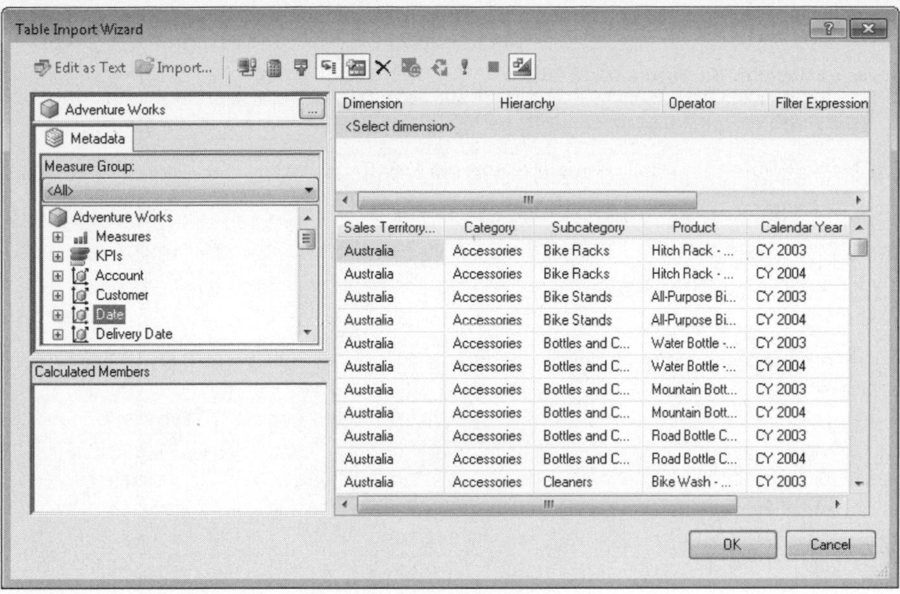


**FIGURE 5-18** The MDX editor in the Table Import Wizard.

The first interesting feature is the measure group selector. The measure group selector allows you to select a measure group from which you want to load data. It is very useful because, if the cube contains several dimensions, not all of which are linked to all measure groups, selecting a specific measure group hides all the dimensions that are not linked to that measure group. If, for example, you select the Sales Target measure group, (see Figure 5-19), all the dimensions that are not related to the sales targets are hidden, to make it easier to build the query by reducing the number of dimensions.

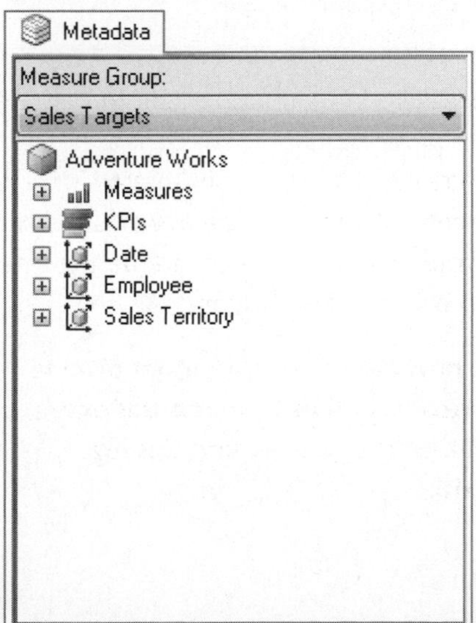


**FIGURE 5-19** The measure group selection automatically filters unrelated dimensions.

Using the MDX editor is pretty simple and looks much like using the PivotTable. To build the query, it is enough to drag measures, dimension attributes, or complete hierarchies from the selector in the query area. The wizard immediately refreshes the query, showing you a preview of the data set you are about to query.

The editor is very similar to an Excel PivotTable. The only noticeable difference is that you cannot put data items in columns; you can retrieve items only in rows. You can better understand it if you compare Figure 5-18 with Figure 5-20, in which you can see the same query using Excel. We put the calendar year, as you are probably used to seeing it, in columns.

| Sum of MeasuresInternet Sales Amount | Column Labels | | |
|---|---|---|---|
| Row Labels | CY 2003 | CY 2004 | Grand Total |
| **⊟Accessories** | **293,709.71** | **407,050.25** | **700,759.96** |
| Bike Racks | 16,440.00 | 22,920.00 | 39,360.00 |
| Bike Stands | 18,921.00 | 20,670.00 | 39,591.00 |
| Bottles and Cages | 23,280.27 | 33,517.92 | 56,798.19 |
| Cleaners | 3,044.85 | 4,173.75 | 7,218.60 |
| Fenders | 19,408.34 | 27,211.24 | 46,619.58 |
| Helmets | 92,583.54 | 132,752.06 | 225,335.60 |
| Hydration Packs | 16,771.95 | 23,535.72 | 40,307.67 |
| Tires and Tubes | 103,259.76 | 142,269.56 | 245,529.32 |

**FIGURE 5-20** We are accustomed to using columns for dates or other dimensions in Excel reporting.

If you put the calendar year in PivotTable rows instead of columns, (see Figure 5-21), you get a result identical to that produced by the query editor.

| Row Labels | Sum of MeasuresInternet Sales Amount |
|---|---|
| **⊟Accessories** | **700,759.96** |
| **⊟Bike Racks** | **39,360.00** |
| ⊟Hitch Rack - 4-Bike | 39,360.00 |
| CY 2003 | 16,440.00 |
| CY 2004 | 22,920.00 |
| **⊟Bike Stands** | **39,591.00** |
| ⊟All-Purpose Bike Stand | 39,591.00 |
| CY 2003 | 18,921.00 |
| CY 2004 | 20,670.00 |

**FIGURE 5-21** If you put dimensions only in rows, you get the same result from the wizard and from Excel.

You can see that, from the point of view of the data, there is no difference at all between the two representations; it is just a matter of pivoting information.

**Note** The MDX editor uses the latter method of querying data because it needs to define the number of columns in the destination table. If you put, for example, the date on columns, the number of columns of the resulting table might vary, depending on when you execute the query (as the number of years increases, so does the number of columns). When you impose the restriction of putting dimensions on rows only, the MDX editor grants that the number of columns is invariant and can be used to determine the structure of the PowerPivot destination table, which needs a fixed number of columns.

After you have designed the query and clicked OK, the user interface returns to the query editor, showing the complex MDX code that executes the query against the server. We do not think it is at all interesting or necessary for you to understand the complexities of MDX; you can safely trust that the strange code shown in Figure 5-22 will indeed return the correct values.

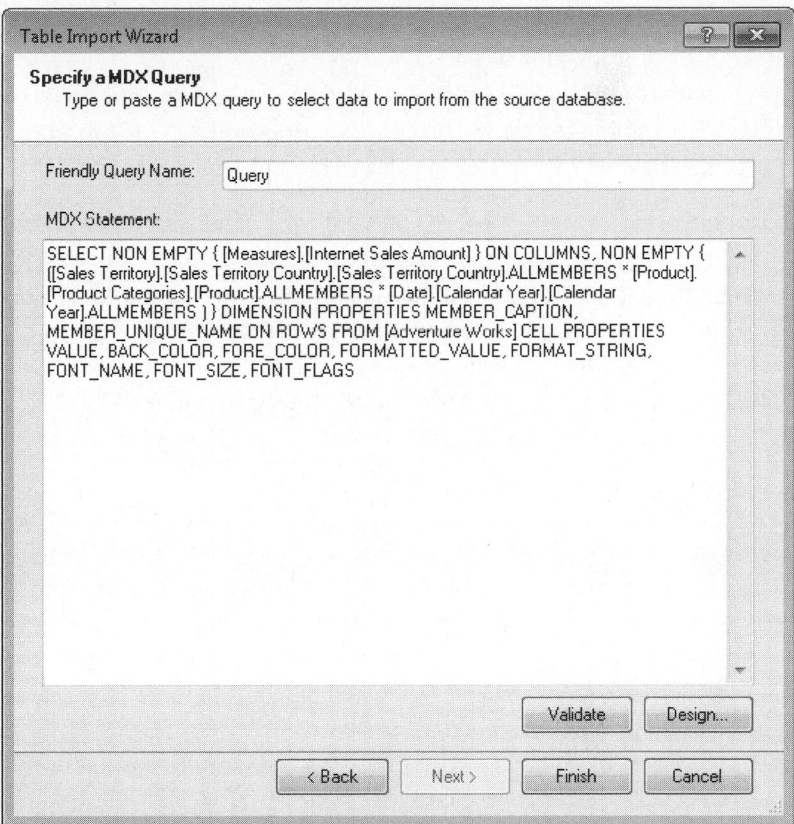


**FIGURE 5-22** The MDX code generated by the editor.

If you now click Finish, PowerPivot begins loading the data. Nevertheless, if you look at the imported table, you discover that some work is yet to be done. Let us look at Figure 5-23, where you can see the imported table.

| Sales TerritorySales Territory CountrySales Territory Country | ProductProduct CategoriesCategory | ProductProduct CategoriesSubcategory |
|---|---|---|
| Australia | Bikes | Road Bikes |
| Australia | Bikes | Road Bikes |
| Australia | Bikes | Road Bikes |
| Australia | Bikes | Road Bikes |
| Australia | Bikes | Road Bikes |

**FIGURE 5-23** The table created from an MDX query has some pretty long column names.

You can see that the names chosen by PowerPivot for the columns are far from being user friendly. PowerPivot uses a pattern to assign column names that includes the name of the dimension, the hierarchy, and finally the attribute, all concatenated. This leads to some very funny names, such as SalesTerritorySalesTerritoryCountrySalesTerritoryCountry, something that you will surely rename Country in the PowerPivot window.

There is no way to define friendly names in the MDX editor, so you just need to remember to create some order after loading the table. Furthermore, if you refresh the table later, the columns retain the correct new names, so this work needs to be done only once.

The last step you need to take to have a clean table is to review the data types of the imported columns. The Analysis Services data source loads all the data as strings, which might not be the correct representation. To correct the data types, you just need to use the Data Type box in the PowerPivot window, and in case of any error, correct it by setting the right type for each column. This is particularly important for all the numeric measures, which are not aggregated unless you change their type to the correct numeric type in PowerPivot.

## Handling of Keys in the OLAP Cube

You have seen that by using the MDX editor, you can easily load data from Analysis Services. Nevertheless, when loading data from an OLAP cube, you need to face a subtle problem, which we are going to describe now. OLAP cube programmers often design the cube structure so that it is easy for people to query. So the programmers tend to expose textual attributes that are easy to understand from a human point of view and hide all the more technical attributes, which are not useful when you are pivoting data. In other words, they follow the same process of hiding technical columns that you learned in Chapter 2. This data model is well suited for pivoting data but it is seldom the best one for further processing, as you want to do in PowerPivot.

An example will surely help to clarify this concept. If, for example, you want to load the average unit price per year for each product, you can easily create a query that returns a table like the one shown in Figure 5-24.

| Product Key | Year | Average Unit Price |
|---|---|---|
| BB-7421 | CY 2003 | $32.394 |
| BB-9108 | CY 2003 | $72.894 |
| BC-M005 | CY 2003 | $9.99 |
| BC-R205 | CY 2003 | $8.99 |
| BK-M18B-40 | CY 2003 | $392.0475 |
| BK-M18B-42 | CY 2003 | $363.926 |
| BK-M18B-44 | CY 2003 | $374.4604 |

**FIGURE 5-24** Average unit price per product and year.

You probably created this table to integrate its information with other tables in the same PowerPivot workbook. Nevertheless, to relate this table with other ones—for example, by product—you need a product key. Now the OLAP cube lets you easily load the product name because this is what people want to see to identify a product. On the other hand, in the PowerPivot tables, tables tend to use the ProductID as the product key. The ProductID is not useful in reporting, so cube designers do not normally show this instance of data, even if they store it in the database for technical reasons.

**Note** You can include the ProductID in the MDX query, but this requires the ability to manually change the MDX query code created by the query designer, and after that query has been modified, the designer cannot be used anymore to change that query. You might ask your IT department to help you create these MDX queries, if necessary.

All this means that, if you want to create relationships with this table, you need to use the product name and not the product ID because the product ID is not available. Sometimes you will find it hard to detect a valid key to create relationships; it all depends on the availability of good candidates for the key column in OLAP cubes.

### Investigate the Presence of a Data Mart

If you can load data from an OLAP cube, it is highly likely that the OLAP cube is fed from a SQL data mart. Normally, the data mart contains a lot more information than that made available through the cube, and table identifiers are among the items. Data marts store identifiers as the internal key even if they are hidden in the final OLAP structure.

If you face such a situation, it is surely worth investigating whether you can load data directly from the data mart so that you can have access to all the technical information and make relationships using identifiers.

## Using Linked Tables

Now we continue our discovery of the most interesting ways to load data into PowerPivot. The next topic deals with linked tables. Linked tables are probably the easiest way to load data into PowerPivot, even if they do not belong to the family of data sources. If you need a table that is not already loaded in any of your databases, you can simply create an Excel worksheet, load data into it, and then link the worksheet to a PowerPivot table.

Because the creation of a linked table is so easy, we want to show you not only how to create a linked table, but also, by means of a full example, how you can use linked tables to immediately update PowerPivot values and produce interactive reports.

Let us suppose that at the start of 2005, you performed an analysis of the sales increase month by month, computing values based on your personal experience, external market analysis, and various meetings with your sales departments. You ended up with an Excel worksheet that contains, for each month, a percentage that indicates how you thought sales would vary during the year 2005 (see Figure 5-25). You can find this example in the companion workbook CH05-02-LinkTables.xlsx.

**Sales in 2005**

| Month | Increase |
|---|---|
| January | 5% |
| February | 5% |
| March | 6% |
| April | 7% |
| May | 7% |
| June | 5% |
| July | 4% |
| August | -2% |
| September | -3% |
| October | 0% |
| November | 2% |
| December | 5% |

**FIGURE 5-25** Increase in sales in 2005, in an Excel worksheet.

Now you would like to use this information to create a PivotTable that applies these corrective factors to the sales in 2004, to make some kind of projection of the sales in 2005. The first step is to load sales from 2004 into PowerPivot, to have a starting set of figures. You can query the OLAP cube to get the sales amount in 2004, producing, for example, a table that contains the value for each month, category, and subcategory. The resulting table is shown in Figure 5-26.

| Month | Category | Subcategory | SalesAmount |
|---|---|---|---|
| January | Accessories | Bike Racks | 2,160.00 |
| January | Accessories | Bike Stands | 2,544.00 |
| January | Accessories | Bottles and Cages | 4,797.28 |
| January | Accessories | Cleaners | 715.50 |
| January | Accessories | Fenders | 4,352.04 |
| January | Accessories | Helmets | 17,704.94 |
| January | Accessories | Hydration Packs | 3,244.41 |
| January | Accessories | Tires and Tubes | 20,938.76 |
| January | Bikes | Mountain Bikes | 516,610.67 |

**FIGURE 5-26** Sales in 2004, divided by month, category, and subcategory.

To use the predictive values in PowerPivot, you need to load the worksheet in Figure 5-20 into PowerPivot and then make some computations to get the prediction to work. To load the table in PowerPivot, it is enough to put the cursor in it and click the Create Linked Table button on the PowerPivot ribbon. This immediately loads the table into the PowerPivot database and gives it the same name as the table in Excel, which by default could be Table1. You can see the loaded table in Figure 5-27.

| Month | Increase |
|---|---|
| January | 0.05 |
| February | 0.05 |
| March | 0.06 |
| April | 0.07 |
| May | 0.07 |
| June | 0.05 |
| July | 0.04 |
| August | -0.02 |
| September | -0.03 |
| October | 0 |
| November | 0.02 |
| December | 0.05 |

**FIGURE 5-27** The predictive table loaded into PowerPivot.

If you did not define a name for these tables in Excel, you rename them Sales and Prediction in PowerPivot, to give them meaningful names. However, we suggest that you name these tables correctly in Excel, too, so that you have the same names for these tables in both Excel and PowerPivot.

**Note** You can rename a table in Excel from the Design tab on the Table Tools contextual tab of the ribbon, to arrive at the Table Name text box that is displayed in the Properties group.

At this point, the missing link is a relationship between the Sales and the Prediction tables so that you can use the predictive factor in the Sales table. You can do that in PowerPivot by clicking the Create Relationship button and configuring it as it is shown in Figure 5-28.

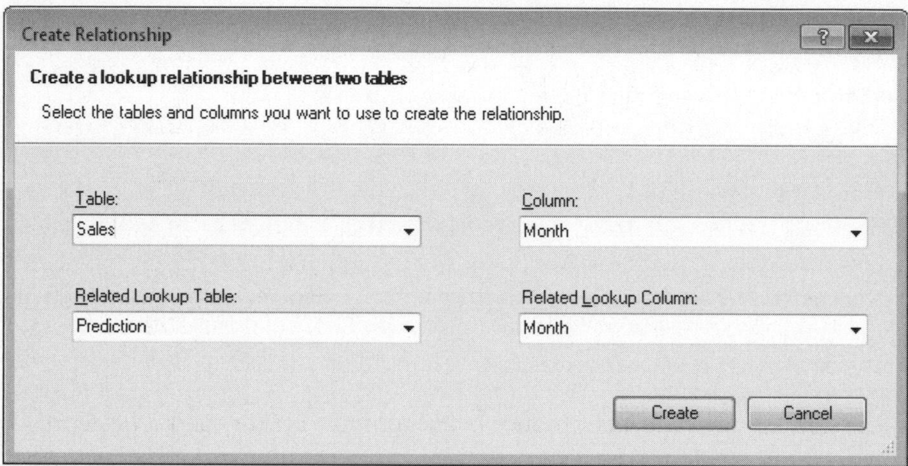


**FIGURE 5-28** The relationship between the Sales and Prediction tables.

Now you can use PowerPivot relationships to define two new columns in the Sales table; you can call them PredictiveFactor and PredictedSales. The formulas, shown in Table 5-1, are pretty easy.

**TABLE 5-1 Formulas to predict sales in 2005 based on 2004 data.**

| Column | Formula |
|---|---|
| PredictiveFactor | =RELATED(Prediction[Increase]) |
| PredictedSales | =Sales[SalesAmount]*(1+Sales[PredictiveFactor]) |

The PredictiveFactor column computes the increase in sales of the month, by using the RELATED function. The PredictedSales column uses the predictive factor to compute the value of sales, correcting in this way the sales in 2004 with the predictive factor.

It is now very easy to create a PivotTable based on the PowerPivot data model, add it to a worksheet, and produce the report shown in Figure 5-29.

**Sales in 2005**

| Month | Increase |
|---|---|
| January | 5% |
| February | 5% |
| March | 6% |
| April | 7% |
| May | 7% |
| June | 5% |
| July | 4% |
| August | -2% |
| September | -3% |
| October | 0% |
| November | 2% |
| December | 5% |

**Sales prediction divided by Category / Subcategory**

| Sum of PredictedSales | Column Labels | | | |
|---|---|---|---|---|
| Row Labels | April | February | January | Grand Total |
| **Accessories** | **67,060.73** | **59,845.70** | **59,279.78** | **186,186.20** |
| Bike Racks | 2,696.40 | 3,024.00 | 2,268.00 | 7,988.40 |
| Bike Stands | 4,933.77 | 3,172.05 | 2,671.20 | 10,777.02 |
| Bottles and Cages | 5,731.42 | 5,324.43 | 5,037.14 | 16,093.00 |
| Cleaners | 586.95 | 651.11 | 751.28 | 1,989.33 |
| Fenders | 4,139.27 | 3,508.01 | 4,569.64 | 12,216.92 |
| Helmets | 22,613.34 | 19,031.06 | 18,590.19 | 60,234.59 |
| Hydration Packs | 2,765.45 | 3,810.81 | 3,406.63 | 9,982.88 |
| Tires and Tubes | 23,594.13 | 21,324.23 | 21,985.70 | 66,904.06 |
| **Bikes** | **1,620,032.14** | **1,446,290.09** | **1,317,296.68** | **4,383,618.91** |
| Mountain Bikes | 625,888.71 | 596,037.70 | 542,441.20 | 1,764,367.61 |
| Road Bikes | 538,873.56 | 458,875.88 | 420,248.61 | 1,417,998.05 |
| Touring Bikes | 455,269.87 | 391,376.51 | 354,606.87 | 1,201,253.25 |
| **Clothing** | **34,270.20** | **29,468.04** | **30,680.74** | **94,418.97** |
| Caps | 1,827.67 | 1,935.10 | 1,680.23 | 5,443.00 |
| Gloves | 3,458.97 | 3,188.60 | 3,008.60 | 9,656.16 |
| Jerseys | 17,086.74 | 14,665.68 | 16,294.96 | 48,047.38 |
| Shorts | 7,339.15 | 5,805.67 | 5,805.67 | 18,950.49 |
| Socks | 480.97 | 405.90 | 490.85 | 1,377.72 |
| Vests | 4,076.70 | 3,467.10 | 3,400.43 | 10,944.23 |
| **Grand Total** | **1,721,363.07** | **1,535,603.82** | **1,407,257.20** | **4,664,224.09** |

**FIGURE 5-29** The integrated report for predicted sales in 2005.

You can now use this report to produce predictions for category and subcategory. Moreover, as you might already imagine, if you want to add more attributes for the product, you have merely to change the source query of the Sales table.

**Caution** The careful reader will notice that the months are not sorted correctly: April comes before February and January is at the end. This is an issue with PowerPivot, which sorts attributes only alphabetically and has no knowledge about a month's need to be sorted by month numbers. You will learn how to address this issue later on in the chapter about the date dimension.

The interesting point here is that you have been able to integrate the original OLAP cube with external information and create new PivotTables on the integrated data model. Although this is a simple example, it shows the power of data integration that PowerPivot provides.

The unique characteristic of linked tables is that they are refreshed immediately and do not need you to reload data. If, for example, you need to change some values in the prediction table, to perform some kind of what-if analysis or compute different scenarios, you need merely to change the values in the Excel worksheet and refresh the PowerPivot data model and the PivotTable to get the new values immediately computed. This leads to your being able to create interactive reports, which use the PowerPivot engine to perform complex computations immediately.

## Loading from Excel Files

You have learned that if a table is stored in an Excel file, it can be used to create PowerPivot linked tables. Nevertheless, linked tables have one big limitation: you can create a linked table only if the table resides in the same Excel file as the PowerPivot data model. You might have another Excel file containing some data—for example, a list of the special offers we plan to give in 2005, such as the one shown in Figure 5-30 that you want to load into PowerPivot. In this case, you cannot create a linked table, thus you will need to use the Excel data source and treat the Excel workbook as if it was a database. This is exactly what we are going to show now.

| Special Offer | Start | End | Category | Discount |
|---|---|---|---|---|
| Christmas Gifts | 12/1/2005 | 12/31/2005 | Accessory | 25% |
| Christmas Gifts | 12/1/2005 | 12/31/2005 | Bykes | 12% |
| Christmas Gifts | 12/1/2005 | 12/31/2005 | Clothing | 24% |
| Summer Specials | 8/1/2005 | 8/15/2005 | Clothing | 10% |
| Summer Specials | 8/1/2005 | 8/15/2005 | Accesory | 10% |

**FIGURE 5-30** Special offers planned for the year 2005, in an external Excel file.

In this example, the Excel range containing data has been formatted as a table to make it easier to refer to in other worksheets because we can use the table name instead of the cell range. Let us suppose that you have saved this table in the CH05-03-2005Plans.xlsx file, which contains several tables with your thoughts about the 2005 budget, and now you want to import the data into PowerPivot. By the way, this Excel file is part of the book's companion material, so you can use the companion workbook to follow this example.

To begin the loading process, you need to select the From Other Sources button in the PowerPivot window, after which you open the Table Import Wizard and then select Excel File, which is near the end of the list, under the Text Files section. When you click Next, PowerPivot opens the Table Import Wizard for Excel files (see Figure 5-31).

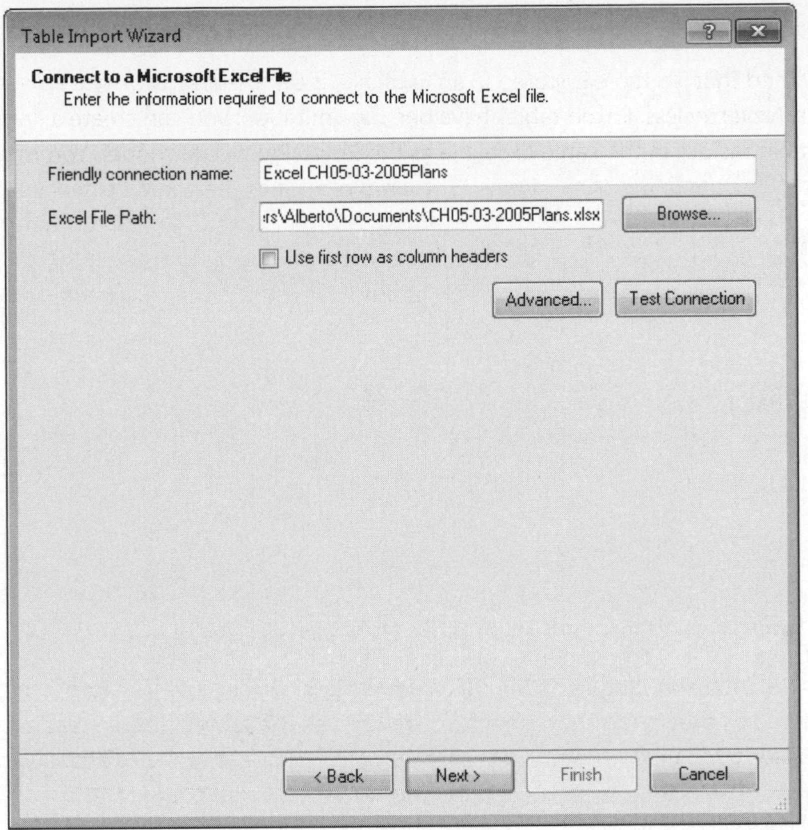


**FIGURE 5-31** The Table Import Wizard for Excel files.

You need to provide the file path of the file containing the data to select an Excel file. An important check box is the Use First Row As Column Headers. If your table contains column names in the first row (as is the case in the example), you need to select this check box so that PowerPivot automatically detects the column names of the table you are about to load. If you now click on Next, the wizard opens the Excel file, searches for worksheets in it, and allows you to choose which one to load, as you see in Figure 5-32.

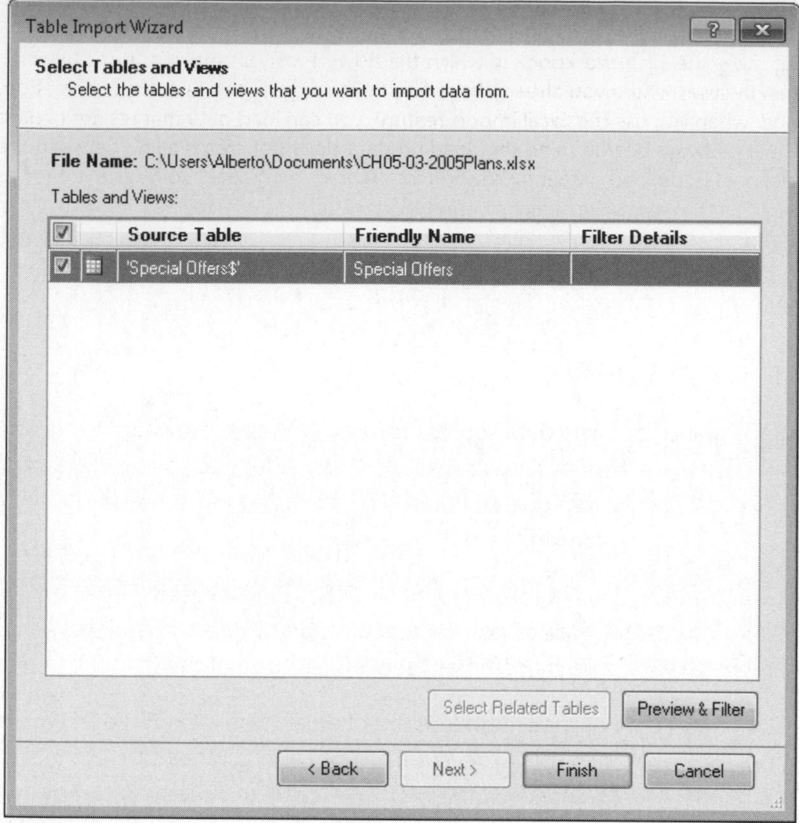


**FIGURE 5-32** Selection of worksheets to load from an Excel file.

**Important** Only worksheets are imported from an external Excel workbook. If there are tables defined in an Excel file, they are not considered. For this reason, it is better to have just one table for each worksheet and no other data in the same worksheet. This version of PowerPivot cannot detect single tables in an external workbook.

After you select the table to import, the wizard loads data into PowerPivot and makes it available for you to perform any kind of computation. Obviously, you can use the Preview & Filter button to have a look at the data before the data loads, and you can apply filtering, if you like, as you have already learned to do with relational tables.

**Note** Let us review the difference between a linked table and an Excel import. Linked tables need to be in the same Excel workbook in which the PowerPivot database is stored, which might be a limitation in cases where you already have files containing all the relevant information. On the other hand, when you use the Excel import feature, you can load data that resides in different Excel worksheets. Always bear in mind that loading data does not create a link between the two files: the process of importing data into PowerPivot creates a copy of it, so data is not refreshed when you update the original Excel file. If you want to refresh data, you need to do it manually, by using the Refresh button in PowerPivot.

## Loading from Text Files

As you can see, the list of possible data sources for PowerPivot is growing very quickly. The PowerPivot team has spent a lot of time to make it possible for you to load data from many different sources because the main goal of PowerPivot is integration. It is now time to analyze another possible source of data: text files.

Data can be stored in text files in a format know as Comma Separated Values (CSV). This widespread format represents data as normal text lines, each one containing a row. Each row contains columns, separated by commas (hence the name of the format).

If you have a CSV file containing some data (see the companion file CH05-04-2005_Plans.txt), you can import it into PowerPivot using the text file data source. Let us suppose that our CSV file contains the special offers planned for the year 2005, (the same data that we used to show the Excel data source). It looks like this:

```
Special Offer,Start,End,Category,Discount
Christmas Gifts,12/1/2005,12/31/2005,Accessory,25%
Christmas Gifts,12/1/2005,12/31/2005,Bykes,12%
Christmas Gifts,12/1/2005,12/31/2005,Clothing,24%
Summer Specials,8/1/2005,8/15/2005,Clothing,10%
Summer Specials,8/1/2005,8/15/2005,Accesory,10%
```

You can see that each line contains a row, and each row contains columns, each separated by a comma from the next. Usually CSV files contain the column header in the first row of the file so that the file contains both the data and the column names. This is the same standard we normally use with Excel tables.

To load this file into PowerPivot, you need to use the From Text button in the PowerPivot window. This action opens the Table Import Wizard for text files (see Figure 5-33), for which you need to provide several parameters.

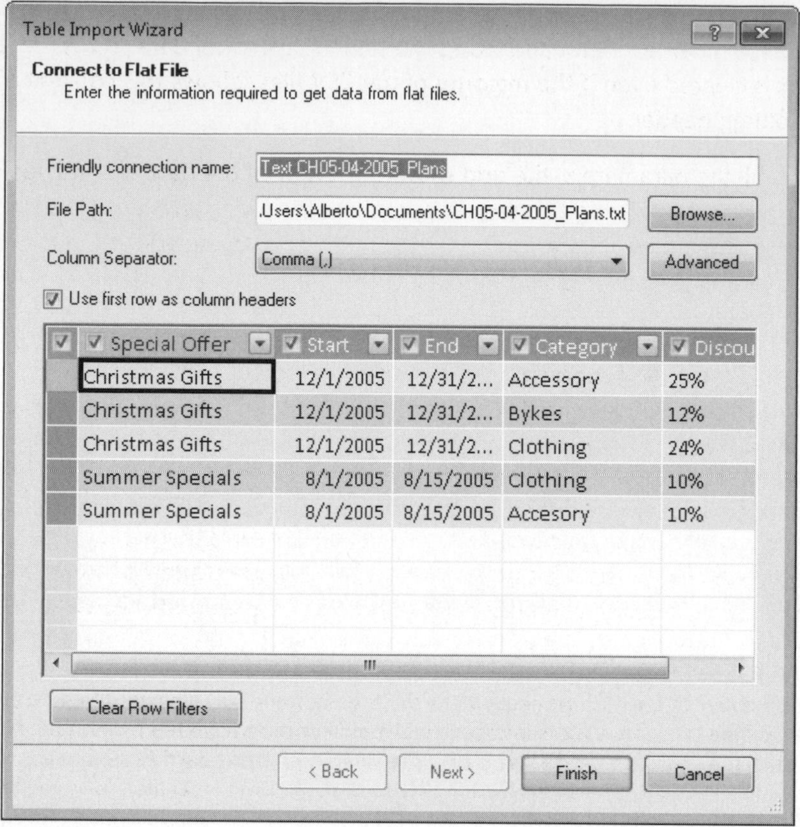


**FIGURE 5-33** Selection of tables to load from an Excel file.

You can choose the column separator, which by default is a comma, from a list that includes colon, semicolon, tab, and several other separators. The right choice depends on the format of the file.

## Handling More Complex CSV Files

You might encounter a CSV file that contains fancy separators, and you might find that the Table Import Wizard cannot correctly load it because you cannot choose just any characters for the separators and file properties. It might be helpful to use the schema.ini file, in which you can define advanced properties of the comma separated file. Please read *http://tinyurl.com/SchemaIniPPG* to learn this advanced technique for loading complex data files.

The Use First Row As Column Headers check box indicates whether the first row of the file contains the column names or not and works the same as the Excel data source. By default, this check box is cleared even if the majority of the CSV files follows this convention and contain the column header.

As soon as you fill the parameters, the grid shows a preview of the data as it will look in PowerPivot; you can use the grid to select or deselect any column and to set row filters, as you can with any other data source you have seen up to now. When you are done with the setup, clicking Finish starts the loading process.

After the loading is finished, you still need to check whether the column types have been correctly detected. CSV files do not contain, for instance, the type of each column, so PowerPivot tries to guess the types by analyzing the file content. Clearly, as with any guess, it might fail to detect the correct type.

In the example, PowerPivot detected the correct type of all the columns except the discount column. PowerPivot missed that one because the flat file contains the percentage symbol after the number, and so PowerPivot treats it as a character string and not a number. If you need to change the column type, you can always do that later using the PowerPivot ribbon.

**Note** If the content of the CSV file needs to be adjusted in some way (as might be true of the sample file we have been discussing, in which you would like to remove the percentage symbol from the Discount column), you can always load the file using the standard Excel functions in an Excel worksheet and then create a linked table. Having the data in an Excel file allows you to modify the data to suit your needs. Always remember that PowerPivot tables are not updatable, so if you need to make any kind of change, you can always use Excel tables as an intermediate step.

## Loading from the Clipboard

Let us move forward in our description of the many ways to load data into PowerPivot and analyze a way to load data without using any data source: the Clipboard. Using the Clipboard, we can load data into PowerPivot from any application, as long as we are able to copy data from that application to the Clipboard.

Let us suppose that you have a Microsoft Word table, like the one shown in Figure 5-34 (which you can also find in the companion Word document CH05-05-Word table.docx).

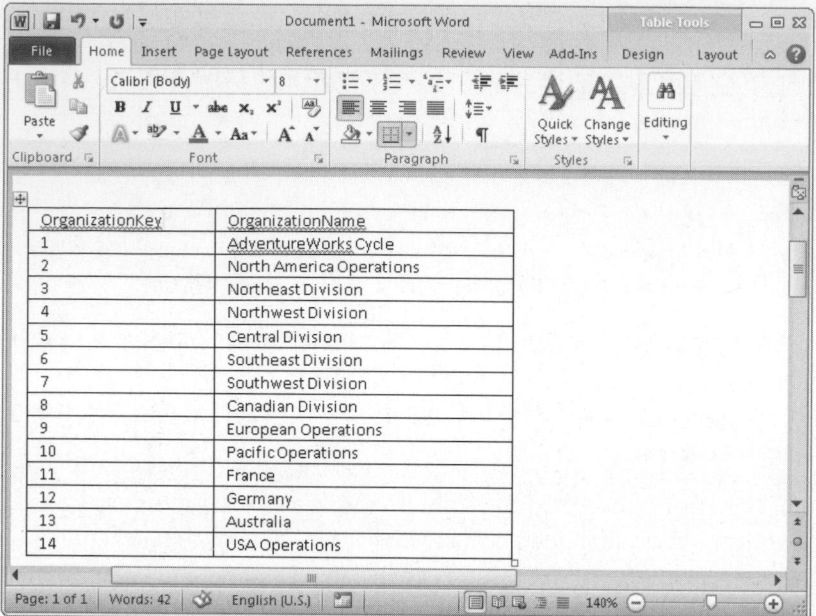


| OrganizationKey | OrganizationName |
|---|---|
| 1 | AdventureWorks Cycle |
| 2 | North America Operations |
| 3 | Northeast Division |
| 4 | Northwest Division |
| 5 | Central Division |
| 6 | Southeast Division |
| 7 | Southwest Division |
| 8 | Canadian Division |
| 9 | European Operations |
| 10 | Pacific Operations |
| 11 | France |
| 12 | Germany |
| 13 | Australia |
| 14 | USA Operations |

**FIGURE 5-34** A Word table containing some information.

Even if PowerPivot has no data source to load from Word documents, you can load this table into PowerPivot if you want to by selecting the full table, copying it to the Clipboard, and then using the Paste button in the PowerPivot window. PowerPivot opens the Paste Preview dialog box, shown in Figure 5-35.

Using this window, you can give the table a friendly name and preview the data before you import into PowerPivot. Clicking OK ends the loading process and places the table in the PowerPivot database.

Clearly the same process can be initiated by copying a selection from an Excel worksheet or any other software that is able to copy data in tabular format to the Clipboard.

It is worth noting that you can use the two buttons Paste Append and Paste Replace. With the first button, you append the content of the Clipboard to an already existing PowerPivot table. With the second, you can replace the contents of a table with that of the Clipboard.

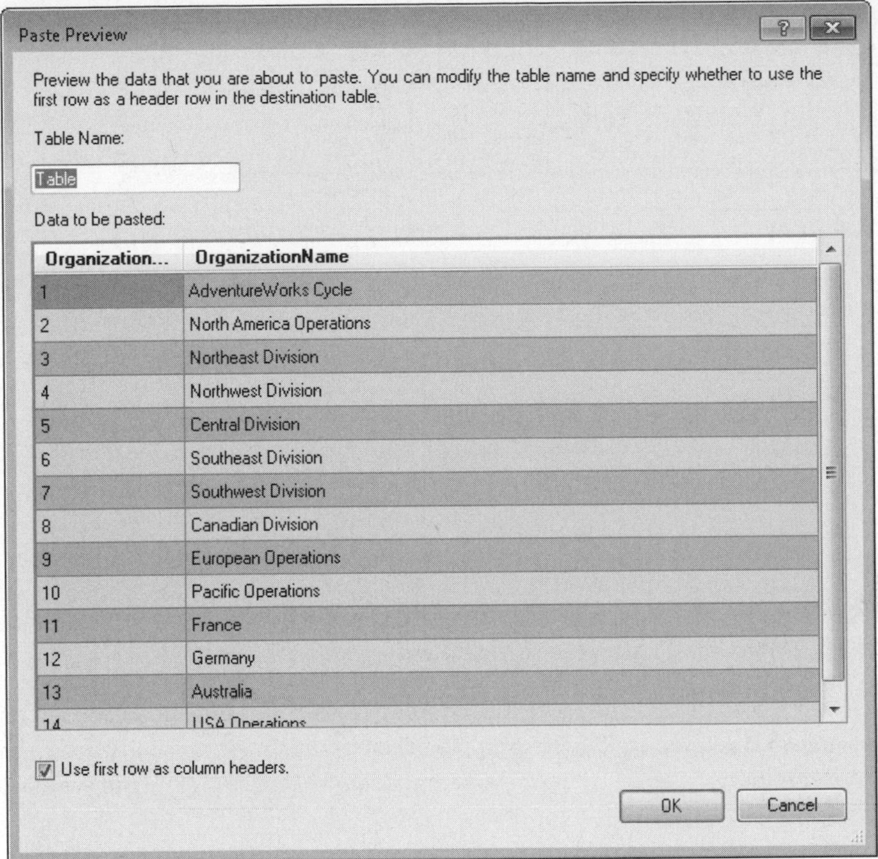


**FIGURE 5-35** The Paste Preview dialog box, before you paste data from the Clipboard.

# Loading from a Report

When you work for a company, you are likely to have many reports available to you. You might want to import part or all of the data of an existing report into your model, using it as a data source for your own report. Most of the time, you import such data by copying it manually or by using copy and paste techniques. However, these methods mean you always load the final output of the report and not the original data that has been used to make the calculations. Moreover, if you use the copy and paste technique, you often have to delete formatting values, such as separators, labels, and so on, from the real data. In this way, building a report that is able to automatically refresh data extracted from another report is hard if not impossible, and most of the time you end up repeating the import process of copying data from your sources.

If you have access to reports published by Microsoft SQL Server Reporting Services 2008 R2, PowerPivot is able to directly connect to the data used by the report. This way, you have access to a more detailed data model that can also be refreshed, and you are not worried by the presence of separators or other decorative items. You get only the data: in fact, you can use a report as a special case of Data Feed, a more general type of data source that we describe in the next section. Because this is a particular case of data feed, there is a dedicated user interface to select data coming from a report.

Look at the report shown in Figure 5-36: the URL points to a sample Reporting Services report. (The URL can be different depending on the installation of Reporting Services sample reports, which you can download from *http://msftrsprodsamples.codeplex.com/*.)

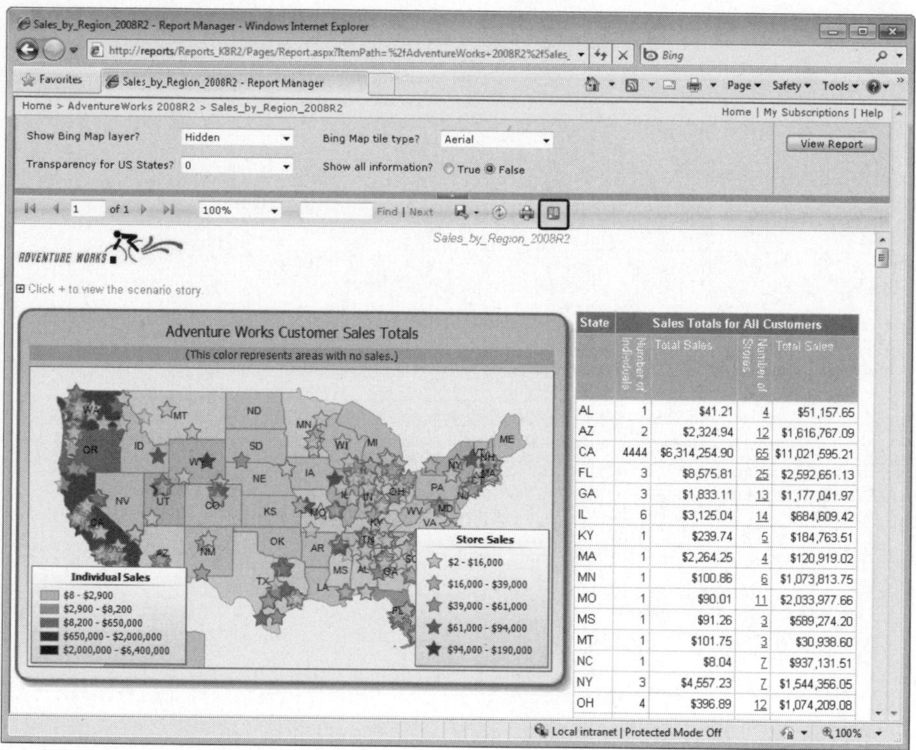


**FIGURE 5-36** Sales by Region report from Reporting Services 2008 R2.

This report shows the sales divided by region and by individual stores, using a chart and a table. Clicking the number-of-shops number of a state, the report scrolls down to the list of shops in the corresponding state. So you see another table, not visible in Figure 5-36, which appears when you scroll down the report. If you click the Export To Data Feed icon that is highlighted in Figure 5-36, your browser asks you to open or save a file with a name that has the .atomsvc extension, as you can see in Figure 5-37.

**Note** The .atomsvc file contains technical information about the source data feeds. Technically speaking, this file is a data service document in an XML format that specifies a connection to one or more data feeds.

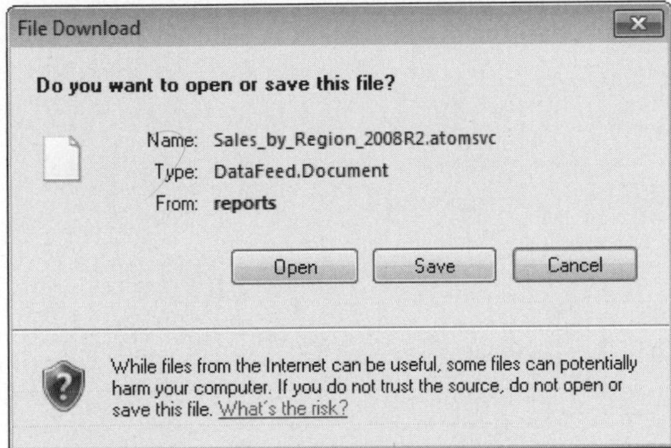


**FIGURE 5-37** The dialog box displayed when you click the Export To Data Feed button in a report.

If you choose to save this file, you can then open it from the PowerPivot window by using the Get External Data From Data Feeds feature that we discuss in the next section. However, if you choose to open this file, the same importing feature is activated automatically, and you see the Table Import Wizard, shown in Figure 5-39.

**Note** If you have one or more Excel files already open, clicking Open produces another dialog box (before showing the wizard you see in Figure 5-39) that asks you whether you want to add the data from the data feed to one of the open files or into a newly created Excel file, as you can see in Figure 5-38.

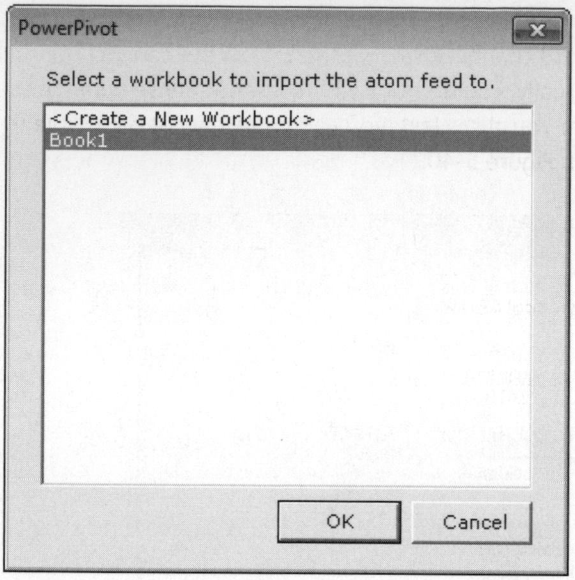

PowerPivot

Select a workbook to import the atom feed to.

<Create a New Workbook>

Book1

OK Cancel

**FIGURE 5-38** Selecting the workbook to which you import data.

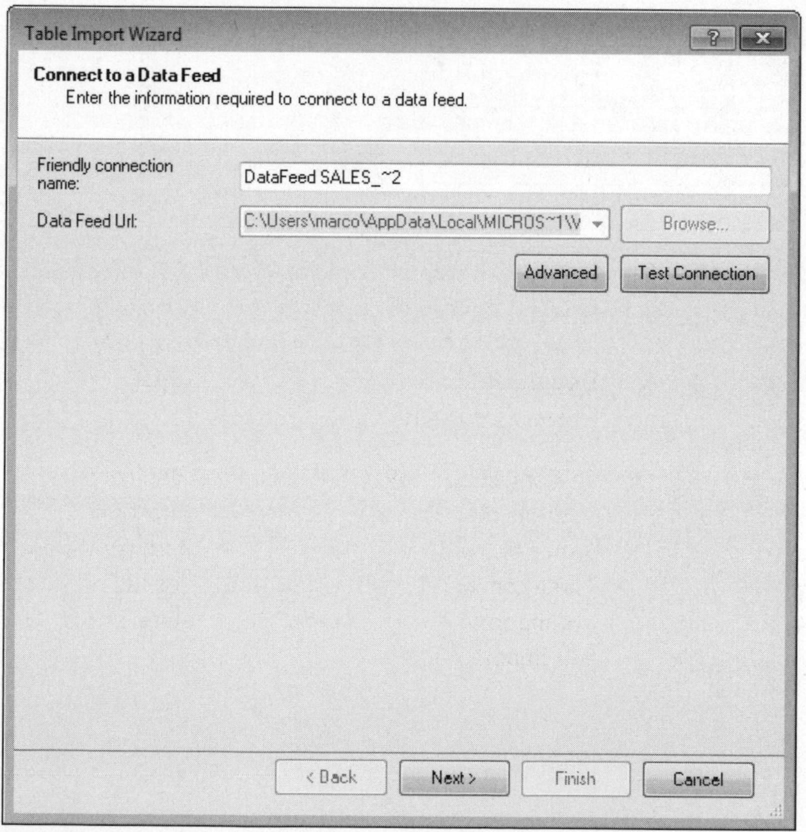


**FIGURE 5-39** Opening an .atomsvc file displays the Table Import Wizard.

You can just change the friendly connection name for this data feed and then click Next. The Advanced button allows you to change some parameters of the connection, such as user credentials and other settings. Usually, you do not need to change these parameters for data feeds coming from a report. After you click Next, you can choose what data table to import from the report, as you can see in Figure 5-40.

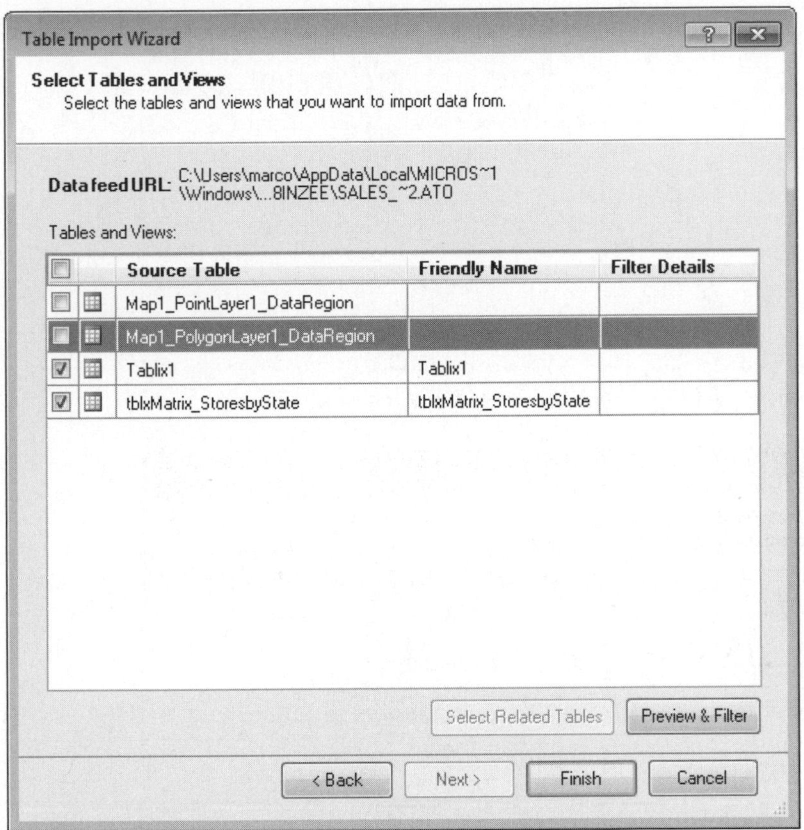


**FIGURE 5-40** Selecting tables to import from a data feed (a report in this case).

The report you saw in Figure 5-36 contains four data tables. The first two contain information about the graphical visualization of the map on the left side of the report. The other two are more interesting: Tablix1 is the source of the table on the right side, which contains sales divided by state, and tblMatrix_StoresbyState contains the sales of each store for each state. You can see in Figure 5-41 the number of rows imported in each of the selected tables, shown after you click Finish in the final stage of the Table Import Wizard.

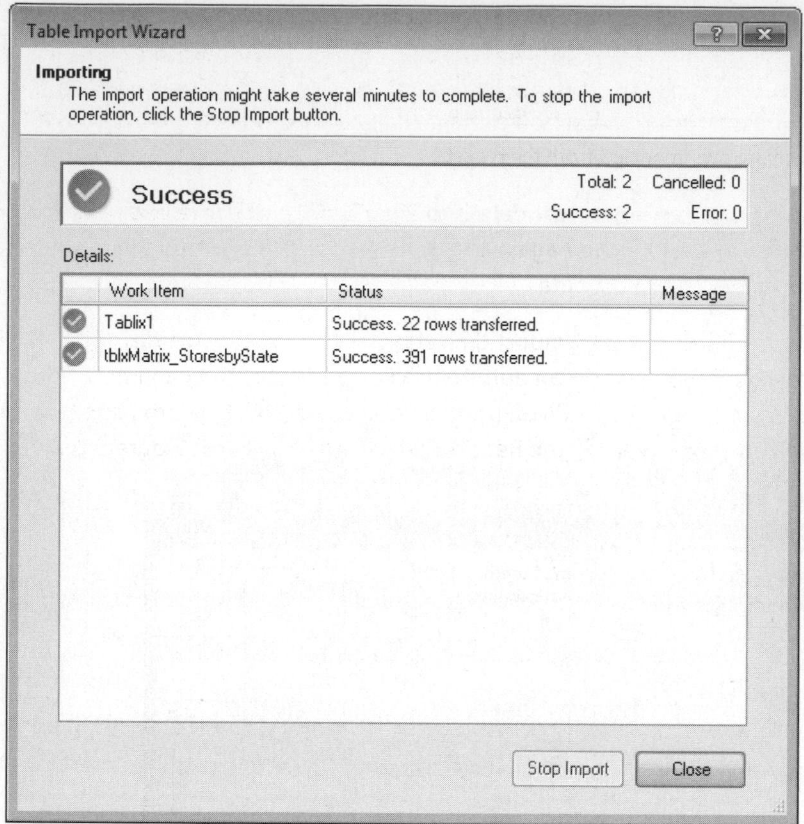


**FIGURE 5-41** End of import data from report.

Clearly, the first time you import data from a report, you might not know the content of each of the tables available: in this case, you can use the preview features available in the Table Import Wizard or simply try to import everything and then remove from PowerPivot all the tables and columns that do not contain useful data. You can see in Figure 5-42 the first few rows of the Tablix1 table.

**Note** You can see in Figure 5-42 that the last two columns do not have meaningful names. These names really depend on the discipline of the report author, and because usually they are just internal names not visible in a report, it is pretty common to have such undescriptive names. In such cases, you should rename these columns before you use these numbers in PowerPivot.

| Distance | ShowBingMaps | BingMapTileT... | USSt... | ShowAll | StateProvin... | CustomerID | TotalDue | Textbox8 | Textbox10 |
|---|---|---|---|---|---|---|---|---|---|
| 50 | Hidden | Aerial | 0 | FALSE | AL | 1 | 41.2055 | 4 | 51157.6464 |
| 50 | Hidden | Aerial | 0 | FALSE | AZ | 2 | 2324.9417 | 12 | 1616767.085 |
| 50 | Hidden | Aerial | 0 | FALSE | CA | 4444 | 6314254.9032 | 65 | 11021595.2057 |
| 50 | Hidden | Aerial | 0 | FALSE | FL | 3 | 8575.8053 | 25 | 2592651.1315 |
| 50 | Hidden | Aerial | 0 | FALSE | GA | 3 | 1833.1067 | 13 | 1177041.9682 |

**FIGURE 5-42** Sample rows imported from the report.

Now that you have imported report data into PivotTable, each time you refresh a table in PowerPivot the report is executed again and updated data is imported to the selected tables, overriding previously imported data.

Until now, you have seen how to import data starting from the report displayed in a browser, opening Excel and PowerPivot in an automatic way. However, you can import data from a report when you are using PowerPivot, using its Get External Data From Report feature. The Table Import Wizard asks you for the Report Path, as you can see in Figure 5-43.

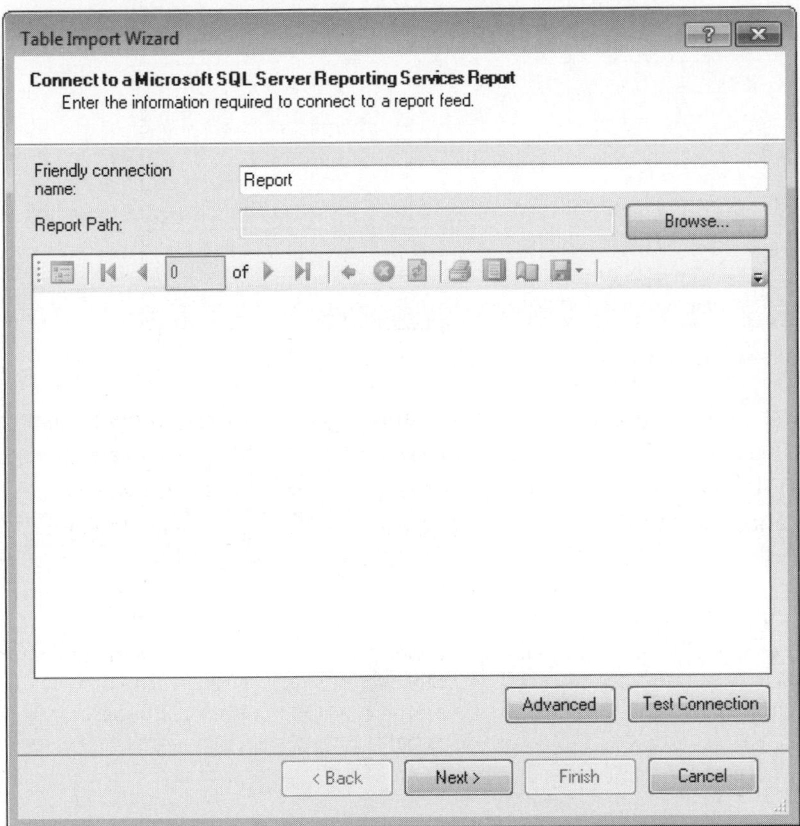


**FIGURE 5-43** Table Import Wizard importing data from a report.

When you click the Browse button, you can choose the report to use, as shown in Figure 5-44.

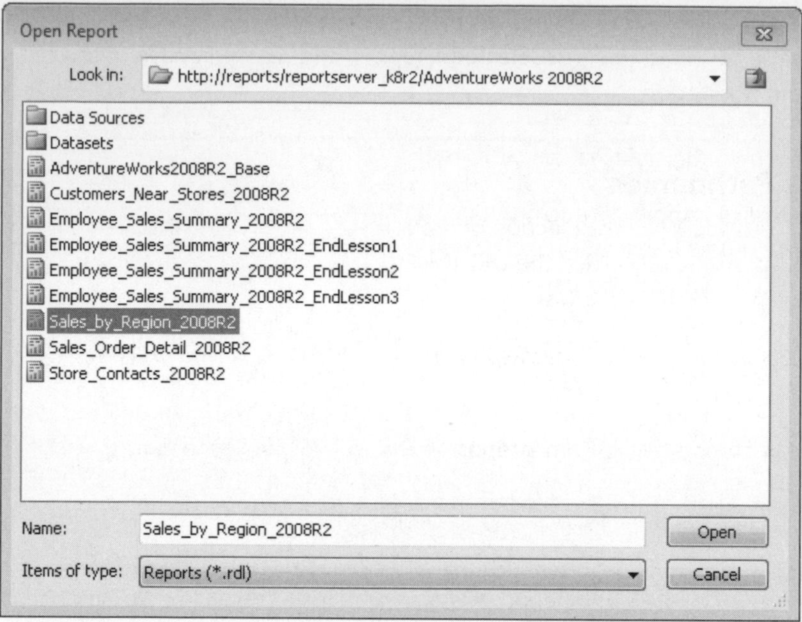


**FIGURE 5-44** Table Import Wizard shown to import data from a report.

When you click Open, the selected report appears in the Table Import Wizard, as you can see in Figure 5-45.

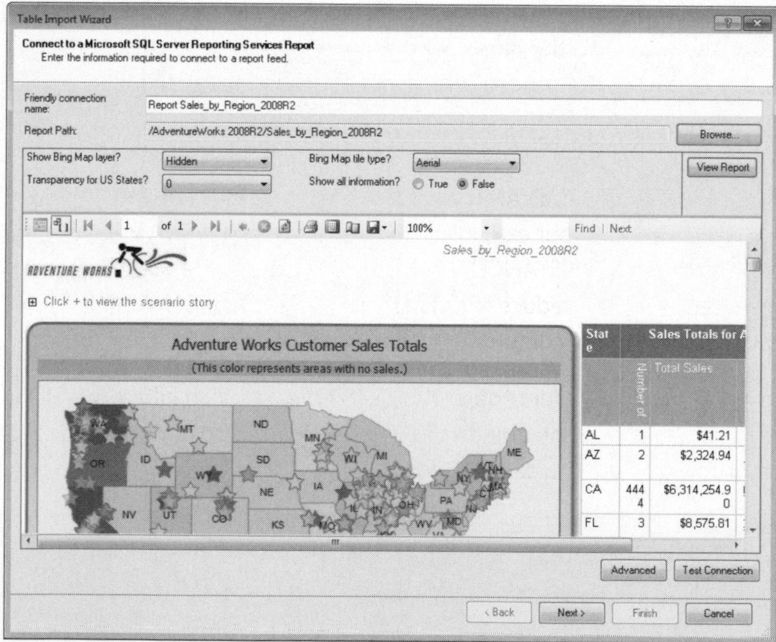


**FIGURE 5-45** Preview of a report from Reporting Services.

At this point, when you click Next you see exactly the same request as in Figure 5-40 because you are at the same point: you just selected a report, and now you have to select the tables to import from that report.

## Reports Pathnames

In Figure 5-44, you saw the selection of the same report previously used in Figure 5-36. However, you should note that the URL is a little bit different. In fact, the URL for the report shown in the browser was

*http://reports/Reports_K8R2/Pages/Report.aspx?ItemPath=%2fAdventureWorks+2008R2%2f Sales_by_Region_2008R2*

Now, the URL to load data from a report in PowerPivot is different:

*http://reports/reportserver_k8r2/AdventureWorks 2008R2*

The difference is that the URL used by PowerPivot is a direct pointer to the report, which bypasses the user interface of Report Manager that you used earlier. You should ask for the assistance of your IT department to get the right URL for your reports.

As a rule of thumb, if you can "navigate" in the reports available through a browser by starting here:

*http://SERVERNAME/Reports_INSTANCENAME*

you can do the same by using the name *ReportServer* in place of *Reports* when you want to navigate into available reports by using the Open Report dialog box:

*http://SERVERNAME/ReportServer_INSTANCENAME*

The SERVERNAME and INSTANCENAME parts of the path need to be replaced by the real names used on your server. In our examples, *Reports* is the SERVERNAME and *K8R2* is the INSTANCENAME. In case the INSTANCENAME is omitted, the underscore character also has to be eliminated. You can deduce SERVERNAME and INSTANCENAME by looking at the URL for the reports in your company.

However, if the URL used for your reports has a different nomenclature and is actually a SharePoint path, you should be able to use the same URL both in the browser and in the Open Report dialog box you saw in Figure 5-44.

# Loading from a Data Feed

In the previous section, you saw how to load a data feed exported by Reporting Services in PowerPivot. In fact, Reporting Services makes data available to PowerPivot by exporting it as a data feed. However, this technique is not exclusive to Reporting Services and can be used to get data from many other services, including Internet sources that support the Open Data Protocol (also known as OData), and data exported as a data feed by SharePoint 2010, which we describe in the next section.

You can click the From Data Feeds button on the ribbon in the PowerPivot window to start the loading operation. The Table Import Wizard dialog box displayed in Figure 5-46 asks for the Data Feed URL. You saw this dialog box in Figure 5-39 when you were getting data from a report. This time, however, the Data Feed URL text box can be modified and does not have a fixed value provided by the report itself.

**FIGURE 5-46** Requesting a Data Feed URL.

You can use the following URL to test this data source:

*http://services.odata.org/Northwind/Northwind.svc/*

After you click Next, you can select the tables to import, just as in Figure 5-47. In that screen, only the Customers, Order_Details, Orders, and Products tables have been selected.

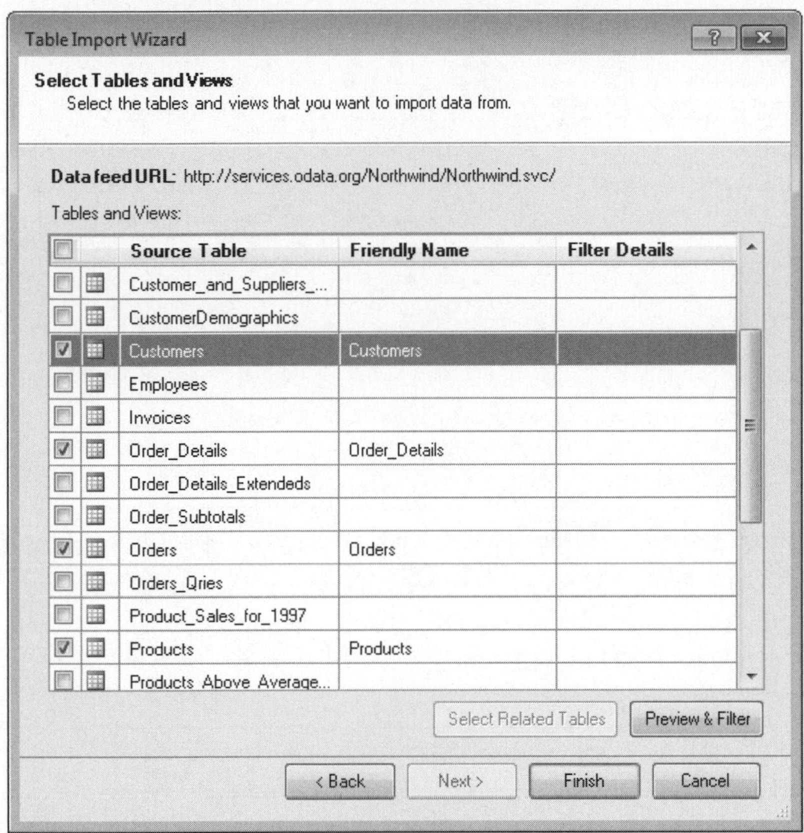


**FIGURE 5-47** Table selection from a Data Feed URL.

After you click Finish, the selected tables are imported into PowerPivot tables. This operation can take a long time when you have a high volume of data to import and the remote service providing data has a slow bandwidth. At the end, you see a report of the import, similar to the one you saw already in Figure 5-41, and the imported data is available as PowerPivot tables, as you can see in Figure 5-48.

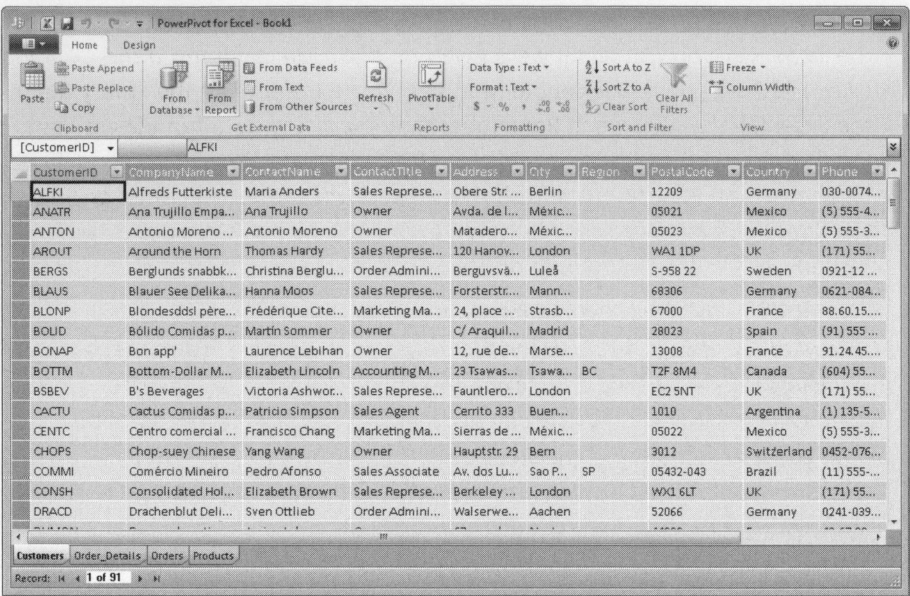


**FIGURE 5-48** Some of Northwind's tables imported in PowerPivot by means of a Data Feed.

# Loading from SharePoint

SharePoint 2010 might contain several instances of data you would like to import into PowerPivot. You cannot find a specific tool dedicated to importing data from SharePoint; depending on the type of data or document you want to use, you can choose to use one of the methods already shown.

This is a list of the most common data sources you can import from SharePoint:

- **Report** A report generated by Reporting Services can be stored and displayed in SharePoint. In this case, you follow the same procedure we described in the "Loading from a Report" section of this chapter.

- **Excel workbook** You can import data from an Excel workbook saved in SharePoint the same way you would if it were saved on disk. You can refer to the "Loading from Excel Files" section in this chapter and simply use the path to the library that contains the Excel file that you want. Remember that importing data from SharePoint (including Excel workbooks) makes it possible to refresh data of a PowerPivot model published on SharePoint; you cannot refresh that PowerPivot model published on SharePoint if the data is imported from a file stored on a local disk, which is not available after the PowerPivot model is published on SharePoint.
- **PowerPivot model embedded into an Excel workbook** If an Excel workbook contains a PowerPivot model, you can choose to extract data from the model by querying it. Working this way, you do not make a copy of the tables of that model. Instead, you query the model published on SharePoint and get a copy of just the result of that query. To do that, you can follow the same steps described in the "Loading from Analysis Services" section earlier in this chapter, with the only difference that you use the complete path to the published Excel file instead of the name of an Analysis Services server. (You do not have a Browse help tool; you probably need to copy and paste the complete URL from a browser.) A complete demonstration of how to use this feature is included in Chapter 9, "PowerPivot DAX Patterns."
- **SharePoint List** Any data included in a SharePoint List can be exported as a Data Feed. So you can use the same instructions described in the preceding "Loading from a Report" and "Loading from a Data Feed" sections.

In Figure 5-49, you can see an example of the user interface that enables you to export a SharePoint List as a Data Feed. The Export As Data Feed button is highlighted. When you click it, an .atomsvc file downloads and you see the same user interface previously shown for reports in Figure 5-37.

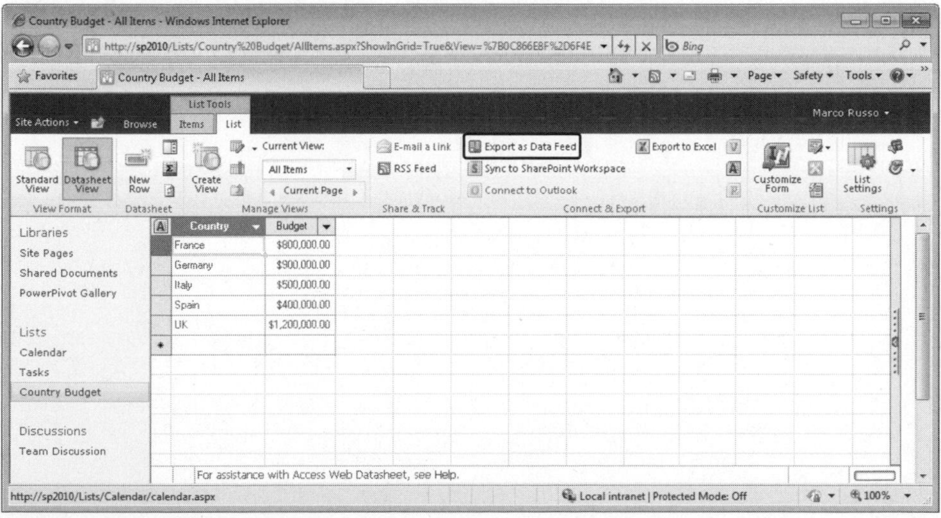


**FIGURE 5-49** The Export As Data Feed feature in a SharePoint List.

# Summary

In this chapter, you took a full tour of the various data loading capabilities of PowerPivot. You can load data from many data sources, which lets you integrate data from the different sources into a single, coherent, view of the information you need to analyze.

Bear in mind that the data loading process is just a technical step needed to provide information to the PowerPivot database. To get the best from the analytical capabilities of PowerPivot, you need to perform both the data loading procedures explained in this chapter and the data modeling step, which we introduced in Chapter 4.

Chapter 6

# Evaluation Context and CALCULATE

To get the best from DAX, you need to understand the evaluation context. We introduced this terminology when we talked about calculated columns and measures in Chapter 3, "Introduction to DAX," mentioning that calculated columns and measures differ mainly in their evaluation context. Now let us look at how the evaluation context is defined, and most important, how it works. In this chapter, we also introduce one of the most important DAX functions: CALCULATE, which allows you to make complex calculations by manipulating the evaluation context.

**Note** Understanding the content of this chapter is important if you want to use DAX in Microsoft SQL Server PowerPivot for Excel. Nevertheless, the topics described here are demanding, so do not be afraid if some concepts seem obscure during your first read. We suggest that you read this chapter again when you start creating your own DAX expressions; you are likely to discover that many concepts are clearer as soon as you implement your own DAX expressions and feel the need to better understand evaluation contexts.

## Understanding Evaluation Context

There are two kinds of evaluation context:

- **Filter Context** The set of active rows in a calculation.
- **Row Context** The current row in a table iteration.

We explain these in detail in the next topics.

### Filter Context in a Single Table

Let us start with the filter context. When a DAX expression is evaluated, you can imagine that for each table in the PowerPivot workbook there is a set of *active rows*, which are the only ones that will be used for the calculation. We call this set of active rows for all the tables in the data model a *filter context*. The filter context is a subset of all the rows, including the special cases of the whole set of all the rows and the empty set.

To better understand the filter context, consider the table shown in Figure 6-1, which is part of the sample workbook CH06-01-EvaluationContext-demo.xlsx in the companion content.

| City | Channel | Color | Size | Quantity | Price |
|---|---|---|---|---|---|
| Paris | Store | Red | Large | 1 | 15 |
| Paris | Store | Red | Small | 2 | 13 |
| Torino | Store | Green | Large | 4 | 11 |
| New York | Store | Green | Small | 8 | 9 |
| | Internet | Red | Large | 16 | 7 |
| | Internet | Red | Small | 32 | 5 |
| | Internet | Green | Large | 64 | 3 |
| | Internet | Green | Small | 128 | 1 |

**FIGURE 6-1** Simple Orders table.

When you use this data in a PivotTable, each cell defines a different filter context, which is used to calculate the value of the measure in that cell. Roughly speaking, the filter context of a cell is determined by its coordinates in the table.

In Figure 6-2, the cell E5 (which has the value of 64) corresponds to a filter context that includes these conditions:

- Color Green (on the row axis)
- Size Large (on the column axis)
- Channel Internet (on the slicer)

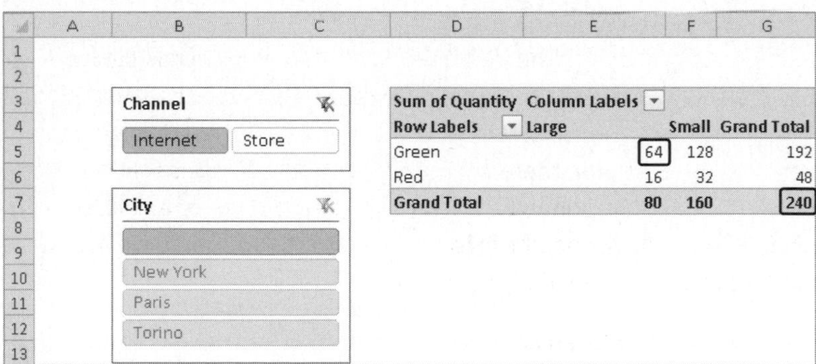


**FIGURE 6-2** Coordinates of cells E5 and G7.

There is no filter on the City attribute. In this example, the filter context corresponds to a single row of the underlying table. The cell G7, on the other hand, is the sum of all the rows that have Internet Channel, regardless of their Color, Size, and City value. The sum of these rows (which are the second half of the table shown in Figure 6-1) has a value of 240. The relationship between table rows and PivotTable cells is graphically shown in Figure 6-3.

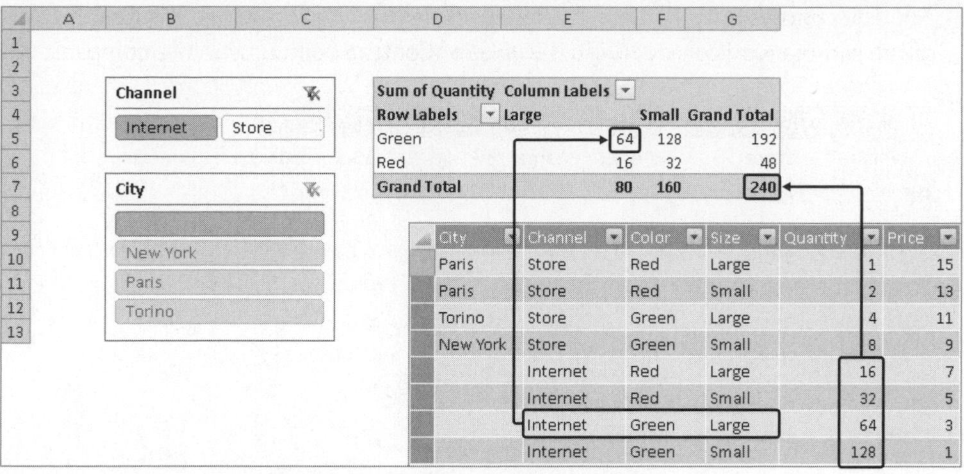


**FIGURE 6-3** The relationships between table rows and PivotTable cells.

So we can say that each selection that you make in a PivotTable (selection on columns, rows, filters, and slicers) corresponds to a filter in the PowerPivot table. If a column of the table is not used in any part of the PivotTable, there is no filter on that column.

In this first example, we considered only one table in the model. If you have more than one table, your work gets more complicated, but before diving into that, let us introduce the second kind of evaluation context: the row context.

## Row Context in a Single Table

*Row context* is conceptually close to the idea of *current row*. When a calculation is applied to a single row in a table, we say that there is a row context active for the calculation. This means that if you reference a column in the table, you want to use the value of that column in the current row. As you see later, there are certain DAX expressions that are meaningful only when there is an active row context (like the simple reference of a column) and other expressions that are valid only in the filter context, regardless of the active row context (for example, the SUM aggregation function).

There are two cases when there is an active row context:

- Evaluation of a calculated column
- Evaluation of a DAX function that iterates over a table

The first case is simple because it is really similar to how Excel works with tables. The expression contained in a calculated column is evaluated once for each row of the table. For each row, the row context contains the row itself and nothing else. When a row context is active, any reference to a column of the same table is valid and returns the value of that column for the same row. In other words, the presence of a row context does not require an aggregation function because the expression returns just the value of the referenced column in the same row.

In Figure 6-4, you can see that the formula for the calculated column Amount computes a product, and for each row, the computation is made using the corresponding values of Quantity and Price in the same row. This is pretty much the same behavior of an Excel table and is truly intuitive.

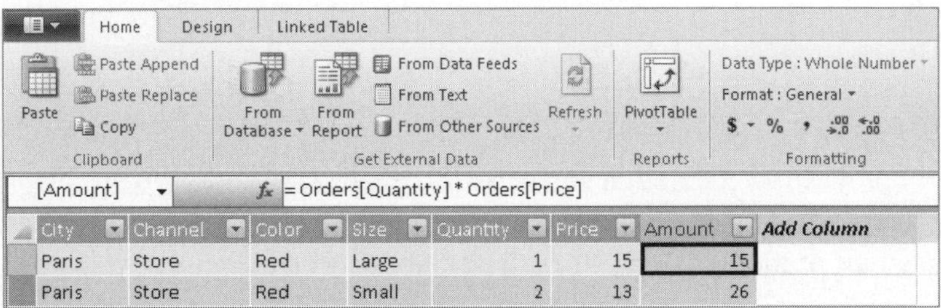


**FIGURE 6-4** Example of a calculated column.

Let us clarify this process with an example: how is the formula evaluated for row 1 in Figure 6-4? PowerPivot creates a row context containing only row 1 and then evaluates the formula, which requires the evaluation of Orders[Quantity]. To get the value of the expression, it searches for the value of the Quantity column in the row context, and this yields a value of 1. The same evaluation process is necessary for Orders[Price], which in the row context has the value of 15.

**Note** The expression defined in a calculated column is evaluated in a row context that is automatically defined for each row of the table.

There are other cases in which you would like to make a calculation for each row of a table, but you do not want to create a calculated column. There are many reasons for avoiding making a calculated column—for example, to create a dynamic expression that changes the calculation depending on the selection made by the end user in the PivotTable.

For example, you could write a measure like this:

```
SUM( Orders[Amount] )
```

This formula calculates the sum of the Amount calculated column. However, if you do not have a calculated column for Amount and you want to create it by using a measure, you might be tempted to use the expression you used previously for the Amount calculated column now for a CalcAmount measure. But this will not work, as you can see in Figure 6-5.

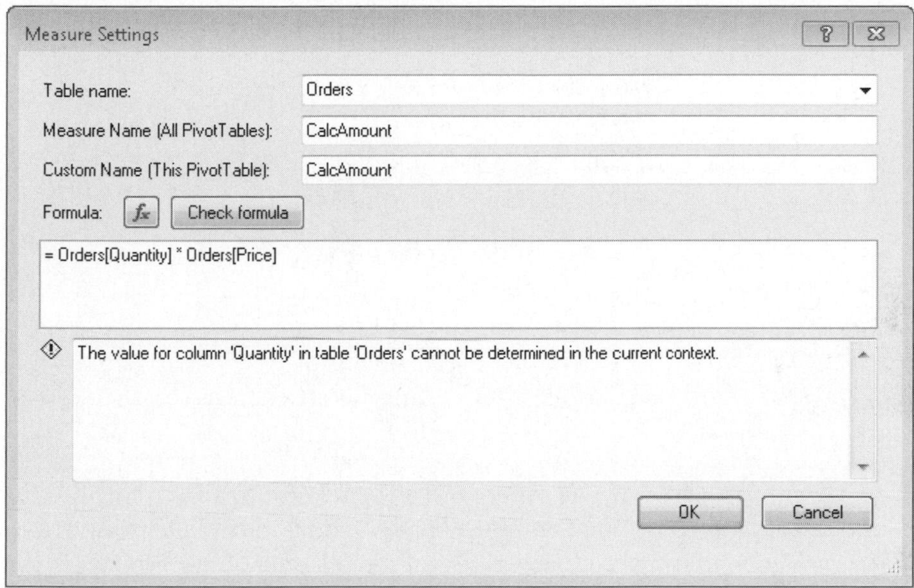


**FIGURE 6-5** You get an error message when you define a measure by referencing a row value.

The error shown in Figure 6-5 indicates a problem related to the evaluation of a column in the current context. Unless you have a clear understanding of evaluation context, you are likely to find the error message very cryptic. Let us try to make it meaningful: when you are browsing a PivotTable, you have a filter context but there is no row context defined. The expression *Orders[Quantity]* requires a row context to be correctly evaluated. So PowerPivot complains about the lack of a context in which the formula can be understood.

If you try to use the SUM function to aggregate the expression, you get another error (see Figure 6-6) although different.

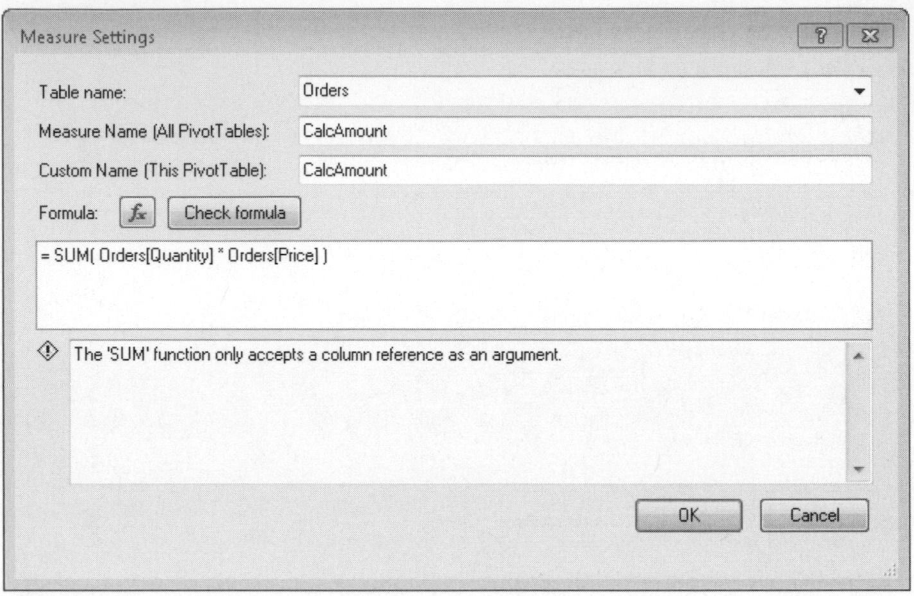


**FIGURE 6-6** You get an error message when you use SUM with an expression as parameter.

As you can see in Figure 6-6, you cannot use an expression as an argument of the SUM function because the SUM function works only with a column as a parameter and does not accept a generic expression. However, you can obtain the result you want by using a different formula:

```
SUMX( Orders, Orders[Quantity] * Orders[Price] )
```

The SUMX aggregation function iterates the table passed as the first parameter (Orders), and for each row of the table makes the calculation specified in the second parameter (Orders[Quantity] * Orders[Price]). The expression is evaluated in a row context corresponding to the current row of the iteration. The result of the expression for each row is summed up for all the rows, and the SUMX function returns the result of this aggregation, as shown in Figure 6-7.

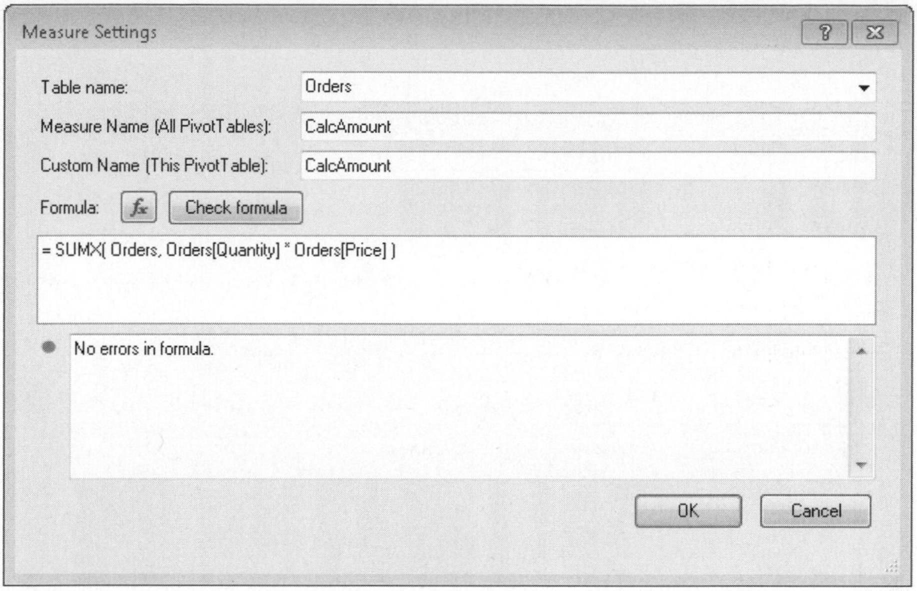

Measure Settings

Table name: Orders

Measure Name (All PivotTables): CalcAmount

Custom Name (This PivotTable): CalcAmount

Formula: Check formula

```
= SUMX( Orders, Orders[Quantity] * Orders[Price] )
```

No errors in formula.

OK Cancel

**FIGURE 6-7** Correct definition of measure using SUMX.

In Figure 6-7, we used the SUMX function to apply our initial expression to each of the rows of the Orders table that are active in the current filter context, and as you can see in Figure 6-8, the CalcAmount measure works fine.

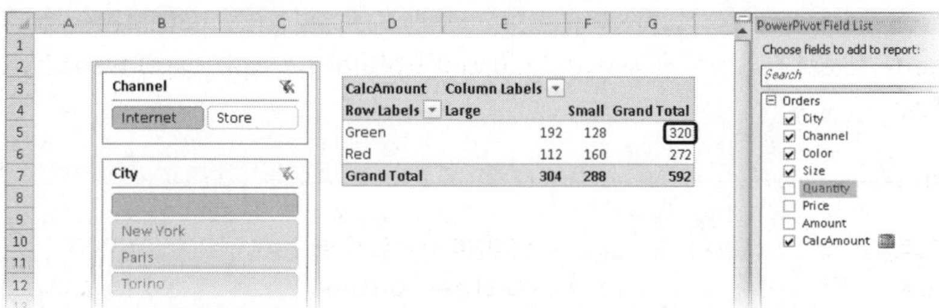


**FIGURE 6-8** Resulting value of the CalcAmount measure.

You need to understand that the filter context defined by the coordinates of each cell in the PivotTable is used, during the computation of the SUMX function, to filter the rows of the Orders table. So this is the crux of the matter: the expression in the SUMX function has been evaluated under both a filter context and a row context.

To understand better what happened, let us look at the exact sequence of operations performed to calculate the value in cell G5, which is highlighted in Figure 6-8:

- The filter context is defined by the coordinates of cell G5, which are <Green, Internet>.
- The value required is CalcAmount, which is the measure defined with this expression: SUMX( Orders, Orders[Quantity] * Orders[Price] ).
- The SUMX function iterates all the rows of the Orders table that are active in the filter context. So only the two rows highlighted in Figure 6-9 are going to be iterated.

| City | Channel | Color | Size | Quantity | Price |
|---|---|---|---|---|---|
| Paris | Store | Red | Large | 1 | 15 |
| Paris | Store | Red | Small | 2 | 13 |
| Torino | Store | Green | Large | 4 | 11 |
| New York | Store | Green | Small | 8 | 9 |
| | Internet | Red | Large | 16 | 7 |
| | Internet | Red | Small | 32 | 5 |
| | Internet | Green | Large | 64 | 3 |
| | Internet | Green | Small | 128 | 1 |

**FIGURE 6-9** Rows iterated by SUMX to calculate cell G5 of the PivotTable.

- For each of these two rows, the calculation Orders[Quantity] * Orders[Price] is performed using that row as the row context.
- The resulting values of these two rows (192 and 128, respectively) are aggregated together, summing them up, because we are using SUMX.
- The final result of 320 is returned by SUMX and is used to fill the G5 cell.

You have a set of functions that show the same behavior as SUMX but use a different aggregation criterion. These functions are named with the name of the aggregation operation and end with an X character.

- AVERAGEX
- COUNTAX
- COUNTX
- MAXX
- MINX
- SUMX

An important concept to remember is that these functions add a row context to the existing filter context, making an iteration on all the rows that are included in the filter context and activating a row context for each of these rows.

## Adding Filters to a Filter Context for a Single Table

The filter context can be modified to evaluate a particular DAX expression, to get a value for a different context. For instance, you might want to sum a value over a subset of the rows of a table, so you need a way to define the rows you want to include in that calculation.

All of the aggX aggregation functions have syntax with two parameters: the first one is the table that will be used to iterate rows (filtered by the current filter context), the second parameter is the expression applied to each of the iterated rows.

```
SUMX( <table>, <expression> )
```

Instead of a table, in the first parameter, you can use a function returning a table. For example, you can use the FILTER function, which gets a table and further restricts the filter context on that table by using the Boolean expression received as the second parameter.

```
FILTER( <table>, <filter expression> )
```

Simply said, the expression passed to a FILTER function adds that filter to the current filter context for that table. As we said, you use FILTER in place of a table in a DAX expression. For example, if you write the following:

```
SUMX( FILTER( Orders, Orders[Quantity] > 0 ), Orders[Amount] )
```

instead of

```
SUMX( Orders, Orders[Amount] )
```

you get the same result because in our sample data there are no rows with a Quantity value that is less than zero. However, you might consider only rows with a price greater than 1:

```
SUMX( FILTER( Orders, Orders[Price] > 1 ), Orders[Amount] )
```

In this case, the FILTER function skips just the <Internet, Green, Small> row from the table we saw in Figure 6-9 (which has a price of 1 and is excluded by the filter condition). Using that formula for your CalcAmount measure, you ignore that row in the PivotTable calculation.

As you can see in Figure 6-10, there is no value for the highlighted F5 cell in the PivotTable, and the total for rows and columns ignores the filtered row, too. So the FILTER function can filter data by restricting the filter context used (for example) to calculate aggregations in a PivotTable.

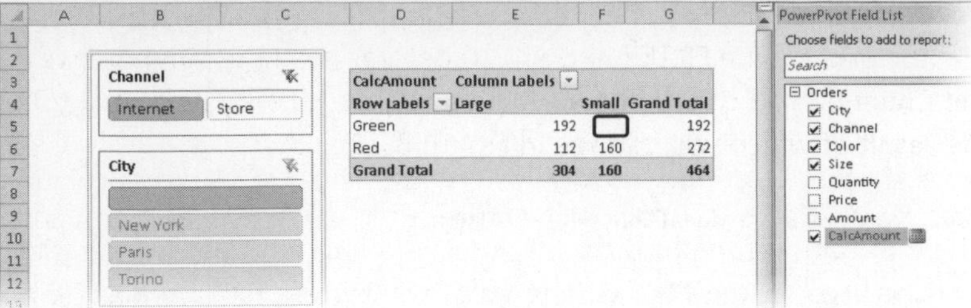


**FIGURE 6-10** The cell F5 is empty because the CalcAmount measure considers only rows with a price greater than 1.

## Removing Filters from a Filter Context for a Single Table

Now that you have seen how to add a filter to the filter context, let us take a look at how to remove one of the existing filters. If you need to remove a filter from the filter context or if you want to remove the filter context on a table altogether, you need a slightly different approach. The first technique is to remove all the filters on a table. For example, if you want to get the value of all the orders, regardless of any selection made by the user in the PivotTable, you can use the ALL function, which returns a table containing all the rows of a table, regardless of the existing filter context, and then passes its result to the SUMX function. For example, you can create an AllAmount measure by using the following expression:

```
SUMX( ALL( Orders ), Orders[Amount] )
```

In Figure 6-11, you can see that for any cell of the PivotTable where AllAmount is calculated, the value is always the same (it is always 749) because the ALL function ignores the filter context.

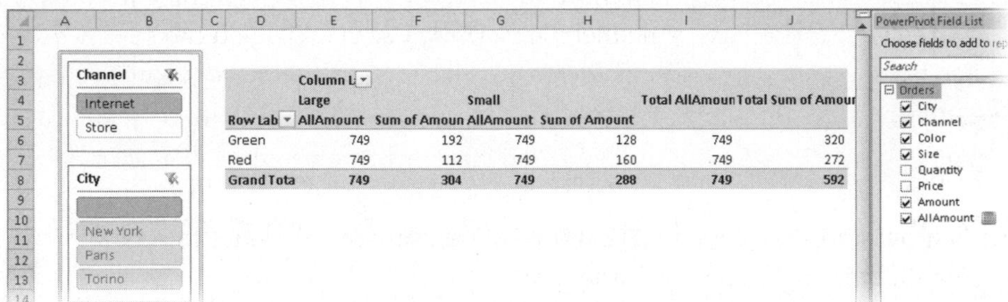


**FIGURE 6-11** The AllAmount measure always considers all the rows in the Order table.

**Note** From a certain point of view, the ALL function does not change the filter context, but it really creates a new one, at least when it is applied to a table. Shortly, you will see that ALL can be used also with a single column as parameter to eliminate a filter from a filter context for just one column.

If you need to filter only some rows, but with criteria that are independent of the current filter context, you can combine FILTER and ALL to get, for example, all the rows in Orders for the Internet Channel. You can define an AllInternet measure by using the following DAX expression (the result of which you can see in Figure 6-12):

```
SUMX( FILTER( ALL( Orders ), Orders[Channel]="Internet" ), Orders[Amount] )
```

| Row Labels | Large AllInternet | Large Sum of Amount | Small AllInternet | Small Sum of Amount | Total AllInter | Total Sum of A |
|---|---|---|---|---|---|---|
| Green | 592 | 192 | 592 | 128 | 592 | 320 |
| Red | 592 | 112 | 592 | 160 | 592 | 272 |
| Grand Total | 592 | 304 | 592 | 288 | 592 | 592 |

**FIGURE 6-12** The AllInternet measure always considers all the rows in the Order table.

In Figure 6-12, the AllInternet value is always 592, which corresponds to the total of Amount for the Internet Channel. However, you can see that this approach has a limitation because you cannot use the existing selection of attributes in your filter condition. In other words, you are replacing the filter context for a table with a new one, but you are not able to change only part of the filter context by using this process. When you want to remove only one selection of the user (for example the Channel) while keeping all the other filters in the filter context, you need to use the CALCULATE function. We more thoroughly describe the CALCULATE function later because it is very powerful and flexible and deserves its own section; nevertheless, it is useful to start taking a look at it now.

Let us imagine that you want to remove the filter on the Channel attribute from the filter context but still want to keep all the other filters. Using CALCULATE, you can specify a filter on a column that overrides any existing filter for that column only. You can define an AllChannels measure with the following expression:

```
CALCULATE( SUMX( Orders, Orders[Amount] ), ALL( Orders[Channel] ) )
```

The first parameter of CALCULATE is the expression that you want to evaluate in a filter context that is modified by the other parameters.

**Note** There could be any number of parameters in the CALCULATE function after the first one, and each of these parameters defines a set of values for a column or a table that clears the existing corresponding filter of the current filter context, replacing it with a new one.

In the example, the ALL function receives a column reference as a parameter (previously we used a table reference) and returns all the values from that column, regardless of the existing filter context. In other words, using CALCULATE and ALL with one or more column parameters clears the existing filter context for those columns for the expression passed to and evaluated by the CALCULATE function.

The AllChannels measure defined in Figure 6-13 returns the total for all the channels, even if you have a different selection in the PivotTable.

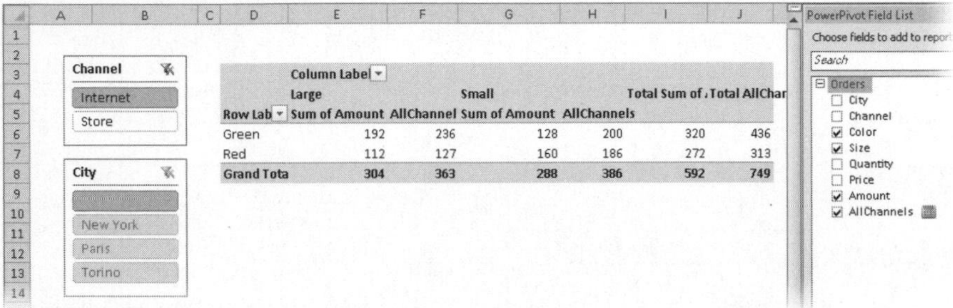


**FIGURE 6-13** The AllChannels measure calculates amount by ignoring the Channel selection.

**Important** When you use CALCULATE, you can replace SUMX with SUM whenever the expression of SUMX is made of a single column. In other words, these two expressions are equivalent:

```
CALCULATE( SUMX( Orders, Orders[Amount] ), ALL( Orders[Channel] ) )
CALCULATE( SUM( Orders[Amount] ), ALL( Orders[Channel] ) )
```

You still need SUMX whenever the expression that has to be aggregated contains more terms:

```
CALCULATE( SUMX( Orders, Orders[Quantity] * Orders[Price] ),
           ALL( Orders[Channel] ) )
```

In that case, you do not have an alternative syntax based on SUM, unless you move the expression in a calculated column, just like the Amount column in the Orders table.

CALCULATE is a fundamental function for operating on the filter context; it calculates rows that are not part of the current selection but that are needed to make comparisons, ratios, and so on.

Finally, we should mention that if you want to remove filters from all but a few columns in a table, you can use ALLEXCEPT. In other words, using the Orders table as an example, the following statements are equivalent:

```
CALCULATE( SUM( Orders[Amount] ),
           ALL( Orders[Channel], Orders[Color], Orders[Size],
                Orders[Quantity], Orders[Price], Orders[Amount] ) )

CALCULATE( SUM( Orders[Amount] ),
           ALLEXCEPT( Orders, Orders[City] ) )
```

**Note** Actually, there is a subtle difference between the two: the expression based on the ALLEXCEPT function operates even when there are relationships with other tables, ignoring possible filters implicitly included by those relationships. If you want to get the same result as ALLEXCEPT, you need to add the entire list of ALL calls—that is, you should include an ALL call for each table related to the one you are basing your calculation on (Orders in this example). The following use of the CALCULATE function is truly equivalent to the one you saw before using the ALLEXCEPT function:

```
CALCULATE( SUM( Orders[Amount] ),
           ALL( Channels ), ALL( Cities ),
           ALL( Orders[Channel], Orders[Color], Orders[Size],
                Orders[Quantity], Orders[Price], Orders[Amount] ) )
```

For this reason, we recommend the use of ALLEXCEPT whenever you want to exclude almost all of the filters from a table.

## Row Context with Multiple Tables

Now, you can take a step further by adding a new related table to the PowerPivot data model—for example, the Channels table, which has a discount percentage for each channel type, as you can see in Figure 6-14.

| Channel | Discount |
|---|---|
| Internet | 0.1 |
| Store | 0.05 |

**FIGURE 6-14** The Channels table added to the PowerPivot model.

You might want to calculate the discounted amount for each transaction by defining a calculated column in the Orders table. So the first idea is to define a formula this way:

```
Orders[Amount] * (1 - Channels[Discount])
```

but this produces an error, as you can see in Figure 6-15.

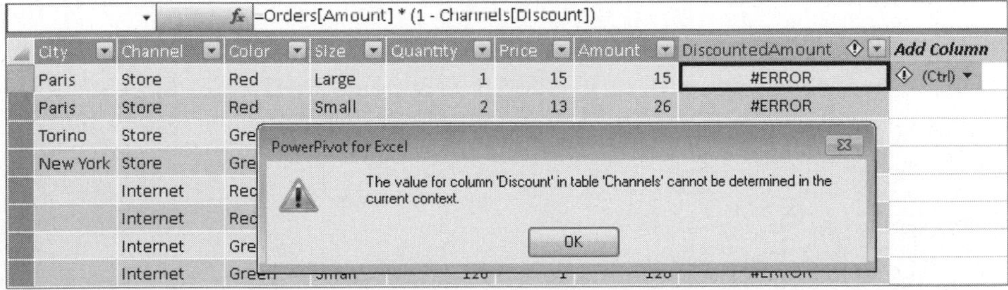


**FIGURE 6-15** An error produced by using the Discount column from the Channels table in a calculated column in Orders.

Let us try to understand what is happening when you try to define this column. The Discount column is in the Channels table, which is not the table in which you are defining the new DiscountedAmount calculated column. For this reason, if you want to read the value from the Channels table (which does not have a row context) you must use the RELATED function, which propagates the row context to the related table, as you can see in the formula used in Figure 6-16.

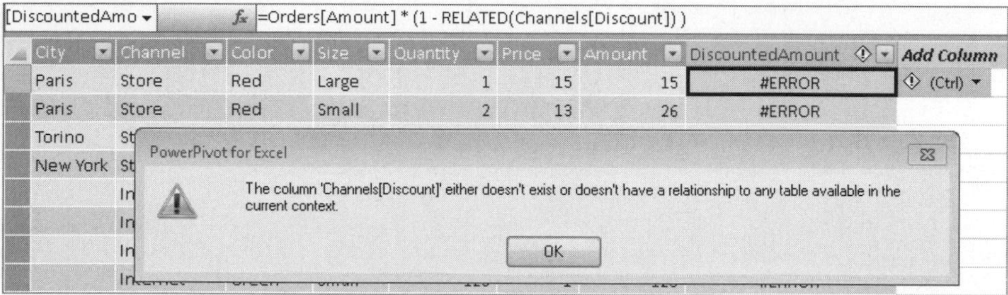


**FIGURE 6-16** An error caused by a missing relationship between the Orders and Channels tables.

However, the RELATED function you used in Figure 6-16 still generates an error, but this time, the reason is that there is no relationship defined between the Orders and the Channels tables.

When you define the relationship as shown in Figure 6-17, the RELATED function evaluates the column passed as the parameter by applying the appropriate row context. For example, an expression in a calculated column of the Orders table is always evaluated in a specific row context. Starting from that row, the relationship you defined is used to choose a row in the Channels lookup table that has the same Channel value as the row evaluated in the Orders table. In other words, you could say that the RELATED function propagates the row context to another table by following the existing relationship.

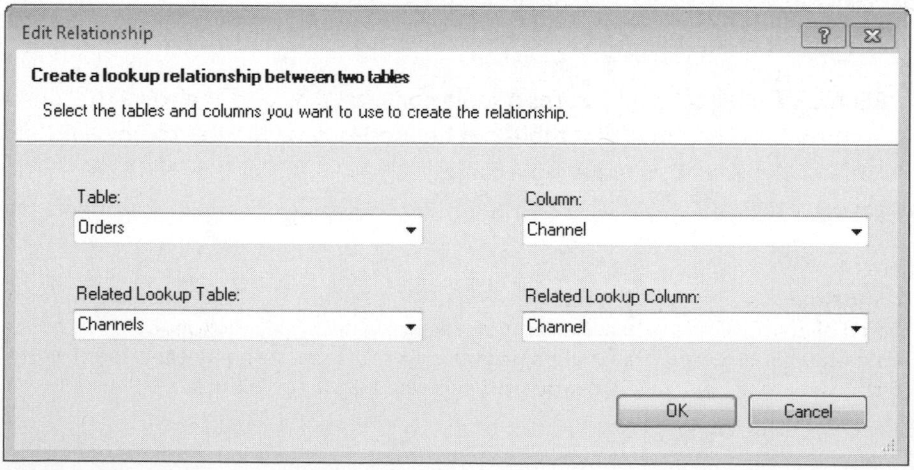

**FIGURE 6-17** The relationship between the Orders and Channels tables.

**Note** The row context is limited to a single row, and relationships between tables do not propagate the row context to other tables by themselves. The RELATED function propagates the effect of row context to a related table, provided that a valid relationship to a related lookup table exists.

After you define the relationship between Orders and Channels, the DiscountedAmount column can be calculated for each row, as you can see in Figure 6-18.

[DiscountedAmo ▾ | =Orders[Amount] * (1 - RELATED(Channels[Discount]) )

| City | Cha... | Color | Size | Quantity | Price | Amount | DiscountedAmount |
|---|---|---|---|---|---|---|---|
| Paris | Store | Red | Large | 1 | 15 | 15 | 14.25 |
| Paris | Store | Red | Small | 2 | 13 | 26 | 24.7 |
| Torino | Store | Green | Large | 4 | 11 | 44 | 41.8 |
| New York | Store | Green | Small | 8 | 9 | 72 | 68.4 |
| | Internet | Red | Large | 16 | 7 | 112 | 100.8 |
| | Internet | Red | Small | 32 | 5 | 160 | 144 |
| | Internet | Green | Large | 64 | 3 | 192 | 172.8 |
| | Internet | Green | Small | 128 | 1 | 128 | 115.2 |

**FIGURE 6-18** Valid calculation for the DiscountedAmount calculated column.

On the opposite side of the relationship, you might want to calculate over the set of rows related to a Channel selection in the Channels table. For example, you might want to calculate the total number of orders for each channel in a calculated column of the Channels table, as in the OrdersCount calculated column shown in Figure 6-19.

[OrdersCount] ▾ | =COUNTROWS( RELATEDTABLE( Orders ) )

| Cha... | Discount | OrdersCount | Add Column |
|---|---|---|---|
| Internet | 0.1 | 4 | |
| Store | 0.05 | 4 | |

Orders | Channels

**FIGURE 6-19** A calculated column in a Channels table using the RELATEDTABLE function.

The RELATEDTABLE function returns a table composed of only the rows that are related to the current row context. That table can be used as a parameter to any aggX function or to other DAX functions requiring a table, such as FILTER or COUNTROWS (which we used in our example).

**Important** You should avoid using the RELATEDTABLE function when there are alternatives based on CALCULATE that get better performance. Although this might be not convenient for calculated columns, it is almost always possible for measures and when it is necessary to manipulate the filter context, as you will see in the following sections.

## Filter Context with Multiple Tables

Now that you have seen how to use row context with related tables, you might find it interesting to note that table relationships directly affect the filter context of involved tables, regardless of DAX expressions used. For example, you can add a Cities table to the model like the one in Figure 6-20, which has a relationship as a lookup table with the Orders table through the City column (see Figure 6-21).

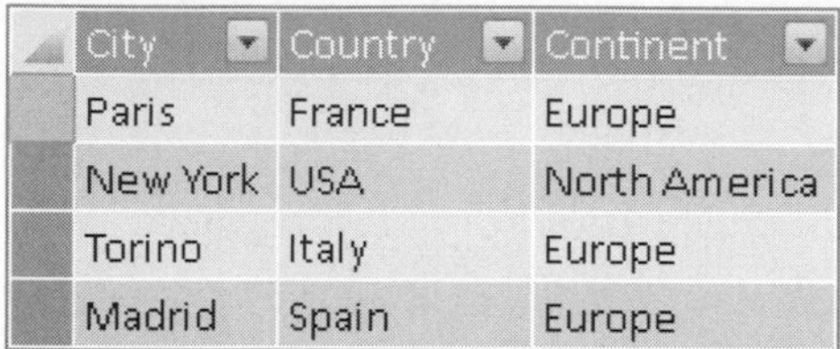

| City | Country | Continent |
|---|---|---|
| Paris | France | Europe |
| New York | USA | North America |
| Torino | Italy | Europe |
| Madrid | Spain | Europe |

**FIGURE 6-20** The Cities table contains Country and Continent columns.

Create Relationship

**Create a lookup relationship between two tables**

Select the tables and columns you want to use to create the relationship.

Table: Orders

Column: City

Related Lookup Table: Cities

Related Lookup Column: City

Create Cancel

**FIGURE 6-21** The relationship between the Orders and Cities tables.

When you browse the data by using a PivotTable, you can choose Continent and Channel as the slicers, DiscountedAmount as a measure, and Color and Size in Rows and Columns, respectively.

In Figure 6-22, you can see the data of all the rows in the Orders table partitioned by Color and Size attributes. Despite the presence of Continent and Channel as slicers, there is no filter active on these slicers because all the members are selected. Keep in mind that the Continent Slicer also contains an empty member that corresponds to all the sales made in the Internet Channel that do not have a corresponding City. (See Figure 6-18 to look at raw data.)

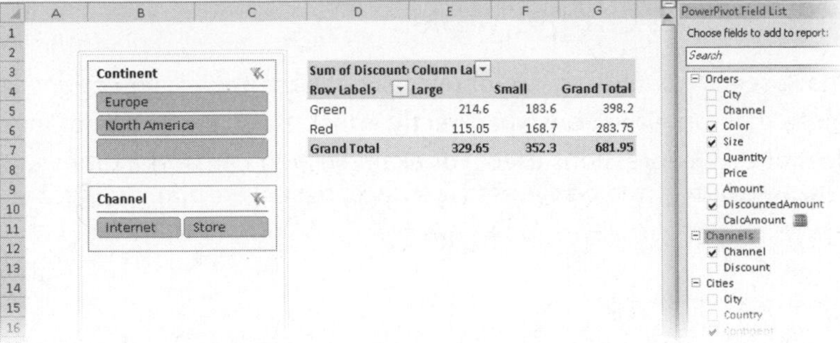


**FIGURE 6-22** Browse data without a filter.

Whenever you make a selection on the Continent Slicer, you also define a filter context on the Cities table that immediately propagates its effects on related tables. In fact, you are making a filter on a lookup table, and this implies that all the tables that have a relationship with that lookup table are also filtered. In our example, the Orders table has a relationship with the Cities table, which contains the Continent column. If you select the North America member, only the row with New York is filtered in the Cities table, and this propagates to the Orders table by filtering only the rows corresponding to New York.

Figure 6-23 illustrates the behavior of the filter context defined by the selection of the North America member in the Continent slicer. The rows in the PowerPivot tables that are included in the filter context are highlighted through a box. Notice that the Channel Slicer is also affected by this filter context because even if there are two members visible and selected (Store and Internet), only Store is colored and Internet is grayed; in fact, in the current filter context, there are no rows in the Orders table that are active in the filter context.

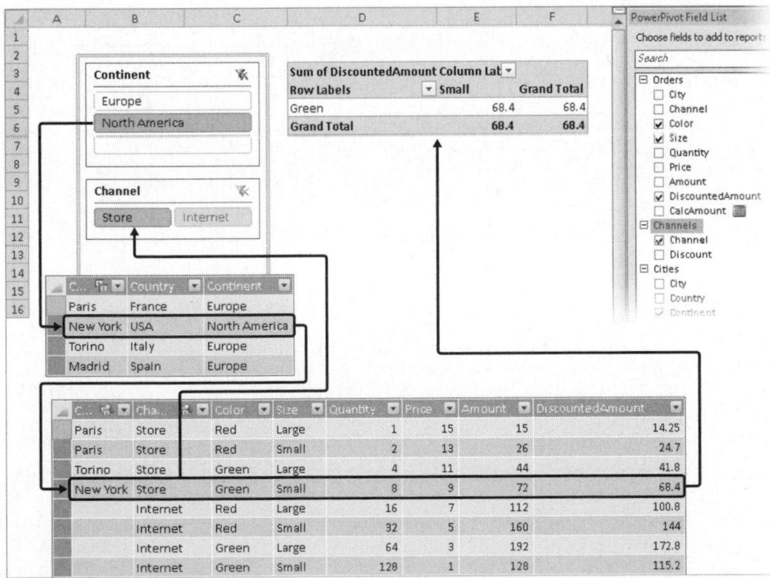


| City | Country | Continent |
|---|---|---|
| Paris | France | Europe |
| New York | USA | North America |
| Torino | Italy | Europe |
| Madrid | Spain | Europe |

| City | Channel | Color | Size | Quantity | Price | Amount | DiscountedAmount |
|---|---|---|---|---|---|---|---|
| Paris | Store | Red | Large | 1 | 15 | 15 | 14.25 |
| Paris | Store | Red | Small | 2 | 13 | 26 | 24.7 |
| Torino | Store | Green | Large | 4 | 11 | 44 | 41.8 |
| New York | Store | Green | Small | 8 | 9 | 72 | 68.4 |
| | Internet | Red | Large | 16 | 7 | 112 | 100.8 |
| | Internet | Red | Small | 32 | 5 | 160 | 144 |
| | Internet | Green | Large | 64 | 3 | 192 | 172.8 |
| | Internet | Green | Small | 128 | 1 | 128 | 115.2 |

**FIGURE 6-23** Filter context defined by the selection of the North America continent.

**Note** An item grayed in a slicer indicates that the selection of that member does not have any effect on the result of the PivotTable because values for that item are already filtered out by selections of other attributes, or in other words, by the filter context.

If you change the selection of the Continent Slicer by choosing Europe, the filter context activates three rows in the Cities table. Only rows corresponding to these cities are active in the Orders table, as you can see in Figure 6-24.

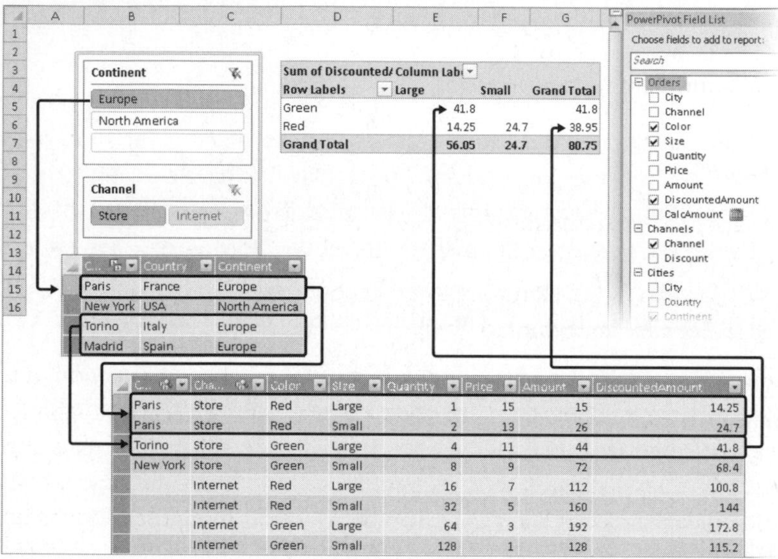


**FIGURE 6-24** Filter context defined by the selection of Europe.

The filter context defined for the Orders table is further reduced when single cells of the PivotTable are evaluated. For example, cell E5 includes only the row <Torino, Store, Green, Large> because it is the only one that satisfies the user filter <Europe, Green, Large> that results from user selection. This type of user filter is <Europe, Red> for cell G6 and includes two rows from the Orders table. We used the term *user filter* because it represents the will of the user, regardless of the number of internal operations that are necessary to define the exact requirements of the filter for the table containing the values to extract.

At this point, you can still add filters to the evaluation context by using FILTER as a parameter of an aggregation function like SUMX, in the same way you have seen is valid for a single table. However, you need to use a different approach if you need to remove filters from the filter context—for example, if you want to calculate a ratio between the amount for a color and the corresponding amount for an item regardless of the color.

## Modifying Filter Context for Multiple Tables

We previously introduced the CALCULATE function to remove filters from filter context for a single table. However, CALCULATE is the most important function for manipulating the filter context.

The CALCULATE function accepts two forms of filter parameters. The first type is a Boolean expression, similar to a filter condition in a FILTER function. This type of filter for CALCULATE is also called *table filter*. For example, this expression calculates the total amount for Europe, regardless of the selection in the Continent Slicer (we call it EuropeSales in Figure 6-25):

```
CALCULATE( SUM( Orders[Amount] ), Cities[Continent] = "Europe" )
```

This expression is equivalent to the following:

```
SUMX( FILTER( Orders, RELATED( Cities[Continent] ) = "Europe" ),
      Orders[Amount] )
```

However, it is always better to write the CALCULATE version because it is faster than the SUMX version. In general, whenever you can write an expression using CALCULATE or FILTER, always prefer CALCULATE instead of FILTER for performance reasons. This is another reason why learning CALCULATE is very important.

**Note** The reason the CALCULATE function is faster than the FILTER function lies in the way the filter is made in the Orders table.

When you use CALCULATE, the filter is applied to the Cities table, and the real filter of the Orders table is made by using the City set that belongs to the Europe Continent data in the Cities table. This operation is pretty fast because it uses internal indexes and does not require a complete iteration over all the rows of the Orders table.

By using SUMX, the filter on the Orders table is made by the FILTER function, which could iterate the Orders table row by row, making an evaluation of the filter condition for each Orders row, without taking advantage of existing internal indexes defined by the relationship between the Cities and Orders tables.

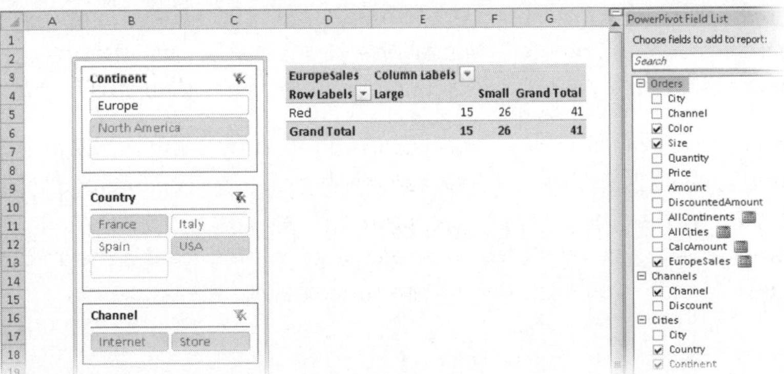


**FIGURE 6-25** The PivotTable calculates only Orders from France, despite the filter on the North America Continent data.

In Figure 6-25, you can see that the filter made on the Europe Continent by the EuropeSales measure returns data only from France: the filter made on the Continent Slicer is ignored for that measure, but the filter on Country is still valid and removes the Italy rows of the Orders table from the filter context.

The second type of filter parameter for the CALCULATE function is a list of values for a column or a list of rows for a table. For example, you could get the total Amount for all the Continents using this expression (we call it AllContinents in Figure 6-26):

```
CALCULATE( SUM( Orders[Amount] ), ALL( Cities[Continent] ) )
```

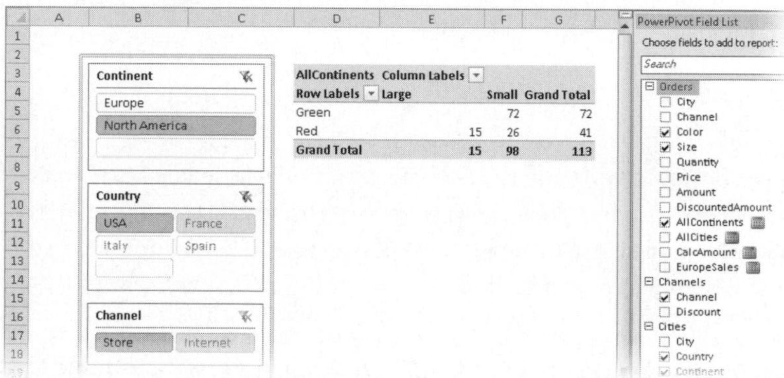


**FIGURE 6-26** The PivotTable excludes Orders from Italy and Spain, despite ignoring the Continent selections.

However, even in this case the measure ignores any selections in the Continent Slicer, but it makes use of the Country Slicer selection in the filter context to calculate the sum of Amount, as you can see in Figure 6-26.

**Important** Actually, the user has to select an existing combination of Continent and Country in the slicers. For example, if you select USA and Europe, there are no valid rows in the Cities table; this stops the calculation for Orders and shows no data at all. This limitation is valid for all the following examples.

If you wanted to ignore any of the selections in the Cities attributes (which are Continent, Country, and City), you have to write this other expression:

```
CALCULATE( SUM( Orders[Amount] ), ALL( Cities ) )
```

As you can see in Figure 6-27, the new AllCities measure ignores any selections made by Country and Continent Slicers.

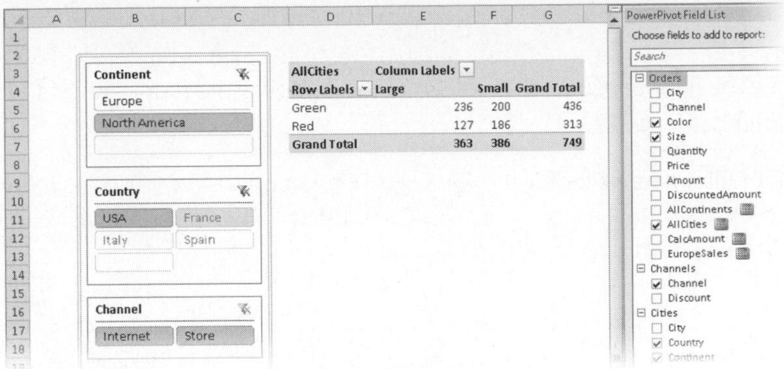


**FIGURE 6-27** The AllCities measure ignores any selections of Continent and Country Slicers.

The CALCULATE function allows you to define a new filter context based on the existing one. However, you can completely overwrite the existing filter context if you specify a new filter for each of the columns of the tables. In fact, you can specify more filters in the same CALCULATE function call, and you could write such an expression, which ignores any selection of Continent, Country (both of these belong to the Cities table), and Channel Slicers:

```
CALCULATE( SUM( Orders[Amount] ), ALL( Cities ), ALL( Channels ) )
```

All the filter conditions that you specify in a CALCULATE function call have to be satisfied to make a row active in the filter context. In other words, all the filter conditions are in logical AND. Usually, mixing ALL on some columns and specifying Boolean conditions for others, you obtain the filter context that you want.

For example, if you wanted to filter Italy and France only (doing just as you did when you selected both those countries in the Country Slicer), and you want to ignore the selection of the City attribute, you can use this expression:

```
CALCULATE( SUM( Orders[Amount] ),
           OR( Cities[Country] = "Italy", Cities[Country] = "France" ),
           ALL( Cities[City] ) )
```

However, sometimes the CALCULATE function syntax cannot be used—for example when you have an OR condition or when you need to compare more columns at a row level in a table. Unfortunately, these kinds of filter conditions cannot be used directly in a CALCULATE filter. For example, the following expression generates the error shown in Figure 6-28.

```
CALCULATE( SUM( Orders[Amount] ),
           Orders[Quantity] * 2 < Orders[Price] )
```

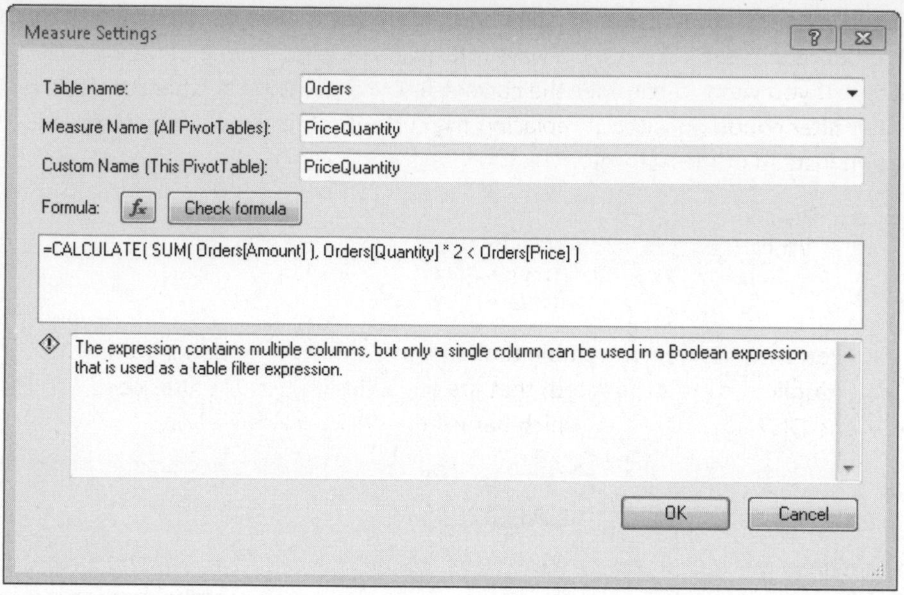

**FIGURE 6-28** The Table filter expression cannot reference more than one column in a Boolean expression.

You can overcome this limitation by using a functionally equivalent FILTER syntax writing this expression:

```
CALCULATE( SUM( Orders[Amount] ),
          FILTER( Orders, Orders[Quantity] * 2 < Orders[Price] ) )
```

In the next section, you see how this technique works. For now, it is enough to say that you can get around some limitations of the filters in the CALCULATE function by using FILTER, which returns the rows that are active in the filter context defined by the CALCULATE function. However, do pay attention to the first parameter passed to the FILTER function included in a CALCULATE call; we explain why in the next paragraphs.

Until now you have seen how to operate with CALCULATE by replacing existing column filters on filter context with a new filter, which is not related to the existing filter condition. In fact, this expression

```
CALCULATE( SUM( Orders[Amount] ),
          OR( Cities[Country] = "Italy", Cities[Country] = "France" ) )
```

is equivalent to this one:

```
CALCULATE( SUM( Orders[Amount] ),
          FILTER( ALL( Cities[Country] ),
                  OR( Cities[Country] = "Italy",
                      Cities[Country] = "France" ) ) )
```

In other words, the condition that filters only cities in Italy or France operates on all the values of the Country column. In fact, it always returns a value, regardless of the user selection of Country. If you want to consider the current filter context and further restrict it by adding another filter condition without replacing the current selection, you need to use the VALUES function instead of the ALL one.

```
CALCULATE( SUM( Orders[Amount] ),
           FILTER( VALUES( Cities[Country] ),
                   OR( Cities[Country] = "Italy",
                       Cities[Country] = "France" ) ) )
```

VALUES returns a one-column table that contains the distinct values from the specified column (duplicates are eliminated) that are active in the current filter context. It is equivalent to the DISTINCT function, which has exactly the same behavior.

### Avoid Using FILTER in CALCULATE

Sometimes you can use alternatives to FILTER in a CALCULATE call. Whenever you have an alternative to FILTER (for example, by using a Boolean condition on a column), use the alternative.

The FILTER function creates a new table in memory, whereas a simple filter condition on a column does not require this and is faster than the FILTER function.

## Final Considerations for Evaluation Context

Filter context and row context are two important concepts that you need to understand well to create advanced DAX expressions.

This is a short list of the more important concepts that you have learned until now about evaluation context:

- RELATED always refers to the row context.
- Column references with the syntax Table[Column] always refer to the row context.
- CALCULATE and RELATEDTABLE convert all row contexts to filter context.
- VALUES is bound to filter context.
- Base tables used as arguments for aggX and FILTER functions are filtered by filter context.
- Use CALCULATE instead of FILTER or RELATEDTABLE to get better performance.

# Understanding the CALCULATE Function

The CALCULATE function is the magic key for many DAX calculations. However, it is not very intuitive, and for these reasons it deserves a section dedicated to it so that you can take the time you need to discover the intricacies of this function.

First of all, let us review the syntax.

```
CALCULATE( <expression>, <filter1>, <filter2>… )
```

- The result of CALCULATE is the evaluation of the expression represented by the first parameter.
- The first parameter expression is evaluated in a context that is modified by the subsequent filters passed as parameters. A key point is that these filters can both enlarge or restrict the filter context.

Because the final result needs to be a value and not a table, the expression is usually an aggregation function such as SUM, MIN, MAX, COUNTROWS, and so on. As we mentioned in previous sections, an aggX function is required whenever the expression that has to be aggregated contains more terms, such as when you want to multiply UnitPrice by Quantity and you do not have a calculated column for that in the table.

Let us try to get a better understanding of how the filters affect the expression evaluation by looking at some examples, which you can find also in the companion workbook CH06-02-Calculate-demo.xlsx.

You start by using the Orders table (see Figure 6-1). If you put the sum of Quantity data in a PivotTable and the Channel attribute on the rows, you get the result shown in Figure 6-29.

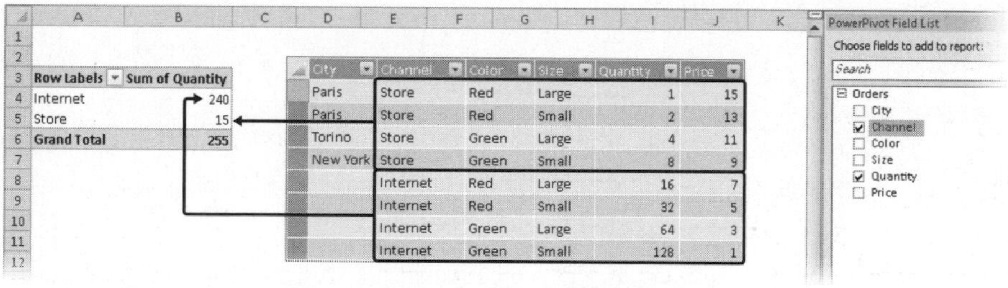
Row Labels
Sum of Quantity
Internet 240
Store 15
Grand Total 255
City
Channel
Color
Size
Quantity
Price
Paris Store Red Large 1 15
Paris Store Red Small 2 13
Torino Store Green Large 4 11
New York Store Green Small 8 9
Internet Red Large 16 7
Internet Red Small 32 5
Internet Green Large 64 3
Internet Green Small 128 1
PowerPivot Field List
Choose fields to add to report:
Search
Orders
City
Channel
Color
Size
Quantity
Price

**FIGURE 6-29** Quantity of orders grouped by Channel.

Now you might need to calculate a measure that is not affected by the selection of the Channel attribute, or in other words, that always calculates the context for all the channels by eliminating the Channel column from the filter context. So you define the QtyAllChannels measure in this way:

```
CALCULATE( SUM( Orders[Quantity] ), ALL( Orders[Channel] ) )
```

You obtain the QtyAllChannels column in the PivotTable that always returns the sum of all the Quantity data from the Orders table, without considering the filter on the Channel attribute, as you can see in Figure 6-30.

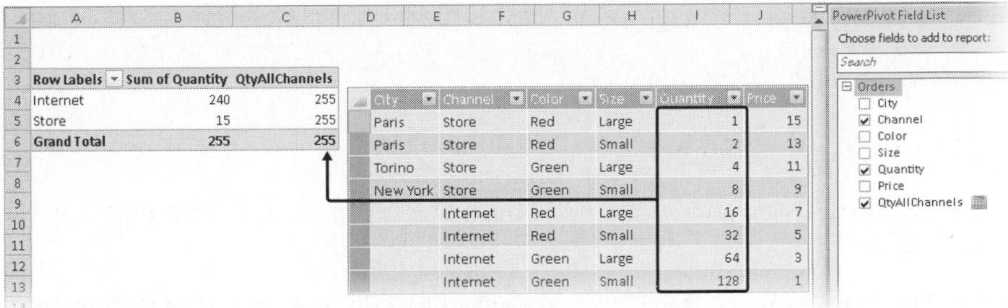


**FIGURE 6-30** Total Quantity for all the channels.

However, if you add the Color attribute to the rows of the PivotTable, the QtyAllChannels is filtered by that attribute, too. In fact, for each color, you have two rows for a Channel and four rows that take into account all the channels. In Figure 6-31, you can see that the sum of Quantity for row 5 of the PivotTable (<Internet, Green>) corresponds to 192, which is the sum of Quantity for the rows that belong to the intersection between the Internet and the Green filters. Meanwhile, the QtyAllChannels calculation is affected by only the Green filter and does not consider the Channel filter on Internet; for this reason, the resulting value of 204 is calculated by summing the Quantity of all four rows that are Green.

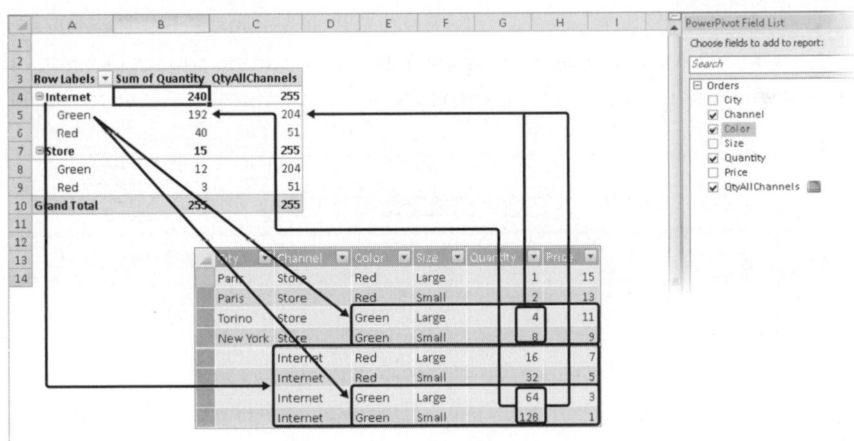


**FIGURE 6-31** The effects of filtering on Channel and Color.

At this point, you might wonder whether the CALCULATE filter parameters are enlarging or restricting the context of evaluation. The rule is the following one.

If the filter context has a filter on a column of a PowerPivot table (which is a selection of a PivotTable, regardless of whether it is a slicer, a report filter, or a row/column selection), *any reference* for that column in one or more filter parameters of the CALCULATE function replaces the existing filter context for that column. Then the filters specified in the CALCULATE parameters are combined by using a logical AND condition among them; in other words, only rows that satisfy all the filter conditions in the filter context are considered.

For instance, consider a filter on the Color Green using a Boolean expression in the CALCULATE function for the QtyGreen measure:

```
CALCULATE( SUM( Orders[Quantity] ), Orders[Color] = "Green" )
```

This is important: a Boolean expression used as a filter parameter in a CALCULATE function corresponds to an equivalent FILTER expression that operates on all the values of a column:

```
CALCULATE( SUM( Orders[Quantity] ),
           FILTER( ALL( Orders[Color]), Orders[Color] = "Green" ) )
```

For this reason, only a single column can be specified in a Boolean expression that is used as a table filter expression in a CALCULATE call.

Now the QtyGreen measure always filters by color Green, and each Channel has only two rows with the color Green, as shown in Figure 6-32.

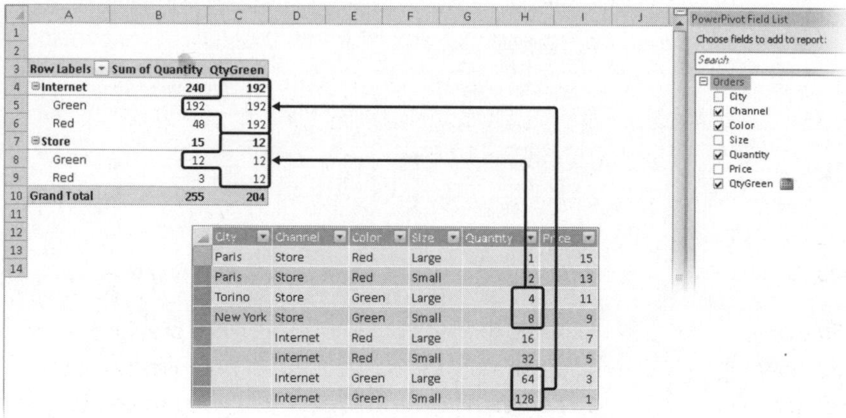


**FIGURE 6-32** The filter on Color in the QtyGreen measure overrides the row filter context defined by the PivotTable.

Any filter expression in a CALCULATE statement overrides the existing selection of the PivotTable for the columns it contains. In the previous rule, we highlighted the reference definition because the FILTER that is internally used in place of the Boolean expression uses a FILTER expression that returns a set of values for the Color column. So the existing selection for the color (the Color is in fact specified in the rows of the PivotTable) is overridden by your filter and only Green rows in the source table are considered for calculating the value of the QtyGreen measure. The reason you lose the current selection on the color attribute is that the ALL( Demo[Color] ) expression returns a set of all the color values and ignores the existing selection.

If you do not want to lose the existing selection of the PivotTable (which means that you do not want to lose the existing filters on the calculation context), you can simply use a function that takes the existing selection into account. So instead of using the ALL( Demo[Color] ) expression, you can use VALUES( Demo[Color] ), which keeps existing selections and returns only the values still available in the color attribute.

In fact, if you create a QtyGreenFiltered measure with the following expression:

```
CALCULATE( SUM( Orders[Quantity] ),
           FILTER( VALUES( Orders[Color]), Orders[Color] = "Green" ) )
```

the Color filter of the PivotTable is still active, and the QtyGreenFiltered column now correctly computes no value for the Red rows, as you can see in Figure 6-33.

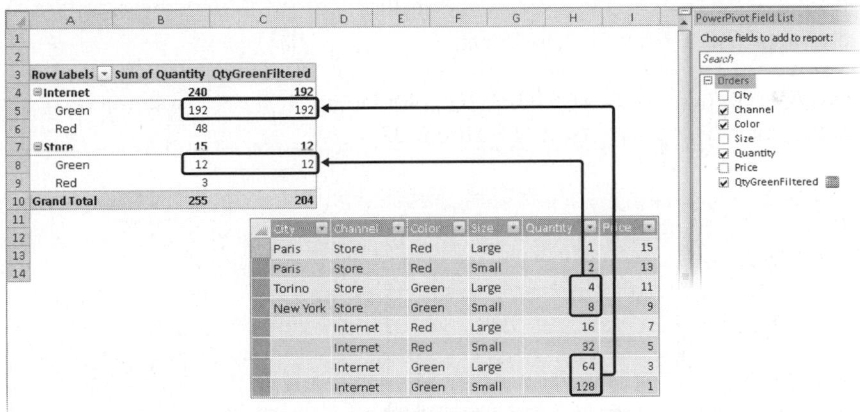


**FIGURE 6-33** The effects of using FILTER( VALUES .. ) in CALCULATE to keep existing selections.

The FILTER expression in a CALCULATE function always replaces the previous context for the referenced columns. However, you can save the existing context by using an expression that uses the existing context and further restricts the members you want to consider for one or more columns. This is what you did when you used the VALUES function instead of ALL as the first parameter of the FILTER call.

At this point, you can summarize the effect of the various combination of FILTER, ALL, and VALUES in a CALCULATE statement.

```
CALCULATE( SUM( Orders[Quantity] ),
           Orders[Color] = "Green" )

CALCULATE( SUM( Orders[Quantity] ),
           FILTER( ALL( Orders[Color] ), Orders[Color] = "Green" ) )
```

The preceding syntaxes are equivalent and both clear the existing Color filter and then set a filter on the Green Color.

```
CALCULATE( SUM( Orders[Quantity] ),
           FILTER( VALUES( Orders[Color] ), Orders[Color] = "Green" ) )
```

The preceding syntax keeps the existing Color filters by adding a further filter on Green.

```
CALCULATE( SUM( Orders[Quantity] ),
           FILTER( ALL( Orders[Color] ), Orders[Color] = "Green" ),
           VALUES( Orders[Color] ) )
```

This syntax is like the one that precedes it and keeps existing Color filters by adding a further filter on Green. Note that the first filter (FILTER( ALL ... )) would consider all the colors, but the second expression (VALUES) considers only the current selection of colors. The two filters work by using an AND condition, and the final result is the same as if you just used VALUES instead of ALL in the first parameter of the FILTER call, as in the previous syntax.

```
CALCULATE( SUM( Orders[Quantity] ),
           FILTER( ALL( Orders ), Orders[Color] = "Green" ) )
```

This new syntax clears existing filters on all the columns of the Orders table, and then sets a filter on *all* the columns (City, Channel, Size, and so on, not just Color) by using the rows of the Orders table that meet the filter condition (in this case, the rows that are Green).

**Important** Notice that a filter parameter for CALCULATE has a slightly different behavior if it represents a set of members of a single column or a set of rows from a table. In this last case, any column filter in the same table existing in the filter context before the CALCULATE call is cleared by the presence of this set of rows. However, there could be other filter parameters that specify other conditions for rows and/or columns of the same table. If the same column or the same table is filtered in more parameters of the same CALCULATE call, the resulting filter context contains only rows that satisfy all of the filter conditions.

Finally, let us caution you about the first parameter you pass to the FILTER function. If you consider this possible definition of the QtyGreen measure

```
CALCULATE( SUM( Orders[Quantity] ),
           FILTER( Orders, Orders[Color] = "Green" ) )
```

you pass the whole Orders table to the FILTER condition, which results in a filter of the filter context with *all the columns of the Orders table!* Accordingly, you apply a restriction on the color Green and you get the same result as before (no rows for any color but green; the selection of color of the PivotTable is still applied so that row for the color Red returns an empty cell), but remember, the FILTER is returning *all* the columns. What does this mean?

Well, consider a further selection on the PivotTable wherein the Size attribute is filtered by Large. In Figure 6-34, you can see the result of this last QtyGreen definition.

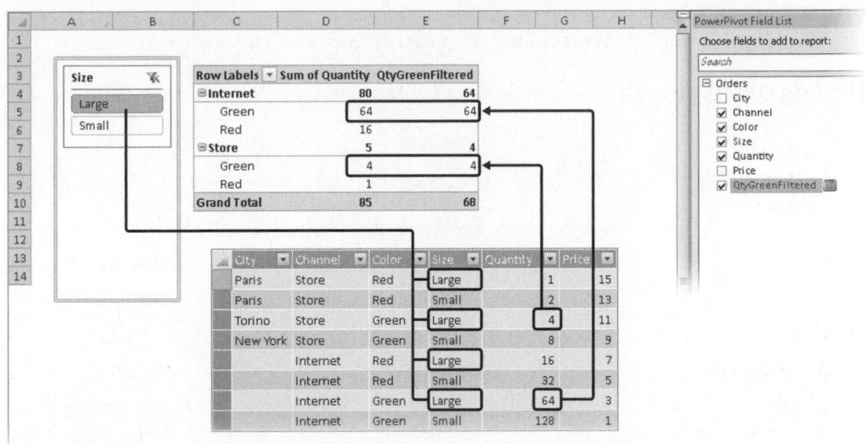


**FIGURE 6-34** The result using the FILTER on the Orders table seems to be the same as the previous definition of QtyGreenFiltered.

Now let us add another filter to the CALCULATE function so that we also filter the rows with Size equal to Small, defining a QtyGreenSmall measure.

```
CALCULATE( SUM( Orders[Quantity] ),
           FILTER( Orders, Orders[Color] = "Green" ),
           Orders[Size] = "Small" )
```

As you have seen before, that definition corresponds to the following:

```
CALCULATE( SUM( Orders[Quantity] ),
           FILTER( Orders, Orders[Color] = "Green" ),
           FILTER( ALL( Orders[Size] ), Orders[Size] = "Small" ) )
```

The result is that the filter for Large defined in the PivotTable plus the filter for Small defined in the QtyGreenSmall measure returns no rows at all in the measure result, as you can see in Figure 6-35. If you think about it, this behavior is not very intuitive.

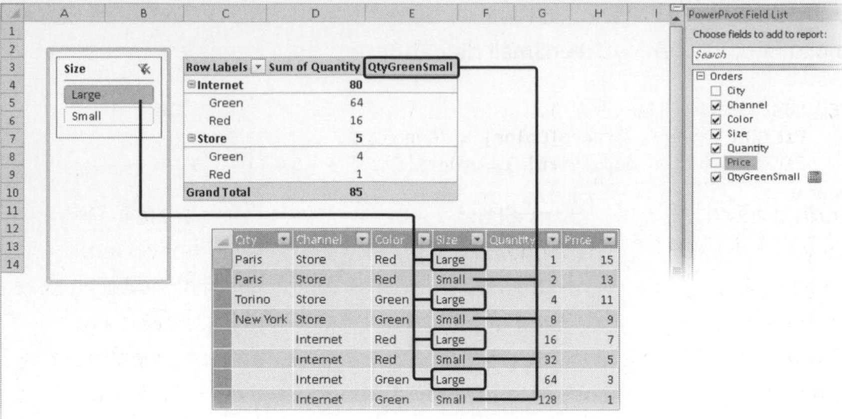


**FIGURE 6-35** Double filter on Large (slicer) and Small (CALCULATE) returns an empty QtyGreenSmall.

Our filter of the Size column in the CALCULATE expression is actually restricting the current selection and is not replacing it. Nevertheless, if you apply the filter just on Size, without the filter on Color, you have this QtySmall measure definition:

```
CALCULATE( SUM( Orders[Quantity] ),
           Orders[Size] = "Small" )
```

It produces the result in Figure 6-36, which replaces the Large selection of the slicer of the PivotTable.

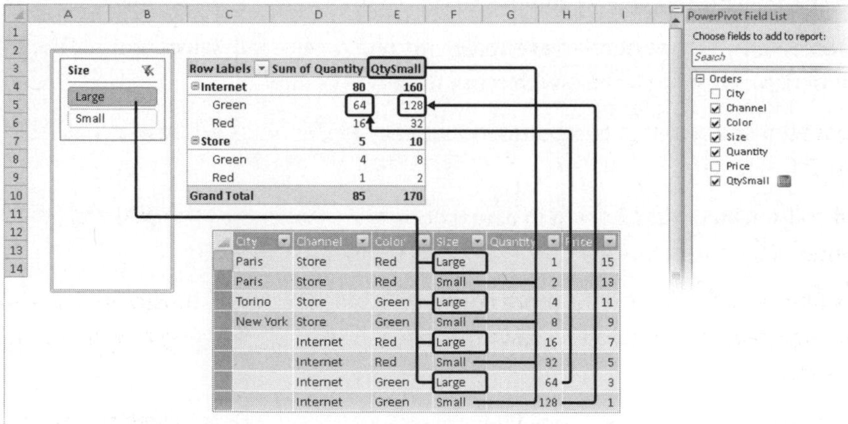


**FIGURE 6-36** The QtySmall measure overrides the Large selection on the Size Slicer.

This last calculation (QtySmall) is simple to explain because it exhibits the same behavior you saw before with the first QtyGreen measure, wherein the filter of the color Green replaced any existing color selection in the PivotTable. The difference in the QtyGreenSmall calculation is the other FILTER parameter, which returns all the columns from the Orders table. Consider the boldface filter in the QtyGreenSmall definition:

```
CALCULATE( SUM( Orders[Quantity] ),
           FILTER( Orders, Orders[Color] = "Green" ),
           FILTER( ALL( Orders[Size] ), Orders[Size] = "Small" ) )
```

The filter on the color Green returns all the columns of the Orders table in the current filter context. If you consider the corresponding rows for the cell D5 of the PivotTable (<Internet, Green, Large>), this is just one row (the one with 64 as Quantity), and this row has the Large value for the Size column. When you apply the second filter, you have a single value for the attribute Size, which is Small. At this point, the intersection between those two sets of Size (one is only Large, the other is only Small) is an empty set. So the result for the QtyGreenSmall measure is empty because there are no corresponding rows for the selection made, as you saw in Figure 6-35.

This can be tricky, but you finally see this behavior:

- The CALCULATE function applies a calculation (the first parameter) for each cell, considering the resulting filter obtained by replacing the filters (the second and following parameters) of the current filter context.
- Each filter constraint in a CALCULATE function can be either a table filter constraint or a column filter constraint.
- A column filter constraint has values for only one column and is defined by using a Boolean filter constraint or a function returning a single column table.
- A table filter constraint can have values for one or more columns and is defined by using a function returning a table with more than one column.
- Each filter constraint is computed individually in the filters expressions of the CALCULATE function.
- If a column value is specified in at least one filter, it replaces the selection of the filter context for that column.
- If a filter expression returns more columns, it is a table filter constraint. The CALCULATE function considers only table rows that have at least a matching row in the table filter constraint.
- If a column is specified in many filter constraints, the resulting values are the intersection of these sets of values (for that column).
- After all the filters have been evaluated, the intersection of all the filter constraints determines the filter context for the expression passed as the first parameter to the CALCULATE function.

Despite its complexity, this calculation is pretty fast. The key point is to understand all the side effects when a filter returns more columns than those you explicitly specified in the filter condition itself, which is something you have to consider carefully each time you use one or more FILTER functions in a CALCULATE expression.

## Understanding the EARLIER Function

You have seen that there are two distinct concepts in evaluation context: the row context and the filter context. The CALCULATE function can change the evaluation context, and functions such as FILTER, SUMX, and other aggregation functions ending with an X character define a new row context for each iterated value. It is interesting to note that a new row context might be generated while an external operation in the same expression was using another row context. In other words, a row context might be nested within another one while you use several DAX functions nested in each other. However, only the innermost row context is the one that remains active; none of the others is considered anymore, by default.

For example, consider the table shown in Figure 6-37, which you can find in the companion workbook CH06-03-Earlier-demo.xlsx:

| | A | B |
|---|---|---|
| 1 | Date | Value |
| 2 | 1/1/2009 | 10 |
| 3 | 2/28/2009 | 20 |
| 4 | 3/31/2009 | 30 |
| 5 | 4/30/2009 | 40 |
| 6 | 11/30/2009 | 50 |
| 7 | 12/31/2009 | 60 |
| 8 | 1/31/2010 | 70 |
| 9 | 2/28/2010 | 80 |
| 10 | 3/31/2010 | 90 |
| 11 | 4/30/2010 | 100 |

**FIGURE 6-37** The table used to demonstrate the EARLIER behavior.

You can create a linked table in PowerPivot and then define a calculated column with the year-to-date value updated for each row. This is just a theoretical example because we see later in Chapter 7, "Date Calculations in DAX," that there are specific functions to calculate year-to-date values, and most of the time it is better to use a measure instead of a calculated column to do this type of calculation. Nevertheless, trying to solve the year-to-date issue by writing a DAX expression can be helpful for understanding the EARLIER function behavior.

If you look at the Figure 6-38, you can see a YTD column with the correct value already calculated. First of all, to create the necessary DAX formula, you need to describe the required algorithm. A simple (and not complete) definition might be *sum all the values of the rows with a date less than or equal to the date of the row considered for the calculation.* However, this is not enough because in this case the values for year 2010 would also include all the values of rows belonging to year 2009. A better definition is *sum all the values of the rows with a year equal to the year of the row considered and with a date less than or equal to the date of the row considered for the calculation.*

| Date | Value | YTD |
|---|---|---|
| 1/1/2009 | 10 | 10 |
| 2/28/2009 | 20 | 30 |
| 3/31/2009 | 30 | 60 |
| 4/30/2009 | 40 | 100 |
| 11/30/2009 | 50 | 150 |
| 12/31/2009 | 60 | 210 |
| 1/31/2010 | 70 | 70 |
| 2/28/2010 | 80 | 150 |
| 3/31/2010 | 90 | 240 |
| 4/30/2010 | 100 | 340 |

**FIGURE 6-38** A linked table in PowerPivot, with the calculated column YTD.

To get this result, you have to define the YTD formula in DAX. If you try to translate into DAX the statement you just read in the English language, the problem to solve would be how to define the FILTER condition because you have to compare the value of a column during the FILTER operation with the value of the current row that is used to make the whole YTD calculation. In other words, you might write something like this:

```
= SUMX( FILTER( Sales table, condition ),
        Sales[Value] )
```

where *condition* determines whether the row iterated in the FILTER condition is filtered or not, comparing its date with the date of the current row in the external loop (which is the iteration of the rows in the Sales table with which you calculate the value of YTD for each row).

It is important to remember what is going to happen: there will be a loop over all of the rows of the Sales table. For each of these rows, the DAX expression is evaluated. The presence of a FILTER function to get the subset of rows that have to be summed determines another loop, and this means a new row context. At this point, every access to a column of this linked table operates in the new row context, but this is a problem if you want to get the value of the previous row context, the one that invoked the calculation of the YTD column.

The EARLIER function in DAX provides exactly this behavior: getting data from the previous row context. Any column referenced in an EARLIER function call returns the value of that column, ignoring the current row context.

### EARLIER Parameters and the EARLIEST Function

The EARLIER function has a second optional parameter that specifies how many evaluation passes have to be discarded. This is useful when you have multiple, iterating, nested functions, changing the row context multiple times. If the second parameter is omitted, it defaults to 1, which indicates the previous row context.

A similar function, named EARLIEST, has a single parameter, which is the column name. It returns the column value out of any evaluation pass (in other words, it is the first row context of the whole DAX expression). You can get the same result of EARLIEST by passing -1 to the second parameter of EARLIER.

So because you need the Date value of the current row before the execution of the FILTER statement, you can use the EARLIER syntax:

```
EARLIER( Sales[Date] )
```

So the right DAX definition of the YTD calculated column is the following one:

```
= SUMX( FILTER( Sales, Sales[Date] <= EARLIER( Sales[Date] )
                       && YEAR( Sales[Date] ) = YEAR( EARLIER( Sales[Date] ) ) ),
        Sales[Value])
```

### EARLIER and Filter Context

The EARLIER function operates only on row contexts. There are no DAX functions (other than CALCULATE) that can return an expression value for a different (previous) filter context because filter context is not modified when you use this approach.

## Summary

In this chapter, you have seen how the evaluation context works and how it can be manipulated when you use the CALCULATE function in a DAX expression. The evaluation context can be defined by a filter context and a row context. Each of these contexts has an effect on DAX expressions and they are also affected by the presence of relationships between tables in a PowerPivot model.

Chapter 7

# Date Calculations in DAX

Many analyses of data have to deal with dates. Microsoft SQL Server PowerPivot for Excel offers a number of functions that simplify many calculations on dates that are typical in a business scenario, but using the right function in the right way requires some explanation. As you see in this chapter, the first step in date calculations is to create a separate Dates table that supports most of the requirements.

## Working with a Dates Table

In some examples in the previous chapters, we defined calculated columns that extracted parts of the date that we used to group dates, such as the year and the month. This technique might be applied to each table containing a date, but it would quickly become hard to manage. It is better to create a separate table containing a row for each date, using the date as a key to link that Dates table with other tables that contain data related to a date. In this way, you obtain a model wherein all attributes about dates are included in a separate table and are easy to access when you browse data with a PivotTable, as you can see in Figure 7-1.

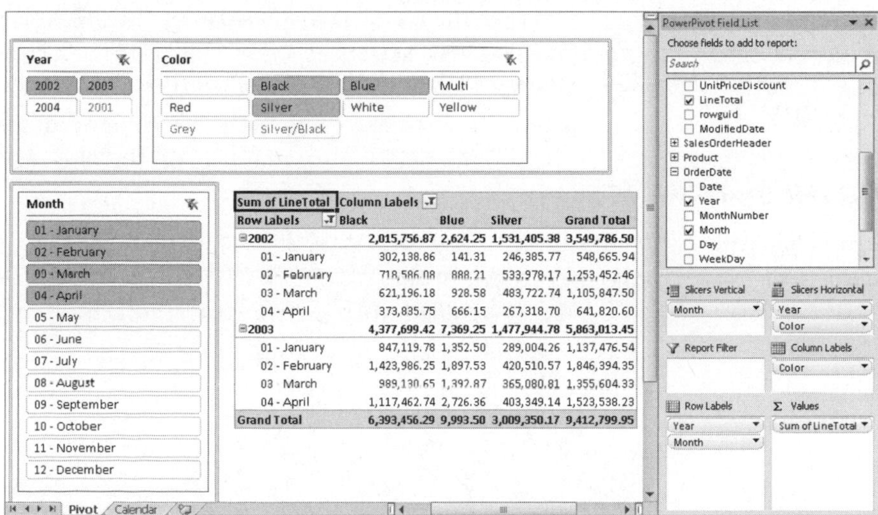


**FIGURE 7-1** PivotTable browsing Order data by using a Dates table named OrderDate.

A Dates table is also useful for making calculations using special DAX functions that operate on Dates. These functions, of which DATEADD is an example, often require that all the days in a given range exist in the data table—otherwise, a missing day might result in a wrong calculation. You might have no sales for a day (in fact, it is pretty common to have no sales on nonworking days), so the separate Dates table allows you to make the right calculations without requiring any modification of the original table that contains measures to analyze.

The only side effect of this technique is that you need to create a Dates table in PowerPivot for each date attribute you want to analyze in a single table because there can be only one relationship between two tables in PowerPivot.

**Tip** Creating multiple relationships with the same lookup table is not supported in PowerPivot. For this reason, you must duplicate the Dates table whenever you have more date columns that you want to analyze in the same table, such as Order Date and Ship Date attributes in a Sales table.

## How to Build a Dates Table

To create a Dates table in PowerPivot, you need a data source that contains at least a column with all days included in the period of time you want to analyze. For example, if the minimum and maximum date contained in Sales data is July 3, 2001 and July 27, 2004, respectively, the range of dates you should consider is between January 1, 2001 and December 31, 2004. In this way, you have all the days for all the years containing sales data.

In Chapter 3, "Introduction to DAX," you saw how to create Day, Month, and Year calculated columns for a Calendar table that has just the Date column as existing data. However, if you do not have an external source providing you with a valid Dates table (such as a corresponding table in SQL Server), we suggest that you create all the calculated columns for a Dates table in Excel. In this way, it will be easier to copy and paste the entire contents of that table into a new one when you have to handle more dates—for example, Order Date and Ship Date—in your PowerPivot model.

To create your Dates table, you can start by typing Date in a cell and 1/1/2001 in the cell below it, as you can see in Figure 7-2.

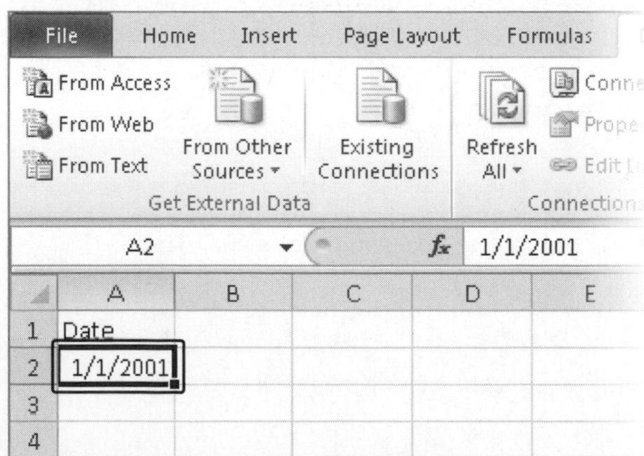


**FIGURE 7-2** Creating a Dates table in Excel.

Then in the bottom-right corner of the cell containing the 1/1/2001 date (which is highlighted in Figure 7-2), you can drag down until you reach the date of 12/31/2004, as you can see in Figure 7-3.

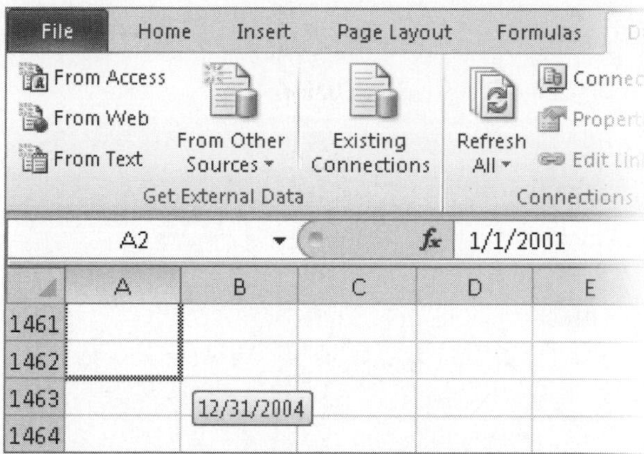


**FIGURE 7-3** Selecting end range for creating a Dates table in Excel.

At this point, you can release the mouse. You just created a list of all the days included from the beginning of 2001 to the end of 2004. Now you can click the Date cell, click the Format As Table button on the Home tab of the ribbon, and then confirm that your table has headers, as you can see in Figure 7-4.

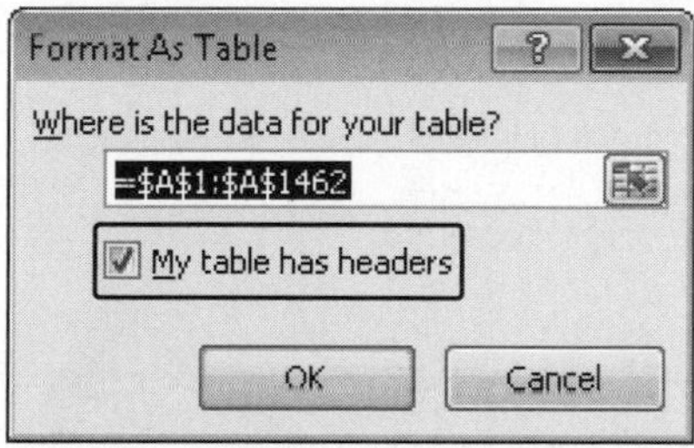


**FIGURE 7-4** Confirming the range of the Table and confirming that your table has headers.

In Figure 7-5, you can see how to give the Calendar name to the table by using the text box available on the Design tab of the Table Tools contextual tab of the Excel ribbon and how to start adding new columns by right-clicking a cell in the table and selecting the InsertTable Column To The Right item from the Insert context menu.

In Figure 7-6, you can see how to define a formula in an empty cell of the new column to calculate the Year. After you type **=YEAR(**, you can click the Date column to get the right syntax to read that column, as shown in Figure 7-6.

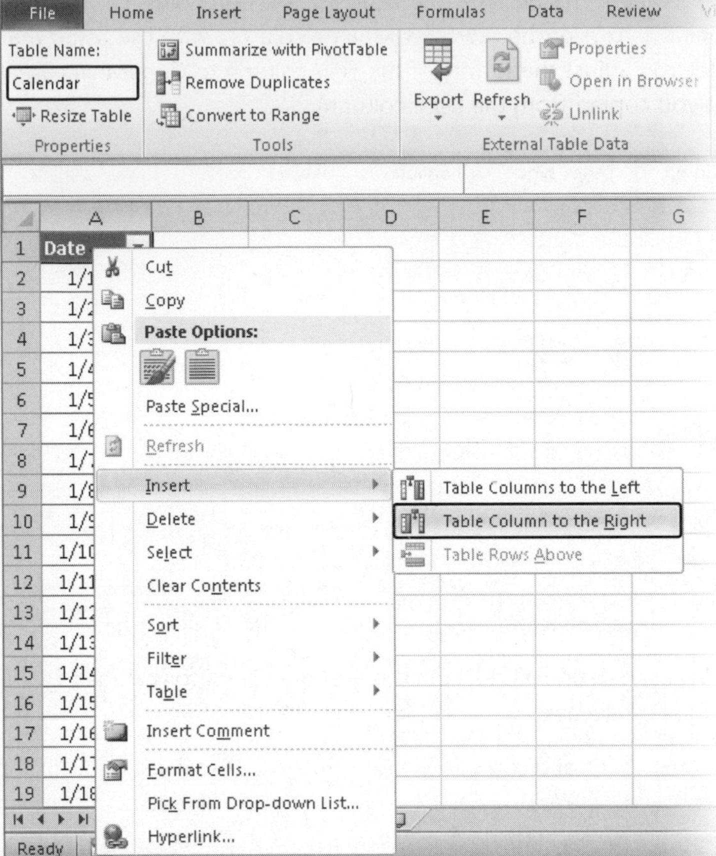


**FIGURE 7-5** Inserting a new column in the Dates table.

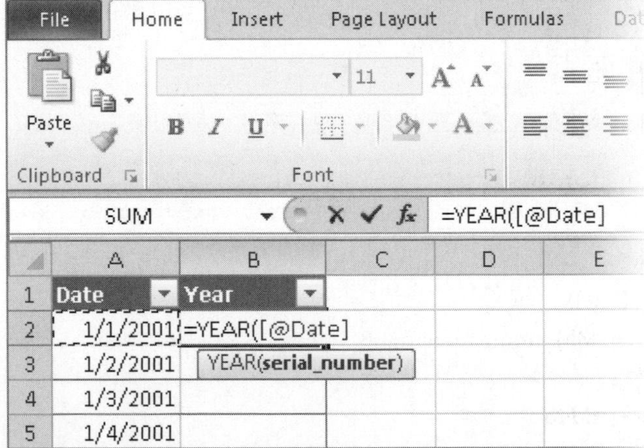


**FIGURE 7-6** Defining the formula for the Year column in Excel.

At this point, you can type the closing parenthesis and then press Enter. The formula is automatically copied for all the rows of the table in the same column, with the result that you can see in Figure 7-7 (after you adjust the format of the Year column to General in case it was a different format that you copied from the Date column).

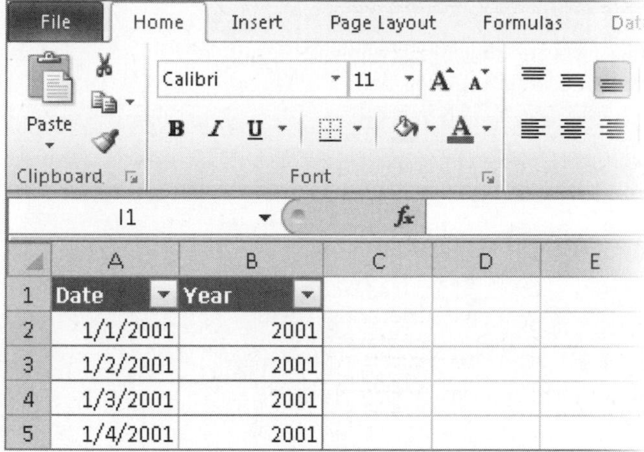


**FIGURE 7-7** The Year column calculated for all the rows.

With this technique, you can define all the columns that are useful for navigating the data that aggregate date in several ways.

Figure 7-8 shows the final result of a complete Dates table with fiscal year starting on July 1. You can find this table in the CH07-01-Calendar.xlsx workbook included on the companion DVD. Table 7-1 contains the formula definitions for all of the columns.

| | Date | Year | MonthNumber | Month | Day | WeekDay | Quarter | FiscalYear | FiscalQuarter |
|---|---|---|---|---|---|---|---|---|---|
| 545 | 6/28/2002 | 2002 | 6 | 06 - June | 28 | Friday | Q2 | FY-2002 | FQ4 |
| 546 | 6/29/2002 | 2002 | 6 | 06 - June | 29 | Saturday | Q2 | FY-2002 | FQ4 |
| 547 | 6/30/2002 | 2002 | 6 | 06 - June | 30 | Sunday | Q2 | FY-2002 | FQ4 |
| 548 | 7/1/2002 | 2002 | 7 | 07 - July | 1 | Monday | Q3 | FY-2003 | FQ1 |
| 549 | 7/2/2002 | 2002 | 7 | 07 - July | 2 | Tuesday | Q3 | FY-2003 | FQ1 |
| 550 | 7/3/2002 | 2002 | 7 | 07 - July | 3 | Wednesday | Q3 | FY-2003 | FQ1 |
| 551 | 7/4/2002 | 2002 | 7 | 07 - July | 4 | Thursday | Q3 | FY-2003 | FQ1 |
| 552 | 7/5/2002 | 2002 | 7 | 07 - July | 5 | Friday | Q3 | FY-2003 | FQ1 |

**FIGURE 7-8** A complete Dates table with fiscal year starting on July 1.

**TABLE 7-1 Formula definitions for the Dates table in Excel.**

| Column | Formula |
|---|---|
| Year | =YEAR([@Date]) |
| MonthNumber | =MONTH([@Date]) |
| Month | =TEXT([@Date],"MM - mmmm") |
| Day | =DAY([@Date]) |
| WeekDay | =TEXT([@Date],"dddd") |
| Quarter | ="Q" & ROUNDUP(MONTH([@Date]) /3,0) |
| FiscalYear | ="FY-" & [@Year]+IF([@MonthNumber]<7,0,1) |
| FiscalQuarter | ="FQ" &MOD(CEILING(22+[@MonthNumber]-6-1,3)/3,4)+1 |

**Note** Table 7-1 does not include a column for week number. The table omits it because there are several techniques for calculating the week number in a year, and different businesses have different ways to make this calculation. More important, sometimes a week belongs to a year that is different from the calendar year—the fiscal year, for example—even if only for a few days of a year. In that case, you also need to define a WeekYear column that must be used for browsing the weeks in a meaningful way. We preferred not to include a specific week calculation to keep the Dates table simple and to avoid possible confusion introducing an algorithm that might be different than that used in your company.

Now you can import this table in PowerPivot as a linked table. The result is shown in Figure 7-9.

| Date | Year | MonthNumber | Month | Day | WeekDay | Quarter | FiscalYear | FiscalQuarter |
|---|---|---|---|---|---|---|---|---|
| 1/1/2001 | 2001 | 1 | 01 - January | 1 | Monday | Q1 | FY-2001 | FQ3 |
| 1/2/2001 | 2001 | 1 | 01 - January | 2 | Tuesday | Q1 | FY-2001 | FQ3 |
| 1/3/2001 | 2001 | 1 | 01 - January | 3 | Wednesday | Q1 | FY-2001 | FQ3 |
| 1/4/2001 | 2001 | 1 | 01 - January | 4 | Thursday | Q1 | FY-2001 | FQ3 |
| 1/5/2001 | 2001 | 1 | 01 - January | 5 | Friday | Q1 | FY-2001 | FQ3 |
| 1/6/2001 | 2001 | 1 | 01 - January | 6 | Saturday | Q1 | FY-2001 | FQ3 |

**FIGURE 7-9** The Dates table imported in PowerPivot as a linked table.

You can see that the month name contains the month number in front of it, so December is described as *12 – December*. It is useful to have the month names automatically sorted. However, if you want to sort month names but also want to avoid the initial number, please take a look at the section "Custom Sorting in PivotTables" in Chapter 8, "Mastering PivotTables," where we describe how to sort columns of a Dates table in a PivotTable.

You might want to change the data types of some columns in the Dates table. Whenever you import the Excel table into PowerPivot, columns like Year, MonthNumber, and Day are usually defined as Whole Number data types. For this reason, when you select one of these columns in the PivotTable, the selected attribute is placed by default in the Values area of the PivotTable and is aggregated when you use the Sum function. You might prefer to change the data types of these columns to Text so that by default they are used to group data in rows.

If you want to test your new Calendar table, you should now import the SalesOrderHeader, SalesOrderDetail, Customer, and Product tables from the AdventureWorks database into the same PowerPivot model. Relationships between these tables are automatically detected during the import. At this point, you need to create a relationship between the OrderDate field of the SalesOrderHeader table and the Date field of the Calendar table you just imported. Before starting, in PowerPivot you have to rename the Calendar table to OrderDate so that it expresses the dates it represents. Then you click the Create Relationship button on the Design tab of the ribbon and fill in the dialog box, as shown in Figure 7-10.

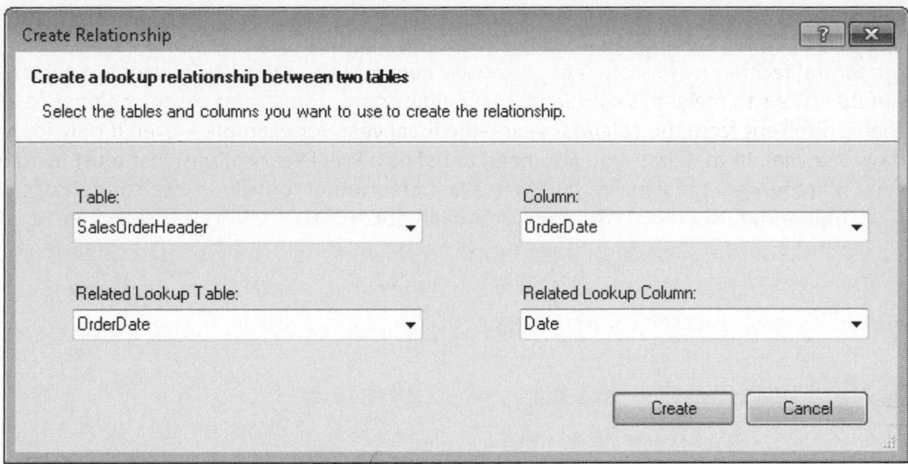


**FIGURE 7-10** Create a relationship between the SalesOrderHeader and OrderDate tables.

At this point, the model is ready to browse data, as you saw at the beginning of this chapter, in Figure 7-1.

## Working with Multiple Dates Tables

In the model you saw in the previous section, each Order has several dates. In case you want to analyze not only the Order Date but also the Ship Date, you need to define a second table in PowerPivot because the same table (that is, the Dates table) cannot have more than one relationship with a given table (SalesOrderHeader).

At this point, you have two options. You can either create a new linked table starting from the same table you used before (shown in Figure 7-8) or copy that table into Excel and create the linked table starting from this copy. The first option is not the best one because in PowerPivot you can have only one linked table for a given Excel table. If you try to create a linked table starting from the same Calendar table you defined before, the warning message shown in Figure 7-11 appears.

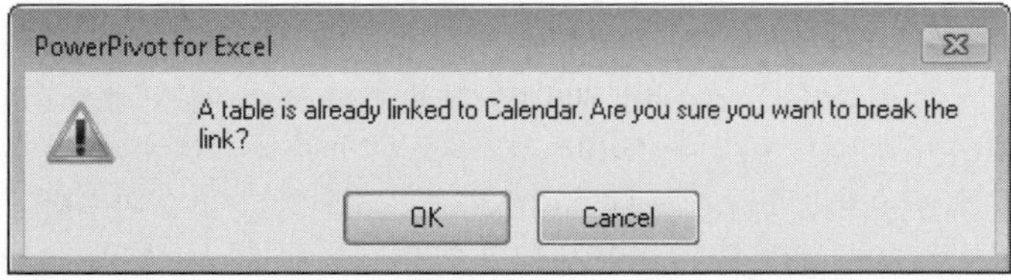


**FIGURE 7-11** A warning against trying to create a linked table for an Excel table already used as a linked table.

If you continue creating a linked table this way, you cannot update the OrderDate table anymore. If you create a model that must be refreshed over time and that is likely to have a life cycle longer than the current year, you are better off using another way, which allows future updates.

The second option requires you to copy and paste the existing Calendar table in Excel. Before you do that, you should rename the Calendar table in Excel, using the same name we used for the corresponding linked table in PowerPivot, which is OrderDate. To do that, you can type the OrderDate name into the Table Name text box available on the Design tab of the Table Tools contextual tab of the Excel ribbon, as you can see in Figure 7-12.

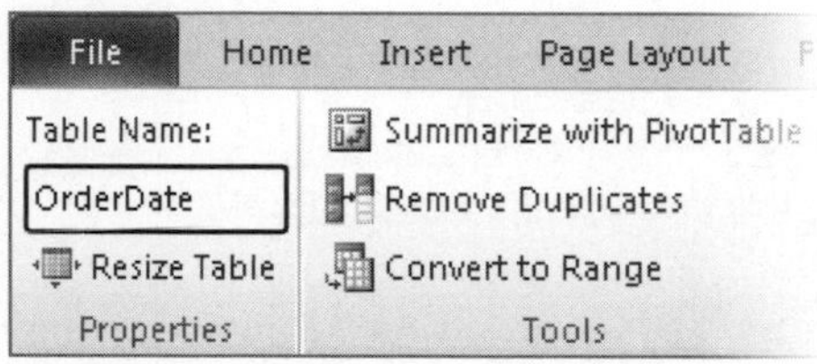


**FIGURE 7-12** Renaming the table OrderDate, in Excel.

At this point, if you try to Update the OrderDate linked table in PowerPivot, you get the error message shown in Figure 7-13.

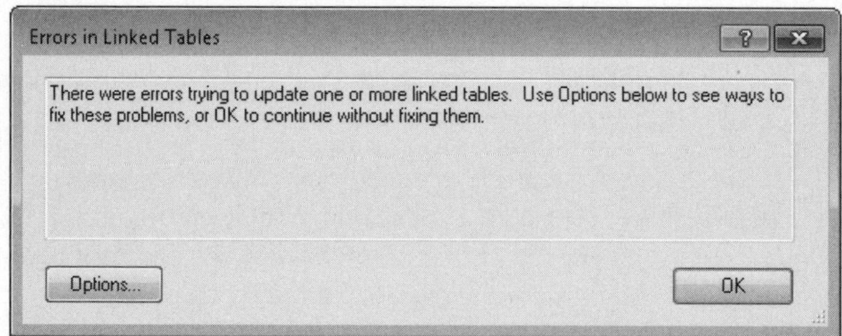


**FIGURE 7-13** The error message you get when you try to update OrderDate after changing the name of the underlying Excel table.

When you click the Options button, you can select the Change Excel Table Name option. Then you choose the OrderDate table in the combo box that shows the available tables in Excel, as you can see in Figure 7-14.

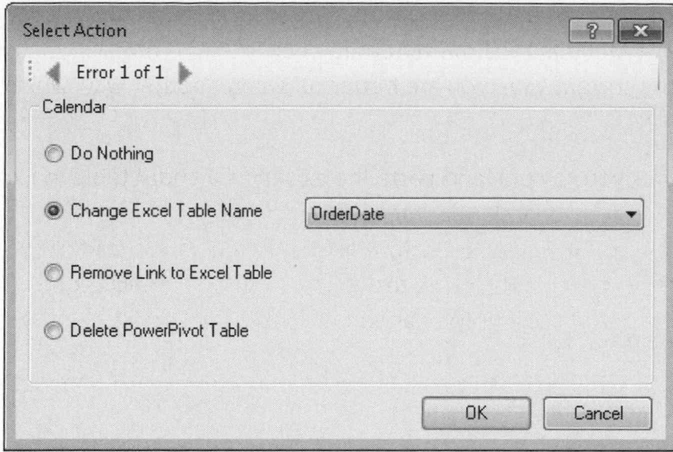


**FIGURE 7-14** Fixing the error in LinkedTable by selecting the correct underlying Excel table.

Now you can copy the OrderDate table in Excel into a new one that we call ShipDate. You might do this by selecting the whole table, copying it, and then pasting it into an empty space of your Excel workbook. However, another option is to use a single dedicated Excel worksheet for each table like these so that you can simply duplicate the worksheet into a new one. In this way, whenever you need to add columns or rows to the table, you never have to move other existing tables. Moreover, tables are easily accessible when you click the corresponding worksheet name in Excel.

To create a copy of the worksheet containing the OrderDate table, you have to right-click the OrderDate label and select Move Or Copy from the context menu that you can see in Figure 7-15.

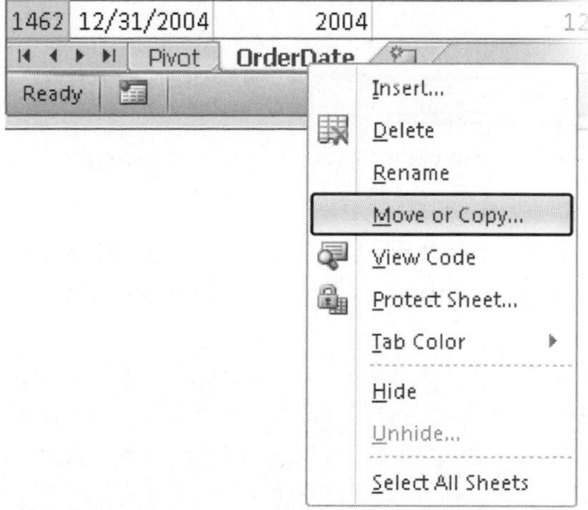


**FIGURE 7-15** Choosing Move Or Copy from the context menu.

The selection displays the dialog box shown in Figure 7-16, in which you have to select the Create A Copy check box and choose the position of the new sheet.

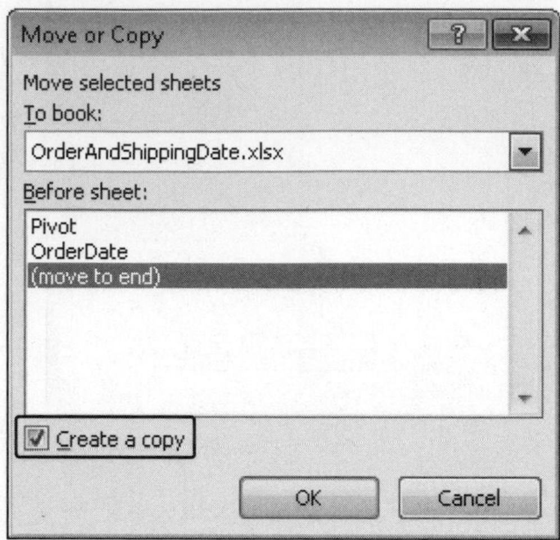


**FIGURE 7-16** Selecting the option to create a copy of the worksheet to place at the end of the list.

At this point, you rename both the table (using the same procedure you saw already in Figure 7-12) and the worksheet (by right-clicking on the OrderDate (2) label and then selecting Rename from the context menu that you can see in Figure 7-17); you use the new ShipDate name.

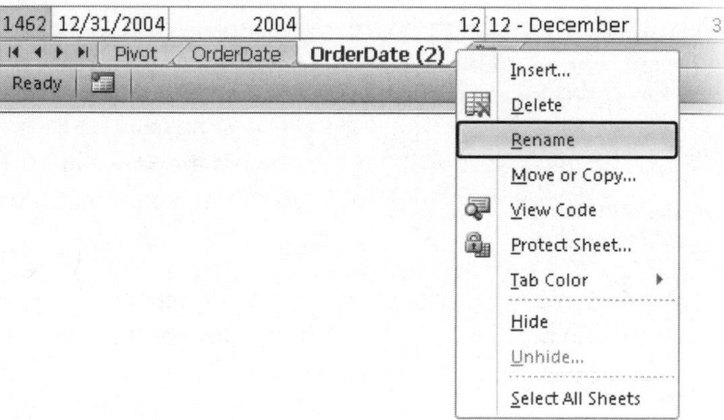


**FIGURE 7-17** The Rename option in the context menu.

Finally, you can create a linked table for the ShipDate table by clicking the Create Linked Table button on the PowerPivot ribbon. Again, you have to create a relationship in PowerPivot between the SalesOrderHeader and ShipDate tables, by using the ShipDate column of the SalesOrderHeader table this time, as you can see in Figure 7-18.

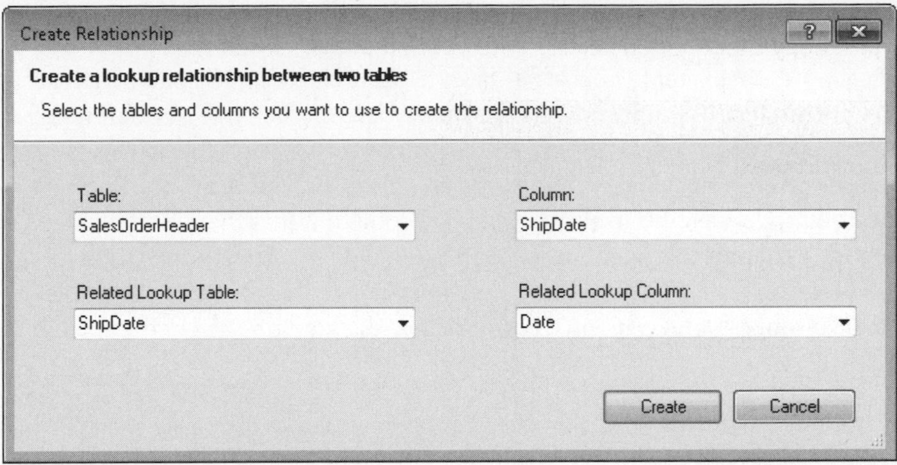


**FIGURE 7-18** Creating a relationship between the SalesOrderHeader and OrderDate tables.

You can find the resulting model in the CH07-02-OrderAndShippingDate.xlsx workbook included on the companion DVD. However, as you can see in the next section, duplicating tables might not be enough. Because Excel does not show the table name to which a column belongs when you use it for Slicers and Filters, you might want to add a prefix to your columns. It is better to do that directly in the source Excel table rather than renaming the columns in PowerPivot only so that the overall model is simpler to understand.

## Dates Columns in Different Tables

You must define a separate Dates table to distinguish the semantics of different dates in your data. This is certainly true whenever different date columns belong to the same table, as in the case of the OrderDate and ShipDate columns in the SalesOrderHeader table. However, when you have dates columns in different tables, you have to evaluate whether the semantics of these dates is the same or not.

Every time you have a different role for a date, you have to create separate Dates tables to browse data, just as you saw in this section. On the other hand, you have to use the same Dates table whenever these dates have the same meaning, at least for your analysis.

For example, if you have an OrderDate in the Sales table and a CallDate in a CallCenterCalls table, you might decide to create two separate data tables named OrderDate and CallDate. But you might also want to create a single Dates table that connects both events, which would ease the browsing over time of data from both tables in the same report. If you have no other dates in your model, no ambiguities arise from that arrangement, but if there are other dates involved in the same model, you should consider a separate model for doing correlation analysis, avoiding misleading names in your model.

## Differentiating Columns in Multiple Dates Tables

Duplicating the same table, such as a Dates table, multiple times in a PowerPivot model makes the resulting PivotTable difficult to read whenever the same attributes are used from different tables. For example, in Figure 7-19, you can see a PivotTable in which the Year from OrderDate has been put in rows and in the first slicer, and the Year from ShipDate has been put in columns and in the second slicer. The problem is that there is no evidence of the table that a column belongs to whenever it is moved into slicers, filters, rows, or columns of the PivotTable. The final model for the example of this section is available in the CH07-03-PrefixedDateColumns.xlsx workbook included on the companion DVD.

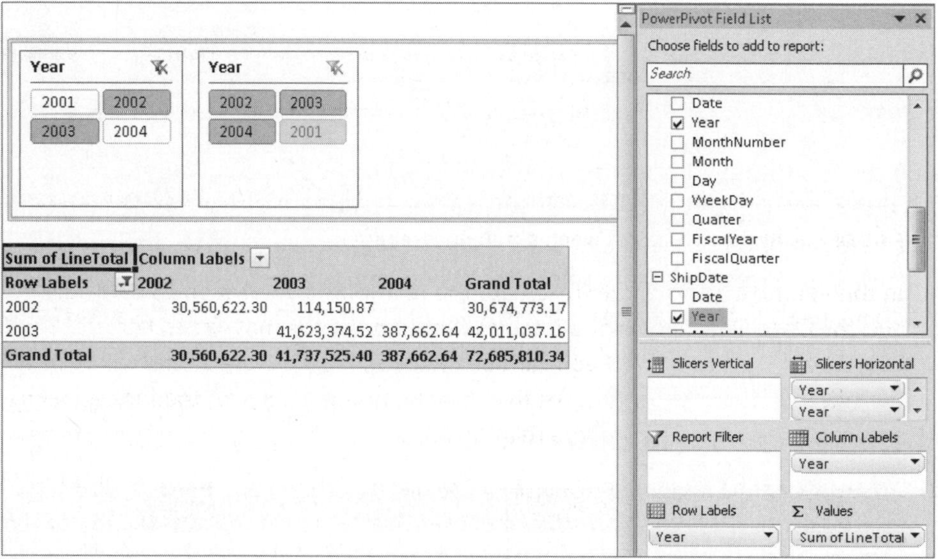


**FIGURE 7-19** Columns with the same name from different tables are not recognizable in a PivotTable.

So in case you create a model with multiple copies of the same tables, you should differentiate the names of the columns so that they are immediately recognizable in a report. You can edit the table names in Excel by adding a prefix to each column. In Figure 7-20, you can see the heading of the OrderDate table, wherein each column has been prefixed with the word *Order*. You can do the same for the ShipDate column by using the *Ship* prefix.

| | A | B | C | D | E | F | G | H | I |
|---|---|---|---|---|---|---|---|---|---|
| 1 | OrderDate | OrderYear | OrderMonthNumber | OrderMonth | OrderDay | OrderWeekDay | OrderQuarter | OrderFiscalYear | OrderFiscalQuarter |
| 2 | 1/1/2001 | 2001 | 1 | 01 - January | 1 | Monday | Q1 | FY-2001 | FQ3 |
| 3 | 1/2/2001 | 2001 | 1 | 01 - January | 2 | Tuesday | Q1 | FY-2001 | FQ3 |
| 4 | 1/3/2001 | 2001 | 1 | 01 - January | 3 | Wednesday | Q1 | FY-2001 | FQ3 |
| 5 | 1/4/2001 | 2001 | 1 | 01 - January | 4 | Thursday | Q1 | FY-2001 | FQ3 |

**FIGURE 7-20** The columns of OrderDate prefixed with *Order*.

## Broken Relationships After Columns Are Renamed

Renaming a column that is part of a relationship breaks that relationship. For example, if you try to update the linked tables after renaming the Date columns, you receive the error message shown in Figure 7-21. The existing relationships were based on a column (Date) that does not exist anymore.

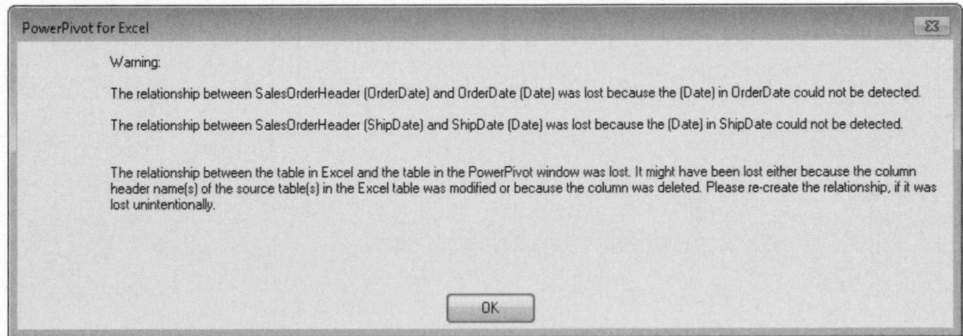


**FIGURE 7-21** Relationships lost when a column is renamed.

In this example, you need to re-create the relationships between SalesOrderHeader and the OrderDate and ShipDate tables (through the columns OrderDate and ShipDate, respectively). In Figure 7-22, you can see the definition of the relationship for OrderDate; the one for ShipDate simply uses the corresponding names for the lookup table name and columns used to define the relationships.

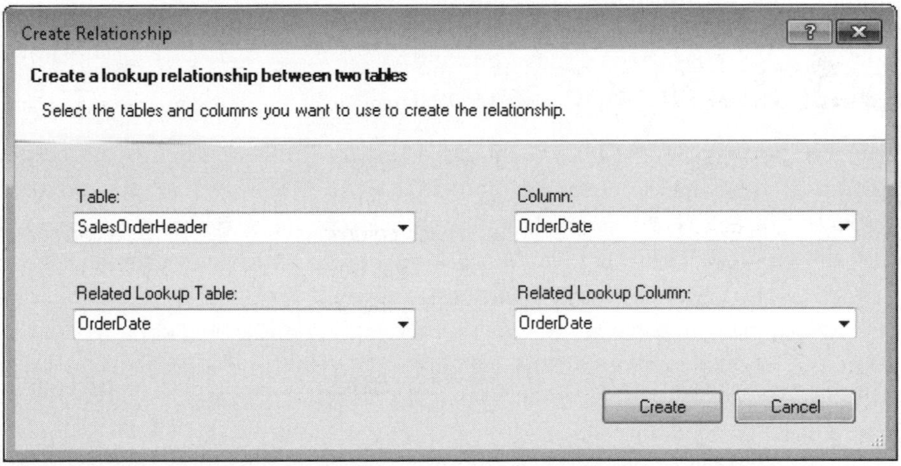

Create Relationship

Create a lookup relationship between two tables

Select the tables and columns you want to use to create the relationship.

Table: SalesOrderHeader

Column: OrderDate

Related Lookup Table: OrderDate

Related Lookup Column: OrderDate

Create Cancel

**FIGURE 7-22** Recreating relationships by using the new lookup column name.

After you rename your column, you can create a report similar to the one you saw in Figure 7-19, but this time, use more meaningful names for columns that were ambiguous before. You can see the result of such a process in Figure 7-23.

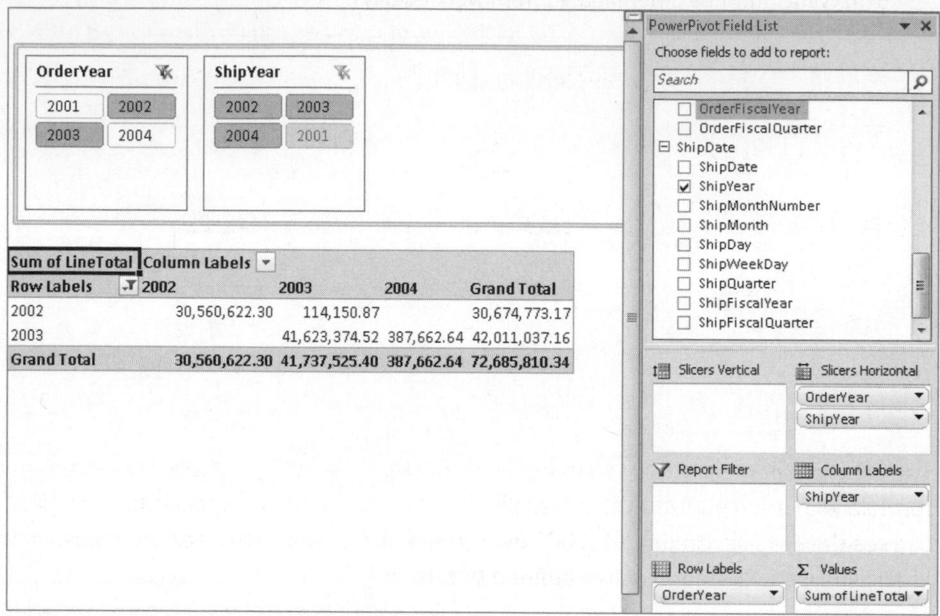


| Sum of LineTotal | Column Labels | | | |
|---|---|---|---|---|
| Row Labels | 2002 | 2003 | 2004 | Grand Total |
| 2002 | 30,560,622.30 | 114,150.87 | | 30,674,773.17 |
| 2003 | | 41,623,374.52 | 387,662.64 | 42,011,037.16 |
| **Grand Total** | **30,560,622.30** | **41,737,525.40** | **387,662.64** | **72,685,810.34** |

**FIGURE 7-23** Column prefixes are more recognizable both in the slicers and in the PowerPivot Field List.

We suggest that you use column prefixes every time you have the same column name in different tables—not just for Dates tables.

## Calculating Working Days

Now that you have learned how to create a calendar table, it is worth pointing out some columns that can be very useful in data analysis and that can be conveniently stored in the calendar table. For example, you might be interested in defining a measure that calculates the average of sales per working days in a given period. (You can find the complete example in the CH07-04-WorkingDays.xlsx workbook included on the companion DVD.) To do that, you have to calculate the number of working days, which in turn requires knowing whether a day is a working day. The simpler way to do this is to add a WorkingDays column to the Excel OrderDate table. That column should have the value 1 for working days, and 0 for holidays, weekends, and other nonworking days. Instead of compiling this column by hand, you might define it by using the following Excel formula that assigns 1 to all week days between Monday and Friday, leaving 0 to Saturday and Sunday:

```
= IF( WEEKDAY([@Date],2) > 5, 0, 1 )
```

**Tip** You might want to use a separate NonWorkingDays table to configure the working days in the week. In that case, you use the VLOOKUP Excel function in the preceding expression. You see a similar example later in this section, when we discuss how to create a table that defines public holidays that must be differentiated from working days.

This formula is automatically copied into all the rows of the OrderDate table, as you can see in Figure 7-24.

J2 fx =IF( WEEKDAY([@Date],2) > 5, 0, 1 )

| Date | Year | MonthNumber | Month | Day | WeekDay | Quarter | FiscalYear | FiscalQuarter | WorkingDays |
|---|---|---|---|---|---|---|---|---|---|
| 1/1/2001 | 2001 | 1 | 01 - January | 1 | Monday | Q1 | FY-2001 | FQ3 | 1 |
| 1/2/2001 | 2001 | 1 | 01 - January | 2 | Tuesday | Q1 | FY-2001 | FQ3 | 1 |
| 1/3/2001 | 2001 | 1 | 01 - January | 3 | Wednesday | Q1 | FY-2001 | FQ3 | 1 |
| 1/4/2001 | 2001 | 1 | 01 - January | 4 | Thursday | Q1 | FY-2001 | FQ3 | 1 |
| 1/5/2001 | 2001 | 1 | 01 - January | 5 | Friday | Q1 | FY-2001 | FQ3 | 1 |
| 1/6/2001 | 2001 | 1 | 01 - January | 6 | Saturday | Q1 | FY-2001 | FQ3 | 0 |
| 1/7/2001 | 2001 | 1 | 01 - January | 7 | Sunday | Q1 | FY-2001 | FQ3 | 0 |
| 1/8/2001 | 2001 | 1 | 01 - January | 8 | Monday | Q1 | FY-2001 | FQ3 | 1 |

**FIGURE 7-24** The WorkingDays column added to the OrderDate table in Excel.

You can modify single values for other nonworking days, such as public holidays, overriding the formula with a forced fixed value (usually 0) just for these days. For example, in Figure 7-25, you can see the value for January 1, 2001 overridden by a 0 value, whereas the following dates are still evaluated by the formula we defined before.

J2 fx 0

| Date | Year | MonthNumber | Month | Day | WeekDay | Quarter | FiscalYear | FiscalQuarte | WorkingDays |
|---|---|---|---|---|---|---|---|---|---|
| 1/1/2001 | 2001 | 1 | 01 - January | 1 | Monday | Q1 | FY-2001 | FQ3 | 0 |
| 1/2/2001 | 2001 | 1 | 01 - January | 2 | Tuesday | Q1 | FY-2001 | FQ3 | 1 |
| 1/3/2001 | 2001 | 1 | 01 - January | 3 | Wednesday | Q1 | FY-2001 | FQ3 | 1 |
| 1/4/2001 | 2001 | 1 | 01 - January | 4 | Thursday | Q1 | FY-2001 | FQ3 | 1 |
| 1/5/2001 | 2001 | 1 | 01 - January | 5 | Friday | Q1 | FY-2001 | FQ3 | 1 |
| 1/6/2001 | 2001 | 1 | 01 - January | 6 | Saturday | Q1 | FY-2001 | FQ3 | 0 |
| 1/7/2001 | 2001 | 1 | 01 - January | 7 | Sunday | Q1 | FY-2001 | FQ3 | 0 |
| 1/8/2001 | 2001 | 1 | 01 - January | 8 | Monday | Q1 | FY-2001 | FQ3 | 1 |

**FIGURE 7-25** The value 0 overriding the formula for January 1, 2001.

**Note** The warning shown in Figure 7-25 to the left of cell J2 indicates a possible inconsistency in a column that contains a formula. You can click the Ignore Error item in the context menu to turn off the warning.

You can update the OrderDate linked table in PowerPivot, and the WorkingDays column shows up in the PivotTable too. At this point, you can define a measure belonging to the SalesOrderDetail table named DailySales, which divides the sum of LineTotal by the sum of working days, as you can see in Figure 7-26.

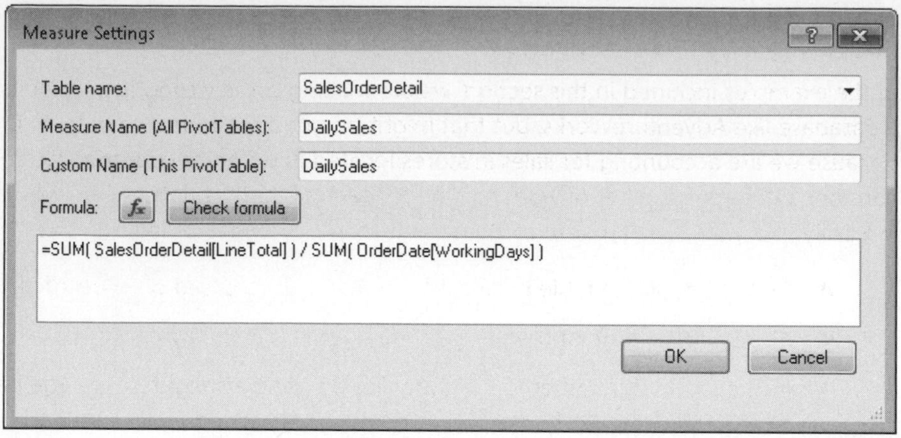

Measure Settings

Table name: SalesOrderDetail

Measure Name (All PivotTables): DailySales

Custom Name (This PivotTable): DailySales

Formula: Check formula

```
=SUM( SalesOrderDetail[LineTotal] ) / SUM( OrderDate[WorkingDays] )
```

OK Cancel

**FIGURE 7-26** The definition of DailySales measure.

The final result is shown in Figure 7-27, where both WorkingDays and DailySales measures are exposed in the PivotTable. However, in a real report, you usually do not show the working days number but just the average measures, such as Daily Sales.

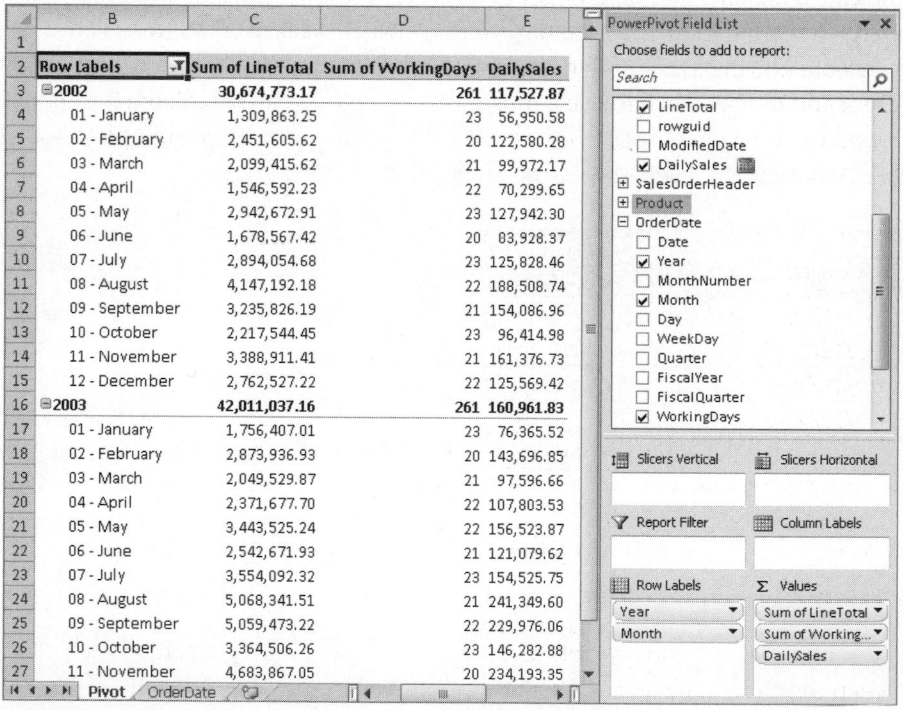

| Row Labels | Sum of LineTotal | Sum of WorkingDays | DailySales |
|---|---|---|---|
| **2002** | **30,674,773.17** | **261** | **117,527.87** |
| 01 - January | 1,309,863.25 | 23 | 56,950.58 |
| 02 - February | 2,451,605.62 | 20 | 122,580.28 |
| 03 - March | 2,099,415.62 | 21 | 99,972.17 |
| 04 - April | 1,546,592.23 | 22 | 70,299.65 |
| 05 - May | 2,942,672.91 | 23 | 127,942.30 |
| 06 - June | 1,678,567.42 | 20 | 83,928.37 |
| 07 - July | 2,894,054.68 | 23 | 125,828.46 |
| 08 - August | 4,147,192.18 | 22 | 188,508.74 |
| 09 - September | 3,235,826.19 | 21 | 154,086.96 |
| 10 - October | 2,217,544.45 | 23 | 96,414.98 |
| 11 - November | 3,388,911.41 | 21 | 161,376.73 |
| 12 - December | 2,762,527.22 | 22 | 125,569.42 |
| **2003** | **42,011,037.16** | **261** | **160,961.83** |
| 01 - January | 1,756,407.01 | 23 | 76,365.52 |
| 02 - February | 2,873,936.93 | 20 | 143,696.85 |
| 03 - March | 2,049,529.87 | 21 | 97,596.66 |
| 04 - April | 2,371,677.70 | 22 | 107,803.53 |
| 05 - May | 3,443,525.24 | 22 | 156,523.87 |
| 06 - June | 2,542,671.93 | 21 | 121,079.62 |
| 07 - July | 3,554,092.32 | 23 | 154,525.75 |
| 08 - August | 5,068,341.51 | 21 | 241,349.60 |
| 09 - September | 5,059,473.22 | 22 | 229,976.06 |
| 10 - October | 3,364,506.26 | 23 | 146,282.88 |
| 11 - November | 4,683,867.05 | 20 | 234,193.35 |

PowerPivot Field List

Choose fields to add to report:

LineTotal, rowguid, ModifiedDate, DailySales, SalesOrderHeader, Product, OrderDate, Date, Year, MonthNumber, Month, Day, WeekDay, Quarter, FiscalYear, FiscalQuarter, WorkingDays

Slicers Vertical | Slicers Horizontal | Report Filter | Column Labels

Row Labels: Year, Month

Values: Sum of LineTotal, Sum of Working..., DailySales

**FIGURE 7-27** PivotTable showing results for WorkingDays and DailySales.

### Working Days in Different Countries

In the examples included in this section, we are making some wrong assumptions for a database like AdventureWorks, but that might be good for your own data. In fact, because we are accounting for sales in stores located in different countries, we should consider a different number of working days for each of these countries. This would make the DailySales measure harder to calculate. In fact, we should accomplish all this as well:

- Define a separate table to calculate working days, based on country and date.
- Make a calculation of the required DailySales average by country.
- Aggregate that number for all countries by using a weighted average based on the sales amount for that country in a given period.

Although this calculation is still possible, it is very complex and it is seldom used because this measure is probably not the same for different countries in the same report.

Our technique up to now is really error prone because we write directly into a cell a value of 0 to indicate a holiday, without any further explanation. If we make an error, it is really hard to identify; furthermore, we make no distinction between weekend days (which are automatically calculated) and holidays. A better solution is to define a separate Holidays table, which is easier to check and to maintain because it moves into a single calculated column the logic to merge weekend evaluation and holiday definition using a single formula. In Figure 7-28, you can see such a Holidays table, defined in Excel.

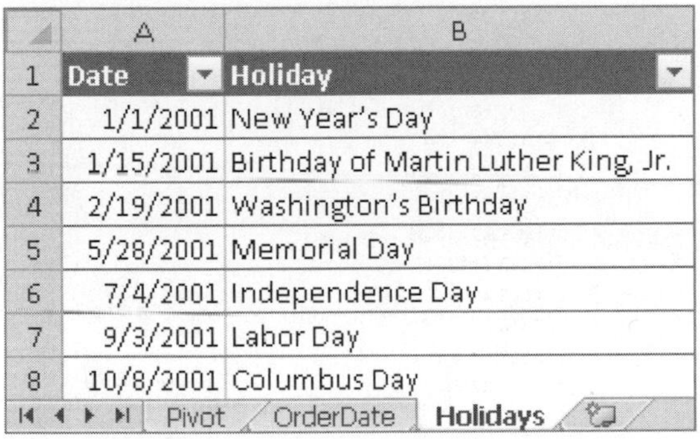

| | A | B |
|---|---|---|
| 1 | Date | Holiday |
| 2 | 1/1/2001 | New Year's Day |
| 3 | 1/15/2001 | Birthday of Martin Luther King, Jr. |
| 4 | 2/19/2001 | Washington's Birthday |
| 5 | 5/28/2001 | Memorial Day |
| 6 | 7/4/2001 | Independence Day |
| 7 | 9/3/2001 | Labor Day |
| 8 | 10/8/2001 | Columbus Day |

Pivot / OrderDate / **Holidays**

**FIGURE 7-28** Holidays table in Excel.

You can import this Holidays table as a linked table in PowerPivot and define a relationship between the OrderDate and Holidays tables, as shown in Figure 7-29.

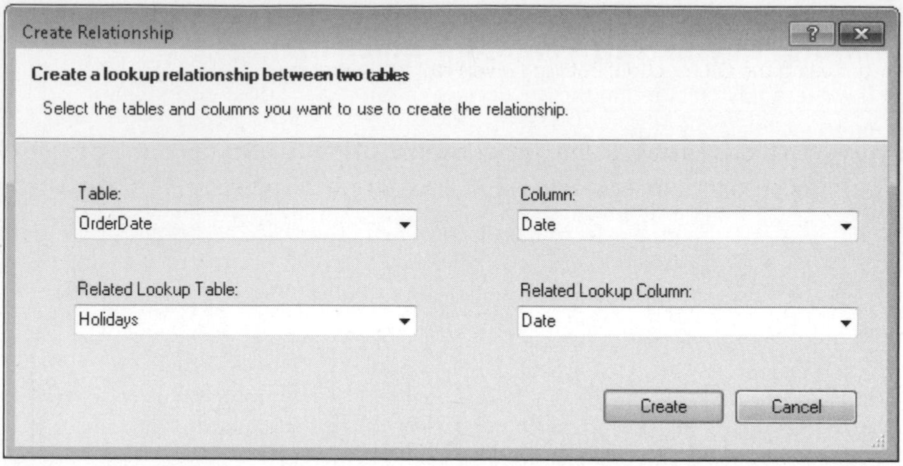

Create Relationship

**Create a lookup relationship between two tables**

Select the tables and columns you want to use to create the relationship.

Table: OrderDate

Column: Date

Related Lookup Table: Holidays

Related Lookup Column: Date

Create Cancel

**FIGURE 7-29** The relationship between the OrderDate and Holidays tables.

You can remove the WorkingDays column because you are moving the whole logic into PowerPivot. Because you need to use the RELATE function to get holiday information in PowerPivot, you should move all the business logic into one simple place: avoid splitting it half and half between Excel and and PowerPivot. After you update the OrderDate table in PowerPivot by removing the WorkingDays data column, you can define a new WorkingDays calculated column by using the DAX formula that you can see in Figure 7-30.

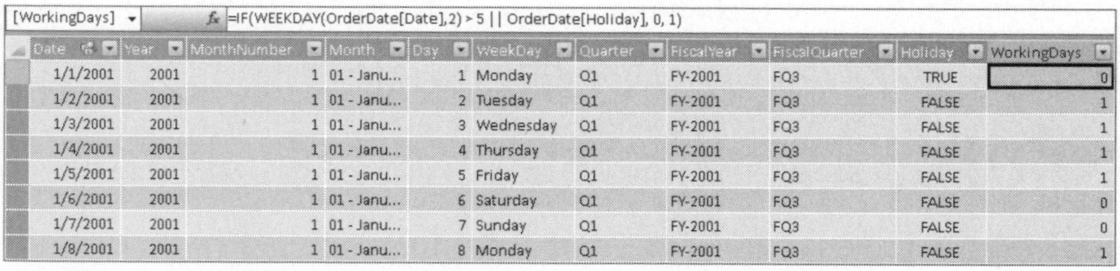

[WorkingDays] =IF(WEEKDAY(OrderDate[Date],2) > 5 || OrderDate[Holiday], 0, 1)

| Date | Year | MonthNumber | Month | Day | WeekDay | Quarter | FiscalYear | FiscalQuarter | Holiday | WorkingDays |
|---|---|---|---|---|---|---|---|---|---|---|
| 1/1/2001 | 2001 | 1 | 01 - Janu... | 1 | Monday | Q1 | FY-2001 | FQ3 | TRUE | 0 |
| 1/2/2001 | 2001 | 1 | 01 - Janu... | 2 | Tuesday | Q1 | FY-2001 | FQ3 | FALSE | 1 |
| 1/3/2001 | 2001 | 1 | 01 - Janu... | 3 | Wednesday | Q1 | FY-2001 | FQ3 | FALSE | 1 |
| 1/4/2001 | 2001 | 1 | 01 - Janu... | 4 | Thursday | Q1 | FY-2001 | FQ3 | FALSE | 1 |
| 1/5/2001 | 2001 | 1 | 01 - Janu... | 5 | Friday | Q1 | FY-2001 | FQ3 | FALSE | 1 |
| 1/6/2001 | 2001 | 1 | 01 - Janu... | 6 | Saturday | Q1 | FY-2001 | FQ3 | FALSE | 0 |
| 1/7/2001 | 2001 | 1 | 01 - Janu... | 7 | Sunday | Q1 | FY-2001 | FQ3 | FALSE | 0 |
| 1/8/2001 | 2001 | 1 | 01 - Janu... | 8 | Monday | Q1 | FY-2001 | FQ3 | FALSE | 1 |

**FIGURE 7-30** The WorkingDays calculated column in the OrderDate table.

Let us examine the DAX formula in Figure 7-30. First of all, you can see a new Holiday calculated column defined by the following formula:

```
Holiday = IF( ISBLANK( RELATED(Holidays[Date]) ), FALSE, TRUE )
```

The Holiday column has a TRUE value for every day that corresponds to a holiday in the Holidays table. Using this information, we extend the previously defined Excel formula that considers whether a nonworking day is a Saturday, a Sunday, or a holiday by using the following DAX formula:

```
WorkingDays = IF( WEEKDAY( OrderDate[Date], 2 ) > 5 || OrderDate[Holiday],
                 0, 1)
```

**Tip** Remember that the || operator corresponds to the OR Boolean operator, which also can be written using the OR function, both in PowerPivot and Excel.

Finally, you can browse data with the right calculation of WorkingDays, according to the Holidays table we included in the model. In Figure 7-31, you can see the resulting PivotTable, which you can find along with the complete model in the CH07-05-WorkingDays-HolidaysTable.xlsx workbook included on the companion DVD.

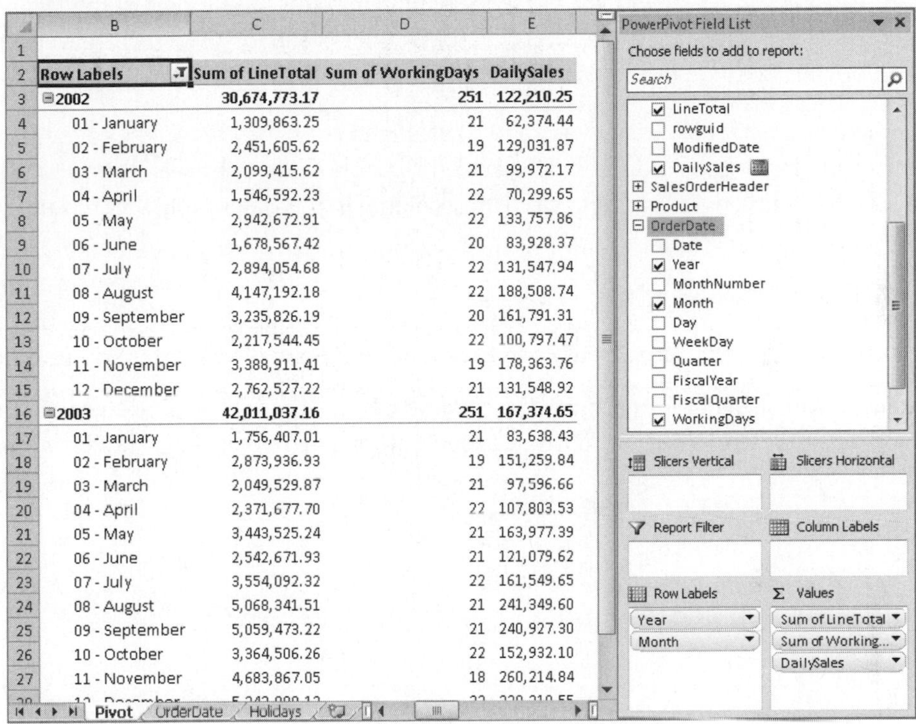

| Row Labels | Sum of LineTotal | Sum of WorkingDays | DailySales |
|---|---|---|---|
| **2002** | **30,674,773.17** | **251** | **122,210.25** |
| 01 - January | 1,309,863.25 | 21 | 62,374.44 |
| 02 - February | 2,451,605.62 | 19 | 129,031.87 |
| 03 - March | 2,099,415.62 | 21 | 99,972.17 |
| 04 - April | 1,546,592.23 | 22 | 70,299.65 |
| 05 - May | 2,942,672.91 | 22 | 133,757.86 |
| 06 - June | 1,678,567.42 | 20 | 83,928.37 |
| 07 - July | 2,894,054.68 | 22 | 131,547.94 |
| 08 - August | 4,147,192.18 | 22 | 188,508.74 |
| 09 - September | 3,235,826.19 | 20 | 161,791.31 |
| 10 - October | 2,217,544.45 | 22 | 100,797.47 |
| 11 - November | 3,388,911.41 | 19 | 178,363.76 |
| 12 - December | 2,762,527.22 | 21 | 131,548.92 |
| **2003** | **42,011,037.16** | **251** | **167,374.65** |
| 01 - January | 1,756,407.01 | 21 | 83,638.43 |
| 02 - February | 2,873,936.93 | 19 | 151,259.84 |
| 03 - March | 2,049,529.87 | 21 | 97,596.66 |
| 04 - April | 2,371,677.70 | 22 | 107,803.53 |
| 05 - May | 3,443,525.24 | 21 | 163,977.39 |
| 06 - June | 2,542,671.93 | 21 | 121,079.62 |
| 07 - July | 3,554,092.32 | 22 | 161,549.65 |
| 08 - August | 5,068,341.51 | 21 | 241,349.60 |
| 09 - September | 5,059,473.22 | 21 | 240,927.30 |
| 10 - October | 3,364,506.26 | 22 | 152,932.10 |
| 11 - November | 4,683,867.05 | 18 | 260,214.84 |



**FIGURE 7-31** The PivotTable showing final results using the Holidays table support.

Another common calculation involving working days is the delta between two dates. For example, in the SalesOrderHeader table of the model used in this chapter, there are three dates, which you can also see in Figure 7-32:

- OrderDate: The date of the order
- DueDate: When the customer expects the order to be delivered
- ShipDate: The date of order shipment

| SalesOrderID | RevisionNumber | OrderDate | DueDate | ShipDate | Status |
|---|---|---|---|---|---|
| 43702 | 1 | 7/2/2001 | 7/14/2001 | 7/9/2001 | 5 |
| 43706 | 1 | 7/3/2001 | 7/15/2001 | 7/10/2001 | 5 |
| 43707 | 1 | 7/3/2001 | 7/15/2001 | 7/10/2001 | 5 |

**FIGURE 7-32** The Dates column in the SalesOrderHeader table.

Calculating whether an order has been shipped on time seems pretty easy: you should just compare the DueDate and ShipDate columns. However, if you consider a standard delivery time of four working days, you should calculate how many orders have been shipped after DueDate minus four working days. This calculation requires the support of the Dates table. The complete model of the following example is available in the CH07-06-DeliveryDays.xlsx workbook included on the companion DVD.

To make the calculation, we need to add a calculated column in the SalesOrderHeader table that calculates for each order the difference (in working dates) between the two dates. You can create a WorkingDayNumber calculated column in the Dates table that has the following formula:

```
WorkingDayNumber =SUMX( FILTER( OrderDate,
                            OrderDate[Date] <= EARLIER(OrderDate[Date]) ),
                       OrderDate[WorkingDays] )
```

This number calculates for each day the number of working days elapsed since the first date in the Dates table. In Figure 7-33, you can see how this number is calculated for a few rows.

| Date | Year | MonthNum... | Month | Day | WeekDay | Qu... | Holiday | WorkingDays | WorkingDayNumber |
|---|---|---|---|---|---|---|---|---|---|
| 1/1/2001 | 2001 | 1 | 01 - Janu... | 1 | Monday | Q1 | TRUE | 0 | 0 |
| 1/2/2001 | 2001 | 1 | 01 - Janu... | 2 | Tuesday | Q1 | FALSE | 1 | 1 |
| 1/3/2001 | 2001 | 1 | 01 - Janu... | 3 | Wednesday | Q1 | FALSE | 1 | 2 |
| 1/4/2001 | 2001 | 1 | 01 - Janu... | 4 | Thursday | Q1 | FALSE | 1 | 3 |
| 1/5/2001 | 2001 | 1 | 01 - Janu... | 5 | Friday | Q1 | FALSE | 1 | 4 |
| 1/6/2001 | 2001 | 1 | 01 - Janu... | 6 | Saturday | Q1 | FALSE | 0 | 4 |
| 1/7/2001 | 2001 | 1 | 01 - Janu... | 7 | Sunday | Q1 | FALSE | 0 | 4 |
| 1/8/2001 | 2001 | 1 | 01 - Janu... | 8 | Monday | Q1 | FALSE | 1 | 5 |
| 1/9/2001 | 2001 | 1 | 01 - Janu... | 9 | Tuesday | Q1 | FALSE | 1 | 6 |
| 1/10/2001 | 2001 | 1 | 01 - Janu... | 10 | Wednesday | Q1 | FALSE | 1 | 7 |

**FIGURE 7-33** The WorkingDayNumber calculation.

At this point, you can define the number of working days between two dates using the difference of WorkingDayNumber for the correspondent dates. Because you might not want to add too many tables to the PowerPivot model, you may reuse the same OrderDate table already imported into the model to get the WorkingDayNumber for both DueDate and ShipDate dates of an order. For example, this number for ShipDate can be obtained by using the following DAX expression:

```
CALCULATE( VALUES( OrderDate[WorkingDayNumber] ),
           FILTER( OrderDate,
                   OrderDate[Date] = SalesOrderHeader[ShipDate] ) )
```

The FILTER call filters only the ShipDate row in the OrderDate table. Using this filter, the CALCULATE function returns the value of WorkingDayNumber for that row. The use of VALUES grants that an error message is raised if the FILTER returns more than one row (in which case, the filter condition contains an error).

So using this DAX expression for both ShipDate and DueDate, we can define a DueDeltaDays calculated column in SalesOrderHeader by using the following formula:

```
DueDeltaDays = CALCULATE( VALUES( OrderDate[WorkingDayNumber] ),
                   FILTER( OrderDate,
                       OrderDate[Date] = SalesOrderHeader[ShipDate])) + 4
             - CALCULATE( VALUES( OrderDate[WorkingDayNumber] ),
                   FILTER( OrderDate,
                       OrderDate[Date] = SalesOrderHeader[DueDate]))
```

The DueDeltaDays column shows a positive number in the case of a delay, representing the number of delay days. Negative numbers indicate an early delivery (measured always in days). In Figure 7-34, you can see values for this column and for another calculated column named DeliveryDelayDays, which displays a value only for delayed orders.

| SalesOrderID | RevisionNumber | OrderDate | DueDate | ShipDate | DueDeltaDays | DeliveryDelayDays |
|---|---|---|---|---|---|---|
| 44224 | 1 | 9/20/2001 | 10/2/2001 | 9/27/2001 | 1 | 1 |
| 44234 | 1 | 9/22/2001 | 10/4/2001 | 9/29/2001 | 0 | |
| 44241 | 1 | 9/23/2001 | 10/5/2001 | 9/30/2001 | -1 | |
| 44250 | 1 | 9/25/2001 | 10/7/2001 | 10/2/2001 | 1 | 1 |
| 44251 | 1 | 9/25/2001 | 10/7/2001 | 10/2/2001 | 1 | 1 |
| 44253 | 1 | 9/26/2001 | 10/8/2001 | 10/3/2001 | 2 | 2 |
| 44273 | 1 | 9/30/2001 | 10/12/2001 | 10/7/2001 | 0 | |
| 44274 | 1 | 9/30/2001 | 10/12/2001 | 10/7/2001 | 0 | |
| 44327 | 1 | 10/3/2001 | 10/15/2001 | 10/10/2001 | 1 | 1 |
| 44330 | 1 | 10/3/2001 | 10/15/2001 | 10/10/2001 | 1 | 1 |
| 44334 | 1 | 10/5/2001 | 10/17/2001 | 10/12/2001 | 1 | 1 |

**FIGURE 7-34** The DueDeltaDays and DeliveryDelayDays calculated columns in the SalesOrderHeader.

With this information, you can calculate some measures in the PivotTable, such as the ratio of delayed deliveries:

```
DeliveryDelayRation = COUNT( SalesOrderHeader[DeliveryDelayDays] )
                      / COUNTROWS( SalesOrderHeader )
```

You can also calculate the average delay (in days) for delayed orders, by simply selecting the Summarize By Average item on the DeliveryDelayDays column. In Figure 7-35, you can see a PivotTable displaying both these measures.

| Row Labels | Sum of LineTotal | DeliveryDelayRatio | Average of DeliveryDelayDays |
|---|---|---|---|
| **⊟2002** | **30,674,773.17** | **61.08%** | **1.15** |
| 01 - January | 1,309,863.25 | 73.68% | 1.11 |
| 02 - February | 2,451,605.62 | 72.00% | 1.11 |
| 03 - March | 2,099,415.62 | 65.78% | 1.00 |
| 04 - April | 1,546,592.23 | 48.36% | 1.00 |
| 05 - May | 2,942,672.91 | 72.24% | 1.13 |
| 06 - June | 1,678,567.42 | 46.45% | 1.09 |
| 07 - July | 2,894,054.68 | 44.62% | 1.00 |
| 08 - August | 4,147,192.18 | 75.00% | 1.08 |
| 09 - September | 3,235,826.19 | 37.22% | 1.00 |
| 10 - October | 2,217,544.45 | 68.87% | 1.19 |
| 11 - November | 3,388,911.41 | 79.45% | 1.59 |
| 12 - December | 2,762,527.22 | 51.13% | 1.22 |

**FIGURE 7-35** The DeliveryDelayRatio and average of DeliveryDelayDays columns in PivotTable.

### Calculating WorkingDays by Using Table Relationships

You might wonder why we have not used table relationships to relate SalesDate and DueDate tables with corresponding SalesDates and DueDates tables; why have we used a more complicated DAX expression instead? We have two reasons for that. First, we would have needed to duplicate these two tables both in Excel and in PowerPivot. Second, the need to duplicate would have been propagated to the Holidays table too, requiring three Holidays tables in Excel that would have been imported in three different linked tables in PowerPivot. You can look at an example of such a model in the CH07-07-DeliveryDays-UsingRelationships.xlsx workbook included on the companion DVD.

Because PowerPivot does not support more than one relationship between two tables, it follows in an indirect way that you cannot relate the same Holiday table from two or more different tables (such as SalesDates and DueDates) if these tables are both related to the same table (such as SalesOrderHeader), even if the relationship is through different columns.

## Aggregating and Comparing over Time

Working days calculation is only the first step in the benefits that you can obtain by using a calendar table. In the next sections, we introduce other useful techniques. It is often required that you analyze particular aggregations of values over time. For example, you might want to calculate the aggregated value of a measure from the beginning of the year up to the period you are selecting. (This is commonly called *year-to-date aggregation*.) You might want to look at the Sales Amount for the month of March but also want to look at the total Sales Amount from January to March. Having a Dates table is an important prerequisite for making this calculation in PivotTable.

## Year-to-Date, Quarter-to-Date, and Month-to-Date

The calculation of year-to-date (YTD), quarter-to-date, (QTD) and month-to-date (MTD) are all very similar. Obviously, month-to-date is meaningful only when you are looking at data at the day level, whereas year-to-date and quarter-to-date calculations are often used to look at data at the month level.

For example, in Figure 7-36, you can see the LineTotal measure aggregated by year, quarter, and month.

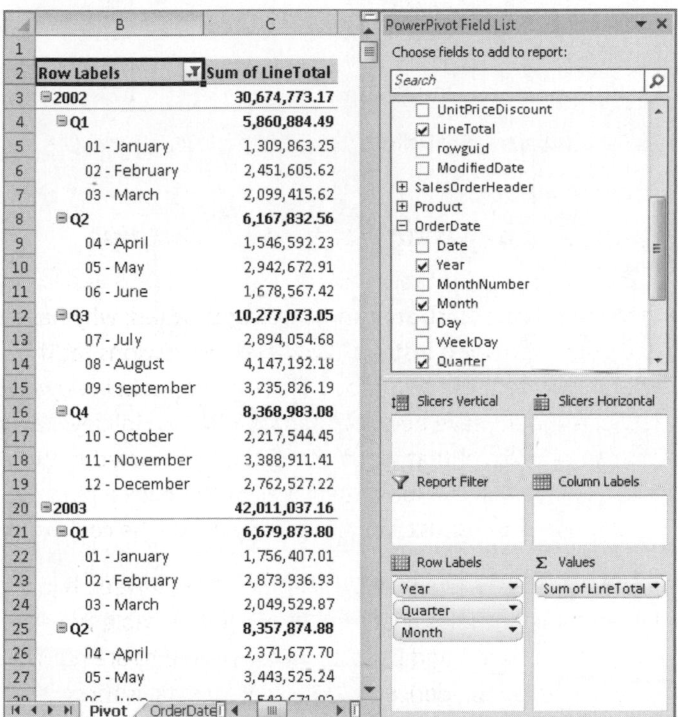


**FIGURE 7-36** The LineTotal measure aggregated by the corresponding period in a row.

You can calculate the year-to-date value of LineTotal for each month and quarter by using a measure that operates on the filter context, modifying the filter context on dates for a range that starts on January 1 and ends on the month corresponding to the calculated cell. You can define a YtdLineTotal measure by using the following DAX formula:

```
YtdLineTotal = CALCULATE( SUM( SalesOrderDetail[LineTotal] ),
                         DATESYTD( OrderDate[Date] ) )
```

The CALCULATE function receives in its second parameter a table that contains the dates of the year-to-date period that has to be considered in the aggregation. This set of dates is returned by the built-in DATESYTD function, which is a Time Intelligence function that returns a list of all the dates from the beginning of the year until the last date included in the current filter context.

You can see the new measure in action in Figure 7-37.

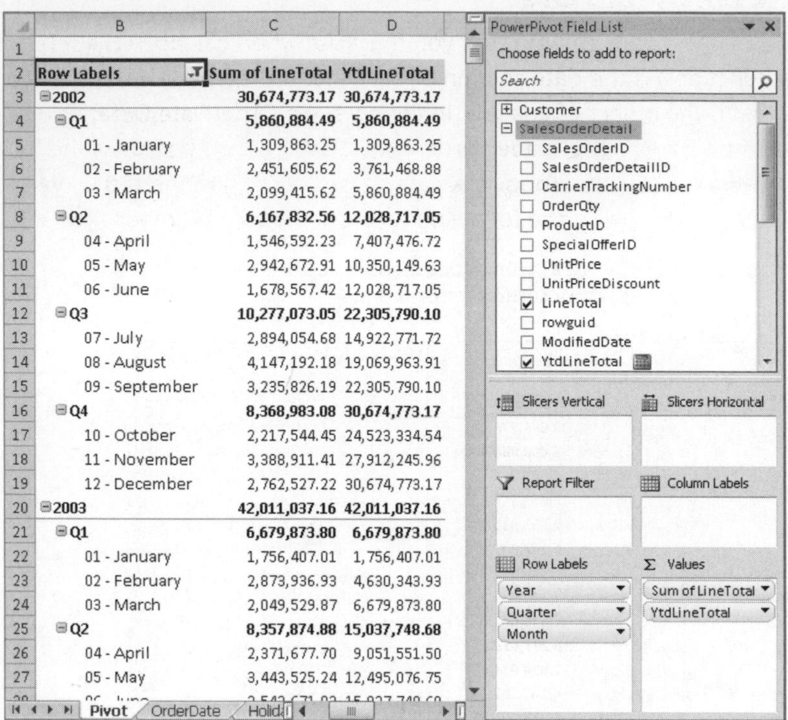


| Row Labels | Sum of LineTotal | YtdLineTotal |
|---|---|---|
| **2002** | **30,674,773.17** | **30,674,773.17** |
| **Q1** | **5,860,884.49** | **5,860,884.49** |
| 01 - January | 1,309,863.25 | 1,309,863.25 |
| 02 - February | 2,451,605.62 | 3,761,468.88 |
| 03 - March | 2,099,415.62 | 5,860,884.49 |
| **Q2** | **6,167,832.56** | **12,028,717.05** |
| 04 - April | 1,546,592.23 | 7,407,476.72 |
| 05 - May | 2,942,672.91 | 10,350,149.63 |
| 06 - June | 1,678,567.42 | 12,028,717.05 |
| **Q3** | **10,277,073.05** | **22,305,790.10** |
| 07 - July | 2,894,054.68 | 14,922,771.72 |
| 08 - August | 4,147,192.18 | 19,069,963.91 |
| 09 - September | 3,235,826.19 | 22,305,790.10 |
| **Q4** | **8,368,983.08** | **30,674,773.17** |
| 10 - October | 2,217,544.45 | 24,523,334.54 |
| 11 - November | 3,388,911.41 | 27,912,245.96 |
| 12 - December | 2,762,527.22 | 30,674,773.17 |
| **2003** | **42,011,037.16** | **42,011,037.16** |
| **Q1** | **6,679,873.80** | **6,679,873.80** |
| 01 - January | 1,756,407.01 | 1,756,407.01 |
| 02 - February | 2,873,936.93 | 4,630,343.93 |
| 03 - March | 2,049,529.87 | 6,679,873.80 |
| **Q2** | **8,357,874.88** | **15,037,748.68** |
| 04 - April | 2,371,677.70 | 9,051,551.50 |
| 05 - May | 3,443,525.24 | 12,495,076.75 |

**FIGURE 7-37** The LineTotal year-to-date measure side-by-side with a regular measure.

This approach requires that you deal with the CALCULATE function, but because this pattern (using a CALCULATE and a DATESYTD function) is very common, PowerPivot offers a dedicated DAX function that simplifies (and makes more readable) the syntax of the YTD calculation, TOTALYTD:

```
YtdLineTotal = TOTALYTD( SUM( SalesOrderDetail[LineTotal] ),
                         OrderDate[Date] )
```

As you can see, the syntax requires the hoped-for aggregation as the first parameter and then just the date column as the second parameter. The behavior is identical to the original measure, but the name of the TOTALYTD function immediately communicates the intention of the formula. However, you need to know the behavior of the original CALCULATE syntax because it allows a more complex calculation that you define later in this chapter.

## What Date Column to Use

Keep in mind that the date column that you must use when calling TOTALYTD (and other similar functions) is the date column of the Dates table, and not the date column of the table that is the object of analysis. In this case, the OrderDate[Date] column was used instead of the SalesOrderHeader[OrderDate] column. If we had used the latter, the calculation would have been wrong. You can see in Figure 7-38 the result that would have been produced by using the following formula for the YTD measure:

```
YtdLineTotal = TOTALYTD( SUM( SalesOrderDetail[LineTotal] ),
                         SalesOrderHeader[OrderDate] )
```

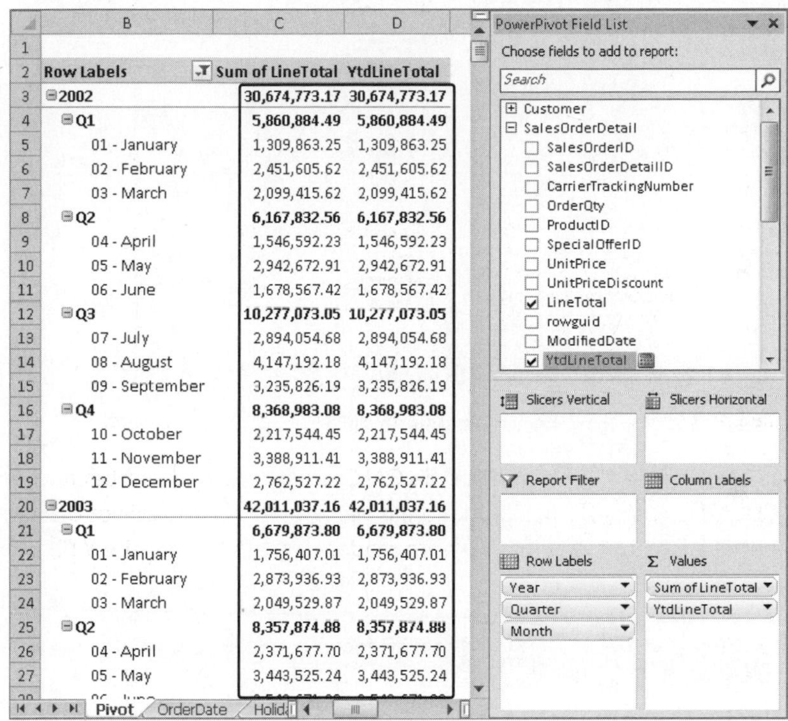

| Row Labels | Sum of LineTotal | YtdLineTotal |
|---|---|---|
| **2002** | **30,674,773.17** | **30,674,773.17** |
| **Q1** | **5,860,884.49** | **5,860,884.49** |
| 01 - January | 1,309,863.25 | 1,309,863.25 |
| 02 - February | 2,451,605.62 | 2,451,605.62 |
| 03 - March | 2,099,415.62 | 2,099,415.62 |
| **Q2** | **6,167,832.56** | **6,167,832.56** |
| 04 - April | 1,546,592.23 | 1,546,592.23 |
| 05 - May | 2,942,672.91 | 2,942,672.91 |
| 06 - June | 1,678,567.42 | 1,678,567.42 |
| **Q3** | **10,277,073.05** | **10,277,073.05** |
| 07 - July | 2,894,054.68 | 2,894,054.68 |
| 08 - August | 4,147,192.18 | 4,147,192.18 |
| 09 - September | 3,235,826.19 | 3,235,826.19 |
| **Q4** | **8,368,983.08** | **8,368,983.08** |
| 10 - October | 2,217,544.45 | 2,217,544.45 |
| 11 - November | 3,388,911.41 | 3,388,911.41 |
| 12 - December | 2,762,527.22 | 2,762,527.22 |
| **2003** | **42,011,037.16** | **42,011,037.16** |
| **Q1** | **6,679,873.80** | **6,679,873.80** |
| 01 - January | 1,756,407.01 | 1,756,407.01 |
| 02 - February | 2,873,936.93 | 2,873,936.93 |
| 03 - March | 2,049,529.87 | 2,049,529.87 |
| **Q2** | **8,357,874.88** | **8,357,874.88** |
| 04 - April | 2,371,677.70 | 2,371,677.70 |
| 05 - May | 3,443,525.24 | 3,443,525.24 |



**FIGURE 7-38** The wrong year-to-date calculation returns the same value as the LineTotal measure.

The problem is that the existing filter on year and month would be still applied. There are possible workarounds that you might use, but our suggestion is to always define and use a Dates table. Further details on the issue and possible workarounds are available in this blog post written by Kasper de Jonge: *http://tinyurl.com/DaxTimeAll.*

As you can for the year-to-date calculation, you can also define quarter-to-date and month-to-date calculations with built-in functions, as in these measures:

```
QtdLineTotal = TOTALQTD( SUM( SalesOrderDetail[LineTotal] ),
                         OrderDate[Date] )

MtdLineTotal = TOTALMTD( SUM( SalesOrderDetail[LineTotal] ),
                         OrderDate[Date] )
```

In Figure 7-39, you can see the year-to-date and quarter-to-date measures used in a PivotTable. Note that the quarter-to-date measure makes the year total equal to the last quarter of the year.

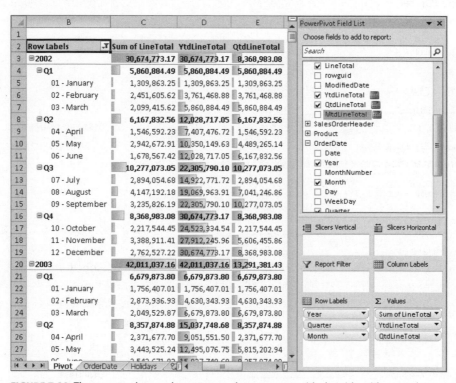

| Row Labels | Sum of LineTotal | YtdLineTotal | QtdLineTotal |
|---|---|---|---|
| **2002** | **30,674,773.17** | **30,674,773.17** | **8,368,983.08** |
| **Q1** | **5,860,884.49** | **5,860,884.49** | **5,860,884.49** |
| 01 - January | 1,309,863.25 | 1,309,863.25 | 1,309,863.25 |
| 02 - February | 2,451,605.62 | 3,761,468.88 | 3,761,468.88 |
| 03 - March | 2,099,415.62 | 5,860,884.49 | 5,860,884.49 |
| **Q2** | **6,167,832.56** | **12,028,717.05** | **6,167,832.56** |
| 04 - April | 1,546,592.23 | 7,407,476.72 | 1,546,592.23 |
| 05 - May | 2,942,672.91 | 10,350,149.63 | 4,489,265.14 |
| 06 - June | 1,678,567.42 | 12,028,717.05 | 6,167,832.56 |
| **Q3** | **10,277,073.05** | **22,305,790.10** | **10,277,073.05** |
| 07 - July | 2,894,054.68 | 14,922,771.72 | 2,894,054.68 |
| 08 - August | 4,147,192.18 | 19,069,963.91 | 7,041,246.86 |
| 09 - September | 3,235,826.19 | 22,305,790.10 | 10,277,073.05 |
| **Q4** | **8,368,983.08** | **30,674,773.17** | **8,368,983.08** |
| 10 - October | 2,217,544.45 | 24,523,334.54 | 2,217,544.45 |
| 11 - November | 3,388,911.41 | 27,912,245.96 | 5,606,455.86 |
| 12 - December | 2,762,527.22 | 30,674,773.17 | 8,368,983.08 |
| **2003** | **42,011,037.16** | **42,011,037.16** | **13,291,381.43** |
| **Q1** | **6,679,873.80** | **6,679,873.80** | **6,679,873.80** |
| 01 - January | 1,756,407.01 | 1,756,407.01 | 1,756,407.01 |
| 02 - February | 2,873,936.93 | 4,630,343.93 | 4,630,343.93 |
| 03 - March | 2,049,529.87 | 6,679,873.80 | 6,679,873.80 |
| **Q2** | **8,357,874.88** | **15,037,748.68** | **8,357,874.88** |
| 04 - April | 2,371,677.70 | 9,051,551.50 | 2,371,677.70 |
| 05 - May | 3,443,525.24 | 12,495,076.75 | 5,815,202.94 |

FIGURE 7-39 The year-to-date and quarter-to-date measures side-by-side with a regular measure.

To calculate a year-to-date measure over the fiscal year, you need to use an optional parameter that specifies the end day of the fiscal year. For example, you can calculate the fiscal year-to-date for LineTotal by using the following expression:

```
FiscalYtdLineTotal = TOTALYTD( SUM( SalesOrderDetail[LineTotal] ),
                               OrderDate[Date],
                               "06-30" )
```

The last parameter corresponds to June 30, which in our OrderDate table corresponds to the end of the fiscal year. You can find several Time Intelligence functions that have a last, optional YE_Date parameter for this purpose: STARTOFYEAR, ENDOFYEAR, PREVIOUSYEAR, NEXTYEAR, DATESYTD, TOTALYTD, OPENINGBALANCEYEAR, and CLOSINGBALANCEYEAR.

## Periods from the Prior Year

People commonly need to get a value from a period of the prior year (PY). This can be useful for making comparisons of trends, during a period last year to the same period this year, as you can see in the CH07-08-Aggregation.xlsx workbook included on the companion DVD. This is the DAX expression you need to calculate that value:

```
PyLineTotal = CALCULATE( SUM( SalesOrderDetail[LineTotal] ),
                         SAMEPERIODLASTYEAR( OrderDate[Date] ) )
```

The CALCULATE function changes the filter by using the SAMEPERIODLASTYEAR function, which returns a set of dates shifted one year back in time. The SAMEPERIODLASTYEAR function is a specialized version of the more generic DATEADD function, which can be used by specifying the number and type of periods to shift. For example, the same PyLineTotal measure can be defined by this equivalent expression:

```
PyLineTotal = CALCULATE( SUM( SalesOrderDetail[LineTotal] ),
                         DATEADD( OrderDate[Date], -1, YEAR ) )
```

Sometimes you must look at the total amount of a measure for the previous year, usually to compare it with the year-to-date total. To do that, you can use the PARALLELPERIOD function, which is similar to DATEADD but returns the full period specified in the third parameter instead of the partial period returned by DATEADD. The PyTotLineTotal measure that calculates the total sum of LineTotal for the previous year can be defined this way:

```
PyTotLineTotal = CALCULATE( SUM( SalesOrderDetail[LineTotal] ),
                            PARALLELPERIOD( OrderDate[Date], -1, YEAR ) )
```

In Figure 7-40, you can see the result of the PyLineTotal and PyTotLineTotal measures. The quarters data in 2002 for the Sum Of LineTotal column has been copied into the respective quarters of year 2003 in the PyLineTotal column. The PyTotLineTotal simply reports for every period the total amount of the LineTotal column for the year before.

| Row Labels | Sum of LineTotal | PyLineTotal | PyTotLineTotal |
|---|---|---|---|
| **2002** | **30,674,773.17** | **11,331,808.96** | **11,331,808.96** |
| Q1 | 5,860,884.49 | | 11,331,808.96 |
| Q2 | 6,167,832.56 | | 11,331,808.96 |
| Q3 | 10,277,073.05 | 4,647,156.85 | 11,331,808.96 |
| Q4 | 8,368,983.08 | 6,684,652.11 | 11,331,808.96 |
| **2003** | **42,011,037.16** | **30,674,773.17** | **30,674,773.17** |
| Q1 | 6,679,873.80 | 5,860,884.49 | 30,674,773.17 |
| Q2 | 8,357,874.88 | 6,167,832.56 | 30,674,773.17 |
| Q3 | 13,681,907.05 | 10,277,073.05 | 30,674,773.17 |
| Q4 | 13,291,381.43 | 8,368,983.08 | 30,674,773.17 |
| **Grand Total** | **72,685,810.34** | **42,006,582.14** | **42,006,582.14** |

**FIGURE 7-40** Prior Year simple calculations.

When you want to calculate the year-to-date of the prior year because, typically, you want to compare it with the current year-to-date measure, you have to mix the two techniques. Instead of passing the OrderDate[Date] parameter to SAMEPERIODLASTYEAR, which corresponds to the list of dates that are active in the current filter context, you can use the DATESYTD function to make a transformation of these dates, defining the year-to-date group first. However, you might also invert the order of these calls. In fact, the two following definitions of PyYtdLineTotal are equivalent:

```
PyYtdLineTotal = CALCULATE( SUM( SalesOrderDetail[LineTotal] ),
                            SAMEPERIODLASTYEAR( DATESYTD( OrderDate[Date] ) ) )

PyYtdLineTotal = CALCULATE( SUM( SalesOrderDetail[LineTotal] ),
                            DATESYTD( SAMEPERIODLASTYEAR( OrderDate[Date] ) ) )
```

You can see the results of the PyYtdLineTotal in Figure 7-41. The values of YtdLineTotal are reported for PyYtdLineTotal shifted by one year. In the same screen, you can also see the FiscalYtdLineTotal measure that you saw at the end of the previous section: the horizontal lines between Q2 and Q3 in that column highlight the points at which the year-to-date calculation restarts.

| Row Labels | Sum of LineTotal | YtdLineTotal | PyYtdLineTotal | FiscalYtdLineTotal |
|---|---|---|---|---|
| **2002** | **30,674,773.17** | **30,674,773.17** | **11,331,808.96** | **18,646,056.13** |
| Q1 | 5,860,884.49 | 5,860,884.49 | | 17,192,693.45 |
| Q2 | 6,167,832.56 | 12,028,717.05 | | 23,360,526.01 |
| Q3 | 10,277,073.05 | 22,305,790.10 | 4,647,156.85 | 10,277,073.05 |
| Q4 | 8,368,983.08 | 30,674,773.17 | 11,331,808.96 | 18,646,056.13 |
| **2003** | **42,011,037.16** | **42,011,037.16** | **30,674,773.17** | **26,973,288.48** |
| Q1 | 6,679,873.80 | 6,679,873.80 | 5,860,884.49 | 25,325,929.93 |
| Q2 | 8,357,874.88 | 15,037,748.68 | 12,028,717.05 | 33,683,804.81 |
| Q3 | 13,681,907.05 | 28,719,655.73 | 22,305,790.10 | 13,681,907.05 |
| Q4 | 13,291,381.43 | 42,011,037.16 | 30,674,773.17 | 26,973,288.48 |
| **Grand Total** | **72,685,810.34** | **42,011,037.16** | **30,674,773.17** | **26,973,288.48** |

**FIGURE 7-41** The year-to-date calculation for Prior Year and Fiscal Year.

Another commonly requested calculation that eliminates seasonal changes in sales is the moving annual total (MAT), which always considers the last 12 months. For example, the value of MatLineTotal for March 2002 is calculated by summing the range of dates from April 2001 to March 2002. Consider the following MatLineTotal measure definition, which calculates the moving annual total for LineTotal:

```
MatLineTotal = CALCULATE( SUM( SalesOrderDetail[LineTotal] ),
                          DATESBETWEEN(
                              OrderDate[Date],
                                  NEXTDAY(
                                      SAMEPERIODLASTYEAR(
                                          LASTDATE( OrderDate[Date] ) ) ),
                                  LASTDATE( OrderDate[Date] ) ) )
```

The implementation of this measure requires some attention. You need to use the DATESBETWEEN function, which returns the dates from a column included between two specified dates. Because this calculation is always made at the day level, even if the PivotTable is browsing data at the month level, you must calculate the first day and the last day of the interval you want. The last day can be obtained by calling the LASTDATE function, which returns the last date of a given column (always considering the current filter context). Starting from this date, you can get the first day of the interval by requesting the following day (by calling NEXTDAY) of the corresponding last date one year before. (You can do this by using SAMEPERIODLASTYEAR, as we did before.)

In Figure 7-42, you can see a PivotTable using the moving annual total calculation. For example, the 2003 Q2 data has been calculated by summing Q3 and Q4 of 2002, plus Q1 and Q2 of 2003. In the middle, you see the classic year-to-date calculation, which has the same value of moving annual total only for the last period of each year (in this case Q4).

| Row Labels | Sum of LineTotal | YtdLineTotal | MatLineTotal |
|---|---|---|---|
| **2002** | **30,674,773.17** | **30,674,773.17** | **30,674,773.17** |
| Q1 | 5,860,004.49 | 5,860,884.49 | 17,192,693.45 |
| Q2 | 6,167,832.56 | 12,028,717.05 | 23,360,526.01 |
| Q3 | 10,277,073.05 | 22,305,790.10 | 28,990,442.21 |
| Q4 | 8,368,983.08 | 30,674,773.17 | 30,674,773.17 |
| **2003** | **42,011,037.16** | **42,011,037.16** | **42,011,037.16** |
| Q1 | 6,679,873.80 | 6,679,873.80 | 31,493,762.49 |
| Q2 | 8,357,874.88 | 15,037,748.68 | 33,683,804.81 |
| Q3 | 13,681,907.05 | 28,719,655.73 | 37,088,638.81 |
| Q4 | 13,291,381.43 | 42,011,037.16 | 42,011,037.16 |
| **Grand Total** | **72,685,810.34** | **42,011,037.16** | **42,011,037.16** |

**FIGURE 7-42** The moving Annual Total vs. year-to-date calculation.

## Other Aggregation Functions and the CALCULATE Syntax

In all the examples, we have used the SUM aggregation function. You might need to use other aggregation functions, such as AVERAGE, or more complex formulas. Whenever you saw SUM( SalesOrderDetail[LineTotal] ) in the previous example, consider that you can always replace such expressions with another DAX formula, also by simply replacing the aggregation function.

In case your calculation becomes more complex, you might prefer to specify that calculation, which can be shared across several other measures, into a separated measure, containing just this operation. In this way, you can avoid the duplication of the aggregation function in all the formulas for measures that make special calculations for dates.

For example, you might want to calculate the weighted average price with the following formula, assigned to measure AveragePrice:

```
AveragePrice = SUM( SalesOrderDetail[LineTotal] ) / SUM( SalesOrderDetail[OrderQty] )
```

You can use a direct reference to that measure, without using an aggregation function, whenever you use formulas such as CALCULATE or special Time Intelligence functions that behave like CALCULATE, as in the year-to-date calculation defined in YtdAveragePrice measure:

```
YtdAveragePrice = TOTALYTD( SalesOrderDetail[AveragePrice], OrderDate[Date] )
```

The calculation for the prior year can be written by using the CALCULATE function:

```
PyAveragePrice = CALCULATE( SalesOrderDetail[AveragePrice],
                            SAMEPERIODLASTYEAR( OrderDate[Date] ) )
```

In Figure 7-43, you can see the results of these formulas in a PivotTable.

| Row Labels | Sum of LineTotal | Sum of OrderQty | AveragePrice | YtdAveragePrice | PyAveragePrice |
|---|---|---|---|---|---|
| **⊟2002** | **30,674,773.17** | **60,918.00** | **503.54** | **503.54** | **956.43** |
| Q1 | 5,860,884.49 | 5,184.00 | 1,130.57 | 1,130.57 | |
| Q2 | 6,167,832.56 | 7,064.00 | 873.14 | 982.10 | |
| Q3 | 10,277,073.05 | 28,146.00 | 365.13 | 552.21 | 961.55 |
| Q4 | 8,368,983.08 | 20,524.00 | 407.77 | 503.54 | 952.91 |
| **⊟2003** | **42,011,037.16** | **124,699.00** | **336.90** | **336.90** | **503.54** |
| Q1 | 6,679,873.80 | 13,095.00 | 510.11 | 510.11 | 1,130.57 |
| Q2 | 8,357,874.88 | 20,416.00 | 409.38 | 448.74 | 873.14 |
| Q3 | 13,681,907.05 | 48,955.00 | 279.48 | 348.26 | 365.13 |
| Q4 | 13,291,381.43 | 42,233.00 | 314.72 | 336.90 | 407.77 |
| **Grand Total** | **72,685,810.34** | **185,617.00** | **391.59** | **336.90** | **577.28** |

**FIGURE 7-43** The year-to-date and prior year calculations for Average Price.

In case you want to make a monthly average of the total sales, you should use the number of months in the denominator of the ratio, as in the following expression that you can use to define the MonthlyAverage measure:

```
MonthlyAverage = IF( COUNTROWS( VALUES( OrderDate[Month] ) ) > 0,
                     SUM( SalesOrderDetail[LineTotal] )
                         / COUNTROWS( VALUES( OrderDate[Month] ) ),
                     BLANK() )
```

*Please note that this definition does not work with a selection of more than one year.* To avoid this issue, you need to create a calculated column in the OrderDate table with a concatenation of year and month so that the distinct number of values over a period take account also of the year and not just the month. If you do that, you must replace that column to the Month column used in the formula above.

To make a monthly average of the year-to-date sales, you have to replace the corresponding YtdLineTotal measure at the numerator and you need a CALCULATE expression at the denominator so that you can calculate the number of months included in the year-to-date calculation:

```
YtdMonthlyAverage = IF( COUNTROWS( VALUES( OrderDate[Month] ) ) > 0,
                        SalesOrderDetail[YtdLineTotal]
                            / CALCULATE( COUNTROWS( VALUES( OrderDate[Month] ) ),
                                         DATESYTD( OrderDate[Date] ) ),
                        BLANK() )
```

As you can see, the expression might be different according to the calculation you have to do. You have to pay particular attention to the calculation necessary for numerators and denominators of any ratio and average measure.

## Difference over Previous Year

A common operation that compares a measure with its value in the prior year is to calculate the difference of these values. That difference might be expressed as an absolute value or by using a percentage, as you can see in the CH07-09-Yoy.xlsx workbook included on the companion DVD. To make these calculations, you need the value for the prior year that you already defined in PyLineTotal:

```
PyLineTotal = CALCULATE( SUM( SalesOrderDetail[LineTotal] ),
                         SAMEPERIODLASTYEAR( OrderDate[Date] ) )
```

The absolute difference of LineTotal over previous year (year-over-year, YOY) is a simple subtraction. You can define a YoyLineTotal measure with the following expression:

```
YoyLineTotal = SUM( SalesOrderDetail[LineTotal] ) - SalesOrderDetail[PyLineTotal]
```

You calculate the value of the selected year by using the SUM aggregation; the measure corresponding to the value of the prior year does not need to be summed because the aggregation is already done as part of the underlying measure expression.

The analogous calculation for comparing the year-to-date measure with a corresponding value in the prior year is a simple subtraction of two measures, YtdLineTotal and PyYtdLineTotal, which you saw in the previous section; we report it here just as reminder:

```
PyYtdLineTotal = CALCULATE( SUM( SalesOrderDetail[LineTotal] ),
                            SAMEPERIODLASTYEAR( DATESYTD( OrderDate[Date] ) ) )

YoyYtdLineTotal = SalesOrderDetail[YtdLineTotal] - SalesOrderDetail[PyYtdLineTotal]
```

Most of the time, the year-over-year difference is better expressed as a percentage in a report. You can define this calculation by dividing YoyLineTotal by the PyLineTotal; in this way, the difference uses the prior read value as a reference for the percentage difference (100 percent corresponds to a value that is doubled in one year). In the following expression that defines the YoyPercLineTotal measure, the IF statement avoids a divide-by-zero error in case there is no corresponding data in the prior year:

```
YoyPercLineTotal = IF( SalesOrderDetail[PyLineTotal] = 0,
                       BLANK(),
                       SalesOrderDetail[YoyLineTotal] / SalesOrderDetail[PyLineTotal] )
```

A similar calculation can be made to display the percentage difference of a year-over-year comparison for the year-to-date aggregation. You can define YoyPercYtdLineTotal by using the following formula:

```
YoyPercYtdLineTotal = IF( SalesOrderDetail[PyYtdLineTotal] = 0,
                          BLANK(),
                          SalesOrderDetail[YoYYtdLineTotal]
                              / SalesOrderDetail[PyYtdLineTotal] )
```

In Figure 7-44, you can see the results of these measures in a PivotTable.

| Row Labels | Sum of LineTotal | PyLineTotal | YoyLineTotal | YoyYtdLineTotal | YoyPercLineTotal | YoyPercYtdLineTotal | PyYtdLineTotal | YtdLineTotal |
|---|---|---|---|---|---|---|---|---|
| **2001** | **11,331,808.96** | | **11,331,808.96** | **11,331,808.96** | | | | **11,331,808.96** |
| Q3 | 4,647,156.85 | | 4,647,156.85 | 4,647,156.85 | | | | 4,647,156.85 |
| Q4 | 6,684,652.11 | | 6,684,652.11 | 11,331,808.96 | | | | 11,331,808.96 |
| **2002** | **30,674,773.17** | **11,331,808.96** | **19,342,964.21** | **19,342,964.21** | **170.70%** | **170.70%** | **11,331,808.96** | **30,674,773.17** |
| Q1 | 5,860,884.49 | | 5,860,884.49 | 5,860,884.49 | | | | 5,860,884.49 |
| Q2 | 6,167,832.56 | | 6,167,832.56 | 12,028,717.05 | | | | 12,028,717.05 |
| Q3 | 10,277,073.05 | 4,647,156.85 | 5,629,916.20 | 17,658,633.24 | 121.15% | 379.99% | 4,647,156.85 | 22,305,790.10 |
| Q4 | 8,368,983.08 | 6,684,652.11 | 1,684,330.97 | 19,342,964.21 | 25.20% | 170.70% | 11,331,808.96 | 30,674,773.17 |
| **2003** | **42,011,037.16** | **30,674,773.17** | **11,336,263.99** | **11,336,263.99** | **36.96%** | **36.96%** | **30,674,773.17** | **42,011,037.16** |
| Q1 | 6,679,873.80 | 5,860,884.49 | 818,989.31 | 818,989.31 | 13.97% | 13.97% | 5,860,884.49 | 6,679,873.80 |
| Q2 | 8,357,874.88 | 6,167,832.56 | 2,190,042.32 | 3,009,031.64 | 35.51% | 25.02% | 12,028,717.05 | 15,037,748.68 |
| Q3 | 13,681,907.05 | 10,277,073.05 | 3,404,833.99 | 6,413,865.63 | 33.13% | 28.75% | 22,305,790.10 | 28,719,655.73 |
| Q4 | 13,291,381.43 | 8,368,983.08 | 4,922,398.36 | 11,336,263.99 | 58.82% | 36.96% | 30,674,773.17 | 42,011,037.16 |
| **2004** | **25,828,762.10** | **42,011,037.16** | **-16,182,275.06** | **-16,182,275.06** | **-38.52%** | **-38.52%** | **42,011,037.16** | **25,828,762.10** |
| Q1 | 11,398,376.28 | 6,679,873.80 | 4,718,502.47 | 4,718,502.47 | 70.64% | 70.64% | 6,679,873.80 | 11,398,376.28 |
| Q2 | 14,379,545.19 | 8,357,874.88 | 6,021,670.32 | 10,740,172.79 | 72.05% | 71.42% | 15,037,748.68 | 25,777,921.47 |
| Q3 | 50,840.63 | 13,681,907.05 | -13,631,066.42 | -2,890,893.63 | -99.63% | -10.07% | 28,719,655.73 | 25,828,762.10 |
| Q4 | | 13,291,381.43 | -13,291,381.43 | -16,182,275.06 | -100.00% | -38.52% | 42,011,037.16 | 25,828,762.10 |
| **Grand Total** | **109,846,381.40** | **84,017,619.30** | **25,828,762.10** | **-16,182,275.06** | **30.74%** | **-38.52%** | **42,011,037.16** | **25,828,762.10** |

**FIGURE 7-44** The year-over-year (YOY) measures used in a PivotTable.

## Simplifying Browsing with a Period Table

In this chapter, you have seen how to create single measures with special calculations over time, such as year-to-date, year-over-year, and so on. One drawback of this approach is that you have to define one measure for each of these calculations, and the list of the measures in your model might grow too long.

A possible solution to this issue, which is also an interesting generic modeling solution, is to create a special table containing one line for each of the calculations you might want to apply to a measure. In this way, the end user has a shorter list of measures and possible operations on them, instead of having the Cartesian product of these two sets. However, you can also see that this solution has its own drawbacks, and maybe it is better to create just the measures you really want to use in your model, trying to expose only the combinations of measures and calculations that are meaningful for the expected analysis of your data.

First of all, you create a Period table in Excel, which contains the list of possible calculations that should be applied to a measure, as you can see in Figure 7-45. The complete model used for this example is available in the CH07-10-PeriodTable.xlsx workbook included on the companion DVD.

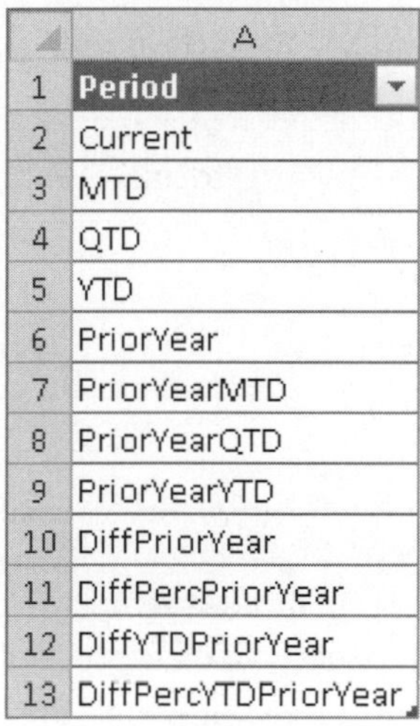

| | A |
|---|---|
| 1 | Period |
| 2 | Current |
| 3 | MTD |
| 4 | QTD |
| 5 | YTD |
| 6 | PriorYear |
| 7 | PriorYearMTD |
| 8 | PriorYearQTD |
| 9 | PriorYearYTD |
| 10 | DiffPriorYear |
| 11 | DiffPercPriorYear |
| 12 | DiffYTDPriorYear |
| 13 | DiffPercYTDPriorYear |

**FIGURE 7-45** A Period table in Excel.

The same table has to be imported as a linked table into PowerPivot. However, you do not have to define any relationships between this table and other tables in your model because you use the selected member of the Period table to change the behavior of a measure through its DAX definition. Nevertheless, PowerPivot warns you of a missing relationship when you browse data in a PivotTable, as you can see in Figure 7-46.

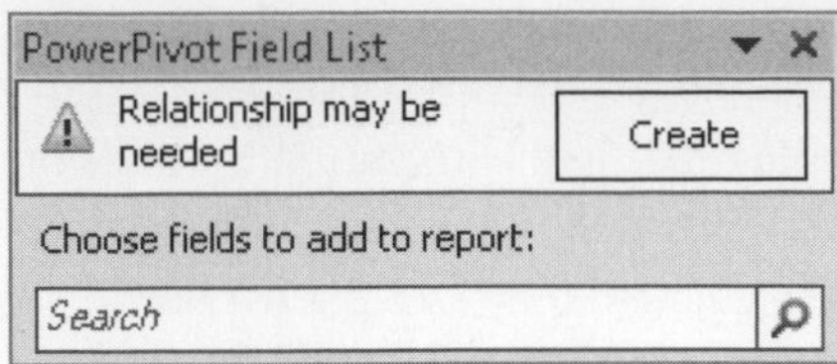


**FIGURE 7-46** A warning about a missing relationship caused by the Period table.

This warning is provoked by the Period table, which does not have any relationships with other tables in the model. You can disable this warning by pressing the Detection button on the PowerPivot tab of the ribbon, which is the one highlighted in Figure 7-47.

**FIGURE 7-47** The Detection button on the PowerPivot tab of the ribbon disables the detection of missing relationships.

At this point, you can define a single measure that checks the selected value of the Period table and uses a DAX expression to return the corresponding calculation. Because there are no relationships with the Period table, the selected value in the Period table is always the one chosen by the user whenever that table is used as a filter, or the selected value is the corresponding value in a row or a column whenever Period is used in Row or Column labels. In general, we follow this generic pattern:

```
= IF( COUNTROWS( VALUES( Period[Period] ) ) = 1,
      IF( VALUES( Period[Period] ) = "Current", <expression>,
      IF( VALUES( Period[Period] ) = "MTD", <expression>,
      ...
```

The first condition checks that there are not multiple values active in the filter context. In such a case, you should avoid any calculation because of the ambiguity of having multiple active values; otherwise, you should generate an error in the calculation, instead of returning a wrong value without warning the user. Then in the next step, each value is checked by a different IF statement, which evaluates the correct expression corresponding to the Period value. Assuming you have all the measures previously defined in this chapter, you need to replace the expression tag with the corresponding specific measure. For example, you can define a generic CalcLineTotal measure, which is used to apply one or more of the operations described in the Period table to the LineTotal measure:

```
CalcLineTotal = IF( COUNTROWS( VALUES( Period[Period] ) ) = 1,
      IF( VALUES( Period[Period] ) = "Current", SUM( SalesOrderDetail[LineTotal] ),
      IF( VALUES( Period[Period] ) = "MTD", SalesOrderDetail[MtdLineTotal],
      IF( VALUES( Period[Period] ) = "QTD", SalesOrderDetail[QtdLineTotal],
      IF( VALUES( Period[Period] ) = "YTD", SalesOrderDetail[YtdLineTotal],
      IF( VALUES( Period[Period] ) = "PriorYear", SalesOrderDetail[PyLineTotal],
      IF( VALUES( Period[Period] ) = "PriorYearMTD", SalesOrderDetail[PyMtdLineTotal],
      IF( VALUES( Period[Period] ) = "PriorYearQTD", SalesOrderDetail[PyQtdLineTotal],
      IF( VALUES( Period[Period] ) = "PriorYearYTD", SalesOrderDetail[PyYtdLineTotal],
      IF( VALUES( Period[Period] ) = "DiffPriorYear", SalesOrderDetail[YoyLineTotal],
      IF( VALUES( Period[Period] ) = "DiffPercPriorYear",
                                          SalesOrderDetail[YoyPercLineTotal],
      IF( VALUES( Period[Period] ) = "DiffYTDPriorYear", SalesOrderDetail[YoyYtdLineTotal],
      IF( VALUES( Period[Period] ) = "DiffPercYTDPriorYear",
                                          SalesOrderDetail[YoyPercYtdLineTotal],
  BLANK() ) ) ) ) ) ) ) ) ) ) ) ) ),
      BLANK() )
```

You have to repeat this definition for each of the measures to which you want to apply the Period calculations. You might avoid defining all the internal measures by replacing each reference to a measure with its corresponding DAX definition. This would make the CalcLineTotal definition longer and hard to maintain, but it is a design choice you might follow.

**Tip** Remember that you cannot hide a measure from a PivotTable (you can hide only calculated columns). So if you do not want to expose internal calculations, you should expand all the measures included in the preceding CalcLineTotal expression.

At this point, you can browse data by using the Period values crossed with the CalcLineTotal measure. In Figure 7-48, only the CalcLineTotal measure has been selected; the Period values are in the columns, and a selection of years and quarters is in the rows.

| CalcLine' Column L | | | | | | | | | | | | |
|---|---|---|---|---|---|---|---|---|---|---|---|---|
| Row L | Current | DiffPer | DiffPercYTE | DiffPriorYear | DiffYTDPriorYear | MTD | PriorYear | PriorYearMTD | PriorYearQTD | PriorYearYTD | QTD | YTD |
| **⊟2002** | **30,674,773** | **2** | **2** | **19,342,964** | **19,342,964** | **2,762,527** | **11,331,809** | **2,458,472** | **6,684,652** | **11,331,809** | **8,368,983** | **30,674,773** |
| Q1 | 5,860,884 | | | 5,860,884 | 5,860,884 | 2,099,416 | | | | | 5,860,884 | 5,860,884 |
| Q2 | 6,167,833 | | | 6,167,833 | 12,028,717 | 1,678,567 | | | | | 6,167,833 | 12,028,717 |
| Q3 | 10,277,073 | 1 | 4 | 5,629,916 | 17,658,633 | 3,235,826 | 4,647,157 | 1,639,840 | 4,647,157 | 4,647,157 | 10,277,073 | 22,305,790 |
| Q4 | 8,368,983 | 0 | 2 | 1,684,331 | 19,342,964 | 2,762,527 | 6,684,652 | 2,458,472 | 6,684,652 | 11,331,809 | 8,368,983 | 30,674,773 |
| **⊟2003** | **42,011,037** | **0** | **0** | **11,336,264** | **11,336,264** | **5,243,008** | **30,674,773** | **2,762,527** | **8,368,983** | **30,674,773** | **13,291,381** | **42,011,037** |
| Q1 | 6,679,874 | 0 | 0 | 818,989 | 818,989 | 2,049,530 | 5,860,884 | 2,099,416 | 5,860,884 | 5,860,884 | 6,679,874 | 6,679,874 |
| Q2 | 8,357,875 | 0 | 0 | 2,190,042 | 3,009,032 | 2,542,672 | 6,167,833 | 1,678,567 | 6,167,833 | 12,028,717 | 8,357,875 | 15,037,749 |
| Q3 | 13,681,907 | 0 | 0 | 3,404,834 | 6,413,866 | 5,059,473 | 10,277,073 | 3,235,826 | 10,277,073 | 22,305,790 | 13,681,907 | 28,719,656 |
| Q4 | 13,291,381 | 1 | 0 | 4,922,398 | 11,336,264 | 5,243,008 | 8,368,983 | 2,762,527 | 8,368,983 | 30,674,773 | 13,291,381 | 42,011,037 |

**FIGURE 7-48** The Period calculations applied to the CalcLineTotal measure.

As we anticipated, this solution has several drawbacks.

- After you put Period in rows or columns, you cannot change the order of its members. Actually, you can do this by using some Excel features, but it is not as immediate and intuitive as moving the list of measures into the Values list in the PowerPivot Field List panel.
- The number format of the measure cannot change for particular calculations requested through some Period values. For example, in Figure 7-48, you can see that the DiffPercPriorYear and DiffPercYTDPriorYear calculations do not display the CalcLineTotal value as a percentage because you can define a single number format for a measure in a PivotTable. A possible workaround is to change the number format directly in Excel cells, but this change is lost as soon as you navigate into the PivotTable.
- If you use more than one measure in the PivotTable, you must create a set based on column items in Excel, choosing only the combination of measures and Period values that you really want to see in the PivotTable. You can see an example of how to create these sets in the "Defining Sets" section of Chapter 8, "Mastering PivotTables."
- You have to create a specific DAX expression for each combination of Period calculations and measures that you want to support. This is not flexible and scalable as a more generic solution could be.

You have to evaluate case by case whether or not these drawbacks make the implementation of a Period table a good option.

### Calculation Parameters Using an Unrelated Table

In the last section, you saw us apply a technique that depends on a table in the PowerPivot model that does not have any relationships with other tables in the same model. In general, this technique might be useful as a way to pass information to a measure as if it were a parameter. For example, imagine that you define a table in Excel that contains all the integers from 1 to 10, and then you import this table into PowerPivot, calling it SimulationParameter. At this point, you might use the value selected in this table in the DAX expressions of your measures, using that number as if it were a parameter passed to your formula. Moving that table into a slicer would be a convenient way for an end user to look at results by changing the selected value.

# Closing Balance over Time

In a PivotTable, each cell contains the result of applying an aggregation function to a measure. Whenever that function is SUM, the measure is called an additive measure because SUM is applied over all dimensions. Whenever another function is applied, such as AVERAGE, MIN, or MAX, the measure is called a nonadditive measure because an aggregation function other than SUM is applied over all dimensions. However, it is important to note that both for additive and nonadditive measures, the same aggregation function is always applied over all dimensions, without exception.

## Semiadditive Measures

Some measures should behave in a different way. For example, think about the balance for a bank account. If you consider several accounts, you can calculate the total balance for an occupation by summing up all the balances of customers grouped by occupation. However, you cannot sum the same balance twice, and you probably have several balances of the same account that measure it over time. For example, in Figure 7-49, you can see a Balance table in Excel: the same account has a balance value for each date. This type of measure is called a semiadditive measure, because it can be aggregated using SUM over some dimensions but requires a different aggregation algorithm over other dimensions. You can find the following example in the CH07-11-SemiAdditive.xlsx workbook included on the companion DVD.

| Name | Occupation | Country | Date | Balance |
|---|---|---|---|---|
| Katie Jordan | Farmer | USA | 2/28/2010 | 2,812.00 |
| Luis Bonifaz | IT Consultant | Argentina | 2/28/2010 | 2,450.00 |
| Maurizio Macagno | IT Consultant | Italy | 2/28/2010 | 2,500.00 |
| Katie Jordan | Farmer | USA | 3/31/2010 | 3,737.00 |
| Luis Bonifaz | IT Consultant | Argentina | 3/31/2010 | 3,430.00 |
| Maurizio Macagno | IT Consultant | Italy | 3/31/2010 | 3,500.00 |
| Katie Jordan | Farmer | USA | 4/30/2010 | 2,250.00 |
| Luis Bonifaz | IT Consultant | Argentina | 4/30/2010 | 1,960.00 |
| Maurizio Macagno | IT Consultant | Italy | 4/30/2010 | 2,000.00 |

**FIGURE 7-49** The raw balance account data.

In the case of account balance data, the only dimension that cannot be summed is the Date. With the term *dimension Date,* we include all the attributes of a Dates table related to the table containing the real measures. The logic that has to be implemented for the Date attributes is to consider only the values belonging to the last date in the evaluated period. In other words, you must implement a logic that can produce the same results that you see in Figure 7-50.

| LastBalance | Column Labels | | |
|---|---|---|---|
| Row Labels | Farmer | IT Consultant | Grand Total |
| **Q1** | **3,737.00** | **6,930.00** | **10,667.00** |
| 01 - January | 1,687.00 | 2,970.00 | 4,657.00 |
| 02 - February | 2,812.00 | 4,950.00 | 7,762.00 |
| 03 - March | 3,737.00 | 6,930.00 | 10,667.00 |
| **Q2** | **2,700.00** | **4,752.00** | **7,452.00** |
| 04 - April | 2,250.00 | 3,960.00 | 6,210.00 |
| 05 - May | 2,025.00 | 3,564.00 | 5,589.00 |
| 06 - June | 2,700.00 | 4,752.00 | 7,452.00 |
| **Q3** | **2,812.00** | **4,950.00** | **7,762.00** |
| 07 - July | 3,600.00 | 6,336.00 | 9,936.00 |
| 08 - August | 5,062.00 | 8,910.00 | 13,972.00 |
| 09 - September | 2,812.00 | 4,950.00 | 7,762.00 |
| **Q4** | **2,531.00** | **4,155.00** | **6,686.00** |
| 10 - October | 2,250.00 | 3,960.00 | 6,210.00 |
| 11 - November | 2,081.00 | 3,663.00 | 5,744.00 |
| 12 - December | 2,531.00 | 4,155.00 | 6,686.00 |
| **Grand Total** | **2,531.00** | **4,155.00** | **6,686.00** |

**FIGURE 7-50** The result of applying the LastBalance measure.

The LastBalance measure used in Figure 7-50 calculates the total of a quarter by using just the last month available in that period. For each month, only the last date for that month is considered. So the total of a quarter is calculated using only the last day of that quarter. You can define the LastBalance measure in this way:

```
LastBalance = CALCULATE( SUM( Balances[Balance] ), LASTDATE( BalanceDate[Date] ) )
```

The definition of the LastBalance measure uses the LASTDATE function to keep just the last date that is active in the current filter context. So only the last date in the selected period is considered in the CALCULATE call.

As usual, you must use a separate Dates table. Remember that the last date in a period is the last date available in the BalanceDate table (mentioned in the preceding formula) and not the last date for which there is raw data. This might have unwanted consequences. If your data does not have values for the last day of a month and the Dates table contains all the days for that month, the LastBalance formula you have used returns no data (a blank value) for that month. Consider the last two months available in the Balances table, as shown in Figure 7-51.

| Name | Occupation | Country | Date | Balance |
|---|---|---|---|---|
| Katie Jordan | Farmer | USA | 11/30/2010 | 2,081.00 |
| Luis Bonifaz | IT Consultant | Argentina | 11/30/2010 | 1,813.00 |
| Maurizio Macagno | IT Consultant | Italy | 11/30/2010 | 1,850.00 |
| Katie Jordan | Farmer | USA | 12/15/2010 | 2,531.00 |
| Luis Bonifaz | IT Consultant | Argentina | 12/15/2010 | 2,205.00 |
| Maurizio Macagno | IT Consultant | Italy | 12/15/2010 | 1,950.00 |

**FIGURE 7-51** The last two months of balance account data.

The Balances table contains a balance for each account and each last day of the month, but for December the last day available is December 15. If the BalanceDate table contains all the days for year 2010, including 31 days for December, the LastBalance measure tries to filter balance data for December 31, which is not available, resulting in a PivotTable like the one shown in Figure 7-52, where the row for December is missing.

| LastBalance | Column Labels | | |
|---|---|---|---|
| Row Labels | Farmer | IT Consultant | Grand Total |
| **Q1** | **3,737.00** | **6,930.00** | **10,667.00** |
| 01 - January | 1,687.00 | 2,970.00 | 4,657.00 |
| 02 - February | 2,812.00 | 4,950.00 | 7,762.00 |
| 03 - March | 3,737.00 | 6,930.00 | 10,667.00 |
| **Q2** | **2,700.00** | **4,752.00** | **7,452.00** |
| 04 - April | 2,250.00 | 3,960.00 | 6,210.00 |
| 05 - May | 2,025.00 | 3,564.00 | 5,589.00 |
| 06 - June | 2,700.00 | 4,752.00 | 7,452.00 |
| **Q3** | **2,812.00** | **4,950.00** | **7,762.00** |
| 07 - July | 3,600.00 | 6,336.00 | 9,936.00 |
| 08 - August | 5,062.00 | 8,910.00 | 13,972.00 |
| 09 - September | 2,812.00 | 4,950.00 | 7,762.00 |
| **Q4** | | | |
| 10 - October | 2,250.00 | 3,960.00 | 6,210.00 |
| 11 - November | 2,081.00 | 3,663.00 | 5,744.00 |

**FIGURE 7-52** December and 4th Quarter totals are missing.

A possible solution is to delete rows from the BalanceDate from December 16 through December 31. In this way, the LastBalance measure returns values as previously shown in Figure 7-50. Another option is to use the LASTNONBLANK function, which returns the last date for which a particular expression is not blank. The use of this function is not very intuitive when the Dates column and the expression you want to evaluate manage different tables. First of all, this is a formula for a LastBalanceNonBlank measure that works also with the BalanceDate complete with all the dates through December 31.

```
LastBalancaNonBlank = CALCULATE( SUM( Balances[Balance] ),
                                 LASTNONBLANK( BalanceDate[Date],
                                               COUNTROWS( RELATEDTABLE(Balances) ) ) )
```

The preceding formula produces exactly the result you saw in Figure 7-50, without your needing to remove rows from the BalanceDate table.

### Using FIRSTNONBLANK and LASTNONBLANK Functions

The LASTNONBLANK function you have just seen has a particular behavior, shared also by FIRSTNONBLANK. The syntax of these functions is the following one:

```
FIRSTNONBLANK( <column>, <expression> )
LASTNONBLANK( <column>, <expression> )
```

These functions return the first or last value in <column>, filtered by the current context, wherein the <expression> is not blank. So these functions behave like SUMX or similar functions in this regard. They set a row context for a value of <column> and then evaluate the <expression> by using that row context. If <expression> and <column> manage data of the same table, everything works fine. However, whenever <expression> uses columns of tables other than the one to which <column> belongs, you need to transform a row context into a filter context by using RELATEDTABLE or CALCULATE. This is a very common situation every time you have a separate Dates table, which is the best practice for every date-related calculation.

To get the right value for the last nonblank date for a given measure/table, you have to use something like this:

```
=LASTNONBLANK( Dates[Date], CALCULATE( COUNT( Balances[Balance] ) ) )
```

It returns the last date (in the current filter context) for which there are values for the Balance column in the Balances table. You can also use an equivalent formula:

```
=LASTNONBLANK( Dates[Date], COUNTROWS( RELATEDTABLE( Sales ) ) )
```

This formula returns the last date (in the current filter context) for which there is a related row in the Sales table.

## OPENINGBALANCE and CLOSINGBALANCE Functions

DAX provides several functions to get the first and last date of a period (year, quarter, or month) that are useful whenever you need to get that value of a selection that is smaller than the whole period considered. For example, looking at the month level (which may be displayed in rows), you might want to display also the value of the end of the quarter and the end of the year in the same row, as you can see in Figure 7-53. (The examples shown in this section are also available in the CH07-12-ClosingBalance.xlsx workbook included on the companion DVD.)

**Note** Please note that raw data used in this example includes balances for dates through December 31. For this reason, the DAX function we are going to use provides complete results because the data based on the LASTDATE function would not work if the last day of a period (such as month, quarter, or year) were missing.

| Row Labels | LastBalance | ClosingBalanceMonth | ClosingBalanceQuarter | ClosingBalanceYear |
|---|---|---|---|---|
| **⊟2010** | **6,686.00** | **6,686.00** | **6,686.00** | **6,686.00** |
| **⊟Q1** | **10,667.00** | **10,667.00** | **10,667.00** | **6,686.00** |
| 01 - January | 4,657.00 | 4,657.00 | 10,667.00 | 6,686.00 |
| 02 - February | 7,762.00 | 7,762.00 | 10,667.00 | 6,686.00 |
| 03 - March | 10,667.00 | 10,667.00 | 10,667.00 | 6,686.00 |
| **⊟Q2** | **7,452.00** | **7,452.00** | **7,452.00** | **6,686.00** |
| 04 - April | 6,210.00 | 6,210.00 | 7,452.00 | 6,686.00 |
| 05 - May | 5,589.00 | 5,589.00 | 7,452.00 | 6,686.00 |
| 06 - June | 7,452.00 | 7,452.00 | 7,452.00 | 6,686.00 |
| **⊟Q3** | **7,762.00** | **7,762.00** | **7,762.00** | **6,686.00** |
| 07 - July | 9,936.00 | 9,936.00 | 7,762.00 | 6,686.00 |
| 08 - August | 13,972.00 | 13,972.00 | 7,762.00 | 6,686.00 |
| 09 - September | 7,762.00 | 7,762.00 | 7,762.00 | 6,686.00 |
| **⊟Q4** | **6,686.00** | **6,686.00** | **6,686.00** | **6,686.00** |
| 10 - October | 6,210.00 | 6,210.00 | 6,686.00 | 6,686.00 |
| 11 - November | 5,744.00 | 5,744.00 | 6,686.00 | 6,686.00 |
| 12 - December | 6,686.00 | 6,686.00 | 6,686.00 | 6,686.00 |
| **Grand Total** | **6,686.00** | **6,686.00** | **6,686.00** | **6,686.00** |

**FIGURE 7-53** The balance data at end of month, quarter, and year for each month.

The formulas used to calculate ClosingBalanceMonth, ClosingBalanceQuarter, and ClosingBalanceYear measures are the following:

```
ClosingBalanceMonth = CLOSINGBALANCEMONTH( SUM( Balances[Balance] ), BalanceDate[Date] )
ClosingBalanceQuarter = CLOSINGBALANCEQUARTER( SUM( Balances[Balance] ), BalanceDate[Date] )
ClosingBalanceYear = CLOSINGBALANCEYEAR( SUM( Balances[Balance] ), BalanceDate[Date] )
```

These formulas use the LASTDATE function internally, but they operate on a set of dates that can extend the current selection in the PivotTable. For example, the CLOSINGBALANCEYEAR function considers the LASTDATE of Balance[Date], which is applied to the last year period of the dates included in the filter context. So for February 2010 (and for any month or quarter of 2010), this date is December 31, 2010. The CLOSINGBALANCEYEAR function behaves like a CALCULATE expression using the ENDOFYEAR function as a filter. As usual, the use of CALCULATE is more generic and flexible, but specific DAX functions like CLOSINGBALANCEYEAR better express the intention of the measure designer. The following are measures equivalent to the ones previously shown using CALCULATE syntax.

```
ClosingBalanceEOM = CALCULATE( SUM( Balances[Balance] ), ENDOFMONTH( BalanceDate[Date] ) )
ClosingBalanceEOQ = CALCULATE( SUM( Balances[Balance] ), ENDOFQUARTER( BalanceDate[Date] ) )
ClosingBalanceEOY = CALCULATE( SUM( Balances[Balance] ), ENDOFYEAR( BalanceDate[Date] ) )
```

**Tip** The DAX functions OPENINGBALANCEMONTH, OPENINGBALANCEQUARTER, and OPENINGBALANCEYEAR use the FIRSTDATE internally instead of the LASTDATE of the considered period. They correspond to the CALCULATE formula, which uses STARTOFMONTH, STARTOFQUARTER, and STARTOFYEAR internally as its filter, respectively.

An important consideration has to be made about dates for which there is available data in your model. You can see this if you drill down to data at the day level in the PivotTable. Before doing that, consider the raw data set we used in this example, shown in Figure 7-54. As you can see, there are more balances for each month. For example, in January there are balances for days 8, 15, 22, and 31.

| Name | Occupation | Country | Date | Balance |
|---|---|---|---|---|
| Katie Jordan | Farmer | USA | 1/8/2010 | 1,540.00 |
| Luis Bonifaz | IT Consultant | Argentina | 1/8/2010 | 2,310.00 |
| Maurizio Macagno | IT Consultant | Italy | 1/8/2010 | 1,450.00 |
| Katie Jordan | Farmer | USA | 1/15/2010 | 1,230.00 |
| Luis Bonifaz | IT Consultant | Argentina | 1/15/2010 | 2,020.00 |
| Maurizio Macagno | IT Consultant | Italy | 1/15/2010 | 1,120.00 |
| Katie Jordan | Farmer | USA | 1/22/2010 | 980.00 |
| Luis Bonifaz | IT Consultant | Argentina | 1/22/2010 | 1,850.00 |
| Maurizio Macagno | IT Consultant | Italy | 1/22/2010 | 630.00 |
| Katie Jordan | Farmer | USA | 1/31/2010 | 1,687.00 |
| Luis Bonifaz | IT Consultant | Argentina | 1/31/2010 | 1,470.00 |
| Maurizio Macagno | IT Consultant | Italy | 1/31/2010 | 1,500.00 |
| Katie Jordan | Farmer | USA | 2/10/2010 | 2,150.00 |
| Luis Bonifaz | IT Consultant | Argentina | 2/10/2010 | 1,230.00 |
| Maurizio Macagno | IT Consultant | Italy | 2/10/2010 | 2,830.00 |
| Katie Jordan | Farmer | USA | 2/19/2010 | 2,030.00 |
| Luis Bonifaz | IT Consultant | Argentina | 2/19/2010 | 1,020.00 |
| Maurizio Macagno | IT Consultant | Italy | 2/19/2010 | 2,140.00 |
| Katie Jordan | Farmer | USA | 2/28/2010 | 2,812.00 |
| Luis Bonifaz | IT Consultant | Argentina | 2/28/2010 | 2,450.00 |
| Maurizio Macagno | IT Consultant | Italy | 2/28/2010 | 2,500.00 |
| Katie Jordan | Farmer | USA | 3/10/2010 | 2,650.00 |
| Luis Bonifaz | IT Consultant | Argentina | 3/10/2010 | 2,180.00 |
| Maurizio Macagno | IT Consultant | Italy | 3/10/2010 | 2,400.00 |

**FIGURE 7-54** The raw balance data with more balances for each month.

**Note** In this example, we always have a balance value for each account, as if we took a snapshot on a certain date for every account available, even if it has not changed its value since the previous date. We see in the next section what to do whenever this condition is not true.

If you browse this data at the day level in the PivotTable by using the same measures as the previous example, you see the results shown in Figure 7-55.

| Row Labels | LastBalance | ClosingBalanceMonth | ClosingBalanceQuarter | ClosingBalanceYear |
|---|---|---|---|---|
| **2010** | **6,686.00** | **6,686.00** | **6,686.00** | **6,686.00** |
| **Q1** | **10,667.00** | **10,667.00** | **10,667.00** | **6,686.00** |
| 01 - January | 4,657.00 | 4,657.00 | 10,667.00 | 6,686.00 |
| 1/1/2010 | | 4,657.00 | 10,667.00 | 6,686.00 |
| 1/2/2010 | | 4,657.00 | 10,667.00 | 6,686.00 |
| 1/3/2010 | | 4,657.00 | 10,667.00 | 6,686.00 |
| 1/4/2010 | | 4,657.00 | 10,667.00 | 6,686.00 |
| 1/5/2010 | | 4,657.00 | 10,667.00 | 6,686.00 |
| 1/6/2010 | | 4,657.00 | 10,667.00 | 6,686.00 |
| 1/7/2010 | | 4,657.00 | 10,667.00 | 6,686.00 |
| 1/8/2010 | 5,300.00 | 4,657.00 | 10,667.00 | 6,686.00 |
| 1/9/2010 | | 4,657.00 | 10,667.00 | 6,686.00 |
| 1/10/2010 | | 4,657.00 | 10,667.00 | 6,686.00 |
| 1/11/2010 | | 4,657.00 | 10,667.00 | 6,686.00 |
| 1/12/2010 | | 4,657.00 | 10,667.00 | 6,686.00 |
| 1/13/2010 | | 4,657.00 | 10,667.00 | 6,686.00 |
| 1/14/2010 | | 4,657.00 | 10,667.00 | 6,686.00 |
| 1/15/2010 | 4,370.00 | 4,657.00 | 10,667.00 | 6,686.00 |
| 1/16/2010 | | 4,657.00 | 10,667.00 | 6,686.00 |
| 1/17/2010 | | 4,657.00 | 10,667.00 | 6,686.00 |

**FIGURE 7-55** Browsing data at the day level displays rows with no balance data.

As you can see, the measures defined to display values at the end of the period suffer an unpleasant side effect: all the dates are visible, even those for which there are no balance data available. If you want to display just the rows corresponding to dates with balance data defined, you have to modify the measures, checking the existence of data in the Balances table, in this way:

```
ClosingBalanceMonth2
    = IF( COUNTROWS( Balances ) > 0,
          CLOSINGBALANCEMONTH( SUM( Balances[Balance] ), BalanceDate[Date] ),
          BLANK() )

ClosingBalanceQuarter2
    = IF( COUNTROWS( Balances ) > 0,
          CLOSINGBALANCEQUARTER( SUM( Balances[Balance] ), BalanceDate[Date] ),
          BLANK() )

ClosingBalanceYear2
    = IF( COUNTROWS( Balances ) > 0,
          CLOSINGBALANCEYEAR( SUM( Balances[Balance] ), BalanceDate[Date] ),
          BLANK() )
```

Browsing data using these measures results in a report like the one shown in Figure 7-56.

| Row Labels | LastBalance | ClosingBalanceMonth2 | ClosingBalanceQuarter2 | ClosingBalanceYear2 |
|---|---|---|---|---|
| **2010** | **6,686.00** | **6,686.00** | **6,686.00** | **6,686.00** |
| **Q1** | **10,667.00** | **10,667.00** | **10,667.00** | **6,686.00** |
| 01 - January | 4,657.00 | 4,657.00 | 10,667.00 | 6,686.00 |
| 1/8/2010 | 5,300.00 | 4,657.00 | 10,667.00 | 6,686.00 |
| 1/15/2010 | 4,370.00 | 4,657.00 | 10,667.00 | 6,686.00 |
| 1/22/2010 | 3,460.00 | 4,657.00 | 10,667.00 | 6,686.00 |
| 1/31/2010 | 4,657.00 | 4,657.00 | 10,667.00 | 6,686.00 |
| 02 - February | 7,762.00 | 7,762.00 | 10,667.00 | 6,686.00 |
| 2/10/2010 | 6,210.00 | 7,762.00 | 10,667.00 | 6,686.00 |
| 2/19/2010 | 5,190.00 | 7,762.00 | 10,667.00 | 6,686.00 |
| 2/28/2010 | 7,762.00 | 7,762.00 | 10,667.00 | 6,686.00 |
| 03 - March | 10,667.00 | 10,667.00 | 10,667.00 | 6,686.00 |
| 3/10/2010 | 7,230.00 | 10,667.00 | 10,667.00 | 6,686.00 |
| 3/31/2010 | 10,667.00 | 10,667.00 | 10,667.00 | 6,686.00 |

**FIGURE 7-56** Using measures that display only days for which there is balance data.

By default, the PivotTable in Excel does not display empty rows and columns. For this reason, the days containing no balance date are not shown: all the measures used in the PivotTable return BLANK for those days, removing them from the report.

## Updating Balances by Using Transactions

The balance account model you saw in the previous section makes an important assumption: for a given date, either data is not present at all or all the accounts have a balance value for that date. In case an account does not have a balance value for a date that other accounts are measured, that account is considered to have a zero balance for that date. This assumption is good for certain data structures, which are generated by a system that makes a snapshot of the situation (all balance accounts values) on a given date.

However, some scenarios have a different data model in which the previous assumption is not valid. For example, consider this other way to collect data about balance accounts. In the Balances table shown in Figure 7-57, data has been normalized by means of an Accounts table, which can be seen on the right side of the same figure. (The model used in this section is available in the CH07-13-ClosingTransaction.xlsx workbook included on the companion DVD.) Moreover, you can find a balance row for an account only for dates when a transaction made some changes in the account balance.

| Account | Date | Balance |
|---|---|---|
| A001 | 1/1/2010 | 1,540.00 |
| A002 | 1/1/2010 | 2,310.00 |
| A003 | 1/1/2010 | 1,450.00 |
| A001 | 1/12/2010 | 1,230.00 |
| A002 | 1/14/2010 | 2,020.00 |
| A003 | 1/15/2010 | 1,120.00 |
| A001 | 1/20/2010 | 980.00 |
| A002 | 1/21/2010 | 1,850.00 |
| A003 | 1/22/2010 | 630.00 |
| A001 | 1/25/2010 | 1,687.00 |
| A002 | 1/26/2010 | 1,470.00 |
| A003 | 1/30/2010 | 1,500.00 |
| A001 | 2/8/2010 | 2,150.00 |
| A002 | 2/9/2010 | 1,230.00 |
| A003 | 2/10/2010 | 2,830.00 |

| Account | Name | Occupation | Country |
|---|---|---|---|
| A001 | Katie Jord | Farmer | USA |
| A002 | Luis Bonif | IT Consultant | Argentina |
| A003 | Maurizio M | IT Consultant | Italy |

**FIGURE 7-57** Raw balance account data updated for transactions and not in snapshots.

As you can see, account A001 changes its value on January 1, 12, 20, and 25; account A002 changes on January 1, 14, 21, and 26; and account A003 changes on January 1, 15, 22, and 30. There is no data at the end of month (January 31), and there is no data for all accounts on a given date (for example, January 12 has an account balance only for account A001). So neither LastBalance nor ClosingBalance measures we have seen before can work with this data because their initial assumptions are not valid anymore. We must create a more complex calculation.

The basic idea is that, for each account, you must get the last nonblank date included in the selected period. The calculation for a single account can be made by using the CALCULATE function and by filtering data on the LASTNONBLANK date included in the period between the first date available and the last date in the period. Notice that the date range considered begins even outside the period: you might request the balance for February and there might be no rows in that month, so previous dates also must be considered for the interval. You use a SUMX function to iterate all the available accounts.

```
SUMX( ALL( Balances[Account] ),
     CALCULATE( SUM( Balances[Balance] ),
                LASTNONBLANK( DATESBETWEEN( BalanceDate[Date],
                                            BLANK(),
                                            LASTDATE( BalanceDate[Date] ) ),
                          CALCULATE( COUNT( Balances[Balance] ) ) ) ) )
```

This expression calculates a value for each date in the BalanceDate table. To get the calculation only for dates that have at least one transaction (for any account), you must make a test similar to the one you saw already in the previous section for ClosingBalance measures. Finally, you can define the complete LastBalanceTx measure by using this DAX formula:

```
LastBalanceTx
  = IF( COUNTX( BalanceDate,
                CALCULATE( COUNT( Balances[Balance] ),
                           ALLEXCEPT( Balances, BalanceDate[Date] ) ) ) > 0,
        SUMX( ALL( Balances[Account] ),
              CALCULATE( SUM( Balances[Balance] ),
                         LASTNONBLANK( DATESBETWEEN( BalanceDate[Date],
                                                     BLANK(),
                                                     LASTDATE( BalanceDate[Date] ) ),
                                       CALCULATE( COUNT( Balances[Balance] ) ) ) ) ),
        BLANK() )
```

This formula produces the result shown in Figure 7-58, in which you can see the balance updated for each account (one for each column) only for days in which at least one new balance is present in the Balances table.

| LastBalanceTx | Column Labels | | | |
|---|---|---|---|---|
| Row Labels | A001 | A002 | A003 | Grand Total |
| **2010** | **2,531.00** | **2,205.00** | **1,950.00** | **6,686.00** |
| **Q1** | **3,737.00** | **3,430.00** | **3,500.00** | **10,667.00** |
| 01 - January | 1,687.00 | 1,470.00 | 1,500.00 | 4,657.00 |
| 1/1/2010 | 1,540.00 | 2,310.00 | 1,450.00 | 5,300.00 |
| 1/12/2010 | 1,230.00 | 2,310.00 | 1,450.00 | 4,990.00 |
| 1/14/2010 | 1,230.00 | 2,020.00 | 1,450.00 | 4,700.00 |
| 1/15/2010 | 1,230.00 | 2,020.00 | 1,120.00 | 4,370.00 |
| 1/20/2010 | 980.00 | 2,020.00 | 1,120.00 | 4,120.00 |
| 1/21/2010 | 980.00 | 1,850.00 | 1,120.00 | 3,950.00 |
| 1/22/2010 | 980.00 | 1,850.00 | 630.00 | 3,460.00 |
| 1/25/2010 | 1,687.00 | 1,850.00 | 630.00 | 4,167.00 |
| 1/26/2010 | 1,687.00 | 1,470.00 | 630.00 | 3,787.00 |
| 1/30/2010 | 1,687.00 | 1,470.00 | 1,500.00 | 4,657.00 |
| 02 - February | 2,812.00 | 2,450.00 | 2,500.00 | 7,762.00 |
| 2/8/2010 | 2,150.00 | 1,470.00 | 1,500.00 | 5,120.00 |
| 2/9/2010 | 2,150.00 | 1,230.00 | 1,500.00 | 4,880.00 |
| 2/10/2010 | 2,150.00 | 1,230.00 | 2,830.00 | 6,210.00 |

**FIGURE 7-58** Results of LastBalanceTx measure.

**Tip** This scenario requires a particularly complex DAX calculation, which becomes much more complicated if other tables are added to the model. The document available in the Microsoft PowerPivot for Excel 2010 Data Analysis Expressions Sample (which can be downloaded at *http://tinyurl.com/DaxSample*) shows a similar example in the Time Intelligence Functions section involving an Inventory Scenario with two tables other than the Dates table. Take a look at that document if you have a similar scenario.

Keep in mind that the Balances[Account] column used to make the relationship with the Accounts table is used in the LastBalanceTx formula and should not be selected in the PivotTable. Instead of that, you should use the Accounts[Account] column; otherwise, you could see wrong data in the PivotTable. The reason is similar to the case for which we suggest you use a Dates table instead of denormalizing all dates information in the same table that contains the measures. So a best practice is to hide in PivotTable all the columns that you use to relate Balances (the table containing measures) to other tables such as BalanceDate and Accounts (which are the tables containing attributes for browsing data).

## Summary

In this chapter, you saw how to create a Dates table for a PowerPivot model and how to use that table to support several types of calculations: number of working days, aggregation and comparison over time, and closing balance over time.

Chapter 8

# Mastering PivotTables

Now that you are acquainted with the DAX language and Microsoft SQL Server PowerPivot for Excel basics, it is time to move into some advanced topics. In this chapter, you are going to learn in deep detail most of the advanced features of PivotTables.

Some of the features we analyze are not exclusive to PowerPivot—they are Excel features that might be applied to any PivotTable. Nevertheless, we feel that it is very important to see how these features can improve the reporting capabilities of PowerPivot.

Please note that this chapter is quite an advanced one, so we will describe formulas and scenarios taking for granted that the reader has sufficient knowledge of DAX and data models. If, during some scenario, you feel the need to better understand a topic, we suggest going back to the chapter where we have explained it, moving forward and backward until you understand the scenario well.

## Understanding Different Types of PivotTables

Excel is able to handle three different types of PivotTables, which seems identical but have some differences that are worth noting. These are the three PivotTables:

- **Classical PivotTable** A PivotTable that uses an Excel worksheet as the data source. This PivotTable has basic functionalities. The calculations are carried on in Excel, and its main limitation is that you can have a single worksheet as the source.
- **PivotTable on an OLAP cube** A PivotTable that uses an OLAP cube running under Microsoft SQL Server Analysis Services (SSAS). This PivotTable has very powerful functionalities that are exposed by the SSAS server. The calculations are made by the Analysis Services server; Excel acts as an interface between the user and the server, and it has no control over how values are computed. The functionalities of this type of PivotTable strongly depend on the Analysis Services data model.
- **PowerPivot PivotTable** This PivotTable is linked to the PowerPivot database engine. In this case, Excel uses the internal PowerPivot engine to perform calculations. The engine is very similar to Analysis Services, although it runs in Excel and not on a remote server. Moreover, in PowerPivot tables, the data model is stored in the Excel workbook, and Excel defines and maintains it.

So even if the user interface of the three PivotTables looks similar, they actually run on completely different engines and provide very different performance and features. Let us review the differences in higher detail.

## File Size

First of all, let us perform a quick analysis of file size. Even if—for modern hard disks—file size seems not to be an important parameter, we need to point out that file size is a good indicator of how much data Excel needs to scan to provide the results of the PivotTable. Clearly, the differing file sizes of the standard PivotTable and PowerPivot matter when the computation is carried on by Excel. When you use SSAS PivotTables, the computation is carried on by the server, so you cannot have any information about the OLAP cube size and memory management. Moreover, for SSAS PivotTables, the Excel file contains only the results of the query, not the original data.

To perform a comparison, we made a very simple test with a worksheet with 121,318 rows and 19 columns (see CH08-01-FileSizeClassical.xlsx on the companion DVD). We saved this data in a standard Excel workbook, and then we loaded it into a PowerPivot table, saving the workbook with a different name (see CH08-02-FileSizePowerPivot.xlsx).

The original Excel workbook occupies 17,170 kilobytes (KB), whereas the PowerPivot workbook occupies only 1,811 KB, resulting in an 88 percent space saving. So if you ever need to share a workbook with somebody else, through Microsoft SharePoint or a simple e-mail message, reducing the size of the workbook is very sensible.

### About Columnar Data Storage

The reason for the very compact PowerPivot file size is that PowerPivot is a columnar data store with automatic deduplication of data. If a value is found more than once in a column, it is stored only once, and all the other occurrences are replaced by a reference to the first value. So if the product color Black occurs 1,000 times, it does not occupy the size of Black multiplied by 1,000 but a much smaller amount of memory.

The rationale behind this data deduplication algorithm is that databases that need to be analyzed through a PivotTable normally contain a lot of duplications. If a column contains many different values, it is not very useful in a PivotTable because we cannot produce interesting aggregates over it. Apart from the key columns, all other attributes in a table should end up with a low number of different values to make them useful aggregators. Because PowerPivot performs data deduplication, it does not matter how many rows are present in the source table: if the number of distinct values of a column is low, the file size is small.

We are not particularly concerned with computation speed because it is hard to measure. Both Excel and PowerPivot engines run at a blazing speed, and from the user point of view, the difference between 0.5 seconds and 0.05 is not noticeable.

## Handling Slicers

Another difference between the types of PivotTables is in the handling of slicers. Slicers are not a PowerPivot-specific feature—they are a standard feature of Excel. Nevertheless, when connected to a PowerPivot database, slicers have a slightly easier user interface, both for their creation (they can be easily created through the Vertical and Horizontal Slicers panes in the PowerPivot Field List) and for their management (PowerPivot slicers are created in a *slicer box* that is easily moveable in the report).

A slicer can be connected to several PivotTables of the same type at the same time, but it cannot be connected to PivotTables of different types. This means that if you have, for example, two PivotTables in the same workbook, one of which is based on SSAS and the other one on PowerPivot, you cannot add a slicer that filters both PivotTables at the same time.

## Flattened PivotTable

You might be used to looking at PivotTables in their classic, browsable shape, wherein each row and column label can be expanded and reduced, as you can see in Figure 8-1. You can find this example in the worksheet CH08-03-Flattened.xlsx on the companion DVD.

| Sum of SalesAmount 1 | Column Labels | | | | |
|---|---|---|---|---|---|
| Row Labels | 2001 | 2002 | 2003 | 2004 | Grand Total |
| Europe | 709,947.20 | 1,627,759.71 | 3,382,979.27 | 3,209,356.08 | 8,930,042.26 |
| France | 180,571.69 | 514,942.01 | 1,026,324.97 | 922,179.04 | 2,644,017.71 |
| Germany | 237,784.99 | 521,230.85 | 1,058,405.73 | 1,076,890.77 | 2,894,312.34 |
| United Kingdom | 291,590.52 | 591,586.85 | 1,298,248.57 | 1,210,286.27 | 3,391,712.21 |
| North America | 1,247,379.26 | 2,748,298.93 | 3,374,296.82 | 3,997,659.37 | 11,367,634.37 |
| Canada | 146,829.81 | 621,602.38 | 535,784.46 | 673,628.21 | 1,977,844.86 |
| United States | 1,100,549.45 | 2,126,696.55 | 2,838,512.36 | 3,324,031.16 | 9,389,789.51 |
| Central | | | 2,768.12 | 232.71 | 3,000.83 |
| Northeast | | | 3,966.81 | 2,565.66 | 6,532.47 |
| Northwest | 415,203.49 | 847,839.26 | 1,094,829.47 | 1,291,994.33 | 3,649,866.55 |
| Southeast | | 782.99 | 3,013.46 | 8,442.40 | 12,238.85 |
| Southwest | 685,345.96 | 1,270,074.30 | 1,733,934.50 | 2,020,796.06 | 5,718,150.81 |
| Pacific | 1,309,047.20 | 2,154,284.88 | 3,033,784.21 | 2,563,884.29 | 9,061,000.58 |
| Grand Total | 3,266,373.66 | 6,530,343.53 | 9,791,060.30 | 9,770,899.74 | 29,358,677.22 |

**FIGURE 8-1** The PivotTable classic layout.

This type of layout is very convenient when browsing data, but it could present some problems if you want to copy the table information into a new Excel file or any other application (including PowerPivot itself) because not all the child rows contain full information. For example, in Figure 8-1, the row for United States does not contain a column for North America because it should be implied by the previous rows. For this reason, PowerPivot introduces a new type of PivotTable, called Flattened Pivot Table, which replicates the data in each row, resulting in a standard tabular format. In Figure 8-2, you can see the same data in a flattened PivotTable.

| Sum of SalesAmount 1 | | | CalendarYe | | | |
|---|---|---|---|---|---|---|
| SalesTerritoryGroup | SalesTerritoryC | SalesTerrito | 2001 | 2002 | 2003 | 2004 |
| Europe | France | France | 180,571.69 | 514,942.01 | 1,026,324.97 | 922,179.04 |
| Europe | Germany | Germany | 237,784.99 | 521,230.85 | 1,058,405.73 | 1,076,890.77 |
| Europe | United Kingdom | United Kingdoı | 291,590.52 | 591,586.85 | 1,298,248.57 | 1,210,286.27 |
| North America | Canada | Canada | 146,829.81 | 621,602.38 | 535,784.46 | 673,628.21 |
| North America | United States | Central | | | 2,768.12 | 232.71 |
| North America | United States | Northeast | | | 3,966.81 | 2,565.66 |
| North America | United States | Northwest | 415,203.49 | 847,839.26 | 1,094,829.47 | 1,291,994.33 |
| North America | United States | Southeast | | 782.99 | 3,013.46 | 8,442.40 |
| North America | United States | Southwest | 685,345.96 | 1,278,074.30 | 1,733,934.50 | 2,020,796.06 |
| Pacific | Australia | Australia | 1,309,047.20 | 2,154,284.88 | 3,033,784.21 | 2,563,884.29 |

**FIGURE 8-2** A flattened PivotTable.

Flattened PivotTables are available only with PowerPivot. You can still mimic the behavior of a classic PivotTable by using the Field Settings dialog box (available by right-clicking the row values of the PivotTable): on the Layout & Print tab, you can configure the PivotTable to show data in tabular form and repeat the line item labels, as you see in Figure 8-3.

**FIGURE 8-3** The Field Settings dialog box lets you change many PivotTable options.

Finally, in Figure 8-4, you can see the classic PivotTable that mimics the flattened PivotTable of PowerPivot.

| Sum of SalesAmount | | | Column Labels | | |
|---|---|---|---|---|---|
| Row Labels | SalesTerritoryCountry | SalesTerritoryRegion | 2002 | 2003 | 2004 |
| ⊟Europe | ⊟France | France | | 1,428,020.38 | 3,179,517.56 |
| Europe | ⊟Germany | Germany | | | 1,983,988.04 |
| Europe | ⊟United Kingdom | United Kingdom | | 1,406,491.96 | 2,872,516.87 |
| ⊟North America | ⊟Canada | Canada | 3,079,806.81 | 5,615,169.14 | 5,682,949.64 |
| North America | ⊟United States | Central | 2,024,175.80 | 2,810,586.67 | 3,071,245.71 |
| North America | United States | Northeast | 1,182,920.47 | 3,352,228.07 | 2,397,693.48 |
| North America | United States | Northwest | 3,255,251.43 | 3,386,959.80 | 5,792,864.77 |
| North America | United States | Southeast | 2,857,047.77 | 2,480,188.69 | 2,530,179.76 |
| North America | United States | Southwest | 3,889,239.48 | 7,442,025.82 | 7,135,193.50 |
| ⊟Pacific | ⊟Australia | Australia | | | 1,594,335.38 |
| Grand Total | | | 16,288,441.77 | 27,921,670.52 | 36,240,484.70 |

**FIGURE 8-4** The classic PivotTable that mimics the flattened PivotTable.

So if you need flattened PivotTables, using the PowerPivot user interface is easier because it simply requires you to choose that kind of PivotTable and produces a slightly better result.

## Comparing Features

Table 8-1 is useful for comparing the different features of the types of PivotTables available in Excel.

**TABLE 8-1 Comparison of features for different PivotTables.**

| Feature | Standard | OLAP | PowerPivot |
|---|---|---|---|
| File Size | Very Big | Does not store data | Very compact |
| Number of tables | 1 | Many (Dimensions) | Many (Tables) |
| Processing | Excel on local PC | SSAS on remote server | PowerPivot on local PC |
| Slicers | From menu | From menu | From Field List |
| Flattened Pivot Tables | Field Settings | Field Settings | Easy creation |

# Custom Sorting in PivotTables

Sorting is useful, no doubt about that; users are accustomed to reading sorted reports, and most of the time, alphabetical order is preferred. So PowerPivot automatically sorts all reports into alphabetical order.

Nevertheless, for some specific columns, alphabetical sorting might not be the right choice. For example, if you have a column that contains three different sizes (small, medium, large), alphabetical sorting would be large, medium, small, which is exactly opposite of what the user normally expects. Moreover, month names are a major issue in this situation: the alphabetical order of month names is obviously wrong because nobody would ever think that April ought to come first.

Luckily, Excel has a very useful feature—Custom Lists—to provide custom sorting. Unluckily, this feature is very well hidden in the Excel user interface. Nevertheless, let us describe it. The Custom Lists feature, as its name suggests, is simply a list of sorted values that Excel can use to show a different sorting.

You can find the Excel Custom Lists item among the Excel options, at the end of the Advanced page, as you can see in Figure 8-5.

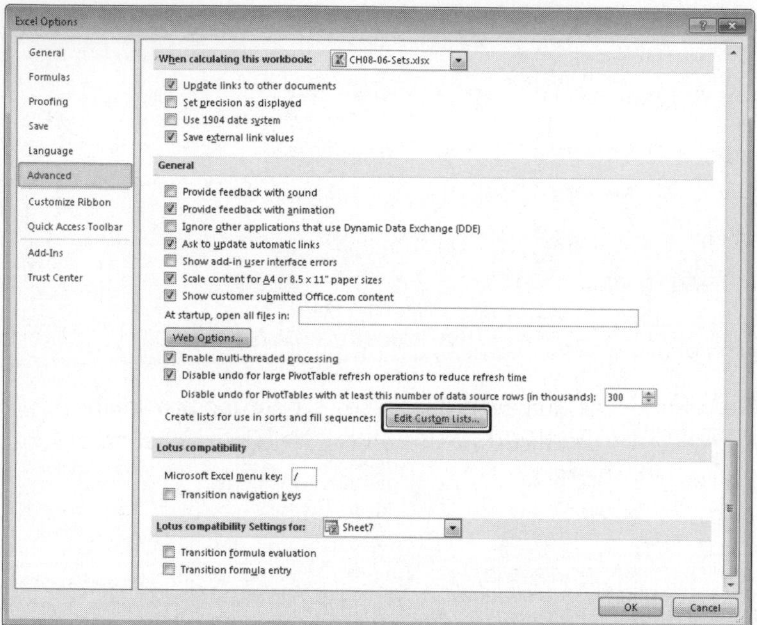


**FIGURE 8-5** Excel Custom Lists is located on the Advanced page of the Excel Options dialog box.

When you open the Custom List dialog box, you can see some custom lists that are shipped with Excel and provide custom sorting for weekdays and month names, localized in your Excel language, as you can see in Figure 8-6.

You can add as many custom lists as you need by listing the values directly into this window or by using an Excel workbook that already contains the sorted list. Now the interesting part of this procedure is that even if month names are present in this window, PowerPivot still refuses to sort month names using the custom list and uses alphabetical ordering instead.

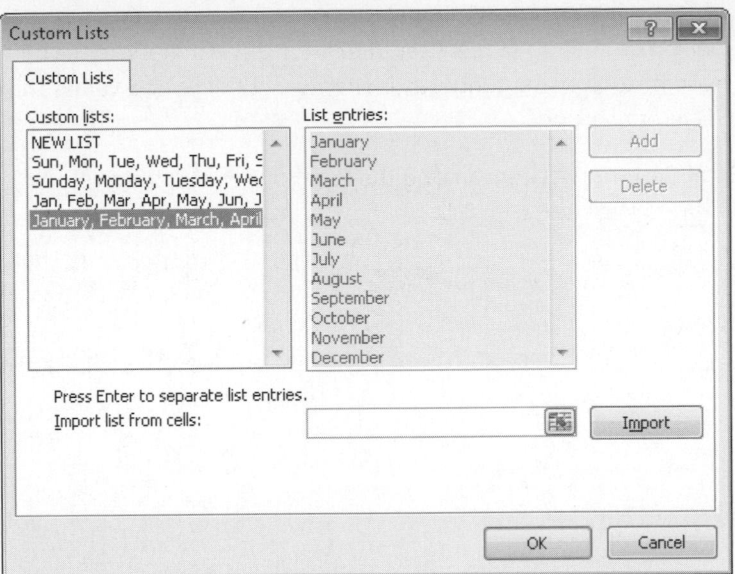


**FIGURE 8-6** The Custom Lists dialog box.

The reason for this is that by default PowerPivot uses the sorting provided by the internal engine, which is not aware of Excel custom lists and always uses alphabetical sorting for strings, as you can see in Figure 8-7.

| Sum of SalesAmount1 | Column Labels | | | | |
|---|---|---|---|---|---|
| **Row Labels** | **2001** | **2002** | **2003** | **2004** | **Grand Total** |
| April | | 882,899.94 | 1,865,278.43 | 2,204,623.41 | 4,952,801.79 |
| August | 1,538,408.31 | 3,601,190.71 | 4,212,971.51 | | 9,352,570.54 |
| December | 1,702,944.54 | 2,185,213.21 | 3,510,948.73 | | 7,399,106.49 |
| February | | 1,900,788.93 | 2,384,846.59 | 2,700,766.80 | 6,986,402.32 |
| January | | 713,116.69 | 1,317,541.83 | 1,662,547.32 | 3,693,205.85 |
| July | 489,328.58 | 2,393,689.53 | 2,665,650.54 | | 5,548,668.64 |
| June | | 1,001,803.77 | 1,987,872.71 | 3,415,479.07 | 6,405,155.55 |
| March | | 1,455,200.41 | 1,563,955.08 | 2,739,370.98 | 5,758,606.48 |
| May | | 2,269,116.71 | 2,880,752.68 | 3,315,275.00 | 8,465,144.40 |
| November | 2,324,135.80 | 3,053,816.33 | 3,483,161.40 | | 8,861,113.53 |
| October | 844,721.00 | 1,802,154.21 | 2,282,115.88 | | 4,928,991.09 |
| September | 1,165,897.08 | 2,885,359.20 | 4,047,574.04 | | 8,098,830.31 |
| **Grand Total** | **8,065,435.31** | **24,144,429.65** | **32,202,669.43** | **16,038,062.60** | **80,450,596.98** |

**FIGURE 8-7** By default, the PivotTable always uses alphabetical sorting.

So you need to do something counterintuitive: you need to tell Excel to sort alphabetically by month name so that it ignores the sorting provided by the internal engine and uses its sorting algorithm. Even if you ask Excel to perform an alphabetical sorting, it still searches its custom lists settings, and because the list of months is present there, it does not perform an alphabetical sorting but the custom sort. To accomplish this, you need to activate the menu shown in Figure 8-8 to sort row values.

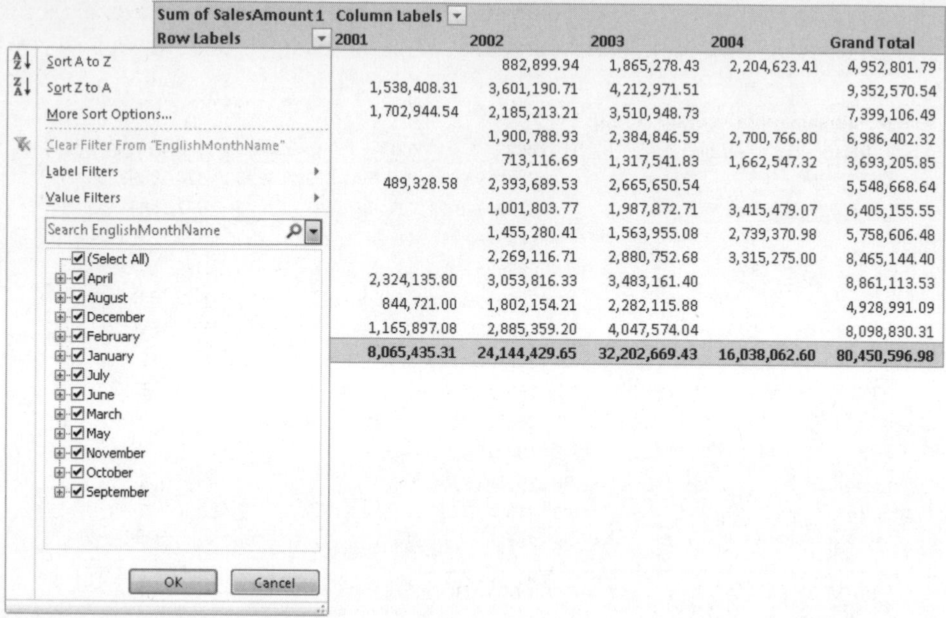


**FIGURE 8-8** The menu for sorting row values.

When you select More Sort Options from this menu, you get the Sort dialog box, from which you need to select the Ascending (A to Z) option, shown in Figure 8-9.

Sort (EnglishMonthName)

Sort options

Data source order

Manual (you can drag items to rearrange them)

Ascending (A to Z) by:

EnglishMonthName

Descending (Z to A) by:

EnglishMonthName

Summary

Sort EnglishMonthName in ascending order

More Options... OK Cancel

**FIGURE 8-9** The Sort dialog box.

As we said, this activates the ascending sort, but if the list of values is present in a custom list, that list takes over the sorting, resulting in a nice report like the one shown in Figure 8-10.

| Sum of SalesAmount1 | Column Labels | | | | |
|---|---|---|---|---|---|
| Row Labels | 2001 | 2002 | 2003 | 2004 | Grand Total |
| January | | 713116.6943 | 1317541.833 | 1662547.324 | 3693205.852 |
| February | | 1900788.93 | 2384846.591 | 2700766.803 | 6986402.325 |
| March | | 1455280.414 | 1563955.081 | 2739370.984 | 5758606.478 |
| April | | 882899.9424 | 1865278.434 | 2204623.412 | 4952801.789 |
| May | | 2269116.712 | 2880752.681 | 3315275.005 | 8465144.397 |
| June | | 1001803.77 | 1987872.707 | 3415479.07 | 6405155.546 |
| July | 489328.5787 | 2393689.526 | 2665650.539 | | 5548668.644 |
| August | 1538408.312 | 3601190.714 | 4212971.51 | | 9352570.536 |
| September | 1165897.078 | 2885359.199 | 4047574.038 | | 8098830.315 |
| October | 844720.9963 | 1802154.213 | 2282115.877 | | 4928991.085 |
| November | 2324135.798 | 3053816.326 | 3483161.403 | | 8861113.527 |
| December | 1702944.543 | 2185213.215 | 3510948.732 | | 7399106.489 |
| **Grand Total** | **8065435.305** | **24144429.65** | **32202669.43** | **16038062.6** | **80450596.98** |

**FIGURE 8-10** When you use custom lists, month names are sorted correctly.

As you see, custom lists are powerful and useful, even if their functionalities are hard to find in the Excel user interface. Now that you know where to find them, you can take care of most of your sorting needs.

**Tip** In Chapter 7, "Date Calculations in DAX," you saw how to add a prefix to the Month column in a Dates table, to get the proper sort order whenever data are displayed. The custom sort in a PivotTable that you see in this section can be used instead, but it requires you to activate it every time you create a new PivotTable.

# Computing Ratios and Percentage in PivotTables

A frequent need, in reporting, is the computation of ratios and percentages. You encounter many situations in which you want to focus more on the percentage each value contributes to other values, than on the value itself. Analyzing the percentage of contribution of geographical areas to the total sales is a common scenario. In this situation, graphs are useful because they provide a simple representation of data. For example, take a look at Figure 8-11. You can find this example in the workbook CH08-04-RatiosPercentage.xlsx on the companion DVD.

| Sum of SalesAmount | Column Labels | | | | |
|---|---|---|---|---|---|
| Row Labels | 2001 | 2002 | 2003 | 2004 | Grand Total |
| Australia | 1,309,047.20 | 2,154,284.88 | 3,033,784.21 | 2,563,884.29 | 9,061,000.58 |
| Canada | 146,829.81 | 621,602.38 | 535,784.46 | 673,628.21 | 1,977,844.86 |
| France | 180,571.69 | 514,942.01 | 1,026,324.97 | 922,179.04 | 2,644,017.71 |
| Germany | 237,784.99 | 521,230.85 | 1,058,405.73 | 1,076,890.77 | 2,894,312.34 |
| United Kingdom | 291,590.52 | 591,586.85 | 1,298,248.57 | 1,210,286.27 | 3,391,712.21 |
| United States | 1,100,549.45 | 2,126,696.55 | 2,838,512.36 | 3,324,031.16 | 9,389,789.51 |
| **Grand Total** | **3,266,373.66** | **6,530,343.53** | **9,791,060.30** | **9,770,899.74** | **29,358,677.22** |

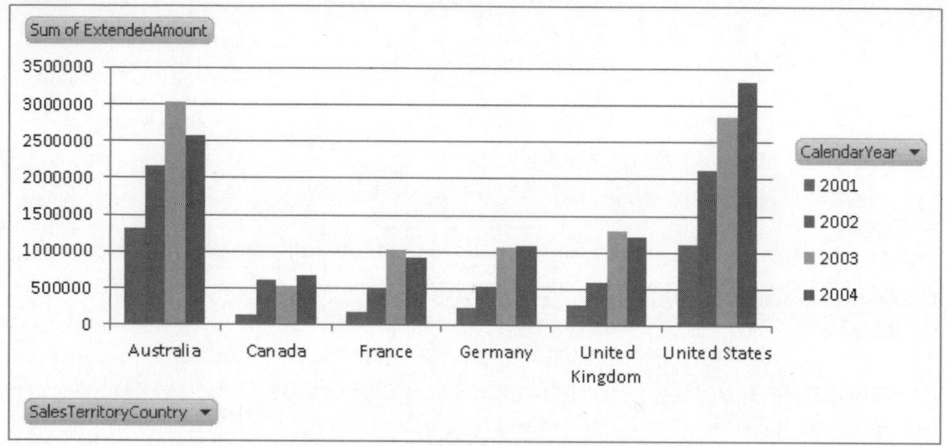


**FIGURE 8-11** Adding a graph greatly increases the expressiveness of a report.

The same report is showing both raw values and a graph that helps you understand how sales moved over years in each country. Nevertheless, neither graph nor raw values give an immediate perception of the percentage change in each country.

In a PivotTable, you can use a powerful feature that lets you convert raw values into percentages and perform several kinds of computation. You can find this feature on the Options tab of the Excel ribbon, on the Show Values As menu, as you see in Figure 8-12.

You can choose from many different options. We are not going to explain all of them in detail; our interest is in describing the overall algorithm that is performed by this feature.

When you select one of these options, Excel first queries the PivotTable to get raw results and then performs a second round of calculations to transform the raw results into ratios, percentages, running totals, or ranking, depending on your request.

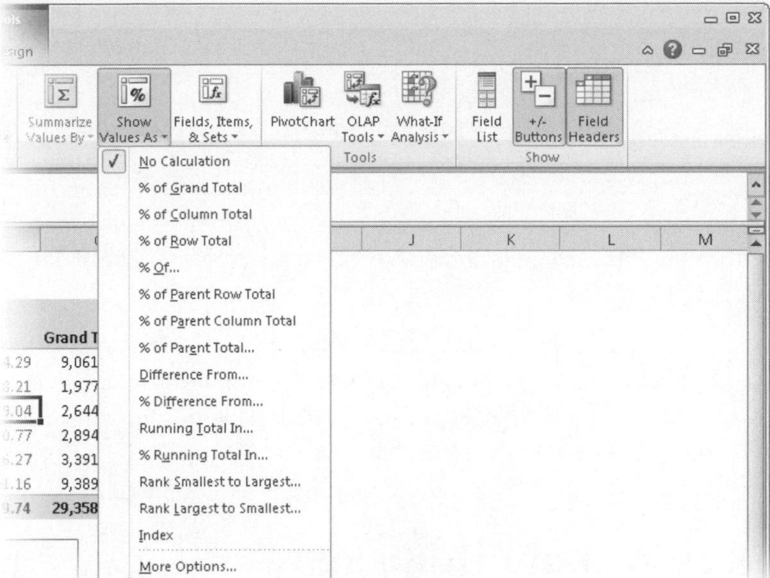


**FIGURE 8-12** The Show Values As menu of Excel 2010.

To better understand how this works, look at Figure 8-13 to see the result of selecting, for example, the % Of Column Total in the previous report.

| Sum of SalesAmount | Column Labels | | | | |
|---|---|---|---|---|---|
| **Row Labels** | **2001** | **2002** | **2003** | **2004** | **Grand Total** |
| Australia | 40.08% | 32.99% | 30.99% | 26.24% | 30.86% |
| Canada | 4.50% | 9.52% | 5.47% | 6.89% | 6.74% |
| France | 5.53% | 7.89% | 10.48% | 9.44% | 9.01% |
| Germany | 7.28% | 7.98% | 10.81% | 11.02% | 9.86% |
| United Kingdom | 8.93% | 9.06% | 13.26% | 12.39% | 11.55% |
| United States | 33.69% | 32.57% | 28.99% | 34.02% | 31.98% |
| **Grand Total** | **100.00%** | **100.00%** | **100.00%** | **100.00%** | **100.00%** |

**FIGURE 8-13** Showing values as percentages of Column Total.

When you select this option, each value is replaced with the percentage of the value over the total of the column. It is now much clearer, for example, that the Australia percentage has a descending path even if the raw value of sales is growing.

It is not fruitful to describe all the different options in this area; the interested reader can easily try them and look at the different results that can be obtained with different kinds of calculations. Instead, we want to note a couple of things:

- Because the calculation is carried on by Excel after the PivotTable has returned the results, this feature works with any type of PivotTable.
- This is an Excel setting, which means that the measures can be shown in the PivotTable, but you cannot use this technique to perform any kind of further computation based on these values.

This last point might be an issue if you ever need to compute such a ratio and then use it further. Excel does not help you get past this potential shortcoming. You definitely need to exploit DAX power. You learn how to make these calculations in both calculated columns and measure in Chapter 9, "PowerPivot DAX Patterns."

## Aggregating Data Without Using Sum

In most of the examples that you have seen up to now, you used the SUM function to summarize data over attributes. For example, if you think about the various date attributes, the aggregate of sales amounts over a year or over a month is the sum of all the sales amounts in that period. The same aggregation applies to any other attribute in any other table. It does not matter whether you want to aggregate by the product color or the sales territory, the aggregate value has always been the sum.

Nevertheless, there are some situations in which you should not sum up all the values to get the total. Instead, you need different aggregators. You saw some examples of this when you learned how to handle the distinct count measure. Distinct count does not aggregate by sum; it uses a special aggregation instead. So it needs to be computed as a measure and cannot be implemented as a calculated column.

The distinct count example clearly shows that the aggregation function depends on the measure—that is, different measures might need different aggregators. These measures are called *nonadditive,* and they require aggregators that are not the simple sum.

Moreover, there are frequent cases in which the aggregation function depends not only on the measure, but on the dimension used to slice data too. When we face such a situation, we speak about *semiadditive measures*. Usually, semiadditive measures are related to calculation over time, and you can read how to handle these scenarios in the last part of Chapter 7, "Date Calculations in DAX."

PowerPivot, by default, handles only additive measures. It uses the SUM aggregation on all numeric columns and COUNT on all strings of all tables. Because PowerPivot does not distinguish additive from nonadditive measures, it needs a default behavior.

If you are facing a regular nonadditive measure, one solution might be to change the function used by PowerPivot to perform the aggregation.

**Note** Beware that this solution works only for nonadditive measures and does not address the problem of semiadditive ones, which we already explained in Chapter 7.

As an example (see CH08-05-OrdersWeight.xlsm companion workbook), let us consider a PowerPivot model in which we gather for each line of the orders, the weight of the item shipped, along with some other useful columns that you can see in Figure 8-14.

| Year | Month | OrderNumber | Product | Freight | Ord... | Weight | ProductCat... | ProductSubc... |
|---|---|---|---|---|---|---|---|---|
| CY 2003 | December | SO59884 | Road-250 Black, 58 | 61.0838 | 1 | 15.68 | Bikes | Road Bikes |
| CY 2003 | December | SO59994 | Road-250 Black, 58 | 61.0838 | 1 | 15.68 | Bikes | Road Bikes |
| CY 2003 | December | SO60164 | Road-250 Black, 58 | 61.0838 | 1 | 15.68 | Bikes | Road Bikes |
| CY 2003 | December | SO60850 | Road-250 Black, 58 | 61.0838 | 1 | 15.68 | Bikes | Road Bikes |
| CY 2003 | December | SO60873 | Road-250 Black, 58 | 61.0838 | 1 | 15.68 | Bikes | Road Bikes |
| CY 2003 | December | SO60880 | Road-250 Black, 58 | 61.0838 | 1 | 15.68 | Bikes | Road Bikes |
| CY 2003 | December | SO61079 | Road-250 Black, 58 | 61.0838 | 1 | 15.68 | Bikes | Road Bikes |
| CY 2004 | January | SO61308 | Road-250 Red, 58 | 61.0838 | 1 | 15.79 | Bikes | Road Bikes |
| CY 2004 | January | SO61429 | Road-250 Red, 58 | 61.0838 | 1 | 15.79 | Bikes | Road Bikes |
| CY 2004 | January | SO61639 | Road-250 Red, 58 | 61.0838 | 1 | 15.79 | Bikes | Road Bikes |

**FIGURE 8-14** Sample data model with order lines and weight.

You can easily build a PivotTable on this model and produce the report in Figure 8-15 where, for each month, we summarize the total number of orders (computed using a measure that performs the distinct count) and the weight.

| Row Labels | NumOfOrders | Sum of Weight |
|---|---|---|
| ⊟ CY 2001 | 1,013.00 | 16,299.36 |
| August | 156.00 | 2,538.04 |
| December | 235.00 | 3,772.89 |
| July | 146.00 | 2,377.08 |
| November | 169.00 | 2,740.56 |
| October | 161.00 | 2,604.09 |
| September | 146.00 | 2,266.70 |
| ⊞ CY 2002 | 2,677.00 | 46,894.27 |
| ⊞ CY 2003 | 10,919.00 | 136,496.27 |
| ⊞ CY 2004 | 13,050.00 | 150,315.81 |
| Grand Total | 27,659.00 | 350,005.71 |

**FIGURE 8-15** A sample PivotTable showing number of orders and weight.

Nevertheless, when it comes to the analysis of weight, the sum of all weights might be not so interesting; it is generally more useful to analyze the average, minimum, and maximum of the weights so that you can make decisions based on this information. To get these different values, you simply need to change the aggregation function.

To change the aggregation function for a measure, you need to click on the column in the ∑ Values pane. From there, you can open a menu in which you select the Summarize By option and then choose among the various aggregator functions that PowerPivot can compute, as you can see in Figure 8-16.

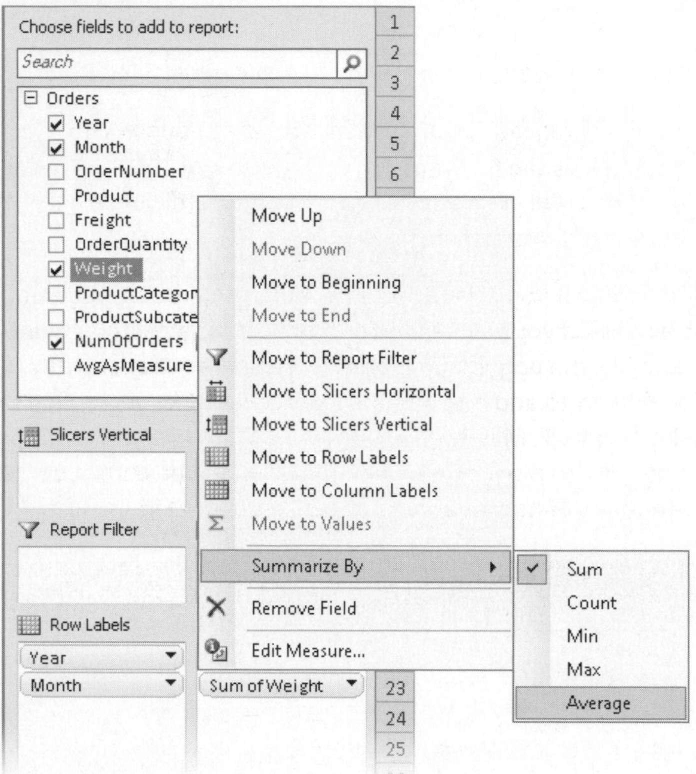


**FIGURE 8-16** You can select among several aggregator functions for each measure.

You can choose Average, for example, to get the average weight of each shipment. Then, by adding the same measure to the values, you can choose another aggregation function. In Figure 8-17, we add the weight three times and have chosen MIN, MAX, and AVERAGE as the aggregators.

| Row Labels | NumOfOrders | Minimum of Weight | Maximum of Weight | Average of Weight |
|---|---|---|---|---|
| **⊟ CY 2001** | **1.013** | **13,77** | **21,42** | **16,09** |
| August | 156 | 13,77 | 21,42 | 16,27 |
| December | 235 | 13,77 | 21,42 | 16,05 |
| July | 146 | 13,77 | 21,42 | 16,28 |
| November | 169 | 13,77 | 21,42 | 16,22 |
| October | 161 | 13,77 | 21,42 | 16,17 |
| September | 146 | 13,77 | 21,42 | 15,53 |
| **⊞ CY 2002** | **2.677** | **13,77** | **24,13** | **17,52** |
| **⊞ CY 2003** | **10.919** | **0,75** | **30,00** | **5,58** |
| **⊞ CY 2004** | **13.050** | **0,75** | **30,00** | **4,66** |
| **Grand Total** | **27.659** | **0,75** | **30,00** | **5,79** |

**FIGURE 8-17** When you select different aggregation functions, you get different results.

Obviously, you can use other aggregators in different situations. Although COUNT is frequently used to get the number of rows (as can be the case for the number of orders or the number of products sold), MIN and MAX can be useful, for example, to get the minimum and maximum discounted price of a product sold over time or, as in the example, for weights.

This procedure is easy to follow if you have a measure that should be aggregated with a specific function. Nevertheless, if you want an easier model, it is better to define a new measure that already contains the aggregation function instead of changing the default aggregator each time you need to add it to a report. Moreover, after you define the new measure, if the aggregation with SUM is not meaningful, you can hide the original column from the PivotTable so that you can select only the measure with the correct aggregation. In our example, you can easily define a new measure, as you see in Figure 8-18.

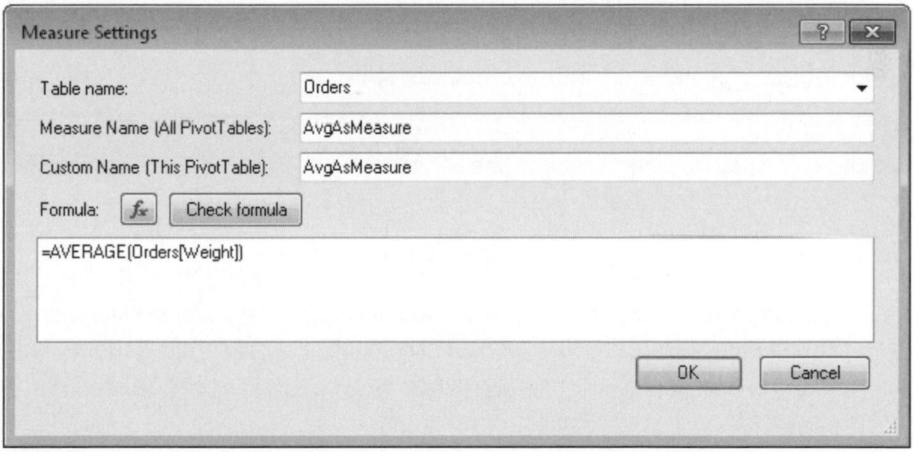

**FIGURE 8-18** A new calculated measure is useful for automatically choosing the correct aggregator.

# Creating Dashboards

Pivot tables are really powerful tools for exploring data. Nevertheless, they often serve as the first step in the production of complex reports that gather data from a PivotTable, and then perform computations, format findings, and provide the final results in compact reports, sometimes called dashboards. Roughly speaking, a dashboard is nothing but a report that contains several pieces of information, each one taken from a query to the database; the result is a compact representation of the company status.

Let us suppose that you want to produce a report that contains the total sales, the growth in percentage of the total sales, and the shares of Internet and reseller sales of the last three years. The report should contain information divided by region so that you can use it to find which regions need your attention.

In Figure 8-19, we show such a report in its final form. You can find the report in the companion workbook CH08-06-Dashboard.xlsx.

| | Total Sales | | | Growth | | 2002 | | 2003 | | 2004 | |
|---|---|---|---|---|---|---|---|---|---|---|---|
| | 2002 | 2003 | 2004 | 2003 | 2004 | Internet | Resell | Internet | Resell | Internet | Resell |
| Europe | 1,478,106 | 4,757,754 | 13,553,399 | 221.88% | 184.87% | 100% | | 40% | 60% | 41% | 59% |
| France | 414,245 | 2,061,420 | 4,772,398 | 397.63% | 131.51% | 100% | | 31% | 69% | 33% | 67% |
| Germany | 513,353 | 593,247 | 3,768,095 | 15.56% | 535.16% | 100% | | 100% | | 47% | 53% |
| United Kingdom | 550,507 | 2,103,087 | 5,012,905 | 282.03% | 138.36% | 100% | | 33% | 67% | 43% | 57% |
| North America | 19,313,719 | 26,826,465 | 33,182,889 | 38.90% | 23.69% | 16% | 84% | 6% | 94% | 20% | 80% |
| Canada | 3,652,908 | 5,920,180 | 6,771,829 | 62.07% | 14.39% | 16% | 84% | 5% | 95% | 16% | 84% |
| United States | 15,660,811 | 20,906,285 | 26,411,060 | 33.49% | 26.33% | 16% | 84% | 7% | 93% | 21% | 79% |
| Central | 2,024,176 | 2,812,658 | 3,072,175 | 38.95% | 9.23% | | 100% | 0% | 100% | 0% | 100% |
| Northeast | 1,182,920 | 3,354,277 | 2,402,177 | 183.56% | -28.38% | | 100% | 0% | 100% | 0% | 100% |
| Northwest | 4,181,083 | 4,006,507 | 7,887,187 | -4.18% | 96.86% | 22% | 78% | 15% | 85% | 27% | 73% |
| Southeast | 2,857,048 | 2,483,826 | 2,538,667 | -13.06% | 2.21% | | 100% | 0% | 100% | 0% | 100% |
| Southwest | 5,415,584 | 8,249,017 | 10,510,854 | 52.32% | 27.42% | 28% | 72% | 10% | 90% | 32% | 68% |
| Pacific | 2,568,701 | 2,099,585 | 5,977,815 | -18.26% | 184.71% | 100% | | 100% | | 73% | 27% |
| Australia | 2,568,701 | 2,099,585 | 5,977,815 | -18.26% | 184.71% | 100% | | 100% | | 73% | 27% |

**FIGURE 8-19** AdventureWorks dashboard for sales by region.

As usual, we are more interested in technique than we are in the real results. So, with a clear idea of the results you want to produce, let us take a closer look at the problems you need to solve.

- The first issue is with the geographical slicing. In the final report, you have data at the group, country, and regional level, but the countries that have only one region have been compacted, removing the region level, which is useless. A PivotTable does not handle this sort of compacting by itself, even though it is a very common request for reports.
- The headers contain total sales and growth divided by year (and the selection of years in the two is different because growth is not shown for the 2002 year). Moreover, in the columns header, you want to show years divided by sales type (Internet and reseller). This mixed kind of slicing is not something that can be realized by a PivotTable.
- Data in the cells is a mix of Internet and reseller sales for some cells (the total sales cells) and a mix of computations in others.
- Moreover, using the conditional formatting option in Excel, the report shows cells of various colors to attract the attention of the reader to the most interesting ones. Clearly, the conditional formatting uses different formulas for different cells.

Needless to say, you cannot produce such a report by using any type of PivotTable. But you can produce the original values needed to compute every single cell by using one or more PivotTables. Just create some PivotTables that perform the computation and then use standard Excel formulas to move the original data to the dashboard.

We are not going to show every step you need to follow to build the report. We just want to focus on the particular characteristics of the dashboard building process. You start by loading tables from the database in PowerPivot and then build a very simple PivotTable that contains the basic information. In Figure 8-20, you can see the PivotTable that contains the report for the reseller sales.

| Sum of SalesAmount | Column Labels | | |
|---|---|---|---|
| Row Labels | 2002 | 2003 | 2004 |
| **⊟Europe** | | **2,834,512.33** | **8,036,022.46** |
| **⊟France** | | **1,428,020.38** | **3,179,517.56** |
| France | | 1,428,020.38 | 3,179,517.56 |
| **⊟Germany** | | | **1,983,988.04** |
| Germany | | | 1,983,988.04 |
| **⊟United Kingdom** | | **1,406,491.96** | **2,872,516.87** |
| United Kingdom | | 1,406,491.96 | 2,872,516.87 |
| **⊟North America** | **16,288,441.77** | **25,087,158.18** | **26,610,126.86** |
| **⊟Canada** | **3,079,806.81** | **5,615,169.14** | **5,682,949.64** |
| Canada | 3,079,806.81 | 5,615,169.14 | 5,682,949.64 |
| **⊟United States** | **13,208,634.95** | **19,471,989.04** | **20,927,177.22** |
| Central | 2,024,175.80 | 2,810,586.67 | 3,071,245.71 |
| Northeast | 1,182,920.47 | 3,352,228.07 | 2,397,693.48 |
| Northwest | 3,255,251.43 | 3,386,959.80 | 5,792,864.77 |
| Southeast | 2,857,047.77 | 2,480,188.69 | 2,530,179.76 |
| Southwest | 3,889,239.48 | 7,442,025.82 | 7,135,193.50 |
| **⊟Pacific** | | | **1,594,335.38** |
| **⊟Australia** | | | **1,594,335.38** |
| Australia | | | 1,594,335.38 |
| **Grand Total** | **16,288,441.77** | **27,921,670.52** | **36,240,404.70** |

**FIGURE 8-20** The original PivotTable that contains reseller sales.

This PivotTable, together with a very similar one built on top of Internet sales, contains the basic information that you need to build the dashboard. Because this is a PowerPivot workbook, you might expect to build a very complex DAX formula that magically produces the dashboard, but this is not the case. PivotTables are useful for exploring data in an interactive way, but there is no need to push them too far from their nature. After you have data available, it is an Excel task to move it to the dashboard and perform further computations.

You can base your dashboard on the PivotTable you just created, creating formulas that move information from the PivotTable to the dashboard. Nevertheless, PivotTables are, by their very nature, dynamic. They can change their size if new values appear in the source tables. So if you reference the cells in the PivotTable directly, you risk needing to update formulas as the source data is updated. It would be much better if you find a way to fix the PivotTable so that it cannot dynamically change its size.

Luckily, an option in Excel helps you convert the dynamic PivotTable in a set of static formulas that show the same data but without the dynamic nature of the PivotTable. You lose the ability to navigate your data, but you gain the immobility of cells.

On the Options tab, a button named OLAP Tools contains a number of features, one of which is Convert To Formulas, as you can see in Figure 8-21.

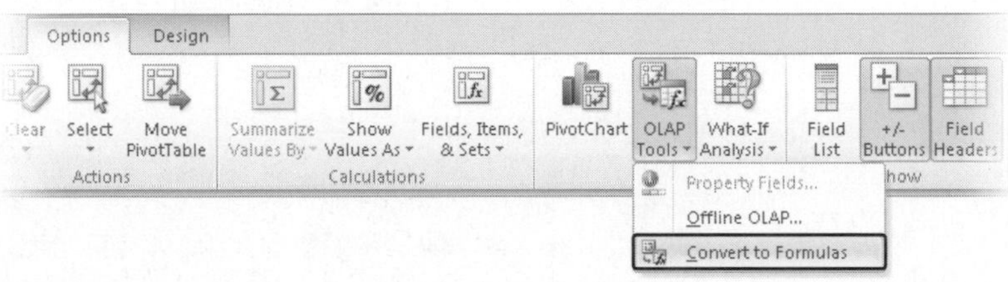


**FIGURE 8-21** The Convert To Formulas option.

If you choose this option, the PivotTable is deleted and returns to being a standard Excel worksheet that contains a formula for each of the original cells, as you can see in Figure 8-22.

| | Column Labels | | |
|---|---|---|---|
| | 2002 | 2003 | 2004 |
| Row Labels | Sum of SalesAmount | Sum of SalesAmount | Sum of SalesAmount |
| Europe | | 2,834,512.33 | 8,036,022.46 |
| France | | 1,428,020.38 | 3,179,517.56 |
| France | | 1,428,020.38 | 3,179,517.56 |
| Germany | | | 1,983,988.04 |
| Germany | | | 1,983,988.04 |
| United Kingdom | | 1,406,491.96 | 2,872,516.87 |
| United Kingdom | | 1,406,491.96 | 2,872,516.87 |
| North America | 16,288,441.77 | 25,087,158.18 | 26,610,126.86 |
| Canada | 3,079,806.81 | 5,615,169.14 | 5,682,949.64 |
| Canada | 3,079,806.81 | 5,615,169.14 | 5,682,949.64 |
| United States | 13,208,634.95 | 19,471,989.04 | 20,927,177.22 |
| Central | 2,024,175.80 | 2,810,586.67 | 3,071,245.71 |
| Northeast | 1,182,920.47 | 3,352,228.07 | 2,397,693.48 |
| Northwest | 3,255,251.43 | 3,386,959.80 | 5,792,864.77 |
| Southeast | 2,857,047.77 | 2,480,188.69 | 2,530,179.76 |
| Southwest | 3,889,239.48 | 7,442,025.82 | 7,135,193.50 |
| Pacific | | | 1,594,335.38 |
| Australia | | | 1,594,335.38 |
| Australia | | | 1,594,335.38 |
| Grand Total | 16,288,441.77 | 27,921,670.52 | 36,240,484.70 |

**FIGURE 8-22** The worksheet that contains PivotTable, after Convert To Formulas has been applied.

Now take a look at the formulas inside the cells. They are of two different types:

- **CUBEMEMBER** This type of formula is used for headers of both columns and rows. It returns an object, called *a member*, which is basically the value of a column in a table. For example, the formula in the 2002 header contains

  ```
  = CUBEMEMBER( "PowerPivot Data", "[DimTime].[FiscalYear].&[2002]" )
  ```

  and it can be read as *return the value of the column FiscalYear in table DimTime where the value is 2002*. The formula might be confusing because we are asking for something whose value is 2002 and provide 2002 as the final parameter. This has to do with the internals of PowerPivot, which reasons in terms of members and values of an OLAP cube.
- **CUBEVALUE** This type of formula is used for the cells in the table. Each cell asks for a value that gives the set of members that form the coordinates of the requested value. For example, in the case of sales in North America for the 2002 year, these are the coordinates:
  - [Measures].[Sum of SalesAmount]
  - [DimTime].[FiscalYear].&[2002]
  - [DimSalesTerritory].[SalesTerritoryGroup].&[North America]

  The result is the value of the measure SalesAmount in 2002 for North America.

Readers used to OLAP databases recognize in these formulas the standard set of coordinates used to navigate OLAP cubes. In fact, at the very end, PowerPivot stores its data in cubes that are automatically processed by PowerPivot itself, which we show later in this chapter.

The really interesting part of all this is that now the worksheet is composed of formulas (the PivotTable disappeared), and the formulas can be moved wherever you want them. Moreover, even if the source data changes, Excel does not change the position of any cell.

You can now create a new worksheet and proceed to write your dashboard, referencing the values in this new set of cells. But be careful: if a cube does not return any data, it is returned by CUBEMEMBER as an empty string. So whenever you need to reference its value, you need to surround it with an IF, as in the cell Total Sales in Europe for 2002 of Figure 8-14, which contains this formula:

```
= IF( Internet!C6 = "", 0, Internet!C6 ) + IF( Resellers!C6 = "", 0, Resellers!C6 )
```

This is the only particular care you need to take when using values coming from an OLAP cube—that is, you need to remember that empty values are empty strings, not numbers. The remainder of the dashboard can be easily created by using standard Excel formulas and some formatting, all things that are already well known and documented.

**Note** Results from OLAP cubes are always strings, so the ISBLANK function does not help here.

The really interesting part of this section is not in the dashboard itself but in the fact that when you convert a PivotTable into formulas, you can use data coming from PowerPivot as the first layer of a more complex workbook, which uses the original data to provide values, indicators, and other information that can be later processed with the full power of Excel.

## Using Complex Queries as Linked Tables

Let us suppose that you have an OLAP query that produces interesting results that you want to import to PowerPivot. If the results are already present in the query, you know that you can easily reproduce the query in MDX using the designer and directly import data into PowerPivot. Nevertheless, PivotTables are frequently used as the source of data for more complex or customized calculations, which might be not handled by the OLAP cube.

In Figure 8-23, you can see a simple PivotTable that shows quantity and sales for a product category (Bikes) divided into months. We added two columns that compute the contribution of every month to the year total as a percentage. You can see this example in the companion workbook CH08-07-LinkedTables.xlsx.

Product Categories Bikes

| Row Labels | Internet Order Quantity | Sales Amount | Quantity % | Amount % |
|---|---|---|---|---|
| July 2003 | 514 | $2,789,429.42 | 5.26% | 6.29% |
| August 2003 | 495 | $3,873,895.93 | 5.06% | 8.73% |
| September 2003 | 585 | $3,839,855.71 | 5.98% | 8.66% |
| October 2003 | 622 | $2,873,877.41 | 6.36% | 6.48% |
| November 2003 | 698 | $3,922,568.55 | 7.14% | 8.84% |
| December 2003 | 1,058 | $4,489,158.85 | 10.82% | 10.12% |
| January 2004 | 779 | $2,707,692.98 | 7.97% | 6.11% |
| February 2004 | 847 | $3,732,702.39 | 8.66% | 8.42% |
| March 2004 | 881 | $3,821,921.24 | 9.01% | 8.62% |
| April 2004 | 975 | $3,299,529.19 | 9.97% | 7.44% |
| May 2004 | 1,137 | $4,434,639.66 | 11.63% | 10.00% |
| June 2004 | 1,186 | $4,565,082.56 | 12.13% | 10.29% |
| **Grand Total** | **9,777** | **$44,350,353.90** | 100.00% | 100.00% |

**FIGURE 8-23** An Excel worksheet that mixes OLAP queries and Excel calculations.

Now, let us suppose that you want to import this data to PowerPivot. Obviously, because the worksheet is not the result of a simple OLAP query, you cannot import the values directly to PowerPivot by using the MDX query designer. You have no way to express the complexity of the Excel computations in an MDX query by using just the built-in query designer.

You can try to use the Create Linked Table option of PowerPivot, but it will complain that no table exists, and if you try to format the PivotTable as an Excel table, Excel itself refuses to do that because a PivotTable cannot be the source of an Excel table.

You can always use the copy and paste operation, but this strategy prevents you from automatically refreshing data in PowerPivot later.

So it seems that the task of importing complex calculations involving a PivotTable in PowerPivot is harder than expected. Nevertheless, a simple trick makes it an easy procedure.

You can use standard Excel formulas to copy the values from the original cells into another part of the same workbook, which is then a standard Excel range, with no PivotTable in it. At that point, this new range can be formatted as an Excel table and consequently imported into PowerPivot. Please note that we are not using anything fancy here, just copying data from a cell to another one, to move it into a place in which we can leverage PowerPivot linked tables.

In Figure 8-24, you can see that the Excel table contains exactly the same information that is computed in the PivotTable, but because it is an Excel table, it can be easily imported to PowerPivot.

Product Categories Bikes

| Row Labels | Internet | Sales Amount | Quantity % | Amount % |
|---|---|---|---|---|
| July 2003 | 514 | $2,789,429.42 | 5.26% | 6.29% |
| August 2003 | 495 | $3,873,895.93 | 5.06% | 8.73% |
| September 2003 | 585 | $3,839,855.71 | 5.98% | 8.66% |
| October 2003 | 622 | $2,873,877.41 | 6.36% | 6.48% |
| November 2003 | 698 | $3,922,568.55 | 7.14% | 8.84% |
| December 2003 | 1,058 | $4,489,158.85 | 10.82% | 10.12% |
| January 2004 | 779 | $2,707,692.90 | 7.97% | 6.11% |
| February 2004 | 847 | $3,732,702.39 | 8.66% | 8.42% |
| March 2004 | 881 | $3,821,921.24 | 9.01% | 8.62% |
| April 2004 | 975 | $3,299,529.19 | 9.97% | 7.44% |
| May 2004 | 1,137 | $4,434,639.66 | 11.63% | 10.00% |
| June 2004 | 1,186 | $4,565,082.56 | 12.13% | 10.29% |
| **Grand Total** | **9,777** | **$44,350,353.90** | 100.00% | 100.00% |

| Month | Quantity | Amount | Quantity % | Amount % |
|---|---|---|---|---|
| July 2003 | 514.00 | 2,789,429.42 | 5% | 6% |
| August 2003 | 495.00 | 3,873,895.93 | 5% | 9% |
| September 2003 | 585.00 | 3,839,855.71 | 6% | 9% |
| October 2003 | 622.00 | 2,873,877.41 | 6% | 6% |
| November 2003 | 698.00 | 3,922,568.55 | 7% | 9% |
| December 2003 | 1,058.00 | 4,489,158.85 | 11% | 10% |
| January 2004 | 779.00 | 2,707,692.98 | 8% | 6% |
| February 2004 | 847.00 | 3,732,702.39 | 9% | 8% |
| March 2004 | 881.00 | 3,821,921.24 | 9% | 9% |
| April 2004 | 975.00 | 3,299,529.19 | 10% | 7% |
| May 2004 | 1,137.00 | 4,434,639.66 | 12% | 10% |
| June 2004 | 1,186.00 | 4,565,082.56 | 12% | 10% |
| Grand Total | 9,777.00 | 44,350,353.90 | 100% | 100% |

**FIGURE 8-24** A PivotTable converted to an Excel table to let PowerPivot load its data.

**Note** The same technique might be used to reload data from a PivotTable computed by PowerPivot. Having the ability to reload data already computed by PowerPivot lets you create very complex workbooks that perform the final computation in more than one step. First, data is loaded into PowerPivot and used to create PivotTables that perform the first steps of the computation. Then, data is fed again to the PowerPivot engine to build more complex data structures.

# Performing Analysis of Old and New Data Together

Another common scenario occurs when you need to add information to an existing table. For example, when you analyze a budget, you can gather historical information based on previous sales of existing items. Let us suppose that you have access to an OLAP cube that contains all the old stuff. That said, to compute correct data, you frequently need to add some anticipatory information about new items that are going to be introduced to the market. These new products are not part of the existing database because, by their very definition, they are new.

You cannot perform this type of analysis on standard OLAP cubes because there is no way to add new items to their existing dimensions or fact tables. Nevertheless, using PowerPivot you can load the original data, add the new information, and then recompute new PivotTables that take new data into account.

Let us suppose that, at the end of 2004, you want to forecast sales, using both last year sales, with a correction factor, and predicted sales about new bikes that you plan to introduce to the market. To perform this task, you start loading the original data, update it with the correction factor so that they reflect your predicted sales, and then you are ready to add more information to the table, to reflect the introduction of new products.

The first set of data is captured from the OLAP cube, using the query shown in Figure 8-25. You can follow this example in the companion workbook CH08-08-NewProducts.xlsx.

| Dimension | Hierarchy | Operator | Filter Expression | Parame... |
|---|---|---|---|---|
| Date | Date.Fiscal | Equal | { FY 2004 } | ☐ |
| Product | Product Model Categ... | Equal | { Bikes } | ☐ |
| <Select dimension> | | | | |

| Category | Subcategory | Model | Fiscal Year | Month | Internet Sales Amount | Internet Order Quant... |
|---|---|---|---|---|---|---|
| Bikes | Mountain Bikes | Mountain-200 | FY 2004 | July 2003 | 346048.5 | 150 |
| Bikes | Mountain Bikes | Mountain-200 | FY 2004 | August 2003 | 279043.79 | 121 |
| Bikes | Mountain Bikes | Mountain-200 | FY 2004 | September 2003 | 357648.45 | 155 |
| Bikes | Mountain Bikes | Mountain-200 | FY 2004 | October 2003 | 366953.41 | 159 |
| Bikes | Mountain Bikes | Mountain-200 | FY 2004 | November 2003 | 415173.2 | 180 |
| Bikes | Mountain Bikes | Mountain-200 | FY 2004 | December 2003 | 551302.61 | 239 |
| Bikes | Mountain Bikes | Mountain-200 | FY 2004 | January 2004 | 461473 | 200 |
| Bikes | Mountain Bikes | Mountain-200 | FY 2004 | February 2004 | 512212.78 | 222 |
| Bikes | Mountain Bikes | Mountain-200 | FY 2004 | March 2004 | 507572.8 | 220 |
| Bikes | Mountain Bikes | Mountain-200 | FY 2004 | April 2004 | 514482.77 | 223 |
| Bikes | Mountain Bikes | Mountain-200 | FY 2004 | May 2004 | 694616.99 | 301 |
| Bikes | Mountain Bikes | Mountain-200 | FY 2004 | June 2004 | 708536.93 | 307 |
| Bikes | Mountain Bikes | Mountain-400-W | FY 2004 | July 2003 | 15389.8 | 20 |
| Bikes | Mountain Bikes | Mountain-400-W | FY 2004 | August 2003 | 20006.74 | 26 |
| Bikes | Mountain Bikes | Mountain-400-W | FY 2004 | September 2003 | 20776.23 | 27 |
| Bikes | Mountain Bikes | Mountain-400-W | FY 2004 | October 2003 | 26162.66 | 34 |
| Bikes | Mountain Bikes | Mountain-400-W | FY 2004 | November 2003 | 27701.64 | 36 |
| Bikes | Mountain Bikes | Mountain-400-W | FY 2004 | December 2003 | 49247.36 | 64 |
| Bikes | Mountain Bikes | Mountain-400-W | FY 2004 | January 2004 | 33088.07 | 43 |
| Bikes | Mountain Bikes | Mountain-400-W | FY 2004 | February 2004 | 33857.56 | 44 |

**FIGURE 8-25** The 2004 sales taken from the OLAP cube.

You end up with a table that contains the sales for the fiscal year 2004. To change it to fit your needs, you rename some columns. Year becomes OriginalYear, amount becomes OriginalAmount, and you add new columns, which are computed based on the original ones, to move time one year forward, to which you apply the 7.5 percent increase. The only tricky column is the month name, which requires some string acrobatics to be computed. The formula for the month name is this:

```
= LEFT( OriginalSales[OriginalMonth],
        FIND( " ", OriginalSales[OriginalMonth] ) )
  & ( VALUE( RIGHT( OriginalSales[OriginalMonth], 4 ) + 1 )
```

Now you end up with a table, shown in Figure 8-26, that contains the predicted sales for the next fiscal year. Please note that in the figure we already hid the original columns, retaining only the predicted columns.

| Category | SubCategory | Model | Month | Year | Amount | Quantity |
|---|---|---|---|---|---|---|
| Bikes | Mountain Bikes | Mountain-200 | July 2004 | 2005 | 372,002.14 | 161 |
| Bikes | Mountain Bikes | Mountain-200 | August 2004 | 2005 | 299,972.07 | 130 |
| Bikes | Mountain Bikes | Mountain-200 | September 2004 | 2005 | 384,472.08 | 167 |
| Bikes | Mountain Bikes | Mountain-200 | October 2004 | 2005 | 394,474.92 | 171 |
| Bikes | Mountain Bikes | Mountain-200 | November 2004 | 2005 | 446,311.19 | 194 |
| Bikes | Mountain Bikes | Mountain-200 | December 2004 | 2005 | 592,650.31 | 257 |
| Bikes | Mountain Bikes | Mountain-200 | January 2005 | 2005 | 496,083.48 | 215 |
| Bikes | Mountain Bikes | Mountain-200 | February 2005 | 2005 | 550,628.74 | 239 |
| Bikes | Mountain Bikes | Mountain-200 | March 2005 | 2005 | 545,640.76 | 237 |

**FIGURE 8-26** The table that contains predicted sales.

As you see, applying the corrective factor is easy. The next step is to add some rows to this table so that you can simulate the existence of products that are not stored in the original database.

You have a couple of options here. If the original table is a small one, such as this example, you can simply copy the table from PowerPivot into a new Excel worksheet, update it with new data, and then create a new linked table based on that worksheet, which in turn is the source for your PivotTable.

Although this technique works pretty well for small amounts of data, it has the disadvantage of being inappropriate when the number of rows grows too much because you can easily end up with very big workbooks. (Remember that Excel files with millions of rows are slow and big.) Moreover, if the original data changes for some reason, updating it with new data becomes difficult because you must perform a complex process to re-create the merged table.

A better way to accomplish this task is to create an Excel worksheet that contains only the new products and then merge it with the table that contains old data. In this way, the original table can be updated by simply reloading it from the data source, and the only part of the process that needs to be redone in case of update is the merging procedure.

So now we need to create a worksheet that can be appended to our table. The easiest way to perform this task is to copy the original table from PowerPivot, paste it into a new Excel worksheet, and then delete all the rows, retaining only the structure. When you do this, you must be sure that column names are exactly the same and in the same order as the original PowerPivot table. To perform this task, it is enough to open the PowerPivot window, select the whole table, and do a copy and paste operation in Excel.

The resulting table, already filled with new data, is shown in Figure 8-27.

| Category | SubCategory | Model | Month | Year | Amount | Quantity |
|---|---|---|---|---|---|---|
| Bikes | Mountain Bikes | Mountain-900 | July 2004 | 2005 | 0.00 | 0 |
| Bikes | Mountain Bikes | Mountain-900 | August 2004 | 2005 | 0.00 | 0 |
| Bikes | Mountain Bikes | Mountain-900 | September 2004 | 2005 | 0.00 | 0 |
| Bikes | Mountain Bikes | Mountain-900 | October 2004 | 2005 | 171,500.00 | 70 |
| Bikes | Mountain Bikes | Mountain-900 | November 2004 | 2005 | 220,500.00 | 90 |
| Bikes | Mountain Bikes | Mountain-900 | December 2004 | 2005 | 294,000.00 | 120 |
| Bikes | Mountain Bikes | Mountain-900 | January 2005 | 2005 | 367,500.00 | 150 |
| Bikes | Mountain Bikes | Mountain-900 | February 2005 | 2005 | 343,000.00 | 140 |
| Bikes | Mountain Bikes | Mountain-900 | March 2005 | 2005 | 294,000.00 | 120 |
| Bikes | Mountain Bikes | Mountain-900 | April 2005 | 2005 | 245,000.00 | 100 |
| Bikes | Mountain Bikes | Mountain-900 | May 2005 | 2005 | 220,500.00 | 90 |
| Bikes | Mountain Bikes | Mountain-900 | June 2005 | 2005 | 269,500.00 | 110 |

**FIGURE 8-27** The Excel table is ready to be appended to the original PowerPivot table.

Now you could be tempted to copy and paste it directly to the original table. Unfortunately, that does not work because the original table is tied to an external data source, and you cannot add any rows to it. If you could to that, PowerPivot would not be able to refresh it later. To merge the two tables, you need to create a new one and copy data from both the prediction table and the new products table within it.

To create that table, you can simply copy the whole original table and then paste it into a new table, which you call MergedSales. As soon as you click the Paste button, the Paste Preview dialog box appears (see Figure 8-28).

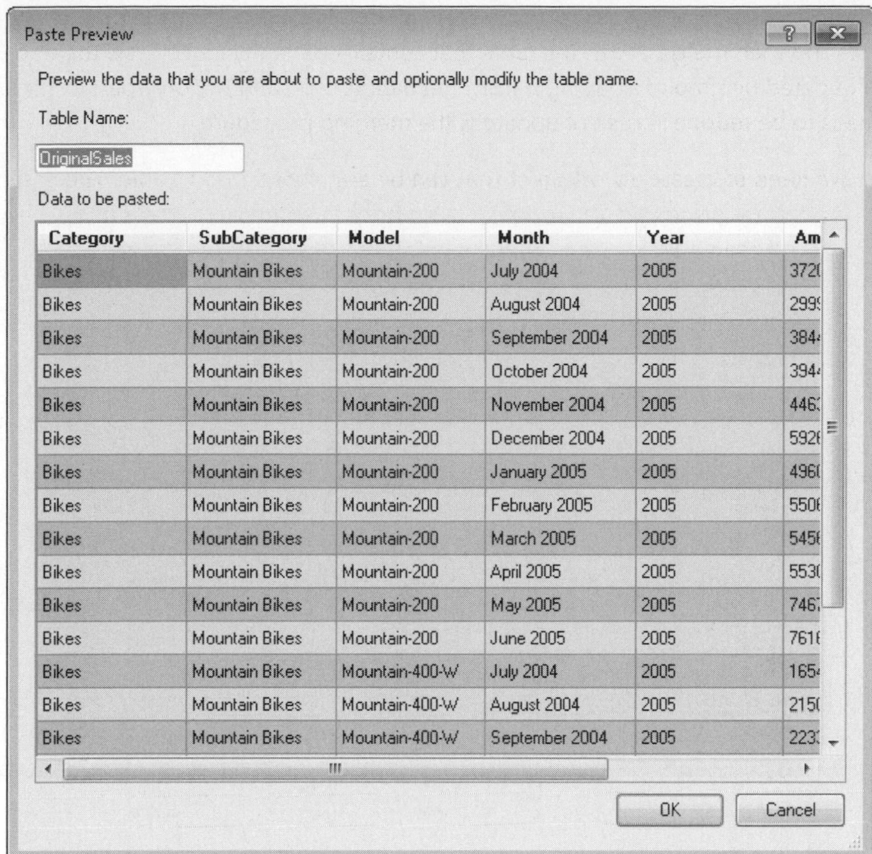


**FIGURE 8-28** The Paste Preview dialog box does not show hidden columns.

Please note that the copy and paste operation does not show any hidden columns, resulting in a table that is missing them. Moreover, all the columns that are calculated in the original table retain only their value, losing the formula. This behavior is correct because the formulas used the hidden columns that are no longer available.

You can now create a Linked Table by using the NewSales table, which contains the new sales from the Excel worksheet. After you have the table, you can use a copy and paste operation in PowerPivot, but this time you choose Paste Append. The rows from the copied table are appended to the destination row, which is evident in Figure 8-29, where you can see that the Paste Preview window shows both source and destination tables.

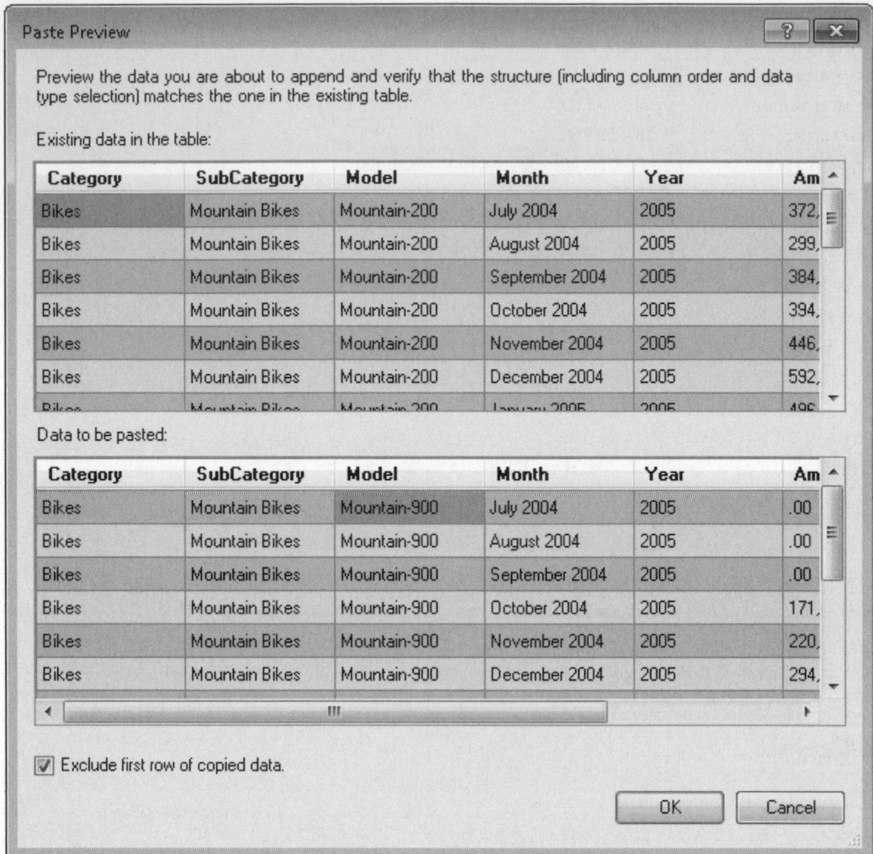


**FIGURE 8-29** The Paste Preview window shows both tables when you use Paste Append.

As you can see, the product model in the Data to be pasted contains the new bike Mountain-900, which does not exist in the original table because it is a new product.

After you paste the data in the existing table, you can analyze the merged information, as you can see in Figure 8-30, where the Mountain Bikes category also includes the new 900 model.

Although this example is a simple one, the very same technique might be applied to a much more complex scenario that includes many PowerPivot tables, some of which might be enriched with Excel data.

| Row Labels | Sum of Amount | Sum of Quantity |
|---|---|---|
| **⊟Mountain Bikes** | **9,302,520.65** | **4,754.00** |
| Mountain-200 | 6,143,695.12 | 2,665.00 |
| Mountain-400-W | 449,170.55 | 584.00 |
| Mountain-500 | 284,154.98 | 515.00 |
| Mountain-900 | 2,425,500.00 | 990.00 |
| **⊟Road Bikes** | **5,635,038.79** | **4,419.00** |
| Road-250 | 1,854,380.48 | 760.00 |
| Road-350-W | 1,698,736.19 | 999.00 |
| Road-550-W | 1,244,276.13 | 1,110.00 |
| Road-750 | 837,645.99 | 1,550.00 |
| **⊟Touring Bikes** | **4,133,161.13** | **2,331.00** |
| Touring-1000 | 3,216,408.44 | 1,351.00 |
| Touring-2000 | 485,818.52 | 401.00 |
| Touring-3000 | 430,934.18 | 579.00 |
| **Grand Total** | **19,070,720.57** | **11,504.00** |

**FIGURE 8-30** The merged table shows information coming from both OLAP and Excel.

Once again, the real power of PowerPivot remains in the capability to integrate data coming from different sources. As simple as it is, the Paste Append option lets you build complex forecasting scenarios.

# Defining Sets

Let us continue our coverage of advanced Excel features by analyzing another useful option of Excel 2010—the ability to define sets. Like many of the other functions described in this chapter, this feature is tied not only to PowerPivot but is an Excel feature that works on any PivotTable type. Before we go on speaking about how sets work, let us explain what a set is.

Intuitively, a set is a list of items, where *item* might be anything we would like to think about. You can define a set by enumerating the items in it, as you normally do with your shopping list, where each item is listed separately. Or you can define a set by giving a description of what belongs to it, such as the set of all countries in North America. Both are good definitions of a set.

Nevertheless, because this is a PowerPivot book, we need to understand the meaning that PowerPivot gives to a set. A PivotTable is made up of cells, and each cell is defined by the filter context that determines which rows to take from the underlying PowerPivot tables to compute its value.

So you might think that each cell defines a filter context. The contrary is true as well: a filter context defines a cell. Moreover, if you move a step forward, you might think of a filter context as something that defines the set of rows that need to be accessed so that you can compute the formula that gives a value to a cell.

At the end, it seems that a filter context is a perfectly good candidate for defining a set. Let us see it with an example; start by looking at Figure 8-31, where you can see a PivotTable working with data. You can find this example in the companion workbook CH08-09-Sets.xlsx.

| Sum of OrderQuantity | Column Labels | | | | |
|---|---|---|---|---|---|
| Row Labels | 2001 | 2002 | 2003 | 2004 | Grand Total |
| **Europe** | **231.00** | **731.00** | **7,511.00** | **9,616.00** | **18,089.00** |
| Accessories | | | 4,457.00 | 6,217.00 | 10,674.00 |
| Bikes | 231.00 | 731.00 | 1,983.00 | 1,957.00 | 4,902.00 |
| Clothing | | | 1,071.00 | 1,442.00 | 2,513.00 |
| **North America** | **388.00** | **1,087.00** | **11,597.00** | **15,892.00** | **28,964.00** |
| Accessories | | | 7,683.00 | 10,731.00 | 18,414.00 |
| Bikes | 388.00 | 1,087.00 | 2,040.00 | 2,316.00 | 5,831.00 |
| Clothing | | | 1,874.00 | 2,845.00 | 4,719.00 |
| **Pacific** | **394.00** | **859.00** | **5,335.00** | **6,757.00** | **13,345.00** |
| Accessories | | | 2,885.00 | 4,119.00 | 7,004.00 |
| Bikes | 394.00 | 859.00 | 1,687.00 | 1,532.00 | 4,472.00 |
| Clothing | | | 763.00 | 1,106.00 | 1,869.00 |
| **Grand Total** | **1,013.00** | **2,677.00** | **24,443.00** | **32,265.00** | **60,398.00** |

**FIGURE 8-31** A simple PivotTable, useful for understanding sets.

Let us analyze Figure 8-31 to try to figure out how we can define it in terms of sets. The sales in North America in year 2002 have a value of 1,087. This value is computed by analyzing *the set of all the sales that have been made in North America in the year 2002*. You can apply the same technique to each cell, to discover that each cell is computed by means of analyzing a set. Because you already know that a cell is defined by its filter context, you can think that each cell is computed analyzing the set of values that satisfy the filter context of the cell. This way of thinking leads you to a first definition of set, which identifies a set with a filter context.

You might be tempted to believe that a set is nothing but a filter context. Even if this were true, we think that it is better to think of a filter context as one member of a set. So when we define a set, we can enumerate a list of filter contexts, and the list of all those filters defines a set. We can make an example of this using the previous figure.

We can define a set containing both *Accessories in Europe for the year 2003* and *Clothing in North America in 2002*. Each item in the set defines a filter context, and the union of both filter contexts (which is, in turn, a more complex filter context) is the set.

As you might have noticed, the definition of a set is given, providing values for some attributes of the data model. You can, for example, fix the year to 2003 and define the set of all sales in 2003. In addition, you can fix another attribute—for example, the territory group—to *North America*, and define the *sales in North America in the year 2003*. Each time you fix the value of an attribute, you narrow the number of elements covered by the set. Whenever you do not restrict the value of an attribute, you mean *any value is good*.

With all this theory in mind, you can now learn how to define a set by using Excel. On the Options tab of the Excel ribbon, you can find a button named Fields, Items, & Sets that contains the links to the feature we are interested in. Look at Figure 8-32.

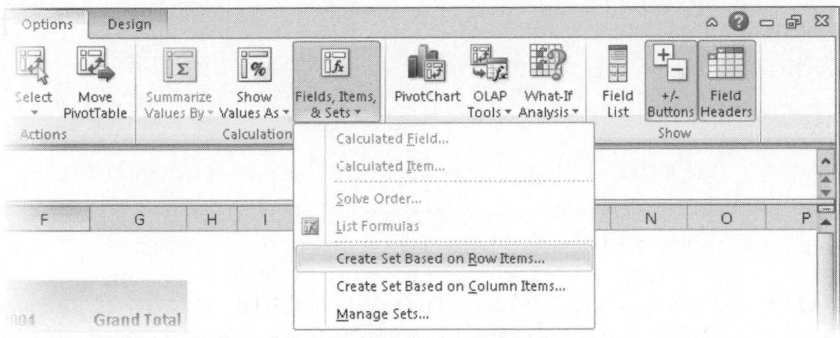


**FIGURE 8-32** The various options for creating sets in Excel.

By means of this menu, you can create a set using the values in the rows or columns of the PivotTable. If you select Create Set Based On Row Items in your PivotTable, Excel opens the Set Editor dialog box shown in Figure 8-33.

New Set (Sandbox)

Set name: Set1

Display folder (optional):

Add Row | Delete Row | Copy Row

| SalesTerritoryGroup | ProductCategory |
|---|---|
| Europe | All |
| Europe | Accessories |
| Europe | Bikes |
| Europe | Clothing |
| North America | All |
| North America | Accessories |
| North America | Bikes |
| North America | Clothing |
| Pacific | All |

Display items from different levels in separate fields

Replace the fields currently in the row area with the new set

Edit MDX...

OK Cancel

**FIGURE 8-33** Set Editor dialog box.

Because you have two attributes on the rows (SalesTerritoryGroup and ProductCategory), the dialog box contains two columns. Each row in the set contains a filter context that defines one of the members of the set. All filter contexts together define the set.

It is interesting to see that the first row in the set defines the following:

- SalesTerritoryGroup = Europe
- ProductCategory = All

This means that the first element forces a constraint on the SalesTerritoryGroup but leaves the ProductCategory free to have any value. In fact, if you look carefully at the first row of the PivotTable, it contains sales made in Europe for all the categories together.

So because there are three values for SalesTerritoryGroup and three values for ProductCategory, our set contains 13 elements: 9 for the different combinations of a single sales territory and product category, 3 for the different combinations of sales territories with the unconstrained category and a final one (the grand total) for the combination of unconstrained territory and unconstrained category. These elements are exactly the number of rows of the PivotTable. If you open this dialog box on a complex PivotTable with hundreds (or thousands) of rows, the number of elements in the set would become very large and hard to manage.

Using this dialog box, you can name the set, provide it with a folder from which to show it, and update the set definition. For an example, let us edit the set to leave only four elements, as shown in Figure 8-34.

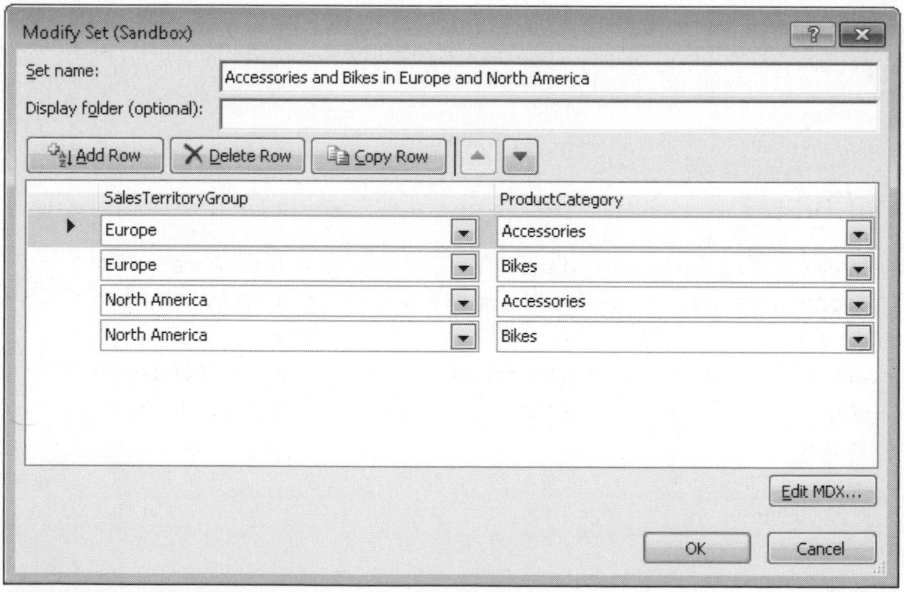

**FIGURE 8-34** Definition of a set made of four elements.

Now the set represents a selection of combinations of sales territories and product categories, as its name suggests. You can save it and look at what happens in the PivotTable Field List. After you define a set, it appears in the special folder Sets at the bottom of the table list. In Figure 8-35, you can see the PivotTable with the set placed on the rows.

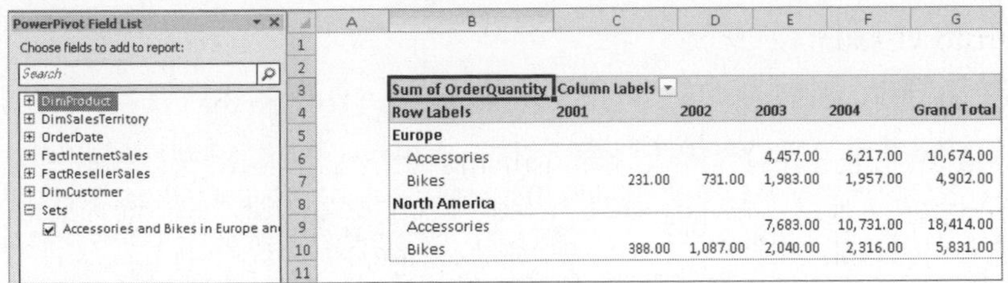


**FIGURE 8-35** The set represents our selection.

When you put a set on rows or columns, you filter the data, which imposes a filter context that makes only the data in the set visible.

If you look carefully at the PivotTable, you might notice that something is missing: you have no total for the territory group, nor any grand total. As strange as that might seem, this is perfectly correct. You have removed from the set the items containing the member All for the ProductCategory. This means that the set does not contain a filter context for *Europe, any category*. So the cells that represent this selection are empty. The same obviously applies to the grand total.

Sets are commonly used with dates. If, for example, you define a set that contains data for the last two years, it is easy to quickly select the last two years in a report. Moreover, when you want to update all reports to show, for example, the last three years, it is enough to update the set, and all the reports are automatically updated to reflect the change in the underlying set.

## Creating Dynamic Sets with MDX

In the previous pages, you learned the basics of set definition. Now we take a step further and look at some advanced uses of sets. The sets that can be defined by means of the standard user interface are statically defined. This means that you enumerate a list of filter contexts and then create a set based on them. The items contained in the set do not change, whatever selection you perform in the PivotTable. Moreover, to create the set, you need to know in advance which items to put in.

Even if this condition might seem obvious, sometimes you need to define a set that changes dynamically, based on your selection, without knowing in advance what it contains. Think, for example, if you could define a set containing the 10 top-selling products. You do not know in advance which these products are. Moreover, the set changes, depending on your filtering because you expect that the top-selling products in 2003 are different from the top-selling products in 2004.

These kinds of sets are called *dynamic sets* because they can change their content based on user selection. To create them, you need take a deep dive into the internals of PowerPivot and discover the OLAP cube that lives well hidden in PowerPivot. Because a PowerPivot database is essentially an OLAP cube, you need to use MDX to create dynamic sets. In this section, we demonstrate what can be done by using MDX to query PowerPivot and create dynamic sets.

**Note** The topic of MDX requires a book of its own, so we are not showing all the details of what you can do using this exciting query language. Our goal is just to bring its possibilities to the attention of the interested reader by letting you see what happens when you query PowerPivot with MDX.

To create a dynamic set, you need to select the Manage Set option of the Fields, Items & Sets menu, which opens the Set Manager dialog box shown in Figure 8-36.

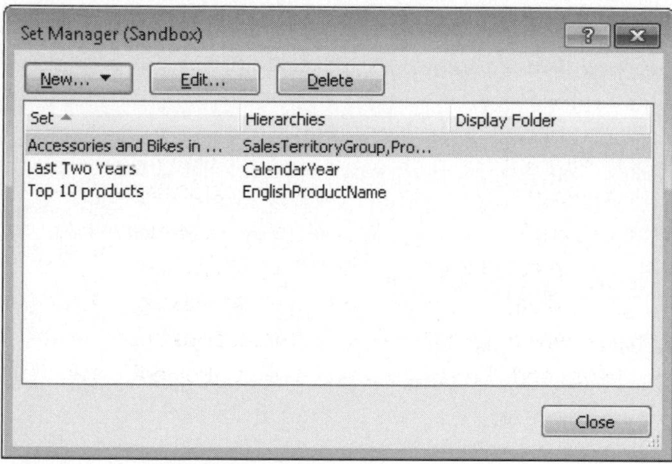


**FIGURE 8-36** The Set Manager window.

Using this window you can create, delete, or update set definitions. Moreover, using the New button, you can create a new set based on rows, columns, or the MDX editor. You already know what happens with the simpler options of rows and columns, so it is time to go deeper and choose the new MDX option. Excel opens a new window, which is the MDX Set Editor, shown in Figure 8-37.

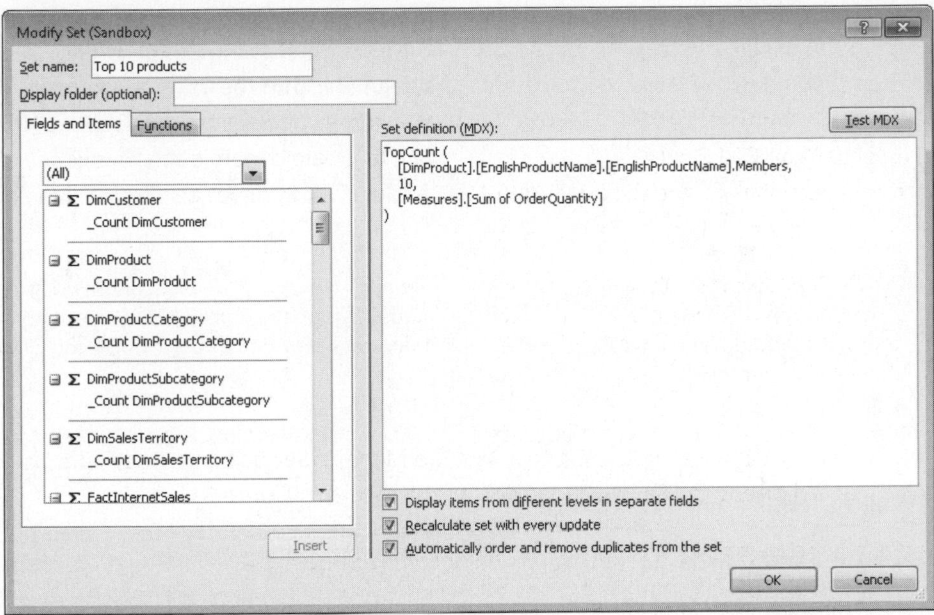


**FIGURE 8-37** The MDX Set Editor window.

This window lets you create an MDX expression that queries the PowerPivot OLAP cube in the PowerPivot database. The PowerPivot database internally creates an OLAP cube based on the tables and relationships that it holds. The user interface of PowerPivot hides the complexity of the OLAP cube and so gives you an easy interface that lets you select columns from tables, but when it comes to computing the values, it converts your selection into an MDX query that it sends to the internal OLAP cube, which performs all the computations and provides the result. This OLAP cube is named *Sandbox* and is completely managed by PowerPivot internally.

**Note** In Chapter 5, "Loading Data and Models," we told you that when you want to query an Excel workbook published on SharePoint that contains PowerPivot data, you need to use the MDX editor to query the internal OLAP cube. You are now discovering what this cube is.

If you need to create dynamic sets, you need to directly query the Sandbox cube and leverage the full power of MDX. It is not an easy task, and to get the best from it, you need to know the MDX language. Nevertheless, it exploits an analytic power that cannot be reached by using the standard PowerPivot user interface.

The Sandbox OLAP cube contains one dimension and one fact table for each PowerPivot table. The dimensions contain the fields used to perform slicing, whereas the fact tables contain the values that can be aggregated. In our example, you have a DimProduct fact table, which lets you count the products (count is a measure that can be shown in cells), and you have a DimProduct dimension, which contains the attributes used to slice data.

With a bit of knowledge of MDX, you can define a new set called *Top 10 products* with this formula:

```
TopCount (
    [DimProduct].[EnglishProductName].[EnglishProductName].Members,
    10,
    [Measures].[Sum of OrderQuantity]
)
```

We do not have space in this book to explain MDX in detail, so for the sake of this example it is enough to understand that the TopCount function call returns the first 10 products after having sorted them by OrderQuantity.

The real power of this feature is that you do not know in advance which these 10 products will be. You ask the OLAP cube to compute them and to return the set of those 10 products, whichever they will be.

You can now create a PivotTable and select this set to discover which these products are, as you see in Figure 8-38.

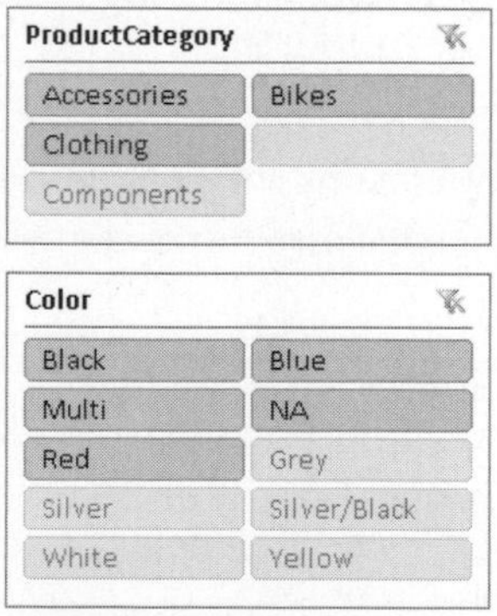

| ProductCategory | |
|---|---|
| Accessories | Bikes |
| Clothing | |
| Components | |

| Color | |
|---|---|
| Black | Blue |
| Multi | NA |
| Red | Grey |
| Silver | Silver/Black |
| White | Yellow |

| Sum of OrderQuantity | Column Labels | | |
|---|---|---|---|
| Row Labels | 2003 | 2004 | Grand Total |
| **Accessories** | | | |
| Water Bottle - 30 oz. | 1,742.00 | 2,502.00 | 4,244.00 |
| Patch Kit/8 Patches | 1,356.00 | 1,835.00 | 3,191.00 |
| Mountain Tire Tube | 1,313.00 | 1,782.00 | 3,095.00 |
| Road Tire Tube | 999.00 | 1,377.00 | 2,376.00 |
| Sport-100 Helmet, Red | 898.00 | 1,332.00 | 2,230.00 |
| Sport-100 Helmet, Blue | 857.00 | 1,268.00 | 2,125.00 |
| Fender Set - Mountain | 883.00 | 1,238.00 | 2,121.00 |
| Sport-100 Helmet, Black | 891.00 | 1,194.00 | 2,085.00 |
| Mountain Bottle Cage | 824.00 | 1,201.00 | 2,025.00 |
| **Clothing** | | | |
| AWC Logo Cap | 885.00 | 1,305.00 | 2,190.00 |

**FIGURE 8-38** The top 10 products set at work.

In this PivotTable, we added a couple of slicers to filter for product category and product color. Nevertheless, if you select, for example, the blue color, the PivotTable does not compute the top 10 blue products; it instead filters the top 10 products showing only the blue ones, as you can see in Figure 8-39.

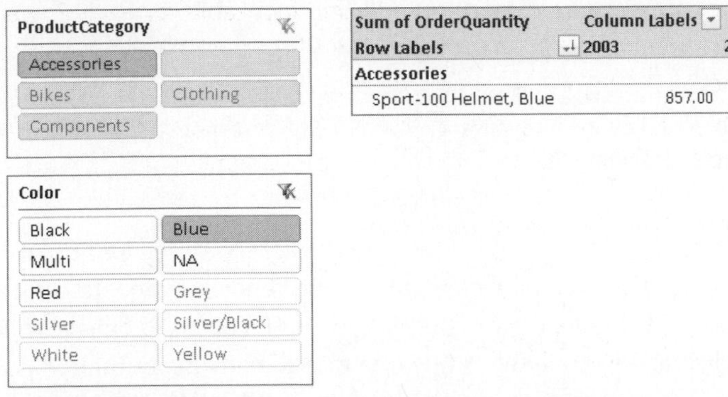


| Sum of OrderQuantity | Column Labels | | |
|---|---|---|---|
| Row Labels | 2003 | 2004 | Grand Total |
| **Accessories** | | | |
| Sport-100 Helmet, Blue | 857.00 | 1,268.00 | 2,125.00 |

**FIGURE 8-39** When a color is selected, the top 10 product set is filtered and not recomputed.

The reason for this behavior is that by default the set, even if defined with MDX, is still a static one. Even if you do not know in advance its content and used MDX to define it, the set is evaluated once during the first query after data is refreshed in the PowerPivot workbook. So it is not recomputed for each query. When you apply a filter, that filter is applied to the set too, reducing its content.

You can convert a standard set to a dynamic one using the Recalculate Set With Every Update check box in the MDX Set Editor window. If you check this box, the set is marked as dynamic and is computed for each query, reflecting the filtering made on the PivotTable.

In Figure 8-40, you can see the same query with the blue color selected, but this time the set is marked as dynamic. Its behavior is different: the set now contains the 10 top-selling products, which are blue.

ProductCategory
Accessories
Bikes
Clothing
Components

Color
Black
Blue
Multi
NA
Red
Grey
Silver
Silver/Black
White
Yellow

| Sum of OrderQuantity | Column Labels | | |
|---|---|---|---|
| Row Labels | 2003 | 2004 | Grand Total |
| **Accessories** | | | |
| Sport-100 Helmet, Blue | 857.00 | 1,268.00 | 2,125.00 |
| **Bikes** | | | |
| Touring-1000 Blue, 46 | 58.00 | 119.00 | 177.00 |
| Touring-1000 Blue, 54 | 53.00 | 107.00 | 160.00 |
| Touring-1000 Blue, 50 | 61.00 | 89.00 | 150.00 |
| Touring-1000 Blue, 60 | 53.00 | 94.00 | 147.00 |
| Touring-2000 Blue, 50 | 42.00 | 64.00 | 106.00 |
| Touring-2000 Blue, 46 | 48.00 | 49.00 | 97.00 |
| **Clothing** | | | |
| Classic Vest, M | 72.00 | 127.00 | 199.00 |
| Classic Vest, L | 67.00 | 128.00 | 195.00 |
| Classic Vest, S | 66.00 | 102.00 | 168.00 |

**FIGURE 8-40** When a color is selected in the top-10-products dynamic set, the set is correctly recomputed.

Using this feature, you can produce a report that gives you the set of the 10 top-selling products that changes whenever you change the filtering condition.

**Note** Please remember that the set is conditioned by the filters and the slicers, not by the selection of rows and columns. This means that the set produces the 10 top-selling products over all time, and then the PivotTable shows the sales in the different years. If you are interested in the top-selling products in a specific year, you need to move the year to a slicer or to the filter part of the PivotTable so that the year acts as a filter and operates over the dynamic set too. Dynamic sets obey the filter context imposed by the filters over the whole PivotTable, not the ones imposed by the rows and columns to each single cell.

This small example just scratches the surface of the power of MDX. When you use MDX to query a cube, you can produce very complex and interesting reports, even if to create them, you definitely need to learn MDX and the structure of an OLAP cube. We believe that when you are a PowerPivot power user, you want to buy one of the many beautiful books about MDX and start learning it if you want to get the best out of PowerPivot. Nevertheless, PowerPivot can still produce great reports without your ever opening an MDX editor, so the message is this: if you need to use MDX, get prepared for a very heavy period of study; on the other hand, if you can get the results you need with the PowerPivot user interface only, life is certainly easier.

# Creating Sets of Measures with MDX

The MDX editing feature that we discussed in the previous sections comes in very handy for defining a different type of set: the measures set. You previously learned how to create a set filtering some values (such as the product category or the year), but it might be interesting to create a set that filters measures. If, for example, you normally look at order quantity and sales amounts together, you could use the standard way of adding both measures to the PivotTable each time, or you could be tempted to create the set of both measures so that it becomes easier to create frequent reports containing both values.

You cannot create measure sets by using the Excel user interface, but you can easily create them by using the MDX editor. In fact, in the OLAP data model, measures belong to a special dimension called *measures* and can be treated much the same way as dimension attributes.

You can, for example, define a set such as the one shown in Figure 8-41, which contains three measures (order quantity, sales amount, and tax amount) as members of the special measures dimension.

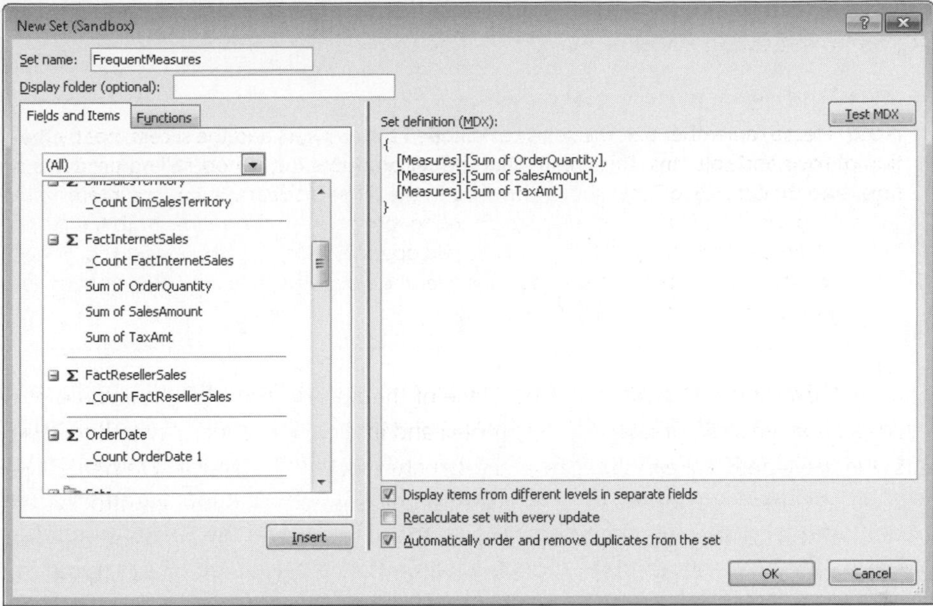


**FIGURE 8-41** A measure set definition.

After you define this set, you can use it and the PivotTable automatically selects all the measures included in the set. Moreover, when you use this technique, you can put the measure set in rows and obtain the listing of measures in rows instead of columns, as you can see in Figure 8-42.

| | Column Labels | | | | |
|---|---|---|---|---|---|
| **Row Labels** | **2001** | **2002** | **2003** | **2004** | **Grand Total** |
| **Europe** | | | | | |
| Sum of SalesAmount | 709.947,20 | 1.627.759,71 | 3.382.979,27 | 3.209.356,08 | 8.930.042,26 |
| Sum of TaxAmt | 56.795,78 | 130.220,78 | 270.638,35 | 256.748,49 | 714.403,40 |
| Sum of OrderQuantity | 231,00 | 731,00 | 7.511,00 | 9.616,00 | 18.089,00 |
| **North America** | | | | | |
| Sum of SalesAmount | 1.247.379,26 | 2.748.298,93 | 3.374.296,82 | 3.997.659,37 | 11.367.634,37 |
| Sum of TaxAmt | 99.790,34 | 219.863,92 | 269.943,75 | 319.812,75 | 909.410,77 |
| Sum of OrderQuantity | 388,00 | 1.087,00 | 11.597,00 | 15.892,00 | 28.964,00 |
| **Pacific** | | | | | |
| Sum of SalesAmount | 1.309.047,20 | 2.154.284,88 | 3.033.784,21 | 2.563.884,29 | 9.061.000,58 |
| Sum of TaxAmt | 104.723,78 | 172.342,80 | 242.702,75 | 205.110,74 | 724.880,07 |
| Sum of OrderQuantity | 394,00 | 859,00 | 5.335,00 | 6.757,00 | 13.345,00 |
| **Total Sum of SalesAmount** | **3.266.373,66** | **6.530.343,53** | **9.791.060,30** | **9.770.899,74** | **29.358.677,22** |
| **Total Sum of TaxAmt** | **261.309,90** | **522.427,50** | **783.284,85** | **781.671,98** | **2.348.694,23** |
| **Total Sum of OrderQuantity** | **1.013,00** | **2.677,00** | **24.443,00** | **32.265,00** | **60.398,00** |

**FIGURE 8-42** A measure set can be placed in rows and produce interesting reports.

**Note** Please note that the current release of PowerPivot handles measure sets gracefully, when you put them in rows or columns, but it does not let you add new measures to the values pane of the PivotTable, if a measure set is used.

In case you want to put measures in rows instead of columns, you can do that by opening the classic PivotTable Field List and moving the Values item in rows or columns, as it is clearly explained at this URL: *http://tinyurl.com/PowerPivotFieldList*.

## Summary

In this chapter, you saw how to master PivotTables in Excel; you learned how to choose between PivotTable types, how to use features such as slicers and flattened PivotTables, how to handle custom sorting, how to display data as ratios and percentages, and how to handle nonadditive measures. You also saw demonstrations of important techniques for creating dashboards in Excel and how to use linked tables and the Paste Append feature of PowerPivot to create complex models wherein data is calculated or generated in Excel. Finally, you learned how to take advantage of fixed and dynamic sets in a PivotTable.

Chapter 9

# PowerPivot DAX Patterns

In this chapter, we show you many common DAX calculations using techniques that can be easily applied to your own Microsoft SQL Server PowerPivot for Excel models. As you will see, DAX calculations might have significant differences from one another, depending on the underlying data model. For this reason, you should be sure that you understand the data modeling concepts presented in Chapter 4, "Data Models," of this book.

## Calculating Ratio and Percentage

In Chapter 8, "Mastering PivotTables," you saw some of the Excel features that allow you to show a value as a percentage of a total. However, you might need to make this calculation in a measure or in a calculated column, for example, because you need that number as part of another calculation.

Calculating the percentage of a total for a given value requires a simple ratio operation:

$$Percentage = \frac{Value}{Total}$$

The resulting percentage should be a decimal number between 0 and 1. To get it as a percentage, you should just set the display format as Percentage. Do not multiply that number by 100—that is not the right way to calculate a percentage. In fact, when you use the percentage format, the number is already multiplied by 100 by the formatting function, just for display purposes. Moreover, you might need to use that value in other expressions (for example, to calculate a weighted average) and in such a case, you usually need just the value between 0 and 1.

### Calculating Ratio on a Single Denormalized Table

Consider a set of data in a single table, like the one shown in Figure 9-1. You have the total amount of sales for products, which can be grouped by product model. Each product is unique and has only one row in this table. The CH09-01-RatioSingleTable.xlsx workbook on the companion DVD contains this example.

| Model | Product | SalesAmount |
|---|---|---|
| LL Touring Seat/Saddle | LL Touring Seat/Saddle | 1,480.75 |
| Long-Sleeve Logo Jersey | Long-Sleeve Logo Jersey, L | 191,606.41 |
| Long-Sleeve Logo Jersey | Long-Sleeve Logo Jersey, M | 107,750.71 |
| Long-Sleeve Logo Jersey | Long-Sleeve Logo Jersey, S | 14,597.08 |
| Long-Sleeve Logo Jersey | Long-Sleeve Logo Jersey, XL | 88,562.61 |
| Men's Bib-Shorts | Men's Bib-Shorts, L | 34,178.20 |
| Men's Bib-Shorts | Men's Bib-Shorts, M | 86,166.05 |
| Men's Bib-Shorts | Men's Bib-Shorts, S | 47,214.37 |
| Men's Sports Shorts | Men's Sports Shorts, L | 16,017.33 |
| Men's Sports Shorts | Men's Sports Shorts, M | 45,594.28 |
| Men's Sports Shorts | Men's Sports Shorts, S | 20,365.00 |

**FIGURE 9-1** Sample data in a single table for ratio calculation.

You can create a PercentageOnTotal measure in the PivotTable that calculates the percentage of sales for each product compared to the total of all the products.

```
PercentageOnTotal = SUM( Sales[SalesAmount] )
                  / CALCULATE( SUM( Sales[SalesAmount] ),
                               ALL( Sales ) )
```

The calculation is a ratio that has a numerator with the SUM for all sales for the products that are active in the filter context. In this way, if you select a group of products (such as all the products of a certain model), that ratio still works. The denominator is also a SUM of the SalesAmount measure, but it is included in a CALCULATE call, which removes any filter context from the whole Sales table, using the ALL function.

In a similar way, you can also define a PercentageOnModel measure, which differs from the previous only in its denominator.

```
PercentageOnModel = SUM( Sales[SalesAmount] )
                  / CALCULATE( SUM( Sales[SalesAmount] ),
                               ALL( Sales[Product] ) )
```

In this case, the CALCULATE statement alters the filter context by removing filters only from the Product column. Because the Model column is not affected, any filters on the Model column still apply. So the CALCULATE statement applies the SUM aggregation on all the products of the Model column to which the current products belong in the PivotTable. In Figure 9-2, you can see the results of these two measures.

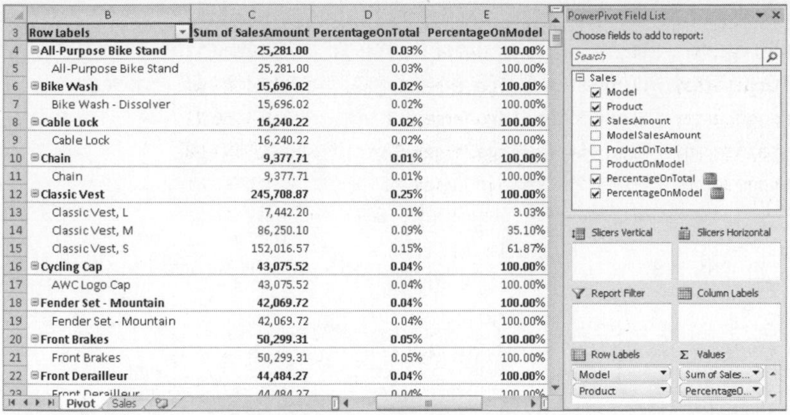

FIGURE 9-2 Browsing data with percentage measures.

The advantage of defining the PercentageOnTotal and PercentageOnModel measures in the PivotTable is that they are calculated dynamically when you apply any other filters on data for both numerator and denominator of the ratios. Usually this is all that you need, but sometimes you might want to make this calculation ignoring any filters made in the PivotTable. This might be necessary, for example, when such a calculation is also used as part of another formula. In these cases, you might consider defining calculated columns so that the calculation is made at data-loading time.

The definition of the calculated column that returns the value of a product as a percentage of all the products is similar to a measure you have seen before:

```
ProductOnTotal = Sales[SalesAmount] / SUM( Sales[SalesAmount] )
```

In this case, the numerator does not require a SUM aggregation because it needs to operate only on the current row. The denominator contains simply the SUM aggregation of SalesAmount, which in this case always sums all the rows of the Sales table.

To calculate the percentage on model, you first need to calculate the SalesAmount value for the model. You use the ModelSalesAmount calculated column as the denominator of the ProductOnModel ratio.

```
ModelSalesAmount = CALCULATE( SUM( Sales[SalesAmount] ),
                              ALLEXCEPT( Sales, Sales[Model] ) )
```

Because you are defining a calculated column, you do not want any filter other than the Model column. For this reason, the ALLEXCEPT function has to be used as the filter parameter of the CALCULATE call so that only the rows that have the same Model column of the current row are considered in that calculation. So the ProductOnModel calculated column just requires a simple ratio:

```
ProductOnModel = Sales[SalesAmount] / Sales[ModelSalesAmount]
```

In Figure 9-3, you can see the results of the calculated columns defined in the Sales table.

| Model | Product | SalesAmount | ModelSalesAmount | ProductOnTotal | ProductOnModel |
|---|---|---|---|---|---|
| LL Touring Seat/Saddle | LL Touring Seat/Saddle | 1,480.75 | 1,480.75 | 0.00 % | 100.00 % |
| Long-Sleeve Logo Jersey | Long-Sleeve Logo Jersey, L | 191,606.41 | 402,516.81 | 0.19 % | 47.60 % |
| Long-Sleeve Logo Jersey | Long-Sleeve Logo Jersey, M | 107,750.71 | 402,516.81 | 0.11 % | 26.77 % |
| Long-Sleeve Logo Jersey | Long-Sleeve Logo Jersey, S | 14,597.08 | 402,516.81 | 0.01 % | 3.63 % |
| Long-Sleeve Logo Jersey | Long-Sleeve Logo Jersey, XL | 88,562.61 | 402,516.81 | 0.09 % | 22.00 % |
| Men's Bib-Shorts | Men's Bib-Shorts, L | 34,178.20 | 167,558.62 | 0.03 % | 20.40 % |
| Men's Bib-Shorts | Men's Bib-Shorts, M | 86,166.05 | 167,558.62 | 0.09 % | 51.42 % |
| Men's Bib-Shorts | Men's Bib-Shorts, S | 47,214.37 | 167,558.62 | 0.05 % | 28.18 % |
| Men's Sports Shorts | Men's Sports Shorts, L | 16,017.33 | 81,976.61 | 0.02 % | 19.54 % |
| Men's Sports Shorts | Men's Sports Shorts, M | 45,594.28 | 81,976.61 | 0.05 % | 55.62 % |
| Men's Sports Shorts | Men's Sports Shorts, S | 20,365.00 | 81,976.61 | 0.02 % | 24.84 % |

**FIGURE 9-3** Calculated columns for product percentages of total and model.

The formulas you have seen in this section can be easily adapted to any scenario where data is stored in a single denormalized table. Having normalized data in more tables requires some changes in the formula, which you are going to learn in the next section.

## Calculating Ratio on Multiple Normalized Tables

Let us consider a different scenario, in which data is normalized in multiple tables. Most of the time, you have a table containing numeric measures that you want to aggregate, and you have other tables describing attributes of these measures in a more verbose way. For example, in Figure 9-4, you can see the SalesAmount measure in the Sales table. For each row, there is a ProductID column that refers to the corresponding row in the Products table, which is shown in Figure 9-5. You can find the following example in the CH09-02-RatioMultipleTables.xlsx workbook on the companion DVD.

| OrderDate | ProductID | SalesAmount |
|---|---|---|
| 7/31/2001 | 750 | 3,578.27 |
| 7/31/2001 | 762 | 699.10 |
| 7/31/2001 | 753 | 3,578.27 |
| 7/31/2001 | 751 | 3,578.27 |
| 8/1/2001 | 774 | 4,079.99 |
| 8/1/2001 | 778 | 4,049.99 |
| 8/1/2001 | 742 | 1,445.19 |

Sales | Products

**FIGURE 9-4** Sample data in a Sales Table.

| P... | Product | Model |
|---|---|---|
| 680 | HL Road Frame - Black, 58 | HL Road Frame |
| 706 | HL Road Frame - Red, 58 | HL Road Frame |
| 707 | Sport-100 Helmet, Red | Sport-100 |
| 708 | Sport-100 Helmet, Black | Sport-100 |
| 709 | Mountain Bike Socks, M | Mountain Bike Socks |
| 710 | Mountain Bike Socks, L | Mountain Bike Socks |
| 711 | Sport-100 Helmet, Blue | Sport-100 |
| 712 | AWC Logo Cap | Cycling Cap |

Sales | **Products**

**FIGURE 9-5** Sample data in a Products table linked to a Sales table.

The measures PercentageOnTotal and PercentageOnModel are very similar to the ones previously defined in the single table scenario.

```
PercentageOnTotal = SUM( Sales[SalesAmount] )
                    / CALCULATE( SUM( Sales[SalesAmount] ),
                                 ALL( Products ) )
```

The only difference in PercentageOnTotal is that the Products table is used to extend the filter through the ALL function. In this way, a possible filter on the OrderDate column would still apply, maintaining the dynamic calculation in the PivotTable.

In the PercentageOnModel measure, the only difference is that the Product column passed to the ALL call belongs to the Products table and no longer to the Sales table.

```
PercentageOnModel = SUM( Sales[SalesAmount] )
                    / CALCULATE( SUM( Sales[SalesAmount] ),
                                 ALL( Products[Product] ) )
```

The results of these two measures are identical to those shown in Figure 9-2.

Now that you see how to define measures, which are dynamic by their nature, we look at what you need to make a similar calculation using calculated columns, to get a calculation that is not dynamically influenced by the selection in the PivotTable. In this scenario, you usually have many rows in the Sales table for each row in the Product table. Because the calculation needs to be at the Product level, you have to follow the relationship between Product and Sales to compute the right value of SalesAmount for each product and each model. First of all, you can calculate the total sales amount for each product by defining the following ProductSalesAmount calculated column in the Products table:

```
ProductSalesAmount = CALCULATE( SUM( Sales[SalesAmount] ) )
```

### CALCULATE vs. SUMX

Remember that the CALCULATE call transforms the row context into a filter context. For this reason, the current row of the Products table (to which ProductSalesAmount belongs) defines a filter for all the related rows in the Sales table, following the relationship between Products and Sales. In other words, the ProductSalesAmount definition returns the same results of the following expression:

```
= SUMX( RELATEDTABLE( Sales ), Sales[SalesAmount] )
```

However, you should prefer the CALCULATE version for performance reasons. You use the SUMX version whenever you need to define a more complex expression for each row of the table specified in the first parameter (something that would not be possible by using CALCULATE).

The ProductOnTotal calculated column can be defined by using the SUM of the sales for all the products in the denominator or the ratio:

```
ProductOnTotal = Products[ProductSalesAmount] / SUM( Products[ProductSalesAmount] )
```

**Note** Even if it were possible to use SUM( Sales[SalesAmount] ) instead of SUM( Products[ProductSalesAmount] ) in the ProductOnTotalDefinition, in this case, it is faster to use the column that has a lower number of rows.

The calculation of ProductOnModel still requires that you define the value of the sales for each model in advance. The ModelSalesAmount column can be defined in the same way as in the single table example, just by using the Products table instead of the Sales table in the ALLEXCEPT filter. In the same way, the ProductOnModel has a definition similar to that for a single table—you can just change the name of the referenced table.

```
ModelSalesAmount = CALCULATE( SUM( Sales[SalesAmount] ),
                              ALLEXCEPT( Products, Products[Model] ) )

ProductOnModel = Products[ProductSalesAmount] / Products[ModelSalesAmount]
```

Finally, the Products table shown in Figure 9-6 contains all the new calculated measures, including the percentages that you might use in other calculations.

| P... | Product | Model | ProductSalesAmount | ModelSalesAmount | ProductOnTotal | ProductOnModel |
|---|---|---|---|---|---|---|
| 707 | Sport-100 Helmet, Red | Sport-100 | 157,772.39 | 484,048.53 | 0.14 % | 32.59 % |
| 708 | Sport-100 Helmet, Black | Sport-100 | 160,869.52 | 484,048.53 | 0.15 % | 33.23 % |
| 711 | Sport-100 Helmet, Blue | Sport-100 | 165,406.62 | 484,048.53 | 0.15 % | 34.17 % |
| 846 | Taillights - Battery-Power... | Taillight | | | | |
| 821 | Touring Front Wheel | Touring Front Wheel | | | | |
| 941 | Touring Pedal | Touring Pedal | 7,143.32 | 7,143.32 | 0.01 % | 100.00 % |
| 829 | Touring Rear Wheel | Touring Rear Wheel | | | | |
| 934 | Touring Tire | Touring Tire | 27,105.65 | 27,105.65 | 0.02 % | 100.00 % |
| 923 | Touring Tire Tube | Touring Tire Tube | 7,425.12 | 7,425.12 | 0.01 % | 100.00 % |

**FIGURE 9-6** Calculated columns for product percentages of total and model.

# Computing Standard Deviation

A common calculation in many statistical and distribution analysis is the standard deviation. For example, you might want to calculate the standard deviation from the mean price.

Because the standard deviation is not an easy formula to compute, we show you an example with a few values so that you can better understand the formula.

Let us start with a very simple set of values, divided into two periods in time, as you can see in Figure 9-7. You can find this example in the CH09-03-StandardDeviation.xlsx workbook included on the companion DVD.

| Category | Row | Value |
|---|---|---|
| A | 1 | 12 |
| A | 2 | 13 |
| A | 3 | 17 |
| B | 4 | 10 |
| B | 5 | 14 |
| B | 6 | 24 |

**FIGURE 9-7** Sample data for the standard deviation calculation.

You can easily import the data into PowerPivot, and then after you add a calculated measure that computes the AVERAGE of Value, you can perform the first simple analysis, shown in Figure 9-8.

| Row Labels | Average of Value |
|---|---|
| **⊟A** | **14** |
| 1 | 12 |
| 2 | 13 |
| 3 | 17 |
| **⊟B** | **16** |
| 4 | 10 |
| 5 | 14 |
| 6 | 24 |
| **Grand Total** | **15** |

**FIGURE 9-8** Simple analysis of the average value over periods.

Standard deviation shows how much variation there is from the average. In other words, it is an indicator of how far the values are from their mean.

The classic formula for the standard deviation is the following:

$$\sigma = \sqrt{\frac{1}{N}\sum_{i=1}^{N}(x_i - \bar{x})^2}$$

We indicate with $\bar{x}$ the average of the values and with $\sigma$ the resulting value of the standard deviation.

The problem with this formula is that you cannot compute it row by row because the value of $\bar{x}$ is an aggregate and cannot be used in a calculated column. Moreover, the value of $\bar{x}$ changes for each aggregate you compute. In the example in Figure 9-8, you can see that there are three different values of $\bar{x}$, depending on the evaluation context: one for each Category and one for the Grand Total. The average over all the values is different from both averages over the two categories. So there is no way to compute the average at the row level, and this brings us to an issue with the innermost term in our formula.

Luckily, the formula can be easily simplified, thanks to thousands of years of statistical theory that is available to us, to this equivalent formula (the interested reader can look at *http://en.wikipedia.org/wiki/Standard_deviation* for the details):

$$\sigma = \sqrt{\frac{1}{N}\left(\sum_{i=1}^{N}x_i^2\right) - \bar{x}^2}$$

The big difference between the two formulas is that the average now appears outside the loop that you need to compute the sum of all squares of values. Now you do not need to know the value of the average at each row level. Instead, the only value you need at the row level is the square of the value, which can be very easily computed by PowerPivot.

You can add a new calculated column to the PowerPivot table named Events, for which the formula is the following:

```
ValueSquared = Events[Value] ^ 2
```

To compute the standard deviation now, you need to add a measure to the PivotTable. The formula is the following:

```
StandardDeviation = SQRT( SUM( Events[ValueSquared] ) / COUNTROWS( Events )
                        - AVERAGE( Events[Value] ) ^ 2 )
```

The formula uses the COUNTROWS function, which counts the rows in a table and performs the same computation shown before. With this new calculated measure, you can perform the interesting analysis shown in Figure 9-9.

| Row Labels | AverageOfValue | StandardDeviation |
|---|---|---|
| ⊟A | **14.00** | **2.16** |
| 1 | 12.00 | - |
| 2 | 13.00 | - |
| 3 | 17.00 | - |
| ⊟B | **16.00** | **5.89** |
| 4 | 10.00 | - |
| 5 | 14.00 | - |
| 6 | 24.00 | - |
| **Grand Total** | **15.00** | **4.55** |

**FIGURE 9-9** Standard deviation analysis.

The standard deviation gives important information. Rows in Category A have a distribution of Value that is usually nearer to the Category average than rows in Category B.

# Ranking over a Measure

The ranking of products, customers, or other entities is sometimes an implicit action of the user interface (like the PivotTable) that is obtained by sorting data using a specific criteria (for example, the sales amount). However, you might need to explicitly use the rank of an entity to make further calculations or to do particular presentations of data (for example, highlighting entities with specific rank conditions). So in this section, you see how to define DAX expressions to calculate the ranking of an attribute over a particular measure. You use the same sets of data previously used in the section "Calculating Ratio and Percentage" at the beginning of this chapter.

## Calculating Ranking on a Single Denormalized Table

For example, consider a set of data in a single table, like the one you saw in Figure 9-1. You can calculate the ranking for products and models over sales amount. Remember that each product is unique and has only one row in this table, but there are several products (thus, rows) for each model. Moreover, notice that there are a few changes in the calculation, depending on whether or not the attribute to be ranked and the values used for ranking are in the same table. In this first example, all the data is in the same table because it is the easiest situation. You can find this example in the CH09-04-RankingSingleTable.xlsx workbook on the companion DVD.

You can define a ProductRank measure using the following DAX expression:

```
ProductRank = COUNTROWS( FILTER( ALL( Sales[Product] ),
                             CALCULATE( SUM( Sales[SalesAmount] ) )
                                > CALCULATE( SUM( Sales[SalesAmount] ),
                                             VALUES( Sales[Product] ) ) )
                       ) + 1
```

The idea is to count how many products have a SalesAmount value higher than the current product. (The formula computes the ranking for a single product, so it does not work if many products are active in the PivotTable for the calculated cell.)

## Explaining the ProductRank Measure

The first parameter passed to FILTER removes the filter on the Product column and makes the FILTER function iterate over the list of all the products, regardless of other filters active in the PivotTable. However, these filters determine whether the following filter expression passed to the FILTER function calculates or does not calculate a value for each product. The CALCULATE( SUM( Sales[SalesAmount] ) ) expression returns the value for the product iterated by FILTER only if this product is visible in the current filters of the PivotTable. For example, if there is a filter on the product model in the PivotTable, only products of that model are calculated. Then a comparison is made against the SalesAmount of the products that are active in the evaluated cell of the PivotTable.

You might wonder why an EARLIER function is not used here. The reason is that EARLIER needs a previous row context, and in this case, there is no row context outside of the FILTER call. In fact, you use EARLIER later for calculated columns. In this case, the SalesAmount of the current product in the PivotTable is obtained by filtering the CALCULATE function with the expression VALUES( Sales[Product] ), which is evaluated before the FILTER function and returns the list of the products that are active for the evaluated cell. (In theory, there should be just one of these.)

In Figure 9-10, you can see an example of the ProductRank measure in a PivotTable that contains all the products sorted by SalesAmount in descending order.

| Row Labels | Sum of SalesAmount | ProductRank |
|---|---|---|
| Mountain-200 Black, 38 | 4,239,861.54 | 1 |
| Mountain-200 Black, 42 | 3,825,977.53 | 2 |
| Mountain-200 Silver, 38 | 3,507,995.97 | 3 |
| Mountain-200 Silver, 42 | 3,289,668.08 | 4 |
| Mountain-200 Silver, 46 | 3,251,889.16 | 5 |
| Mountain-200 Black, 46 | 3,137,630.93 | 6 |
| Road-250 Black, 44 | 2,240,235.19 | 7 |
| Road-250 Black, 48 | 2,036,303.35 | 8 |
| Road-250 Black, 52 | 1,659,907.28 | 9 |
| Road-350-W Yellow, 48 | 1,603,083.57 | 10 |

**FIGURE 9-10** The first top-10 products sorted by SalesAmount with the ProductRank measure shown in the last column.

You can see in Figure 9-11 that the same ProductRank works dynamically over the other selections that are active in the PivotTable. In this case, there are two models selected in the slicer, and the ranking is calculated by considering only the products that are active in the filter context determined by these two models.

**Model**

Road Bottle Cage
Road Tire Tube
Road-150
Road-250
Road-350-W
Road-450
Road-550-W
Road-650
Road-750
Short-Sleeve Classi...
Sport-100
Touring Pedal
Touring Tire
Touring Tire Tube
Touring-1000
Touring-2000

| Row Labels | Sum of SalesAmount | ProductRank |
|---|---|---|
| Road-250 Black, 44 | 2,240,235.19 | 1 |
| Road-250 Black, 48 | 2,036,303.35 | 2 |
| Road-250 Black, 52 | 1,659,907.28 | 3 |
| Road-150 Red, 56 | 1,475,678.55 | 4 |
| Road-150 Red, 62 | 1,314,656.40 | 5 |
| Road-250 Red, 44 | 1,301,521.48 | 6 |
| Road-250 Red, 58 | 1,259,424.76 | 7 |
| Road-250 Black, 58 | 1,225,915.96 | 8 |
| Road-250 Red, 48 | 1,165,508.25 | 9 |
| Road-150 Red, 48 | 1,075,627.96 | 10 |
| Road-150 Red, 52 | 1,011,219.10 | 11 |
| Road-150 Red, 44 | 996,906.02 | 12 |
| Road-250 Red, 52 | 929,939.01 | 13 |
| **Grand Total** | **17,692,843.30** | **1** |

**FIGURE 9-11** Ranking for products in two selected models.

As you can see, the Grand Total value is incorrect because more than one product is active in the filter context, so the ranking formula does not work as expected. A possible solution is to intercept that condition and return NULL instead, as in the following ProductRank definition (we will not repeat this check in following measures, just for the sake of simplicity):

```
ProductRank = IF ( COUNTROWS (VALUES (Sales[Product])) > 1,
                   BLANK (),
                   COUNTROWS( FILTER( ALL( Sales[Product] ),
                              CALCULATE( SUM( Sales[SalesAmount] ) )
                                 > CALCULATE( SUM( Sales[SalesAmount] ),
                                              VALUES( Sales[Product] ) ) )
                            ) + 1
                  )
```

A similar ModelRank measure can be defined by means of the following formula, which is conceptually identical to ProductRank but references Sales[Model] instead of Sales[Product]:

```
ModelRank = COUNTROWS( FILTER( ALL( Sales[Model] ),
                               CALCULATE( SUM( Sales[SalesAmount] ) )
                                  > CALCULATE( SUM( Sales[SalesAmount] ),
                                               VALUES( Sales[Model] ) ) )
                     ) + 1
```

In Figure 9-12, you can see the ModelRank measure in action. In this case, product models in the rows are sorted by name, but the ModelRank column displays the right ranking regardless of the order of the rows.

| Row Labels | Sum of SalesAmount | ModelRank |
|---|---|---|
| All-Purpose Bike Stand | 25,281.00 | 61 |
| Bike Wash | 15,696.02 | 76 |
| Cable Lock | 16,240.22 | 74 |
| Chain | 9,377.71 | 92 |
| Classic Vest | 245,708.87 | 29 |
| Cycling Cap | 43,075.52 | 51 |
| Fender Set - Mountain | 42,069.72 | 52 |
| Front Brakes | 50,299.31 | 46 |
| Front Derailleur | 44,484.27 | 49 |
| Full-Finger Gloves | 129,563.69 | 35 |
| Half-Finger Gloves | 100,184.92 | 39 |
| Hitch Rack - 4-Bike | 225,936.16 | 30 |
| HL Bottom Bracket | 39,581.44 | 55 |

**FIGURE 9-12** Ranking for product models sorted alphabetically.

In case you want to make a fixed calculation of the ranking instead of a dynamic one, or if you want to use the ranking as a filter for browsing data in the PivotTable, you might want to get it through a calculated column in the PowerPivot table. Such a column can be used to get a fixed attribute for each product/model, which is not going to change following the selection made in the PivotTable. You can use the following DAX expression for a ProductRankTotal calculated column:

```
ProductRankTotal = COUNTROWS( FILTER( ALL( Sales ),
                                  Sales[SalesAmount] > EARLIER( Sales[SalesAmount] ) )
                     ) + 1
```

This formula is simpler than the one used for the corresponding measure in the PivotTable because it can make use of the EARLIER function, having a row context external to the FILTER call.

**Explaining the ProductRankTotal Calculated Column**

The formula counts the rows that have a value of SalesAmount greater than the SalesAmount of the current row for which the ProductRankTotal column is calculated. The EARLIER function returns the value of SalesAmount for that current row instead of using the row context defined by the FILTER iteration over the Sales table.

The calculation that is required to define a ranked calculated column for a product model is a little bit more complex in this case because there can be more rows for each model. (Previously, the assumption that there is a single row for each product simplified the calculation.) First of all, you have to calculate the sales amount for the model, which is a group of products, by using the same ModelSalesAmount calculated column you used in the "Calculating Ratio and Percentage" section, earlier in this chapter:

```
ModelSalesAmount = CALCULATE( SUM( Sales[SalesAmount] ),
                     ALLEXCEPT( Sales, Sales[Model] ) )
```

If you look carefully at the preceding formula, you will see a similar statement in the definition of the ModelRankTotal calculated column:

```
ModelRankTotal = COUNTROWS( FILTER( ALL( Sales[Model] ),
                            CALCULATE( VALUES( Sales[ModelSalesAmount] ),
                                       ALLEXCEPT( Sales, Sales[Model]) )
                                           > Sales[ModelSalesAmount])
                   ) + 1
```

The technique is always to count the rows returned by a FILTER call. The predicate of the filter compares the value of the ModelSalesAmount of the row iterated by the FILTER call with the ModelSalesAmount value of the current row.

## Explaining the ModelRankTotal Calculated Column

The purpose of the CALCULATE call in the predicate is to transfer the current row context of the table into a filter context. The FILTER defines an iteration in just the Model column, so the result of the ALLEXCEPT call to the CALCULATE function is to define a filter context formed by just the Model column values iterated by the FILTER call and no filter at all on other columns. (Otherwise, the current row filter for the ModelRankTotal calculation would be applied instead.) There could be several rows in the Sales table for a model, but the CALCULATE statement requires VALUES( Sales[ModelSalesAmount] ), which returns just one value because all the rows filtered are of the same product model and have the same value for ModelSalesAmount. Thus, the CALCULATE statement returns the ModelSalesAmount value of the row iterated by FILTER, which is compared with the ModelSalesAmount value of the current row for which the ModelRankTotal calculated column is computed. Because the filter just iterates all the Model column values, it does not affect the current row of the ModelSalesAmount column, even if these columns are on the same table.

An example of the resulting PowerPivot table is shown in Figure 9-13.

| Model | Product | SalesAmount | ProductRankTotal | ModelSalesAmount | ModelRankTotal |
|---|---|---|---|---|---|
| Mountain-200 | Mountain-200 Silver, 46 | 3,251,889.16 | 5 | 21,253,023.20 | 1 |
| Mountain-200 | Mountain-200 Silver, 42 | 3,289,668.08 | 4 | 21,253,023.20 | 1 |
| Mountain-200 | Mountain-200 Silver, 38 | 3,507,995.97 | 3 | 21,253,023.20 | 1 |
| Mountain-200 | Mountain-200 Black, 46 | 3,137,630.93 | 6 | 21,253,023.20 | 1 |
| Mountain-200 | Mountain-200 Black, 42 | 3,825,977.53 | 2 | 21,253,023.20 | 1 |
| Mountain-200 | Mountain-200 Black, 38 | 4,239,861.54 | 1 | 21,253,023.20 | 1 |
| Road-250 | Road-250 Red, 58 | 1,259,424.76 | 20 | 11,818,755.27 | 2 |
| Road-250 | Road-250 Red, 52 | 929,939.01 | 39 | 11,818,755.27 | 2 |
| Road-250 | Road-250 Red, 48 | 1,165,508.25 | 27 | 11,818,755.27 | 2 |
| Road-250 | Road-250 Red, 44 | 1,301,521.48 | 17 | 11,818,755.27 | 2 |
| Road-250 | Road-250 Black, 58 | 1,225,915.96 | 22 | 11,818,755.27 | 2 |
| Road-250 | Road-250 Black, 52 | 1,659,907.28 | 9 | 11,818,755.27 | 2 |
| Road-250 | Road-250 Black, 48 | 2,036,303.35 | 8 | 11,818,755.27 | 2 |
| Road-250 | Road-250 Black, 44 | 2,240,235.19 | 7 | 11,818,755.27 | 2 |
| Mountain-100 | Mountain-100 Silver, 48 | 985,657.10 | 36 | 9,432,630.72 | 3 |
| Mountain-100 | Mountain-100 Silver, 44 | 1,173,010.49 | 26 | 9,432,630.72 | 3 |

**FIGURE 9-13** Ranking for product and models in calculated columns of a PowerPivot table.

The ranking calculations shown in this section can be easily adapted to other scenarios in which data is stored in a single denormalized table. If you have normalized data in other tables, the following section describes a few differences in procedure.

## Calculating Ranking in Multiple Normalized Tables

The scenario of data normalized in multiple tables is identical to the one you saw in Figures 9-4 and 9-5 in the first part of this chapter: you have a Sales and a Products table. In this scenario, you have a unique product for each row of the Products table and several sales transactions for each product in the Sales table. You can find the complete example in CH09-05-RankingMultipleTables.xlsx workbook on the companion DVD.

The ProductRank measure in this case refers to the Product column of the Products table:

```
ProductRank = IF( COUNTROWS( VALUES( Sales[SalesAmount] ) ) > 0,
                  COUNTROWS( FILTER( ALL( Products[Product] ),
                                     CALCULATE( SUM( Sales[SalesAmount] ) )
                                        > SUM( Sales[SalesAmount] ) )
                           ) + 1,
                  BLANK() )
```

There are two other differences in the ProductRank measure for data in a single table that you saw in the previous section. First, there is an initial IF call that returns BLANK in case there are no rows in the Sales table for a given product. Second, the predicate of the FILTER call calculates the value of the current product by using the SUM( Sales[SalesAmount] ) statement: because data reside in a separate table, you no longer need to use the CALCULATE statement to apply the filter context.

In this scenario, the ModelRank measure is pretty similar to the ProductRank one, with the only difference that the FILTER uses ALL( Products[Model] ) instead of ALL( Products[Product] ) to iterate over all the models instead of over all the products:

```
ModelRank = IF( COUNTROWS( VALUES( Sales[SalesAmount] ) ) > 0,
                COUNTROWS( FILTER( ALL( Products[Model] ),
                                   CALCULATE( SUM( Sales[SalesAmount] ) )
                                      > SUM( Sales[SalesAmount] ) )
                         ) + 1,
                BLANK() )
```

The results of these two measures are visually identical to those you saw in Figures 9-10, 9-11, and 9-12. The only relevant information here is that you have to adapt your DAX formula according to the underlying data model.

Moreover, even in this scenario you can define calculated columns to get a fixed ranking instead of a dynamic one. To define ProductRankTotal in the Products table, you must create a ProductSalesAmount calculated column first:

```
ProductSalesAmount = CALCULATE( SUM( Sales[SalesAmount] ) )
```

The availability of ProductSalesAmount makes it possible to define a ProductRankTotal calculated column that is conceptually identical to the one you saw in the previous section, using a single table with denormalized data:

```
ProductRankTotal = COUNTROWS( FILTER( ALL( Products ),
                                      Products[ProductSalesAmount]
                                          > EARLIER( Products[ProductSalesAmount] ) )
                            ) + 1
```

The main difference is the use of Products instead of a Sales table. So a calculation identical to that in the previous example is required for ModelSalesAmount and ModelRankTotal calculated columns:

```
ModelSalesAmount = CALCULATE( SUM( Sales[SalesAmount] ),
                              ALLEXCEPT( Products, Products[Model] ) )

ModelRankTotal = COUNTROWS( FILTER( ALL( Products[Model] ),
                                    CALCULATE( VALUES( Products[ModelSalesAmount] ),
                                               ALLEXCEPT( Products, Products[Model] ) )
                                        > Products[ModelSalesAmount] )
                          ) + 1
```

Also in these calculations, the reference is to a Products table instead of Sales, except for the reference to the SalesAmount value, which always belongs to the Sales table.

The final results of these calculated columns are visually identical to the Products table you saw in Figure 9-13.

**Tip** Always consider the underlying data model and the uniqueness of the column in the PowerPivot table before you choose the calculation template to apply for ranking. This rule is, in general, valid for any calculation that has to aggregate data by using a different selection than the one made by the user in the PivotTable, as well as for any calculated column that has to aggregate data other than that reachable through standard table relationships.

# Computing ABC and Pareto Analyses

The Pareto principle states that 80 percent of the effects usually come from 20 percent of the causes. A common application of this principle is that 80 percent of the sales come from 20 percent of the customers (or from 20 percent of the products). This rule is also known as the 80-20 rule. The *Pareto analysis* is a technique based on this principle, and it is used to categorize items. For example, you might want to determine the fewest number of customers who account for 80 percent of the sales. These customers might receive particular offers or a particular service, allowing a bigger investment for retention of these customers than for other customers.

The Pareto principle is also the basis for a similar type of classification known as *ABC analysis*. The concept is to classify items (usually products) using three classes:

- Class A, which contains items that account for 70 percent of the total value
- Class B, which contains items that account for another 20 percent of the total value
- Class C, which contains items that account for the remaining 10 percent of the total value

This classification may vary in its definition—for example, someone uses different percentages for ABC classes (80/15/5 instead of 70/20/10) and someone makes a division based on the number of items (for example, 20/30/50 for classes A/B/C).

The ABC analysis is used to create an attribute that can be used to filter items (like Products and Customers). In other words, if a product belongs to Class A, you want to add a column to the products table that contains A so that it can be used in slicers, filters, rows, and columns of a PivotTable. For this reason, you cannot rely on measures to perform ABC analysis.

The calculation for ABC analysis can be made in PowerPivot by using calculated columns. In this way, each row can have an attribute with the appropriate ABC class. The ABC calculation has to be made in consideration of a particular grouping and sort order.

Suppose you want to define an ABC class of Products for sales transactions of AdventureWorks. You might want to classify Products in this way:

- Products that make 70 percent of the sales are in Class A.
- Products that make 20 percent of the sales are in Class B.
- Products that make 10 percent of the sales are in Class C.

Conceptually, you need to group sales transactions by product, sort products by sales amount in descending order, calculate a sort of running sum of products following that order, and define the class for each product by comparing that running sum with the boundaries of the classes (70 percent and 90 percent of sales amounts for all transactions correspond to boundaries of Class B). In the following examples, you see how to implement ABC analysis for Products in several PowerPivot data models.

## ABC Analysis with a Single Denormalized Table

In this first example, you use Sales data in a single table, which is also called a denormalized table. This case might occur whenever you use a query (or a view provided by the IT department) to extract data in a single table. This is a very convenient way to work on data in Excel without PowerPivot. For that reason, you might already have data in this format. However, consider that having data separated in multiple tables is a more convenient way to use PowerPivot, as you will see later.

## Performance Issues in ABC Analysis with a Denormalized Table

Please note that calculating ABC classes in a single denormalized table could perform badly because it requires heavy calculation during data load in PowerPivot. The normalized approach, using one table for each entity (such as Customers, Products, and so on) is far better in terms of performance because the calculation depends only on the size of the related table (such as Products or Customers) and not on the size of the table that contains the sales transactions.

The CH09-06-AbcSingleTable.xlsx workbook included on the companion DVD contains an Excel table with Sales data extracted from AdventureWorks by the IT department, as you can see in Figure 9-14.

| | OrderDate | Customer | EmailAddress | Product | Model | Amount |
|---|---|---|---|---|---|---|
| 52761 | 10/26/2003 | Nathan Martinez | nathan51@adventure-works.cc | Patch Kit/8 Patches | Patch kit | 2.29 |
| 52762 | 10/26/2003 | Marcus James | marcus73@adventure-works.cc | ML Mountain Tire | ML Mountain Tire | 29.99 |
| 52763 | 10/26/2003 | Kristina Chandra | kristina2@adventure-works.co | Women's Mountain Shorts, L | Women's Mountain Shorts | 69.99 |
| 52764 | 10/26/2003 | Kristina Chandra | kristina2@adventure-works.co | Short-Sleeve Classic Jersey, XL | Short-Sleeve Classic Jersey | 53.99 |
| 52765 | 10/26/2003 | Albert Vazquez | albert14@adventure-works.coi | Water Bottle - 30 oz. | Water Bottle | 4.99 |
| 52766 | 10/26/2003 | Shaun Pal | shaun13@adventure-works.coi | Mountain Tire Tube | Mountain Tire Tube | 4.99 |
| 52767 | 10/26/2003 | Ryan Jackson | ryan51@adventure-works.com | Fender Set - Mountain | Fender Set - Mountain | 21.98 |
| 52768 | 10/26/2003 | Hunter Hernande | hunter44@adventure-works.cc | Fender Set - Mountain | Fender Set - Mountain | 21.98 |
| 52769 | 10/26/2003 | Hunter Hernande | hunter44@adventure-works.cc | Sport-100 Helmet, Blue | Sport-100 | 34.99 |

**FIGURE 9-14** Sales data extracted from AdventureWorks in a single Excel table.

You can import this table as a linked table in PowerPivot. At this point, there are several steps to obtain the ABC class that you want for each row; each of them is a new calculated column in the PowerPivot table. Before starting, remember to use the Product and Amount columns in DAX formulas.

The first calculated column you define is SalesAmountProduct: this is the total sales amount for each product. You obtain it by summing up all the sales transactions made for the same product. So the same value is duplicated for each row of the same product.

```
SalesAmountProduct = CALCULATE( SUM( Sales[Amount] ),
                               ALLEXCEPT( Sales, Sales[Product] ) )
```

To make this calculation, you can use the CALCULATE function, which filters only the rows in Sales that belong to the same product of the current row context. In fact, the Sales[Product] in the ALLEXCEPT call does not have a row context provided by the DAX formula, and it uses the row context used to generate the value of the calculated column for each row of the table. Note that this complexity is not required in the normalized version of the ABC calculation. In Figure 9-15, you can see that all transactions of the same product have the same value in the SalesAmountProduct column.

| OrderDate | Cus... | Email... | Product | Model | Amount | SalesAmountProduct |
|---|---|---|---|---|---|---|
| 6/1/2003 | Gregor... | gregory... | ML Mountain Frame - Black, 48 | ML Mou... | 1,255.54 | 200,284.50 |
| 6/1/2003 | Barbar... | barbara... | ML Mountain Frame - Black, 48 | ML Mou... | 1,255.54 | 200,284.50 |
| 9/1/2003 | Franço... | françois... | ML Mountain Frame - Black, 48 | ML Mou... | 258.08 | 200,284.50 |
| 7/1/2003 | Pei Ch... | pei0@a... | ML Mountain Frame-W - Silver, 38 | ML Mou... | 218.45 | 1,529.18 |
| 8/1/2003 | Scott C... | scott3@... | ML Mountain Frame-W - Silver, 38 | ML Mou... | 218.45 | 1,529.18 |
| 8/1/2003 | Jay Ad... | jay1@ad... | ML Mountain Frame-W - Silver, 38 | ML Mou... | 655.36 | 1,529.18 |
| 8/1/2003 | Mae Bl... | mae1@... | ML Mountain Frame-W - Silver, 38 | ML Mou... | 218.45 | 1,529.18 |
| 8/1/2003 | Georg... | george2... | ML Mountain Frame-W - Silver, 38 | ML Mou... | 218.45 | 1,529.18 |
| 7/1/2003 | Jeff Pri... | jeff3@a... | ML Mountain Frame-W - Silver, 40 | ML Mou... | 1,310.72 | 195,826.39 |
| 7/1/2003 | Jo Bro... | jo2@ad... | ML Mountain Frame-W - Silver, 40 | ML Mou... | 436.91 | 195,826.39 |

**FIGURE 9-15** The SalesAmountProduct column has the same value for all the rows of each product.

## Use CALCULATE Whenever Possible

Even if the CALCULATE syntax might not be intuitive when you use it in a calculated column, it is usually faster than possible alternatives based on other aggregation functions. For example, you might use the SUMX function by filtering all the products that correspond to the one in the current row context.

```
SalesAmountProduct = SUMX( FILTER( Sales,
                                   Sales[Product] = EARLIER( Sales[Product] ) ),
                           Sales[Amount] )
```

Because SUMX defines a new row context, you need to use the EARLIER function, which gets the product name of the row context external to the one defined by the SUMX function. However, remember that using CALCULATE is usually better for performance reasons.

The second calculated column is CumulatedProduct: this is the accumulated value of a product, considered in descending order, from the top-seller to the worst.

```
CumulatedProduct = SUMX( FILTER( Sales,
                                 Sales[SalesAmountProduct]
                                     >= EARLIER( Sales[SalesAmountProduct] ) ),
                         Sales[Amount] )
```

You repeat a pattern similar to the one shown in the previous sidebar by using SUMX as a slower alternative to CALCULATE. The SUMX function filters all the sales transactions belonging to a product that has a total sales for the product greater than or equal to the sales of the product in the current row, outside of the SUMX row context. (You have to use EARLIER in the same way you saw in the SalesAmountProduct formula based on SUMX.) In other words, the FILTER function returns all the rows of the products that sold at least the amount value of the current product. You can see in Figure 9-16 that, sorting transactions by SalesAmountProduct in descending order, the CumulatedProduct for the top-selling product has the same value of SalesAmountProduct, and then for the second product in this ranking, the value is the sum of the first two products, and so on.

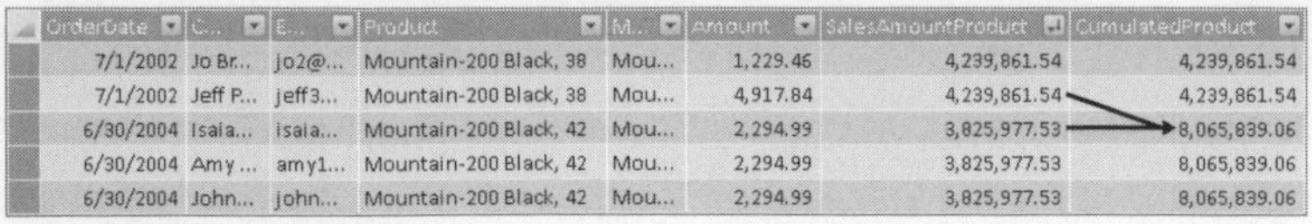

| OrderDate | C... | E... | Product | M... | Amount | SalesAmountProduct | CumulatedProduct |
|---|---|---|---|---|---|---|---|
| 7/1/2002 | Jo Br... | jo2@... | Mountain-200 Black, 38 | Mou... | 1,229.46 | 4,239,861.54 | 4,239,861.54 |
| 7/1/2002 | Jeff P... | jeff3... | Mountain-200 Black, 38 | Mou... | 4,917.84 | 4,239,861.54 | 4,239,861.54 |
| 6/30/2004 | Isaia... | isaia... | Mountain-200 Black, 42 | Mou... | 2,294.99 | 3,825,977.53 | 8,065,839.06 |
| 6/30/2004 | Amy ... | amy1... | Mountain-200 Black, 42 | Mou... | 2,294.99 | 3,825,977.53 | 8,065,839.06 |
| 6/30/2004 | John... | john... | Mountain-200 Black, 42 | Mou... | 2,294.99 | 3,825,977.53 | 8,065,839.06 |

**FIGURE 9-16** CumulatedProduct aggregates all the products that sold more than the current one.

The third calculated column is SortedWeightProduct: this calculation simply transforms the CumulatedProduct value into a percentage. You use this number to filter all the transactions according to the percentage limit that corresponds to ABC classes. (In this case, you use 70 percent for Class A, up to 90 percent for Class B, and the remaining for Class C).

```
SortedWeightProduct = Sales[CumulatedProduct] / SUM( Sales[Amount] )
```

Finally, you can define the last calculated column, named ABC Class Product: this is the final result of the calculation. Depending on the value of SortedWeightProduct, an A, B, or C is displayed. Remember that a percentage is expressed by a number between 0 and 1.

```
[ABC Class Product] = IF( Sales[SortedWeightProduct] <= 0.7,
                          "A",
                          IF( Sales[SortedWeightProduct] <= 0.9,
                              "B",
                              "C" ) )
```

In Figure 9-17, you can see the final result, with an ABC class defined for each transaction.

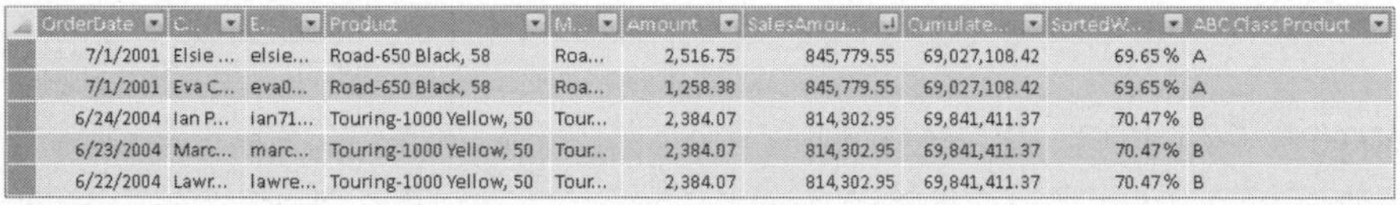

| OrderDate | C... | E... | Product | M... | Amount | SalesAmou... | Cumulate... | SortedW... | ABC Class Product |
|---|---|---|---|---|---|---|---|---|---|
| 7/1/2001 | Elsie ... | elsie... | Road-650 Black, 58 | Roa... | 2,516.75 | 845,779.55 | 69,027,108.42 | 69.65 % | A |
| 7/1/2001 | Eva C... | eva0... | Road-650 Black, 58 | Roa... | 1,258.38 | 845,779.55 | 69,027,108.42 | 69.65 % | A |
| 6/24/2004 | Ian P... | ian71... | Touring-1000 Yellow, 50 | Tour... | 2,384.07 | 814,302.95 | 69,841,411.37 | 70.47 % | B |
| 6/23/2004 | Marc... | marc... | Touring-1000 Yellow, 50 | Tour... | 2,384.07 | 814,302.95 | 69,841,411.37 | 70.47 % | B |
| 6/22/2004 | Lawr... | lawre... | Touring-1000 Yellow, 50 | Tour... | 2,384.07 | 814,302.95 | 69,841,411.37 | 70.47 % | B |

**FIGURE 9-17** ABC Class Product defines the ABC class for each transaction based on SortedWeightProduct.

At this point, you can browse the data with a PivotTable in Excel. In Figure 9-18, for example, you can look at the relevance of the ABC class of products for each customer. (In this case, customers are sorted by total of sales in descending order.)

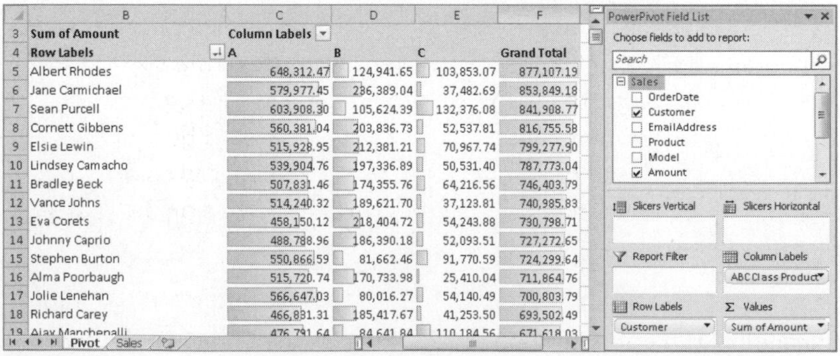

| | B | C | D | E | F |
|---|---|---|---|---|---|
| 3 | Sum of Amount | Column Labels | | | |
| 4 | Row Labels | A | B | C | Grand Total |
| 5 | Albert Rhodes | 648,312.47 | 124,941.65 | 103,853.07 | 877,107.19 |
| 6 | Jane Carmichael | 579,977.45 | 236,389.04 | 37,482.69 | 853,849.18 |
| 7 | Sean Purcell | 603,908.30 | 105,624.39 | 132,376.08 | 841,908.77 |
| 8 | Cornett Gibbens | 560,381.04 | 203,836.73 | 52,537.81 | 816,755.58 |
| 9 | Elsie Lewin | 515,928.95 | 212,381.21 | 70,967.74 | 799,277.90 |
| 10 | Lindsey Camacho | 539,904.76 | 197,336.89 | 50,531.40 | 787,773.04 |
| 11 | Bradley Beck | 507,831.46 | 174,355.76 | 64,216.56 | 746,403.79 |
| 12 | Vance Johns | 514,240.32 | 189,621.70 | 37,123.81 | 740,985.83 |
| 13 | Eva Corets | 458,150.12 | 218,404.72 | 54,243.88 | 730,798.71 |
| 14 | Johnny Caprio | 488,788.96 | 186,390.18 | 52,093.51 | 727,272.65 |
| 15 | Stephen Burton | 550,866.59 | 81,662.46 | 91,770.59 | 724,299.64 |
| 16 | Alma Poorbaugh | 515,720.74 | 170,733.98 | 25,410.04 | 711,864.76 |
| 17 | Jolie Lenehan | 566,647.03 | 80,016.27 | 54,140.49 | 700,803.79 |
| 18 | Richard Carey | 466,831.31 | 185,417.67 | 41,253.50 | 693,502.49 |
| 19 | Ajax Manchenalli | 476,791.64 | 84,641.84 | 110,184.56 | 671,618.03 |

Pivot | Sales

PowerPivot Field List
Choose fields to add to report:
Search
Sales
☐ OrderDate
☑ Customer
☐ EmailAddress
☐ Product
☐ Model
☑ Amount
Slicers Vertical | Slicers Horizontal
Report Filter | Column Labels: ABC Class Product
Row Labels: Customer | Values: Sum of Amount

**FIGURE 9-18** A PivotTable splits customer sales by the ABC class of products.

## ABC Analysis with Multiple Normalized Tables

In this second example, you use five normalized tables; you import from AdventureWorks the following tables: SalesOrderHeader, SalesOrderDetail, Contact, Product, and ProductModel. The CH09-07-AbcMultipleTables.xlsx workbook included on the companion DVD contains the PowerPivot model with these tables already loaded.

**Tip** If you try to make the import by yourself, remember to exclude columns that are not supported by PowerPivot, such as Instructions from the ProductModel table and AdditionalContactInfo from Contact.

In this case, you define the same calculated columns for ABC classification in the Product table instead of the fact table. You use the ProductID column to identify the product and LineTotal (from SalesOrderDetail table) as the measure to use for ABC classification.

This is the definition for the SalesAmountProduct calculated column in the Product table:

```
SalesAmountProduct = CALCULATE( SUM( SalesOrderDetail[LineTotal] ) )
```

In this case, each calculation is different for each row because each row is a single product. The CALCULATE function makes use of the existing relationship between SalesOrderDetail and Product tables, avoiding the need for a filter condition in the CALCULATE function, such as the ALLEXCEPT one used in the previous example with a single denormalized table.

### Slower Alternatives to CALCULATE

An alternative to the CALCULATE function worth mentioning is based on the use of SUMX and RELATEDTABLE. It might appear easier if you are used to working with a relational database, but it is slower than CALCULATE in PowerPivot. For example, consider the following definition for SalesAmountProduct calculated column:

```
SalesAmountProduct = SUMX( RELATEDTABLE( SalesOrderDetail ),
                           SalesOrderDetail[LineTotal] )
```

The RELATEDTABLE function makes use of the existing relationship between SalesOrderDetail and Product tables. However, this is the same logic used by CALCULATE. The only reason to use this version based on SUMX would be if you need to define a more complex calculation that would have to be made on every single row of SalesOrderDetail table without defining a calculated column with such an expression. (The SUM function used in the CALCULATE version accepts only a single column as a parameter.)

The second definition (shown on the following page) is for the CumulatedProduct calculated column, which is always defined in the Product table.

```
CumulatedProduct = SUMX( FILTER( Product,
                                  Product[SalesAmountProduct]
                                        >= EARLIER( Product[SalesAmountProduct] ) ),
                          Product[SalesAmountProduct] )
```

The preceding expression returns the accumulated value of a product, considering products in descending order from the top-seller to the worst. In this case, you use the EARLIER function to get the sales amount for the current product, and the FILTER returns all the rows of the products that sold at least the amount value of the current product. The technique is very similar to the one used for the single denormalized table, but you need to sum the value of SalesAmountProduct instead of the LineTotal of the single transactions because the table you are aggregating is a subset of the Product table and not of the sales transaction table.

Finally, you have to define the two SortedWeightProduct and ABC Class Product calculated columns, which are very similar to those defined in the previous example:

```
SortedWeightProduct = Product[CumulatedProduct] / SUM( Product[SalesAmountProduct] )

[ABC Class Product] = IF( Product[SortedWeightProduct] <= 0.7,
                          "A",
                          IF( Product[SortedWeightProduct] <= 0.9,
                              "B",
                              "C" ) )
```

The only relevant difference is that the denominator of the SortedWeightProduct formula sums the value of SalesAmountProduct from the Product table instead of LineTotal of the SalesOrderDetail table. The result would be identical for both these calculations, but it is faster to aggregate data from a smaller table (Product) than from a larger one (SalesOrderDetail). In Figure 9-19, you can see the calculated columns created in the Product table.

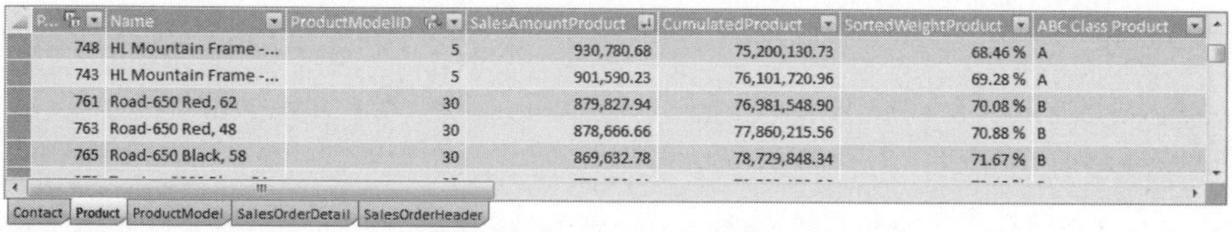

| P... | Name | ProductModelID | SalesAmountProduct | CumulatedProduct | SortedWeightProduct | ABC Class Product |
|---|---|---|---|---|---|---|
| 748 | HL Mountain Frame -... | 5 | 930,780.68 | 75,200,130.73 | 68.46 % | A |
| 743 | HL Mountain Frame -... | 5 | 901,590.23 | 76,101,720.96 | 69.28 % | A |
| 761 | Road-650 Red, 62 | 30 | 879,827.94 | 76,981,548.90 | 70.08 % | B |
| 763 | Road-650 Red, 48 | 30 | 878,666.66 | 77,860,215.56 | 70.88 % | B |
| 765 | Road-650 Black, 58 | 30 | 869,632.78 | 78,729,848.34 | 71.67 % | B |

Contact | Product | ProductModel | SalesOrderDetail | SalesOrderHeader

**FIGURE 9-19** Calculated columns created in the Product table for ABC classification on Products.

Finally, you can do the same ABC analysis that you did for the denormalized table used as a source of data. In this case, you can see in Figure 9-20 the distribution of ABC classification of products grouped by model. As you might expect, there is a strong relationship, which indicates you might classify models instead of products, producing very similar results. But with a few notable exceptions (such as the Road-650 model in row 7), the analysis indicates there are smaller sales divided among a number of very similar products. From a business point of view, you could have an important decision to make (classifying ABC for models instead for products), especially if products differ only in characteristics that do not affect the way they are produced.

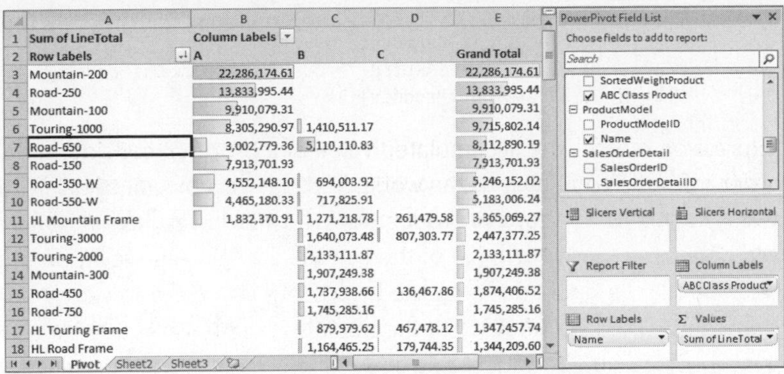

| Sum of LineTotal | Column Labels | | | |
|---|---|---|---|---|
| Row Labels | A | B | C | Grand Total |
| Mountain-200 | 22,286,174.61 | | | 22,286,174.61 |
| Road-250 | 13,833,995.44 | | | 13,833,995.44 |
| Mountain-100 | 9,910,079.31 | | | 9,910,079.31 |
| Touring-1000 | 8,305,290.97 | 1,410,511.17 | | 9,715,802.14 |
| Road-650 | 3,002,779.36 | 5,110,110.83 | | 8,112,890.19 |
| Road-150 | 7,913,701.93 | | | 7,913,701.93 |
| Road-350-W | 4,552,148.10 | 694,003.92 | | 5,246,152.02 |
| Road-550-W | 4,465,180.33 | 717,825.91 | | 5,183,006.24 |
| HL Mountain Frame | 1,832,370.91 | 1,271,218.78 | 261,479.58 | 3,365,069.27 |
| Touring-3000 | | 1,640,073.48 | 807,303.77 | 2,447,377.25 |
| Touring-2000 | | 2,133,111.87 | | 2,133,111.87 |
| Mountain-300 | | 1,907,249.38 | | 1,907,249.38 |
| Road-450 | | 1,737,938.66 | 136,467.86 | 1,874,406.52 |
| Road-750 | | 1,745,285.16 | | 1,745,285.16 |
| HL Touring Frame | | 879,979.62 | 467,478.12 | 1,347,457.74 |
| HL Road Frame | | 1,164,465.25 | 179,744.35 | 1,344,209.60 |



**FIGURE 9-20** A PivotTable splits product model sales by ABC classification of products.

## ABC with Denormalized Attributes on Normalized Tables

In the previous example, the model of a product was described in the ProductModel table, which was referenced by the Product table. However, you might have a scenario in which you want to build an ABC classification for an attribute of the Product table. For example, the model might be a column in the Product table, without being normalized in a separate table. In this case, you need to use a mix of the techniques that we have used in the previous two examples. The Model column is your key to identifying the granularity of ABC classification.

First of all, you still calculate the SalesAmountProducts column by using the same expression we described in the previous scenario. You can find this model in the CH09-08-AbcDenormalizedAttributes.xlsx workbook included on the companion DVD.

```
SalesAmountProduct = CALCULATE( SUM( SalesOrderDetail[LineTotal] ) )
```

You need this calculation to define the SalesAmountModel calculated column, which aggregates the sales of all the products belonging to the same product model:

```
SalesAmountModel = SUMX( FILTER( Product,
                                 Product[Model] = EARLIER( Product[Model] ) ),
                         Product[SalesAmountProduct] )
```

In the SalesAmountModel definition, the EARLIER function gets the model name of the current row (a single product) and the FILTER function returns all the products of the same model. At this point, you can define the CumulatedModel calculated column:

```
CumulatedModel = SUMX( FILTER( Product,
                               Product[SalesAmountModel]
                                    >= EARLIER( Product[SalesAmountModel] ) ),
                       Product[SalesAmountProduct] )
```

That calculation is similar to the CumulatedProduct of the previous example. The only difference is the filter condition because the column to be aggregated is always SalesAmountProduct. (Remember that the FILTER function always operates on the Products table, and for each model there are many products in that table.)

Finally, you can define SortedWeightModel and ABC Class Model calculated columns. These definitions are almost identical to those you saw in the previous example and do not require further comment.

```
SortedWeightModel = Product[CumulatedModel] / SUM( Product[SalesAmountProduct] )

[ABC Class Model] = IF( Product[SortedWeightModel] <= 0.7,
                        "A",
                        IF( Product[SortedWeightModel] <= 0.9,
                            "B",
                            "C" ) )
```

In Figure 9-21, you can see an excerpt of the resulting Product table, which has the new calculated columns required for ABC classification of product models.

| Name | Model | SalesAmountProd... | SalesAmountModel | CumulatedModel | SortedWeigthModel | ABC Class Model |
|---|---|---|---|---|---|---|
| Road-150 Red, 44 | Road-150 | 1,340,419.94 | 7,913,701.93 | 71,772,643.62 | 65.34 % | A |
| Road-150 Red, 62 | Road-150 | 1,769,096.69 | 7,913,701.93 | 71,772,643.62 | 65.34 % | A |
| Road-350-W Yellow, 48 | Road-350-W | 1,774,883.56 | 5,246,152.02 | 77,018,795.64 | 70.12 % | B |
| Road-350-W Yellow, 44 | Road-350-W | 694,003.92 | 5,246,152.02 | 77,018,795.64 | 70.12 % | B |
| Road-350-W Yellow, 42 | Road-350-W | 1,120,066.36 | 5,246,152.02 | 77,018,795.64 | 70.12 % | B |

**FIGURE 9-21** Calculated columns in the Product table for ABC classification of models.

In Figure 9-22, you see a PivotTable that shows the total for each product model crossed with ABC classification of product models. This time, each product model has a value for only one class, which is the one the product model belongs to.

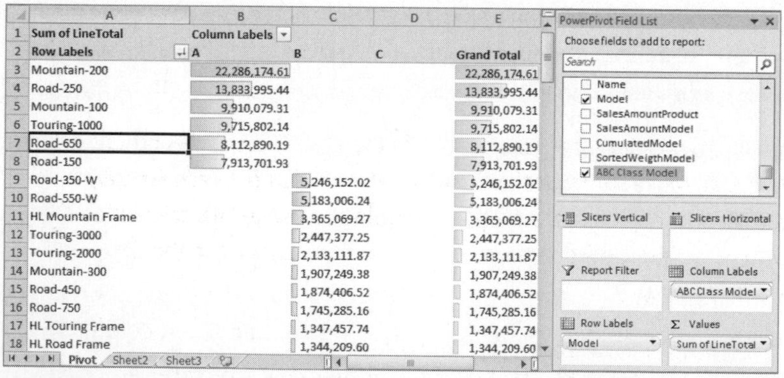

| Sum of LineTotal | Column Labels | | | |
|---|---|---|---|---|
| Row Labels | A | B | C | Grand Total |
| Mountain-200 | 22,286,174.61 | | | 22,286,174.61 |
| Road-250 | 13,833,995.44 | | | 13,833,995.44 |
| Mountain-100 | 9,910,079.31 | | | 9,910,079.31 |
| Touring-1000 | 9,715,802.14 | | | 9,715,802.14 |
| Road-650 | 8,112,890.19 | | | 8,112,890.19 |
| Road-150 | 7,913,701.93 | | | 7,913,701.93 |
| Road-350-W | | 5,246,152.02 | | 5,246,152.02 |
| Road-550-W | | 5,183,006.24 | | 5,183,006.24 |
| HL Mountain Frame | | 3,365,069.27 | | 3,365,069.27 |
| Touring-3000 | | 2,447,377.25 | | 2,447,377.25 |
| Touring-2000 | | 2,133,111.87 | | 2,133,111.87 |
| Mountain-300 | | 1,907,249.38 | | 1,907,249.38 |
| Road-450 | | 1,874,406.52 | | 1,874,406.52 |
| Road-750 | | 1,745,285.16 | | 1,745,285.16 |
| HL Touring Frame | | 1,347,457.74 | | 1,347,457.74 |
| HL Road Frame | | 1,344,209.60 | | 1,344,209.60 |



**FIGURE 9-22** A PivotTable splits product model sales according to ABC classification of models.

### Common Calculations for ABC Analysis

If you consider the three previous examples of ABC classification from a DAX point of view, you can see that they look very similar. However, there are important differences, depending on the data model, and each scenario has some different details in the DAX expressions you use. For this reason, you have to pay attention to the data model first, and then, to retrieve the correct values, you need to use your own tables and columns to replace the correspondent names in the formula we showed you in the previous example.

## Event in Progress

It might be useful to calculate the number of events that are active at a certain date. This value can be used, for example, to plot a chart of the orders in place over time. To make this calculation, you need to import just the SalesOrderHeader table from the AdventureWorks database, and create a Calendar table in Excel as you saw in Chapter 7, "Date Calculations in DAX." That table has to be imported as a linked table in PowerPivot. You can find the complete model for this example in the CH09-09-EventInProgress.xlsx workbook included on the companion DVD.

**Note** The scenario described in this section was originally designed by Chris Webb and described at *http://tinyurl.com/DaxEventInProgress*, which is a post of his blog available at *http://cwebbbi.spaces.live.com/Blog*.

To get the number of orders in place at a certain date, you need to count the number of rows in the SalesOrderHeaders table that have an OrderDate less than or equal to the given date and that have a ShipDate greater than or equal to that same given date. You will see how to make this calculation as both a measure (which is calculated dynamically using active filters in the PivotTable) and a calculated column.

The first calculation is a measure that you can use in the PivotTable browsing Calendar data. Before creating it, *you need to make sure that there are no relationships between SalesOrderHeader and Calendar tables!* This is important because you are going to use a DAX calculation that would not work if a relationship existed between these two tables. You can define the OrdersInPlace measure by using this DAX expression:

```
OrdersInPlace = CALCULATE( COUNTROWS( SalesOrderHeader ),
                           FILTER( VALUES( SalesOrderHeader[OrderDate] ),
                                   MAX( Calendar[Date] ) >= SalesOrderHeader[OrderDate] ),
                           FILTER( VALUES( SalesOrderHeader[ShipDate] ),
                                   MAX( Calendar[Date] ) <= SalesOrderHeader[ShipDate] ) )
```

This formula uses the CALCULATE function by applying a filter context to SalesOrderHeader based on OrderDate and ShipDate so that the rows that are counted by ROWCOUNT are only those that match both filters.

> **Explaining the OrdersInPlace Measure**
>
> We suggest that you use the CALCULATE function in the OrdersInPlace measure for performance reasons. It would be certainly possible to directly use the COUNTROWS function passing a FILTER as a parameter, but this would result in a slower execution.

Using the CALCULATE function, you can modify the filter context on SalesOrderHeader, which is then counted by the COUNTROWS function. Because there are no relationships between the Calendar and SalesOrderHeader tables, without any other filter in the CALCULATE call, the returned value would always be the same, regardless of any Calendar date selected in the PivotTable. The first FILTER returns a set of OrderDate values and the second FILTER returns a set of ShipDate values, using a very similar logic. For each of the OrderDate dates that are available in SalesOrderHeader, which can be filtered by other active filters in the PivotTable, only those that are less than or equal to the selected date are returned. In case of a selection of a single date in Calendar, the MAX( Calendar[Date] ) expression returns just that date. However, in case of a period such as a year or a month, the requirement is to return the same value that would be visible on the last date of that period, which is exactly the date obtained by using the MAX function. The filter for ShipDate works in a similar way, except that only ShipDate dates that are greater than or equal to the selected date are returned.

In Figure 9-23, you can see the resulting PivotTable with a corresponding chart of the OrdersInPlace measure calculated at a day level.

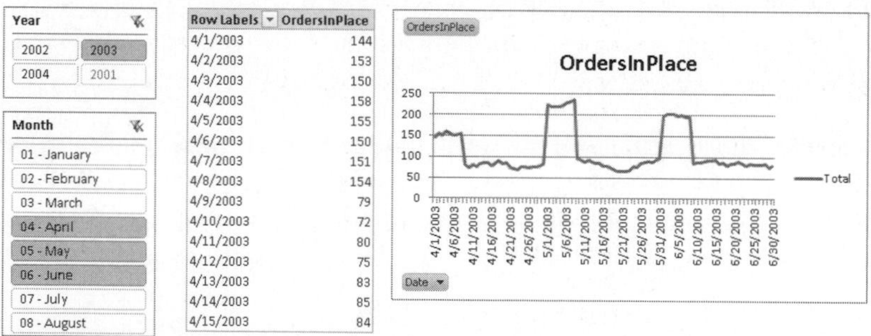


| Row Labels | OrdersInPlace |
|---|---|
| 4/1/2003 | 144 |
| 4/2/2003 | 153 |
| 4/3/2003 | 150 |
| 4/4/2003 | 158 |
| 4/5/2003 | 155 |
| 4/6/2003 | 150 |
| 4/7/2003 | 151 |
| 4/8/2003 | 154 |
| 4/9/2003 | 79 |
| 4/10/2003 | 72 |
| 4/11/2003 | 80 |
| 4/12/2003 | 75 |
| 4/13/2003 | 83 |
| 4/14/2003 | 85 |
| 4/15/2003 | 84 |

**FIGURE 9-23** The OrdersInPlace measure calculated at a day level.

The same calculation can be made at a different granularity, such as the OrdersInPlace measure calculated at a month level in Figure 9-24. Remember that, in this case, you are considering just the last day of each month in this visualization.

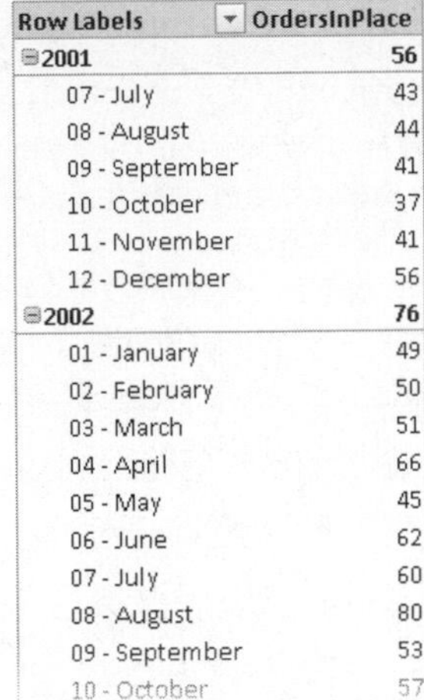

| Row Labels | OrdersInPlace |
|---|---|
| ⊟2001 | 56 |
| 07 - July | 43 |
| 08 - August | 44 |
| 09 - September | 41 |
| 10 - October | 37 |
| 11 - November | 41 |
| 12 - December | 56 |
| ⊟2002 | 76 |
| 01 - January | 49 |
| 02 - February | 50 |
| 03 - March | 51 |
| 04 - April | 66 |
| 05 - May | 45 |
| 06 - June | 62 |
| 07 - July | 60 |
| 08 - August | 80 |
| 09 - September | 53 |
| 10 - October | 57 |

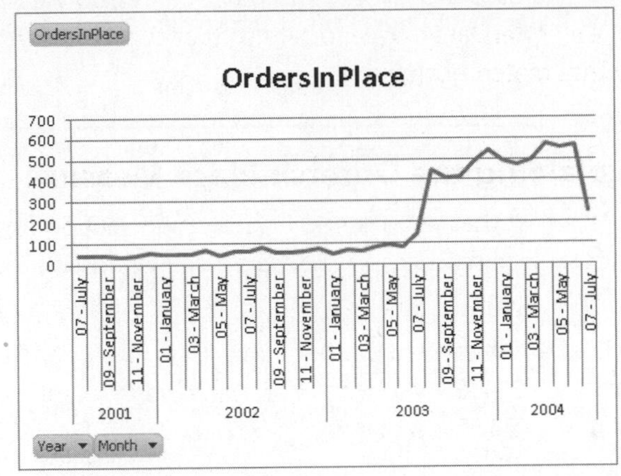


**FIGURE 9-24** The OrdersInPlace measure calculated at a month level.

Sometimes the month calculation you make by using the last day does not satisfy your requirements. For example, you might need a calculation of the monthly average of the OrdersInPlace measure calculated on a daily basis. To do that, you can embed the OrdersInPlace measure in an AVERAGEX call, as in the following definition of OrdersInPlaceDailyAverage:

```
OrdersInPlaceDailyAverage = AVERAGEX( VALUES( Calendar[Date] ),
                                      Calendar[OrdersInPlace] )
```

You can observe the differences between the OrdersInPlaceDailyAverage calculation and the previous one (OrdersInPlace) in Figure 9-25.

Year

2001 | 2002 | 2003 | 2004

| Row Labels | OrdersInPlace | OrdersInPlaceDailyAverage |
|---|---|---|
| 01 - January | 49 | 59.61 |
| 02 - February | 50 | 71.50 |
| 03 - March | 51 | 68.97 |
| 04 - April | 66 | 61.27 |
| 05 - May | 45 | 81.55 |
| 06 - June | 62 | 73.03 |
| 07 - July | 60 | 82.81 |
| 08 - August | 80 | 107.03 |
| 09 - September | 53 | 85.27 |
| 10 - October | 57 | 77.39 |
| 11 - November | 64 | 85.80 |
| 12 - December | 76 | 113.84 |
| **Grand Total** | **76** | **80.79** |

**FIGURE 9-25** OrdersInPlaceDailyAverage compared to OrdersInPlace.

**Note** If you try to replace the OrdersInPlace measure reference with its definition in the OrdersInPlaceDailyAverage expression, you have to remove the MAX calls and obtain the same formula that you use to define the OrdersInPlaceDay calculated column, further along in this section. The reason is that in the AVERAGEX call, there is a row context that makes the MAX call unnecessary and also wrong because it would be resolved outside of the filter context defined by AVERAGEX; that is, it returns the same date instead of using the date iterated by AVERAGEX.

Finally, you can do the same calculation as a calculated column, so that it will not be calculated dynamically; instead, it will be stored as a column in the Calendar table. As a side effect, the average of this measure for a period of dates also will be faster to calculate. However, because performance is usually a minor issue in PowerPivot, it is better to give priority to the requirements of a dynamic calculation, if you need it. You can define the OrdersInPlaceDay calculated column in this way:

```
OrdersInPlaceDay = CALCULATE( COUNTROWS( SalesOrderHeader ),
                              FILTER( VALUES( SalesOrderHeader[OrderDate] ),
                                      Calendar[Date] >= SalesOrderHeader[OrderDate] ),
                              FILTER( VALUES( SalesOrderHeader[ShipDate] ),
                                      Calendar[Date] <= SalesOrderHeader[ShipDate] ) ) )
```

The only difference in the OrdersInPlace measure definition is that there is no MAX aggregation function to get the Calendar[Date] value. In this case, a row context is active (the current row in Calendar table for which the column is calculated) so there is always only one value for that expression. (In the previous definition, if a PivotTable had a selection of a set of dates, you used MAX to get only the last date of that selection.) You can see the OrdersInPlaceDay calculated column in the Calendar table in Figure 9-26.

| Date | Year | MonthNumber | Month | Day | WeekDay | Quarter | FiscalYear | FiscalQuarter | OrdersInPlaceDay |
|---|---|---|---|---|---|---|---|---|---|
| 4/1/2003 | 2003 | 4 | 04 - April | 1 | Tuesday | Q2 | FY-2003 | FQ4 | 144 |
| 4/2/2003 | 2003 | 4 | 04 - April | 2 | Wednesday | Q2 | FY-2003 | FQ4 | 153 |
| 4/3/2003 | 2003 | 4 | 04 - April | 3 | Thursday | Q2 | FY-2003 | FQ4 | 150 |
| 4/4/2003 | 2003 | 4 | 04 - April | 4 | Friday | Q2 | FY-2003 | FQ4 | 158 |
| 4/5/2003 | 2003 | 4 | 04 - April | 5 | Saturday | Q2 | FY-2003 | FQ4 | 155 |
| 4/6/2003 | 2003 | 4 | 04 - April | 6 | Sunday | Q2 | FY-2003 | FQ4 | 150 |
| 4/7/2003 | 2003 | 4 | 04 - April | 7 | Monday | Q2 | FY-2003 | FQ4 | 151 |
| 4/8/2003 | 2003 | 4 | 04 - April | 8 | Tuesday | Q2 | FY-2003 | FQ4 | 154 |
| 4/9/2003 | 2003 | 4 | 04 - April | 9 | Wednesday | Q2 | FY-2003 | FQ4 | 79 |
| 4/10/2003 | 2003 | 4 | 04 - April | 10 | Thursday | Q2 | FY-2003 | FQ4 | 72 |
| 4/11/2003 | 2003 | 4 | 04 - April | 11 | Friday | Q2 | FY-2003 | FQ4 | 80 |
| 4/12/2003 | 2003 | 4 | 04 - April | 12 | Saturday | Q2 | FY-2003 | FQ4 | 75 |

**FIGURE 9-26** The OrdersInPlaceDay calculated column in the Calendar table.

# Summary

In this chapter, you saw how to use DAX in both measures and calculated columns to calculate ratios, percentages, and standard deviation. You also saw how to make ranking and ABC (Pareto) analyses. Finally, you learned a technique for calculating an event in progress over time.

Chapter 10

# PowerPivot Data Model Patterns

Having seen all the features of Microsoft SQL Server PowerPivot for Excel and some advanced models in DAX, we now want to bring all our knowledge to work and analyze ways to use PowerPivot from the data model point of view.

This chapter presents some problematic patterns the PowerPivot user might need to face, and for each pattern, we provide a solution, which makes use of all the techniques we have described to you up to now. Sometimes a problem has more than one solution; when we feel that there are many ways to solve the same problem and all of them are instructive, we present all of them and point out the differences among them.

In Chapter 9, "PowerPivot DAX Patterns," we focused on DAX complex formulas; this chapter deals with different complex data models.

Some patterns might be hard to follow because the data model underlying them is a very complex one. Nevertheless, we suggest that you study all the examples because they serve as a useful toolbox that you can adapt to many different situations. Moreover, as is always the case with examples, it is better to focus on the way a problem is solved than on the problem itself because you are likely to face similar, but not identical, situations.

## Banding

A very common analysis is to convert continuous values into separated bands, to make it easier to perform analysis on them. An example of banding is the analysis of sales divided by price ranges. You might be interested in grouping different prices into categories (for example, high, medium, and low) and analyze sales of products using those categories.

In Figure 10-1, you can see that by using a standard PivotTable, you can put the product price in rows and group sales by product price. Nevertheless, you end up with a lot of rows in which each single price is separated by others. This makes the analysis difficult and the report nearly useless. Moreover, the item price that you use to slice data is the list price, and you cannot use the discounted one, if applicable. You can find this workbook on the companion DVD in the file CH10-01-Banding.xlsm.

| Row Labels | Reseller Order Quantity | Reseller Sales Amount |
|---|---|---|
| 2.29 | 674 | $925.21 |
| 4.99 | 2,571 | $7,476.60 |
| 7.95 | 2,411 | $11,188.37 |
| 8.6442 | 3,289 | $16,779.84 |
| 8.99 | 6,284 | $32,826.92 |
| 9.5 | 1,197 | $6,573.39 |
| 19.99 | 1,130 | $13,514.69 |
| 20.24 | 774 | $9,377.71 |
| 23.5481 | 1,877 | $26,419.61 |
| 24.49 | 3,621 | $52,507.99 |

**FIGURE 10-1** Using the list price, we get a complex PivotTable.

If you use the standard OLAP cube, you cannot slice data using the discounted price. This information is stored as a measure and not as an attribute of a dimension, and the PivotTable would let you slice data based on dimensions only. Nevertheless, using PowerPivot, you are now going to learn how to overcome this limitation.

To get the discounted price for each single sale, you need to load data directly from the database to gather the original reseller sales data so that you have access to each line of the orders with PowerPivot. Moreover, after you load the original data, you need to create a banding table and to define some sort of relationship between the sales and the banding table. As you will see, this relationship cannot use the product code only because the price band for a specific product may vary over time.

Let us show you an example to make the scenario more clear. If you define a price band to range from $20.00 to $30.00 U.S. dollars (USD), you might find that the same product is sometimes sold at $28.00, sometimes at $31.00 because of discounts or price changes over time. So we want to separate these sales into different bands, even if they belong to the very same product.

In Figure 10-2, you can see that after you load the Fact_ResellerSales table into PowerPivot, the discounted prices make the product with code 471 fall inside different price bands as the real price changes over time.

| Product... | OrderDate... | OrderQuantity | UnitPrice | DiscountAmount | SalesAmount | DiscountedPrice |
|---|---|---|---|---|---|---|
| 471 | 793 | 26 | 31.75 | 82.55 | 742.95 | 28.58 |
| 471 | 793 | 25 | 31.75 | 79.375 | 714.38 | 28.58 |
| 471 | 823 | 28 | 31.75 | 88.9 | 800.10 | 28.58 |
| 471 | 884 | 26 | 31.75 | 82.55 | 742.95 | 28.58 |
| 471 | 731 | 29 | 31.75 | 92.075 | 828.68 | 28.58 |
| 471 | 731 | 36 | 31.75 | 114.3 | 1,028.70 | 28.58 |
| 471 | 1036 | 16 | 34.93 | 27.94 | 530.86 | 33.18 |
| 471 | 762 | 15 | 34.93 | 26.1938 | 497.68 | 33.18 |
| 471 | 762 | 15 | 34.93 | 26.1938 | 497.68 | 33.18 |
| 471 | 793 | 15 | 34.93 | 26.1938 | 497.68 | 33.18 |

**FIGURE 10-2** The same product sold under different bands.

Now that the scenario is clear, it is time to search for a data model that makes banding affordable. As we said earlier, to separate prices into bands, you first need a place in which to define the bands. An Excel table is the perfect place to create the price bands, as in Figure 10-3.

| PriceBand | MinPrice | MaxPrice |
|---|---|---|
| VERY LOW | 0 | 5 |
| LOW | 5 | 30 |
| MEDIUM | 30 | 100 |
| HIGH | 100 | 500 |
| VERY HIGH | 500 | 2500 |

**FIGURE 10-3** The Excel table that defines price bands.

It might occur to you to import the price bands table into a PowerPivot linked table, make a relationship between this new table and the sales, and then slice sales by price band. As easy as this solution seems, it cannot work. You need to base the relationship on the price range, not on a single key. In fact, there is no column in the sales table that can act as a key for the price band: the discounted price, $28.50, for example, does not point to any row in the bands table. We definitely need some advanced technique to handle banding because standard PowerPivot relationships are not enough.

## Banding with Band Expansion

A possible solution to the banding problem is to create a new price band table that contains the price band for every single price and then use the DiscountedPrice in the sales table as the key to get into this new table. So if a price band ranges from $1.00 to $10.00 USD, you can create a new table containing 10 rows, one for each price, and each one with the same band description.

Clearly, with ranges varying from $1.00 to $2,500.00 USD, this new table contains 2,500 rows, and we do not even think about filling it by hand; we rely on Excel macros to perform this tedious task.

You can define a new table in the same workbook and name it PriceBandsExpanded, in which the macro loads the rows of the new table. The code of the macro might look like this:

```
Sub Button1_Click()
    Dim PriceBandsExpanded As ListObject
    Set PriceBandsExpanded = ActiveSheet.ListObjects("PriceBandsExpanded")
    Application.ScreenUpdating = False
    If Not (PriceBandsExpanded.DataBodyRange Is Nothing) Then
        PriceBandsExpanded.DataBodyRange.Delete
    End If
    For Each Row In ActiveSheet.ListObjects("PriceBands").ListRows
        Dim MinValue As Integer
        Dim MaxValue As Integer
        Dim Value As Integer
        Dim newRow As ListRow
        MinValue = Row.Range(1, 2).Value
        MaxValue = Row.Range(1, 3).Value - 1
        For Value = MinValue To MaxValue
            Set newRow = PriceBandsExpanded.ListRows.Add
            newRow.Range(1, 1) = Row.Range(1, 1)
            newRow.Range(1, 2) = Value
        Next
    Next
    Application.ScreenUpdating = True
End Sub
```

It is beyond the scope of this book to discuss the details of Microsoft Visual Basic for Applications (VBA) code of the macro, but this simple example iterates over all the rows in the PriceBands original table (the outer loop) and then, for each row, it generates rows in the PriceBandsExpanded table with the values (inner loop).

The two tables are shown side by side in Figure 10-4, where you also can see the Compute button that is linked to the macro shown previously.

| PriceBand | MinPrice | MaxPrice |
|---|---|---|
| VERY LOW | 0 | 5 |
| LOW | 5 | 30 |
| MEDIUM | 30 | 100 |
| HIGH | 100 | 500 |
| VERY HIGH | 500 | 2500 |

| PriceBand | Price |
|---|---|
| VERY LOW | 0 |
| VERY LOW | 1 |
| VERY LOW | 2 |
| VERY LOW | 3 |
| VERY LOW | 4 |
| LOW | 5 |
| LOW | 6 |
| LOW | 7 |
| LOW | 8 |
| LOW | 9 |

Compute

**FIGURE 10-4** The original and expanded price band tables.

Now you can import the new PriceBandsExpanded table as a PowerPivot linked table, and you can use the Price column of the new table as the key and the PriceBand column to slice sales. Because the DiscountedPrice in the Sales table is a floating number, you need to define a calculated column to round it to the nearest integer value, using one of the many rounding functions available in PowerPivot. Last, you can create the relationship, as you can see in Figure 10-5.

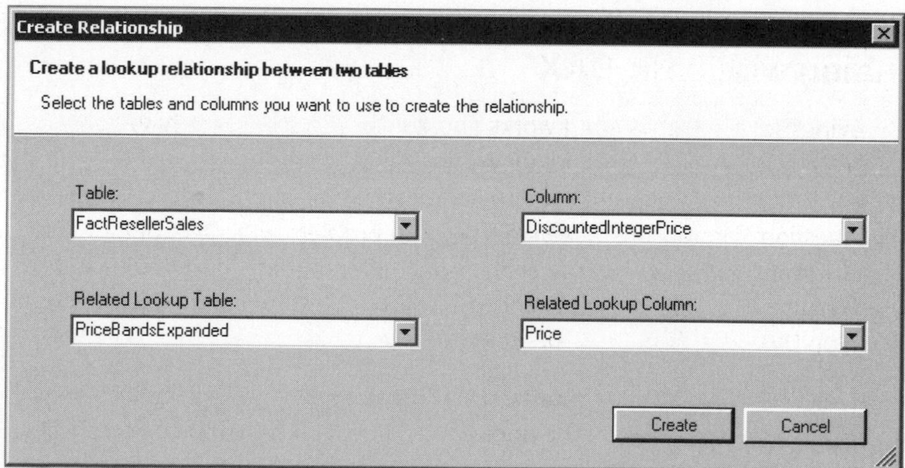


**FIGURE 10-5** The relationship between the sales and price bands expanded table.

Now that you have created the relationship, you can easily analyze sales sliced by price band, like the one shown in Figure 10-6.

| Sum of SalesAmount | Column Labels | | | |
|---|---|---|---|---|
| Row Labels | 2001 | 2002 | 2003 | 2004 |
| HIGH | 1,247,781.88 | 5,738,732.98 | 7,232,714.69 | 2,863,585.30 |
| LOW | 54,500.55 | 315,419.62 | 427,635.21 | 126,761.71 |
| MEDIUM | | 426,967.57 | 1,147,136.25 | 614,501.90 |
| VERY HIGH | 6,763,041.73 | 17,663,075.43 | 23,388,826.86 | 12,429,667.13 |
| VERY LOW | 111.15 | 234.05 | 6,356.43 | 3,546.56 |
| **Grand Total** | **8,065,435.31** | **24,144,429.65** | **32,202,669.43** | **16,038,062.60** |

**FIGURE 10-6** Analysis of sales based on price bands.

If you need to change the price bands, you can easily do it in the original table, recalculate the expanded table, and refresh the PowerPivot data to analyze different banding algorithms.

**Tip** As you might have noticed, bands are sorted alphabetically. To sort them correctly, it might be useful to add a prefix to band names, something like *1-LOW* or *2-MEDIUM* works fine. Another useful option is the one about custom lists discussed in "Custom Sorting in PivotTables" in Chapter 8, "Mastering PivotTables." The choice, obviously, depends entirely on your needs.

Banding is a common problem. We discussed it for prices, but as you might imagine, there are a lot of different situations for which you need to categorize values in different ways, and this technique can be easily adapted to different situations. Nevertheless, before taking banding as a solved problem, let us look at some other techniques that can be used to deal with the same situation.

## Banding with Basic DAX

The previous solution to banding works fine, but it requires you to have some knowledge of Visual Basic for Applications coding. We think that you, as a reader of this book, want to become a DAX expert rather than a Visual Basic for Applications expert. So here is an interesting question: can we solve the same banding problem with DAX only? As you might imagine, the answer is yes, and the analysis of a different data model is indeed very interesting because it involves some advanced DAX coding. You can find this workbook on the companion DVD in the file CH10-02-BandingPricesDAX.xlsm.

In Figure 10-7, you can see the PriceBands table loaded in PowerPivot, where we have already adopted the number in front of the price band name to accomplish correct sorting.

| PriceBand | MinPrice | MaxPrice |
|---|---|---|
| 01 VERY LOW | 0 | 5 |
| 02 LOW | 5 | 30 |
| 03 MEDIUM | 30 | 100 |
| 04 HIGH | 100 | 500 |
| 05 VERY HIGH | 500 | 2500 |

**FIGURE 10-7** The PriceBand table in PowerPivot.

Because you cannot rely on standard relationships, you need to find a different way to relate the Fact_ResellerSales table to the PriceBands table. An interesting solution is to define a calculated column in the Fact_ResellerSales table by using a DAX formula that computes, for each single line of the sales, the band. You might want to write such a DAX formula:

```
= MAXX( FILTER( PriceBands,
                FactResellerSales[DiscountedPrice] >= PriceBands[MinPrice]
                 && FactResellerSales[DiscountedPrice] < PriceBands[MaxPrice] ),
        [PriceBand] )
```

Basically, you filter the PriceBands table searching for the only row that contains the correct band name. FILTER produces a table with only one row, yet it is a table, and because you need to convert the table to a single value, you use the MAXX function to perform this final step.

Unfortunately, this formula does not work because of a limitation of the MAXX function (and the MINX too, in case you are searching for a workaround). Consistent with what happens in Excel, those aggregation functions are designed to work on numbers and dates only, and they raise an error if you try, as in this case, to get the max value of a string column.

Nevertheless, because the idea seems promising, you can adopt a simple trick to make it work anyway. You can add an integer column to the original PriceBands table and name it BandCode. With this small modification, the new PriceBand table looks like Figure 10-8.

| PriceBand | BandCode | MinPrice | MaxPrice |
|---|---|---|---|
| 01 VERY LOW | 1 | 0 | 5 |
| 02 LOW | 2 | 5 | 30 |
| 03 MEDIUM | 3 | 30 | 100 |
| 04 HIGH | 4 | 100 | 500 |
| 05 VERY HIGH | 5 | 500 | 2500 |

**FIGURE 10-8** The PriceBand table with the new BandCode numeric column.

Now that you have a numeric column inside the price band table, you can make the previous formula search for the MAXX of BandCode instead of PriceBand. Because BandCode is numeric, the MAXX function works fine and provides the only code that represents the price band. Clearly, your calculated column now contains a numeric code, not the description of the band, but now you can use the standard relationships of PowerPivot to create a relationship between that code and the price band table, as you can see in Figure 10-9.

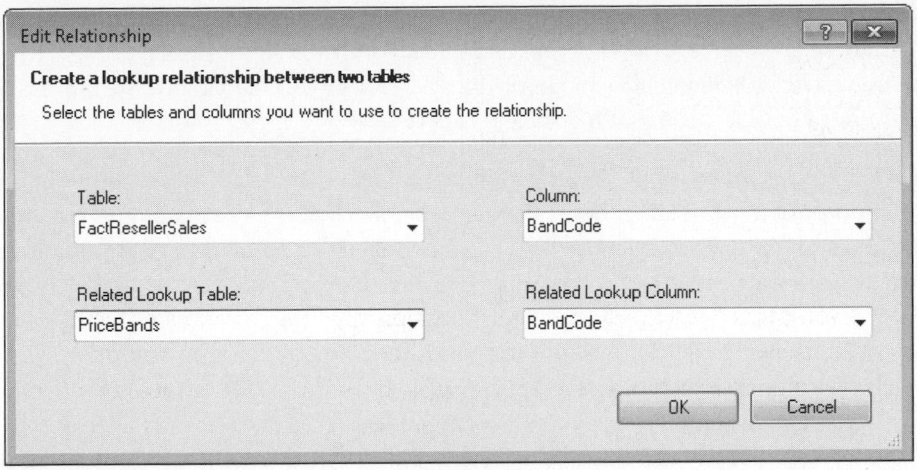

**FIGURE 10-9** The relationship between sales and bands.

This final step makes the full data model work fine.

If you think that you are somehow fooling PowerPivot, well, you are right. Because you cannot make it search for a string by using MAXX, you trick it by asking it to look for a number (which it can do very well) and then use this number to search the string through a relationship. Clearly, this solution works but is far from being either elegant or efficient. So we look for a third solution to the same problem that looks better and works faster too.

## Banding with CALCULATE

The last solution you are going to learn for the banding problem uses the CALCULATE function. We present it as the last solution even if—from the elegance point of view—it is the best.

Using the same data model of the previous example, you can define a new column inside the sales table, whose formula is this:

```
= CALCULATE( VALUES( PriceBands[PriceBand] ),
             FILTER( PriceBands,
                      FactResellerSales[DiscountedPrice] >= PriceBands[MinPrice]
                       && FactResellerSales[DiscountedPrice] < PriceBands[MaxPrice] ) )
```

The logic of computation is the same as above, but this time you use, as we said, the CALCULATE function. You perform a calculation of the values of the PriceBand column (first parameter of CALCULATE) in a filter context specified in the second argument of the CALCULATE function, in which you limit the items visible in the PriceBand table to the only one that satisfies the range condition. The VALUES call is required because CALCULATE needs an aggregation function, even if we know that the FILTER always returns one single row. Because each call to CALCULATE returns just one string, you can safely use this formula in a column definition. The final result is that the calculated column contains the price band of each sale and you can use that column to slice sales.

You might now wonder why we have spent a number of pages explaining different solutions when there is an elegant and compact one that works well. The reason is simply that this last solution is not so evident. It becomes obvious as soon as you read it, but the process of writing this formula does not come at a glance.

As frequently happens with PowerPivot, you can find many solutions to a single problem. We strongly prefer this latter one, but we still believe that the previous ones are interesting to know and understand because they can be applied to several different scenarios, some of which we are going to show in the next section of this chapter.

# Performing Courier Simulation

The previous examples were pretty simple because they concentrated on a single topic. We are now going to present a much more complex situation, in which you adapt the data model to your needs and learn some complicated DAX formulas to get a working report. Let us suppose that, for the next fiscal year, you would like to evaluate a new courier for the shipping of orders your business sells through the Internet. You have two proposals from different couriers (named BlueYonder and WorldWide), and you want to evaluate which one is the best.

Each courier has different shipping charges, all of which are based on both the total weight of the shipment and its destination. Because you do not have provisional information about sales in the next year, you want to perform the analysis based on the past. You would like to carry out a simulation on all the past shipments, applying the different charges of the couriers to each shipment, and you want to obtain a report that shows the freight charge of both couriers. The courier with the lower cost in the simulation of the past is your future courier.

We rely on the AdventureWorks data warehouse to perform such simulation, which you can find on the companion workbook CH10-03-CourierSimulation.xlsm. Unfortunately, the data warehouse does not contain all the information you need to perform the analysis. So you are forced to perform some adjustments to the data.

**Warning** Beware that several of the reports we are going to show are very slow to produce on a standard computer. We suggest that you follow the reports in the book instead of trying to reproduce them. If you want to try them, please be patient and let the computer run for some minutes before the queries are completed. Moreover, if you want to refresh data coming from AdventureWorks, you need to install the AdventureWorks OLAP database on an instance of Analysis Services; otherwise, you get an error every time you try to interact with PivotTables connected to Analysis Services. Ask your IT department whether they can provide such a service.

## Loading the Main Table

To complete your analysis, you need to produce a table that contains all the Internet orders and, for each one, this information:

- Location of shipment
- Total weight of the shipment
- Freight cost

Your final result should look like Figure 10-10.

| OrderNumber | Year | Month | Country | Weight |
|---|---|---|---|---|
| SO43697 | CY 2001 | July | Canada | 15 |
| SO43698 | CY 2001 | July | France | 21.13 |
| SO43699 | CY 2001 | July | United States | 21.13 |
| SO43700 | CY 2001 | July | United States | 20 |
| SO43701 | CY 2001 | July | Australia | 21.13 |
| SO43702 | CY 2001 | July | United States | 13.77 |
| SO43703 | CY 2001 | July | Australia | 15 |
| SO43704 | CY 2001 | July | Australia | 21.42 |
| SO43705 | CY 2001 | July | Australia | 20.35 |

**FIGURE 10-10** The main table needed to perform courier simulation.

As always, you can start with a PivotTable connected to the AdventureWorks OLAP database to build a report that shows all the lines of each order and, for each line, the product sold, the freight cost, and the quantity of products. You can accomplish this easily by using a standard PivotTable connected to the Analysis Services OLAP cube.

Freight cost and location of shipment are pretty easy to get because the OLAP cube lets you slice by geography and summarize the freight cost. The Internet Order Details dimension lets you get the information you need at the order level through the Sales Order Number attribute, as it can be seen in Figure 10-11, where we created a tabular report, ready to be imported to PowerPivot.

Unfortunately, in the Internet Sales measure group, you do not have the weight available as a measure. Weight is instead an attribute of the product dimension, and because it belongs to a dimension, you cannot summarize it by order number to gather the total weight of an order, which is your primary parameter of analysis.

Nevertheless, because weight is an attribute of the product dimension, you can rely on the Show Properties feature of Excel 2010 and make the PivotTable show the freight in the report. By right-clicking in the PivotTable, in a cell that contains a product description, you can select the Show Properties In Report menu and then select the check box beside the weight, as you can see in Figure 10-12.

| Sales Order Number | Product | Internet Freight Cost | Internet Order Quantity |
|---|---|---|---|
| SO51178 | Mountain Bottle Cage | $0.25 | 1 |
| **SO51178 Total** | | **$58.37** | **3** |
| SO51180 | Road-250 Black, 44 | $61.08 | 1 |
| SO51180 | Long-Sleeve Logo Jersey, M | $1.25 | 1 |
| SO51180 | Water Bottle - 30 oz. | $0.12 | 1 |
| SO51180 | Road Bottle Cage | $0.22 | 1 |
| SO51180 | Sport-100 Helmet, Red | $0.87 | 1 |
| **SO51180 Total** | | **$63.56** | **5** |
| SO51185 | Touring-3000 Yellow, 58 | $18.56 | 1 |
| SO51185 | Touring Tire Tube | $0.12 | 1 |
| SO51185 | Touring Tire | $0.72 | 1 |
| **SO51185 Total** | | **$19.41** | **3** |
| SO51188 | Road-750 Black, 52 | $13.50 | 1 |
| **SO51188 Total** | | **$13.50** | **1** |
| SO51191 | Mountain-200 Black, 46 | $57.37 | 1 |
| SO51191 | Water Bottle - 30 oz. | $0.12 | 1 |
| SO51191 | Mountain Bottle Cage | $0.25 | 1 |
| SO51191 | Sport-100 Helmet, Red | $0.87 | 1 |

**FIGURE 10-11** Complete report at the order line level, to perform freight analysis.

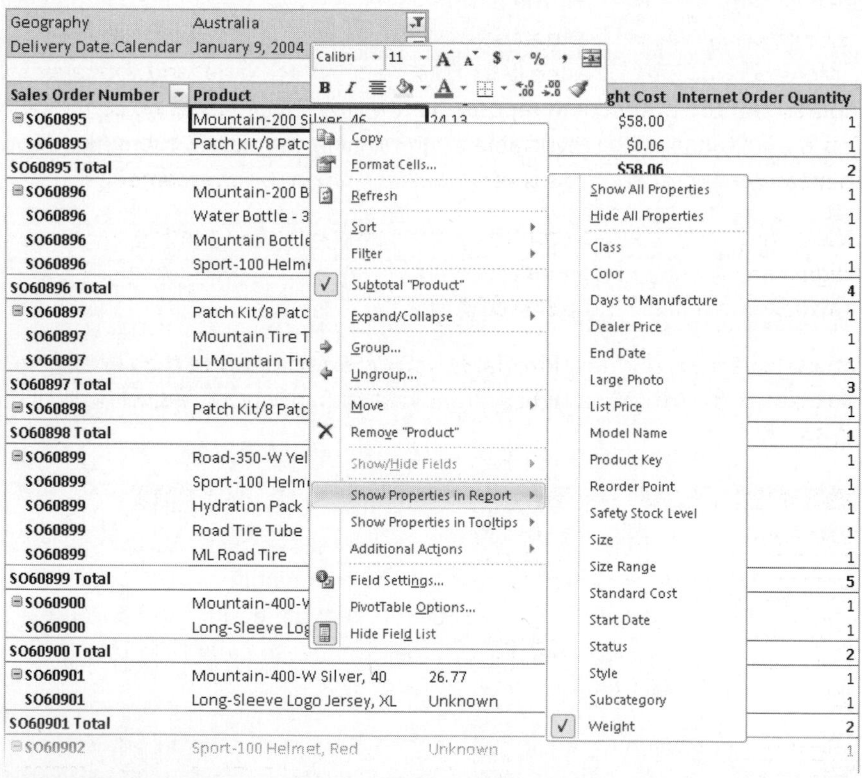


**FIGURE 10-12** The Show Properties In Report menu.

The report now contains the weight of the product, as you can see in Figure 10-13.

| Sales Order Number | Product | Weight | Internet Freight Cost | Internet Order Quantity |
|---|---|---|---|---|
| SO51178 | Mountain Bottle Cage | Unknown | $0.25 | 1 |
| **SO51178 Total** | | | **$58.37** | **3** |
| ⊟SO51180 | Road-250 Black, 44 | 14.77 | $61.08 | 1 |
| SO51180 | Long-Sleeve Logo Jersey, M | Unknown | $1.25 | 1 |
| SO51180 | Water Bottle - 30 oz. | Unknown | $0.12 | 1 |
| SO51180 | Road Bottle Cage | Unknown | $0.22 | 1 |
| SO51180 | Sport-100 Helmet, Red | Unknown | $0.87 | 1 |
| **SO51180 Total** | | | **$63.56** | **5** |
| ⊟SO51185 | Touring-3000 Yellow, 58 | 29.79 | $18.56 | 1 |
| SO51185 | Touring Tire Tube | Unknown | $0.12 | 1 |
| SO51185 | Touring Tire | Unknown | $0.72 | 1 |
| **SO51185 Total** | | | **$19.41** | **3** |
| ⊟SO51188 | Road-750 Black, 52 | 20.42 | $13.50 | 1 |
| **SO51188 Total** | | | **$13.50** | **1** |
| ⊟SO51191 | Mountain-200 Black, 46 | 24.13 | $57.37 | 1 |
| SO51191 | Water Bottle - 30 oz. | Unknown | $0.12 | 1 |
| SO51191 | Mountain Bottle Cage | Unknown | $0.25 | 1 |
| SO51191 | Sport-100 Helmet, Red | Unknown | $0.87 | 1 |

**FIGURE 10-13** You can add the weight as an additional property in the report.

Yet, there are still some problems. The product weight, when you do not have a value for it, is shown as Unknown, which makes aggregations pretty difficult because this description is not a number. Moreover, you are interested in the total weight of the order and you cannot summarize attributes; you can put them in reports, but the PivotTable makes no computations over them. This is a limitation of the PivotTable when working with OLAP cubes: the distinction between measures and dimensions is very rigid and cannot be overcome.

Nevertheless, this report seems to contain all the information you need to perform the analysis, so you might naturally hope that when you import all the data into PowerPivot, you can handle the information with a much more powerful tool.

Now that you have the report in a PivotTable, you need to reproduce the same query with the MDX query editor to import data directly from Analysis Services into PowerPivot, as shown in Figure 10-14.

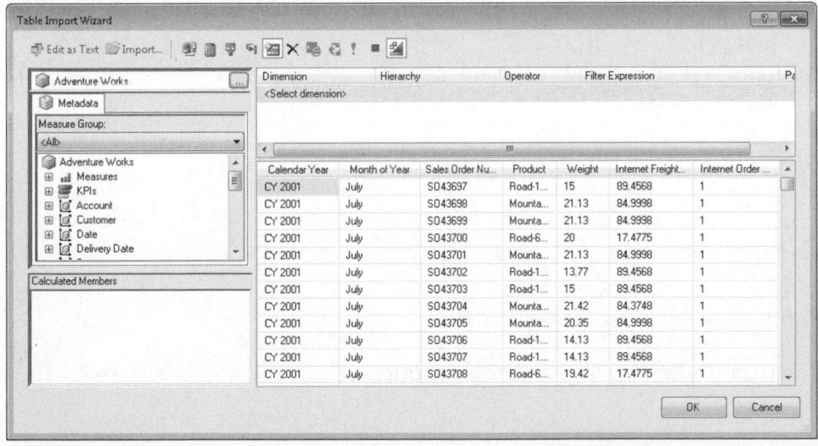


**FIGURE 10-14** The query in the MDX editor to import data in PowerPivot.

After you import the table into PowerPivot, you can now appreciate one big difference between the PivotTable report shown in Figure 10-13 and the PowerPivot table shown in Figure 10-15: the freight, which was an attribute of the product dimension in the PivotTable, is now a column like the others in the table and can be used to slice data. PowerPivot does not make any distinction between measures and attributes; it works on any column.

| Year | Month | OrderNumber | Product | Weight | Freight | OrderQuantity |
|---|---|---|---|---|---|---|
| CY 2004 | June | SO71956 | Water Bottle - 30 oz. | Unknown | 0.1248 | 1 |
| CY 2004 | June | SO71959 | Water Bottle - 30 oz. | Unknown | 0.1248 | 1 |
| CY 2004 | June | SO71960 | Water Bottle - 30 oz. | Unknown | 0.1248 | 1 |
| CY 2004 | June | SO71961 | Water Bottle - 30 oz. | Unknown | 0.1248 | 1 |
| CY 2004 | June | SO71968 | Water Bottle - 30 oz. | Unknown | 0.1248 | 1 |
| CY 2004 | June | SO71971 | Water Bottle - 30 oz. | Unknown | 0.1248 | 1 |
| CY 2004 | June | SO71973 | Water Bottle - 30 oz. | Unknown | 0.1248 | 1 |
| CY 2004 | June | SO71994 | Water Bottle - 30 oz. | Unknown | 0.1248 | 1 |
| CY 2004 | June | SO71995 | Water Bottle - 30 oz. | Unknown | 0.1248 | 1 |
| CY 2004 | June | SO71997 | Water Bottle - 30 oz. | Unknown | 0.1248 | 1 |
| CY 2004 | June | SO72011 | Water Bottle - 30 oz. | Unknown | 0.1248 | 1 |
| CY 2004 | June | SO72018 | Water Bottle - 30 oz. | Unknown | 0.1248 | 1 |
| CY 2004 | June | SO72021 | Water Bottle - 30 oz. | Unknown | 0.1248 | 1 |
| CY 2004 | June | SO72022 | Water Bottle - 30 oz. | Unknown | 0.1248 | 1 |

**FIGURE 10-15** The result of the query in Figure 10-14 imported to PowerPivot.

You are moving towards a solution, but you still have problems to solve. The first issue you need to face is that the weight, as it has been imported, is a string value and not a number. To summarize it, you definitely need to transform it into a number. Because you cannot change the data type of the column (trying to do that would raise an error because the column contains the unknown value), you can add a new column that contains the conversion of the Weight column into a number. When the value is unknown, you assume a 0.75 value as a default. Please note that this assumption might well be wrong. Nevertheless, for what concerns us in this example, you can safely do it.

You can now rename the Weight column OriginalWeight and add a new column, named Weight, which is computed by this formula:

```
Weight = IF( NOT( ISERROR( VALUE( Orders[OriginalWeight] ) ) ),
             VALUE( Orders[OriginalWeight] ),
             0.75 )
```

With this new column in the table, it is now very easy to produce a report such as the one shown in Figure 10-16, where you are able to aggregate the weight per order. (In the report, we show the details of products even if, for the purpose of our analysis, it is useless to go into the details.)

| Row Labels | Sum of Weight | Sum of Freight |
|---|---|---|
| **⊟SO51877** | **26.38** | **59.8744** |
| HL Mountain Tire | 0.75 | 0.875 |
| Mountain Tire Tube | 0.75 | 0.1248 |
| Mountain-200 Silver, 46 | 24.13 | 57.9998 |
| Sport-100 Helmet, Red | 0.75 | 0.8748 |
| **⊟SO51878** | **23.35** | **57.9998** |
| Mountain-200 Silver, 38 | 23.35 | 57.9998 |
| **⊟SO51879** | **0.75** | **0.2248** |
| AWC Logo Cap | 0.75 | 0.2248 |
| **⊟SO51880** | **2.25** | **0.5744** |
| Racing Socks, M | 0.75 | 0.2248 |
| Road Bottle Cage | 0.75 | 0.2248 |
| Water Bottle - 30 oz. | 0.75 | 0.1248 |

**FIGURE 10-16** Using PowerPivot, you are now able to aggregate the weight per order.

It might seem that you have solved the problem, but you are not at the end of the trip. Even if you can easily produce this report, aggregating data by order number, this is not what you really want to do. You want to add the total weight of an order as a new calculated column in the PowerPivot table so that you can compute the freight cost for different couriers. Up to now, you succeeded only in computing the value in a PivotTable, but your needs are quite different.

To compute the total weight, you should compute, for each order, the sum of all the weights of the rows that have the same order number. Nevertheless, it is not easy to perform such a computation over a single table because you need a table that is related to itself, which is not handled by PowerPivot.

The quick-and-dirty solution is straightforward, even if it is not very elegant. You can create a PivotTable that contains the order number and the sum of weight, as shown in Figure 10-17.

| OrderNumber | Sum of Weight |
|---|---|
| SO43697 | 15 |
| SO43698 | 21.13 |
| SO43699 | 21.13 |
| SO43700 | 20 |
| SO43701 | 21.13 |
| SO43702 | 13.77 |
| SO43703 | 15 |

**FIGURE 10-17** Orders and total weight, in a PivotTable.

Then you can select the whole PivotTable, copy it to the Clipboard, and use the Paste button in PowerPivot to have a new table filled with the data. This solution is very simple for small tables (in our example we have 27,662 rows to select), but it might be a problem for medium-size tables, in which you could face millions of rows and selecting them also might be not feasible because of memory constraints. Moreover, the biggest issue with this approach is that, if the source data is updated, you need to repeat the copy and paste operation to refresh data. In the end, this solution works fine for a simple data set, but probably you want a better one.

There are two solutions to this problem, one involving DAX and the other one involving a small change in the data model. As usual, we are going to present both. The data model solution is easy but not very intuitive. Even if you cannot create a relationship in a table with itself, you can still load the same table twice and set up a relationship between the two instances of the same table. You need to load two different tables into PowerPivot, one that has the granularity of the order number and one that has the granularity of the order line. Let us call them Orders and OrderDetails. You compute the weight of a single line at the detail level and then, through a relationship between orders and details, you can summarize the weight in the orders table, which has the correct granularity.

You can load the Orders table with the basic information needed for our analysis, as you see in Figure 10-18.

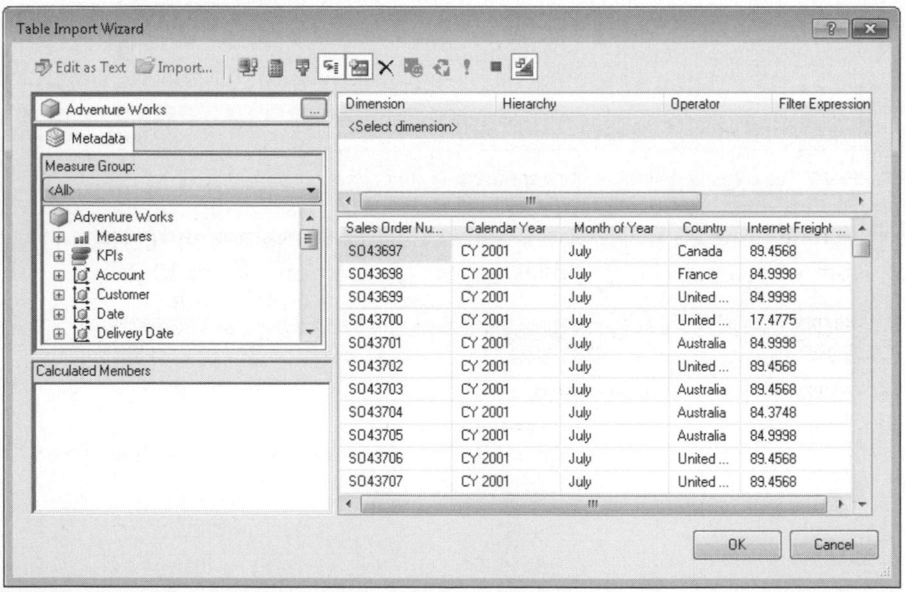


**FIGURE 10-18** The Orders query, with basic information.

Loading this data results in a summarized table, shown in Figure 10-19, which contains information at the order level, with no details about single products. So in this table, you are missing the weight of the order.

| OrderNu... | Year | Month | Country | Freight |
|---|---|---|---|---|
| SO43697 | CY 2001 | July | Canada | 89.46 |
| SO43698 | CY 2001 | July | France | 85.00 |
| SO43699 | CY 2001 | July | United States | 85.00 |
| SO43700 | CY 2001 | July | United States | 17.48 |
| SO43701 | CY 2001 | July | Australia | 85.00 |
| SO43702 | CY 2001 | July | United States | 89.46 |
| SO43703 | CY 2001 | July | Australia | 89.46 |
| SO43704 | CY 2001 | July | Australia | 84.37 |
| SO43705 | CY 2001 | July | Australia | 85.00 |

**FIGURE 10-19** The Orders table, with basic information for analysis.

Now you need to load the order details. You need to add, after the OrderNumber, the OrderLine number, which makes the query work at the granularity of the single line of the order. Moreover, because you are going to use only the weight, you can load only the sales order number, the line number, the weight, and the quantity. Figure 10-20 shows the detail table, with the weight computed using the 0.75 default, as we showed you, and the TotalWeight computed by a simple multiplication of the weight by the quantity.

| OrderNumber | OrderLine | OriginalWeight | OrderQuantity | Weight | TotalWeight |
|---|---|---|---|---|---|
| SO72656 | 8 | Unknown | 1 | 0.75 | 0.75 |
| SO72927 | 7 | Unknown | 1 | 0.75 | 0.75 |
| SO74869 | 7 | Unknown | 1 | 0.75 | 0.75 |
| SO51331 | 2 | 25.9 | 1 | 25.9 | 25.9 |
| SO51669 | 2 | 30 | 1 | 30 | 30 |
| SO51960 | 2 | 27.13 | 1 | 27.13 | 27.13 |
| SO52062 | 2 | 27.68 | 1 | 27.68 | 27.68 |

**FIGURE 10-20** The order detail table, with some computed columns.

Now it is time to set up the relationship between these two tables by linking the OrderNumber column of both tables, as you can see from Figure 10-21.

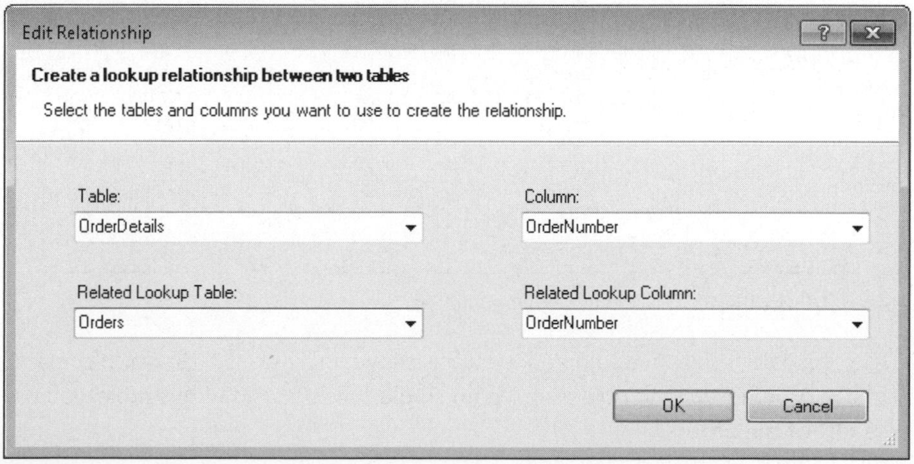

Edit Relationship

**Create a lookup relationship between two tables**

Select the tables and columns you want to use to create the relationship.

Table: OrderDetails

Column: OrderNumber

Related Lookup Table: Orders

Related Lookup Column: OrderNumber

OK Cancel

**FIGURE 10-21** The relationship between the two tables in the OrderNumber column.

With the relationship active, you can now easily build a PivotTable that computes the total weight of an order, as you can see in Figure 10-22.

| Row Labels | Sum of TotalWeight | Sum of Freight |
|---|---|---|
| SO51877 | 26.38 | 59.8744 |
| SO51878 | 23.35 | 57.9998 |
| SO51879 | 0.75 | 0.2248 |
| SO51880 | 2.25 | 0.5744 |
| **Grand Total** | **52.73** | **118.6734** |

**FIGURE 10-22** The total weight in a PivotTable.

The table looks very similar to the one computed before (see Figure 10-17); the big difference is that now the total weight is stored in a separate table (the data model is changed) and you can use simple DAX calculations to bring it into the Orders table as a computed column.

Using the existing relationship, you can take, for each row of the Orders table, all the rows of the OrderDetails table that are in relationship with an order row. If you sum up the TotalWeight column for all of the related rows, you can compute the total weight at the order level. The DAX formula for the Weight column shown in Figure 10-24 is the following:

```
Weight = CALCULATE( SUM( OrderDetails[TotalWeight] ) )
```

**Note** As you have seen previously in the book, the CALCULATE formula uses the existing relationship between Orders and OrderDetails table to transform the row context of the Orders row for which Weight is calculated into a filter context for the OrderDetails table. In this way, the SUM function operates only on related tables. An equivalent way to write the same DAX operation is the following formula that uses SUMX and RELATEDTABLE functions. That pattern is also important to know because it is the only one that can be used whenever you have a more complex expression to calculate for each line of the order:

```
Weight = SUMX( RELATEDTABLE( OrderDetails ),
               OrderDetails[TotalWeight] )
```

The final form of the Order table looks like Figure 10-23.

| OrderNu... | Year | Month | Country | Freight | Weight |
|---|---|---|---|---|---|
| SO43697 | CY 2001 | July | Canada | 89.46 | 15.00 |
| SO43698 | CY 2001 | July | France | 85.00 | 21.13 |
| SO43699 | CY 2001 | July | United States | 85.00 | 21.13 |
| SO43700 | CY 2001 | July | United States | 17.48 | 20.00 |
| SO43701 | CY 2001 | July | Australia | 85.00 | 21.13 |
| SO43702 | CY 2001 | July | United States | 89.46 | 13.77 |

**FIGURE 10-23** The Order weight computed at the OrderNumber level.

The first step in your analysis is solved—you now have a table that contains the basic information you need to perform the simulation, and that data will be refreshed correctly whenever the source data changes. It is now time to perform the courier simulation over this table, something that is harder than expected.

### A More Elegant Solution with CALCULATE and EARLIER

For the brave reader, we have another solution to the same problem, which involves your using the CALCULATE function with only one table (the OrderDetails table) to perform the total weight per order computation. Using CALCULATE and the EARLIER functions, you can summarize the total order weight with this formula:

```
= CALCULATE( SUM( OrderDetails[Weight] ),
             ALL( OrderDetails ),
             OrderDetails[OrderNumber] = EARLIER( OrderDetails[OrderNumber] ) )
```

This solution is easier to implement but requires of you a better understanding of the DAX language. Because we believe that the solution presented before is easier to understand, we provided that one first. Using CALCULATE and EARLIER is much harder to understand, but it gives you a very elegant and neat solution like the one we just showed you. More information about how this technique works can be found in Chapter 6, "Evaluation Context and CALCULATE."

## Adding Courier Information

The next step in the simulation example is to add the information about the courier proposals. To be able to compute, for each order, the freight cost charged by each different courier, you should prepare an Excel workbook that contains the proposal details. Because the variables are the geographical location and the weight of the order, you can end up with a worksheet like the one shown in Figure 10-24.

| Courier | Country | MinWeight | MaxWeight | Freight |
|---|---|---|---|---|
| WorldWide | United States | 5 | 10 | 4 |
| WorldWide | United States | 10 | 20 | 8 |
| WorldWide | United States | 20 | 99 | 18 |
| BlueYonder | Australia | 0 | 2 | 4 |
| BlueYonder | Australia | 2 | 3 | 8 |
| BlueYonder | Australia | 3 | 5 | 12 |
| BlueYonder | Australia | 5 | 15 | 35 |
| BlueYonder | Australia | 15 | 99 | 60 |

**FIGURE 10-24** The configuration worksheet for the couriers.

Please note that the minimum and maximum weight ranges are different for the two couriers shown. This makes the analysis pretty complex because you need to determine, for every single order, which range of weight it belongs to and this will be a different computation for each courier.

This situation is technically known as a *range lookup* and is in some ways similar to the banding process. You need to create a relationship between two tables and the key is not a single column that should match by exact value; instead the match occurs when the key falls within a defined range of values. Moreover, to make the situation slightly more complex, you now need to have both a range lookup for the weight and a standard lookup for the courier name and the country. As we did with the banding, we are going to show more than one solution to the same problem, for educational purposes.

## Using DAX to Resolve Complex Relationships

Because you cannot resolve the relationship between the couriers and the orders tables using the standard PowerPivot relationship model, you need to leverage your DAX knowledge to build an expression that performs the computation.

Let us start with a simple algorithm, which you would use if you needed to perform the computation by hand. Given a specific order, you can compute the freight for the BlueYonder courier searching through the couriers table for a row for which these conditions are true:

- The country is the same as the order.
- The courier name is BlueYonder.
- The order weight falls within the range specified by MinWeight and MaxWeight.

You are confident that, if such a row exists, it will be unique because of how you built the couriers table. When you find that row, its Freight value is the freight cost you were looking for.

To express this in DAX, you use the FILTER function that, as its name suggests, performs a filter on a table returning another table, which is the result of filtering the original table under the condition specified. We refer to this table as the *filtered table*. The expression to obtain the filtered table is the following one:

```
FILTER( Couriers,
        Couriers[Country] = Orders[Country]
         && Couriers[MinWeight] <= Orders[Weight]
         && Orders[Weight] < Couriers[MaxWeight]
         && Couriers[Courier] = "BlueYonder" )
```

The result of this function is still a table, which we already know contains exactly one row. Nevertheless, it is a table and you cannot define a column to contain a table. Because you want to get the Freight value from the filtered table, you can use an aggregation function, such as the SUMX function, to compute the sum of all the rows in the filtered table. Because the filtered table contains only one row, the result is exactly the freight value for the only row in the filtered table.

The complete formula is the following:

```
BlueYonderFreight = SUMX( FILTER( Couriers,
                                  Couriers[Country] = Orders[Country]
                                   && Couriers[MinWeight] <= Orders[Weight]
                                   && Orders[Weight] < Couriers[MaxWeight]
                                   && Couriers[Courier] = "BlueYonder" ),
                          Couriers[Freight] )
```

You can define a new calculated column in the orders table with this formula and another one replacing BlueYonder with WorldWide to get the freight cost of both couriers in two distinct columns.

The resulting table is shown in Figure 10-25.

| OrderNu... | Year | Month | Country | Freight | Weight | WorldWideFreight | BlueYonderFreight |
|---|---|---|---|---|---|---|---|
| SO43697 | CY 2001 | July | Canada | 89.46 | 15.00 | 12.00 | 35.00 |
| SO43698 | CY 2001 | July | France | 85.00 | 21.13 | 64.00 | 36.00 |
| SO43699 | CY 2001 | July | United States | 85.00 | 21.13 | 18.00 | 15.00 |
| SO43700 | CY 2001 | July | United States | 17.48 | 20.00 | 18.00 | 15.00 |
| SO43701 | CY 2001 | July | Australia | 85.00 | 21.13 | 35.00 | 60.00 |
| SO43702 | CY 2001 | July | United States | 89.46 | 13.77 | 8.00 | 0.00 |
| SO43703 | CY 2001 | July | Australia | 89.46 | 15.00 | 18.00 | 60.00 |
| SO43704 | CY 2001 | July | Australia | 84.37 | 21.42 | 35.00 | 60.00 |
| SO43705 | CY 2001 | July | Australia | 85.00 | 20.35 | 35.00 | 60.00 |

**FIGURE 10-25** The complete Orders table, with computed columns for the freights.

With these two columns, now the task of comparing the different freights is very easy. You can check it on single orders, as in Figure 10-26.

| Row Labels | Sum of WorldWideFreight | Sum of BlueYonderFreight |
|---|---|---|
| SO43700 | 18 | 15 |
| SO43701 | 35 | 60 |
| SO43702 | 8 | 8 |
| SO43703 | 18 | 60 |
| SO43704 | 35 | 60 |
| SO43705 | 35 | 60 |
| **Grand Total** | **149** | **263** |

**FIGURE 10-26** Comparison of freights from different couriers.

Moreover, you can easily perform more complex computations—for example, at the country level for some years, as in Figure 10-27.

| Row Labels | Sum of Freight | Sum of WorldWideFreight | Sum of BlueYonderFreight |
|---|---|---|---|
| **CY 2003** | **244,777.58** | **169,158.00** | **220,054.00** |
| Australia | 75,844.84 | 49,546.00 | 104,931.00 |
| Canada | 13,394.74 | 9,576.00 | 12,583.00 |
| France | 25,658.23 | 29,854.00 | 22,208.00 |
| Germany | 26,460.24 | 31,293.00 | 22,988.00 |
| United Kingdom | 32,456.35 | 20,570.00 | 28,734.00 |
| United States | 70,963.17 | 28,319.00 | 28,610.00 |
| **CY 2004** | **244,273.95** | **187,005.00** | **223,660.00** |
| Australia | 64,097.42 | 48,728.00 | 99,216.00 |
| Canada | 16,840.89 | 12,120.00 | 15,116.00 |
| France | 23,054.62 | 31,706.00 | 22,113.00 |
| Germany | 26,922.41 | 39,275.00 | 25,782.00 |
| United Kingdom | 30,257.33 | 21,082.00 | 28,261.00 |
| United States | 83,101.29 | 34,094.00 | 33,172.00 |
| **Grand Total** | **489,051.52** | **356,163.00** | **443,714.00** |

**FIGURE 10-27** Comparison of freights from different couriers.

This solution is very simple to implement, and if you need to analyze further, you can add all the columns that interest you in the Orders table to get more complex and interesting analyses.

## Same Solution with CALCULATE

Before we end this section, it is worth noting that the previous formula to compute the freight for a single courier, might be expressed with CALCULATE, as was the case in the banding example.

```
BlueYonderFreight = CALCULATE( VALUES( Couriers[Freight] ),
                       FILTER( Couriers,
                               Couriers[Country] = Orders[Country]
                                && Couriers[MinWeight] <= Orders[Weight]
                                && Orders[Weight] < Couriers[MaxWeight]
                                && Couriers[Courier] = "BlueYonder" ) )
```

This formula is slightly harder to understand because it makes use of the CALCULATE function. It basically retrieves the values of the Freight column from the Couriers table after having applied a filter context that filters only the relevant rows. Because you use it to define a column, this formula raises an error if the number of values returned is more than one, providing a safer environment whenever errors are detected. The use of CALCULATE might be slightly better also from a performance point of view. Nevertheless, the formula is less intuitive than the previous one. It is up to you to choose the best for your environment.

A big issue with this solution is that you need to define a column for each courier. This works fine when you need to analyze a small number of couriers, but if you need to perform analysis with a variable number of couriers or a very high number of them, you might encounter some usability problems. So because we are striving for perfection, we can study a different data model that solves this problem, too.

## Using Many-to-Many Relationships

A very interesting solution to the same scenario, which solves the problem of hardcoding the courier name in the formula, is to use many-to-many relationships, which we introduced in Chapter 4, "Data Models." This last solution, although very elegant and powerful, is complex.

Before we describe the solution, let us briefly review the problem from the data model point of view. In Figure 10-28, you can see a simplified version of the tables we have been using up to now so that you can better understand the data model. Please note that, for the price list, we are using an expanded version of the price list, wherein we removed the min and max weights and expanded them to the granularity level, as we previously did with the banding example.

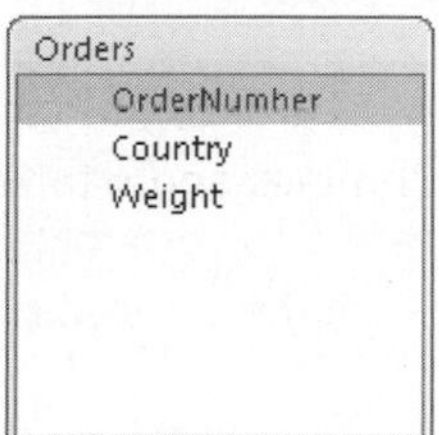

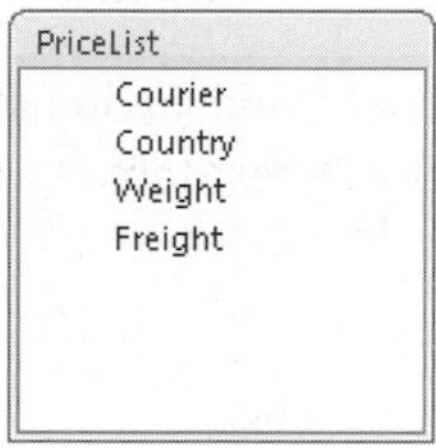

**FIGURE 10-28** The first data model for the courier simulation.

You have only two tables:

- **Orders** Contains the order with all its relevant information. In the diagram, we show only country and weight, which are the useful information for freight computation.
- **PriceList** Contains the price that each courier applies for a specific weight shipped to a specific country. This table is slightly different from the one we used before (in which we had a range of weights), but the information content is basically the same.

From the data model point of view, you would like to create a relationship between the two tables using the columns country and weight. Unfortunately, this cannot be done because country and weight are not unique keys for the tables: they are repeated both in Orders and PriceList, so you cannot create a standard relationship between them. The reason country and weight are repeated is that they appear once for each courier. In other words, a single order refers to many price list rows and the contrary happens also: a single price list applies to many orders.

To use the PowerPivot relationship model, you need an intermediate table that can be used to relate both tables. We call this new table CountryWeight because it can contain all the different combinations of countries and weight. If you introduce such a table, country and weight are keys in that table and you can then set up relationships for both Orders and PriceList to the new CountryWeight table. You can see the new data model in Figure 10-29.

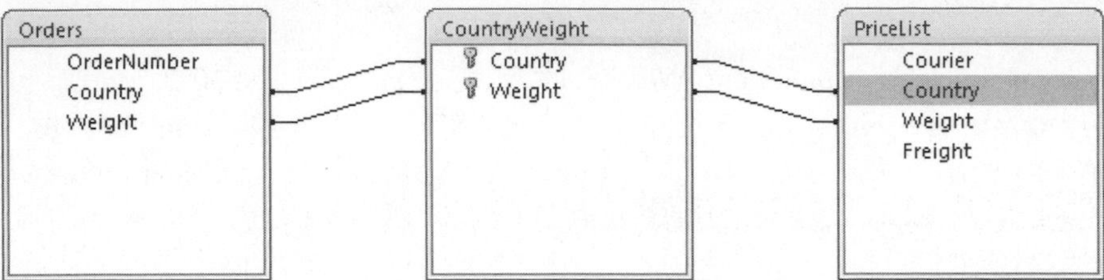


**FIGURE 10-29** The many-to-many data model for the courier simulation. Double lines between tables indicate that relationships are made by using two columns.

The new table has no information in it; it is just a technical table that you need to create the relationship between PriceList and Orders. As you can see, you are changing the data model to make it suit your needs.

Now that you have a data model that could be implemented in PowerPivot, you need to face a simple problem: there is neither a PriceList table nor CountryWeight one. Nevertheless, you can build both tables by starting from the original Excel table, using a modified version of the VBA script that we used previously for banding. In Figure 10-30, you can see the Excel worksheet with the computed tables that you will link in PowerPivot.

| Courier | Country | MinWeight | MaxWeight | Freight |
|---|---|---|---|---|
| BlueYonder | Australia | 0 | 5 | 3 |
| BlueYonder | Australia | 5 | 10 | 5 |
| BlueYonder | Australia | 10 | 20 | 18 |
| BlueYonder | Australia | 20 | 99 | 35 |
| BlueYonder | Canada | 0 | 5 | 2 |
| BlueYonder | Canada | 5 | 10 | 4 |
| BlueYonder | Canada | 10 | 20 | 12 |
| BlueYonder | Canada | 20 | 99 | 30 |
| BlueYonder | France | 0 | 5 | 3 |
| BlueYonder | France | 5 | 10 | 8 |
| BlueYonder | France | 10 | 20 | 25 |
| BlueYonder | France | 20 | 99 | 64 |
| BlueYonder | Germany | 0 | 5 | 4 |
| BlueYonder | Germany | 5 | 10 | 12 |
| BlueYonder | Germany | 10 | 20 | 25 |

| Courier | Country | Weight | Freight |
|---|---|---|---|
| BlueYonder | Australia | 1 | 3 |
| BlueYonder | Australia | 2 | 3 |
| BlueYonder | Australia | 3 | 3 |
| BlueYonder | Australia | 4 | 3 |
| BlueYonder | Australia | 5 | 3 |
| BlueYonder | Australia | 6 | 5 |
| BlueYonder | Australia | 7 | 5 |
| BlueYonder | Australia | 8 | 5 |
| BlueYonder | Australia | 9 | 5 |
| BlueYonder | Australia | 10 | 5 |
| BlueYonder | Australia | 11 | 18 |
| BlueYonder | Australia | 12 | 18 |
| BlueYonder | Australia | 13 | 18 |
| BlueYonder | Australia | 14 | 18 |
| BlueYonder | Australia | 15 | 18 |

Compute

| Country | Weight |
|---|---|
| Australia | 1 |
| Australia | 2 |
| Australia | 3 |
| Australia | 4 |
| Australia | 5 |
| Australia | 6 |
| Australia | 7 |
| Australia | 8 |
| Australia | 9 |
| Australia | 10 |
| Australia | 11 |
| Australia | 12 |
| Australia | 13 |

**FIGURE 10-30** The three tables for the many-to-many solution, computed by a macro.

The VBA code of the macro used in this workbook is slightly more complex than the one we used for banding. Nevertheless, it uses the same approach. The interested reader can find the source code in the companion workbook CH10-04-CourierSimulationM2M.xlsm.

You can create linked tables for the two rightmost tables in PowerPivot to have both the PriceList and the CountryWeight tables available in the PowerPivot database.

Now you need to face another simple issue: the relationship you want to create is based on two columns (country and weight) although, in PowerPivot, you can use only one column to define a relationship. This problem is easily solved by creating new calculated columns in all three tables with appropriate formulas that concatenate the country to the weight. The formula is very easy:

```
CountryWeight = PriceList[Country] & FORMAT( PriceList[Weight], "00" )
```

You can call those columns CountryWeight, and you can see in Figure 10-31 the CountryWeight column for the PriceList table.

| Courier | Country | Weight | Freight | CountryWeight |
|---|---|---|---|---|
| BlueYonder | Australia | 1 | 3 | Australia01 |
| BlueYonder | Australia | 2 | 3 | Australia02 |
| BlueYonder | Australia | 3 | 3 | Australia03 |
| BlueYonder | Australia | 4 | 3 | Australia04 |
| BlueYonder | Australia | 5 | 3 | Australia05 |
| BlueYonder | Australia | 6 | 5 | Australia06 |
| BlueYonder | Australia | 7 | 5 | Australia07 |
| BlueYonder | Australia | 8 | 5 | Australia08 |

**FIGURE 10-31** The PriceList table with the new CountryWeight column.

Using the CountryWeight column, you can create the relationships for the three tables and create the many-to-many data model. You can see the three relationships in Figure 10-32.

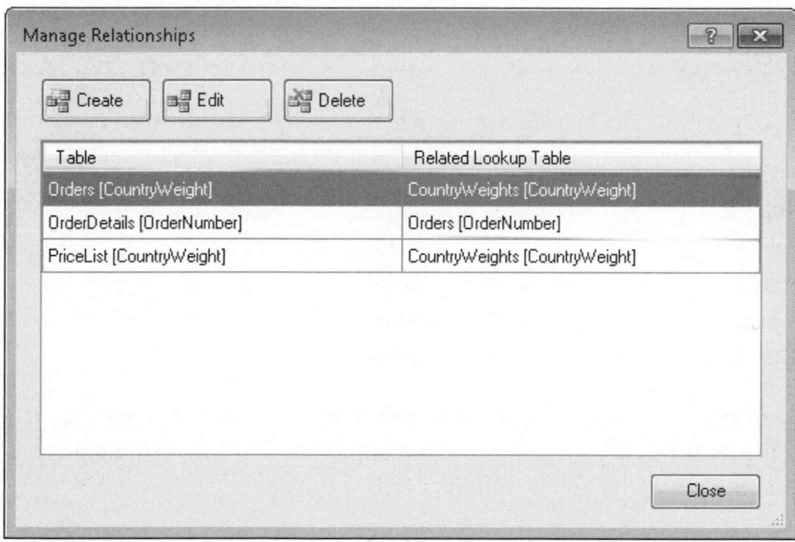


**FIGURE 10-32** The relationship you need for the many-to-many data model.

Now you are ready to study the complex part of the model—that is, the DAX formula that makes the computation work. PowerPivot does not handle many-to-many relationships by itself. It needs some help from you to be able to correctly query a data model that contains many-to-many relationships. You need to instruct PowerPivot to follow the relationship in the correct way to provide the result you want.

To make this model work, you need to take these two steps:

- You need to get the freight cost for a specific order and courier. The PriceList table contains two different prices for each order (one for each courier), although you want to get only one.
- You need to summarize this computed value by summing it up.

It should be clear that you cannot define calculated columns for this data model because a calculated column does not inherit the context filter imposed by the PivotTable. Moreover, many-to-many relationships always define nonadditive measures. So you need to work with measures only.

To help you understand the final formula, we are going to refine it step by step. You can start defining a first measure, following the same example you learned with banding, as follows:

```
CalculatedFreight = VALUES( PriceList[Freight] )
```

The VALUES function returns a table that contains all the distinct values of the PriceList[Freight]. Clearly, this formula returns all the possible values of the freight and not a specific one for a single courier and order. Nevertheless, if PowerPivot is forced to evaluate the formula in the context of a single order and a single courier, the chain of relationships makes the formula return a single value—that is, the freight charged for the order by the courier.

If you try to add this measure to a PivotTable, without solving the multiple values, you get an error because the formula returns multiple values. So the next step is to find a suitable filter context that makes the VALUES formula return a singleton.

To evaluate the formula in a context that restricts the evaluation to a single order, you can use the SUMX function. If you make SUMX iterate over the Orders table and provide the measure CalculatedFreight as the expression, the measure is evaluated once per order, in a context that filters a single order. So you can define a new measure as this:

```
CalculatedOrderFreightFirstTrial = SUMX( Orders, PriceList[CalculatedFreight] )
```

The SUMX formula iterates over all the orders and, for each one, calculates the CalculatedFreight measure we previously defined. However, for each single order, the value of CalculatedFreight is not yet unique, so the formula still does not work as we want. Nevertheless, if the formula is computed in a PivotTable that filters a single courier, the CalculatedFreight returns a single value and can be summed up. If more than one courier was selected, the formula would return a meaningless aggregate for more than one courier, but it would not produce errors.

Even if the CalculatedOrderFreightFirstTrial formula works as expected, it is very interesting to investigate a bit more to try to understand why it has been necessary to define two distinct measures. To reach your goal, you had to define a measure (CalculatedFreight) that seems useless because a simple substitution would lead you to this more compact definition:

```
CalculatedOrderFreightSecondTrial = SUMX( Orders, VALUES( PriceList[Freight] ) )
```

Nevertheless, if you tried to use this second formula, PowerPivot would raise an error and would not be able to perform the computation because SUMX creates a row context and evaluates its second parameter without modifying the filter context. You should remember, from Chapter 6, that the presence of a row context does not modify the filter context, so the expression VALUES (PriceList[Freight]) is evaluated in a context wherein it returns multiple rows, yielding to an error. On the other hand, when you pass the measure CalculatedFreight as the second parameter to SUMX, you request the evaluation of a measure, so a new filter context is created for its evaluation, wherein any row context is automatically transformed into a correspondent filter context.

If a light suddenly turns on in your brain and says CALCULATE, you are one of the most careful readers we could ever dream of. If not, do not worry, it is absolutely normal—it took us a really long time to discover (and remember at the right time) that the CALCULATE function does exactly this: it opens a new filter context that transforms any row context into a filter context. So a more compact representation of the same formula might be this:

```
CalculatedOrderFreightThirdTrial = SUMX( Orders, CALCULATE( VALUES( PriceList[Freight] ) ) )
```

Unfortunately, even this formula does not work as expected; to discover the reason, you need to study the question a little longer. It turns out that simply adding the measure to a PivotTable raises the error shown in Figure 10-33.

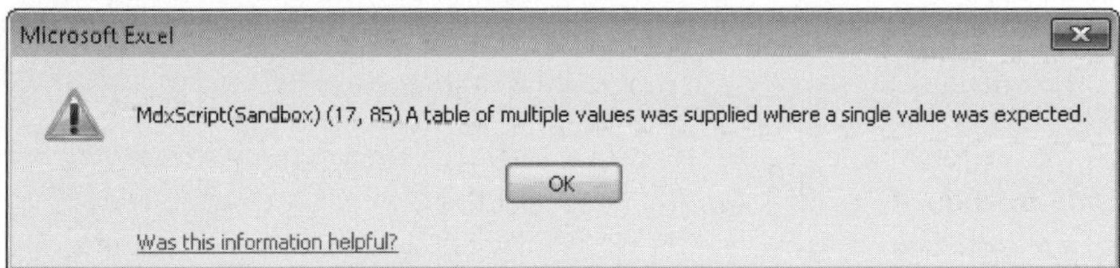


**FIGURE 10-33** Trying to compact a formula sometimes raises unexpected errors.

It seems that, even if CALCULATE opens a correct filter context, the VALUES function still returns multiple values. But if you try to add the formula after having filtered the couriers to show only one of them, the formula works correctly, as you can see in Figure 10-34.

| Courier | BlueYonder |
|---|---|

| Row Labels | CalculatedOrderFreightThirdTrial | CourierFreight |
|---|---|---|
| Australia | 124,277.00 | 124,277.00 |
| Canada | 25,386.00 | 25,386.00 |
| France | 70,108.00 | 70,108.00 |
| Germany | 79,182.00 | 79,182.00 |
| United Kingdom | 95,442.00 | 95,442.00 |
| United States | 77,776.00 | 77,776.00 |
| **Grand Total** | **472,171.00** | **472,171.00** |

**FIGURE 10-34** Imposing a filter on the PivotTable suddenly makes the formula work.

So it seems that the formula is working fine, but only under some circumstances. It turns out that, when you evaluate the grand total of the PivotTable, the courier is not filtered in any way. The evaluation context, even under the CALCULATE call, contains more than one row, creating the multiple rows returned by the VALUES function. If you add some logic to check whether the VALUES call returns only one value, you can slightly change the formula definition and provide the final, correct formula:

```
CalculatedOrderFreight = SUMX( Orders,
                              CALCULATE( IF( COUNT( PriceList[Freight] ) = 1,
                                             VALUES( PriceList[Freight] ),
                                             BLANK() ) ) )
```

The IF call checks to see whether the VALUES call returns only one row and, if this is not what happens, it returns BLANK, avoiding the error that happens for the grand total.

If all the descriptions up to now seem too complex, well, you are right, they are! Nevertheless, it might be clarifying to show a report (see Figure 10-35) produced by means of this data model and explain in great detail what happens under the covers to compute it.

| CourierFreight | Column Labels | | | | | | | |
|---|---|---|---|---|---|---|---|---|
| | CY 2001 | | CY 2002 | | CY 2003 | | CY 2004 | |
| Row Labels | BlueYonder | WorldWide | BlueYonder | WorldWide | BlueYonder | WorldWide | BlueYonder | WorldWide |
| Australia | 8,248.00 | 14,980.00 | 19,253.00 | 34,615.00 | 48,762.00 | 78,153.00 | 48,014.00 | 74,510.00 |
| Canada | 636.00 | 863.00 | 3,180.00 | 4,253.00 | 9,504.00 | 12,005.50 | 12,066.00 | 14,548.50 |
| France | 1,709.00 | 1,244.00 | 7,424.00 | 6,166.00 | 29,464.00 | 20,927.00 | 31,511.00 | 21,439.00 |
| Germany | 2,251.00 | 1,592.00 | 7,424.00 | 6,056.00 | 30,864.00 | 21,574.00 | 38,643.00 | 25,234.00 |
| United Kingdom | 1,848.00 | 2,070.00 | 5,478.00 | 7,076.00 | 39,870.00 | 27,467.00 | 48,246.00 | 27,513.00 |
| United States | 2,988.00 | 3,274.00 | 8,568.00 | 9,793.00 | 29,798.00 | 35,113.00 | 36,422.00 | 42,335.00 |
| **Grand Total** | **17,680.00** | **24,023.00** | **51,327.00** | **67,959.00** | **188,262.00** | **195,239.50** | **214,902.00** | **205,579.50** |

**FIGURE 10-35** Sample report built with the many-to-many model.

Notice that this PivotTable does not have the grand total for the columns because it is blanked by the inner IF function. To better understand how this formula works, let us try to follow the whole path of computation for a single cell.

Let us take, as an example, the cell for <Australia, CY 2001, BlueYonder>, the value of which is 8,248.00. How did PowerPivot reach this result?

- The filter context of execution is given by the coordinates of the cell—that is, <Australia, CY 2001, BlueYonder>.
- The value required is CalculatedOrderFreight, which is the last measure defined in this section. It contains a SUMX over Orders for the complex expression that evaluates the freight cost for the courier.
- Because the formula is a SUMX, PowerPivot iterates over all the orders, satisfying the filter context, and for each row in the Orders table, it evaluates the expression provided in the second parameter. The orders taken into account are orders in Australia and for the CY 2001, the only part of the filter context that actively filters the Orders table.
- During the evaluation of the expression, in the inner loop of SUMX, the evaluation context changes. It adds a row context (the iterated order in the Orders table) to the original filter context imposed by the PivotTable.
- Now, because the next part of the expression is CALCULATE, the row context in the Orders table is transformed into a filter context (propagating the selected row to all the related rows in other tables) that is merged with the existing one, creating a new filter context that is composed by the intersection of both. Under this new filter context, PowerPivot initiates the evaluation of the inner IF.
- The PriceList table is not in direct relationship with the Orders table, so it seems that it will not be filtered. Nevertheless, before going on, PowerPivot needs to apply the complete filter context to all the tables, and here comes into play the CountryWeight table.
- The Orders table contains the Freight column, and it is in relationship with the bridge table CountryWeight. Because we are on a specific row, the Freight value of the row has been added to the filter, and so PowerPivot behaves as if the CountryWeight table contains only one value, defined by the country of the order (which happens to be Australia because of the filter context) and the weight of the order. (Whatever value it has, it is defined by the row context transformed into a filter context.)
- The relationship between PriceList and CountryWeight (which, filtered, contains only one row) forces the PriceList table to consider only two rows, one for each courier. Moreover, because the filter context contains <BlueYonder>, only one of the two rows survives the complete filter, so PowerPivot behaves as if the PriceList table contained only one row.

- Now PowerPivot can proceed with the evaluation of the COUNT of PriceList[Freight], and in accordance with all we said before, it counts only one row. In other words, the filter context applied to the PriceList is composed by these elements:
    - Country = Australia. This value comes from the PivotTable coordinates (which filtered Orders), then it has been propagated to the CountryWeight table due to the first relationship and then again to PriceList due to the relationship with CountryWeight.
    - Weight = <the weight of the specific order>. This value comes from the Orders table, which has selected only one row due to the behavior of the SUMX function. That row has been then propagated to the CountryWeight table and from there, following the same relationship as before, to PriceList.
    - Courier = BlueYonder. This filter is coming directly from the PivotTable coordinates of the cell being evaluated.
- So the count of different Freight values in the PriceList table yields only one because, after the filter, the PriceList table contains only one row. The value of the freight for that order and courier is returned by the function.
- This process is repeated once for each row in the Orders table, summing up all the results until the table is completely scanned. At this point, SUMX returns the final value.

As you can see, the complete evaluation algorithm is pretty complex, but is it based on very simple steps that, mixed together, yield the correct evaluation of the cell.

Mastering all these steps takes time and experience but it lets you build very interesting data models that provide complex simulation tables. We strongly suggest that you follow the complete flow of evaluation until you understand it well because it will transform this data model from something "magically working" into a clear view of the internals of PowerPivot.

# Summary

In this chapter, you saw how to create complex models that let you solve many problems with PowerPivot. We used complex data models, such as many-to-many relationships, and complex DAX formulas, which use CALCULATE, VALUES, EARLIER, error handling, and most of the functions available in PowerPivot.

The final result, when used with the PivotTable, is easy and hides the technical complexity of the data model. As a PowerPivot expert, you have learned how to create complex models that are easy to use.

Chapter 11

# Publishing to SharePoint

After you design your Microsoft Excel reports based on Microsoft SQL Server PowerPivot for Excel, you can publish them to Microsoft SharePoint and share them with other people in your company using just a Web browser. Once published, the PivotTables are still interactive and you can schedule PowerPivot data to be automatically refreshed. In this chapter, you see what features are available to publish your workbooks to SharePoint without your depending on the IT department. However, the installation of SharePoint and its maintenance (there is some administrative effort required, even if just for security policies) is still the responsibility of the IT department, and it is not covered in this book. In this chapter, we assume you already have access to a Microsoft SharePoint 2010 server that has PowerPivot for SharePoint already installed.

## SharePoint 2010 and PowerPivot Integration

SharePoint 2010 is a platform that makes it easier for people to work together; it offers a set of services for sharing information, managing workflows, publishing reports, and so on. You can save your Microsoft Office files to a SharePoint site and, most important, you can publish an Excel workbook on SharePoint, which means that the workbook is shown as a Web page that can be read using just a Web browser. The service that allows this publishing is called Excel Services and is included in SharePoint 2010. Your IT department can add PowerPivot for SharePoint to a SharePoint 2010 installation. With that installed, you can also publish Excel workbooks that contain PowerPivot data.

### Licensing for PowerPivot for SharePoint

SharePoint 2010 requires an Enterprise Client Access License to use Excel Services. PowerPivot for SharePoint also requires a license for Microsoft SQL Server 2008 R2 Enterprise Edition or higher.

An Excel workbook that contains PowerPivot data can be published to a SharePoint site in a standard document library. In this way, your document does not preview any of its content but shows just a line that includes the document name and some other information. In Figure 11-1, you can see a document library that contains a few sample workbooks from Chapter 9, "PowerPivot DAX Patterns."

**Note** The URL available to you to use depends on the location of your SharePoint 2010 server. Ask to your IT department which URL to use if you do not know it.

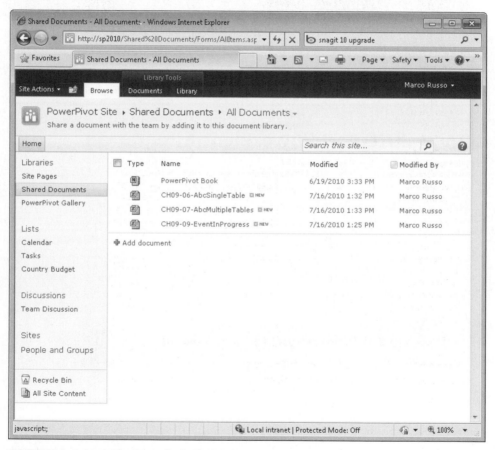

**FIGURE 11-1** A simple document list in SharePoint.

For example, if you click the CH09-07-AbcMultipleTables name, you see the contents of this workbook rendered in a Web page. You can browse the PivotTable by interacting with a filter and slicers (which are not present in this case). In Figure 11-2, you can see the product models sorted by sales amount in descending order, which was the order selected at the moment the workbook was saved.

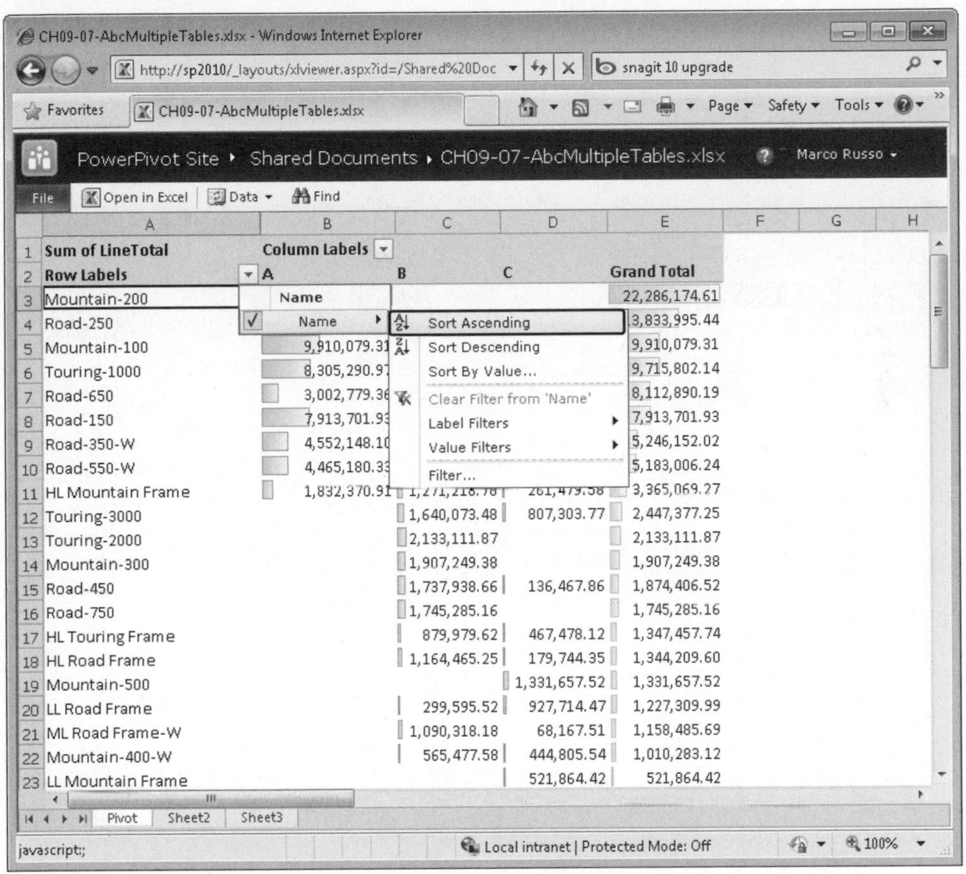


**FIGURE 11-2** Initial view of the workbook and menu for changing sort order.

Notice the highlighted Sort Ascending menu that allows you to change this sort order. You get to that menu by clicking the arrow next to the Row Labels caption. Figure 11-3 shows the result after you choose the Sort Ascending menu item, which sorts models by name in ascending order.

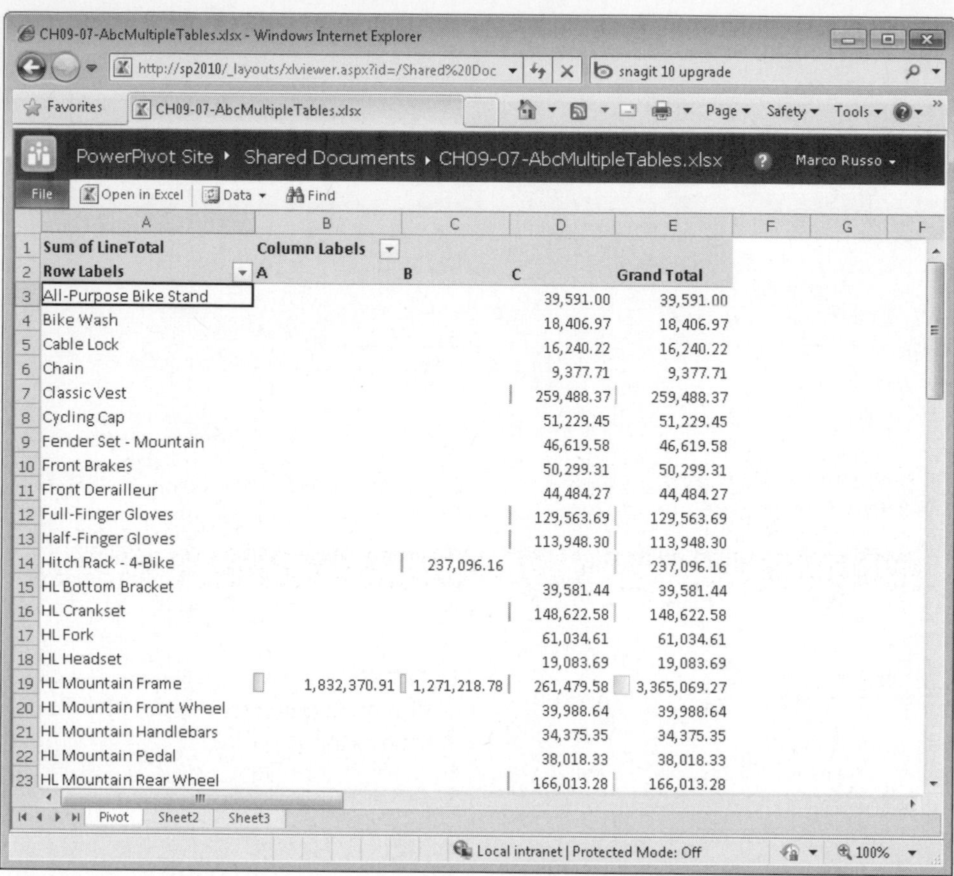


**FIGURE 11-3** The PivotTable has been sorted by model name in ascending order.

As you can see in the preceding figures, saving an Excel workbook in a document library on a SharePoint site publishes the entire contents of the workbook. In this case, all three worksheets are visible, including those that do not have data to show (such as Sheet2 and Sheet3). You see later in this chapter how to publish only parts of the workbook on SharePoint.

## PowerPivot Gallery

A better option for storing workbooks based on PowerPivot data is to use a particular type of document library known as the PowerPivot Gallery. You can create many PowerPivot Gallery libraries, but at least one default PowerPivot Gallery (with this same name) is usually available by default. This type of document library shows a preview of each of the visible worksheets of a published Excel workbook. This preview service is available regardless the presence of PowerPivot data in the published workbook: it works on any Excel workbook. The preview is available in three different views:

- Gallery view
- Theater view
- Carousel view

In Figure 11-4, you can see the Gallery view, in which each workbook has a horizontal band with a big picture of the worksheet that has been selected; you can also see a smaller preview for every other worksheet of the workbook.

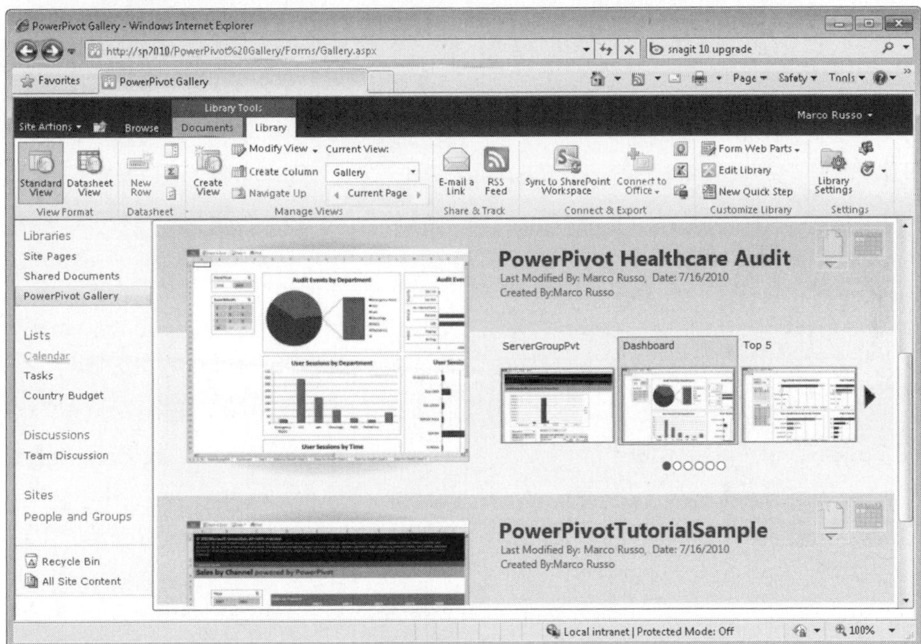


**FIGURE 11-4** The PowerPivot Gallery in default Gallery view.

In Figure 11-5, you can see the Theater view, which shows in the lower pane a horizontal scrollable list of the previews of all the worksheets of all the workbooks in the document library. You can see in the central pane a bigger picture of the worksheet that you selected in the lower pane. The name of the workbook that the selected worksheet belongs to is displayed on the left of the list of worksheets.

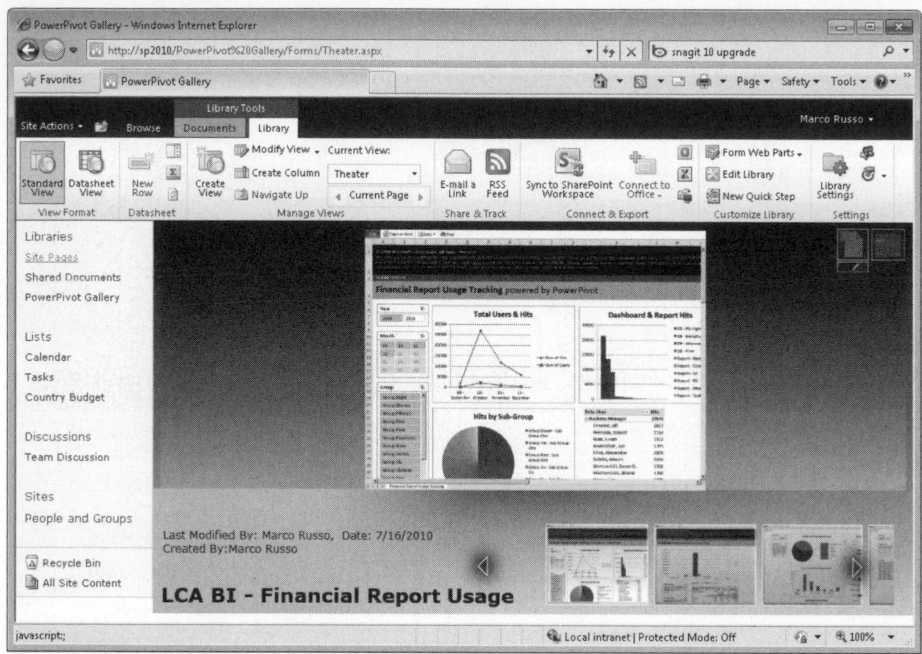


**FIGURE 11-5** The PowerPivot Gallery in Theater view.

Finally, Figure 11-6 shows the Carousel view, which is similar to the Theater view in having a single scrollable list of all the worksheets of all the published workbooks, but it also uses a three-dimensional effect to scroll and present the worksheet previews.

The PowerPivot Gallery does not execute the workbooks while you are browsing the list through one of the available views. A background process opens the workbooks and gets a snapshot of every worksheet so that the preview can be made using ready-to-use screenshots.

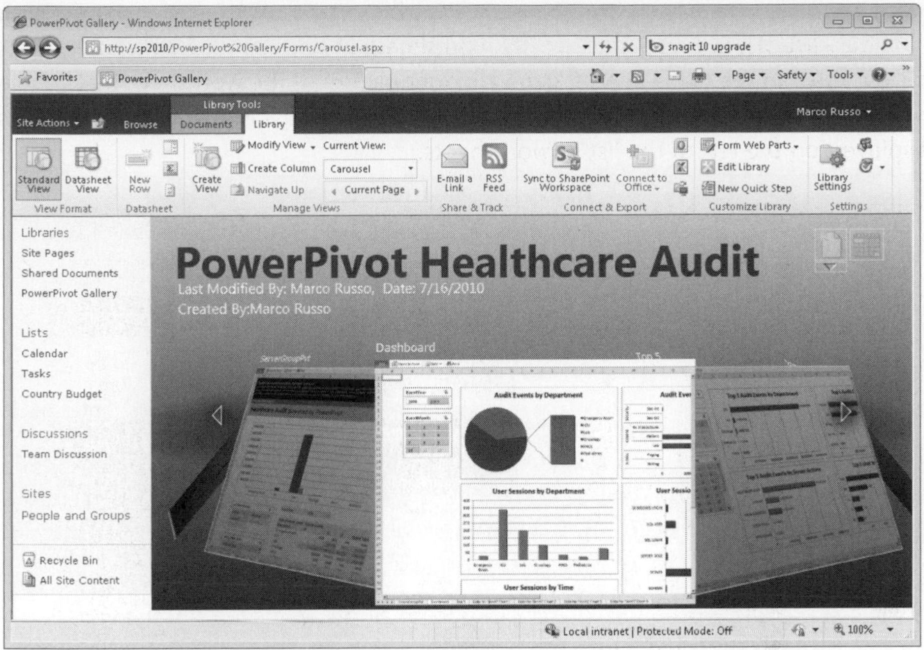

FIGURE 11-6 The PowerPivot Gallery in Carousel view.

**Note** Only Excel files can be previewed in a PowerPivot Gallery. Other file types are not supported. If you try to view other kinds of files in the PowerPivot Gallery, you see an image with an indicator that the preview is not supported instead.

All the views available in a PowerPivot Gallery allow you to view the selected worksheet in the browser by simply clicking on it, just as you can do when you click the name of a file in a standard document library, as you saw in Figure 11-1.

## Publishing an Excel Workbook

You can publish an Excel Workbook in several ways. As you will see, publishing a workbook by using the specific feature available in Excel is the most powerful and flexible option. However, you can also publish a document without even opening Excel, which might be useful in particular circumstances.

When you are in a PowerPivot Gallery or in a standard document library in SharePoint, you can upload an Excel workbook by using the Upload Document command available on the Documents tab of the Library Tools contextual tab of the SharePoint ribbon, which is highlighted in Figure 11-7.

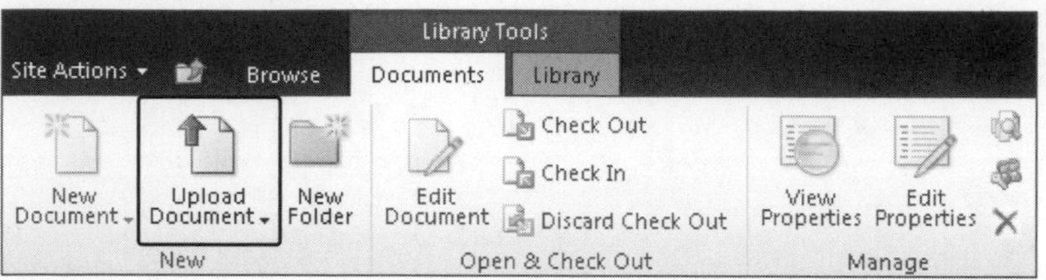


**FIGURE 11-7** Upload Document command on the Documents tab of the Library Tools contextual tab.

**Note** When you upload an Excel workbook in a PowerPivot Gallery, its preview is available in the gallery after a few seconds or minutes, depending on the current workload on the server.

When you use this procedure, you usually publish all the worksheets of the workbook. If you want to publish only some parts of the workbook, you have to modify the Publish Options of the document from within Excel. These options are available as part of the Save To SharePoint command, a pane that you can see in Figure 11-8. You find these options by selecting Save & Send on the File menu and then by clicking Save To SharePoint. The Publish Options button in this pane is highlighted in the figure.

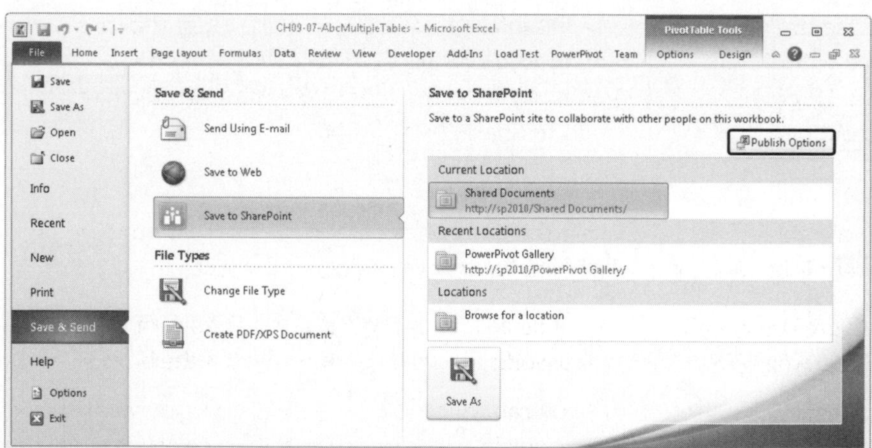


**FIGURE 11-8** Public Options button in the Save To SharePoint pane.

The Publish Options dialog box (shown in Figure 11-9) has two tabs, Show and Parameters.

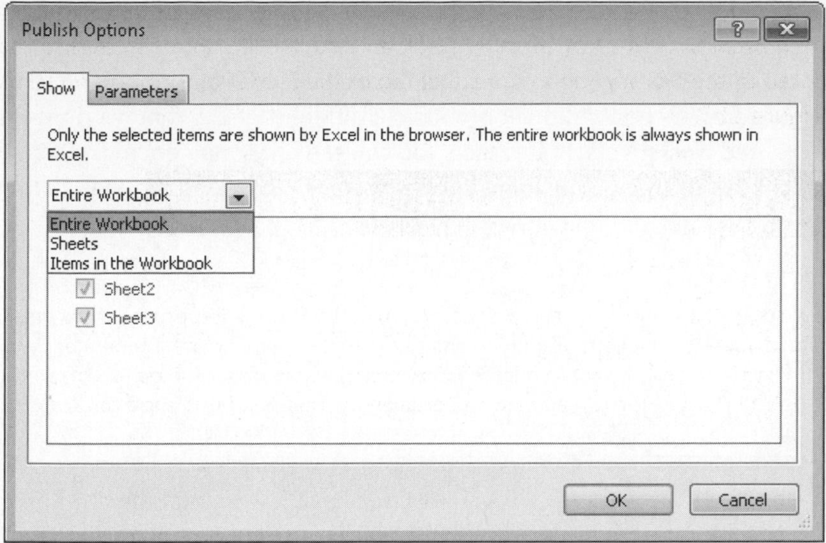


**FIGURE 11-9** The Show tab of the Publish Options dialog box.

## The Parameters Tab in the Publish Options Dialog Box

The Parameters tab allows you to select what parameters to make available to the user in the Web browser. A parameter is a named range corresponding to a single cell of the workbook, which is usually used in other Excel calculations. For example, imagine a loan amortization table that is calculated on a base interest rate. You might want to give to the user the option to change this interest rate in the Web browser, showing the updated table without the user needing to open the workbook in Excel. This is not a feature directly related to PowerPivot, but it can be used as part of the calculation made in a dashboard that is published to SharePoint.

The Show tab allows you to select the parts of the workbook you want to publish after the document is opened into SharePoint. You can choose among these:

- **Entire Workbook** This is the default for any new document. Each of the worksheets of the Excel workbook is shown as a worksheet when displayed inside the browser by SharePoint.
- **Sheets** Using this option, you can choose the worksheets that you want users to see after SharePoint displays the workbook in the browser. The default selection is All Sheets (which corresponds to the Entire Workbook option), but you can choose to make visible or invisible every single worksheet. You have to choose at least one worksheet to be visible.
- **Items in the Workbook** This option allows you to select only a few items of the workbook, such as a selection of Tables, Charts, Named Ranges, and so on. PivotTables and PivotCharts are also items that you can publish.

Whenever you choose to publish Entire Workbook or a selection of Sheets, you see in the Web browser the same arrangement of columns, rows, and worksheets that you are used to seeing in Excel, as you already saw in Figure 11-2 and Figure 11-3. However, choosing to publish any number of Items In The Workbook produces a different result, removing the display of columns, rows, and worksheets. In this case, you can see only one item in the Web browser, and you can choose to change the item you are displaying by using the View combo box to select the item you want, as you can see in Figure 11-10.

**Tip** Be sure to give a meaningful name to each item in the Excel workbook because meaningful names help you select what items to publish and to show. The default names generated by Excel are not so helpful whenever you want to publish more than one item of the same type in a workbook.

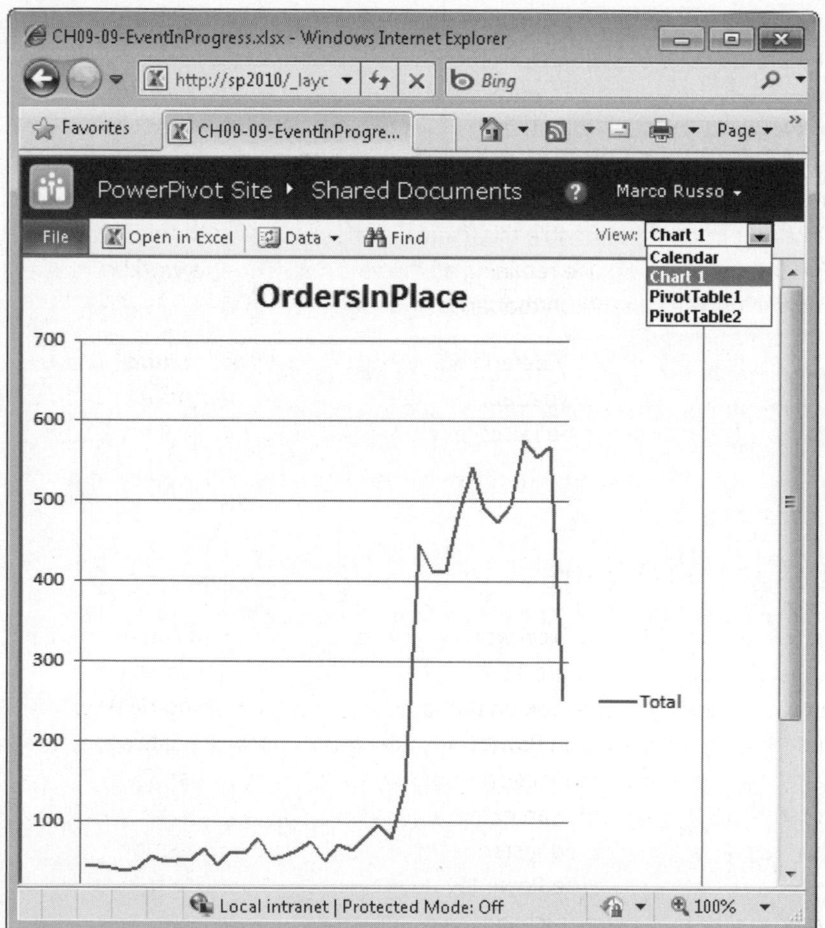


**FIGURE 11-10** The View combo box lets you select the item to display.

After you make your selection in Publish Options, you usually want to save the file to SharePoint by using the Save As button in the same pane that you saw in Figure 11-8. It is very handy to select the location you want by using the list above that button, which displays the last-used paths along with a generic Browse For A Location option.

**Note** Publish Options are saved in the Excel workbook whether or not the file is saved to SharePoint. In other words, if you save the file in your local documents folder after you choose the item to publish and then plan to upload the document to a SharePoint document library without using Excel, the Publish Options you set will still be considered by SharePoint.

### Versioning and File Size

Every time you save or upload a document to SharePoint, you are placing that document in a document library, which might have a setting that automatically creates a new version every time a file is saved. In other words, older versions of the same file are retained in the same document library. By default, this setting is disabled in a PowerPivot Gallery, but it can be changed as it can be in any other document library. An Excel workbook containing PowerPivot data might be hundreds of megabytes in size. In that case, you should be careful about deciding to enable this feature in the document library in which you want to store your Excel files because retaining all the versions of such a workbook might be very expensive for the storage on the server.

Moreover, also consider that by default a SharePoint server has a limit of 50 MB for the size of a file that can be uploaded. To change this limit, you have to contact your IT department. That limit can be raised to a maximum of 2 GB.

## PowerPivot Data Refresh

Each time you request to view an Excel workbook in the browser, you can request (through the Data menu that you can see in Figure 11-2) to refresh data coming from external connections, and you can recalculate the workbook on demand. However, refreshing data from an external connection does not update data in PowerPivot tables. Conceptually, data stored in PowerPivot tables are already an external connection from the point of view of an Excel PivotTable. If a PowerPivot table got its rows from an external database, such as SQL Server, that table is not refreshed just because the user requested refreshed data for a connection in Excel. To update that table, you need to instruct the PowerPivot for SharePoint service to do that job for you, and this requires a different approach and user interface.

In Figure 11-11, you can see the Open menu that is available in a standard document library in SharePoint.

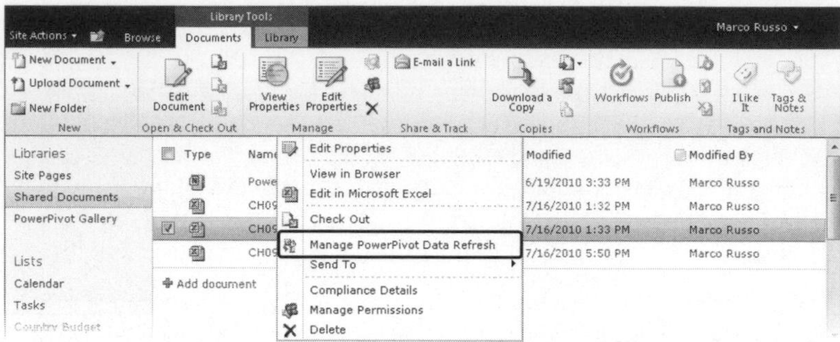


**FIGURE 11-11** The Manage PowerPivot Data Refresh command in the Open menu for an Excel document.

The Manage PowerPivot Data Refresh command call opens a configuration window like the one that you see later, in Figure 11-13. This same configuration window can be opened by clicking the Manage Data Refresh button in the PowerPivot Gallery. These buttons are highlighted in Figure 11-12.

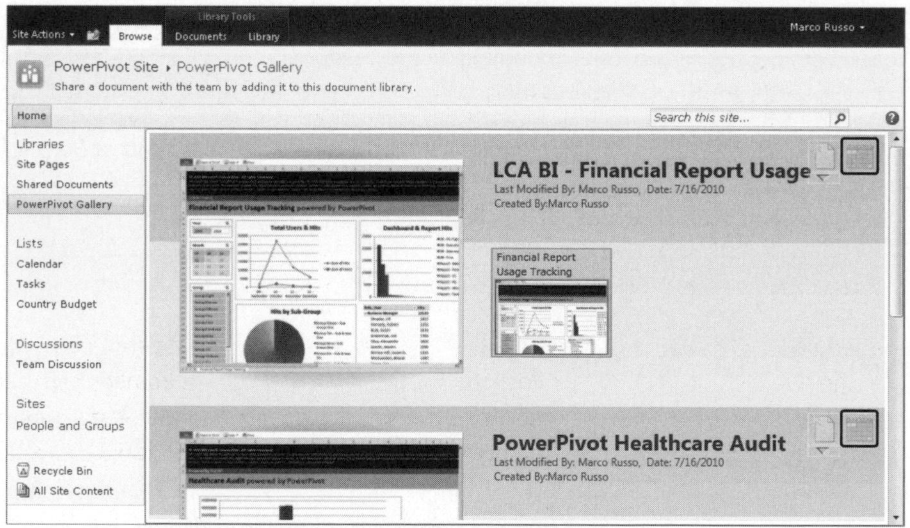


**FIGURE 11-12** The Manage Data Refresh buttons in the PowerPivot Gallery.

The Data Refresh operation is not enabled by default in a workbook published to SharePoint. The first check box you have in the configuration window, shown in Figure 11-13, is just this setting, which must be enabled to schedule an automatic refresh of PivotTable tables contained in the workbook.

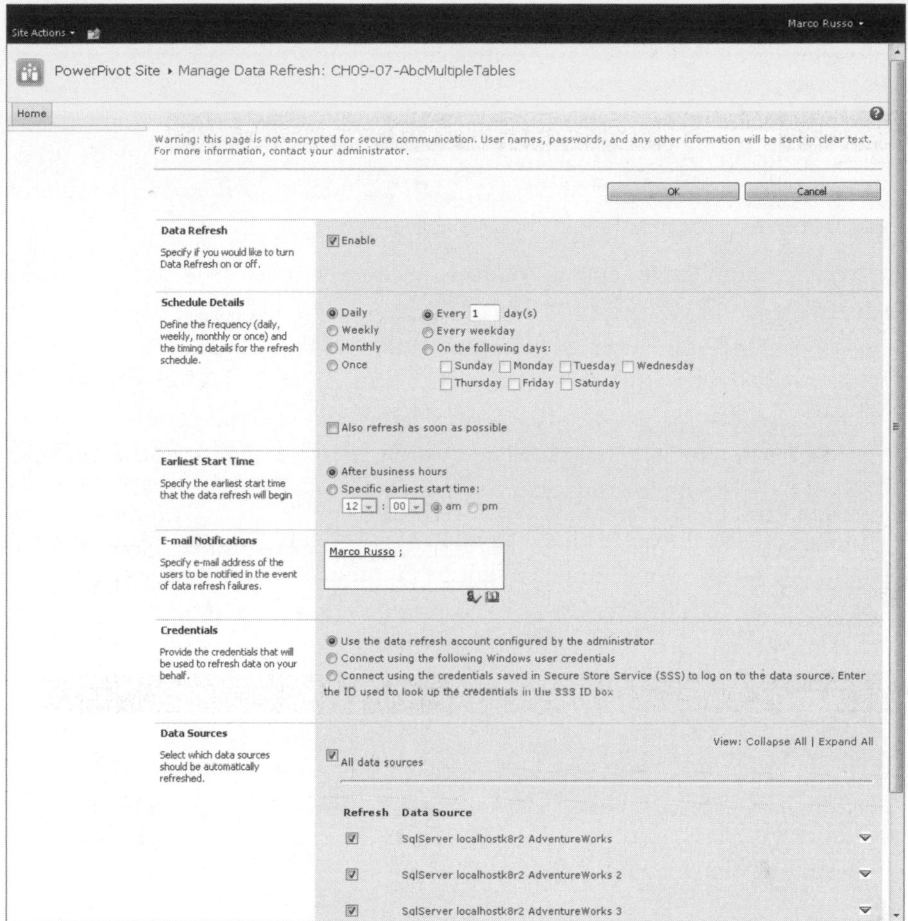


**FIGURE 11-13** Data Refresh configuration.

The Schedule Details section controls the time interval of data refresh operations. You can also choose the Also Refresh As Soon As Possible check box if you want an immediate data refresh of PowerPivot tables. What *immediate* means is explained in the Earliest Start Time section of the configuration window; this section defines the time you have to wait before an *immediate* operation starts.

The E-mail Notifications section simply defines users who have to receive automated e-mail from SharePoint every time a data refresh is completed (with or without errors).

The most important section is Credentials. This is the definition of the credentials that you need to connect to the data source for PowerPivot tables. You have to pay attention to this setting because when you created the PowerPivot tables, you probably used your own user credentials to connect with data sources, but this might not be possible any longer when the refresh is automatically made by the server. Let us take a look at the options available.

- **Use the data refresh account configured by administrator** When this setting, which is the default, is selected, the connection to data sources is made by using a user defined by SharePoint system administrators. It is called the PowerPivot Unattended Data Refresh Account, and you have to ask your IT department whether or not this user is able to connect to your data source. Usually, this account can be used just to connect to data sources that do not run the Windows operating system but have their own authentication system.
- **Connect using the following Windows user credentials** This setting allows you to specify a user name and a password for users to connect to the data source. In theory, you might use your own credentials to connect to the data sources you used to build the PowerPivot model because it should be an account with sufficient rights to do that. However, we do not suggest that you use your own credentials here. It would be better to use a dedicated account provided by your system administrators that has rights of access only to data sources used by the Excel workbook.
- **Connect using the credentials stored in Secure Store Services** You have to use this setting whenever your system administrator provides you with a Secure Store ID. This allows you to enable users to access required data without a password. The infrastructure required to use this service has to be configured by your system administrators and is not discussed in this book.

In the lowest part of Figure 11-13, you can choose, for each of the data sources of your PowerPivot model, whether to use the default settings you defined in the previous section of the configuration window or to use a custom schedule or system credential, as you can see in Figure 11-14.

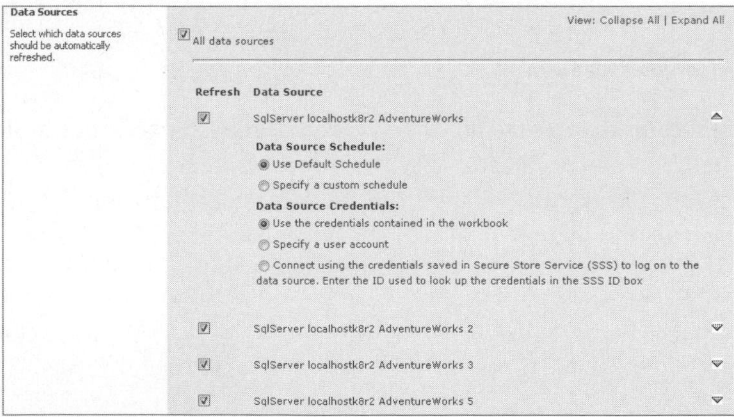


**FIGURE 11-14** Data Refresh configuration.

You can disable the refresh of a single data source by clearing the corresponding check box, which you can see in Figure 11-14.

After you confirm your settings, the next time you call Manage Data Refresh, you see a Data Refresh History page, like the one shown in Figure 11-15.

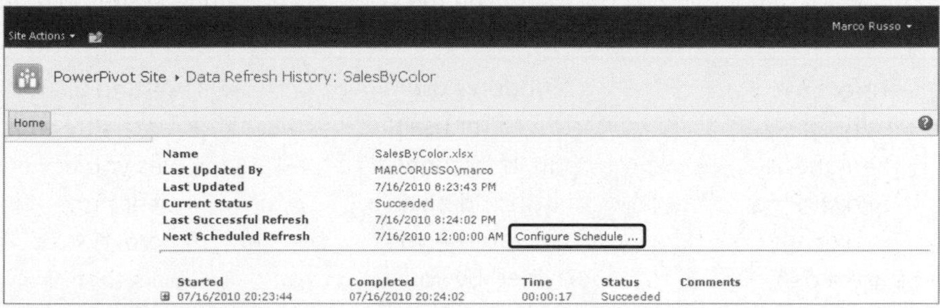


**FIGURE 11-15** Data Refresh History.

The Data Refresh History page shows the state of the last refresh operations and, in case of errors, you also see more details about the reason for each error. By clicking the Configure Schedule link (which is highlighted in Figure 11-15), you return to the Manage Data Refresh page that you saw in Figure 11-13.

# Summary

In this chapter, you saw how to publish an Excel workbook to SharePoint, how to use the PowerPivot Gallery feature, and how to schedule an automatic data refresh of PowerPivot tables.

Appendix

# DAX Functions Reference

This appendix lists functions available in DAX, complete with their syntax. You can find the complete syntax of DAX functions at

*http://technet.microsoft.com/en-us/library/ff452127.aspx*

which is part of the complete DAX Reference in the documentation at

*http://technet.microsoft.com/library/ee835533.aspx.*

## Statistical Functions

Statistical functions aggregate data that returns a scalar value. Usually these functions operate on all the rows of the table that contain the specified column, which has to be of numeric or date type. The 'A' suffix identifies functions that also operate on any other type of column. The 'X' suffix identifies functions that allow you to aggregate the result of an expression applied to each row of the specified table.

**TABLE A-1 Statistical Numeric Functions**

| Function | Description |
|---|---|
| AVERAGE( <column> ) | Returns the arithmetic mean of all the numbers in a column.<br><column> must be of a date or number type. |
| AVERAGEA( <column> ) | Returns the arithmetic mean of all the values in a column.<br>It always returns 0 for text columns, and it returns the same value of AVERAGE for numeric columns.<br><column> can be of any type. |
| AVERAGEX( <table>, <expression> ) | Returns the arithmetic mean of <expression> evaluated for each row of <table>. The <expression> must return a numeric type; otherwise, it returns an error. |
| COUNT( <column> ) | Returns the number of cells in a column containing numbers.<br><column> must be of a numeric type. |
| COUNTA( <column> ) | Returns the number of cells in a column that are not empty.<br>It returns the same value as COUNT for numeric columns.<br><column> can be of any type. |

*(continued)*

| Function | Description |
|---|---|
| COUNTAX( <table>, <expression> ) | Returns the number of nonblank results of <expression> evaluated for each row of <table>. The <expression> can return any type. |
| COUNTBLANK( <column> ) | Returns the number of empty cells in a column. |
| COUNTROWS( <table> ) | Returns the number of rows in a table. <table> can be a PowerPivot table or an expression that returns a table (such as RELATEDTABLE, FILTER, and so on). |
| COUNTX( <table>, <expression> ) | Returns the number of nonblank numeric results of <expression> evaluated for each row of <table>. The <expression> must return a numeric type; otherwise, it returns an error. |
| MAX( <column> ) | Returns the largest numeric value in a column.<br><column> must be of a date or number type. |
| MAXA( <column> ) | Returns the largest numeric value in a column. It always returns 0 for text columns, and it returns the same value of MAX for numeric columns.<br><column> can be of any type. |
| MAXX( <table>, <expression> ) | Returns the largest numeric value of <expression> evaluated for each row of <table>. The <expression> must return a numeric type; otherwise, it returns an error. |
| MIN( <column> ) | Returns the smallest numeric value in a column.<br><column> must be of a date or number type. |
| MINA( <column> ) | Returns the smallest numeric value in a column. It always returns 0 for text columns, and it returns the same value of MIN for numeric columns.<br><column> can be of any type. |
| MINX( <table>, <expression> ) | Returns the smallest numeric value of <expression> evaluated for each row of <table>. The <expression> must return a numeric type; otherwise, it returns an error. |
| SUM( <column> ) | Adds all the numbers in a column.<br><column> must be of a date or number type. |
| SUMX( <table>, <expression> ) | Returns the sum of <expression> evaluated for each row of <table>. The <expression> must return a numeric type; otherwise, it returns an error. |

# Logical Functions

Logical functions return a TRUE/FALSE value and are used to implement logical conditions in a DAX expression—for example, to implement different calculations depending on the value of a column or to intercept an error condition.

**TABLE A-2 Logical Functions**

| Function | Description |
|---|---|
| AND( <logical1>, <logical2> ) | Returns TRUE if both parameters are TRUE.<br>Returns FALSE if any of the parameters is FALSE. |
| FALSE( ) | Returns the logical value FALSE. (It is a TRUE/FALSE type value.) |
| IF( <logical_test>, <value_if_true>, <value_if_false> ) | Returns the <value_if_true> parameter if <logical_test> is TRUE; otherwise, it returns <value_if_false>. It always returns a single data type in a column. (Implicit conversion is used if the two values are of different types.) |
| IFERROR( <value>, <value_if_error> ) | Returns <value_if_error> if <value> is an error; otherwise, it returns <value>. |
| NOT( <logical> ) | Returns TRUE if <logical> is FALSE.<br>Returns FALSE if <logical> is TRUE. |
| OR( <logical1>, <logical2>) | Returns TRUE if any of the parameters is TRUE.<br>Returns FALSE if both parameters are TRUE. |
| TRUE() | Returns the logical value TRUE. (It is a TRUE/FALSE type value.) |

# Information Functions

Information functions are used to analyze the type of an expression. All of these functions return a TRUE/FALSE value and can be used in any logical expression.

**TABLE A-3 Information Functions**

| Function | Description |
|---|---|
| ISBLANK( <value> ) | Returns TRUE if <value> is BLANK (empty cell); otherwise, it returns FALSE. |
| ISERROR( <value> ) | Returns TRUE if <value> is an error; otherwise, it returns FALSE. |
| ISLOGICAL( <value> ) | Returns TRUE if <value> is of TRUE/FALSE type (Boolean); otherwise, it returns FALSE. |
| ISNONTEXT( <value> ) | Returns TRUE if <value> is not text; otherwise, it returns FALSE. A BLANK value (that is, an empty cell) is not text and returns TRUE. |
| ISNUMBER( <value> ) | Returns TRUE if <value> is a number; otherwise, it returns FALSE. A BLANK value (that is, an empty cell) is not text and returns FALSE. |
| ISTEXT( <value> ) | Returns TRUE if <value> is text; otherwise, it returns FALSE. A BLANK value (that is, an empty cell) is not text and returns FALSE. |

## Mathematical Functions

The set of math and trigonometric functions available in DAX is just a subset of the mathematical functions available in Excel. In particular, trigonometric function like COS, SIN, and TAN are missing, and only PI is available.

**TABLE A-4 Math and Trigonometric Functions**

| Function | Description |
|---|---|
| ABS( <number> ) | Absolute value of <number>. |
| CEILING( <number> , <significance> ) | Rounds <number> to the nearest integer or to the nearest multiple of <significance>. It differs from ISO.CEILING just for negative numbers of <significance>. |
| EXP( <number> ) | Returns *e* (which is the base of the natural logarithm) raised to the power of <number>. |
| FACT( <number> ) | Factorial of <number>. It is like 1 * 2 * 3 * ... * <number>. |
| FLOOR( <number>, <significance> ) | Rounds <number> down to the nearest multiple of <significance>. Use 1 for <significance> if you want to round the number to the nearest whole integer, use 0.1 for rounding to one decimal, and so on. |
| INT( <number> ) | Rounds <number> down to the nearest integer. It always removes the decimal part. |
| ISO.CEILING( <number> , <significance> ) | Rounds <number> to the nearest integer or to the nearest multiple of <significance>. It differs from CEILING just for negative numbers of <significance>. |
| LN( <number> ) | Natural logarithm of <number>. |
| LOG( <number>, <base> ) | Logarithm of <number> to the specified <base>. |
| LOG10( <number> ) | Base-10 logarithm of <number>. |
| MOD( <number>, <divisor> ) | Remainder of <number> after it is divided by <divisor>. |
| MROUND( <number>, <multiple> ) | Rounds <number> to the desired <multiple>. |
| PI() | Returns the value of Pi, 3.14159265358979. |
| POWER( <number>, <power> ) | Returns <number> raised to <power>. |
| QUOTIENT( <numerator>, <denominator> ) | Returns the integer portion of the result of <numerator> divided by <denominator>. |
| RAND() | Random number greater than or equal to 0 and less than 1. The number changes on recalculation. |
| RANDBETWEEN( <bottom>, <top> ) | Random *integer* number greater than or equal to <bottom> and less than or equal to <top>. |

| Function | Description |
|---|---|
| ROUND( <number>, <num_digits> ) | Rounds <number> to the number of digits specified by <num_digits>.<br>If <num_digits> is greater than 0, the number is rounded to the specified number of decimal places.<br>If <num_digits> is less than 0, the number is rounded to the left of decimal point (that is, use 2 to round on multiples of 100). If <num_digits> is 0, the number is rounded to the nearest integer. |
| ROUNDDOWN( <number>, <num_digits> ) | Rounds <number> down to zero, using the number of digits specified by <num_digits>. See ROUND description for the meaning of <num_digits>. |
| ROUNDUP( <number>, <num_digits> ) | Rounds <number> up, away from zero, using the number of digits specified by <num_digits>. See ROUND description for the meaning of <num_digits>. |
| SIGN( <number> ) | Returns 1 if <number> is positive, 0 if <number> is 0, and -1 if <number> is negative. |
| SQRT( <number> ) | Square root of <number>. |
| TRUNC( <number> [,<num_digits>] ) | Truncates <number> to an integer by removing the decimal part of the number. The <num_digits> parameter is optional and it is 0 by default. See ROUND description for the meaning of <num_digits>. |

# Text Functions

Text functions available in DAX to manipulate text strings are like those available in Excel 2010, with just a few exceptions.

**TABLE A-5 Text Functions**

| Function | Description |
|---|---|
| CONCATENATE( <text1>, <text2> ) | Concatenates <text1> and <text2> into a single string. Converts argument types to string if necessary. It is like writing <text1> & <text2>. |
| EXACT( <text1>, <text2> ) | Compares two strings, returning TRUE if they are identical; otherwise, FALSE. EXACT is case sensitive. |
| FIND( <find_text>, <within_text> [,<start_num>] ) | Returns the initial position of <find_text> in <within_text> string. If <start_num> is specified, the search begins from character <start_num> in <within_text>. FIND is case sensitive. |

*(continued)*

| Function | Description |
|---|---|
| FIXED( <number> [,<decimals> [,<no_commas>] ] ) | Rounds <number> to the specified number of <decimals> and returns the result as text type. If <decimals> is omitted, two decimals are used by default. The third optional parameter can be TRUE to eliminate commas in the returned text; by default, it is FALSE (so commas are included by default). |
| FORMAT( <value>, <format_string> ) | Formats <value> according to <format_string>. Look for "Custom numeric formats for the FORMAT function" in the PowerPivot help. This function corresponds to the Excel TEXT() function. |
| LEFT( <text>, <num_chars> ) | Returns the first <num_chars> characters from the start of <text> string. |
| LEN( <text> ) | Number of characters of <text> string. |
| LOWER( <text> ) | Convert all letters of <text> to lowercase. |
| MID( <text>, <start_num>, <num_chars> ) | Returns the <num_chars> number of characters from <text> string starting from position <start_num>, where the first character of <text> has position 1. |
| REPLACE( <old_text>, <start_num>, <num_chars>, <new_text> ) | Replaces the part of the <old_text> string starting at the <start_num> position for the <num_chars> character with the <new_text> string. |
| REPT( <text>, <num_times> ) | Repeats <text> for <num_times> times. |
| RIGHT( <text>, <num_chars> ) | Returns the last <num_chars> characters from the end of the <text> string. |
| SEARCH( <search_text>, <within_text> [,<start_num>] ) | Returns the initial position of <search_text> in the <within_text> string. If <start_num> is specified, the search begins from character <start_num> in <within_text>. SEARCH is not case sensitive. |
| SUBSTITUTE( <text>, <old_text>, <new_text> [,<instance_num>] ) | Substitutes <new_text> for <old_text> in the <text> string. If <instance_num> is specified, it indicates the occurrence of <old_text> to replace. By default, every instance of <old_text> is replaced. |
| TRIM( <text> ) | Removes all the spaces from <text> except for single spaces between words. |
| UPPER ( <text> ) | Convert all letters of <text> to uppercase. |
| VALUE( <text> ) | Converts the <text> string that represents a number to a number. If the text does not contain a valid number, it returns an error. To safely convert a text column into a numeric one, converting all non-numeric values into empty values, use IFERROR, as in this example:<br>= IFERROR( VALUE( Table[Column] ), BLANK() ) |

# Date and Time Functions

The basic date and time functions available in PowerPivot mainly operate as converters between text and datetime types. There are also other "time intelligence" functions that are specific to PowerPivot and are covered later in Table A-8, "Time Intelligence Functions."

**TABLE A-6 Date and Time Functions**

| Function | Description |
| --- | --- |
| DATE( <year>, <month>, <day> ) | Returns a value of datetime type corresponding to the date defined by <year>, <month>, and <day>. Because the return is of datetime data type, the hour, minute, and second are set to 0. |
| DATEVALUE( <date_text> ) | Converts a date contained in <date_text> into a value of datetime type. Format of <date_text> depends on system settings. |
| DAY( <date> ) | Day of month (number from 1 through 31) of <date>. |
| EDATE( <start_date>, <months> ) | Returns the date that is indicated by the number of <months> before or after the <start_date>. Positive values for <months> are considered after <start_date>; negative values are considered before <start_date>. |
| EOMONTH( <start_date>, <months> ) | Returns the last day of the month before or after the <start_date> for a specified number of <months>. Positive values for <months> are considered after <start_date>; negative values are considered before <start_date>. |
| HOUR( <datetime> ) | Hour (number from 0 through 23) of <datetime>. |
| MINUTE( <datetime> ) | Minute (number from 0 through 59) of <datetime>. |
| MONTH( <datetime> ) | Month (number from 1 through 12) of <datetime>. |
| NOW() | Returns current date and time. |
| SECOND( <datetime> ) | Second (number from 0 through 59) of <datetime>. |
| TIME( <hour>, <minute>, <second> ) | Returns a value of datetime type corresponding to the time defined by <hour>, <minute>, and <second>. Because the return is of datetime data type, the year, month, and day are set to a reference date (which is December 30, 1899). |
| TIMEVALUE( <time_text> ) | Converts a time contained in <time_text> into a value of datetime type. Format of <time_text> depends on system settings. |
| TODAY( ) | Returns the current date. Because the return is of datetime data type, the hour, minute, and second are set to 0. |
| WEEKDAY( <date> [,<return_type>] ) | Day of week (number from 1 through 7) of <date>. The optional <return_type> parameter determines the return value: for Sunday=1 through Saturday=7, use 1; for Monday=1 through Sunday=7, use 2; for Monday=0 through Sunday=6, use 3. By default, it is 1. |

*(continued)*

| Function | Description |
|---|---|
| WEEKNUM( <date> [,<return_type>] ) | Week number of <date>. The optional <return_type> parameter determines what day to consider for week beginning. With 1, the week begins on Sunday; with 2, the week begins on Monday. By default, it is 1. See WEEKNUM help in Excel to get a complete list of possible values. |
| YEAR( <date> ) | Year (number from 1900 through 9999) of <date>. |
| YEARFRAC( <start_date>, <end_date> [,<basis>] ) | Calculates the fraction of the year represented by the number of whole days from <start_date> through <end_date> dates. The optional <basis> parameter defines the type of day count basis. (See YEARFRAC help in Excel to get a complete list of possible values.) |

# Filter and Value Functions

The functions that manipulate row context and filter context in DAX calculations are explained in detail in Chapter 6, "Evaluation Context and CALCULATE."

**TABLE A-7 Filter and Value Functions**

| Function | Description |
|---|---|
| ALL(<table_or_column>) | Returns all the rows in a table, or all the values in a column, ignoring any filters that might have been applied. |
| ALLEXCEPT( <table> [,<column1> [,<column2> [,...] ] ] ) | Overrides all context filters in the table except filters that have been applied to the specified columns. |
| ALLNONBLANKROW( <table_or_column> ) | Returns all the rows, except for blank rows, in a table or column; disregards any context filters that might exist. |
| BLANK( ) | Returns a blank. |
| CALCULATE( <expression> [,<filter1> [,<filter2> [,...] ] ] ) | Evaluates an expression in a context that is modified by the specified filters. |
| CALCULATETABLE( <expression> [,<filter1> [,<filter2> [,...] ] ] ) | Evaluates a table expression in a context modified by filters. |
| DISTINCT( <column> ) | Returns a one-column table that contains the distinct values from the specified column. |
| EARLIER( <column> [,<number>] ) | Returns the current value of the specified column in a previous evaluation pass of the mentioned column. |
| EARLIEST( <table_or_column> ) | Returns the current value of the specified column in the first evaluation pass of the mentioned column. |
| FILTER( <table>, <filter> ) | Returns a table that represents a subset of another table or expression. |
| RELATED( <column> ) | Returns a related value from another table. |

| Function | Description |
| --- | --- |
| RELATEDTABLE( <table> ) | Follows an existing relationship, in either direction, and returns a table that contains all matching rows from the specified table. |
| VALUES( <column> ) | Returns a one-column table that contains the distinct values from the specified column. This function is similar to the DISTINCT function, but the VALUES function can also return any unknown member as a single BLANK row. |

# Time Intelligence Functions

There are special functions to make complex operations on dates, such as comparing aggregated values year over year or calculating the year-to-date value of a measure. This set of functions is called "Time Intelligence Functions" and is described in Chapter 7, "Date Calculations in DAX."

**TABLE A-8 Time Intelligence Functions**

| Function | Description |
| --- | --- |
| CLOSINGBALANCEMONTH( <expression>, <dates> [,<filter>] ) | Evaluates the specified expression at the calendar end of the given month. The given month is calculated as the month of the latest date in the dates argument, after applying all filters. |
| CLOSINGBALANCEQUARTER( <expression>, <dates> [,<filter>] ) | Evaluates the specified expression at the calendar end of the given quarter. The given quarter is calculated as the quarter of the latest date in the dates argument, after applying all filters. |
| CLOSINGBALANCEYEAR( <expression>, <dates> [,<filter>] [,<year_end_date>] ) | Evaluates the specified expression at the calendar end of the given year. The given year is calculated as the year of the latest date in the dates argument, after applying all filters. |
| DATEADD( <date_column>, <number_of_intervals>, <interval> ) | Returns a table that contains a column of dates, shifted either forward in time or back in time from the dates in the specified date column. |
| DATESBETWEEN( <column>, <start_date>, <end_date> ) | Returns a table of dates that can be found in the specified date column, beginning with the start date and ending with the end date. |
| DATESINPERIOD( <date_column>, <start_date>, <number_of_intervals>, <intervals> ) | Returns a table of dates that can be found in the specified date column, beginning with the start date and continuing for the specified number of intervals. |
| DATESMTD( <date_column> ) | Returns the subset of dates, from date_column, for the interval that starts at the first day of the month and ends at the latest date in the specified dates column for the month that is the corresponding month of the latest date. |

*(continued)*

| Function | Description |
|---|---|
| DATESQTD( <date_column> ) | Returns the subset of dates from <date_column> for the interval that starts at the first day of the quarter and ends at the latest date in the specified dates column for the quarter that is the corresponding quarter of the latest date. |
| DATESYTD( <date_column> [,<year_end_date>] ) | Returns the subset of dates from <date_column> for the interval that starts the first day of the year and ends at the latest date in the specified dates' column for the quarter that is the corresponding quarter of the latest date. |
| ENDOFMONTH( <date_column> ) | Returns the last day of the month in the specified date column. |
| ENDOFQUARTER( <date_column> ) | Returns the last day of the quarter in the specified date column. |
| ENDOFYEAR( <date_column> [,<year_end_date>] ) | Returns the last day of the year in the specified date column. |
| FIRSTDATE( <date_column> ) | Returns the first date in the current context for the specified date column. |
| FIRSTNONBLANK( <column>, <expression> ) | Returns the first value in the <column> filtered by the current context, where the <expression> is not blank. |
| LASTDATE( <date_column> ) | Returns the last date in the current context for the specified date column. |
| LASTNONBLANK( <column>, <expression> ) | Returns the last value in the <column> filtered by the current context, where the <expression> is not blank. |
| NEXTDAY( <date_column> ) | Returns the next day date from date_column. |
| NEXTMONTH( <date_column> ) | Returns the set of dates in the next month from date_column. |
| NEXTQUARTER( <date_column> ) | Returns the set of dates for the next quarter from date_column. |
| NEXTYEAR( <date_column> [,<year_end_date>] ) | Returns the set of dates for the next year from date_column. |
| OPENINGBALANCEMONTH( <expression>, <dates> [,<filter>] ) | Evaluates the specified expression at the calendar end of the month prior the given month. The given month is calculated as the month of the latest date in the dates argument, after applying all filters. |
| OPENINGBALANCEQUARTER( <expression>, <dates> [,<filter>] ) | Evaluates the specified expression at the calendar end of the quarter prior to the given quarter. The given quarter is calculated as the quarter of the latest date in the dates argument, after applying all filters. |
| OPENINGBALANCEYEAR( <expression>, <dates> [,<filter>] [,<year_end_date>] ) | Evaluates the specified expression at the calendar end of the year prior to the given year. The given year is calculated as the year of the latest date in the dates argument, after applying all filters. |
| PARALLELPERIOD( <date_column>, <number_of_intervals>, <intervals> ) | This function moves the specified number of intervals and then returns all contiguous full months that contain any values after that shift. Gaps between the first and last dates are filled in, and months are also filled in. |
| PREVIOUSDAY( <date_column> ) | Returns the previous day date from date_column. |

| Function | Description |
|---|---|
| PREVIOUSMONTH( <date_column> ) | Returns the set of dates in the previous month from date_column. |
| PREVIOUSQUARTER( <date_column> ) | Returns the set of dates in the previous quarter from date_column. |
| PREVIOUSYEAR( <date_column> [,<year_end_date>] ) | Returns the set of dates in the previous year from date_column. |
| SAMEPERIODLASTYEAR( <date_column> ) | Returns a table of dates that can be found in the specified date column. |
| STARTOFMONTH( <date_column> ) | Returns the first day of the month in the specified date column. |
| STARTOFQUARTER( <date_column> ) | Returns the first day of the quarter in the specified date column. |
| STARTOFYEAR( <date_column> [,<year_end_date>] ) | Returns the first day of the year in the specified date column. |
| TOTALMTD( <expression>, <dates> [,<filter>] ) | Evaluates the specified expression for the interval that starts at the first day of the month and ends at the latest date in the specified dates column, after applying all filters. |
| TOTALQTD( <expression>, <dates> [,<filter>] ) | Evaluates the specified expression for the interval that starts at the first day of the quarter and ends at the latest date in the specified dates column, after applying all filters. |
| TOTALYTD( <expression>, <dates> [,<filter>] [,<year_end_date>] ) | Evaluates the specified expression for the interval that starts at the first day of the year and ends at the latest date in the specified dates column, after applying all filters. |

# Index

# D

# E



# F

## G



## H



## I



## J

## K



## L



## M

# N



# O



# P

# Q

## R



## S

# T

## U



## V



## W



## X



## Y

# Biography

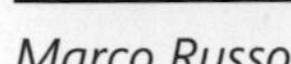

*Marco Russo* *Alberto Ferrari*

**Marco Russo** (*marco.russo@sqlbi.com*) and **Alberto Ferrari** (*alberto.ferrari@sqlbi.com*) are the two founders of SQLBI.COM. They both provide consultancy and training on Business Intelligence (BI), with a particular specialization in the Microsoft Technologies related to BI. They have written several papers about these topics, with a particular mention for "SQLBI Methodology," which is a complete methodology for designing and implementing the back-end of a BI solution (from OLTP to OLAP cubes through Data Warehouse and Data Marts) using the Microsoft BI stack of technologies, and "The Many-to-Many Revolution," which is a paper dedicated to modeling patterns using many-to-many dimension relationships in Analysis Services.

In 2009, Marco, Alberto, and Chris Webb wrote *Expert Cube Development with Microsoft SQL Server 2008 Analysis Services*, which is considered an important set of guidelines and best practices for using Microsoft Analysis Services in the real world.

Marco and Alberto are also regular speakers at major international conferences about Microsoft SQL Server PowerPivot for Excel and Microsoft SQL Server Analysis Services.

They have been working with PowerPivot since the first beta version in 2009.

# Resources for SQL Server 2008

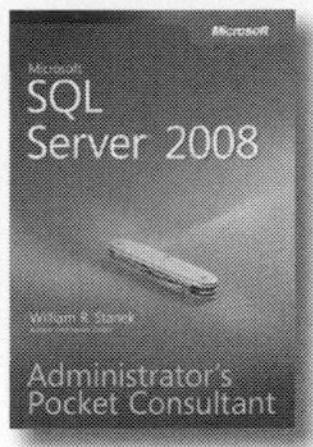


**Microsoft® SQL Server® 2008 Administrator's Pocket Consultant**
William R. Stanek
ISBN 9780735625891

**Programming Microsoft SQL Server 2008**
Leonard Lobel, Andrew J. Brust, Stephen Forte
ISBN 9780735625990

**Microsoft SQL Server 2008 Step by Step**
Mike Hotek
ISBN 9780735626041

**Microsoft SQL Server 2008 T-SQL Fundamentals**
Itzik Ben-Gan
ISBN 9780735626010

**EXAM 70-432**
**MCTS Self-Paced Training Kit Microsoft SQL Server 2008 Implementation and Maintenance**
Mike Hotek
ISBN 9780735626058

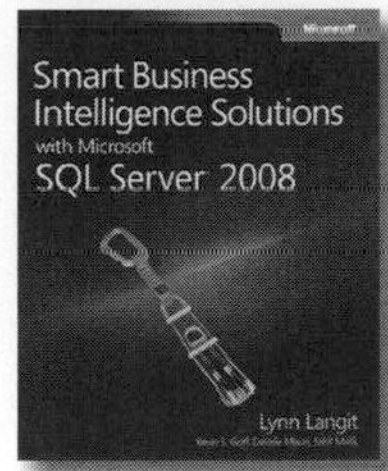


**Smart Business Intelligence Solutions with Microsoft SQL Server 2008**
Lynn Langit, Kevin S. Goff, Davide Mauri, Sahil Malik
ISBN 9780735625808

## ALSO SEE

**Microsoft SQL Server 2008 Internals**
Kalen Delaney *et al.*
ISBN 9780735626249

**Inside Microsoft SQL Server 2008: T-SQL Querying**
Itzik Ben-Gan, Lubor Kollar, Dejan Sarka, Steve Kass
ISBN 9780735626034

**Inside Microsoft SQL Server 2008: T-SQL Programming**
Itzik Ben-Gan, Dejan Sarka, Roger Wolter, Greg Low, Ed Katibah, Isaac Kunen
ISBN 9780735626027

**Microsoft SQL Server 2008 MDX Step by Step**
Bryan C. Smith, C. Ryan Clay, Hitachi Consulting
ISBN 9780735626188

**Microsoft SQL Server 2008 Reporting Services Step by Step**
Stacia Misner
ISBN 9780735626478

**Microsoft SQL Server 2008 Analysis Services Step by Step**
Scott Cameron, Hitachi Consulting
ISBN 9780735626201

**microsoft.com/mspress**